57th Annual Meeting of the Association for Computational Linguistics (ACL 2019)

Student Research Workshop

Florence, Italy
28 July – 2 August 2019

ISBN: 978-1-5108-9097-8

ACL 2019

**The 57th Annual Meeting of the
Association for Computational Linguistics**

Proceedings of the Student Research Workshop

July 28 - August 2, 2019
Florence, Italy

Introduction

Welcome to the ACL 2019 Student Research Workshop! The ACL 2019 Student Research Workshop (SRW) is a forum for student researchers in computational linguistics and natural language processing. The workshop provides a unique opportunity for student participants to present their work and receive valuable feedback from the international research community as well as from faculty mentors.

Following the tradition of the previous years' student research workshops, we have two tracks: research papers and research proposals. The research paper track is a venue for Ph.D. students, Masters students, and advanced undergraduates to describe completed work or work-in-progress along with preliminary results. The research proposal track is offered for advanced Masters and Ph.D. students who have decided on a thesis topic and are interested in feedback on their proposal and ideas about future directions for their work.

This year, the student research workshop has received a great attention, reflecting the growth of the field. We received 214 submissions in total: 27 research proposals and 147 research papers. Among these, 7 research proposals and 22 research papers were non-archival. We accepted 71 papers, for an acceptance rate of 33%. After withdrawals and excluding non-archival papers, 61 papers are appearing in these proceedings, including 14 research proposals and 47 research papers. All of the accepted papers will be presented as posters in late morning sessions as a part of the main conference, split across three days (July 29th-31th).

Mentoring is at the heart of the SRW. In keeping with previous years, students had the opportunity for pre-submission mentoring prior to the submission deadline. Total of 64 papers participated in pre-submission mentoring program. This program offered students a chance to receive comments from an experienced researcher, in order to improve the quality of the writing and presentation before making their submission. In addition, authors of accepted SRW papers are matched with mentors who will meet with the students in person during the poster presentations. Each mentor prepares in-depth comments and questions prior to the student's presentation, and provides discussion and feedback during the workshop.

We are deeply grateful to our sponsors whose support will enable a number of students to attend the conference. We would also like to thank our program committee members for their careful reviews of each paper, and all of our mentors for donating their time to provide feedback to our student authors. Thank you to our faculty advisors Hannaneh Hajishirzi, Aurelie Herbelot, Scott Yih, Yue Zhang for their essential advice and guidance, and to the members of the ACL 2018 organizing committee, in particular David Traum, Anna Korhonen and Lluís Màrquez for their helpful support. Finally, kudos to our student participants!

Organizers:
Fernando Alva-Manchego, University of Sheffield
Eunsol Choi, Univeristy of Washington
Daniel Khashabi, University of Pennsylvania

Faculty Advisor:
Hannaneh Hajishirzi, University of Washington
Aurelie Herbelot, University of Trento
Scott Yih, Facebook AI Research
Yue Zhang, Westlake University

Faculty Mentors:
Andreas Vlachos - U of Cambridge
Arkaitz Zubiaga - University of Warwick
Aurelie Herbelot - University of Trento
Bonnie Webber - U of Edinburgh
David Chiang - University of Notre Dame
Diyi Yang - CMU
Ekaterina Kochmar - U of Cambridge
Emily M. Bender - U of Washington
Gerald Penn - U of Toronto
Greg Durrett - University of Texas, Austin
Ivan Vulić - U of Cambridge
Jacob Andreas - MIT
Jacob Eisenstein - Georgia Tech
Masoud Rouhizadeh - Johns Hopkins University
Matt Gardner - AI2
Melissa Roemmele - SDL
Carolina Scarton - University of Sheffield
Natalie Schluter - U of Copenhagen
Giovanni Semeraro - University of Bari Aldo Moro
Gunhee Kim - Seoul National University
Parisa Kordjamshidi - Tulane University
Saif M. Mohammad - National Research Council Canada
Paul Rayson - Lancaster University
Stephen Roller - Facebook
Valerio Basile - U of Turin
Wei Wang - University of New South Wales
Yue Zhang - Westlake University
Zhou Yu - UC Davis

Program Committee:
Abigail See - Stanford U
Adam Fisch - MIT
Aida Amini - UW
Alexandra Balahur - European Commission
Ali Emami - McGill
Alice Lai - Microsoft
Alina Karakanta - U of Saarland

Amir Yazdavar - Wright State U
Amrita Saha - IBM
Antonio Toral - U of Groningen
Anusha Balakrishnan - FB
Ari Holtzman - UW
Arun Tejasvi Chaganty - Stanford U
Avinesh P.V.S - TU Darmstadt
Ben Zhou - U of Pennsylvania
Bernd Bohnet - Google AI
Bharat Ram Ambati - Apple
Bill Yuchen Lin - USC
Bruno Martins - U of Lisbon
Chandra Bhagavatula - AI2
Chen-Tse Tsai - Bloomberg
Chuan-Jie Lin - National Taiwan Ocean University
Dallas Card - U of Washington
Dat Quoc Nguyen - U of Edinburgh
Dayne Freitag - SRI
Divyansh Kaushik - CMU
Douwe Kiela - U of Cambridge
Ehsan Kamalloo - U of Alberta
Ehsaneddin Asgari - UC Berkeley
Elaheh Raisi - VT
Erfan Sadeqi Azer - Indiana U
Gabriel Satanovsky - AI2
Ge Gao - UW
Hardy - U of Sheffield
Ivan Vulić - U of Cambridge
Jeenu Grover - IIT
Jeff Jacobs - Columbia U
Jiangming Liu - U of Edinburgh
Jiawei Wu - UCSB
John Hewitt - Stanford
Jonathan P. Chang - Cornell U
Julien Plu - EuroCom
Justine Zhang - Cornell U
Kalpesh Krishna - UMASS
Kartikeya Upasani - FB
Kevin Lin - UW
Kevin Small - Amazon
Kun Xu - PKU
Kurt Espinosa - U of Manchester
Leo Wanner - Pompeu Fabra U
Leon Bergen - UCSD
Luciano Del Corro - MPI
Maarten Sap - UW
Madhumita Sushil - University of Antwerp
Malihe Alikhani - Rutgers U
Manex Agirrezabal - U of Copenhagen
Manish Shrivastava - IIT
Marco Turchi - U of Bristol

Marco Antonio Sobrevilla Cabezudo - Universidade de São Paulo
Marcos Garcia - University of Santiago de Compostela
Michael Sejr Schlichtkrull - U of Amsterdam
Miguel Ballesteros - IBM research
Miguel A. Alonso - University of A Coruña
Mohammad Sadegh Rasooli - Columbia U
Mona Jalal - Boston U
Najoung Kim - JHU
Negin Ghasemi - Amirkabir University of Technology
Nelson F. Liu - UW
Omid Memarrast - U of Illinois, Chicago
Omnia Zayed - Insight Center (NUI Galway)
Pradeep Dasigi - AI2
Reza Ghaeini - Oregon State
Rezvaneh Rezapour - U of Illinois, Urbana-Champaign
Rob Voigt - Stanford
Roberto Basili - University of Roma
Roee Aharoni - Bar-Ilan U
Rui Meng - U Pitt
Ruken Cakici - Middle East Technical University
Saadia Gabriel - UW
Sanjay Subramanian - UPenn
Sebastian Schuster - Stanford U
Sedeeq Al-khazraji - RIT
Sepideh Sadeghi - Tufts U
Sewon Min - UW
Shabnam Tafreshi - George Washington U
Shamil Chollampatt - National University of Singapore (NUS)
Shuai Yuan - Google
Shyam Upadhyay - Google
Sihao Chen - U of Pennsylvania
Sina Sheikholeslami - KTH
Sowmya Vajjala - Iowa State U
Sudipta Kar - U of Houston
Thomas Kober - U of Sussex
Valentina Pyatkin - U of Rome
Vasu Sharma - CMU
Vivek Gupta - U of Utah
Vlad Niculae - Instituto de Telecomunicações, Lisbon
Wuwei Lan - Ohio State U
Yanai Elazar - BIU
Zeerak Waseem - U of Sheffield
Ziyu Yao - OSU

Table of Contents

Conference Program

Monday, July 29, 2019

Poster Session 1 : Research Proposals

10:30–12:10   *Distributed Knowledge Based Clinical Auto-Coding System*
Rajvir Kaur

10:30–12:10   *Robust to Noise Models in Natural Language Processing Tasks*
Valentin Malykh

10:30–12:10   *A Computational Linguistic Study of Personal Recovery in Bipolar Disorder*
Glorianna Jagfeld

10:30–12:10   *Measuring the Value of Linguistics: A Case Study from St. Lawrence Island Yupik*
Emily Chen

10:30–12:10   *Not All Reviews Are Equal: Towards Addressing Reviewer Biases for Opinion Summarization*
Wenyi Tay

10:30–12:10   *Towards Turkish Abstract Meaning Representation*
Zahra Azin and Gülşen Eryiğit

10:30–12:10   *Gender Stereotypes Differ between Male and Female Writings*
Yusu Qian

10:30–12:10   *Question Answering in the Biomedical Domain*
Vincent Nguyen

10:30–12:10   *Knowledge Discovery and Hypothesis Generation from Online Patient Forums: A Research Proposal*
Anne Dirkson

10:30–12:10   *Automated Cross-language Intelligibility Analysis of Parkinson's Disease Patients Using Speech Recognition Technologies*
Nina Hosseini-Kivanani, Juan Camilo Vásquez-Correa, Manfred Stede and Elmar Nöth

10:30–12:10   *Natural Language Generation: Recently Learned Lessons, Directions for Semantic Representation-based Approaches, and the Case of Brazilian Portuguese Language*
Marco Antonio Sobrevilla Cabezudo and Thiago Pardo

10:30–12:10   *Long-Distance Dependencies Don't Have to Be Long: Simplifying through Provably (Approximately) Optimal Permutations*
Rishi Bommasani

10:30–12:10   *Predicting the Outcome of Deliberative Democracy: A Research Proposal*
Conor McKillop

10:30–12:10   *Active Reading Comprehension: A Dataset for Learning the Question-Answer Relationship Strategy*
Diana Galván-Sosa

Poster Session 1 (continued) : Non-Archival Research Papers and Proposals

10:30–12:10   *Developing OntoSenseNet: A Verb-Centric Ontological Resource for Indian Languages and Analysing Stylometric Difference in Men and Women Writing using the Resource*

10:30–12:10   *Imperceptible Adversarial Examples for Automatic Speech Recognition*

10:30–12:10   *Public Mood Variations in Russia based on Vkontakte Content*

10:30–12:10   *Analyzing and Mitigating Gender Bias in Languages with Grammatical Gender and Bilingual Word Embeddings*

10:30–12:10   *Multilingual Model Using Cross-Task Embedding Projection*

10:30–12:10   *Sentence Level Curriculum Learning for Improved Neural Conversational Models*

10:30–12:10   *On the impressive performance of randomly weighted encoders in summarization tasks*

10:30–12:10   *Automatic Data-Driven Approaches for Evaluating the Phonemic Verbal Fluency Task with Healthy Adults*

10:30–12:10   *On Dimensional Linguistic Properties of the Word Embedding Space*

10:30–12:10 *Sentiment Analysis on Naija-Tweets*
Taiwo Kolajo, Olawande Daramola and Ayodele Adebiyi

10:30–12:10 *Fact or Factitious? Contextualized Opinion Spam Detection*
Stefan Kennedy, Niall Walsh, Kirils Sloka, Andrew McCarren and Jennifer Foster

10:30–12:10 *Scheduled Sampling for Transformers*
Tsvetomila Mihaylova and André F. T. Martins

10:30–12:10 *BREAKING! Presenting Fake News Corpus for Automated Fact Checking*
Archita Pathak and Rohini Srihari

10:30–12:10 *Cross-domain and Cross-lingual Abusive Language Detection: A Hybrid Approach with Deep Learning and a Multilingual Lexicon*
Endang Wahyu Pamungkas and Viviana Patti

10:30–12:10 *De-Mixing Sentiment from Code-Mixed Text*
Yash Kumar Lal, Vaibhav Kumar, Mrinal Dhar, Manish Shrivastava and Philipp Koehn

10:30–12:10 *Unsupervised Learning of Discourse-Aware Text Representation for Essay Scoring*
Farjana Sultana Mim, Naoya Inoue, Paul Reisert, Hiroki Ouchi and Kentaro Inui

10:30–12:10 *Multimodal Logical Inference System for Visual-Textual Entailment*
Riko Suzuki, Hitomi Yanaka, Masashi Yoshikawa, Koji Mineshima and Daisuke Bekki

10:30–12:10 *Deep Neural Models for Medical Concept Normalization in User-Generated Texts*
Zulfat Miftahutdinov and Elena Tutubalina

10:30–12:10 *Using Semantic Similarity as Reward for Reinforcement Learning in Sentence Generation*
Go Yasui, Yoshimasa Tsuruoka and Masaaki Nagata

10:30–12:10 *Sentiment Classification Using Document Embeddings Trained with Cosine Similarity*
Tan Thongtan and Tanasanee Phienthrakul

10:30–12:10 *Detecting Adverse Drug Reactions from Biomedical Texts with Neural Networks*
Ilseyar Alimova and Elena Tutubalina

Distributed Knowledge Based Clinical Auto-Coding System

Rajvir Kaur

School of Computing, Engineering and Mathematics
Western Sydney University, Australia
18531738@student.westernsydney.edu.au

Abstract

Codification of free-text clinical narratives have long been recognised to be beneficial for secondary uses such as funding, insurance claim processing and research. In recent years, many researchers have studied the use of Natural Language Processing (NLP), related Machine Learning (ML) methods and techniques to resolve the problem of manual coding of clinical narratives. Most of the studies are focused on classification systems relevant to the U.S and there is a scarcity of studies relevant to Australian classification systems such as ICD-10-AM and ACHI. Therefore, we aim to develop a knowledge-based clinical auto-coding system, that utilise appropriate NLP and ML techniques to assign ICD-10-AM and ACHI codes to clinical records, while adhering to both local coding standards (Australian Coding Standard) and international guidelines that get updated and validated continuously.

1   Introduction

Documentation related to an episode of care of a patient, commonly referred to as a medical record, contains clinical findings, diagnoses, interventions, and medication details which are invaluable information for clinical decisions making. To carry out meaningful statistical analysis, these medical records are converted into a special set of codes which are called *Clinical codes* as per the clinical coding standards set by the World Health Organisation (WHO). The International Classification of Diseases (ICD) codes are a special set of alphanumeric codes, assigned to an episode of care of a patient, based on which reimbursement is done in some countries (Kaur and Ginige, 2018). Clinical codes are assigned by trained professionals, known as *clinical coders*, who have a sound knowledge of medical terminologies, clinical classification systems, and coding rules and guidelines. The current scenario of assigning clinical codes is a manual process which is very expensive, time-consuming, and error-prone (Xie and Xing, 2018). The wrong assignment of codes leads to issues such as reviewing of whole process, financial losses, increased labour costs as well as delays in reimbursement process. The coded data is not only used by insurance companies for reimbursement purposes, but also by government agencies and policy makers to analyse healthcare systems, justify investments done in the healthcare industry and plan future investments based on these statistics (Kaur and Ginige, 2018).

With the transition from ICD-9 to ICD-10 in 1992, the number of codes increased from 3,882 codes to approximately 70,000, which further makes manual coding a non-trivial task (Subotin and Davis, 2014). On an average, a clinical coder codes 3 to 4 clinical records per hour, resulting in 15-42 records per day depending on the experience and efficiency of the human coder (Santos et al., 2008; Kaur and Ginige, 2018). The cost incurred in assigning clinical codes and their follow up corrections are estimated to be 25 billion dollars per year in the United States (Farkas and Szarvas, 2008; Xie and Xing, 2018). There are several reasons behind the wrong assignment of codes. First, assignment of ICD codes to patient's records is highly erroneous due to subjective nature of human perception (Arifoğlu et al., 2014). Second, manual process of assigning codes is a tedious task which leads to inability to locate critical and subtle findings due to fatigue. Third, in many cases, physicians or doctors often use abbreviations or synonyms, which causes ambiguity (Xie and Xing, 2018).

A study by (McKenzie and Walker, 2003), describes changes that have occurred in the coder workforce over the last eight years in terms of employment conditions, duties, resources, and access to and need for continuous education. Similarly,

1

Proceedings of the ACL 2019, Student Research Workshop, pages 1–9
Florence, Italy, July 28th-August 2nd, 2019. ©2019 Association for Computational Linguistics

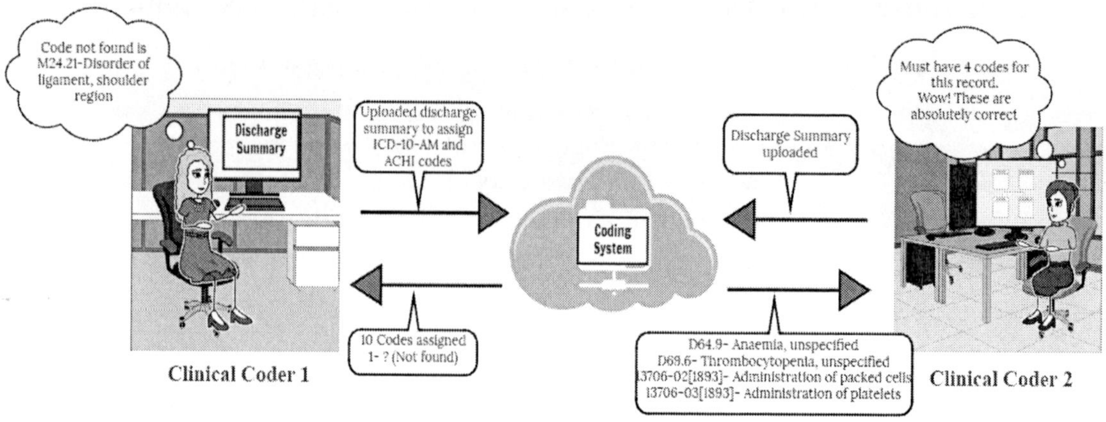

Figure 1: A distributed knowledge-based clinical auto-coding system

another study (Butler-Henderson, 2017), highlights major future challenges that health information management practitioners and academics will face with an ageing workforce, where more than 50% of the workforce is aged 45 years or older.

To reduce coding errors and cost, research is being conducted to develop methods for automated coding. Most of the research in auto-coding is focused on ICD-9-CM (Clinical Modification), ICD-10-CM, ICD-10-PCS (Procedure Coding System) which are US modifications. Very limited studies are focused on ICD-10-AM (Australian Modification) and Australian Classification of Health Intervention (ACHI).Hence, our research aims to develop a distributed knowledge-based clinical autocoding system that would leverage on NLP and ML techniques, where a human coders will give their queries to the coding system and in revert the system will suggest a set of clinical codes. Figure 1 shows a possible scenario, how a distributed knowledge-based coding system will be used in practice.

2   Related Work

In early 19th century, a French statistician Jacques Bertillon, developed a classification system to record causes of death. Later in 1948, the WHO started maintaining the Bertillon classification and named it as International Statistical Classification of Disease, Injuries and Causes of Death (Cumerlato et al., 2010). Since then, roughly every ten years, this classification had been revised and in 1992, ICD-10 was approved. Twenty-six (26)

years after the introduction of ICD-10, the next generation of classification ICD-11 is released in May 2019 but not yet implemented (Kaur and Ginige, 2018). ICD-11 increases the complexity by introducing a new code structure, a new chapter on X-Extension Codes, dimensions of external causes (histopathology, consciousness, temporality, and etiology), and a new chapters on sleep-awake disorder, conditions related to sexual health, and traditional medicine conditions (Organisation, 2016; Hargreaves and Njeru, 2014; Reed et al., 2016).

In previous research related to clinical narrative analysis, different methods and techniques ranging from pattern matching to deep learning approaches are applied to categorise clinical narratives into different categories (Mujtaba et al., 2019). Several researchers across the globe have employed text classification to categorise clinical narratives into various categories using machine learning approaches including supervised (Hastie et al., 2009), unsupervised (Ko and Seo, 2000), semi-supervised (Zhu and Goldberg, 2009), ontology-based (Hotho et al., 2002), rule-based (Deng et al., 2015), transfer (Pan and Yang, 2010), and multi-view learning (Amini et al., 2009).

(Cai et al., 2016) reviewed the fundamentals of NLP and describe various techniques such as pattern matching, linguistic approach, statistical and machine learning approaches that constitute NLP in radiology, along with some key applications. (Larkey and Croft, 1995) studied three different classifiers namely: k-nearest neighbor, relevance feedback and Bayesian independence classifiers for assigning ICD-9 codes to dictated inpatient discharge summaries. The study found that a combination of different classifiers produced better results than any single type of classifier. (Farkas and Szarvas, 2008) proposed a rule-based ICD-9-CM coding system for radiology reports and achieved good classification performances on a limited number of ICD-9-CM codes (45 in total). Similarly, (Goldstein et al., 2007; Pestian et al., 2007b; Crammer et al., 2007) also proposed automated system for assigning ICD-9-CM codes to free text radiology reports.

(Koopman et al., 2015) proposed a system for automatic ICD-10 classification of cancer from free-text death certificates. The classifiers were deployed in a two-level cascaded architecture, where the first level identifies the presence of cancer (i.e., binary form cancer/no cancer), and the second level identifies the type of cancer. However, all ICD-10 codes were truncated into three character level.

All the above mentioned research studies are based on some type of deep learning, machine learning or statistical approach, where the information contained in the training data is distillate into mathematical models, which can be successfully employed for assigning ICD codes (Chiaravalloti et al., 2014). One of the main flaws in these approaches is that training data is annotated by human coders. Thus, there is a possibility of inaccurate ICD codes. Therefore, if clinical records labelled with incorrect ICD codes are given as an input to an algorithm, it is likely that the model will also provide incorrect predictions.

2.1 Standard Pipeline for Clinical Text Classification

Various research studies have used different methods and techniques to handle and process clinical text, but the standard pipeline is utilised in some shape or form. This section details the steps in the standard pipeline in machine learning, as it is required for the auto-coding.

2.1.1 Types of clinical record

Clinical text classification techniques have been employed on different types of clinical records such as surgical reports (Stocker et al., 2014; Raja et al., 2012), radiology reports (Mendona et al., 2005), autopsy reports (Mujtaba et al., 2018), death certificates (Koopman et al., 2015), clinical narratives (Meystre and Haug, 2006; Friedlin and McDonald, 2008), progress notes (Frost et al., 2005), laboratory reports (Friedlin and McDonald, 2008; Liu et al., 2012), admission notes and patient summaries (Jensen et al., 2012), pathology reports (Imler et al., 2013), and unstructured electronic text (Portet et al., 2009). In this research, we aim to primarily use clinical discharge summaries as the input text data.

2.1.2 Datasets available

The data sources used in various research studies can be categorised into two types: homogeneous sources and heterogeneous sources, which can further be divided into three subtypes: binary class, multi-class single labeled, multi-class multi-labeled datasets (Mujtaba et al., 2019). There are few datasets that are publicly available such as PhysioNet[1], i2b2 NLP dataset[2], and OHSUMED[3]. In this research, we aim to use both publicly available and data acquired from hospitals.

2.1.3 Preprocessing

Preprocessing is done to remove meaningless information from the dataset as the clinical narratives may contain high level of noise, sparsity, mispelled words, grammatical errors (Nguyen and Patrick, 2016; Mujtaba et al., 2019). Different preprocessing techniques are applied in research studies including sentence splitting, tokenisation, spell error detection and correction, stemming and lemmatisation, normalisation (Manning et al., 2008), removal of stop words, removal of punctuation or special symbols, abbreviation expansion, chunking, named entity recognition (Bird et al., 2009), negation detection (Chapman et al., 2001).

2.1.4 Feature Engineering

Feature engineering is the combination of feature extraction, feature representation, and feature selection (Mujtaba et al., 2019). Feature extraction is the process of extracting useful features which includes Bag of Words (BoW), n-gram, Word2Vec, and GloVe. Once features are extracted, next step is to represent in numeric form to feature vectors using either binary representation, term frequency (tf), term frequency with inverse document frequency (tf-idf), or normalised tf-idf.

---

[1]https://physionet.org/mimic2/
[2]https://www.i2b2.org/NLP/DataSets/
[3]http://davis.wpi.edu/xmdv/datasets/ohsumed.html

2.1.5 Classification

For classification, various research studies have used classifiers such as Support Vector Machine (SVM) (Cortes and Vapnik, 1995), k-Nearest Neighbor (kNN) (Altman, 1992), Convolutional Neural Network (CNN) (Karimi et al., 2017), Recurrent Neural Network (RNN), Long short-term memory (LSTM)(Luo, 2017), and Gated Recurrent Unit (GRU) (Jagannatha and Yu, 2016).

2.1.6 Evaluation Metrics

The performance of clinical text classification models can be measured using standard evaluation metrics which include precision, recall, F-measure (or F-score), accuracy, precision (micro and macro-average), recall (micro and macro-average), F-measure (micro and macro-average), and area under the curve (AUC). These metrics can be computed by using values of true positive (TP), false positive (FP), true negative (TN), and false negative (FN) in the standard confusion matrix (Mujtaba et al., 2019).

3 Experimental Framework

3.1 Data collection and ethics approval

This research has ethics approval from Western Sydney University Human Research Ethics Committee (HREC) under reference No: H12628 to use 1,200 clinical records. The ethics approval is valid for the next four years until 11th April, 2023. In addition, we also have access to publicly available dataset such as MIMIC-III and Computational Medicine Center (CMC) (Pestian et al., 2007a). Apart from this, more clinical records from acute or sub-acute hospitals will also be collected.

3.2 Proposed Research

Within the broader scope of this proposal, the work will be focused on the research questions given below:

How to optimise the use of computerised algorithms to assign ICD-10-AM and ACHI codes to clinical records, while adhering to local coding standard (for example, Australian Coding Standard (ACS)) and international guidelines, leveraging on a distributed knowledge-base?

To address main research question, the following sub-research questions will be investigated:

Why do certain algorithms perform differently with similar dataset?

The *No free lunch theorem* (Wolpert, 1996) states that there is no such algorithm that is universally best for every problem. If one algorithm does really good for a given dataset, it may not do really well for other dataset. For example, one cannot say that SVM always does better prediction than Naïve Bayes or Decision Tree all the times. The intention of ML or statistical learning research is not to find the universally best algorithm, but the reason is that most of the algorithms work on the sample data and then make predictions or inference out of that. We cannot make proper truthful prediction just by working on a sample data. In fact, the results are all probabilistic in nature, not 100% true or certain. The study (Kaur and Ginige, 2018), performed comparative analysis on different approaches such as pattern matching, rule-based, ML, and hybrid. Each of the above mentioned methods and techniques performed differently in every case, but there was no explanations given behind the performance of each algorithm. Moreover, this study did not used ACS rules while assigning ICD-10-AM and ACHI codes.

There are few reasons that may have effected the algorithms performance used for codification of ICD-10-AM and ACHI codes in the previous study (Kaur and Ginige, 2018). Firstly, domain knowledge is very essential before assigning codes. In Australia, coding standards are used for clinical coding purpose to provide consistency of data collection, and support secondary classifications based on ICD such as the Australian Refined Diagnosis Related Groups (AR-DRGs). Therefore, during ICD-10-AM and ACHI code assignment, ACS rules are considered. If these ACS rules are not considered, then there is a possibility of wrong assignment of codes. Secondly, the study (Kaur and Ginige, 2018) had very limited number of medical records due to which the algorithms were unable to learn and predict correct codes properly. A similar study (Kaur and Ginige, 2019) done by the same set of authors using the same dataset describes that the dataset contains 420 unique labels, out of which 221 labels appeared only once in the whole dataset, 77 labels appeared twice, and only 24 labels appeared more than 15 times. Therefore, it lowers the learning rate of the algorithms.

To overcome the above stated problems, we

will make use of ACS in conjunction in ICD-10-AM and ACHI codes, and use large-scale data so that the algorithms can learn properly and make correct predictions. In order to process raw data, feature engineering will be carried out to transform the raw data into feature vectors. Moreover, in NLP, word embeddings has the ability to capture high-level semantic and syntactic properties of text. A study by (Henriksson et al., 2015) leverages word embeddings to identify adverse drug events from clinical notes and shows that using word embeddings can improve the predictive performance of machine learning methods. Therefore, in our research, we will explore semantic and syntactic properties of text to improve the performance of algorithms which give different performance on the same dataset.

How to assign ICD codes before referring to local and international standards and guidelines?

In the U.S, the Centers for Medicare and Medicaid Services (CMS) and the National Center for Health Statistics (NCHS), provide the guidelines for coding and reporting using the ICD-10-CM. These guidelines are a set of rules that have been approved by the four organisations: American Hospital Association (AHA), the American Health Information Association (AHIMA), CMS, and NCHS (for Health Statistics). Similarly, in Australia, the clinical coding standards *i.e.,* ACS rules are designed to be used in conjunction with ICD-10-AM and ACHI and are applicable to all public and private hospitals in Australia (for Classification Development, 2017). The clinical codes are not only assigned based on the information provided on the front sheet or the discharge summary but a complete analysis is performed by following the guidelines given in the ACS.

Since the introduction of ICD-10 in 1992, many countries have modified the WHO's ICD-10 classification system into their country specific reporting purpose. For example, ICD-10-CA (Canadian Modification) and ICD-10-GM (German Modification). There are few major difference between the US and Australian classification systems. Firstly, there are few additional ICD-10-AM codes that are more specific (approximately $4,915$ codes) that are coded only in Australia and 15 other countries including Ireland, and Saudi Arabia that use Australian classification system as their national classification system. For exam-

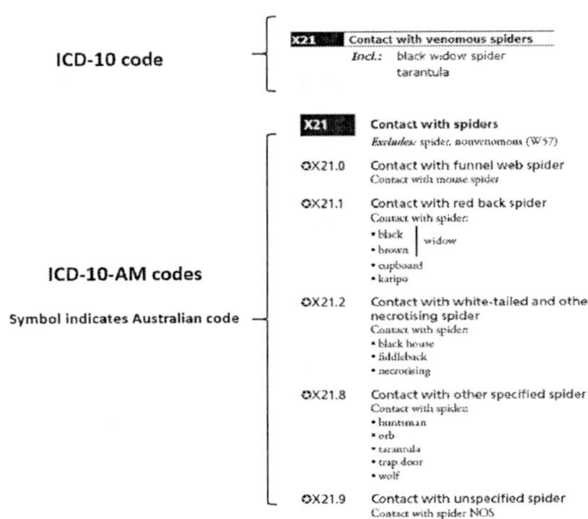

Figure 2: Difference between ICD-10 and ICD-10-AM codes.

ple, in the U.S, *contact with venomous spiders* is coded as $X21$, whereas in Australia, it is more specific by adding fourth character level as shown in Figure 2. There are 12% ICD-10-AM specific codes that do not exist in ICD-10-CM, ICD-9-CM or any other classification system. Secondly, countries that have developed their own national classification system use different coding practices. For example, in the U.S, Pulmonary oedema is coded as $J81$, whereas in Australia, to assign code for Pulmonary oedema, there is ACS rule 0920 which says,"When *acute pulmonary oedema* is documented without further qualification about the underlying cause, assign *I50.1 Left ventricular failure*". Therefore, in our research, we will find methods and techniques to represent the coding standards and guidelines in a computerised format before assigning ICD codes. In addition, we will also explore mechanisms to manage the evolving nature of coding standards.

How to pre-process heterogeneous dataset?

Collecting data in health-care domain is a challenge in itself. Though, there are few publicly available repositories, there are certain issues to be resolved before using these in our research. For example, MIMIC dataset contains de-identified health data based on ICD-9 codes and Current Procedural Terminology (CPT) codes. As our research is focused on assigning ICD-10-AM and ACHI codes to clinical records, there is a need of mapping between ICD-9 to ICD-10 and vice-versa and ICD-10-CM to ICD-10-AM.

There are some existing look-up, translators, or mapping tools, which will translate ICD-9 codes into ICD-10 codes and vice versa (Butler, 2007). Therefore, we will explore and use the existing mapping tools to convert ICD-9 to ICD-10 codes, ICD-10 to ICD-10-AM codes or another classification system in order to train the model that is not annotated using ICD-10-AM and ACHI codes.

What sort of a distributed knowledge-based system would support the assigning clinical codes?

The majority of studies have used ML, hybrid, and deep learning approaches for clinical text classification. There are two main challenges that one has to face while doing research in health-care domain. First, to train the model when data is scarce. The ML based algorithms for classification and automated ICD code assignment are characterised by many limitations. For example, knowledge acquisition bottleneck, in which ML algorithms require a large number of annotated data for constructing an accurate classification model. Therefore, many believe that the quality of ML based algorithms highly depended on data rather than algorithms (Mujtaba et al., 2019). Even after a great efforts, researchers are able to collect millions of data, there is still a possibility that the occurrence of some diseases and interventions will not be enough to train the model properly and give correct codes. However, when data is insufficient, transfer learning or fine tuning are other possible options to look into (Singh, 2018). Secondly, it is difficult and expensive to assign ground truth codes (or label) to the clinical records. Although, the above mentioned approaches are capable of providing good results, but these approaches require annotated data in order to train the model. The labelling process requires human expert to assign labels (or ICD codes) to each clinical record. For example, the study (Kaur and Ginige, 2018) contains 190 de-identified discharge summaries belonging to diseases and interventions of respiratory and digestive system. The discharge summaries were in the hand written form, which were later converted into digital form and assigned ground truth codes with the help of a human expert. Thus, a considerable amount of effort was exerted in preparing the training data.

Therefore, in our research we aim to develop a distributed knowledge-base system where humans (clinical coders) and machines can work together to overcome the above mentioned challenges. If machine is unable to predict the correct ICD code for a given disease or intervention then humans input will be considered. Moreover, the human coder can also verify the codes assigned by machine.

3.3 Baseline Methods

There are three main approaches for automated ICD codes assignment: (1) machine learning; (2) hybrid (combining machine learning and rule-base); and (3) deep learning. Deep learning models have demonstrated successful results in many NLP tasks such as language translation (Zhang and Zong, 2015), image captioning (LeCun et al., 2015) and sentiment analysis (Socher et al., 2013). We will work on different ML and deep learning models including LSTM, CNN-RNN, and GRU. Pre-processing will be done using standard pipeline and convert the assigned labels based on Australian classification system using existing mapping tools. Feature extraction will be done using non-sequential and sequential features followed by training and testing of the model using baseline models and deep learning models.

4 Conclusion

In this research proposal, we aim to develop a knowledge-based clinical auto-coding system that uses computerised algorithms to assign ICD-10-AM, ACHI, ICD-11, and ICHI codes to an episode of care of a patient while adhering coding guidelines. Further, we will explore how ML models can be trained with limited dataset, mapping between different classification systems, and avoiding labelling efforts.

Acknowledgments

I would like to thank my supervisors, Dr. Jeewani Anupama Ginige, Dr. Oliver Obst and Vera Dimitropoulos for their feedback that greatly improved the paper. This research is supported by Western Sydney University Postgraduate Research Scholarship.

References

N. S. Altman. 1992. An introduction to kernel and nearest-neighbor nonparametric regression. *The American Statistician*, 46(3):175–185.

M.R. Amini, N. Usunier, and C. Goutte. 2009. Learning from multiple partially observed views - an application to multilingual text categorization. pages 28–36, Vancouver, BC. Conference of 23rd Annual Conference on Neural Information Processing Systems, NIPS 2009 ; Conference Date: 7 December 2009 - 10 December 2009.

Damla Arifoğlu, Onur Deniz, Kemal Aleçakır, and Meltem Yöndem. 2014. Codemagic: Semiautomatic assignment of ICD-10-AM codes to patient records. In *Information Sciences and Systems 2014*, pages 259–268. Springer International Publishing.

Steven Bird, Ewan Klein, and Edward Loper. 2009. *Natural Language Processing with Python: analyzing text with the natural language toolkit.* " O'Reilly Media, Inc.".

Rhonda R Butler. 2007. ICD-10 general equivalence mappings: Bridging the translation gap from ICD-9. *Journal of American Health Information Management Association*, 78(9):84–86.

Kerryn Butler-Henderson. 2017. Health information management 2025. what is required to create a sustainable profession in the face of digital transformation?

Tianrun Cai, Andreas A. Giannopoulos, Sheng Yu, Tatiana Kelil, Beth Ripley, Kanako K. Kumamaru, Frank J. Rybicki, and Dimitrios Mitsouras. 2016. Natural language processing technologies in radiology research and clinical applications. *RadioGraphics*, 36(1):176–191. PMID: 26761536.

Wendy W. Chapman, Will Bridewell, Paul Hanbury, Gregory F. Cooper, and Bruce G. Buchanan. 2001. A Simple Algorithm for Identifying Negated Findings and Diseases in Discharge Summaries. *Journal of Biomedical Informatics*, 34(5):301 – 310.

Maria Teresa Chiaravalloti, Roberto Guarasci, Vincenzo Lagani, Erika Pasceri, and Roberto Trunfio. 2014. A coding support system for the icd-9-cm standard. In *2014 IEEE International Conference on Healthcare Informatics*, pages 71–78.

Australian Consortium for Classification Development. 2017. *Australian Coding Standards for ICD-10-AM and ACHI*. Independent Hospital Pricing Authority.

Corinna Cortes and Vladimir Vapnik. 1995. Support-Vector Networks. *Machine Learning*, 20(3):273–297.

Koby Crammer, Mark Dredze, Kuzman Ganchev, Partha Pratim Talukdar, and Steven Carroll. 2007. Automatic code assignment to medical text. In *Proceedings of the Workshop on BioNLP 2007: Biological, Translational, and Clinical Language Processing*, BioNLP '07, pages 129–136, Stroudsburg, PA, USA. Association for Computational Linguistics.

Megan Cumerlato, Lindy Best, Belinda Saad, and N.S.W.) National Centre for Classification in Health (Sydney. 2010. *Fundamentals of morbidity coding using ICD-10-AM, ACHI, and ACS seventh edition*. Sydney : National Centre for Classification in Health. "June 2010"–T.p.

Y. Deng, M.J. Groll, and K. Denecke. 2015. Rule-based cervical spine defect classification using medical narratives. *Studies in Health Technology and Informatics*, 216:1038. Conference of 15th World Congress on Health and Biomedical Informatics, MEDINFO 2015 ; Conference Date: 19 August 2015-23 August 2015.

Richárd Farkas and György Szarvas. 2008. Automatic construction of rule-based ICD-9-CM coding systems. *BMC Bioinformatics*, 9(3):S10.

F. Jeff Friedlin and Clement J. McDonald. 2008. A Software Tool for Removing Patient Identifying Information from Clinical Documents. *Journal of the American Medical Informatics Association*, 15(5):601–610.

H. Robert Frost, Dean F. Sittig, Victor J. Stevens, and Brian Hazlehurst. 2005. MediClass: A System for Detecting and Classifying Encounter-based Clinical Events in Any Electronic Medical Record. *Journal of the American Medical Informatics Association*, 12(5):517–529.

Ira Goldstein, Anna Arzumtsyan, and Özlem Uzuner. 2007. Three approaches to automatic assignment of icd-9-cm codes to radiology reports. In *AMIA Annual Symposium Proceedings*, volume 2007, page 279. American Medical Informatics Association.

Jenny Hargreaves and Jodee Njeru. 2014. ICD-11: A dynamic classification for the information age.

Trevor Hastie, Robert Tibshirani, and Jerome Friedman. 2009. *Overview of Supervised Learning*, pages 9–41. Springer New York, New York, NY.

National Center for Health Statistics. ICD-10-CM Official Guidelines for Coding and Reporting.

Aron Henriksson, Maria Kvist, Hercules Dalianis, and Martin Duneld. 2015. Identifying adverse drug event information in clinical notes with distributional semantic representations of context. *Journal of Biomedical Informatics*, 57:333 – 349.

Andreas Hotho, Alexander Maedche, and Steffen Staab. 2002. Ontology-based text document clustering. *KI*, 16(4):48–54.

Timothy D. Imler, Justin Morea, Charles Kahi, and Thomas F. Imperiale. 2013. Natural language processing accurately categorizes findings from colonoscopy and pathology reports. *Clinical Gastroenterology and Hepatology*, 11(6):689 – 694.

Abhyuday N Jagannatha and Hong Yu. 2016. Bidirectional RNN for medical event detection in electronic health records. In *Proceedings of the conference. Association for Computational Linguistics. North American Chapter. Meeting*, volume 2016, page 473. NIH Public Access.

Peter B Jensen, Lars J Jensen, and Søren Brunak. 2012. Mining electronic health records: towards better research applications and clinical care. *Nature Reviews Genetics*, 13(6):395.

Sarvnaz Karimi, Xiang Dai, Hamedh Hassanzadeh, and Anthony Nguyen. 2017. Automatic diagnosis coding of radiology reports: A comparison of deep learning and conventional classification methods. In *BioNLP 2017*, pages 328–332. Association for Computational Linguistics.

Rajvir Kaur and Jeewani Anupama Ginige. 2018. Comparative Analysis of Algorithmic Approaches for Auto-Coding with ICD-10-AM and ACHI. *Studies in Health Technology and Informatics*, 252:73–79.

Rajvir Kaur and Jeewani Anupama Ginige. 2019. Analysing effectiveness of multi-label classification in clinical coding. In *Proceedings of the Australasian Computer Science Week Multiconference*, ACSW 2019, pages 24:1–24:9, New York, NY, USA. ACM.

Youngjoong Ko and Jungyun Seo. 2000. Automatic text categorization by unsupervised learning. In *Proceedings of the 18th Conference on Computational Linguistics - Volume 1*, COLING '00, pages 453–459, Stroudsburg, PA, USA. Association for Computational Linguistics.

Bevan Koopman, Guido Zuccon, Anthony Nguyen, Anton Bergheim, and Narelle Grayson. 2015. Automatic ICD-10 classification of cancers from free-text death certificates. *International Journal of Medical Informatics*, 84(11):956 – 965.

Leah S Larkey and W Bruce Croft. 1995. Automatic assignment of ICD-9 codes to discharge summaries. Technical report, Technical report, University of Massachusetts at Amherst, Amherst, MA.

Yann LeCun, Yoshua Bengio, and Geoffrey Hinton. 2015. Deep learning. *Nature*, 521(7553):436.

Hongfang Liu, Kavishwar B Wagholikar, Kathy L MacLaughlin, Michael R Henry, Robert A Greenes, Ronald A Hankey, and Rajeev Chaudhry. 2012. Clinical decision support with automated text processing for cervical cancer screening. *Journal of the American Medical Informatics Association*, 19(5):833–839.

Yuan Luo. 2017. Recurrent neural networks for classifying relations in clinical notes. *Journal of Biomedical Informatics*, 72:85 – 95.

Christopher D. Manning, Prabhakar Raghavan, and Hinrich Schütze. 2008. *Introduction to Information Retrieval*. Cambridge University Press, New York, NY, USA.

Kirsten McKenzie and Sue M Walker. 2003. *The Australian coder workforce 2002: a report of the National Clinical Coder Survey*. National Centre for Classification in Health.

Eneida A. Mendona, Janet Haas, Lyudmila Shagina, Elaine Larson, and Carol Friedman. 2005. Extracting information on pneumonia in infants using natural language processing of radiology reports. *Journal of Biomedical Informatics*, 38(4):314 – 321.

Stphane Meystre and Peter J. Haug. 2006. Natural language processing to extract medical problems from electronic clinical documents: Performance evaluation. *Journal of Biomedical Informatics*, 39(6):589 – 599.

Ghulam Mujtaba, Liyana Shuib, Norisma Idris, Wai Lam Hoo, Ram Gopal Raj, Kamran Khowaja, Khairunisa Shaikh, and Henry Friday Nweke. 2019. Clinical text classification research trends: Systematic literature review and open issues. *Expert Systems with Applications*, 116:494 – 520.

Ghulam Mujtaba, Liyana Shuib, Ram Gopal Raj, Retnagowri Rajandram, and Khairunisa Shaikh. 2018. Prediction of cause of death from forensic autopsy reports using text classification techniques: A comparative study. *Journal of Forensic and Legal Medicine*, 57:41 – 50. Thematic section: Big dataGuest editor: Thomas LefvreThematic section: Health issues in police custodyGuest editors: Patrick Chariot and Steffen Heide.

Hoang Nguyen and Jon Patrick. 2016. Text mining in clinical domain: Dealing with noise. In *Proceedings of the 22Nd ACM SIGKDD International Conference on Knowledge Discovery and Data Mining*, KDD '16, pages 549–558, New York, NY, USA. ACM.

World Health Organisation. 2016. ICD-11 Revision Conference Report.

Sinno Jialin Pan and Qiang Yang. 2010. A survey on transfer learning. *IEEE Transactions on Knowledge and Data Engineering*, 22(10):1345–1359.

John P. Pestian, Chris Brew, Pawel Matykiewicz, DJ Hovermale, Neil Johnson, K. Bretonnel Cohen, and Wlodzislaw Duch. 2007a. A shared task involving multi-label classification of clinical free text. In *Biological, translational, and clinical language processing*, pages 97–104. Association for Computational Linguistics.

John P. Pestian, Christopher Brew, PawelMatykiewicz, D. J. Hovermale, Neil Johnson, K. Bretonnel Cohen, and WDuch. 2007b. A shared task involving multi-label classification of clinical free text. In *Proceedings of the Workshop on BioNLP 2007: Biological, Translational, and Clinical Language Processing*, BioNLP '07, pages 97–104, Stroudsburg, PA, USA. Association for Computational Linguistics.

François Portet, Ehud Reiter, Albert Gatt, Jim Hunter, Somayajulu Sripada, Yvonne Freer, and Cindy Sykes. 2009. Automatic generation of textual summaries from neonatal intensive care data. *Artificial Intelligence*, 173(7-8):789–816. AvImpFact=2.566 estim. in 2012.

Ali S. Raja, Ivan K. Ip, Luciano M. Prevedello, Aaron D. Sodickson, Cameron Farkas, Richard D. Zane, Richard Hanson, Samuel Z. Goldhaber, Ritu R. Gill, and Ramin Khorasani. 2012. Effect of computerized clinical decision support on the use and yield of ct pulmonary angiography in the emergency department. *Radiology*, 262(2):468–474. PMID: 22187633.

Geoffrey M. Reed, Jack Drescher, Richard B. Krueger, Elham Atalla, Susan D. Cochran, Michael B. First, Peggy T. Cohen-Kettenis, Ivn Arango-de Montis, Sharon J. Parish, Sara Cottler, Peer Briken, and Shekhar Saxena. 2016. Disorders related to sexuality and gender identity in the icd-11: revising the icd-10 classification based on current scientific evidence, best clinical practices, and human rights considerations. *World Psychiatry*, 15(3):205–221.

Suong Santos, Gregory Murphy, Kathryn Baxter, and Kerin M Robinson. 2008. Organisational factors affecting the quality of hospital clinical coding. *Health Information Management Journal*, 37(1):25–37.

Sonit Singh. 2018. Pushing the limits of radiology with joint modeling of visual and textual information. In *Proceedings of ACL 2018, Student Research Workshop*, pages 28–36. Association for Computational Linguistics.

Richard Socher, Alex Perelygin, Jean Wu, Jason Chuang, Christopher D. Manning, Andrew Ng, and Christopher Potts. 2013. Recursive deep models for semantic compositionality over a sentiment treebank. In *Proceedings of the 2013 Conference on Empirical Methods in Natural Language Processing*, pages 1631–1642. Association for Computational Linguistics.

Christof Stocker, Leopold-Michael Marzi, Christian Matula, Johannes Schantl, Gottfried Prohaska, Aberto Brabenetz, and Andreas Holzinger. 2014. Enhancing patient safety through human-computer information retrieval on the example of german-speaking surgical reports. In *2014 25th International Workshop on Database and Expert Systems Applications*, pages 216–220.

Michael Subotin and Anthony Davis. 2014. A system for predicting icd-10-pcs codes from electronic health records. In *Proceedings of BioNLP 2014*, pages 59–67, Baltimore, Maryland. Association for Computational Linguistics.

David H. Wolpert. 1996. The lack of a priori distinctions between learning algorithms. *Neural Computation*, 8(7):1341–1390.

Pengtao Xie and Eric Xing. 2018. A neural architecture for automated icd coding. In *Proceedings of the 56th Annual Meeting of the Association for Computational Linguistics (Volume 1: Long Papers)*, pages 1066–1076. Association for Computational Linguistics.

J. Zhang and C. Zong. 2015. Deep neural networks in machine translation: An overview. *IEEE Intelligent Systems*, 30(5):16–25.

Xiaojin Zhu and Andrew B Goldberg. 2009. Introduction to semi-supervised learning. *Synthesis lectures on artificial intelligence and machine learning*, 3(1):1–130.

Robust-to-Noise Models in Natural Language Processing Tasks

Valentin Malykh
Neural Systems and Deep Learning Laboratory, Moscow Institute of Physics and Technology,
Samsung-PDMI Joint AI Center, Steklov Mathematical Institute at St. Petersburg
valentin.malykh@phystech.edu

Abstract

There are a lot of noisy texts surrounding a person in modern life. A traditional approach is to use spelling correction, yet the existing solutions are far from perfect. We propose a robust to noise word embeddings model which outperforms existing commonly used models like fasttext and word2vec in different tasks. In addition, we investigate the noise robustness of current models in different natural language processing tasks. We propose extensions for modern models in three downstream tasks, i.e. text classification, named entity recognition and aspect extraction, these extensions show improvement in noise robustness over existing solutions.

1 Introduction

The rapid growth of the usage of mobile electronic devices has increased the number of user input text issues such as typos. This happens because typing on a small screen and in transport (or while walking) is difficult, and people accidentally hit wrong keys more often than when using a standard keyboard. Spell-checking systems widely used in web services can handle this issue, but they can also make mistakes. These typos are considered to be noise in original text. Such noise is a widely known issue and to mitigate its presence there were developed spelling correcting systems, e.g. (Cucerzan and Brill, 2004). Although spelling correction systems have been developed for decades up to this day, their quality is still far from perfect, e.g. for the Russian language it is 85% (Sorokin, 2017). So we propose a new way to handle noise i.e. to make models themselves robust to noise.

This work is considering the main area of noise robustness in natural language processing and, in particular, in four related subareas which are described in corresponding sections. All the subar-

eas share the same research questions applied to a particular downstream task:

RQ1. Are the existing state of the art models robust to noise?

RQ2. How to make these models more robust to noise?

In order to answer these RQs, we describe the commonly used approaches in a subarea of interest and specify their features which could improve or deteriorate the performance of these models. Then we define a methodology for testing existing models and proposed extensions. The methodology includes the experiment setup with quality measure and datasets on which the experiments should be run.

This work is organized as follows: in Section 2 the research on word embeddings is motivated and proposed, in further sections, i.e. 3, 4, 5, there are propositions to conduct research in the area of text classification, named entity recognition and aspect extraction respectively. In Section 6 we present preliminary conclusions and propose further research directions in the mentioned areas and other NLP areas.

2 Word Embeddings

Any text processing system is now impossible to imagine without word embeddings — vectors encode semantic and syntactic properties of individual words (Arora et al., 2016). However, to use these word vectors user input should be clean (i.e. free of misspellings), because a word vector model trained on clean data will not have misspelled versions of words. There are examples of models trained on noisy data (Li et al., 2017), but this approach does not fully solve the problem, because typos are unpredictable and a corpus cannot contain all possible incorrectly spelled versions of a word. Instead, we suggest that we should make

Proceedings of the ACL 2019, Student Research Workshop, pages 10–16
Florence, Italy, July 28th-August 2nd, 2019. ©2019 Association for Computational Linguistics

algorithms for word vector modelling robust to noise.

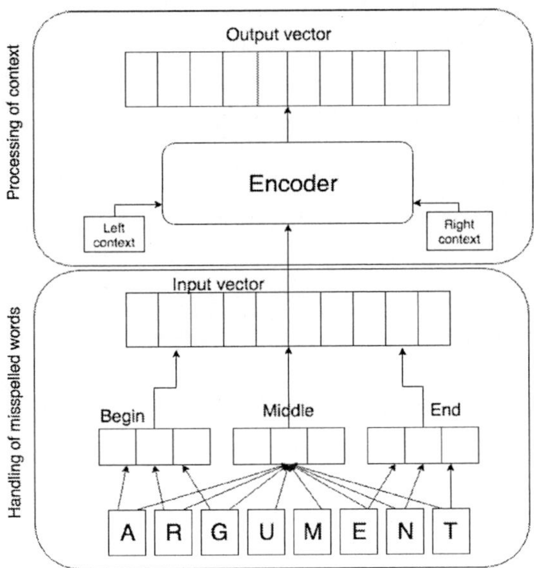

Figure 1: RoVe model architecture.

We suggest a new architecture **RoVe** (Robust Vectors).[1] It is presented on Fig. 1. The main feature of this model is open vocabulary. It encodes words as sequences of symbols. This enables the model to produce embeddings for out-of-vocabulary (OOV) words. The idea as such is not new, many other models use character-level embeddings (Ling et al., 2015) or encode the most common ngrams to assemble unknown words from them (Bojanowski et al., 2016). However, unlike analogous models, RoVe is specifically targeted at typos — it is invariant to swaps of symbols in a word. This property is ensured by the fact that each word is encoded as a bag of characters. At the same time, word prefixes and suffixes are encoded separately, which enables RoVe to produce meaningful embeddings for unseen word forms in morphologically rich languages. Notably, this is done without explicit morphological analysis. This mechanism is depicted on Fig. 2.

Another feature of RoVe is context dependency — in order to generate an embedding for a word one should encode its context (the top part of Fig. 1). The motivation for such architecture is the following. Our intuition is that when processing an OOV word our model should produce an embedding similar to that of some similar word

from the training data. This behaviour is suitable for typos as well as unseen forms of known words. In the latter case we want a word to get an embedding similar to the embedding of its initial form. This process reminds lemmatisation (reduction of a word to its initial form). Lemmatisation is context-dependent since it often needs to resolve homonymy based on word's context. By making RoVe model context-dependent we enable it to do such implicit lemmatisation.

At the same time, it has been shown that embeddings which are generated considering word's context in a particular sentence are more informative and accurate, because a word's immediate context informs a model of the word's grammatical features (Peters et al., 2018). On the other hand, use of context-dependent representations allowed us to eliminate character-level embeddings. As a result, we do not need to train a model that converts a sequence of character-level embeddings to an embedding for a word, as it was done in (Ling et al., 2015).

2.1 Methodology

We suppose to compare RoVe with common word vector tools: word2vec (Mikolov et al., 2013) and fasttext (Bojanowski et al., 2016).

We score the performance of word vectors generated with RoVe and baseline models on three tasks: paraphrase detection, sentiment analysis, identification of text entailment. We consider these tasks to be binary classification ones, so we use ROC AUC measure for model quality evaluation.

For all tasks we suppose to train simple baseline models. This is done deliberately to make sure that the performance is largely defined by the quality of vectors that we use. For all the tasks we will compare word vectors generated by different modifications of RoVe with vectors produced by word2vec and fasttext models.

We presume to conduct the experiments on datasets for three languages: English (analytical language), Russian (synthetic fusional), and Turkish (synthetic agglutinative). Affixes have different structures and purposes in these types of languages, and in our experiments we show that our character-based representation is effective for all of them.

For the above mentioned tasks we are going to use the following corpora: Paraphraser.ru

---

[1]An open-source implementation is available here: `https://gitlab.com/madrugado/robust-w2v`

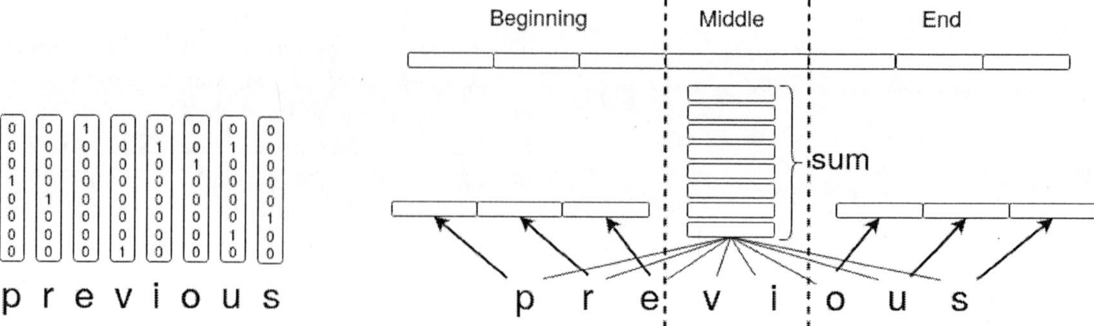

Figure 2: Generation of input embedding for the word *previous*. Left: generation of character-level one-hot vectors, right: generation of BME representation.

	English			Russian		
noise (%)	0	10	20	0	10	20
BASELINES						
word2vec	0.649	0.611	0.554	0.649	0.576	0.524
fasttext	**0.662**	0.615	0.524	0.703	0.625	0.524
RoVe						
stackedLSTM	0.621	0.593	0.586	0.690	0.632	0.584
SRU	0.627	0.590	0.568	0.712	0.680	0.598
biSRU	0.656	**0.621**	**0.598**	**0.721**	**0.699**	**0.621**

Table 1: Results of the sentiment analysis task in terms of ROC AUC.

(Pronoza et al., 2016) for the Russian language paraphrase identification task, Microsoft Research Paraphrase Corpus (Dolan et al., 2004) for the English language paraphrase identification task, Turkish Paraphrase Corpus (Demir et al., 2012) for the Turkish language paraphrase identification task; Russian Twitter Sentiment Corpus (Rubtsova, 2014) for the Russian language sentiment analysis task, Stanford Sentiment Treebank (Socher et al., 2013) for the English language sentiment analysis task; and Stanford Natural Language Inference (Bowman et al., 2015) for the English language natural language inference task.

2.2 Results

Due to lack of space we provide the results only for sentiment analysis task for the Russian and English languages and for natural language inference task for the English language.

There are three variants of the proposed RoVe model listed in Tables 1 and 2, these are ones using different recurrent neural networks for context encoding. The whole results are published in (hidden).

For both mentioned tables the robust word embedding model Rove shows better results for all noise level and both tasks, with the exception of zero noise for English language sentiment analy-

	English		
noise (%)	0	10	20
BASELINES			
word2vec	0.624	0.593	0.574
fasttext	0.642	0.563	0.517
RoVe			
stackedLSTM	0.617	0.590	0.516
SRU	0.627	0.590	0.568
biSRU	**0.651**	**0.621**	**0.598**

Table 2: Results of the task on identification of textual entailment.

sis task for which the fasttext word embeddings are showing better results. The latter could be explained as fasttext has been explicitly trained for this zero noise level, which is unnatural for human generated text.

3 Text Classification

A lot of text classification applications like sentiment analysis or intent recognition are performed on user-generated data, where no correct spelling or grammar may be guaranteed.

Classical text vectorisation approach such as bag of words with one-hot or TF-IDF encoding encounters out-of-vocabulary problem given vast variety of spelling errors. Although there are successful applications to low-noise tasks on common datasets (Bojanowski et al., 2016; Howard and Ruder, 2018), not all models behave well with real-world data like comments or tweets.

3.1 Methodology

We do experiments on two corpora: Airline Twitter Sentiment [2] and Movie Review (Maas et al., 2011), which are marked up for sentiment analysis task.

We conduct three types of experiments: (a) the train- and testsets are spell-checked and artificial noise in inserted; (b) the train- and testsets are not changed (with the above mentioned exception for Russian corpus) and no artificial noise is added; and (c) the trainset is spell-checked and noised, the testset is unchanged.

These experimental setups are meant to demonstrate the robustness of tested architectures to artificial and natural noise.

As baselines we use architectures based on fasttext word embedding model (Bojanowski et al., 2016) and an architecture which follows (Kim et al., 2016). Another baseline, which is purely character-level, will be adopted from the work (Kim, 2014).

3.2 Results

Fig. 3 contains results for 4 models:

- FastText, which is recurrent neural network using fasttext word embeddings,

- CharCNN, which is a character-based convolutional neural network, based on work (Kim, 2014),

- CharCNN-WordRNN - a character-based convolutional neural network for word embeddings with recurrent neural network for entire text processing; it follows (Kim et al., 2016),

- and RoVe, which is a recurrent neural network using robust to noise word embeddings.

One could see in the figure that the model which uses robust word embeddings is more robust to noise itself starting from 0.075 (7.5%) noise level.

4 Named Entity Recognition

The field of named entity recognition (NER) received a lot of attention in past years. This task

is an important part of dialog systems (Béchet, 2011). Nowadays dialog systems become more and more popular. Due to that the number of dialog system users is increased and also many users communicate with such systems in inconvenient environments, like being in transport. This makes a user to be less concentrated during a conversation and thus causes typos and grammatical errors. Considering this we need to pay more attention to NER models robustness to this type of noise.

4.1 Methodology

We conduct three types of experiments: (a) the trainset and testset are not changed and no artificial noise is induced; (b) the artificial noise is inserted into trainset and testset simultaneously; and (c) the trainset is being noised, the testset is unchanged.

These experimental setups are meant to demonstrate the robustness of tested architectures to artificial and natural noise (i.e. typos).

The proposed corpora to use are: English and Russian news corpora, CoNLL'03 (Tjong Kim Sang and De Meulder, 2003) and Persons-1000 (Mozharova and Loukachevitch, 2016) respectively, and French social media corpus CAp'2017 (Lopez et al., 2017).

We investigate variations of the state of the art architecture for Russian (Anh et al., 2017) and English (Lample et al., 2016) languages and apply the same architecture to the French language corpus.

5 Aspect Extraction

Aspect extraction task could provide information to make dialogue systems more engaging for user (Liu et al., 2010).

Therefore, we have decided to study the Attention-Based Aspect Extraction (ABAE) model (He et al., 2017) robustness using artificially generated noise. We propose three extensions for an ABAE model, which are supposedly more noise robust. There are:

- CharEmb - a convolutional neural network over characters in addition to word as a whole embeddings; these two embeddings are concatenated and used in ABAE model;

- FastText - an ABAE model using fasttext word embeddings;

---

[2]Publicly available here: https://www.kaggle.com/crowdflower/twitter-airline-sentimen

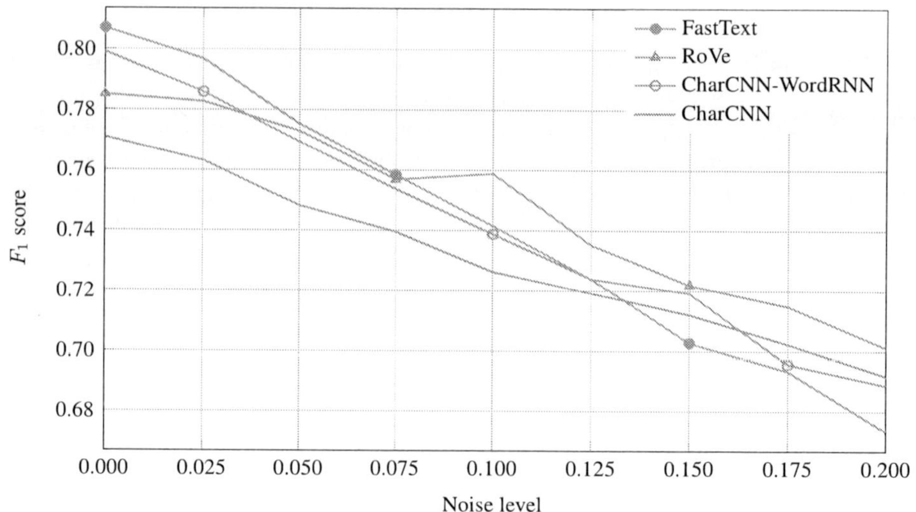

Figure 3: Airline Twitter Sentiment Dataset. Trained on spell-checked and noised data, tested on spell-checked and noised with the same noise level as the training set.

- RoVe - an ABAE model using robust word embeddings.

5.1 Methodology

As the noise model, we took simple character swapping with some probability, i.e. for any given string we go through it character by character and randomly decide if we need to replace this particular letter of the input with some random character.

As a quality measure we take F_1 (weighted by class representativity) score following (He et al., 2017). The authors of the original paper used data from the Citysearch corpus with user reviews on restaurants in New York city originally described in (Ganu et al., 2009). The reviews were labeled by human annotators with a set of categories, like "Food" or "Stuff". The authors used only reviews with exactly one labeled category. So in the end a model predicts a label for a review in the unsupervised way. The label is considered to be the most probable aspect label.

5.2 Results

In Fig. 4 we show both the baseline ABAE model and its extended version proposed in this work. The original model has shown lower results for all lower noise levels, while all extensions show improvement over the original model. The RoVe extensions shows improvement for all noise levels over the original model and the other extensions. The full results for aspect extraction task are published in (Malykh and Khakhulin, 2018).

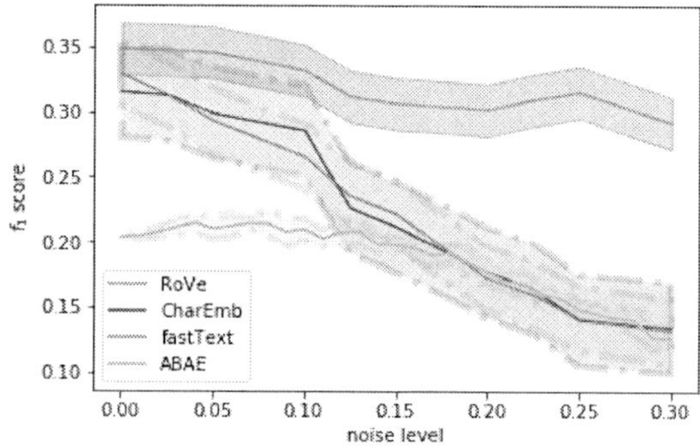

Figure 4: F_1 measure for ABAE model and proposed extensions.

6 Preliminary Results and Future Research Directions

In this work the research in four related subareas is proposed, these are word embeddings, text classification and named entity recognition and aspect extraction.

Preliminary experiments for the robust to noise word embeddings showed that explicit noise handling is better than implicit like in fasttext model. The preliminary results for the word embeddings had been published in (Malykh, 2017). The possible further research in that direction could be an investigation of embeddings for infix morphology languages, like Arabic and Hebrew.

In the downstream tasks experiments show that designed noise robustness improves quality on noisy data. For named entity recognition task the

14

preliminary results are published in (Malykh and Lyalin, 2018), and for aspect extraction task the results are published in (Malykh and Khakhulin, 2018). The further research could be done in three directions. Firstly, all of the tasks could be applied to more languages. Secondly, for classification task corpora with more marked up classes could be used. This task is harder in general case, and there are some available corpora with dozens of classes. And last but not least, thirdly, the suggested methodology could be applied to the other subareas of natural language processing, like Automatic Speech Recognition and Optical Character Recognition, and achieve results in noise robustness improvement there.

References

Thanh L Anh, Mikhail Y Arkhipov, and Mikhail S Burtsev. 2017. Application of a hybrid bi-lstm-crf model to the task of russian named entity recognition. In *Conference on Artificial Intelligence and Natural Language*, pages 91–103. Springer.

Sanjeev Arora, Yuanzhi Li, Yingyu Liang, Tengyu Ma, and Andrej Risteski. 2016. Linear algebraic structure of word senses, with applications to polysemy.

Frédéric Béchet. 2011. Named entity recognition. *Spoken Language Understanding: systems for extracting semantic information from speech*, pages 257–290.

Piotr Bojanowski, Edouard Grave, Armand Joulin, and Tomas Mikolov. 2016. Enriching word vectors with subword information.

Samuel R. Bowman, Gabor Angeli, Christopher Potts, and Christoper Manning. 2015. A large annotated corpus for learning natural language inference.

Silviu Cucerzan and Eric Brill. 2004. Spelling correction as an iterative process that exploits the collective knowledge of web users. In *Proceedings of the 2004 Conference on Empirical Methods in Natural Language Processing*.

Seniz Demir, Ilknur Durgar El-Kahlout, Erdem Unal, and Hamza Kaya. 2012. Turkish paraphrase corpus. In *Proceedings of the Eight International Conference on Language Resources and Evaluation (LREC'12)*, Istanbul, Turkey. European Language Resources Association (ELRA).

Bill Dolan, Chris Quirk, and Chris Brockett. 2004. Unsupervised construction of large paraphrase corpora: Exploiting massively parallel news sources.

Gayatree Ganu, Noemie Elhadad, and Amélie Marian. 2009. Beyond the stars: improving rating predictions using review text content. In *WebDB*, volume 9, pages 1–6. Citeseer.

Ruidan He, Wee Sun Lee, Hwee Tou Ng, and Daniel Dahlmeier. 2017. An unsupervised neural attention model for aspect extraction. In *Proceedings of the 55th Annual Meeting of the Association for Computational Linguistics (Volume 1: Long Papers)*, volume 1, pages 388–397.

Jeremy Howard and Sebastian Ruder. 2018. Fine-tuned language models for text classification. *arXiv preprint arXiv:1801.06146*.

Yoon Kim. 2014. Convolutional neural networks for sentence classification. pages 1746–1751.

Yoon Kim, Yacine Jernite, David Sontag, and Alexander M Rush. 2016. Character-aware neural language models.

Guillaume Lample, Miguel Ballesteros, Sandeep Subramanian, Kazuya Kawakami, and Chris Dyer. 2016. Neural architectures for named entity recognition. In *Proceedings of NAACL-HLT*, pages 260–270.

Quanzhi Li, Sameena Shah, Xiaomo Liu, and Armineh Nourbakhsh. 2017. Data sets: Word embeddings learned from tweets and general data.

Wang Ling, Tiago Luís, Luís Marujo, Ramón Fernández Astudillo, Silvio Amir, Chris Dyer, Alan W. Black, and Isabel Trancoso. 2015. Finding function in form: Compositional character models for open vocabulary word representation. *CoRR*, abs/1508.02096.

Jingjing Liu, Stephanie Seneff, and Victor Zue. 2010. Dialogue-oriented review summary generation for spoken dialogue recommendation systems. In *Human Language Technologies: The 2010 Annual Conference of the North American Chapter of the Association for Computational Linguistics*, pages 64–72. Association for Computational Linguistics.

Cédric Lopez, Ioannis Partalas, Georgios Balikas, Nadia Derbas, Amélie Martin, Coralie Reutenauer, Frédérique Segond, and Massih-Reza Amini. 2017. Cap 2017 challenge: Twitter named entity recognition. *arXiv preprint arXiv:1707.07568*.

Andrew L Maas, Raymond E Daly, Peter T Pham, Dan Huang, Andrew Y Ng, and Christopher Potts. 2011. Learning word vectors for sentiment analysis. In *Proceedings of the 49th annual meeting of the association for computational linguistics: Human language technologies-volume 1*, pages 142–150. Association for Computational Linguistics.

V. Malykh. 2017. Generalizable architecture for robust word vectors tested by noisy paraphrases. In *Supplementary Proceedings of the Sixth International Conference on Analysis of Images, Social Networks and Texts (AIST 2017)*, pages 111–121.

Valentin Malykh and Taras Khakhulin. 2018. Noise robustness in aspect extraction task. In *The Proceedings of the 2018 Ivannikov ISP RAS Open Conference*.

Valentin Malykh and Vladislav Lyalin. 2018. Named entity recognition in noisy domains. In *The Proceedings of the 2018 International Conference on Artificial Intelligence: Applications and Innovations.*

Tomas Mikolov, Ilya Sutskever, Kai Chen, G.s Corrado, and Jeffrey Dean. 2013. Distributed representations of words and phrases and their compositionality. 26.

Valerie Mozharova and Natalia Loukachevitch. 2016. Two-stage approach in russian named entity recognition. In *Intelligence, Social Media and Web (ISMW FRUCT), 2016 International FRUCT Conference on*, pages 1–6. IEEE.

Matthew E. Peters, Mark Neumann, Mohit Iyyer, Matt Gardner, Christopher Clark, Kenton Lee, and Luke Zettlemoyer. 2018. Deep contextualized word representations. *CoRR*, abs/1802.05365.

Ekaterina Pronoza, Elena Yagunova, and Anton Pronoza. 2016. Construction of a russian paraphrase corpus: Unsupervised paraphrase extraction. 573:146–157.

Yuliya Rubtsova. 2014. Automatic term extraction for sentiment classification of dynamically updated text collections into three classes. In *International Conference on Knowledge Engineering and the Semantic Web*, pages 140–149. Springer.

R Socher, A Perelygin, J.Y. Wu, J Chuang, C.D. Manning, A.Y. Ng, and C Potts. 2013. Recursive deep models for semantic compositionality over a sentiment treebank. 1631:1631–1642.

Alexey Sorokin. 2017. Spelling correction for morphologically rich language: a case study of russian. In *Proceedings of the 6th Workshop on Balto-Slavic Natural Language Processing*, pages 45–53.

Erik F Tjong Kim Sang and Fien De Meulder. 2003. Introduction to the conll-2003 shared task: Language-independent named entity recognition. In *Proceedings of the seventh conference on Natural language learning at HLT-NAACL 2003-Volume 4*, pages 142–147. Association for Computational Linguistics.

A computational linguistic study of personal recovery in bipolar disorder

Glorianna Jagfeld
Spectrum Centre for Mental Health Research
Lancaster University
United Kingdom
`g.jagfeld@lancaster.ac.uk`

Abstract

Mental health research can benefit increasingly fruitfully from computational linguistics methods, given the abundant availability of language data in the internet and advances of computational tools. This interdisciplinary project will collect and analyse social media data of individuals diagnosed with bipolar disorder with regard to their recovery experiences. Personal recovery - living a satisfying and contributing life along symptoms of severe mental health issues - so far has only been investigated qualitatively with structured interviews and quantitatively with standardised questionnaires with mainly English-speaking participants in Western countries. Complementary to this evidence, computational linguistic methods allow us to analyse first-person accounts shared online in large quantities, representing unstructured settings and a more heterogeneous, multilingual population, to draw a more complete picture of the aspects and mechanisms of personal recovery in bipolar disorder.

1 Introduction and background

Recent years have witnessed increased performance in many computational linguistics tasks such as syntactic and semantic parsing (Collobert et al., 2011; Zeman et al., 2018), emotion classification (Becker et al., 2017), and sentiment analysis (Barnes et al., 2017, 2018a,b), especially concerning the applicability of such tools to noisy online data. Moreover, the field has made substantial progress in developing multilingual models and extending semantic annotation resources to languages beyond English (Pianta et al., 2002; Boas, 2009; Piao et al., 2016; Boot et al., 2017).

Concurrently, it has been argued for mental health research that it would constitute a 'valuable critical step' (Stuart et al., 2017) to analyse first-hand accounts by individuals with lived experience of severe mental health issues in blog posts, tweets, and discussion forums. Several severe mental health difficulties, e.g., bipolar disorder (BD) and schizophrenia are considered as chronic and clinical recovery, defined as being relapse and symptom free for a sustained period of time (Chengappa et al., 2005), is considered difficult to achieve (Forster, 2014; Heylighen et al., 2014; U.S. Department of Health and Human Services: The National Institute of Mental Health, 2016). Moreover, clinically recovered individuals often do not regain full social and educational/vocational functioning (Strakowski et al., 1998; Tohen et al., 2003). Therefore, research originating from initiatives by people with lived experience of mental health issues has been advocating emphasis on the individual's goals in recovery (Deegan, 1988; Anthony, 1993). This movement gave rise to the concept of personal recovery (Andresen et al., 2011; van Os et al., 2019), loosely defined as a 'way of living a satisfying, hopeful, and contributing life even with limitations caused by illness' (Anthony, 1993). The aspects of personal recovery have been conceptualised in various ways (Young and Ensing, 1999; Mansell et al., 2010; Morrison et al., 2016). According to the frequently used CHIME model (Leamy et al., 2011), its main components are Connectedness, Hope and optimism, Identity, Meaning and purpose, and Empowerment.

Here, we focus on BD, which is characterised by recurring episodes of depressed and elated (hypomanic or manic) mood (Jones et al., 2010; Forster, 2014). Bipolar spectrum disorders were estimated to affect approximately 2% of the UK population (Heylighen et al., 2014) with rates ranging from 0.1%-4.4% across 11 other European, American and Asian countries (Merikangas et al., 2011). Moreover, BD is associated with a

Proceedings of the ACL 2019, Student Research Workshop, pages 17–26
Florence, Italy, July 28th-August 2nd, 2019. ©2019 Association for Computational Linguistics

high risk of suicide (Novick et al., 2010), making its prevention and treatment important tasks for society. BD-specific personal recovery research is motivated by mainly two facts: First, the pole of positive/elevated mood and ongoing mood instability constitute core features of BD and pose special challenges compared to other mental health issues, such as unipolar depression (Jones et al., 2010). Second, unlike for some other severe mental health difficulties, return to normal functioning is achievable given appropriate treatment (Coryell et al., 1998; Tohen et al., 2003; Goldberg and Harrow, 2004).

A substantial body of qualitative and quantitative research has shown the importance of personal recovery for individuals diagnosed with BD (Mansell et al., 2010; Jones et al., 2010, 2012, 2015; Morrison et al., 2016). Qualitative evidence mainly comes from (semi-)structured interviews and focus groups and has been criticised for small numbers of participants (Stuart et al., 2017), lacking complementary quantitative evidence from larger samples (Slade et al., 2012). Some quantitative evidence stems from the standardised bipolar recovery questionnaire (Jones et al., 2012) and a randomised control trial for recovery-focused cognitive-behavioural therapy (Jones et al., 2015). Critically, previous research has taken place only in structured settings.

What is more, the recovery concept emerged from research primarily conducted in English-speaking countries, mainly involving researchers and participants of Western ethnicity. This might have led to a lack of non-Western notions of well-being in the concept, such as those found in indigenous peoples (Slade et al., 2012), limiting its the applicability to a general population. Indeed, the variation in BD prevalence rates from 0.1% in India to 4.4% in the US is striking. It has been shown that culture is an important factor in the diagnosis of BD (Mackin et al., 2006), as well as on the causes attributed to mental health difficulties in general and treatments considered appropriate (Sanches and Jorge, 2004; Chentsova-Dutton et al., 2014). While approaches to mental health classification from texts have long ignored the cultural dimension (Loveys et al., 2018), first studies show that online language of individuals affected by depression or related mental health difficulties differs significantly across cultures (De Choudhury et al., 2017; Loveys et al., 2018).

Hence, it seems timely to take into account the wealth of accounts of mental health difficulties and recovery stories from individuals of diverse ethnic and cultural backgrounds that are available in a multitude of languages on the internet. Corpus and computational linguistic methods are explicitly designed for processing large amounts of linguistic data (Jurafsky and Martin, 2009; O'Keeffe and McCarthy, 2010; McEnery and Hardie, 2011; Rayson, 2015), and as discussed above, recent advances have made it feasible to apply them to noisy user-generated texts from diverse domains, including mental health (Resnik et al., 2014; Benton et al., 2017b). Computer-aided analysis of public social media data enables us to address several shortcomings in the scientific underpinning of personal recovery in BD by overcoming the small sample sizes of lab-collected data and including accounts from a more heterogeneous population.

In sum, our research questions are as follows: (1) How is personal recovery discussed online by individuals meeting criteria for BD? (2) What new insights do we get about personal recovery and factors that facilitate or hinder it? We will investigate these questions in two parts, looking at English-language data by westerners and at multilingual data by individuals of diverse ethnicities.

2 Data

Previous work in computational linguistics and clinical psychology has tended to focus on the detection of mental health issues as classification tasks (Arseniev-Koehler et al., 2018). Datasets have been collected for various conditions including BD using publicly available social-media data from Twitter (Coppersmith et al., 2015) and Reddit (Sekulić et al., 2018; Cohan et al., 2018). Unfortunately, the Twitter dataset is unavailable for further research.[1] In both Reddit datasets, mental health-related content was deliberately removed. This allows the training of classifiers that try to predict the mental health of authors from excerpts that do not explicitly address mental health, yet it renders the data useless for analyses on how mental health is talked about online. Due to this lack of appropriate existing publicly accessible datasets, we will create such resources and make them available to subsequent researchers.

We plan to collect data relevant for BD in gen-

---

[1] Email communication with the first author of Coppersmith et al. (2015).

eral as well as for personal recovery in BD from three sources varying in their available amount versus depth of the accounts we expect to find: 1) Twitter, 2) Reddit (focusing on mental health-related content unlike previous work), 3) blogs authored by affected individuals. Twitter and Reddit users with a BD diagnosis will be identified automatically via self-reported diagnosis statements, such as 'I was diagnosed with BD-I last week'. To do so, we will extend on the diagnosis patterns and terms for BD provided by Cohan et al. (2018)[2]. Implicit consent is assumed from users on these platforms to use their public tweets and posts.[3] Relevant blogs will be manually identified, and their authors will be contacted to obtain informed consent for using their texts.

Since language and culture are important factors in our research questions, we need information on the language of the texts and the country of residence of their authors[3], which is not provided in a structured format in the three data sources. For language identification, Twitter employs an automatic tool (Trampus, 2015), which can be used to filter tweets according to 60 language codes, and there are free, fairly accurate tools such as the Google Compact Language Detector[4], which can be applied to Reddit and blog posts. The location of Twitter users can be automatically inferred from their tweets (Cheng et al., 2010) or the (albeit noisy) location field in their user profiles (Hecht et al., 2011). Only one attempt to classify the location of Reddit users has been published so far (Harrigian, 2018) showing meagre results, indicating that the development of robust location classification approaches on this platform would constitute a valuable contribution.

Some companies collect mental health-related online data and make them available to researchers subject to approval of their internal review boards, e.g., OurDataHelps[5] by Qntfy or the peer-support forum provider 7 Cups[6]. Unlike 'raw' social media data, these datasets have richer user-provided metadata and explicit consent for research usage. On the other hand, less data is available, the process to obtain access might be tedious within the short timeline of a PhD project and it might be im-

possible to share the used portions of the data with other researchers. Therefore, we will follow up the possibilities of obtaining access to these datasets, but in parallel also collect our own datasets to avoid dependence on external data providers.

3 Methodology and Resources

As explained in the introduction, the overarching aim of this project is to investigate in how far information conveyed in social media posts can complement more traditional research methods in clinical psychology to get insights into the recovery experience of individuals with a BD diagnosis. Therefore, we will first conduct a systematic literature review of qualitative evidence to establish a solid base of what is already known about personal recovery experiences in BD for the subsequent social media studies.

Our research questions, which regard the experiences of different populations, lend themselves to several subprojects. First, we will collect and analyse English-language data from westerners. Then, we will address ethnically diverse English-speaking populations and finally multilingual accounts. This has the advantage that we can build data processing and methodological workflows along an increase in complexity of the data collection and analysis throughout the project.

In each project phase, we will employ a mixed-methods approach to combine the advantages of quantitative and qualitative methods (Tashakkori and Teddlie, 1998; Creswell and Plano Clark, 2011), which is established in mental health research (Steckler et al., 1992; Baum, 1995; Sale et al., 2002; Lund, 2012) and specifically recommended to investigate personal recovery (Leonhardt et al., 2017). Quantitative methods are suitable to study observable behaviour such as language and yield more generalisable results by taking into account large samples. However, they fall short of capturing the subjective, idiosyncratic meaning of socially constructed reality, which is important when studying individuals' recovery experience (Russell and Browne, 2005; Mansell et al., 2010; Morrison et al., 2016; Crowe and Inder, 2018). Therefore, we will apply an explanatory sequential research design (Creswell and Plano Clark, 2011), starting with statistical analysis of the full dataset followed by a manual investigation of fewer examples, similar to 'distant reading' (Moretti, 2013) in digital humanities.

---

[2] http://ir.cs.georgetown.edu/data/smhd/
[3] See Section 4 for ethical considerations on this.
[4] https://github.com/CLD2Owners/cld2
[5] https://ourdatahelps.org/
[6] https://7cups.com/

Since previous research mainly employed (semi-)structured interviews and we do not expect to necessarily find the same aspects emphasised in unstructured settings, even less so when looking at a more diverse and non-English speaking population, we will not derive hypotheses from existing recovery models for testing on the online data. Instead, we will start off with exploratory quantitative research using comparative analysis tools such as Wmatrix (Rayson, 2008) to uncover important linguistic features, e.g., on keywords and key concepts that occur with unexpected frequency in our collected datasets relative to reference corpora. The underlying assumption is that keywords and key concepts are indicative of certain aspects of personal recovery, such as those specified in the CHIME model (Leamy et al., 2011), other previous research (Mansell et al., 2010; Morrison et al., 2016; Crowe and Inder, 2018), or novel ones. Comparing online sources with transcripts of structured interviews or subcorpora originating from different cultural backgrounds might uncover aspects that were not prominently represented in the accounts studied in prior research.

A specific challenge will be to narrow down the data to parts relevant for personal recovery, since there is no control over the discussed topics compared to structured interviews. To investigate how individuals discuss personal recovery online and what (potentially unrecorded) aspects they associate with it, without a priori narrowing down the search-space to specific known keywords seems like a chicken-and-egg problem. We propose to address this challenge by an iterative approach similar to the one taken in a corpus linguistic study of cancer metaphors (Semino et al., 2017). Drawing on results from previous qualitative research (Leamy et al., 2011; Morrison et al., 2016), we will compile an initial dictionary of recovery-related terms. Next, we will examine a small portion of the dataset manually, which will be partly randomly sampled and partly selected to contain recovery-related terms. Based on this, we will be able to expand the dictionary and additionally automatically annotate semantic concepts of the identified relevant text passages using a semantic tagging approach such as the UCREL Semantic Analysis System (USAS) (Rayson et al., 2004). Crucially for the multilingual aspect of the project, USAS can tag semantic categories in eight languages (Piao et al., 2016). Then, semantic tagging will be applied to the full corpus to retrieve all text passages mentioning relevant concepts. Furthermore, distributional semantics methods (Lenci, 2008; Turney and Pantel, 2010) can be used to find terms that frequently co-occur with words from our keyword dictionary. Occurrences of the identified keywords or concepts can be quantified in the full corpus to identify the importance of the related personal recovery aspects.

Linguistic Inquiry and Word Count (LIWC) (Pennebaker et al., 2015) is a frequently used tool in social-science text analysis to analyse emotional and cognitive components of texts and derive features for classification models (Cohan et al., 2018; Sekulić et al., 2018; Tackman et al., 2018; Wang and Jurgens, 2018). LIWC counts target words organised in a manually constructed hierarchical dictionary without contextual disambiguation in the texts under analysis and has been psychometrically validated and developed for English exclusively. While translations for several languages exist, e.g., Dutch (Boot et al., 2017), and it is questionable to what extent LIWC concepts can be transferred to other languages and cultures by mere translation. We therefore aim to apply and develop methods that require less manual labour and are applicable to many languages and cultures. One option constitute unsupervised methods, such as topic modelling, which has been applied to explore cultural differences in mental-health related online data already (De Choudhury et al., 2017; Loveys et al., 2018). The Differential Language Analysis ToolKit (DLATK) (Schwartz et al., 2017) facilitates social-scientific language analyses, including tools for preprocessing, such as emoticon-aware tokenisers, filtering according to meta data, and analysis, e.g. via robust topic modelling methods.

Furthermore, emotion and sentiment analysis constitute useful tools to investigate the emotions involved in talking about recovery and identify factors that facilitate or hinder it. There are many annotated datasets to train supervised classifiers (Bostan and Klinger, 2018; Barnes et al., 2017) for these actively researched NLP tasks. Machine learning methods were found to usually outperform rule-based approaches based on look-ups in dictionaries such as LIWC. Again, most annotated resources are English, but state of the art approaches based on multilingual embeddings allow transferring models between languages (Barnes et al., 2018a).

4 Ethical considerations

Ethical considerations are established as essential part in planning mental health research and most research projects undergo approval by an ethics committee. On the contrary, the computational linguistics community has started only recently to consider ethical questions (Hovy and Spruit, 2016; Hovy et al., 2017). Likely, this is because computational linguistics was traditionally concerned with publicly available, impersonal texts such as newspapers or texts published with some temporal distance, which left a distance between the text and author. Conversely, recent social media research often deals with highly personal information of living individuals, who can be directly affected by the outcomes (Hovy and Spruit, 2016).

Hovy and Spruit (2016) discuss issues that can arise when constructing datasets from social media and conducting analyses or developing predictive models based on these data, which we review here in relation to our project: Demographic bias in sampling the data can lead to exclusion of minority groups, resulting in overgeneralisation of models based on these data. As discussed in the introduction, personal recovery research suffers from a bias towards English-speaking Western individuals of white ethnicity. By studying multilingual accounts of ethnically diverse populations we explicitly address the demographic bias of previous research. Topic overexposure is tricky to address, where certain groups are perceived as abnormal when research repeatedly finds that their language is different or more difficult to process. Unlike previous research (Coppersmith et al., 2015; Cohan et al., 2018; Sekulić et al., 2018) our goal is not to reveal particularities in the language of individuals affected by mental health problems. Instead, we will compare accounts of individuals with BD from different settings (structured interviews versus informal online discourse) and of different backgrounds. While the latter bears the risk to overexpose certain minority groups, we will pay special attention to this in the dissemination of our results.

Lastly, most research, even when conducted with the best intentions, suffers from the dual-use problem (Jonas, 1984), in that it can be misused or have consequences that affect people's life nega-

tively. For this reason, we refrain from publishing mental health classification methods, which could be used, for example, by health insurance companies for the risk assessment of applicants based on their social media profiles.

If and how informed consent needs to be obtained for research on social media data is a debated issue (Eysenbach and Till, 2001; Beninger et al., 2014; Paul and Dredze, 2017), mainly because it is not straightforward to determine if posts are made in a public or private context. From a legal point of view, the privacy policies of Twitter[7] and Reddit[8], explicitly allow analysis of the user contents by third party, but it is unclear to what extent users are aware of this when posting to these platforms (Ahmed et al., 2017). However, in practice it is often infeasible to seek retrospective consent from hundreds or thousands of social media users. According to current ethical guidelines for social media research (Benton et al., 2017a; Williams et al., 2017) and practice in comparable research projects (O'Dea et al., 2015; Ahmed et al., 2017), it is regarded as acceptable to waive explicit consent if the anonymity of the users is preserved. Therefore, we will not ask the account holders of Twitter and Reddit posts included in our datasets for their consent.

Benton et al. (2017a) formulate guidelines for ethical social media health research that pertain especially to data collection and sharing. In line with these, we will only share anonymised and paraphrased excerpts from the texts, as it is often possible to recover a user name via a web search for the verbatim text of a post. However, we will make the original texts available as datasets to subsequent research under a data usage agreement. Since the (automatic) annotation of demographic variables in parts of our dataset constitutes especially sensitive information on minority status in conjunction with mental health, we will only share these annotations with researchers that demonstrate a genuine need for them, i.e. to verify our results or to investigate certain research questions.

Another important question is in which situations of encountering content indicative of a risk of self-harm or harm to others it would be appro-

---

[7]https://cdn.cms-twdigitalassets.com/content/dam/legal-twitter/site-assets/privacy-policy-new/Privacy-Policy-Terms-of-Service_EN.pdf

[8]www.redditinc.com/policies/privacy-policy

priate or even required by duty of care for the research team to pass on information to authorities. Surprisingly, we could only find two mentions of this issue in social media research (O'Dea et al., 2015; Young and Garett, 2018). Acknowledging that suicidal ideation fluctuates (Prinstein et al., 2008), we accord with the ethical review board's requirement in O'Dea et al. (2015) to only analyse content posted at least three months ago. If the research team, which includes clinical psychologists, still perceives users at risk we will make use of the reporting facilities of Twitter and Reddit.

As a central component we consider the involvement of individuals with lived experience in our project, an aspect which is missing in the discussion of ethical social media health research so far. The proposal has been presented to an advisory board of individuals with a BD diagnosis and was received positively. The advisory board will be consulted at several stages of the project to inform the research design, analysis, and publication of results. We believe that board members can help to address several of the raised ethical problems, e.g., shaping the research questions to avoid feeding into existing biases or overexposing certain groups and highlighting potentially harmful interpretations and uses of our results.

5   Impact and conclusion

The importance of the recovery concept in the design of mental health services has recently been prominently reinforced, suggesting recovery-oriented social enterprises as key component of the integrated service (van Os et al., 2019). We think that a recovery approach as leading principle for national or global health service strategies, should be informed by voices of individuals as diverse as those it is supposed to serve. Therefore, we expect the proposed investigations of views on recovery by previously under-researched ethnic, language, and cultural groups to yield valuable insights on the appropriateness of the recovery approach for a wider population. The datasets collected in this project can serve as useful resources for future research. More generally, our social-media data-driven approach could be applied to investigate other areas of mental health if it proves successful in leading to relevant new insights.

Finally, this project is an interdisciplinary endeavour, combining clinical psychology, input from individuals with lived experience of BD, and computational linguistics. While this comes with the challenges of cross-disciplinary research, it has the potential to apply and develop state-of-the-art NLP methods in a way that is psychologically and ethically sound as well as informed and approved by affected people to increase our knowledge of severe mental illnesses such as BD.

Acknowledgments

I would like to thank my supervisors Steven Jones, Fiona Lobban, and Paul Rayson for their guidance in this project. My heartfelt thanks go also to Chris Lodge, service user researcher at the Spectrum Centre, and the members of the advisory panel he coordinates that offer feedback on this project based on their lived experience of BD. Further, I would like to thank Masoud Rouhizadeh for his helpful comments during pre-submission mentoring and the anonymous reviewers. This project is funded by the Faculty of Health and Medicine at Lancaster University as part of a doctoral scholarship.

References

Wasim Ahmed, Peter A. Bath, and Gianluca Demartini. 2017. Using Twitter as a data source: an overview of ethical, legal and methodological challenges. In Kandy Woodfield, editor, *The Ethics of Online Research*, pages 79–107. Emerald Books.

Retta Andresen, Peter Caputi, and Lindsay G Oades. 2011. *Psychological Recovery: Beyond Mental Illness*. John Wiley & Sons, Ltd, Chichester, West Sussex.

William A. Anthony. 1993. Recovery from mental illness: the guiding vision of the mental health system in the 1990s. *Psychosocial Rehabilitation Journal*, 16(4):11–23.

Alina Arseniev-Koehler, Sharon Mozgai, and Stefan Scherer. 2018. What type of happiness are you looking for? - A closer look at detecting mental health from language. In *Proceedings of the Fifth Workshop on Computational Linguistics and Clinical Psychology: From Keyboard to Clinic*, pages 1–12.

Jeremy Barnes, Roman Klinger, and Sabine Schulte im Walde. 2017. Assessing State-of-the-Art Sentiment Models on State-of-the-Art Sentiment Datasets. In *Proceedings of the 8th Workshop on Computational Approaches to Subjectivity, Sentiment and Social Media Analysis*, pages 2–12.

Jeremy Barnes, Roman Klinger, and Sabine Schulte im Walde. 2018a. Bilingual Sentiment Embeddings:

Joint Projection of Sentiment Across Languages. In *Proceedings of the 56th Annual Meeting of the Association for Computational Linguistics (ACL)*, pages 2483–2493, Melbourne.

Jeremy Barnes, Roman Klinger, and Sabine Schulte im Walde. 2018b. Projecting Embeddings for Domain Adaptation: Joint Modeling of Sentiment Analysis in Diverse Domains. In *Proceedings of the 27th International Conference on Computational Linguistics*, pages 818–830.

Frances Baum. 1995. Researching public health: Behind the qualitative-quantitative methodological debate. *Social Science and Medicine*, 40(4):459–468.

Karin Becker, Viviane P. Moreira, and Aline G. L. dos Santos. 2017. Multilingual emotion classification using supervised learning: comparative experiments. *Information Processing and Management*, 53(3):684–704.

Kelsey Beninger, Alexandra Fry, Natalie Jago, Hayley Lepps, Laura Nass, and Hannah Silvester. 2014. Research using Social Media; Users' Views.

Adrian Benton, Glen Coppersmith, and Mark Dredze. 2017a. Ethical Research Protocols for Social Media Health Research. *Proceedings of the First Workshop on Ethics in Natural Language Processing*, page 94102.

Adrian Benton, Margaret Mitchell, and Dirk Hovy. 2017b. Multi-Task Learning for Mental Health using Social Media Text. In *Proceedings of the 15th Conference of the European Chapter of the Association for Computational Linguistics (EACL)*, volume 1, pages 152–162.

Hans C. Boas, editor. 2009. *Multilingual FrameNets in Computational Lexicography: Methods and Applications*. Mouton de Gruyter, Berlin.

Peter Boot, Hanna Zijlstra, and Rinie Geenen. 2017. The Dutch translation of the Linguistic Inquiry and Word Count (LIWC) 2007 dictionary. *Dutch Journal of Applied Linguistics*, 6(1):65 – 76.

Laura-Ana-Maria Ana Maria Bostan and Roman Klinger. 2018. An Analysis of Annotated Corpora for Emotion Classification in Text. In *Proceedings of the 27th International Conference on Computational Linguistics*, pages 2104–2119. Association for Computational Linguistics.

Zhiyuan Cheng, James Caverlee, and Kyumin Lee. 2010. You are where you tweet: A content-based approach to geo-locating Twitter users. *Proceedings of the 19th ACM International Conference on Information and Knowledge Management*, pages 759–768.

K. N. Roy Chengappa, John Hennen, Ross J. Baldessarini, David J. Kupfer, Lakshmi N. Yatham, Samuel Gershon, Robert W. Baker, and Mauricio Tohen. 2005. Recovery and functional outcomes following olanzapine treatment for bipolar I mania. *Bipolar Disorders*, 7(1):68–76.

Yulia E. Chentsova-Dutton, Andrew G. Ryder, and Jeanne Tsai. 2014. Understanding depression across cultural contexts. In Ian H. Gotlib and Constance L. Hammen, editors, *Handbook of Depression*, pages 337–354. Guilford Press.

Arman Cohan, Bart Desmet, Sean Macavaney, Andrew Yates, Luca Soldaini, Sean Macavaney, and Nazli Goharian. 2018. SMHD: A Large-Scale Resource for Exploring Online Language Usage for Multiple Mental Health Conditions. In *Proceedings of the 27th International Conference on Computational Linguistics (COLING)*, pages 1485–1497, Santa Fe. Association for Computational Linguistics.

Ronan Collobert, Jason Weston, Lon Bottou, Michael Karlen, Koray Kavukcuoglu, and Pavel Kuksa. 2011. Natural language processing (almost) from scratch. *Journal of Machine Learning Research*, 12:2493–2537.

Glen Coppersmith, Mark Dredze, Craig Harman, and Kristy Hollingshead. 2015. From ADHD to SAD: Analyzing the Language of Mental Health on Twitter through Self-Reported Diagnoses. In *Conference of the North American Chapter of the Association for Computational Linguistics Human Language Technologies (NAACL)*, pages 1–10.

William Coryell, Carolyn Turvey, Jean Endicott, Andrew C. Leon, Timothy Mueller, David Solomon, and Martin Keller. 1998. Bipolar I affective disorder: Predictors of outcome after 15 years. *Journal of Affective Disorders*, 50(2-3):109–116.

John W. Creswell and Vicki L. Plano Clark. 2011. *Designing and Conducting Mixed Methods Research*. SAGE Publications.

Marie Crowe and Maree Inder. 2018. Staying well with bipolar disorder: A qualitative analysis of five-year follow-up interviews with young people. *Journal of Psychiatric and Mental Health Nursing*, 25(4):236–244.

Munmun De Choudhury, Tomaz Logar, Sanket S. Sharma, Wouter Eekhout, and Ren Clausen Nielsen. 2017. Gender and Cross-Cultural Differences in Social Media Disclosures of Mental Illness. In *Proceedings of the 2017 ACM Conference on Computer Supported Cooperative Work and Social Computing*, pages 353–369.

Patricia E. Deegan. 1988. Recovery: The lived experience of rehabilitation. *Psychosocial Rehabilitation Journal*, 11(4):11–19.

Gunther Eysenbach and James E. Till. 2001. Ethical issues in qualitative research on internet communities. *BMJ*, 323(7055):1103–1105.

Peter Forster. 2014. Bipolar Disorder. *Encyclopedia of the Neurological Sciences*, pages 420–424.

Joseph F. Goldberg and Martin Harrow. 2004. Consistency of remission and outcome in bipolar and unipolar mood disorders: A 10-year prospective follow-up. *Journal of Affective Disorders*, 81(2):123–131.

Keith Harrigian. 2018. Geocoding without geotags: a text-based approach for reddit. In *Proceedings of the 2018 EMNLP Workshop W-NUT: The 4th Workshop on Noisy User-generated Text*, pages 17–27.

Brent Hecht, Lichan Hong, Bongwon Suh, and Ed H. Chi. 2011. Tweets from Justin Bieber's heart: the dynamics of the location field in user profiles. In *Proceedings of the SIGCHI Conference on Human Factors in Computing Systems*, pages 237–246.

Ann Heylighen, Herman Neuckermans, Yoko Akazawa-Ogawa, Mototada Shichiri, Keiko Nishio, Yasukazu Yoshida, Etsuo Niki, Yoshihisa Hagihara, R. C. Dempsey, P. A. Gooding, Steven Huntley Jones, Nadia Akers, Jayne Eaton, Elizabeth Tyler, Amanda Gatherer, Alison Brabban, Rita Marie Long, Anne Fiona Lobban, Raya A. Jones, Kallia Apazoglou, Anne-Lise Küng, Paolo Cordera, Jean-Michel Aubry, Alexandre Dayer, Patrik Vuilleumier, Camille Piguet, Russell S.J., Prof Steven Jones, Anne Cooke, Anne Cooke, Karin Falk, I. Marshal, Steven Huntley Jones, Gina Smith, Lee D Mulligan, Fiona Lobban, Heather Law, Graham Dunn, Mary Welford, James Kelly, John Mulligan, Anthony P Morrison, Elizabeth Tyler, Anne Fiona Lobban, Chris Sutton, Colin Depp, Sheri L Johnson, Ken Laidlaw, Steven Huntley Jones, Greg Murray, Nuwan D Leitan, Neil Thomas, Erin E Michalak, Sheri L Johnson, Steven Huntley Jones, Tania Perich, Lesley Berk, Michael Berk, Timothy H. Monk, Joseph F. Flaherty, Ellen Frank, Kathleen Hoskinson, David J. Kupfer, Ailbhe Spillane, Karen Matvienko-Sikar, Celine Larkin, Paul Corcoran, and Ella Arensman. 2014. *Bipolar disorder: assessment and management*, volume 7. National Institute for Health and Care Excellence.

Dirk Hovy, Shannon Spruit, Margaret Mitchell, Emily M Bender, Michael Strube, and Hanna Wallach. 2017. *Proceedings of the First ACL Workshop on Ethics in Natural Language Processing*. Association for Computational Linguistics.

Dirk Hovy and Shannon L. Spruit. 2016. The Social Impact of Natural Language Processing. In *Proceedings of the 54th Annual Meeting of the Association for Computational Linguistics (ACL)*, pages 591–598.

Hans Jonas. 1984. *The Imperative of Responsibility: Foundations of an Ethics for the Technological Age*. University of Chicago Press, Chicago.

Steven Jones, Fiona Lobban, and Anne Cook. 2010. *Understanding Bipolar Disorder - Why some people experience extreme mood states and what can help*. British Psychological Society.

Steven Jones, Lee D. Mulligan, Sally Higginson, Graham Dunn, and Anthony P Morrison. 2012. The bipolar recovery questionnaire: psychometric properties of a quantitative measure of recovery experiences in bipolar disorder. *Journal of Affective Disorders*, 147(1-3):34–43.

Steven H. Jones, Gina Smith, Lee D. Mulligan, Fiona Lobban, Heather Law, Graham Dunn, Mary Welford, James Kelly, John Mulligan, and Anthony P. Morrison. 2015. Recovery-focused cognitive-behavioural therapy for recent-onset bipolar disorder: randomised controlled pilot trial. *British Journal of Psychiatry*, 206(1):58–66.

Daniel Jurafsky and James H. Martin. 2009. *Speech and Language Processing (2nd Edition)*. Prentice-Hall, Inc., Upper Saddle River, USA.

Mary Leamy, Victoria Bird, Clair Le Boutillier, Julie Williams, and Mike Slade. 2011. Conceptual framework for personal recovery in mental health: Systematic review and narrative synthesis. *British Journal of Psychiatry*, 199(6):445–452.

Alessandro Lenci. 2008. Distributional semantics in linguistic and cognitive research. *Italian Journal of Linguistics*, 20(1):1–31.

Bethany L. Leonhardt, Kelsey Huling, Jay A. Hamm, David Roe, Ilanit Hasson-Ohayon, Hamish J. McLeod, and Paul H. Lysaker. 2017. Recovery and serious mental illness: a review of current clinical and research paradigms and future directions. *Expert Review of Neurotherapeutics*, 17(11):1117–1130.

Kate Loveys, Jonathan Torrez, Alex Fine, Glen Moriarty, and Glen Coppersmith. 2018. Cross-cultural differences in language markers of depression online. In *Proceedings of the Fifth Workshop on Computational Linguistics and Clinical Psychology: From Keyboard to Clinic*, pages 78–87.

Thorleif Lund. 2012. Combining Qualitative and Quantitative Approaches: Some Arguments for Mixed Methods Research. *Scandinavian Journal of Educational Research*, 56(2):155–165.

Paul Mackin, Steven D. Targum, Amir Kalali, Dror Rom, and Allan H. Young. 2006. Culture and assessment of manic symptoms. *British Journal of Psychiatry*, 189(04):379–380.

Warren Mansell, Seth Powell, Rebecca Pedley, Nia Thomas, and Sarah Amelia Jones. 2010. The process of recovery from bipolar I disorder: A qualitative analysis of personal accounts in relation to an integrative cognitive model. *British Journal of Clinical Psychology*, 49(2):193–215.

Tony McEnery and Andrew Hardie. 2011. *Corpus Linguistics: Method, Theory and Practice*. Cambridge Textbooks in Linguistics. Cambridge University Press.

Kathleen R. Merikangas, Robert Jin, Jian-ping He, Ronald C. Kessler, Sing Lee, Nancy A. Sampson, Maria Carmen Viana, Laura Helena Andrade, Chiyi Hu, Elie G. Karam, Maria Ladea, Maria Elena Medina Mora, Mark Oakley Browne, Yutaka Ono, Jose Posada-Villa, Rajesh Sagar, and Zahari Zarkov. 2011. Prevalence and correlates of bipolar spectrum disorder in the world mental health survey initiative. *Archives of general psychiatry*, 68(3):241–251.

Franco Moretti. 2013. *Distant reading*. Verso, London.

Anthony P. Morrison, Heather Law, Christine Barrowclough, Richard P. Bentall, Gillian Haddock, Steven Huntley Jones, Martina Kilbride, Elizabeth Pitt, Nicholas Shryane, Nicholas Tarrier, Mary Welford, and Graham Dunn. 2016. Psychological approaches to understanding and promoting recovery in psychosis and bipolar disorder: a mixed-methods approach. *Programme Grants for Applied Research*, 4(5):1–272.

Danielle M. Novick, Holly A. Swartz, and Ellen Frank. 2010. Suicide attempts in bipolar I and bipolar II disorder: a review and meta-analysis of the evidence. *Bipolar disorders*, 12(1):1–9.

Bridianne O'Dea, Stephen Wan, Philip J. Batterham, Alison L. Calear, Cecile Paris, and Helen Christensen. 2015. Detecting suicidality on Twitter. *Internet Interventions*, 2(2):183–188.

Anne O'Keeffe and Michael McCarthy. 2010. *The Routledge Handbook of Corpus Linguistics*. Routledge Handbooks in Applied Linguistics. Routledge.

Jim van Os, Sinan Guloksuz, Thomas Willem Vijn, Anton Hafkenscheid, and Philippe Delespaul. 2019. The evidence-based group-level symptom-reduction model as the organizing principle for mental health care: time for change? *World Psychiatry*, 18(1):88–96.

Michael J. Paul and Mark Dredze. 2017. Social Monitoring for Public Health. *Synthesis Lectures on Information Concepts, Retrieval, and Services*, 9(5):1–183.

James W. Pennebaker, Ryan L. Boyd, Kayla Jordan, and Kate Blackburn. 2015. The Development and Psychometric Properties of LIWC2015. Technical report, University of Texas at Austin, Austin.

Emanuele Pianta, Luisa Bentivogli, and Christian Girardi. 2002. MultiWordNet: developing an aligned multilingual database. In *Proceedings of the 1st International WordNet Conference*, pages 293–302.

Scott Piao, Paul Rayson, Dawn Archer, Francesca Bianchi, Carmen Dayrell, Ricardo-mara Jiménez, Dawn Knight, Michal Křen, Laura Löfberg, Muhammad Adeel Nawab, Jawad Shafi, Phoey Lee Teh, and Olga Mudraya. 2016. Lexical Coverage Evaluation of Large-scale Multilingual Semantic Lexicons for Twelve Languages. *Tenth International Conference on Language Resources and Evaluation*, pages 2614–2619.

Mitchell J. Prinstein, Matthew K. Nock, Valerie Simon, Julie Wargo Aikins, Charissa S. L. Cheah, and Anthony Spirito. 2008. Longitudinal Trajectories and Predictors of Adolescent Suicidal Ideation and Attempts Following Inpatient Hospitalization. *Journal of Consulting and Clinical Psychology*, 76(1):92–103.

Paul Rayson. 2008. From key words to key semantic domains. *International Journal of Corpus Linguistics*, 13(4):519–549.

Paul Rayson. 2015. Computational tools and methods for corpus compilation and analysis. In Douglas Biber and Randi Reppen, editors, *The Cambridge Handbook of English corpus linguistics*, pages 32–49. Cambridge University Press.

Paul Rayson, Dawn Archer, Scott Piao, and Tony McEnery. 2004. The UCREL semantic analysis system. *Proceedings of the beyond named entity recognition semantic labelling for NLP tasks workshop*, (February 2017):7–12.

Philip Resnik, Rebeca Resnik, and Margaret Mitchell. 2014. *Proceedings of the Workshop on Computational Linguistics and Clinical Psychology From Linguistic Signal to Clinical Reality*. Association for Computational Linguistics.

Sarah J. Russell and Jan L. Browne. 2005. Staying well with bipolar. *Australian & New Zealand Journal of Psychiatry*, 39(3):187–193.

Joanna E. M. Sale, Lynne H. Lohfeld, and Kevin Brazil. 2002. Revisiting the Quantitative-Qualitative Debate: Implications for Mixed-Methods Research. *Quality & Quantity*, 36:43–53.

Marsal Sanches and Miguel Roberto Jorge. 2004. Transcultural aspects of bipolar disorder. *Brazilian Journal of Psychiatry*, 26(3):54–56.

H. Andrew Schwartz, Salvatore Giorgi, Maarten Sap, Patrick Crutchley, Johannes C. Eichstaedt, and Lyle Ungar. 2017. DLATK: Differential Language Analysis ToolKit. In *Proceedings of the 2017 EMNLP System Demonstrations*, pages 55–60.

Ivan Sekulić, Matej Gjurković, and Jan Šnajder. 2018. Not Just Depressed: Bipolar Disorder Prediction on Reddit. In *WASSA@EMNLP*, 2001, pages 72–78, Brussels. Association for Computational Linguistics.

Elena Semino, Zsfia Demjén, Andrew Hardie, Sheila Payne, and Paul Rayson. 2017. *Metaphor, Cancer and the End of Life: A Corpus-Based Study*.

M. Slade, M. Leamy, F. Bacon, M. Janosik, C. Le Boutillier, J. Williams, and V. Bird. 2012. International differences in understanding recovery: Systematic review. *Epidemiology and Psychiatric Sciences*, 21(4):353–364.

Allan Steckler, Kenneth R. McLeroy, Robert M. Goodman, Sheryl T. Bird, and Lauri McCormick. 1992. Toward Integrating Qualitative and Quantitative Methods: An Introduction. *Health Education & Behavior*, 19(1):1–8.

Stephen M. Strakowski, Paul E. Keck, Susan L. McElroy, Scott A. West, Kenji W. Sax, John M. Hawkins, Geri F. Kmetz, Vidya H. Upadhyaya, Karen C. Tugrul, and Michelle L. Bourne. 1998. Twelve-Month Outcome After a First Hospitalization for Affective Psychosis. *Archives of General Psychiatry*, 55(1):49–55.

Simon Robertson Stuart, Louise Tansey, and Ethel Quayle. 2017. What we talk about when we talk about recovery: a systematic review and best-fit framework synthesis of qualitative literature. *Journal of Mental Health*, 26(3):291–304.

Allison M. Tackman, David A. Sbarra, Angela L. Carey, M. Brent Donnellan, Andrea B. Horn, Nicholas S. Holtzman, To'Meisha S. Edwards, James W. Pennebaker, and Matthias R. Mehl. 2018. Depression, Negative Emotionality, and Self-Referential Language: A Multi-Lab, Multi-Measure, and Multi-Language-Task Research Synthesis. *Journal of Personality and Social Psychology*, (March).

Abbas Tashakkori and Charles Teddlie. 1998. *Mixed methodology: Combining qualitative and quantitative approaches*, volume 46. Sage.

Mauricio Tohen, Carlos A. Zarate, John Hennen, Hari Mandir Kaur Khalsa, Stephen M. Strakowski, Priscilla Gebre-Medhin, Paola Salvatore, and Ross J. Baldessarini. 2003. The McLean-Harvard first-episode mania study: Prediction of recovery and first recurrence. *American Journal of Psychiatry*, 160(12):2099–2107.

Mitja Trampus. 2015. Evaluating language identification performance.

Peter D. Turney and Patrick Pantel. 2010. From Frequency to Meaning: Vector Space Models of Semantics. *Journal of Artificial Intelligence Research*, 37:141–188.

U.S. Department of Health and Human Services: The National Institute of Mental Health. 2016. Schizophrenia.

Zijian Wang and David Jurgens. 2018. It's going to be okay: Measuring Access to Support in Online Communities. In *Proceedings of the 2018 Conference on Empirical Methods in Natural Language Processing (EMNLP)*, pages 33–45.

Matthew L. Williams, Pete Burnap, and Luke Sloan. 2017. Towards an Ethical Framework for Publishing Twitter Data in Social Research: Taking into Account Users Views, Online Context and Algorithmic Estimation. *Sociology*, 51(6):1149–1168.

Sean D. Young and Renee Garett. 2018. Ethical issues in addressing social media posts about suicidal intentions during an online study among youth: case study. *Journal of Medical Internet Research*, 20(5):1–5.

Sharon L. Young and David S. Ensing. 1999. Exploring recovery from the perspective of people with psychiatric disabilities. *Psychiatric Rehabilitation Journal*, 22(3):219–231.

Daniel Zeman, Jan Hajic, Martin Popel, Milan Straka, Joakim Nivre, Filip Ginter, Slav Petrov, and Stephan Oepen. 2018. Proceedings of the CoNLL 2018 Shared Task: Multilingual Parsing from Raw Text to Universal Dependencies. In *The SIGNLL Conference on Computational Natural Language Learning*.

Measuring the Value of Linguistics:
A Case Study from St. Lawrence Island Yupik

Emily Chen
University of Illinois Urbana-Champaign / Urbana, IL
`echen41@illinois.edu`

Abstract

The adaptation of neural approaches to NLP is a landmark achievement that has called into question the utility of linguistics in the development of computational systems. This research proposal consequently explores this question in the context of a neural morphological analyzer for a polysynthetic language, St. Lawrence Island Yupik. It asks whether incorporating elements of Yupik linguistics into the implementation of the analyzer can improve performance, both in low-resource settings and in high-resource settings, where rich quantities of data are readily available.

1 Introduction

In the years to come, the advent of neural approaches will undoubtedly stand out as a pivotal point in the history of computational linguistics and natural language processing. The introduction of neural techniques has resulted in system implementations that are performant, but highly dependent on algorithms, statistics, and vast quantities of data. Still we consider this work to belong to computational linguistics, which raises the question: Where does *linguistics* fit in?

Researchers have endeavored to answer this question, though some years before the popularization of neural approaches, demonstrating in particular the value of linguistics to morphological and syntactic parsing (Johnson, 2011; Bender, 2013) as well as machine translation (Raskin, 1987). This question is all the more relevant now in light of machine learning; as such, the research proposed herein is an exploration of the value of linguistics and how its pairing with neural techniques consequently affects system performance.

2 Previous Work

As this question is too broad in scope to explore as is, we instead apply it to a specific context, and ask how the use of linguistics can facilitate the development of a neural morphological analyzer for the language St. Lawrence Island Yupik.

St. Lawrence Island Yupik, hereafter *Yupik*, is an endangered, polysynthetic language of the Bering Strait region that exhibits considerable morphological productivity. Yupik words may possess several derivational suffixes, such as **-pig** in (1), which are responsible for deriving new words from existing ones: **mangteghapig-** '*Yupik house*' from **mangteghagh-** '*house*'. Derivational suffixes are then followed by inflectional suffixes which mark grammatical properties such as case, person, and number.

(1)   **mangteghapiput**
      mangteghagh-   -pig-   -put
      house-   -real-   ABS.PL.1PLPOSS
      '*our Yupik houses*' (Nagai, 2001, p.22)

Analyzing a Yupik word into its constituent morphemes thus poses a challenge given the potential length and morphological complexity of that word, as well as the fact that its morphemes' actual forms may have been altered by the language's morphophonology (see § 4.2), as illustrated in (1). Moreover, since there exist few Yupik texts that could qualify as training data for a neural morphological analyzer, Yupik may also be considered a low-resource language.

Low-resource settings offer initial insights into how linguistics impacts a morphological analyzer's performance. While many neural systems perform well when they are trained on a multitude of data points, studies have shown that utilizing linguistic concepts and incorporating language features can enhance performance in settings where training data is scarce.

With respect to the task of morphological analysis in particular, Moeller et al. (2019) demonstrated that when data was limited to 10,000 to

Proceedings of the ACL 2019, Student Research Workshop, pages 27–33
Florence, Italy, July 28th-August 2nd, 2019. ©2019 Association for Computational Linguistics

30,000 training examples, a neural morphological analyzer for Arapaho verbs that considered linguistically-motivated intermediate forms ultimately outperformed the analyzer that did not.

3 Linguistics in Low-Resource Settings

Given the success of Moeller et al. (2019)'s study, we replicated the morphological parsing or analysis experiments for Yupik nouns, studying the extendability of the claim that incorporating linguistics eases the task of morphological analysis.

3.1 Methodology

3.1.1 Morphological Analysis as Machine Translation

Initial steps toward recreating the Arapaho experiments involved recasting morphological analysis as a sequence-to-sequence machine translation task. The input sequence consists of characters that comprise the surface form, such as **whales**, which is *translated* into an output sequence of characters and morphological tags that comprise the glossed form, such as **whale[PL]**:

$$\text{w h a l e s}$$
$$\downarrow$$
$$\text{w h a l e [PL]}$$

The morphological analysis of the Yupik surface form in (2) can consequently be regarded as the following translation:

$$\text{a g h v e g h e t}$$
$$\downarrow$$
$$\text{a g h v e g h [ABS] [PL]}$$

Observe that the glossed form resembles the interlinear morphological gloss, underlined in (2), which offers a lexical or linguistic description of each individual morpheme.

(2) **aghveghet**
  aghvegh- -et
  <u>whale-</u> <u>-ABS.PL</u>
  '*whales*'

While this methodology of training a machine translation system to translate between surface forms and glossed forms (the *direct strategy*) has resulted in fairly successful morphological analyzers (Micher, 2017; Moeller et al., 2018; Schwartz et al., 2019), Moeller et al. (2019) found that supplementing the training procedure with an intermediate translation step (the *intermediate strategy*) improved the performance of the Arapaho

verb analyzer in instances of data scarcity. This intermediate step utilized the second line seen in (2) that is neglected in the direct strategy, but is regarded as significant by linguists for listing constituent morphemes in their full forms. As a result, in addition to training an analyzer via the direct strategy, Moeller et al. (2019) trained a second analyzer via the intermediate strategy, that performed two sequential translation tasks, from *surface form* (SF) to *intermediate form* (IF), and from intermediate form to *glossed form* (GF).

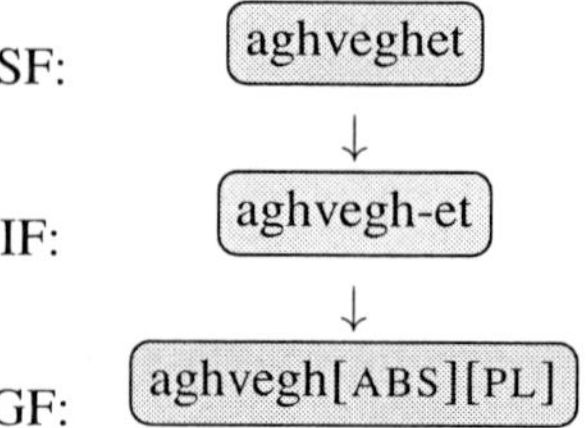

3.1.2 Generating Training Data

The training data in our replicated study consequently consisted of Yupik SF-IF-GF triplets. Like the training sets described in Moeller et al. (2019), the Yupik datasets were generated via the existing finite-state morphological analyzer (Chen and Schwartz, 2018), implemented in the `foma` finite-state toolkit (Hulden, 2009). Since analyzers implemented in `foma` perform both morphological analysis (SF→GF) and generation (GF→SF) and permit access to intermediate forms, the glossed forms were generated first, by pairing a Yupik noun root with a random selection of derivational suffixes, and a nominal case ending, as in (3) (see § 4.1 for a more detailed discussion).

(3) aghvegh-ghllag[ABS][PL]

Each glossed form's intermediate and surface forms were subsequently generated via our Yupik finite-state analyzer (Chen and Schwartz, 2018), resulting in triplets such as the one seen below:

  SF aghveghllaget
  IF aghvegh-ghllag-et
  GF aghvegh-ghllag[ABS][PL]

Each triplet was split into three training sets, consisting of the following parallel data:

1. SF → IF
2. IF → GF
3. SF → GF

The first two sets were used to train the analyzer via the intermediate strategy, and the last set was used to train the analyzer that adhered to the direct strategy. Lastly, whereas Moeller et al. (2019) developed training sets consisting of 14.5K, 18K, 27K, 31.5K, and 36K examples, the Yupik training sets varied from 1K to 20K examples in increments of 5000, to more realistically represent the low-resource setting of Yupik.

3.1.3 Training Parameters

For training, each parallel dataset was tokenized by character and randomly partitioned into a training set, a validation set, and a test set in a 0.8 / 0.1 / 0.1 ratio. The two analyzers trained on each of these datasets were then implemented as bidirectional recurrent encoder-decoder models with attention (Schuster and Paliwal, 1997; Bahdanau et al., 2014) in the Marian Neural Machine Translation framework (Junczys-Dowmunt et al., 2018). We used the default parameters of Marian, described in Sennrich et al. (2016), where the encoder and decoder consisted of one hidden layer each, and the model was trained to convergence via early stopping and holdout cross validation.

3.2 Results

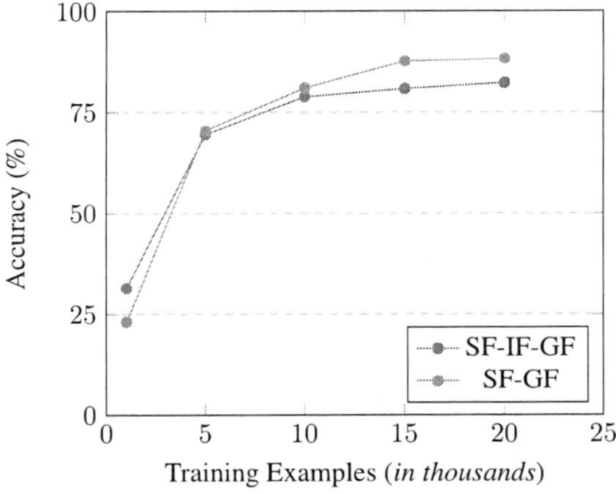

Figure 1: Accuracy scores of the analyzers trained on the intermediate and direct strategies, for all five datasets

The two trained analyzers for each dataset were evaluated on identical held-out test sets in order to compare their performances. As illustrated in Figure 1, it was only in the lowest data setting that the intermediate strategy outperformed the direct strategy with respect to accuracy. In all other instances, the direct strategy emerged as the better training methodology.

We speculate that this disparity in our results and that of Moeller et al. (2019) is due to differences in the morphophonological systems of Arapaho and Yupik and their effects on spelling. Arapaho's morphophonology, in particular, can radically alter the spelling of morphemes in the GF versus SF of a given word, as seen below (Moeller et al., 2019). It is possible that the intermediate step consequently assists the Arapaho analyzer in bridging this orthographical gap.

SF   nonoohobeen
IF   noohoween
GF   [VERB][TA][ANIMATE-OBJECT]
      [AFFIRMATIVE][PRESENT]
      [IC]noohow[1PL-EXCL-SUBJ][2SG-OBJ]

In Yupik, however, there is considerably less variation in the spelling (see § 3.1.2). This may mean the addition of the intermediate step in the Yupik analyzer only creates more room for error, and the direct strategy fares better as a result.

Though the results of our replicated study seem to point to the expendability of linguistics for the task of morphological analysis, calculating the Levenshtein distances between the incorrect outputs of each analyzer and their gold standard outputs offers a novel interpretation.

For every morphological analysis flagged as incorrect, its Levenshtein distance to the correct analysis was calculated, and all such distances were averaged for each analyzer (see Figure 2).

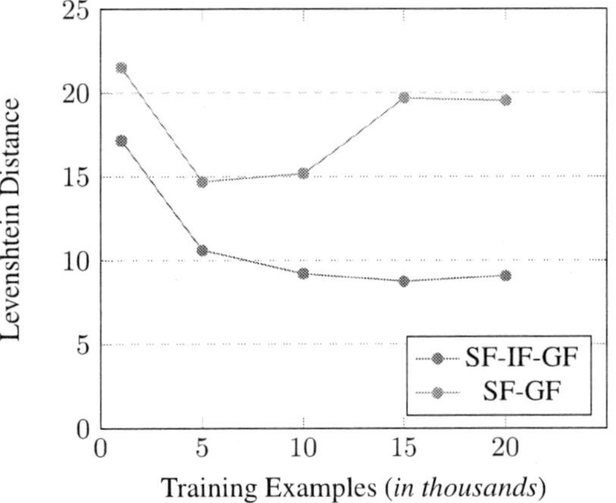

Figure 2: Average Levenshtein distances of the analyzers trained on the intermediate and direct strategies, for all five datasets

(4) **nunivagseghat**
nunivagseghagh-   -t
tundra.vegetation-   -ABS.PL
'*tundra vegetation*' (Nagai, 2001, p.60)

(5) **Sivuqaghhmiinguunga**
Sivuqagh-   -mii-   -ngu-   -u-   -nga
St. Lawrence Island- -resident.of- -to.be.   -INTR.IND-   -1SG
'*I am a St. Lawrence Islander*' (Jacobson, 2001, p.42)

(6) **ilughaghniighunneghtughllagyalghiit**
ilughagh-   -niigh-   -u-   -negh-   -tu-   -ghllag-   -yalghii-   -t
cousin-   -tease-   -do-   -very.many-   -do.habitually-   -very-   -INTR.PTCP_OBL-   -3PL
'*Many cousins used to teach each other a lot*' (Apassingok et al., 1993, p.47)

We found that the average Levenshtein distance for the analyzer trained on the intermediate strategy was statistically less than that of the direct strategy analyzer ($p < 0.0001$), with the exception of the lowest data setting. At 15K and 20K training examples, for instance, the average Levenshtein distances differed by nearly 10 or 11 operations. Furthermore, there did not appear to be a statistically significant difference in the complexity of the analyses being flagged as incorrect; the direct strategy was just as likely as the intermediate strategy to misanalyze simple words with one or two derivational suffixes.

The shorter Levenshtein distances suggest that the analyzers trained on the intermediate strategy consistently returned analyses that better resembled the correct answers as compared to their direct strategy counterparts. Therefore, even though the direct strategy proved superior to the intermediate strategy with respect to general accuracy, the outputs of the intermediate strategy may be more valuable to students of Yupik who are more reliant on the neural analyzer for an initial parse.

4 Linguistics in High-Resource Settings

The replicated study suggests that the accuracy of the analyzer is proportional to the quantity of training examples, especially for the direct strategy, as evidenced in Figure 1. Additional experiments demonstrated, however, that even using the finite-state analyzer to generate as many as 10 million training examples resulted in the accuracy of the neural analyzer plateauing around 88.77% for types and 87.19% for tokens on a blind test set that encompassed 659 types and 796 tokens re-

spectively. This raises the question as to whether it is possible to improve the neural analyzer to competitive accuracy scores above 90% by reinforcing the direct strategy with aspects of Yupik linguistics whose effects have yet to be explored. Thus, the remainder of this proposal introduces these linguistic aspects and suggests means of integrating them into the high-resource implementation of the neural analyzer.

4.1 Integrating Yupik Morphology

One aspect of Yupik that may be useful is its word structure, which typically adheres to the following template, where ( ) denotes optionality:

Root + (Derivational Suffix(es)) + Inflectional Suffix(es) + (Enclitic)

Most roots can be identified as common nouns or verbs and are responsible for the most morphologically complex words in the language, as they are the only roots that can take derivational suffixes. Moreover, all derivational morphology is suffixing in nature, and Yupik words may have anywhere from zero to seven derivational suffixes, with seven being the maximum that has been attested in Yupik literature (de Reuse, 1994). Lastly, there are two types of inflection in Yupik: nominal inflection and verbal inflection.

This word structure consequently results in Yupik words of varying length as well as varying morphological complexity (see (4), (5), and (6)), which in turn constitutes ideal conditions for *curriculum learning*.

Curriculum learning, with respect to machine learning, is a training strategy that "introduces different concepts at different times, exploiting previously learned concepts to ease the learning of new abstractions" (Bengio et al., 2013). As such, "simple" examples are presented in the initial phases of training, with each phase introducing examples that are progressively more complex than the last, until the system has been trained on all phases, that is, the full *curriculum.*

The morphological diversity of Yupik words is naturally suited for curriculum learning, and may positively impact the accuracy of the neural analyzer. One proposed experiment of this paper is to restructure the training dataset, such that the neural analyzer is trained on the simplest Yupik words first, that is, those words consisting of an inflected root with zero derivational suffixes. Each successive phase introduces words with an additional derivational suffix, until the last phase presents the most morphologically complex words attested in the language.

4.2 Integrating Yupik Morphophonology

A second aspect of Yupik linguistics that may be integrated is its complex morphophonological rule system. In particular, the suffixation of derivational and inflectional morphemes in Yupik is conditioned by morphophonological rules that apply at each morpheme boundary and obscure them, rendering a surface form that may be unrecognizable from the glossed form, as in (7):

(7) **kaanneghituq**
    kaate-   -nghite-   -u-   -q
    arrive-   -did.not-   -INTR.IND- -3SG
    '*he/she did not arrive*' (Jacobson, 2001, p.43)

Moreover, each morphophonological rule has been assigned an arbitrary symbol in the Yupik literature (Jacobson, 2001), and so, every derivational and inflectional suffix can be written with all of the rules associated with it, as in (8). Here, @ modifies root-final *-te*, − deletes root-final consonants, $\sim_f$ deletes root-final *-e*, and **(g/t)** designates allomorphs that surface under distinct phonological conditions.

(8) **kaanneghituq**
    kaate-   -@−nghite-   -$\sim_f$(g/t)u- -q
    arrive-   -did.not-   -INTR.IND- -3SG
    '*he/she did not arrive*' (Jacobson, 2001, p.43)

A second proposed experiment will consequently explore the potential insight provided by including these morphophonological symbols in the training examples, studying whether the symbols facilitate learning of the surface form to glossed form mapping or whether these additional characters actually introduce noise. Since minimal pairs do exist to differentiate the phonological conditions under which each symbol applies (see (9)), inclusion of the symbols may in fact assist the system in learning the morphophonological changes that are induced by certain suffixes.

(9)   nuna–ghllak   →   nunaghllak
        qulmesiite–ghllak →   qulmesiiteghllak
        anyagh–ghllak   →   angyaghllak
        sikig–ghllak   →   sikigllak
        kiiw–ghllak   →   kiiwhllagek

Lastly, Yupik morphophonology may also be integrated into a curriculum learning training strategy, where separating the "easy-to-learn" training examples from the "hard-to-learn" training examples can be accomplished in the following ways:

1. Quantifying the number of morphophonological rules associated with a given morpheme, such that the simplest training examples encompass all suffixes with zero symbols attached, such as **-ni** '*the smell of; the odor of; the taste of*' (Badten et al., 2008, p.658). Subsequent phases successively increase this quantity by one.

2. Ranking the morphophonological rules themselves by difficulty, such that the initial phase introduces Yupik suffixes with the rules that have been deemed "easiest to learn", while future phases gradually introduce those that are "harder to learn" [1].

5 Presenting A Holistic Experiment

In summary, the objective of this proposed research is to utilize aspects of the Yupik language to reinforce the direct strategy in high-resource settings, guiding how the training examples are structured and the nature of their content. Previous sections share possible ways in which these linguistic elements of Yupik may be taken into account, but they can in fact be integrated into a single holistic experiment that trains multiple analyzers with varying degrees of linguistic information.

---

[1] A difficulty ranking was elicited from a single student during fieldwork conducted in March 2019, as most Yupik students had not yet mastered the symbols and the rules they represented.

In particular, we propose developing several sets of training data with the following characteristics:

1. Includes the morphophonological symbols (§ 4.2)

2. Ranks the training examples with respect to the number of morphemes (§ 4.1)

3. Ranks the training examples with respect to the number of morphophonological symbols per morpheme (§ 4.2)

4. Ranks the training examples with respect to the learning difficulty of the symbols (§ 4.2)

Each training dataset will incorporate as many or as few of these characteristics as desired, for a total of 15 datasets ($\binom{4}{4} + \binom{4}{3} + \binom{4}{2} + \binom{4}{1}$), and by extension, 15 neural analyzers. We expect any training set that involves morphophonological symbols to improve upon the existing analyzer's ability to distinguish between otherwise homographic suffixes, often a point of confusion. Taking morpheme count into consideration may also improve the analyzer's handling of words with relatively few derivational suffixes ($\sim$0-3), leaving the bulk of errors to instead comprise the most morphologically complex words. Furthermore, by virtue of training on an organized dataset rather than a randomly selected one, we predict that the analyzer will be exposed to a much more equal distribution of Yupik roots and suffixes. It should then be less likely than it is now to invent roots and suffixes that conform morphophonologically, but do not actually exist in the attested lexicon. Lastly, the performance of these analyzers can be compared to the performance of a baseline system, that is simply trained on the direct strategy without any morphophonological symbols or structure to its training data.

6   Conclusion

Moeller et al. (2019) and the replicated study for Yupik presented herein suggest that the use of linguistics can positively impact the performances of neural morphological analyzers, at least in lower resource settings. The proposed research, however, seeks to extend this observation to any data setting, and explore the effects of incorporating varying degrees of linguistic information in the training data, in hopes of shedding light on how best to approach to the task of morphological analysis via machine learning.

Acknowledgments

Portions of this work were funded by NSF Documenting Endangered Languages Grant #BCS 1761680, and a University of Illinois Graduate College *Illinois Distinguished Fellowship*. Special thanks to the Yupik speakers who have shared their language and culture with us.

References

Anders Apassingok, (Iyaaka), Jessie Uglowook, (Ayuqliq), Lorena Koonooka, (Inyiyngaawen), and Edward Tennant, (Tengutkalek), editors. 1993. *Kallagneghet / Drumbeats*. Bering Strait School District, Unalakleet, Alaska.

Linda Womkon Badten, Vera Oovi Kaneshiro, Marie Oovi, and Christopher Koonooka. 2008. *St. Lawrence Island / Siberian Yupik Eskimo Dictionary*. Alaska Native Language Center, University of Alaska Fairbanks.

Dzmitry Bahdanau, Kyunghyun Cho, and Yoshua Bengio. 2014. Neural machine translation by jointly learning to align and translate. *arXiv preprint arXiv:1409.0473*.

Emily M. Bender. 2013. *Linguistic Fundamentals for Natural Language Processing: 100 Essentials from Morphology and Syntax*. Morgan & Claypool Publishers.

Yoshua Bengio, Aaron Courville, and Pascal Vincent. 2013. Representation learning: A review and new perspectives. *IEEE Transactions on Pattern Analysis and Machine Intelligence*, 35(8):1798–1828.

Emily Chen and Lane Schwartz. 2018. A morphological analyzer for St. Lawrence Island / Central Siberian Yupik. In *Proceedings of the 11th Language Resources and Evaluation Conference*, Miyazaki, Japan.

Mans Hulden. 2009. Foma: A finite-state compiler and library. In *Proceedings of the 12th Conference of the European Chapter of the Association for Computational Linguistics*, pages 29–32. Association for Computational Linguistics.

Steven A. Jacobson. 2001. *A Practical Grammar of the St. Lawrence Island / Siberian Yupik Eskimo Language, Preliminary Edition*, 2nd edition. Alaska Native Language Center, Fairbanks, Alaska.

Mark Johnson. 2011. How relevant is linguistics to computational linguistics? *Linguistic Issues in Language Technology*, 6.

Marcin Junczys-Dowmunt, Roman Grundkiewicz, Tomasz Dwojak, Hieu Hoang, Kenneth Heafield, Tom Neckermann, Frank Seide, Ulrich Germann, Alham Fikri Aji, Nikolay Bogoychev, André F. T.

Martins, and Alexandra Birch. 2018. Marian: Fast neural machine translation in C++. In *Proceedings of ACL 2018, System Demonstrations*, pages 116–121, Melbourne, Australia. Association for Computational Linguistics.

Jeffrey Micher. 2017. Improving coverage of an inuktitut morphological analyzer using a segmental recurrent neural network. In *Proceedings of the 2nd Workshop on the Use of Computational Methods in the Study of Endangered Languages*, pages pp. 101–106, Honolulu. Association for Computational Linguistics.

Sarah Moeller, Ghazaleh Kazeminejad, Andrew Cowell, and Mans Hulden. 2018. A neural morphological analyzer for Arapaho verbs learned from a finite state transducer. In *Proceedings of the Workshop on Computational Modeling of Polysynthetic Languages*, Santa Fe, New Mexico. Association for Computational Linguistics.

Sarah Moeller, Ghazaleh Kazeminejad, Andrew Cowell, and Mans Hulden. 2019. Improving low-resource morphological learning with intermediate forms from finite state transducers. *Proceedings of the Workshop on Computational Methods for Endangered Languages: Vol. 1*.

Kayo Nagai. 2001. *Mrs. Della Waghiyi's St. Lawrence Island Yupik Texts with Grammatical Analysis*. Number A2-006 in Endangered Languages of the Pacific Rim. Nakanishi Printing, Kyoto, Japan.

Victor Raskin. 1987. Linguistics and natural language processing. *Machine Translation: Theoretical and Methodological Issues*, pages 42–58.

Willem J. de Reuse. 1994. *Siberian Yupik Eskimo — The Language and Its Contacts with Chukchi*. Studies in Indigenous Languages of the Americas. University of Utah Press, Salt Lake City, Utah.

Mike Schuster and Kuldip K. Paliwal. 1997. Bidirectional recurrent neural networks. *IEEE Transactions on Signal Processing*, 45(11):2673–2681.

Lane Schwartz, Emily Chen, Sylvia Schreiner, and Benjamin Hunt. 2019. Bootstrapping a neural morphological analyzer for St. Lawrence Island Yupik from a finite-state transducer. *Proceedings of the Workshop on Computational Methods for Endangered Languages: Vol. 1*.

Rico Sennrich, Barry Haddow, and Alexandra Birch. 2016. Edinburgh neural machine translation systems for WMT 16. *arXiv preprint arXiv:1606.02891*.

Not All Reviews are Equal:
Towards Addressing Reviewer Biases for Opinion Summarization

Wenyi Tay
RMIT University, Australia
CSIRO Data61, Australia
`wenyi.tay@student.rmit.edu.au`

Abstract

Consumers read online reviews for insights which help them to make decisions. Given the large volumes of reviews, succinct review summaries are important for many applications. Existing research has focused on mining for opinions from only review texts and largely ignores the reviewers. However, reviewers have biases and may write lenient or harsh reviews; they may also have preferences towards some topics over others. Therefore, not all reviews are equal. Ignoring the biases in reviews can generate misleading summaries. We aim for summarization of reviews to include balanced opinions from reviewers of different biases and preferences. We propose to model reviewer biases from their review texts and rating distributions, and learn a *bias-aware opinion representation*. We further devise an approach for *balanced opinion summarization* of reviews using our bias-aware opinion representation.

1 Introduction

Consulting online reviews on products or services is popular among consumers. Opinions in reviews are scrutinised to make an informed decision on which product to buy, what service to use, or which point-of-interest to visit. An opinion is *a view or judgment formed about something, not necessarily based on fact or knowledge.*[1] In the context of online reviews, opinions contain information about the target ("something") and the sentiment ("view or judgment") that is associated with it. There can also be more than one opinion in a review.

Opinion mining research is dedicated to tasks that involves opinions (Pang and Lee, 2008). Current research in opinion mining mostly focuses only on review texts. Some key tasks include sentiment polarity classification (Hu and Liu, 2004b) at levels of words, sentences or documents, and opinion target (e.g., aspect) identification and classification.

Opinion summarization from reviews is an important task related to opinion mining. Early work on opinion summarization aims for structured representation of aspect-sentiment pairs (Hu and Liu, 2004a), where the positive and negative sentiment for each aspect are extracted from review texts and aggregated. Opinion summaries in natural language texts contain richer, detailed description of opinions and are easier for end users to understand. Existing studies mainly use the review texts for summarization.

However, reviewers are unique individuals with beliefs and preferences. Reviewers have preferences towards certain aspects, for example service or cleanliness in hotel reviews (Wang et al., 2010). Different reviewers can have different ways of expressing their opinions (Tang et al., 2015b). Also, some reviewers are lenient in their assessment of products or services, while others are harsher (Lauw et al., 2012). Overall, an opinion is a reflection of the reviewer as it encompasses their *biases*. Thus, not all reviews are equal.

Depending on the application, biases captured in the reviews can be amplified. Hu et al. (2006) suggest that reviewers write reviews when they are extremely satisfied or when they are extremely upset. Existing summarization techniques often treat all reviews equally by selecting salient opinions which may not necessarily be representative for different reviewers. We aim to compensate for biases in reviews, especially for review summarization. We focus on the following research questions:

1. How to model a reviewer's bias? What in-

---

[1] Oxford dictionary

Proceedings of the ACL 2019, Student Research Workshop, pages 34–42
Florence, Italy, July 28th-August 2nd, 2019. ©2019 Association for Computational Linguistics

formation from a reviewer should be used to model a reviewer's bias?

2. How to learn a representation for reviews that captures reviewer biases as well as the opinion?

3. How to generate a balanced opinion summary of reviews written by different reviewers?

Below, we outline the relevant past studies as well as our our research proposal to address these questions.

2   Related Work

Our research is related to two research areas summarized below.

2.1   Opinion and Reviewer Modeling

We identified two studies that jointly model opinions and reviewers. Wang et al. (2010) investigate the problem of decomposing the overall review rating into aspect ratings using a hotel domain dataset. The authors model opinions and reviewers using a generative approach. Reviewers are modeled to reflect their individual emphasis on various aspects. The authors demonstrate that despite giving the same overall review rating, two reviewers can value and rate aspects differently. Meanwhile, Li et al. (2014) present a topic model incorporating reviewer and item information for sentiment analysis. Through probabilistic matrix factorisation of reviewer-item matrix, the latent factors are included in a supervised topic model guided by sentiment labels. The proposed model outperforms baselines in predicting the sentiment label given the review text, reviewer and item on a movie review dataset and a microblog dataset.

Opinion modeling   Opinion can be represented as a aspect-sentiment tuple (Hu and Liu, 2004b). In order to obtain the components of the opinion, aspect identification and sentiment classification are key. Both tasks can be treated separately or combined. For aspect identification, aspects can be identified with the help of experts (Hu and Liu, 2004b; Zhang et al., 2012). The drawback is that it requires input from experts and is specific to a domain. This triggered studies that seek to discover aspects in an unsupervised manner using topic models (Brody and Elhadad, 2010; Moghaddam and Ester, 2010). However, such methods may not always produce interpretable aspects. Subsequent

models are developed to discover interpretable aspects (McAuley and Leskovec, 2013; Titov and McDonald, 2008a,b). To determine opinion polarity, lexicon-based (Hu and Liu, 2004b) and classification (Dave et al., 2003) approaches are often used. However, modeling opinions based on aspects and sentiment separately is not sufficient as the sentiment words can depend on the aspect. More recent models focus on incorporating context to model opinions. Such approaches include joint aspect-sentiment models (Lin and He, 2009), word embeddings (Maas et al., 2011), and neural network models (He et al., 2017).

Alternatively, opinions can potentially be represented as a high-dimensional vector. Opinion representation in this form is a relatively unexplored space. However, in the closely related area of sentiment classification, sentences and documents are represented as vectors to be used as inputs for classification (Conneau et al., 2017; Tang et al., 2015a). The idea is to model a sequence of words as a high-dimensional vector that captures the relationships of words. Similarly, opinions are sequences of sentences, thus it is appropriate to build on the work in sentence and document representation. One of the earliest work is an extension of word2vec (Mikolov et al., 2013) to learn a distributed representation of text (Le and Mikolov, 2014). More recently, pre-trained sentence encoders trained on a large general corpus aim to capture task-invariant properties that can be fine-tuned for downstream tasks (Cer et al., 2018; Conneau et al., 2017; Kiros et al., 2015). On another front, progress in context-aware embeddings (Peters et al., 2018) and pre-trained language models (Devlin et al., 2018; Howard and Ruder, 2018) provide other options to capture context that can be used to obtain sequence representation. All these studies focus on encoding topical semantics of text sequences, where opinions are not explicitly modeled.

Reviewer modeling   Various reviewer characteristics that are modeled include expertise (Liu et al., 2008), reputation (Chen et al., 2011; Shaalan and Zhang, 2016), characteristics of language use (Tang et al., 2015b) and preferences (Zheng et al., 2017). Some of these modelings are achieved using reviewer aggregated statistics and review meta-data. Reviewer expertise is modeled by number of reviews, where larger number of reviews suggests higher expertise (Liu et al., 2008).

Reviewer reputation can be modeled by the number of helpfulness votes and total votes received by the reviewer. A higher ratio of helpfulness votes to total votes suggests a better reputation (Shaalan and Zhang, 2016). In another reviewer reputation model, reviewers are modeled to have domain expertise which corresponds to the product categories that the reviewer reviewed on (Chen et al., 2011).

Review text is also used in reviewer modeling. When predicting ratings from review text, the same sentiment bearing word, for example "good", can mean different sentiment intensity to different reviewers. Tang et al. (2015b) model reviewers' word use by using review text and its corresponding review rating. The resulting reviewer-modified word representations capture variations in reviewers' word use that translates to better rating prediction. Recently, review text is used in addition to review ratings to model users and items together for recommendation (Zheng et al., 2017). Using all the reviews written by the reviewer, the model learns a latent representation of the reviewer. All the above approaches focus on modeling the reviewer. However, our focus is to model opinions, where reviewer information is to be used as a factor during the process of modeling.

For our proposed work, we explore using review text, review ratings and meta data to model reviewers except for helpfulness votes. The helpfulness mechanism is shown to be biased (Liu et al., 2007) and it is still not well understood what we can infer from such votes (Ocampo Diaz and Ng, 2018).

2.2 Opinion Summarization

Opinion summarization aims to capture salient opinions within a collection of document, in our case online reviews. Key challenges in summarizing opinions from a collection of documents are highlighted by Pang and Lee (2008): (1) How to identify documents and parts of the document that are of the same opinion; and (2) How to decide two sentences or texts have the same semantic meaning.

To identify documents and parts of documents of the same opinion, one strategy is to use review ratings as a means to identify similar opinion. However, review ratings have drawbacks such as rating scales differ for different review sources, different assessment criteria among reviewers and reviewers may not share the same opinion despite giving the same overall rating. Review ratings can be adjusted to correct for different assessment criteria by comparing the reviewers' rating behaviour relative to the community rating behaviour (Lauw et al., 2012; Wadbude et al., 2018). The review rating only captures the overall sentiment polarity of the review but not the individual opinions that make up the review. As such, the authors propose to decompose the review rating into aspect ratings according to the review text (Wang et al., 2010). Alternatively, the same opinions can be found by mining aspects and sentiment polarity of each review. Opinion summarization can be seen as a task that builds on top of the opinion mining task.

In deciding if two sentences or texts have the same semantic meaning, the crux lies in the representation of sentences and text. Sentences with the same meaning have good overlap in words (Ganesan et al., 2010). More recent approaches adopt representing sentences or texts as high-dimensional vectors such that similar representations have similar meaning (Le and Mikolov, 2014; Tang et al., 2015a).

The presentation of the opinion summary depends on two considerations, (1) the needs of the reader; and (2) the approach to construct opinion summaries. An opinion summary can be presented in different ways, catering to the different needs of readers. The summary can be on one product (Angelidis and Lapata, 2018; Hu and Liu, 2004a), comparing two products (Sipos and Joachims, 2013) or generate a summary in response to a query (Bonzanini et al., 2013).

There are two main ways of constructing opinion summaries. The extractive opinion summaries are summaries put together by selecting sentences or word segments (Angelidis and Lapata, 2018; Xiong and Litman, 2014). For abstractive summaries, the summary is generated from scratch (Ganesan et al., 2010; Wang et al., 2010).

An early work in opinion summarization proposed an aspect-based summary by organising all opinions according to aspects and their sentiment polarity (Hu and Liu, 2004a). Although there is no textual summarization involved, it inspired future work to focus on including aspects into the generated summary regardless whether it is extractive or abstractive.

For extractive summarization, the objective is to identify salient sentences, at the same time reducing redundancy in the selected sentences. Angelidis and Lapata (2018) score opinion segments according to the aspect and the sentiment polarity. In another work, sentences in the review are scored according to a combination of textual features and latent topics discovered by helpfulness votes (Xiong and Litman, 2014). To reduce redundancy in selected sentences, a greedy algorithm can be applied to add one sentence at a time to form the summary. The greedy algorithm imposes the criterion that the selected sentence must be different from the sentences that are already in the summary (Angelidis and Lapata, 2018). As most extractive summarization techniques are closely coupled with identifying opinions from review texts, the outcome is a set of sentences that are salient in terms of topic coverage, but they may not necessarily be the most representative opinions from reviewers.

On the other hand, abstractive methods first learn to identify the salient opinions before generating a shorter text to reflect the opinion. A graph-based method is proposed by Ganesan et al. (2010) which models a word with its Part-of-Speech (POS) tag as nodes and directed edges to represent the order of words. The edge weights increases when the sequence of words is repeated. The summary is generated by capturing the paths with high edge weights. In a recent study, an encoder-decoder network is employed to generate an abstractive summary of movie reviews (Wang and Ling, 2016).

3 Proposed Methodology

The intuition for our research is that summarization techniques that rely on similarity between opinions to identify salient opinions benefit from clustering similar opinions together and separating different opinions into different clusters. By modeling reviewers with opinions, we aim to capture biases reviewers bring into their opinions. We next elaborate our approaches to modeling user biases, learning *bias-aware opinion representations* and *balanced opinion summarization.*

3.1 Bias-Aware Opinion Representation

To achieve a bias-aware opinion representation, we model opinions and reviewer biases for each sentence in a review. We assume that one sentence contains one opinion (Hu and Liu, 2004b). We envision two possible approaches to learn a bias-aware opinion representation: (1) Two-step process by modeling opinions then adjust the opinions according to reviewer biases; and, (2) Generative approach using text, rating and reviewer information.

Using a two-step process, our main objective is to first learn a representation of the sentences to capture the opinion and this is not a trivial task. Ideally, we expect our opinion representation to exhibit two key characteristics: (1) Similar opinions need to be close in its representation. Using opinions for restaurant reviews as an example, "The soup is rich and creamy" and "Delicious food" are similar opinions but expressed differently; and, (2) Opinion models should be able to tease apart different opinions.

In terms of representing opinions that are similar, a promising technology for us is to make use of pre-trained sentence encoders and language models (Cer et al., 2018; Devlin et al., 2018; Peters et al., 2018; Conneau et al., 2017). These pre-trained models have the advantage of transferring the learned information from large corpora. However, we hypothesize that even with the use of pre-trained models, we are unable to capture sentiment polarity of opinions accurately. It will be similar to the problem that word embeddings are not able to capture sentiment polarity (Maas et al., 2011). One potential direction is to adopt supervised learning using labeled aspect and sentiment polarity labels to improve our opinions representation. But labeled data is expensive to acquire and the granularity of aspect can vary with different aspect annotation guidelines. We propose to use review ratings as supervision signal to improve our opinion representation as ratings can provide a guide to sentiment polarity of opinions.

Towards learning bias-aware opinion representations, we further refine the learnt opinion vectors via modeling reviewer biases from their reviews and ratings. Reviewer biases can influence their star rating and textual expressions. The key to model reviewer biases is learning a distribution of latent factors and sentiment polarity from the reviews and their rating distributions for the reviewer. The refinement will be a user matrix that learn weights corresponding to the opinion representation. This can also be seen as the matrix that represents the biases of reviewers. We plan to explore different ways to learn this matrix. One option to model reviewers' biases is to learn representations from their past reviews such as using techniques in recommender systems literature to model reviewers using review text (Zheng et al., 2017). Alternatively, other associated review information such as review ratings and even metadata of reviews can possibly guide the modeling of biases. We can also explore textual features of review such as the position of opinions may also provide clues to model reviewers.

For our second possible approach, we adopt a generative approach to model opinions as topics using reviewer information as latent factors (Li et al., 2014; Wang et al., 2010). However, the topic model approach is restricted to using words as tokens. The neural topic model (Cao et al., 2015) is a potential technique to utilise word embeddings to improve the learning of topics in the collection of reviews.

3.2 Balanced Opinion Summarization

Summaries generated by the existing summarization techniques are accurate to the collection of reviews it summarizes. They are not a reflection of the true opinion towards the product. In view that opinions capture reviewer biases, we propose a novel way of summarizing opinions.

Instead of the usual summary that is presented as a paragraph of selected sentences, we are inspired by the work of Paul et al. (2010) and Wang et al. (2010), where opposing opinions are contrasted. We propose a *balanced opinion summary*, where we summarize and contrast the opinions of reviewers having different biases. For example, we contrast opinions of a reviewers who are lenient against reviewers who are critical. This allows us to present a balanced summary to the reader. The biases can be latent factors that will be discovered during the modeling process.

We propose to achieve a balanced summary that selects salient opinions from reviewers with different biases. We hypothesize that the bias-aware opinion representation will form clusters of similar opinions from reviewers with similar biases. Building on a graph-based approach to summarization like LexRank (Erkan and Radev, 2004) and Yin and Pei (2015), opinions can be represented as nodes and edges as the similarity between bias-aware opinion representation. The density of the graph can be adjusted by the similarity threshold imposed on the graph. The saliency of the opinions can then be obtained by applying PageRank on the graph. In doing so, we

also model the similar opinions that signals agreement or consensus among reviewers. After ranking opinions based on its salience, we can utilise a diversity objective through a greedy approach or Maximal Marginal Relevance (MMR) to select salient opinions that are different.

4 Evaluation

Datasets Suitable datasets in the restaurant domain for our research questions are: (1) NY city search (Ganu et al., 2013); (2) SemEval 2016 ABSA Restaurant Reviews in English (Pontiki et al., 2016); and, (3) Yelp dataset challenge[2]. All datasets contain user ID, product ID, review text and review rating, which will allow us to model opinions. In addition, datasets (1) and (2) are labeled with aspect and sentiment polarity. Although we choose to work in the restaurant domain for our proposed work, our models are not domain-specific. Other potential review datasets are on product and hotel reviews (McAuley et al., 2015; Wang et al., 2010).

We approach evaluation in a two part process. First, we evaluate our proposed model on how well it learns a representation of opinion sentence. Next, we compare summaries generated with our bias-aware opinion representation with selected baseline models.

4.1 Bias-Aware Opinion Representation

Our objective is to learn a bias-aware opinion representation such that similar opinions from reviewers with similar bias should cluster together and different opinions form different clusters. We apply the evaluation method used to evaluate vector representation of text sequences by Le and Mikolov (2014). We believe this evaluation method is applicable for our representation. We begin with a dataset of labeled opinions. From the labeled dataset, a triplet of opinions is created with the first and second opinions of the triplet to be of the same opinion, and first and third opinions to be of different opinions. We compute the similarity of opinion between a pairs of the triplet of representation. We expect the first and second opinion to produce a higher similarity as compared to the similarity of the first and third opinion. Of all the triplets we create, we will report the error rate. Error rate here refers to the number of triplets that

---

first and third opinion is more similar than first and second opinion over the total number of triplets.

Our second evaluation will be a cluster analysis of opinion representations. We expect homogeneous clusters of similar opinions from reviewers with similar bias and different clusters for different opinions with reviewer biases. A potential approach will be to perform a k-means clustering where the number of clusters k can be determined by an elbow plot. The quality of clusters can be evaluated using the Silhouette Score.

In order to evaluate the bias-aware opinion representation, we look to answer a related question. Suppose each opinion captures the opinion target, the polarity and reviewer bias. Each opinion within the review contributes to the overall rating. The task is to predict the overall rating based on review text. The model will be trained on a training set of review text, reviewer information and rating. If the model accurately captures the opinion and reviewer bias in the representation, the representative should improve the ability to predict the overall rating of the review given the review text and reviewer information.

4.2 Summarization

Evaluating summaries is a challenging problem. There are two options to evaluate summaries. First, an automatic evaluation method using metrics such as ROUGE and BLEU. However, such method requires a gold standard summary. Obtaining a gold standard summary for our purpose is a challenging task. The second method of evaluation is a user-study type evaluation. Users are presented with generated summaries and are asked to judge the summary according to given criteria or to compare between different summaries. Some baseline models to compare against are Lexrank (Erkan and Radev, 2004) to represent word level models and DivSelect+CNNLM to represent vector representation models (Yin and Pei, 2015). We intend to evaluate our summaries using a user-study.

5 Summary

Not all reviews are equal as reviews capture biases of their reviewers. These biases can be amplified when we analyse a collection of reviews that is not representative of the consumers of the product. As such, analysis on the collection of reviews is not representative and can potentially impact readers who depend on the analysis for decision-making. To address this problem, we propose to model opinion with its reviewer using review text and review rating to obtain a bias-aware opinion representation. We plan to demonstrate the utility of the representation in opinion summarization. Specifically, the representation will be useful in the scoring the sentences for saliency and selection of sentences for generating a balanced summary. Although we focus on modeling opinions for opinion summarization, we believe the same modeling concepts can also be applied to recommendation. We leave evaluation of bias-aware opinion representation on recommendations to future work.

Acknowledgments

I thank the anonymous reviewers for their thorough and insightful comments. I am grateful to my supervisors, Xiuzhen Zhang, Sarvnaz Karimi and Stephen Wan for their guidance and support. Wenyi is supported by an Australian Government Research Training Program Scholarship and a CSIRO Data61 Top-up Scholarship.

References

Stefanos Angelidis and Mirella Lapata. 2018. Summarizing Opinions: Aspect Extraction Meets Sentiment Prediction and They Are Both Weakly Supervised. In *Proceedings of the Conference on Empirical Methods in Natural Language Processing*, pages 3675–3686, Brussels, Belgium.

Marco Bonzanini, Miguel Martinez-Alvarez, and Thomas Roelleke. 2013. Extractive Summarisation via Sentence Removal: Condensing Relevant Sentences into a Short Summary. In *Proceedings of the International ACM SIGIR Conference on Research and Development in Information Retrieval*, pages 893–896, Dublin, Ireland.

Samuel Brody and Noemie Elhadad. 2010. An Unsupervised Aspect-sentiment Model for Online Reviews. In *Annual Conference of the North American Chapter of the Association for Computational Linguistics*, pages 804–812, Los Angeles, CA.

Ziqiang Cao, Sujian Li, Yang Liu, Wenjie Li, and Heng Ji. 2015. A Novel Neural Topic Model and Its Supervised Extension. In *Proceedings of the AAAI Conference on Artificial Intelligence*, pages 2210–2216, Austin, TX.

Daniel Cer, Yinfei Yang, Sheng-yi Kong, Nan Hua, Nicole Limtiaco, Rhomni St. John, Noah Constant, Mario Guajardo-Cespedes, Steve Yuan, Chris Tar, Brian Strope, and Ray Kurzweil. 2018. Universal Sentence Encoder for English. In *Proceedings of the*

Conference on Empirical Methods in Natural Language Processing, pages 169–174, Brussels, Belgium.

Bee-Chung Chen, Jian Guo, Belle Tseng, and Jie Yang. 2011. User Reputation in a Comment Rating Environment. In *Proceedings of the ACM SIGKDD International Conference on Knowledge Discovery and Data Mining*, pages 159–167, San Diego, CA.

Alexis Conneau, Douwe Kiela, Holger Schwenk, Loïc Barrault, and Antoine Bordes. 2017. Supervised Learning of Universal Sentence Representations from Natural Language Inference Data. In *Proceedings of the Conference on Empirical Methods in Natural Language Processing*, pages 670–680, Copenhagen, Denmark.

Kushal Dave, Steve Lawrence, and David M. Pennock. 2003. Mining the Peanut Gallery: Opinion Extraction and Semantic Classification of Product Reviews. In *Proceedings of the International Conference on World Wide Web*, pages 519–528, Budapest, Hungary.

Jacob Devlin, Ming-Wei Chang, Kenton Lee, and Kristina Toutanova. 2018. BERT: Pre-training of deep bidirectional transformers for language understanding. *arXiv preprint arXiv:1810.04805*.

Günes Erkan and Dragomir R Radev. 2004. Lexrank: Graph-based Lexical Centrality as Salience in Text Summarization. *Journal of Artificial Intelligence Research*, 22:457–479.

Kavita Ganesan, ChengXiang Zhai, and Jiawei Han. 2010. Opinosis: A Graph Based Approach to Abstractive Summarization of Highly Redundant Opinions. In *Proceedings of the International Conference on Computational Linguistics*, pages 340–348, Beijing, China.

Gayatree Ganu, Yogesh Kakodkar, and AméLie Marian. 2013. Improving the Quality of Predictions Using Textual Information in Online User Reviews. *Information Systems*, 38(1):1–15.

Ruidan He, Wee Sun Lee, Hwee Tou Ng, and Daniel Dahlmeier. 2017. An Unsupervised Neural Attention Model for Aspect Extraction. In *Proceedings of the Annual Meeting of the Association for Computational Linguistics*, pages 388–397, Vancouver, Canada.

Jeremy Howard and Sebastian Ruder. 2018. Universal Language Model Fine-tuning for Text Classification. In *Proceedings of the Annual Meeting of the Association for Computational Linguistics*, pages 328–339, Melbourne, Australia.

Minqing Hu and Bing Liu. 2004a. Mining and Summarizing Customer Reviews. In *Proceedings of the ACM SIGKDD International Conference on Knowledge Discovery and Data Mining*, pages 168–177, Seattle, WA.

Minqing Hu and Bing Liu. 2004b. Mining Opinion Features in Customer Reviews. In *Proceedings of the National Conference on Artifical Intelligence*, pages 755–760, San Jose, CA.

Nan Hu, Paul A. Pavlou, and Jennifer Zhang. 2006. Can Online Reviews Reveal a Product's True Quality?: Empirical Findings and Analytical Modeling of Online Word-of-mouth Communication. In *Proceedings of the ACM Conference on Electronic Commerce*, pages 324–330, Ann Arbor, MI.

Ryan Kiros, Yukun Zhu, Ruslan Salakhutdinov, Richard S. Zemel, Antonio Torralba, Raquel Urtasun, and Sanja Fidler. 2015. Skip-thought Vectors. In *Proceedings of the International Conference on Neural Information Processing Systems - Volume 2*, pages 3294–3302, Montreal, Canada.

Hady W Lauw, Ee-Peng Lim, and Ke Wang. 2012. Quality and Leniency in Online Collaborative Rating Systems. *ACM Transactions on the Web (TWEB)*, 6(1):4.

Quoc Le and Tomas Mikolov. 2014. Distributed Representations of Sentences and Documents. In *Proceedings of the International Conference on International Conference on Machine Learning - Volume 32*, pages II–1188–II–1196, Beijing, China.

Fangtao Li, Sheng Wang, Shenghua Liu, and Ming Zhang. 2014. SUIT: A Supervised User-Item Based Topic Model for Sentiment Analysis. In *Proceedings of the AAAI Conference on Artificial Intelligence*, pages 1636–1642, Quebec, Canada.

Chenghua Lin and Yulan He. 2009. Joint Sentiment/Topic Model for Sentiment Analysis. In *Proceedings of the ACM Conference on Information and Knowledge Management*, pages 375–384, Hong Kong, China.

Jingjing Liu, Yunbo Cao, Chin-Yew Lin, Yalou Huang, and Ming Zhou. 2007. Low-Quality Product Review Detection in Opinion Summarization. In *Proceedings of the Joint Conference on Empirical Methods in Natural Language Processing and Computational Natural Language Learning*, pages 334–342, Prague, Czech Republic.

Yang Liu, Xiangji Huang, Aijun An, and Xiaohui Yu. 2008. Modeling and Predicting the Helpfulness of Online Reviews. In *IEEE International Conference on Data Mining*, pages 443–452, Pisa, Italy.

Andrew L. Maas, Raymond E. Daly, Peter T. Pham, Dan Huang, Andrew Y. Ng, and Christopher Potts. 2011. Learning Word Vectors for Sentiment Analysis. In *Proceedings of the Annual Meeting of the Association for Computational Linguistics: Human Language Technologies*, pages 142–150, Portland, OR.

Julian McAuley and Jure Leskovec. 2013. Hidden Factors and Hidden Topics: Understanding Rating Dimensions with Review Text. In *Proceedings of the*

ACM Conference on Recommender Systems, pages 165–172, Hong Kong, China.

Julian McAuley, Christopher Targett, Qinfeng Shi, and Anton van den Hengel. 2015. Image-Based Recommendations on Styles and Substitutes. In *Proceedings of the International ACM SIGIR Conference on Research and Development in Information Retrieval*, pages 43–52, Santiago, Chile.

Tomas Mikolov, Ilya Sutskever, Kai Chen, Greg Corrado, and Jeffrey Dean. 2013. Distributed Representations of Words and Phrases and Their Compositionality. In *Proceedings of the International Conference on Neural Information Processing Systems - Volume 2*, pages 3111–3119, Lake Tahoe, NV.

Samaneh Moghaddam and Martin Ester. 2010. Opinion Digger: An Unsupervised Opinion Miner from Unstructured Product Reviews. In *Proceedings of the ACM International Conference on Information and Knowledge Management*, pages 1825–1828, Toronto, Canada.

Gerardo Ocampo Diaz and Vincent Ng. 2018. Modeling and Prediction of Online Product Review Helpfulness: A Survey. In *Proceedings of the Annual Meeting of the Association for Computational Linguistics (Volume 1: Long Papers)*, pages 698–708, Melbourne, Australia.

Bo Pang and Lillian Lee. 2008. Opinion mining and sentiment analysis. *Foundations and Trends in Information Retrieval*, 2(12):1–135.

Michael Paul, ChengXiang Zhai, and Roxana Girju. 2010. Summarizing Contrastive Viewpoints in Opinionated Text. In *Proceedings of the Conference on Empirical Methods in Natural Language Processing*, pages 66–76, Cambridge, MA.

Matthew Peters, Mark Neumann, Mohit Iyyer, Matt Gardner, Christopher Clark, Kenton Lee, and Luke Zettlemoyer. 2018. Deep Contextualized Word Representations. In *Proceedings of the Conference of the North American Chapter of the Association for Computational Linguistics: Human Language Technologies*, pages 2227–2237, New Orleans, LA.

Maria Pontiki, Dimitris Galanis, Haris Papageorgiou, Ion Androutsopoulos, Suresh Manandhar, Mohammad AL-Smadi, Mahmoud Al-Ayyoub, Yanyan Zhao, Bing Qin, Orphee De Clercq, Veronique Hoste, Marianna Apidianaki, Xavier Tannier, Natalia Loukachevitch, Evgeniy Kotelnikov, Núria Bel, Salud María Jiménez-Zafra, and Gülşen Eryiğit. 2016. SemEval-2016 Task 5: Aspect Based Sentiment Analysis. In *Proceedings of the International Workshop on Semantic Evaluation*, pages 19–30, San Diego, CA.

Yassien Shaalan and Xiuzhen Zhang. 2016. A time and opinion quality-weighted model for aggregating online reviews. In *Australasian Database Conference*, pages 269–282. Springer.

Ruben Sipos and Thorsten Joachims. 2013. Generating Comparative Summaries from Reviews. In *Proceedings of the ACM International Conference on Information & Knowledge Management*, pages 1853–1856, San Francisco, CA.

Duyu Tang, Bing Qin, and Ting Liu. 2015a. Document Modeling with Gated Recurrent Neural Network for Sentiment Classification. In *Proceedings of the Conference on Empirical Methods in Natural Language Processing*, pages 1422–1432, Lisbon, Portugal.

Duyu Tang, Bing Qin, Ting Liu, and Yuekui Yang. 2015b. User Modeling with Neural Network for Review Rating Prediction. In *Proceedings of the International Conference on Artificial Intelligence*, pages 1340–1346, Buenos Aires, Argentina.

Ivan Titov and Ryan McDonald. 2008a. A Joint Model of Text and Aspect Ratings for Sentiment Summarization. In *Proceedings of the Annual Meeting of the Association for Computational Linguistics: Human Language Technologies*, pages 308–316, Columbus, OH.

Ivan Titov and Ryan McDonald. 2008b. Modeling Online Reviews with Multi-grain Topic Models. In *Proceedings of the International Conference on World Wide Web*, pages 111–120, Beijing, China.

Rahul Wadbude, Vivek Gupta, Dheeraj Mekala, and Harish Karnick. 2018. User Bias Removal in Review Score Prediction. In *Proceedings of the ACM India Joint International Conference on Data Science and Management of Data*, pages 175–179, Goa, India.

Hongning Wang, Yue Lu, and Chengxiang Zhai. 2010. Latent Aspect Rating Analysis on Review Text Data: A Rating Regression Approach. In *Proceedings of the ACM SIGKDD International Conference on Knowledge Discovery and Data Mining*, pages 783–792, Washington, DC.

Lu Wang and Wang Ling. 2016. Neural Network-Based Abstract Generation for Opinions and Arguments. In *Proceedings of the Conference of the North American Chapter of the Association for Computational Linguistics: Human Language Technologies*, pages 47–57, San Diego, CA.

Wenting Xiong and Diane Litman. 2014. Empirical Analysis of Exploiting Review Helpfulness for Extractive Summarization of Online Reviews. In *Proceedings of the International Conference on Computational Linguistics: Technical Papers*, pages 1985–1995, Dublin, Ireland.

Wenpeng Yin and Yulong Pei. 2015. Optimizing Sentence Modeling and Selection for Document Summarization. In *Proceedings of International Conference on Artificial Intelligence*, pages 1383–1389, Buenos Aires, Argentina.

Kunpeng Zhang, Yu Cheng, Wei-keng Liao, and Alok Choudhary. 2012. Mining Millions of Reviews: A Technique to Rank Products Based on Importance of Reviews. In *Proceedings of the International Conference on Electronic Commerce*, pages 12:1–12:8, Liverpool, United Kingdom.

Lei Zheng, Vahid Noroozi, and Philip S. Yu. 2017. Joint Deep Modeling of Users and Items Using Reviews for Recommendation. In *Proceedings of the ACM International Conference on Web Search and Data Mining*, pages 425–434, Cambridge, United Kingdom.

Towards Turkish Abstract Meaning Representation

Zahra Azin
Informatics Institute
Istanbul Technical University
Istanbul, Turkey
azin18@itu.edu.tr

Gülşen Eryiğit
Department of Computer Engineering
Istanbul Technical University
Istanbul, Turkey
gulsen.cebiroglu@itu.edu.tr

Abstract

Using rooted, directed and labeled graphs, Abstract Meaning Representation (AMR) abstracts away from syntactic features such as word order and does not annotate every constituent in a sentence. AMR has been specified for English and was not supposed to be an Interlingua. However, several studies strived to overcome divergences in the annotations between English AMRs and those of their target languages by refining the annotation specification. Following this line of research, we have started to build the first Turkish AMR corpus by hand-annotating 100 sentences of the Turkish translation of the novel "*The Little Prince*" and comparing the results with the English AMRs available for the same corpus. The next step is to prepare the Turkish AMR annotation specification for training future annotators.

1 Introduction

For a long time, semantic annotation of natural language sentences was split into subtasks, i.e. there were independent semantic annotations for named entity recognition, semantic relations, temporal entities, etc. The ultimate goal of Abstract Meaning Representation (AMR) is to build a SemBank of English sentences paired with their whole-sentence logical meaning. To do this, one of the primary rules in AMR annotating sentences is to disregard many syntactic characteristics to unify the semantic annotations into a simple, readable SemBank (Banarescu et al., 2013).

According to the Abstract Meaning Representation specification, AMR is not an Interlingua. The assertion has attracted researchers' attention to sample AMR formalism on different languages. Several researches have been done to examine the compatibility of AMR framework with other languages such as Chinese and Czech (Xue et al., 2014; Hajic et al., 2014; Li et al., 2016). Other studies proposed methods to generate AMR annotations for languages with no gold standard dataset by implementing cross lingual and other rule based methods (Damonte and Cohen, 2017; Vanderwende et al., 2015).

In this work, we have manually annotated 100 sentences from the Turkish translation of the novel "*The Little Prince*" with AMRs to describe the differences between these annotations and their English counterparts. The next step is to prepare the Turkish AMR guideline based on the differences extracted in the previous phase for training future annotators who wish to construct the first Turkish AMR bank by hand-annotating 1562 sentences of "*The Little Prince*" for which the English AMR bank is available.

2 Abstract Meaning Representation

Abstract Meaning Representation is defined as a simple readable semantic representation of sentences with rooted, directional labeled graphs (Flanigan et al., 2014). The main goal was set to build a SemBank resembling the proposition bank which is independent and disregards syntactic idiosyncrasies.

The building blocks of AMR graphs are concepts represented in nodes and relations that hold among these concepts as the edges of the graph. Thus, instead of using syntactic features, AMR focuses on the relationships among concepts, some of which are extracted from PropBank and other words. Example 1 shows the English AMR for the sentence "I have had to grow old." The root of the graph is a reference to the sense *obligate-01* and is extracted from

43

Proceedings of the ACL 2019, Student Research Workshop, pages 43–47
Florence, Italy, July 28th-August 2nd, 2019. ©2019 Association for Computational Linguistics

PropbBank frames as the sentence contains the syntactic modal *had to*.

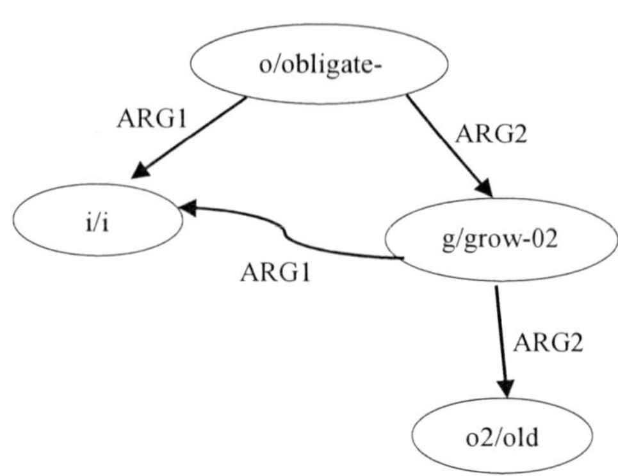

Example 1: The AMR annotation graph for the sentence " *I have had to grow old.*"

AMR does not annotate every single word in the sentence since its goal is to represent the analysis of a sentence in predicative and conceptual levels. Furthermore, AMR does not represent inflectional morphology for syntactic categories like tense which results in the same meaning representation of similar sentences with different wordings or word order. For example, the two sentences *"The boss has decided to fire the employee."* and *"This is the boss decision to fire the employee."* have same AMR annotations.

3   AMR Resources

Inspired by the UNL project[1], a freely downloadable annotated corpus of the novel *"The Little Prince"* containing 1562 sentences has been released by the project initiators[2]. The purpose was to release a corpus so that other researchers could compare their annotated sentences based on the same text. There is another annotated corpus, Bio AMR, freely available on the same website which contains cancer-related articles including about 1000 sentences. Moreover, Abstract Meaning Representation release 2.0 which contains more than 39,260 annotated sentences was developed by the Linguistic Data Consortium (LDC), SDL/language Weaver, Inc., The University of Colorado, and the University of Southern California and is distributed via the LDC catalog.

4   AMR Parsing

The ultimate goal of semantic formalisms such as Abstract Meaning Representation in natural language processing is to automatically map natural language strings to their meaning representations. In an AMR parsing system, we work on graphs which have their own characteristics specified by AMR formalism. These properties like reentrancy in which a single concept participates in multiple relations or the possibility to represent a sentence with different word orders by a single AMR make the parsing phase challenging. On the bright side, similar to dependency trees, AMR has a graph structure in which nodes contain concepts and edges represent linguistic relationships.

Several AMR parsing algorithms have been proposed so far (Wang et al., 2015; Vanderwende et al., 2015; Welch et al., 2018; Damonte et al., 2016; Damonte and Cohen, 2016) among which JAMR is the first open-source automatic parser published by the project initiators[3]. It works based on a two-stage algorithm in which concepts and then relations are identified using statistical methods. On the other hand, the transition-based method which transforms the dependency tree to an AMR graph seems promising because of its use of available dependency trees for different languages (Wang et al., 2015).

Sometimes, in natural language processing, due to limited resources or lack of NLP tools, researchers seek to discover methods to get the most out of it. Cross-lingual Abstract Meaning Representation parsing (Damonte and Cohen, 2017) for which we do not require a standard gold data seems to overcome the structural differences between English and a target language in AMR annotation process using "annotation projection" method. The parser works based on annotation projection from English to a target language and has been trained for Italian, German, Chinese, and Spanish.

---

[1] http://www.unlweb.net/unlweb/
[2] https://amr.isi.edu/download.html
[3] https://github.com/jflanigan/JAMR

Building a semantically hand-annotated corpus like an AMR bank is an arduous time-consuming task. However, annotating a small amount of data manually results in achieving an understanding of the formalism, in the first place, and facilitating the evaluation of AMR parsers. The annotated AMR corpus of this study can be utilized in evaluating future Turkish AMR parsers.

5   Turkish AMR

As AMR is not an interlingua, several studies have examined the differences between AMR annotations of sentences in languages like Chinese and Czech with English AMR annotations (Xue et al., 2014; Hajic et al., 2014; Li et al., 2016) so far and some have introduced cross-lingual and rule based methods to generate AMR graphs for languages other than English (Damonte and Cohen, 2015; Vanderwende et al., 2015). However, none of them had ever tackled an agglutinative language in which there is a possibility to derive and inflect words by cascading suffixes indefinitely.

One of the main challenges in developing language models for morphologically rich languages with productive derivational morphology like Hungarian, Finnish, and modern Turkish is the number of word forms that can be derived from a root. According to Turkish Language Association (TDK)[4], 759 root verbs exist in Turkish. Moreover, 2380 verbs are derived from nouns and 2944 verbs from verbs. Thus, there is almost no limit on suffixes a verb can take which results in tens of possible word formations.

Another challenge in Turkish processing is its free word order that allows sentence constituents to move freely at different phrase levels. One should note that as the word order changes, some pragmatic characteristics such as focus and topics change as well. This property of Turkish might lead to several challenges such as the need for collecting as much data as possible to cover all possible word orders.

For the first step, we have started hand-annotating the Turkish translation of *"The Little Prince"* aligning to its English AMR annotation to find out divergences and at the same time developing the very first Turkish AMR specification based on both English AMR guideline and differences between the two languages. The sentences were annotated by a non-Turkish linguist who aligned the English sentences with their literary translation in Turkish and created the AMR graphs using the Online AMR Editor[5]. Final annotations were proofread by a Turkish speaker.

We annotated 100 sentences and came up with following observations. First, a small number of sentences have exactly the same AMR structure as their English translation. An example is shown in figure 1. As it is illustrated in the textual form of the annotation, which is in the form of PENMAN notation (Matthiessen and Bateman, 1991), concepts and relations are aligned, although objects of the two sentences are different.

```
(t / talk-01

 :ARG0 (i / i)
 :ARG1 (a / and
      :op1 (b / bridge)
      :op2 (g / golf)
      :op3 (p / politics)
      :op4 (n2 / necktie))
 :ARG2 (h / he))
```

```
(k / konuşmak
     :ARG0 (b / ben)
     :ARG1 (v / ve
        :op1 (b2 / briç)
        :op2 (g / golf)
        :op3 (p / politika)
        :op4 (b3 / boyun-bağı))
     :ARG2 (o / onlar))
```

Figure 1: Textual forms of AMR annotations for the sentence *"I would talk to him about bridge, and golf, and politics, and neckties."* and its Turkish translation (*"Onlarla/them-with briç/bridge, golf/golf, politika/politics ve/and boyun bağları/neckties hakkında/about konuştum/I talked."*)

Second, most of the AMR annotations' divergences were due to different word choices in

---

[4] www.tdk.gov.tr

[5] https://www.isi.edu/cgi-bin/div3/mt/amr-editor/login-gen-v1.7.cgi

translating the text. Third, Turkish seems to be more expressive as suffixes add nuances to the words such as possession markers and intensifiers. Figure 2 shows AMR annotations for two sentences from the parallel corpus where ARG0 of *live-01* in English has been changed to a non-core role, *:poss*, which shows possession in Turkish. Although there was the possibility to ignore the possession marker and list the arguments of the predicate, *yaşamak* (to live), like its English counterpart, we chose to leave it as it is to highlight the differences between English and Turkish as an agglutinative language in AMR annotation.

Another important characteristic of Turkish is that unlike English, there are many light verbs and multiword expressions. In English AMR, we simply remove light verb constructions and use onto-notes predicate frames to deal with verb-particle combinations. However, due to the highly productive nature of Turkish and its idiosyncratic features, we need to be more cautious dealing with multiword expressions and light verb constructions. Figure 3 shows the inclination of Turkish toward productivity by duplicating the adjective, *uzun* (long), to be used as an adverb.

In our future study, we will also investigate how morphosemantic features like case markers might help specifying relations between concepts in Turkish and whether adding these properties to the AMR annotation structure may help achieving more accurate results.

```
(s / small
 :degree (v / very)
 :domain (e / everything)
 :location (12 / live-01
      :ARG0 (i / i)))

(k / küçük
   :degree (x / çok)
   :domain (x2 / şey
      :mod (h / her))
   :location (y / yaşamak
      :poss (b / ben)))
```

Figure 2: Textual forms of AMR annotations for the sentence *"Where I live, everything is very small."* and its Turkish translation ("Benim/my yaşadığım/where live-I yerde/place-in her/every şey/thing çok/very küçük/small.")

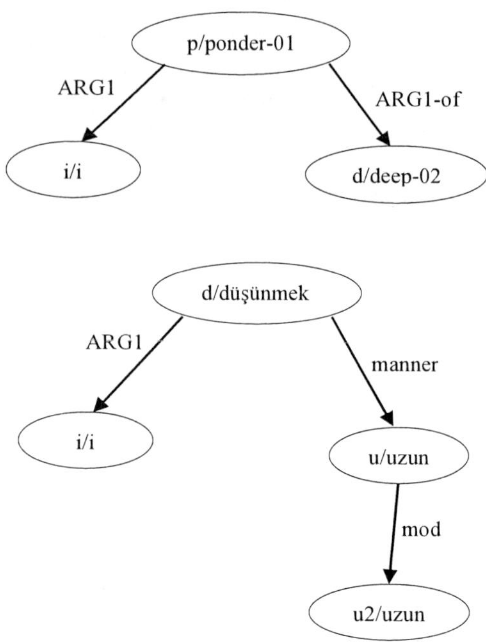

Figure 3: The AMR annotation graph for the sentence *"I pondered deeply"* which is translated as (*"uzun uzun/long long düşündüm/ thought-I."*)

6 Future Work

We have started the Turkish AMR project by annotating the first 100 hundred sentences of our parallel corpus, *"The Little Prince"*, and analyzing the divergences between our annotations and English AMR annotations. Currently, we are developing an AMR annotation guideline to construct the first Turkish Abstract Meaning Representation standard gold data. Finally, based on Turkish language peculiarities, we are going to create a transition-based parser to generate Turkish AMRs, which will be the first AMR parser for an agglutinative language.

Acknowledgments

We would like to thank Tuğba Pamay for her invaluable insights and discussions. We also want to thank Valerio Basile and anonymous reviewers for their comments and suggestions.

References

Atalay, N. B., Oflazer, K., & Say, B. 2003. The annotation process in the Turkish treebank. In *Proceedings of 4th International Workshop on Linguistically Interpreted Corpora (LINC-03) at EACL 1003*. http://aclweb.org/anthology/W03-2405

Banarescu, L., Bonial, C., Cai, S., Georgescu, M., Griffitt, K., Hermjakob, U., ... & Schneider, N. 2013. Abstract meaning representation for sembanking. In *Proceedings of the 7th Linguistic Annotation Workshop and Interoperability with Discourse* (pp.178-186). http://aclweb.org/anthology/W13-2322

Damonte, M., Cohen, S. B., & Satta, G. 2016. An incremental parser for abstract meaning representation. *arXiv preprint arXiv:1608.06111*. http://aclweb.org/anthology/E17-1051

Damonte, M., & Cohen, S. B. 2017. Cross-lingual abstract meaning representation parsing. *arXiv preprint arXiv:1704.04539*. https://doi.org/ 10.18653/v1/N18-1104

Flanigan, J., Thomson, S., Carbonell, J., Dyer, C., & Smith, N. A. 2014. A discriminative graph-based parser for the abstract meaning representation. In *Proceedings of the 52nd Annual Meeting of the Association for Computational Linguistics (Volume 1: Long Papers)* (Vol. 1, pp. 1426-1436). https://doi.org/ 10.3115/v1/P14-1134

Hajic, J., Bojar, O., & Uresova, Z. 2014. Comparing Czech and English AMRs. In *Proceedings of Workshop on Lexical and Grammatical Resources for Language Processing* (pp. 55-64). https://doi.org/ 10.3115/v1/W14-5808

Li, B., Wen, Y., Weiguang, Q. U., Bu, L., & Xue, N. 2016. Annotating the little prince with chinese amrs. In *Proceedings of the 10th linguistic annotation workshop held in conjunction with acl 2016 (law-x 2016)* (pp. 7-15). https://doi.org/ 10.18653/v1/W16-1702

Mathiessen, C. M., & Bateman, J. 1991. Text Generation and Systemic-Functional Linguistics. *London: Pinter*.

Şahin, G. G. 2016. Verb sense annotation for Turkish propbank via crowdsourcing. In *International Conference on Intelligent Text Processing and Computational Linguistics* (pp. 496-506). Springer, Cham.

Vanderwende, L., Menezes, A., & Quirk, C. 2015. An AMR parser for English, French, German, Spanish and Japanese and a new AMR-annotated corpus. In *Proceedings of the 2015 conference of the north american chapter of the association for computational linguistics: Demonstrations* (pp. 26-30). https://doi.org/ 10.3115/v1/N15-3006

Wang, C., Xue, N., & Pradhan, S. 2015. *Boosting transition-based AMR parsing with refined actions and auxiliary analyzers*. In *Proceedings of the 53rd Annual Meeting of the Association for Computational Linguistics and the 7th International Joint Conference on Natural Language Processing (Volume 2: Short Papers)* (Vol. 2, pp. 857-862). https://doi.org/ 10.3115/v1/P15-2141

Wang, C., Xue, N., & Pradhan, S. 2015. A transition-based algorithm for amr parsing. In *Proceedings of the 2015 Conference of the North American Chapter of the Association for Computational Linguistics: Human Language Technologies*(pp. 366-375). https://doi.org/ 10.3115/v1/N15-1040

Welch, C., Kummerfeld, J. K., Feng, S., & Mihalcea, R. 2018. World Knowledge for Abstract Meaning Representation Parsing. In *Proceedings of the Eleventh International Conference on Language Resources and Evaluation (LREC-2018)*. http://aclweb.org/anthology/L18-1492

Xue, N., Bojar, O., Hajic, J., Palmer, M., Uresova, Z., & Zhang, X. 2014. *Not an Interlingua, But Close: Comparison of English AMRs to Chinese and Czech*. In LREC (Vol. 14, pp. 1765-1772). http://www.lrecconf.org/proceedings/lrec2014/pdf/384_Paper.pdf

Gender Stereotypes Differ between Male and Female Writings

Yusu Qian
Tandon School of Engineering
New York University
6 MetroTech Center
Brooklyn, NY 11201
`yq729@nyu.edu`

Abstract

Written language often contains gender stereotypes, typically conveyed unintentionally by the author. Existing methods used to evaluate gender stereotypes in a text compute the difference in the co-occurrence of gender-neutral words with female and male words. To study the difference in how female and male authors portray people of different genders, we quantitatively evaluate and analyze the gender stereotypes in their writings on two different datasets and from multiple aspects, including the overall gender stereotype score, the occupation-gender stereotype score, the emotion-gender stereotype score, and the ratio of male words used to female words. We show that writings by females on average have lower gender stereotype scores. We also find that emotion words in writings by males have much lower stereotype scores than the average score of all words, while in writings by females the scores are similar. We study and interpret the distributions of gender stereotype scores of individual words, and how they differ between male and female writings.

1 Introduction

Gender stereotypes in language have been receiving more and more attention from researchers across different fields. In the past, these studies have been carried out mainly by conducting surveys with humans (Williams and Best, 1977), requiring a large amount of human labor. Garg et al. (2018) quantified gender stereotypes by analyzing word embeddings trained on US Census over the past 100 years. Word embeddings capture gender stereotypes in the training data and transfer them to downstream applications (Bolukbasi et al., 2016). For example, if *programmer* appears more frequently with *he* than *she* in the training corpus, in the word embedding it will have a closer distance to *he* compared with *she*.

In this study, we analyze gender stereotypes directly from writings under different metrics. Specifically, we compare the writings by males and females to see how gender stereotypes differ between writings by the gender of authors. Our results show that writings by female authors contain much fewer gender stereotypes than writings by male authors. We recognize that there are more than two types of gender, but for the sake of simplicity, in this study we consider just female and male.

To the best of our knowledge, this study is the first quantitative analysis of how gender stereotypes differ between writings by authors of different genders. Our contributions are as follows: 1) we show that writings by females contain fewer gender stereotypes; 2) we find that over the past few decades, gender stereotypes in writings by males have decreased.

2 Related Work

Quantifying Gender Stereotypes It has been noticed that stereotypes might be implicitly introduced to image corpora and text corpora in procedures such as data collection (Misra et al., 2016; Gordon and Durme, 2013). Particularly in gender stereotypes, Garg et al. (2018) bridged social science with machine learning when they quantified gender and ethnic stereotypes in word embeddings. Park et al. (2018) measured gender stereotypes on various abusive language models, while analyzing the effect of different pre-trained word embeddings and model architectures. Zhao et al. (2018) showed the effectiveness of measuring and correcting gender stereotypes in co-reference resolution tasks.

Categorizing Text by Author Gender Shimoni et al. (2002) proposed techniques to categorize text by author gender. They selected multiple fea-

Proceedings of the ACL 2019, Student Research Workshop, pages 48–53
Florence, Italy, July 28th-August 2nd, 2019. ©2019 Association for Computational Linguistics

tures, for example, determiners and prepositions, and calculated their frequency means and standard errors in texts. They showed that the distributions of some of these features differ between writings by female and male. Mukherjee and Liu (2010) used POS sequence patterns to capture stylistic regularities in male and female writings. To reduce the number of features, they also proposed a selection method. They showed that author gender can be revealed by multiple features of their writings. Cheng et al. (2011) based on psycholinguistics and gender-preferential cues to build a feature space and trained machine learning models to identify author gender. They pointed out that function words, word-based features and structural features can act as gender discriminators. All these three studies achieved accuracy above 80% for identifying author gender.

3 Methodology

3.1 Dataset

In the first experiment, we use a dataset by Lahiri (2013), which consists of 3,036 English books written by 142 authors. Among these, 189 books were written by 14 female authors, others were produced by male authors.

In the second experiment, we use a dataset by Schler et al. (2006), which consists of 681,288 posts from 19,320 bloggers; approximately 35 posts and 7250 words from each blogger. The blogs are divided into 40 categories, for example, agriculture, arts and science, etc. Female bloggers and male bloggers are of equal number.

3.2 Evaluation Methods

Overall Gender Stereotypes We define the gender stereotype score of a word as:

$$b(w) = \left| \log \frac{c(w,m)}{c(w,f)} \right|,$$

where f is a set of female words, for example, *she*, *girl*, and *woman*. m is a set of male words, for example, *he*, *actor*, and *father*. $c(w,g)$ is the number of times a gender-neutral word w co-occurs with gendered words. The gendered word lists are by Zhao et al. (2018).We use a window size of 10 when calculating co-occurrence.

A word is used in a neutral way if the stereotype score is 0, which means it occurs equally frequently with male words and females word in the text. The overall stereotype score of a text, T_b,
is the sum of stereotype scores of all the gender-neutral by definition words that have more than 10 co-occurrences with gendered words in the text, divided by the total count of words calculated, N.

$$T_b = \frac{1}{N} \sum_{w \in N} b(w)$$

Ratio of Male Words to Female Words To compare the frequency of male words with that of female words in a text, we calculate the ratio of male word count to female word count and denote it by R.

Occupation-Gender Stereotypes Occupation stereotypes are the most common stereotypes in studies on gender stereotypes (Lu et al., 2018). A few decades ago, females normally worked as dairy maids, housemaids and nurses, etc, while males worked as doctors, smiths, and butchers, etc. Nowadays both genders have more choices when looking for a job and for most occupations, there isnt a restriction on gender. Therefore, it is interesting to study how occupation stereotypes change over the years in female and male writings.

Occupation stereotypes score, O_b, in a text is the average stereotype score of a list of 200 gender-neutral occupations, O, in the text.

$$O_b = \frac{1}{|O|} \sum_{w \in O} b(w)$$

Emotion-Gender Stereotypes Emotion stereotypes are another kind of common gender stereotypes. In writings, especially novels, different genders are associated closely with different emotions, resulting in emotion stereotypes.

Emotion stereotypes score, E_b, in a text is the average stereotype score of a list of 200 emotion words, E, in the text.

$$E_b = \frac{1}{|E|} \sum_{w \in E} b(w)$$

Distribution of Stereotype Scores We compare the distributions of stereotype scores to analyze differences in writings by females and writings by males. We consider the following aspects of distributions: mean, variance, skewness, and kurtosis. We use S_v, S_s, and S_k to denote the average of variance, skewness, and kurtosis respectively of the distributions of stereotype scores. We plan to also add directions to individual scores by removing the absolute value function when calculating

Table 1: Statistics of gender stereotypes in female and male writings

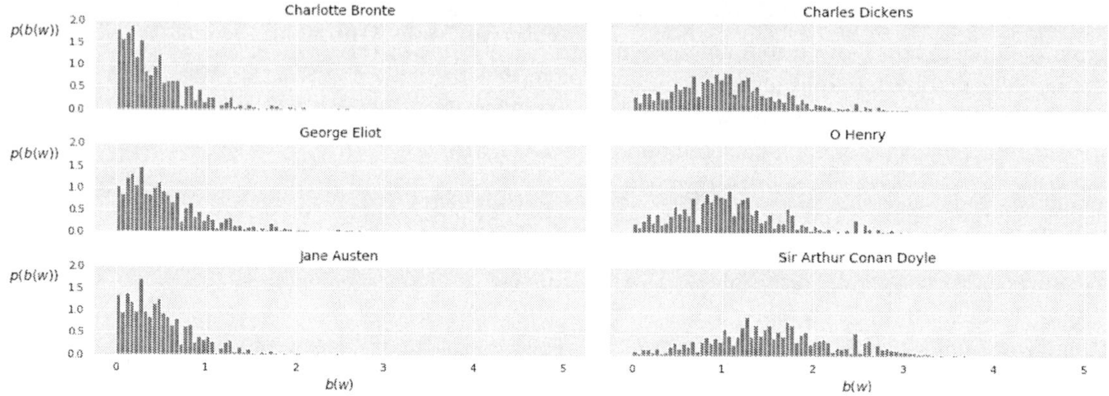

Figure 1: Distribution of stereotype scores in novels written by female(left) and male(right) authors

the scores, and analyze the distribution. We use the absolute function for most of the experiments because positive and negative values will cancel off each other when they are summed up.

Words Most Biased We alter the equation used for evaluating individual stereotype scores by removing the absolute value function, so that words occurring more with female words have negative values and words occurring more with male words have positive values. By sorting individual stereotype scores, we collect lists of words most biased towards the female gender or the male gender.

4 Results

4.1 Gender Stereotypes in Novels

We categorize 3036 books written in English and analyze the overall gender stereotypes in writings by each author. When sorted by overall stereotype scores from low to high, 12 female authors out of 14 are ranked among the top 20, or in another word, top 13.8%.

The average ratio of the total number of male words to female words in novels by female authors is close to 1, indicating that female authors mention the two genders in their novels almost equally frequently. Male authors, on the other hand, tend to write three times more frequently about their own gender.

Figure 1 shows the distribution of stereotype scores in example novels written by female and male authors. Inspection shows that the individual scores of female writings tend to cluster around score value 0 or other small values close to 0, and the percentage of words among all words calculated constantly decreases when stereotype score increases, while the individual scores of male writings tend to cluster around score values between 0.5 and 1.5, and the percentage of words among all words calculated first increases and then decreases.

Statistical analysis on the distributions confirms our observation. Table 1 shows that the average variance of stereotype scores in male writings is much larger than that of female writings, indicating that stereotype scores in female writings tend to gather near the mean while those in male writings spread out more broadly. The distribution of stereotype scores in female writings has both larger average skewness and larger kurtosis, in accordance with our observation that the distribution is skewed right with a sharp peak at a small stereotype score. In contrast, the distribution of stereotype scores in male writings has much smaller average skewness and kurtosis, in accordance with our observation that the distribution has tails on both left and right sides and has a less distinct peak.

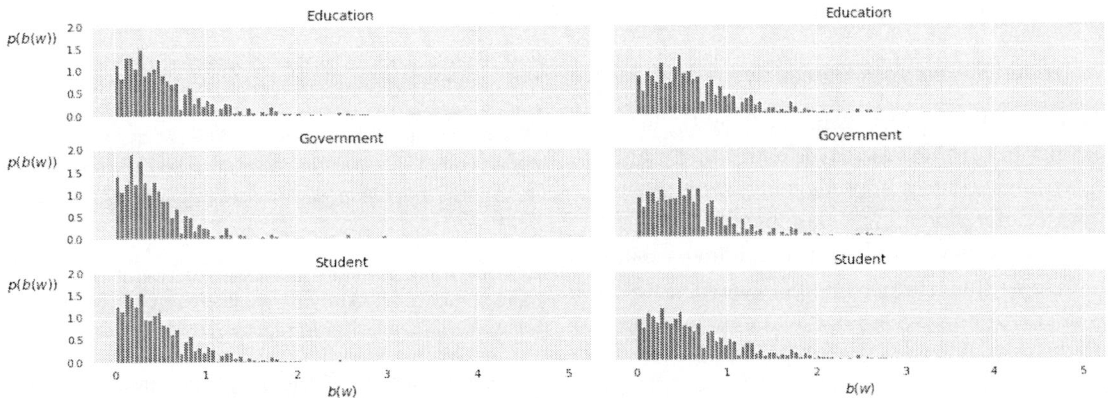

Figure 2: Distribution of stereotype scores in blogs written by female(left) and male(right) authors

Category	Author	Bias Direction	Top 20 Words in the Most Biased Wordlist
novel	male	male	judge, us, speech, friends, much, ask, created, made, never, life, framed, yet, knows, also, like, declared, each, great, believe, political
novel	male	female	necessarily, married, constitution, struck, need, short, votes, before, want, consent, taught, due, but, portion, course, alone, bread, engage, equal, five
novel	female	male	pocket, russian, hands, few, probably, said, round, that, admitted, out, way, caught, read, sure, stared, coming, gravely, began, followed, face
novel	female	female	suppose, bed, set, new, suddenly, door, right, morning, meant, remembered, given, well, up, lay, possible, realized, smiled, kind, lips, eyes
blog	male	male	sure, over, three, saw, got, if, now, did, things, as, two, before, really, this, gets, our, back, being, left, feels
blog	male	female	bring, and, issue, friends, so, said, what, wet, take, telling, wanted, call, going, much, me, always, something, same, little, met
blog	female	male	mail, does, stories, report, lucky, online, beat, imagine, surprised, reply, tonight, reporting, cut, blue, radio, reports, jeans, story, thank, forget
blog	female	female	talk, body, baby, age, death, won, pain, weight, together, later, beautiful, ears, walk, head, large, sees, sexy, dress, passed, family

Table 2: A sample of most biased words in female and male writings from experiments on novels and blogs

4.2 Gender Stereotypes in Blogs

After analyzing blogs on 40 categories written by equal numbers of male and female bloggers, we find out that for 35 categories, writings by males contains more gender stereotypes by 41.39% on average. Only in 5 categories including accounting, agriculture, biotech, construction and military, writings by female contains more gender stereotypes than male writings by 16.29% on average.

The average ratio of the total number of male words to female words in blogs by female authors is around 1.5, while in blogs by male authors, the ratio is around 2.8. Similar to the findings in the first experiment, male authors write more about the male gender.

Figure 2 shows a similar pattern in blogs with the pattern in novels. Individual stereotype scores also cluster closer around 0 or a relatively small value in female writings, while those of male writings cluster around a larger value. This pattern, however, is weaker than that found in experiments on novels. Both Figure 2 and statistics in Table 1 show that difference in blogs written by female and male authors in terms of gender stereotypes is smaller than the difference in novels. It is also worth mentioning that while T_b of blogs written by females is almost the same as that of novels written by females, T_b of blogs written by males is much lower than that of novels written by males. The trend in the ratio of male word count to female word count is similar. One possible interpretation of this is that while the blogs were written in 2004, the novels in the Gutenberg subsample were written decades ago, when the society had more constraints on female and gender equality was not paid as much attention to as it is today.

4.3 Gender Stereotypes Categories

For both two datasets, O_b is larger than T_b, indicating that occupation words in both female and male writings contain more gender stereotypes than most other words. E_b is almost the same as T_b in female writings, while it is much lower than T_b in male writings, indicating that gender stereotypes in emotion words are not the main contributors to the overall gender stereotypes in male writings.

5 Conclusion and Discussion

In this study, we perform experiments on two datasets to analyze how gender stereotypes differ between male and female writings. From our preliminary results we observe that writings by female authors contain fewer gender stereotypes than writings by male authors. This difference appears to have narrowed over time, mainly by the reduction of gender stereotypes in writings by male authors. We plan to: 1)further analyze the typical types of gender stereotypes in writings by authors of different genders and how they resemble with or differ from each other, by studying the most biased words and the average stereotype scores of different categories of words, for example, verbs, adjectives, etc.; 2) perform experiments on more writings from the past century to inspect more closely if there exists a trend in the transformation of gender stereotypes; 3) existing stereotype evaluation methods evaluate every word not in the excluded word lists, in our case, the male and female word lists. Some frequently used words, such as *the*, *one*, and *an*, are not considered to be able to contain stereotypes, unlike words such as *strong*, *doctor*, and *jealous*, which are more closely associated with one gender in writings. We plan to seek a way to filter gender-neutral words and only keep those capable of carrying stereotypes for stereotype quantification.

6 Acknowledgments

Many thanks to Gang Qian, Cuiying Yang, Pedro L. Rodriguez, Hanchen Wang, and Tian Liu for helpful discussion, and reviewers for detailed comments and advice.

References

Tolga Bolukbasi, Kai-Wei Chang, James Zou, Venkatesh Saligrama, and Adam Kalai. 2016. Man is to computer programmer as woman is to homemaker? debiasing word embeddings. In *NIPS'16 Proceedings of the 30th International Conference on Neural Information Processing Systems*, pages 4356–4364.

Na Cheng, Rajarathnam Chandramouli, and K. P. Subbalakshmi. 2011. Author gender identification from text. *Digital Investigation*, 8(1):78–88.

Nikhil Garg, Londa Schiebinger, Dan Jurafsky, and James Zou. 2018. Word embeddings quantify 100 years of gender and ethnic stereotypes. *Proceedings of the National Academy of Sciences*, 115(16):E3635–E3644.

Jonathan Gordon and Benjamin Van Durme. 2013. Reporting bias and knowledge acquisition. In *Proceedings of the 2013 workshop on Automated knowledge base construction, AKBC@CIKM 13, San Francisco, California, USA, October 27-28, 2013*, pages 25–30.

Shibamouli Lahiri. 2013. Complexity of word collocation networks: A preliminary structural analysis. *CoRR*, abs/1310.5111.

Kaiji Lu, Piotr Mardziel, Fangjing Wu, Preetam Amancharla, and Anupam Datta. 2018. Gender bias in neural natural language processing. ArXiv:1807.11714v1.

Ishan Misra, C. Lawrence Zitnick, Margaret Mitchell, and Ross B. Girshick. 2016. Seeing through the human reporting bias: Visual classifiers from noisy human-centric labels. In *2016 IEEE Conference on Computer Vision and Pattern Recognition, CVPR 2016, Las Vegas, NV, USA, June 27-30, 2016*, pages 2930–2939.

Arjun Mukherjee and Bing Liu. 2010. Improving gender classification of blog authors. In *Proceedings of the 2010 Conference on Empirical Methods in Natural Language Processing*, EMNLP '10, pages 207–217, Stroudsburg, PA, USA. Association for Computational Linguistics.

Ji Ho Park, Jamin Shin, and Pascale Fung. 2018. Reducing gender bias in abusive language detection. In *Proceedings of the 2018 Conference on Empirical Methods in Natural Language Processing, Brussels, Belgium, October 31 - November 4, 2018*, pages 2799–2804.

Jonathan Schler, Moshe Koppel, Shlomo Argamon, and James Pennebaker. 2006. Effects of age and gender on blogging. In *Computational Approaches to Analyzing Weblogs - Papers from the AAAI Spring Symposium, Technical Report*, volume SS-06-03, pages 191–197.

Anat Rachel Shimoni, Moshe Koppel, and Shlomo Argamon. 2002. Automatically Categorizing Written Texts by Author Gender. *Literary and Linguistic Computing*, 17(4):401–412.

John E. Williams and Deborah L. Best. 1977. Sex stereotypes and trait favorability on the adjective check list. *Educational and Psychological Measurement*, 37(1):101–110.

Jieyu Zhao, Yichao Zhou, Zeyu Li, Wei Wang, and Chang Kaiwei. 2018. Learning gender-neutral word embeddings. In *Proceedings of the 2018 Conference on Empirical Methods in Natural Language Processing*, page 48474853. Association for Computational Linguistics.

Question Answering in the Biomedical Domain

Vincent Nguyen

Research School of Computer Science, Australian National University
Data61, CSIRO
`vincent.nguyen@anu.edu.au`

Abstract

Question answering techniques have mainly been investigated in open domains. However, there are particular challenges in extending these open-domain techniques to extend into the biomedical domain. Question answering focusing on patients is less studied. We find that there are some challenges in patient question answering such as limited annotated data, lexical gap and quality of answer spans. We aim to address some of these gaps by extending and developing upon the literature to design a question answering system that can decide on the most appropriate answers for patients attempting to *self-diagnose* while including the ability to abstain from answering when confidence is low.

1 Introduction

Question Answering (QA) is the downstream task of information seeking wherein a user presents a question in natural language, Q, and a system finds an answer or a set of answers from a collection of natural language documents or knowledge bases (Lende and Raghuwanshi, 2016), A, that satisfies the user's question (Molla and Gonzlez, 2007).

Questions fall into one of two categories: factoid and non-factoid. Factoid QA provides brief facts to the users' questions; for example, *Question: What day is it? Answer: Monday*. Non-factoid question answering is a more complex task. It involves answering questions that require specific knowledge, common sense or a procedure due to ambiguity or the scope of the question. An example from the Yahoo non-factoid question answer dataset[1] illustrates this: *Question: Why is it considered unlucky to open an umbrella indoors?*. The answer is not apparent and requires specific knowledge about cultural superstitions.

Question answering is fundamental in high-level tools such as chatbots (Qiu et al., 2017; Yan et al., 2016; Amato et al., 2017; Ram et al., 2018), search engines (Kadam et al., 2015), and virtual assistants (Yaghoubzadeh and Kopp, 2012; Austerjost et al., 2018; Bradley et al., 2018). However, being a downstream task, question answering suffers from *pipeline error*, as it often relies on the quality of several upstream tasks such as coreference resolution (Vicedo and Ferrández, 2000), anaphora resolution (Ram et al., 2018), named entity recognition (Aliod et al., 2006), information retrieval (Mao et al., 2014), and tokenisation (Devlin et al., 2019).

Thus, there has been a growing demand for these QA systems to deliver precise question-specific answers (Pudaruth et al., 2016) and consequently has sparked much research into improving upon relevant natural language processing approaches (Malik et al., 2013), datasets (Rajpurkar et al., 2016; Kociský et al., 2017) and information retrieval techniques (Weienborn et al., 2013; Mao et al., 2014). These improvements have allowed the domain to evolve from shallow keyword matching to contextual and semantic retrieval systems (Kadam et al., 2015). However, most of these techniques have been focused on the open-domain (Soares and Parreiras, 2018) and the challenges harbouring the biomedical domain have not been well addressed and remain unsolved. Here, we define biomedical QA as either factoid or non-factoid QA on biomedical literature.

One such challenge is due to the creation of complex medical queries which require expert knowledge and up to four hours per query (Russell-Rose and Chamberlain, 2017) to adequately answer. This requirement of expert knowledge leads to a lack of high-quality, publicly available biomedical QA datasets. Furthermore, medical datasets tend to be locked behind ethical, obligatory agreements and are usually small due to

---

[1] https://ciir.cs.umass.edu/downloads/nfL6/

Proceedings of the ACL 2019, Student Research Workshop, pages 54–63
Florence, Italy, July 28th-August 2nd, 2019. ©2019 Association for Computational Linguistics

cost constraints and lack of domain experts for annotation (Pampari et al., 2018; Shen et al., 2018). Therefore, open-domain techniques which assume data-rich conditions are not suitable for direct application to the biomedical domain.

Another challenge is clinical term ambiguity, which is due to the temporally and spatially varying nature of clinical terminology, and the frequent use of abbreviation and esoteric medical terminology (Lee et al., 2019) (see Table 1 for examples). It is difficult for systems to adequately disambiguate clinical words to be used in downstream QA systems due to the complexity of the ambiguity of medical terminology, such as abbreviations, due to their varying contexts. Though there are existing tools such as MetaMap (Aronson and Lang, 2010) to disambiguate these terms by mapping them to the UMLS (Unified Medical Language System) metathesaurus, coverage of these systems is low and mappings are often inaccurate (Wu et al., 2012).

Furthermore, systems in the open-domain typically retrieve a long answer before extracting a short continuous span of text to present to the user (Soares and Parreiras, 2018; Rajpurkar et al., 2016). However, for biomedical responses, it is not always sufficient to retrieve short answer continuous spans, and *Answer Evidence* spans that are discontinuous that cross the sentence boundary are often required (Pampari et al., 2018; Hunter and Cohen, 2006; Nentidis et al., 2018).

These problems are not yet solved in the biomedical domain and are reflected in the BioASQ challenge (Nentidis et al., 2018), an annual challenge with a biomedical question answering track. Currently, the state-of-the-art systems do not perform much better than random guess with an accuracy of 66.67% for binary question answering (Chandu et al., 2017), 24.24% for factoid (ranked list of named entities as answers) and an F1-score of 0.3312 for list-type (unranked list of named entities) (Peng et al., 2015) suggesting that there is much room for improvement in terms of algorithms and research.

Furthermore, we found that there is a lack of a biomedical question answering system directed for patients. Biomedical question answering for patients is important as studies from the Pew Research Centre have shown that 35% of U.S. adults have diagnosed themselves using the information they found online[2]. Of these adults, 35% said that they did not get a professional opinion on their self-diagnosis, illustrating that patients may blindly trust the results of search engines without consulting a medical professional. This is cause for concern, as search engines tend to display the most severe ailments first which could lead to a potential waste of hospital resources or deterioration in patient health (Korfage et al., 2006).

Furthermore, although there are negatives to searching symptoms via search engine, for the participants who visited doctors after *self-diagnosis*, research has revealed that doctor-patient relationships and patient compliance with treatment improve as the patients have a clearer understanding of their symptoms and potential disease after *self-diagnosis* (Cocco et al., 2018). These studies motivate the need for a strong biomedical question answering question for patients as it will benefit patients who *self-diagnose* and patients who seek medical advice after looking up their symptoms online.

Finally, we highlight that there is a lexical and semantic gap between clinical and patient language. For example, the expression *"hole in lung"* taken literally is about a punctured lung. However, this colloquialism refers to the condition known as *Pleurisy* (Ben Abacha and Demner-Fushman, 2019; Abacha and Demner-Fushman, 2016), illustrating that patients do not have the level of literacy to formulate complex medical queries nor understand them (Graham and Brookey, 2008).

We aim to address the challenges in applying question answering to biomedical question answering for patients. We highlight that the current gaps of biomedical QA research stem from lack of clinical disambiguation tools, lack of high-quality data, the quality of answer spans, weak algorithms and clinical-patient lexical gaps. Our goal is to present a patient biomedical QA system that can address the gaps in biomedical research and allows a patient to query their symptoms, diseases or available treatment options accurately, but will also abstain from providing answers in cases where there is low confidence in the best answer, question malformation or insufficiency of data to answer the question.

---

[2]https://www.pewinternet.org/2013/01/15/health-online-2013/

Type	Example	Explanation
Temporally varying	Flu	The Flu evolves every year and the cause is predicated on the year it is contracted
Spatially varying	Cancer	Cancer is a disease that varies with severity based on location (Late stage brain cancer is much worse than early stage skin cancer)
Abbreviation	HR	A common clinical abbreviation that typically means heart rate, but may mean hazard ratio depending on the context
Esoteric terminology	c.248T>C	A gene mutation that does not appear in any open-domain corpus such as Wikipedia and has no layman definition

Table 1: Examples of ambiguity in biomedical text.

2 Literature Review

Here, we detail a review of question answering in the open and biomedical domains.

2.1 Information Retrieval Approaches

Biomedical QA systems up until 2015 relied heavily on Information Retrieval (IR) techniques such as tf-idf ranking (Lee et al., 2006) and entity extraction tools such as MetaMap (Aronson and Lang, 2010) in order to obtain candidate answers (by querying biomedical databases) and feature extraction before using machine learning models such as logistic regression (Weienborn et al., 2013). While other techniques included using cosine similarity between one-hot encoded vectors of answer and question for candidate re-ranking (Mao et al., 2014). However, these techniques were inherently bag-of-word approaches that ignored the context of words. Furthermore, these techniques relied on complete matches of question terms and answer paragraphs, which is not realistic in practice. Patients use different terminology to that of medical experts and biomedical literature (Graham and Brookey, 2008).

In more recent years, more neural approaches to IR have been used in the biomedical space (Nentidis et al., 2017, 2018) such as *Position-Aware Convolutional Recurrent Relevance Matching* (Hui et al., 2017), *Deep Relevance Matching Model* (Guo et al., 2017) and *Attention Based Convolutional Neural Network* (Yin et al., 2015). However, though these approaches do not rely on complete matching of words and capture semantics, they either ignore local or global contexts which are useful for disambiguation of clinical terminology and comprehension (McDonald et al., 2018).

2.2 Semantic-level Approach

QA requires the retrieval of long answers before summarisation or retrieval of answer spans. Punyakanok et al. (2004) introduced the use of a question's dependency trees and candidate answers' dependency trees and aligning with the Tree Edit Distance metric to augment statistical classifiers such as Logistic Regression and Conditional Random Fields. However, these methods failed to capture complex semantic information due to a reliance on effective part-of-speech tagging and were not attractive end-to-end solutions. Otherwise, WordNet was utilised to extract semantic relationships and estimate semantic distances between answers and questions (Terol et al., 2007). However, WordNet suffered from being open-domain focused and also was not able to capture complex semantic information such as polysemy (Molla and Gonzlez, 2007).

2.3 Neural Approaches

In recent years, approaches that use neural networks have become popular. Word embedding techniques such as Word2vec and GloVe can model the latent semantic distribution of language through unsupervised learning (Chiu et al., 2016). Furthermore, they are quickly adopted into neural networks as these models take fixed-sized vector inputs, where embeddings could be used as encoded inputs into neural networks such as LSTM (Hochreiter and Schmidhuber, 1997) and CNN (LeCun et al., 1999) in the biomedical domain (Nentidis et al., 2017, 2018).

Though these embedding techniques were useful in capturing latent semantics, they did not distinguish between multiple meanings of clinical text (Molla and Gonzlez, 2007; Vine et al., 2015).

There have been several solutions to this problem (Peters et al., 2018; Howard and Ruder, 2018; Devlin et al., 2019) proposed but they are not relevant specifically to the biomedical domain. Instead, we highlight *BioBERT* (Lee et al., 2019), a biomedical version of *BERT* (Devlin et al., 2019) which is a deeply bidirectional transformer (Vaswani et al., 2017) that is able to incorporate rich context into the encoding or embedding process that has pre-trained on the Wikipedia and PubMed corpora. However, this model fails to account for the spatial and temporal aspects of diseases in biomedical literature as temporality is not encoded into its input. Furthermore, Biobert uses a WordPiece tokeniser (Wu et al., 2016) which keeps a fixed-size vocabulary dictionary for learning new words. However, the vocabulary within the model is derived from Wikipedia, a general domain corpus, and thus Biobert is unable to learn distinct morphological semantics of medical terms like *-phobia*, where '-' denotes suffixation, meaning *fear* as it only has the internal representation for *-bia*.

3   Research Plan

We list the research questions to address some of the research gaps in biomedical QA and the system we aim to design, alongside baseline approaches and methodology as starting points. We will also mention future directions to address these research questions.

RQ1:   What are the limitations of current biomedical QA? The limitations in current biomedical QA include the lack of: sufficient ambiguity resolution tools (Wu et al., 2012), robust techniques to using semantic neural approaches (Lee et al., 2019; Nentidis et al., 2018). The lack of strong comprehension from systems to produce sufficient answer spans that cross the sentence boundary as reflected by poor results in *ideal answer production in BioASQ* (Nentidis et al., 2018, 2017) and addressing issues using real-world patient queries rather than artificially curated queries (Pampari et al., 2018; Guo et al., 2006) which contain colloquial ambiguous non-medical terminology such as *hole in lung*.

In our research, we aim to address each of these gaps by researching into: higher coverage clinical ambiguity tools that use contexts in the spatial and temporal domains, summarisation techniques that can translate from biomedical terminology to patient language (Mishra et al., 2014; Shi et al.,

2018) and tuning biomedical models to solve complex answer span tasks that cross sentence boundaries (Kociský et al., 2017) or require common sense (Talmor et al., 2018).

RQ2:   Data-driven approaches require high-quality datasets.   How can we construct or leverage existing datasets to mimic real-world biomedical question answering? By leveraging existing techniques such as variational auto-encoder (Shen et al., 2018) and Snorkel (Bach et al., 2018), we will be able to generate, label and process additional data that can meet stringent data requirements of neural approaches.

However, synthetic datasets generally perform weaker than handcrafted datasets (Bach et al., 2018). In order to bridge this gap in the research, we propose augmenting these data generation methods via crowd-sourcing methods with textual entailment (Abacha and Demner-Fushman, 2016) and natural language inference (Johnson et al., 2016) to improve the quality of the generated labels and data. For instance, we can use forums like Quora or medical specific forums such as Health24[3] and utilise techniques such as question entailment to find questions that are related to ones seen in the dataset in order to generate higher-quality annotated labels.

We will then develop techniques that can combine synthetic and higher-quality labelled datasets that can be utilized downstream in a QA system. We will compare this against baselines such as majority voting and Snorkel to evaluate our approaches.

Allowing the model to abstain from a decision, through comprehension, has been the focus of many datasets as of late (Rajpurkar et al., 2016; Kociský et al., 2017). We can use these datasets as a starting problem to solve before applying these techniques to the biomedical domain. However, we will also develop and research further techniques in order to allow for improved confidence and low uncertainty from the model.

RQ3: How do we indicate the confidence of the answer that the model has provided? Often researchers interpret softmax or confidence scores from the classifier models as direct correlations to probability but often forget about uncertainties in this measurement (Kendall and Gal, 2017). Due to the real-world application and sensitivity of pre-

---

[3] https://www.health24.com/Experts

dictions in a health-based QA system, there needs
to be guarantees that predictions are of both high
accuracy and low uncertainty.

In order to account for uncertainty, techniques
such as *Inductive Conformal Prediction* (Papadopoulos, 2008) and *Deep Bayesian Learning* (Siddhant and Lipton, 2018) can be used to
model *epistemic uncertainty*, which is not inherently captured by the model during training, in order to make the loss function more robust to noise
and uncertainty and thereby strengthen the predictions of the model. This would then allow softmax scores to be used as confidence scores within
a reasonable level of uncertainty.

RQ4: How do we include temporality or locality of diseases into answers? Diseases are
non-static, they evolve such as the flu or are seasonal such as the summer cold. Current models
utilise only static vector inputs, such as word embeddings, that do not account for this temporal aspect of the input. Furthermore, though diseases
are non-static, they may be more likely in different
countries as there is a spatiotemporal relationship
where countries will experience different seasons
and thus different diseases. In order to accommodate for these relationships, we can draw on prior
research as starting points such as space-time local embeddings (Sun et al., 2015), dynamic word
embeddings (Bamler and Mandt, 2017) or time-embeddings (Barbieri et al., 2018) as baselines and
extend them into the biomedical setting.

RQ5: How do we bridge the semantic gap between clinical text and terminology that a patient can understand? Most patients lack the
expertise in utilising resources such as biomedical literature in order to self-diagnose. Therefore, knowledge or answers should be presented
in a form that they can understand (Graham and
Brookey, 2008). Biomedical language and patient language can be construed as two separate languages as biomedical language changes
and evolves over time (Yan and Zhu, 2018) and
also pose the same problems (Hunter and Cohen,
2006). Therefore, we can model this problem as
a language translation problem and thus can use
techniques in neural machine translation (Qi et al.,
2018; Chousa et al., 2018) based on word embeddings.

However, as biomedical language and patient
English are primarily borne of the same language,
this poses unique problems. For instance, a token
in plain English may translate to several tokens in
the biomedical space or vice versa. This is known
as the alignment problem (Qi et al., 2018). We can
potentially remedy this by borrowing ideas from
n-gram embedding (Zhao et al., 2017) as a starting
point or using Biobert (Lee et al., 2019) projected
to a dual-language embedding space and use attention to produce the alignment. Furthermore, there
are biomedical abbreviations that need to be disambiguated before translation (Festag and Spreckelsen, 2017), for which we would use direct, rulebased approaches using thesauri or tools such as
Metamap (Aronson and Lang, 2010) as our baseline approaches and extend upon using data-driven
approaches (Wu et al., 2017).

4 Experimental Framework

4.1 Datasets

High-quality data is required to address the challenges we outlined. We therefore consider the
following datasets: (1) MEDNLI (Johnson et al.,
2016; Goldberger et al., 2000) for medical language inference; (2) i2b2 in the form of emrQA (Pampari et al., 2018) for synthetic question-answer pairs; (3) SQuAD (Rajpurkar et al.,
2016) for open-domain transfer learning; (4) the
question-answering datasets provided on MediQA
2019[4]; (5) the question entailment dataset and
MedQuAD (Ben Abacha and Demner-Fushman,
2019); (5) CLEF eHealth (Suominen et al., 2018)
to utilize and evaluate IR methods; and (6) we will
supplement our datasets by generating labels for
unlabelled data by leveraging the signals from the
labelled datasets through the use of tools such as
Snorkel (Bach et al., 2018) and CVAE (Shen et al.,
2018).

4.2 Evaluation Metrics

In our experiments, we will evaluate our
summarisation strategies with metrics such as
ROGUE (Lin, 2004), in particular, rogue-2 (Owczarzak and Dang, 2009) and BLEU (Papineni et al., 2002). For question-answering, we use
standard ranking metrics such as *Mean Average
Precision* and *Mean Reciprocal Rank* for evaluating candidate ranking and standard metrics such
as *f1-score*, *Precision*, *Accuracy* and more medical targeted metrics such as *sensitivity* and *specificity* (Parikh et al., 2008).

---

[4]https://sites.google.com/view/mediqa2019

4.3 Proposed Framework

From the research questions mentioned, we propose a framework to unify their solutions.

Embeddings   To begin, we need to construct our date/seasonal embeddings (Barbieri et al., 2018), to do this, we will need datasets that have mentions of the seasonality and locality of disease entities. Also, we will require embeddings that are representative of the text, we will consider state-of-the-art word-level context sensitive embeddings (Lee et al., 2019; Peters et al., 2018) and word-level context insensitive embeddings (Chiu et al., 2016) and ensure they properly represent the biomedical datasets. For instance, *BERT* will need to pre-trained with a biomedical vocabulary rather than a general purpose open-domain one, and, in doing so, we will be able to resolve ambiguity in polysemy or abbreviations.

Furthermore, we will also be researching methodologies to handle out-of-vocabulary words as the current *WordPiece* tokenization (Devlin et al., 2019) or character-level embeddings (Barbieri et al., 2018) would not be sufficient to address esoteric terminology (Lee et al., 2019). The time embeddings and the word-level embeddings will be concatenated and used as input to the model.

Model Architecture   Given the success of multi-task learning (Zhao et al., 2018; Liu et al., 2019), and having been proposed as the *blocking task* in NLP (McCann et al., 2018) that needs to be solved. We therefore apply multi-task learning to this problem. From the state of the art multi-task learning models, we borrow the fundamental building blocks such as multi-headed self-attention (Liu et al., 2019) and multi-pointer generation (McCann et al., 2018) to be used as decisions in a Neural Architecture Search (NAS) (Zoph and Le, 2016). NAS will use reinforcement learning techniques to find a suitable architecture for multi-task learning. We elect to find the architecture to represent our problem this way due to one main reason. The reason is that the field of deep learning in NLP is quickly changing, and thus the state-of-the-art techniques will always change. Therefore, by having a tool that builds architectures from the building blocks of state-of-the-art models is vital. However, crucially, we must add *Heteroscedastic Aleatoric Uncertainty* and *Epistemic Uncertainty* minimisation to the model by adjusting the loss function and weight distribution which will allow the model to be more certain about decisions (Kendall and Gal, 2017). One such decision must be the ability to abstain from answering.

Concretely, we use NAS to discover models for NMT from clinical text to the patient language by conditioning to an encoder-decoder structure. From here, using this model a starting point, NAS will add task-specific layers that will minimise the joint loss over the biomedical tasks such as question answering (Nentidis et al., 2018), question entailment (Abacha and Demner-Fushman, 2016) and natural language inference (Johnson et al., 2016). In doing so, multi-task learning will allow for stronger generalisability and end-to-end training (McCann et al., 2018; Liu et al., 2019).

5   Summary

We highlight gaps within the literature in question answering in the biomedical domain. We outline challenges associated with implementing these systems due to the limitations of current work: lack of annotated data, ambiguity in clinical text and lack of comprehension of question/answer text by models.

We motivate this research in the area of patient QA due to the high volume of medical queries in search engines that are trusted by patients. Our research aims to build upon the strengths of the current state-of-the-art and research new strategies in solving technical challenges to support a patient in retrieving the answers they require with low uncertainty and high confidence.

Acknowledgements

I thank for my supervisors, Dr Sarvnaz Karimi and Dr Zhenchang Xing for providing invaluable insight into the writing of this proposal. This research is supported by the Australian Research Training Program and the CSIRO Postgraduate Scholarship.

References

Ben Abacha and Demner-Fushman. 2016. Recognizing Question Entailment for Medical Question Answering. *American Medical Informatics Association Annual Symposium Proceedings*, 2016:310–318.

Diego Aliod, Menno Zaanen, and Daniel Smith. 2006. Named entity recognition for question answering. In *The Australasian Language Technology Association*, Sydney, Australia.

Flora Amato, Stefano Marrone, Vincenzo Moscato, Gabriele Piantadosi, Antonio Picariello, and Carlo Sansone. 2017. Chatbots meet ehealth: Automatizing healthcare. In *Proceedings of the Workshop on Artificial Intelligence with Application in Health co-located with the 16th International Conference of the Italian Association for Artificial Intelligence*, Bari, Italy.

Alan Aronson and François-Michel Lang. 2010. An overview of Metamap: Historical perspective and recent advances. *Journal of the American Medical Informatics Association*, 17(3):229–236.

Jonas Austerjost, Marc Porr, Noah Riedel, Dominik Geier, Thomas Becker, Thomas Scheper, Daniel Marquard, Patrick Lindner, and Sascha Beutel. 2018. Introducing a virtual assistant to the lab: A voice user interface for the intuitive control of laboratory instruments. *SLAS Technology: Translating Life Sciences Innovation*, 23:476–482.

Stephen Bach, Daniel Rodriguez, Yintao Liu, Chong Luo, Haidong Shao, Cassandra Xia, Souvik Sen, Alexander Ratner, Braden Hancock, Houman Alborzi, Rahul Kuchhal, Christopher Ré, and Rob Malkin. 2018. Snorkel drybell: A case study in deploying weak supervision at industrial scale. *Computing Research Repository*, abs/1812.00417.

Robert Bamler and Stephan Mandt. 2017. Dynamic Word Embeddings. *arXiv e-prints*, page arXiv:1702.08359.

Francesco Barbieri, Luís Marujo, Pradeep Karuturi, William Brendel, and Horacio Saggion. 2018. Exploring emoji usage and prediction through a temporal variation lens. *Computing Research Repository*, abs/1805.00731.

Asma Ben Abacha and Dina Demner-Fushman. 2019. A question-entailment approach to question answering. *Computing Research Repository*, abs/1901.08079.

Nick Bradley, Thomas Fritz, and Reid Holmes. 2018. Context-aware conversational developer assistants. In *Proceedings of the 40th International Conference on Software Engineering*, pages 993–1003, New York, NY, US.

Khyathi Chandu, Aakanksha Naik, Aditya Chandrasekar, Zi Yang, Niloy Gupta, and Eric Nyberg. 2017. Tackling biomedical text summarization: OAQA at BioASQ 5B. In *BioNLP 2017*, pages 58–66, Vancouver, Canada,.

Billy Chiu, Gamal Crichton, Anna Korhonen, and Sampo Pyysalo. 2016. How to train good word embeddings for biomedical NLP. In *Proceedings of the 15th Workshop on Biomedical Natural Language Processing*, pages 166–174, Berlin, Germany.

Katsuki Chousa, Katsuhito Sudoh, and Satoshi Nakamura. 2018. Training neural machine translation using word embedding-based loss. *Computing Research Repository*, abs/1807.11219.

Anthony Cocco, Rachel Zordan, David Taylor, Tracey Weiland, Stuart Dilley, Joyce Kant, Mahesha Dombagolla, Andreas Hendarto, Fiona Lai, and Jennie Hutton. 2018. Dr Google in the ED: searching for online health information by adult emergency department patients. *The Medical Journal of Australia*, 209:342–347.

Jacob Devlin, Ming-Wei Chang, Kenton Lee, and Kristina Toutanova. 2019. BERT: Pre-training of deep bidirectional transformers for language understanding. In *Proceedings of the Conference of the North American Chapter of the Association for Computational Linguistics: Human Language Technologies*, Minneapolis, MN.

Sven Festag and Cord Spreckelsen. 2017. *Word Sense Disambiguation of Medical Terms via Recurrent Convolutional Neural Networks*, volume 236. Health Informatics Meets eHealth.

Ary Goldberger, Luis Amaral, Leon Glass, Jeffrey Hausdorff, Plamen Ivanov, Roger Mark, Joseph Mietus, George Moody, Chung-Kang Peng, and Eugene Stanley. 2000. PhysioBank, PhysioToolkit, and PhysioNet: components of a new research resource for complex physiologic signals. *Circulation*, 101(23):E215–220.

Suzanne Graham and John Brookey. 2008. Do patients understand? *The Permanente journal*, 12(3):67–69.

Jiafeng Guo, Yixing Fan, Qingyao Ai, and Bruce Croft. 2017. A deep relevance matching model for ad-hoc retrieval. *Computing Research Repository*, abs/1711.08611.

Yikun Guo, Robert Gaizauskas, Ian Roberts, and George Demetriou. 2006. Identifying personal health information using support vector machines. In *i2b2 Workshop on Challenges in Natural Language Processing for Clinical Data*, Washington, DC, US.

Sepp Hochreiter and Jrgen Schmidhuber. 1997. Long short-term memory. *Neural Computing*, 9(8):1735–1780.

Jeremy Howard and Sebastian Ruder. 2018. Universal language model fine-tuning for text classification. In *Proceedings of the 56th Annual Meeting of the Association for Computational Linguistics (Volume 1: Long Papers)*, pages 328–339, Melbourne, Australia.

Kai Hui, Andrew Yates, Klaus Berberich, and Gerard de Melo. 2017. A position-aware deep model for relevance matching in information retrieval. *Computing Research Repository*, abs/1704.03940.

Lawrence Hunter and Bretonnel Cohen. 2006. Biomedical language processing: what's beyond pubmed? *Molecular Cell*, 21(5):589–594.

Alistair Johnson, Tom Pollard, Lu Shen, Li-wei Lehman, Mengling Feng, Mohammad Ghassemi, Benjamin Moody, Peter Szolovits, Anthony Celi, and Roger Mark. 2016. MIMIC-III, a freely accessible critical care database. *Scientific Data*, 3:160035.

Aniket Kadam, Shashank Joshi, Sachin Shinde, and Sampat Medhane. 2015. Notice of retraction question answering search engine short review and roadmap to future qa search engine. In *International Conference on Electrical, Electronics, Signals, Communication and Optimization*, pages 1–8, Visakhapatnam, India.

Alex Kendall and Yarin Gal. 2017. What uncertainties do we need in bayesian deep learning for computer vision? *Computing Research Repository*, abs/1703.04977.

Tomás Kociský, Jonathan Schwarz, Phil Blunsom, Chris Dyer, Karl Hermann, Gábor Melis, and Edward Grefenstette. 2017. The narrativeqa reading comprehension challenge. *Computing Research Repository*, abs/1712.07040.

Ida Korfage, Harry Koning, Monique Roobol, Fritz Schrder, and Marie-Louise Essink-Bot. 2006. Prostate cancer diagnosis: The impact on patients mental health. *European Journal of Cancer*, 42(2):165 – 170.

Yann LeCun, Patrick Haffner, Léon Bottou, and Yoshua Bengio. 1999. Object recognition with gradient-based learning. In *Shape, Contour and Grouping in Computer Vision*, page 319, London, UK.

Jinhyuk Lee, Wonjin Yoon, Sungdong Kim, Donghyeon Kim, Sunkyu Kim, Chan Ho So, and Jaewoo Kang. 2019. BioBERT: A pre-trained biomedical language representation model for biomedical text mining. *arXiv e-prints*, page arXiv:1901.08746.

Minsuk Lee, James Cimino, Hai Zhu, Carl Sable, Vijay Shanker, John Ely, and Hong Yu. 2006. Beyond information retrieval–medical question answering. *American Medical Informatics Association Annual Symposium Proceedings*, 2006:469–473.

Sweta Lende and Mukesh Raghuwanshi. 2016. Question answering system on education acts using nlp techniques. In *World Conference on Futuristic Trends in Research and Innovation for Social Welfare (Startup Conclave)*, pages 1–6, Coimbatore, India.

Chin-Yew Lin. 2004. ROUGE: A package for automatic evaluation of summaries. In *Text Summarization Branches Out: Proceedings of the Association for Computational Linguistics Workshop*, pages 74–81, Barcelona, Spain.

Xiaodong Liu, Pengcheng He, Weizhu Chen, and Jianfeng Gao. 2019. Improving multi-task deep neural networks via knowledge distillation for natural language understanding. *Computing Research Repository*, arXiv:1904.0948.

Nidhi Malik, Aditi Sharan, and Payal Biswas. 2013. Domain knowledge enriched framework for restricted domain question answering system. In *IEEE International Conference on Computational Intelligence and Computing Research*, pages 1–7, Madurai, Tamilnadu, India.

Yuqing Mao, Chih-Hsuan Wei, and Zhiyong Lu. 2014. NCBI at the 2014 BioASQ challenge task: Large-scale biomedical semantic indexing and question answering. In *Conference and Labs of the Evaluation Forum*, Sheffield, UK.

Bryan McCann, Nitish Shirish Keskar, Caiming Xiong, and Richard Socher. 2018. The natural language decathlon: Multitask learning as question answering. *Computing Research Repository*, abs/1806.08730.

Ryan McDonald, Georgios-Ioannis Brokos, and Ion Androutsopoulos. 2018. Deep relevance ranking using enhanced document-query interactions. *Computing Research Repository*, abs/1809.01682.

Rashmi Mishra, Jiantao Bian, Marcelo Fiszman, Charlene Weir, Siddhartha Jonnalagadda, Javed Mostafa, and Guilherme Del Fiol. 2014. Text summarization in the biomedical domain: a systematic review of recent research. *Journal of Biomedical Informatics*, 52:457–467.

Diego Molla and Jos Gonzlez. 2007. Question answering in restricted domains: An overview. *Computational Linguistics*, 33:41–61.

Anastasios Nentidis, Konstantinos Bougiatiotis, Anastasia Krithara, Georgios Paliouras, and Ioannis Kakadiaris. 2017. Results of the fifth edition of the bioasq challenge. In *Biomedical Natural Language Processing*, pages 48–57, Vancouver, Canada.

Anastasios Nentidis, Anastasia Krithara, Konstantinos Bougiatiotis, Georgios Paliouras, and Ioannis Kakadiaris. 2018. Results of the sixth edition of the BioASQ challenge. In *Proceedings of the 6th BioASQ Workshop A challenge on large-scale biomedical semantic indexing and question answering*, pages 1–10, Brussels, Belgium.

Karolina Owczarzak and Hoa Dang. 2009. Evaluation of automatic summaries: Metrics under varying data conditions. In *Proceedings of the Workshop on Language Generation and Summarisation*, pages 23–30, Stroudsburg, PA, US.

Anusri Pampari, Preethi Raghavan, Jennifer Liang, and Jian Peng. 2018. emrqa: A large corpus for question answering on electronic medical records. *Computing Research Repository*, abs/1809.00732.

Harris Papadopoulos. 2008. *Inductive Conformal Prediction: Theory and Application to Neural Networks*.

Kishore Papineni, Salim Roukos, Todd Ward, and Wei-Jing Zhu. 2002. Bleu: A method for automatic evaluation of machine translation. In *Proceedings of 40th Annual Meeting of the Association for Computational Linguistics*, pages 311–318, Philadelphia, Pennsylvania, US.

Rajul Parikh, Annie Mathai, Shefali Parikh, Chandra Sekhar, and Ravi Thomas. 2008. Understanding and using sensitivity, specificity and predictive values. *Indian Journal of Ophthalmology*, 56(1):45–50.

Shengwen Peng, Ronghui You, Zhikai Xie, Beichen Wang, Yanchun Zhang, and Shanfeng Zhu. 2015. The fudan participation in the 2015 bioasq challenge: Large-scale biomedical semantic indexing and question answering. In *Conference and Labs of the Evaluation Forum 2015: Conference and Labs of the Evaluation Forum Experimental IR meets Multilinguality, Multimodality and Interaction*, volume 1391, Toulouse, France.

Matthew Peters, Mark Neumann, Mohit Iyyer, Matt Gardner, Christopher Clark, Kenton Lee, and Luke Zettlemoyer. 2018. Deep contextualized word representations. *Computing Research Repository*, abs/1802.05365.

Sameerchand Pudaruth, Kajal Boodhoo, and Lushika Goolbudun. 2016. An intelligent question answering system for ICT. In *2016 International Conference on Electrical, Electronics, and Optimization Techniques*, pages 2895–2899, Paralakhemundi, Odisha, India.

Vasin Punyakanok, Dan Roth, and Wen tau Yih. 2004. Mapping dependencies trees: An application to question answering. In *In Proceedings of the 8th International Symposium on Artificial Intelligence and Mathematics, Fort*, Fort Lauderdale, Flordia.

Ye Qi, Devendra Sachan, Matthieu Felix, Sarguna Padmanabhan, and Graham Neubig. 2018. When and why are pre-trained word embeddings useful for neural machine translation? *Computing Research Repository*, abs/1804.06323.

Minghui Qiu, Feng-Lin Li, Siyu Wang, Xing Gao, Yan Chen, Weipeng Zhao, Haiqing Chen, Jun Huang, and Wei deep-multi-task-learning Chu. 2017. AliMe chat: A sequence to sequence and rerank based chatbot engine. In *Proceedings of the 55th Annual Meeting of the Association for Computational Linguistics (Volume 2: Short Papers)*, pages 498–503, Vancouver, Canada.

Pranav Rajpurkar, Jian Zhang, Konstantin Lopyrev, and Percy Liang. 2016. Squad: 100, 000+ questions for machine comprehension of text. *Computing Research Repository*, abs/1606.05250.

Ashwin Ram, Rohit Prasad, Chandra Khatri, Anu Venkatesh, Raefer Gabriel, Qing Liu, Jeff Nunn, Behnam Hedayatnia, Ming Cheng, Ashish Nagar, Eric King, Kate Bland, Amanda Wartick, Yi Pan,

Han Song, Sk Jayadevan, Gene Hwang, and Art Pettigrue. 2018. Conversational AI: the science behind the alexa prize. *Computing Research Repository*, abs/1801.03604.

Tony Russell-Rose and Jon Chamberlain. 2017. Expert search strategies: The information retrieval practices of healthcare information professionals. *JMIR Medical Informatics*, 5(4):e33.

Sheng Shen, Yaliang Li, Nan Du, Xian Wu, Yusheng Xie, Shen Ge, Tao Yang, Kai Wang, Xingzheng Liang, and Wei Fan. 2018. On the generation of medical question-answer pairs. *Computing Research Repository*, abs/1811.00681.

Tian Shi, Yaser Keneshloo, Naren Ramakrishnan, and Chandan Reddy. 2018. Neural abstractive text summarization with sequence-to-sequence models. *Computing Research Repository*, abs/1812.02303.

Aditya Siddhant and Zachary Lipton. 2018. Deep bayesian active learning for natural language processing: Results of a large-scale empirical study. In *Proceedings of the 2018 Conference on Empirical Methods in Natural Language Processing*, pages 2904–2909, Brussels, Belgium.

Marco Soares and Fernando Parreiras. 2018. A literature review on question answering techniques, paradigms and systems. *Journal of King Saud University - Computer and Information Sciences*.

Ke Sun, Jun Wang, Alexandros Kalousis, and Stephane Marchand-Maillet. 2015. Space-time local embeddings. In *Advances in Neural Information Processing Systems 28*, pages 100–108.

Hanna Suominen, Liadh Kelly, Lorraine Goeuriot, Aurélie Névéol, Lionel Ramadier, Aude Robert, Evangelos Kanoulas, Rene Spijker, Leif Azzopardi, Dan Li, Jimmy, João Palotti, and Guido Zuccon. 2018. Overview of the conference and labs of the evaluation forum ehealth evaluation lab 2018. In *Experimental IR Meets Multilinguality, Multimodality, and Interaction*, pages 286–301, Avignon, France.

Alon Talmor, Jonathan Herzig, Nicholas Lourie, and Jonathan Berant. 2018. Commonsenseqa: A question answering challenge targeting commonsense knowledge. *Computing Research Repository*, abs/1811.00937.

Rafael Terol, Patricio Martinez-Barco, and Manuel Palomar. 2007. A knowledge based method for the medical question answering problem. *Computers in Biology and Medicine*, 37(10):1511–1521.

Ashish Vaswani, Noam Shazeer, Niki Parmar, Jakob Uszkoreit, Llion Jones, Aidan Gomez, Lukasz Kaiser, and Illia Polosukhin. 2017. Attention is all you need. *Computing Research Repository*, abs/1706.03762.

José Vicedo and Antonio Ferrández. 2000. Importance of pronominal anaphora resolution in question answering systems. In *Proceedings of the 38th Annual Meeting of the Association for Computational Linguistics*, pages 555–562, Hong Kong.

Lance Vine, Mahnoosh Kholghi, Guido Zuccon, Laurianne Sitbon, and Anthony Nguyen. 2015. Analysis of word embeddings and sequence features for clinical information extraction. In *Proceedings of the Australasian Language Technology Association Workshop 2015*, pages 21–30, Parramatta, Australia.

Dirk Weienborn, George Tsatsaronis, and Michael Schroeder. 2013. Answering factoid questions in the biomedical domain. In *CEUR Workshop Proceedings*, volume 1094, Valencia, Spain.

Yonghui Wu, Joshua Denny, Trent Rosenbloom, Randolph Miller, Dario Giuse, and Hua Xu. 2012. A comparative study of current clinical natural language processing systems on handling abbreviations in discharge summaries. *American Medical Informatics Association Annual Symposium Proceedings*, 2012:997–1003.

Yonghui Wu, Joshua Denny, Rosenbloom Trent, Randolph Miller, Dario Giuse, Lulu Wang, Carmelo Blanquicett, Ergin Soysal, Jun Xu, and Hua Xu. 2017. A long journey to short abbreviations: developing an open-source framework for clinical abbreviation recognition and disambiguation (CARD). *Journal of the American Medical Informatics Association*, 24(e1):e79–e86.

Yonghui Wu, Mike Schuster, Zhifeng Chen, Quoc Le, Mohammad Norouzi, Wolfgang Macherey, Maxim Krikun, Yuan Cao, Qin Gao, Klaus Macherey, Jeff Klingner, Apurva Shah, Melvin Johnson, Xiaobing Liu, Lukasz Kaiser, Stephan Gouws, Yoshikiyo Kato, Taku Kudo, Hideto Kazawa, Keith Stevens, George Kurian, Nishant Patil, Wei Wang, Cliff Young, Jason Smith, Jason Riesa, Alex Rudnick, Oriol Vinyals, Greg Corrado, Macduff Hughes, and Jeffrey Dean. 2016. Google's neural machine translation system: Bridging the gap between human and machine translation. *Computing Research Repository*, abs/1609.08144.

Ramin Yaghoubzadeh and Stefan Kopp. 2012. Toward a virtual assistant for vulnerable users: Designing careful interaction. In *Proceedings of the 1st Workshop on Speech and Multimodal Interaction in Assistive Environments*, pages 13–17, Jeju, Republic of Korea. Association for Computational Linguistics.

Erjia Yan and Yongjun Zhu. 2018. Tracking word semantic change in biomedical literature. *International Journal of Medical Informatics*, 109:76 – 86.

Zhao Yan, Nan Duan, Junwei Bao, Peng Chen, Ming Zhou, Zhoujun Li, and Jianshe Zhou. 2016. DocChat: An information retrieval approach for chatbot engines using unstructured documents. In *Proceedings of the 54th Annual Meeting of the Association for Computational Linguistics (Volume 1: Long Papers)*, pages 516–525, Berlin, Germany. Association for Computational Linguistics.

Wenpeng Yin, Hinrich Schütze, Bing Xiang, and Bowen Zhou. 2015. ABCNN: attention-based convolutional neural network for modeling sentence pairs. *Computing Research Repository*, abs/1512.05193.

Sendong Zhao, Ting Liu, Sicheng Zhao, and Fei Wang. 2018. A neural multi-task learning framework to jointly model medical named entity recognition and normalization. *Computing Research Repository*, abs/1812.06081.

Zhe Zhao, Tao Liu, Shen Li, Bofang Li, and Xiaoyong Du. 2017. Ngram2vec: Learning improved word representations from ngram co-occurrence statistics. In *Proceedings of the 2017 Conference on Empirical Methods in Natural Language Processing*, pages 244–253, Copenhagen, Denmark.

Barret Zoph and Quoc Le. 2016. Neural architecture search with reinforcement learning. *Computing Research Repository*, abs/1611.01578.

Knowledge discovery and hypothesis generation from online patient forums: A research proposal

Anne Dirkson

Leiden Institute of Advanced Computer Science, Leiden University
Niels Bohrweg 1, Leiden, the Netherlands
`a.r.dirkson@liacs.leidenuniv.nl`

Abstract

The unprompted patient experiences shared on patient forums contain a wealth of unexploited knowledge. Mining this knowledge and cross-linking it with biomedical literature, could expose novel insights, which could subsequently provide hypotheses for further clinical research. As of yet, automated methods for open knowledge discovery on patient forum text are lacking. Thus, in this research proposal, we outline future research into methods for mining, aggregating and cross-linking patient knowledge from online forums. Additionally, we aim to address how one could measure the credibility of this extracted knowledge.

1 Introduction

In the biomedical realm, open knowledge discovery from text has traditionally been limited to semi-structured data, such as electronic health records, and biomedical literature (Fleuren and Alkema, 2015). Patient forums (or *discussion groups*), however, contain a wealth of unexploited knowledge: the unprompted experiences of the patients themselves. Patients indicate that they rely heavily on the experiences of others (Smailhodzic et al., 2016), for instance for learning how to cope with their illness on a daily basis (Burda et al., 2016; Hartzler and Pratt, 2011).

In recent years, researchers have begun to acknowledge the value of such knowledge from experience, also called experiential knowledge. It is increasingly recognized as complementary to empirical knowledge (Carter et al., 2013; Knotnerus and Tugwell, 2012). Consequently, patient forum data has been used for a range of health-related applications from tracking public health trends (Sarker et al., 2016b) to detecting adverse drug responses (Sarker et al., 2015). In contrast to other potential sources of patient experiences such as electronic health records or focus groups, patient forums offer uncensored and unsolicited experiences. Moreover, it has been found that patients are more likely to share their experiences with their peers than with a physician (Davison et al., 2000).

Nonetheless, so far, the mining of experiential knowledge from patient forums has been limited to the extraction of adverse drug responses (ADRs) that patients experience when taking prescription drugs. Yet, patient forums contain an abundance of valuable information hidden in other experiences. For example, patients may report effective coping techniques for side effects of medication. Nevertheless, automated methods for *open* knowledge discovery from patient forum text, which could capture a wider range of experiences, have not yet been developed.

Therefore, we aim to develop such automated methods for mining anecdotal medical experiences from patient forums and aggregating them into a knowledge repository. This could then be cross-linked to a comparable repository of curated knowledge from biomedical literature and clinical trials. Such a comparison will expose any novel information present in the patient experiences, which could subsequently provide hypotheses for further clinical research, or valuable aggregate knowledge directly for the patients.

Although hypothesis generation in this manner could potentially advance research for all patient groups, we expect it to be the most promising for patients with rare diseases. Research into these diseases is scarce (Aymé et al., 2008): their rarity obstructs data collection and for-profit industry considers this research too costly. Aggregation of data from online forums could spur the coordinated, trans-geographic effort necessary to attain progress for these patients (Aymé et al., 2008).

Proceedings of the ACL 2019, Student Research Workshop, pages 64–73
Florence, Italy, July 28th-August 2nd, 2019. ©2019 Association for Computational Linguistics

Problem statement Patient experiences are shared in abundance on patient forums. Experiential knowledge expressed in these experiences may be able to advance understanding of the disease and its treatment, but there is currently no method for automatically mining, aggregating, cross-linking and verifying this knowledge.

Research question To what extent can automated text analysis of patient forum posts aid knowledge discovery and yield reliable hypotheses for clinical research?

Contributions Our main contributions to the NLP field will be: (1) methods for extracting of aggregated knowledge from patient experiences on online fora, (2) a method for cross-linking curated knowledge and complementary patient knowledge, and (3) a method for assessing the credibility of claims derived from medical user-generated content. We will release all code and software related to this project. Data will be available upon request to protect the privacy of the patients.

2 Research Challenges

In order to answer this research question, five challenges must be addressed:

- *Data Quality* Knowledge extraction from social media text is complicated by colloquial language, typographical errors, and spelling mistakes (Park et al., 2015). The complex medical domain only aggravates this challenge (Gonzalez-Hernandez et al., 2017).
- *Named Entity Recognition (NER)* Previous work has been limited to extracting drug names and adverse drug responses (ADRs). Consequently, methods for extracting other types of relevant entities, such as those related to coping behaviour, still need to be developed. In general, layman's terms and creative language use hinder NER from user-generated text (Sarker et al., 2018).
- *Automatic Relation Annotation* Relation extraction from forum text has been explored only for ADR-drug relations. A more open extraction approach is currently lacking. The typically small size of patient forum data and the subsequent lack of redundancy is the main challenge for relation extraction. Other challenges include determining the presence,

direction and polarity of relations and normalizing relationships in order to aggregate claims.
- *Cross-linking with Curated Knowledge* In order to extract novel knowledge, the extracted knowledge should be compared with curated sources. Thus, methods need to be developed to build comparable enough knowledge bases from both types of knowledge.
- *Credibility of Medical User-generated Content* In order to assess the trustworthiness of novel, health-related claims from user-generated online content, a method for measuring their relative credibility must be developed.

3 Prior work

In this section, we will highlight the prior work for each of these research challenges. Hereafter, in section 4, we will outline our proposed approach to tackling them in light of current research gaps.

3.1 Data quality

The current state-of-the-art lexical normalization pipeline for social media was developed by Sarker (2017). Their spelling correction method depends on a standard dictionary supplemented with domain-specific terms to *detect* mistakes, and on a language model of generic Twitter data to *correct* these mistakes. For domains that have many out-of-vocabulary terms compared to the available dictionaries and language models, such as medical social media, this is problematic and results in a low precision for correct domain-specific words.

Besides improving data quality through spelling normalization, it is essential to identify which forum posts contain patient experiences before knowledge can be extracted from these experiences. Previous research into systematically distinguishing experiences on patient forums is limited to a single study on Dutch forum data (Verberne et al., 2019). They identified narratives using only lower-cased words as features. Furthermore, specialized classifiers for differentiating factual statements about ADRs and personal experiences of ADRs on social media have also been developed (e.g. Nikfarjam et al. (2015)). However, these are too specialized to be suited for identifying patient experiences in general.

3.2 NER on health-related social media

Named entity recognition on patient forums is currently restricted to the detection of ADRs to prescription drugs (Sarker et al., 2015). Leaman et al. (2010) were the first to extract ADRs from patient forum data by matching tokens to a lexicon of side effects compiled from three medical databases and manually curated colloquial phrases. As lexicon-based approaches are hindered by descriptive and colloquial language use (O'Connor et al., 2014), later studies attempted to use association mining (Nikfarjam and Gonzalez, 2011). Although partially successful, concepts occurring in infrequent or more complex sentences remained a challenge.

Consequently, more recent studies have employed supervised machine learning, which can detect inexact matches. The current state-of-the-art systems use conditional random fields (CRF) with lexicon-based mapping (Nikfarjam et al., 2015; Metke-Jimenez and Karimi, 2015; Sarker et al., 2016a). Key to their success is their ability to incorporate textual information. Information-rich semantic features, such as polarity (Liu et al., 2016); and unsupervised word embeddings (Nikfarjam et al., 2015; Sarker et al., 2016a), were found to aid the supervised extraction of ADRs. As of yet, deep learning methods have not been explored for ADR extraction from patient forums.

For subsequent concept normalization of ADRs i.e. their mapping to concepts in a controlled vocabulary, supervised methods outperform lexicon-based and unsupervised approaches (Sarker et al., 2018). Currently, the state-of-the-art system is an ensemble of a Recurrent Neural Network and Multinomial Logistic Regression (Sarker et al., 2018). In contrast to previous research, we aim to extract a wider variety of entities, such as those related to coping, and thus we will also extend normalization approaches to a wider range of concepts.

3.3 Automated relation extraction on health-related social media

Research on relation extraction from patient forums has been explored to a limited extent in the context of ADR-drug relations. Whereas earlier studies simply used co-occurrence (Leaman et al., 2010), Liu and Chen (2013) opted for a two-step classifier system with a first classifier to determine *whether* entities have a relation and a second to define it. Another study used a Hidden Markov Model (Sampathkumar et al., 2014) to predict the presence of a causal relationship using a list of keywords e.g. 'effects from'. More recently, Chen et al. (2018) opted for a statistical approach: They used the Proportional Reporting Ratio, a statistical measure for signal detection, which compares the proportion of a given symptom mentioned with a certain drug to the proportion in combination with *all* drugs. In order to facilitate more *open* knowledge discovery on patient forums, we aim to investigate how other relations than ADR-drug relations can be extracted.

3.4 Cross-linking medical user-generated content with curated knowledge

Although the integration of data from different biomedical sources has become a booming topic in recent years (Sacchi and Holmes, 2016), only two studies have cross-linked user-generated content from health-related social media with structured databases. Benton et al. (2011) compared co-occurrence of side effects in breast cancer posts to drug package labels, whereas Yeleswarapu et al. (2014) combined user comments with structured databases and MEDLINE abstracts to calculate the strength of associations between drugs and their side effects. We aim to develop cross-linking methods with curated sources that go beyond ADR-drug relations in order to extract divergent novel knowledge from user-generated text.

3.5 Credibility of medical user-generated content

As the Web accumulates user-generated content, it becomes important to know if a specific piece of information is credible or not (Berti-Equille and Ba, 2016). For novel claims, the factual truth can often not be determined, and thus credibility is the highest attainable.

So far, the approaches to automatically assessing credibility of health-related information on social media has been limited to three studies (Viviani and Pasi, 2017a). Firstly, Vydiswaran et al. (2011) used textual features to compute trustworthiness based on community support. They evaluated their approach using simulated data with varying amounts of invalid claims, defined as disapproved or non-specific treatments, e.g. paracetamol. Secondly, Mukherjee et al. (2014) developed a semi-supervised probabilistic graph that uses an expert medical database of known side effects as a ground truth to assess the credibility of rare or

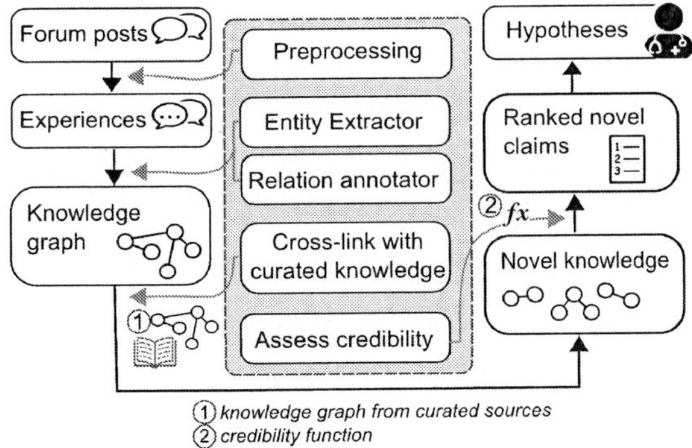

Figure 1: Proposed pipeline

unknown side effects on an online health community. Kinsora et al. (2017) was the first to not focus solely on accessing relations of treatments and side effects. They developed the first labeled data set of misinformative and non-misinformative comments from a health discussion forum, where misinformation is defined as 'medical relations that have not been verified'. By definition, however, the *novel* health-related claims arising from our knowledge discovery process will not be verified. Thus, so far, a methodology for assessing the credibility of novel health-related claims on social media is lacking. We aim to address this gap.

4 Proposed Pipeline

As can be seen in Figure 1, we propose a pipeline that will automatically output a list of medical claims from the knowledge contained in user-generated posts on a patient forum. They will be ranked in order of credibility to allow clinical researchers to focus on the most credible candidate hypotheses.

After preprocessing, we aim to extract relevant entities and their relations from only those posts that contain personal experiences. Therefore, we need a classifier for personal experiences as well as a robust preprocessing system. From the filtered posts, we will subsequently extract a wider range of entities than was done in previous research, such as those related to coping with adverse drug responses, medicine efficacy, comorbidity and lifestyle. Since patients with comorbities, i.e. co-occurring medical conditions, are often excluded from clinical trials (Unger et al., 2019), it is unknown whether medicine efficacy and adverse drug responses might differ for these patients. Moreover, certain lifestyle choices, such as diet, are known to influence both the working of

medication (Bailey et al., 2013) and the severity of side effects. For instance, patients with the rare disease Gastro-Intestinal Stromal Tumor (GIST) provide anecdotal evidence that sweet potato can influence the severity of side effects.[1] These issues greatly impact the quality of life of patients and can be investigated with our approach. However, extending towards a more open information extraction approach instigates various questions. Could, for instance, dependency parsing be employed? Should a pre-specified list of relations be used and if so, which criteria should this list conform to? Which approaches and insights from other NLP domains could help us here?

Answering these questions is complicated by our consecutive aim to cross-link the patient knowledge with curated knowledge: the approach to knowledge extraction and aggregation needs to be similar enough to allow for filtering. A completely open approach may therefore not be possible. A key feature that impedes the generation of comparable data repositories is the difference in terminology. Extracting curated claims is also not trivial, as biomedical literature is at best semi-structured. Yet, comparable repositories are essential, as they will enable us to eliminate presently known facts from our findings.

Finally, we aim to automatically assess the credibility of these novel claims in order to output a ranked list of novel hypotheses to clinical researchers. Our working definition of credibility is the level of trustworthiness of the claim, or how valid the audience perceives the statement itself to be (Hovland et al., 1953). The development of a method for measuring credibility raises interesting points for discussion, such as: which linguistic features could be used to measure the credibility of a claim? And how could support of a statement, or lack thereof, by other forum posts be measured?

In the next two sections, we will elaborate, firstly, on initial results for improving data quality and, secondly, on implementation ideas for our NER and relation extraction system; and for our method for assessing credibility.

5 Initial results

To reduce errors in knowledge extraction, our research initially focused on improving data quality through (1) lexical normalization and (2) identify-

---

[1] https://liferaftgroup.org/
managing-side-effects/

ing messages that contain personal experiences.[2]

Lexical normalization Since the state-of-the-art lexical normalization method (Sarker, 2017) functions poorly for social media in the health domain, we developed a data-driven spelling correction module that is dependent only on a *generic* dictionary and thus capable of dealing with small and niche data sets (Dirkson et al., 2018, 2019b). We developed this method on a rare cancer forum for GIST patients[3] consisting of 36,722 posts. As a second cancer-related forum, we used a subreddit on cancer of 274,532 posts [4].

For *detecting* mistakes, we implemented a decision process that determines whether a token is a mistake by, firstly, checking if it is present in a generic dictionary, and if not, checking for viable candidates. Viable candidates, which are derived from the data, need to have at least double the corpus frequency and a high enough similarity. This relative, as opposed to an absolute, frequency threshold enables the system to detect common spelling mistakes. The underlying assumption is that correct words will occur frequently enough to not have any viable correction candidates: they will thus be marked as correct. Our method attained an $F_{0.5}$ score of 0.888. Additionally, it manages to circumvent the absence of specialized dictionaries and domain- and genre-specific pretrained word embeddings. For *correcting* spelling mistakes, relative weighted edit distance was employed: the weights are derived from frequencies of online spelling errors (Norvig, 2009). Our method attained an accuracy of 62.3% compared to 20.8% for the state-of-the-art method (Sarker, 2017). By pre-selecting viable candidates, this accuracy was further increased by 1.8% point.

This spelling correction pipeline reduced out-of-vocabulary terms by 0.50% and 0.27% in the two cancer-related forums. More importantly, it mainly targeted, and thus corrected, medical concepts. Additionally, it increased classification accuracy on five out of six benchmark data sets of medical forum text (Dredze et al. (2016); Paul and Dredze (2009); Huang et al. (2017); and Task 1 and 4 of the ACL 2019 Social Media Mining 4 Health shared task[5]).

Personal experience classification As research into systematically distinguishing patient experiences was limited to Dutch data with only one feature type (Verberne et al., 2019), we investigated how they could best be identified in English forum data (Dirkson et al., 2019a). Each post was classified as containing a personal experience or not. A personal experience did not need to be about the author but could also be about someone else.

We found that character 3-grams ($F_1 = 0.815$) significantly outperform psycho-linguistic features and document embeddings in this task. Moreover, we found that personal experiences were characterized by the use of past tense, health-related words and first-person pronouns, whereas non-narrative text was associated with the future tense, emotional support words and second-person pronouns. Topic analysis of the patient experiences in a cancer forum uncovered fourteen medical topics, ranging from surgery to side effects. In this project, developing a clear and effective annotation guideline was the major challenge. Although the inter-annotator agreement was substantial ($\kappa = 0.69$), an error analysis revealed that annotators still found it challenging to distinguish a medical fact from a medical experience.

6 Current and Future work

In the upcoming second year of the PhD project, we will focus on developing an NER and relation extraction (RE) system (Section 6.1). After that, we will address the challenge of credibility assessment (Section 6.2).

6.1 Extracting entities and their relations

For named entity recognition, we are currently experimenting with BiLSTMs combined with Conditional Random Fields. Our system builds on the state-of-the-art contextual flair embeddings (Akbik et al., 2018) trained on domain-specific data (Dirkson and Verberne, 2019). Our next step will be to combine these with Glove or Bert Embeddings (Devlin et al., 2018). We may also incorporate domain knowledge from structured databases in our embeddings, as this was shown to improve their quality (Zhang et al., 2019). The extracted entities will be mapped to a subset of preselected categories of the UMLS (Unified Medical Language System) (National Library of Medicine,

---

[2]Code and developed corpora can be found on `https://github.com/AnneDirkson`

[3]`https://www.facebook.com/groups/gistsupport/`

[4]`www.reddit.com/r/cancer`

[5]`https://healthlanguageprocessing.org/`

`smm4h/challenge/`

2009), as this was found to improve precision (Tu et al., 2016).

For relation extraction (RE), our starting point will also be state-of-the-art systems for various benchmark tasks. Particularly the system by Vashishth et al. (2018), RESIDE, is interesting as it focuses on utilizing open IE methods (Angeli et al., 2015) to leverage relevant information from a Knowledge Base (i.e. possible entity types and matching to relation aliases) to improve performance. We may be able to employ similar methods using the UMLS. Nonetheless, as patient forums are typically small in size, recent work in transfer learning for relation extraction (Alt et al., 2019) is also interesting, as such systems may be able to handle smaller data sets better. Recent work on few-shot relation extraction (Han et al., 2018) may also be relevant for this reason. Han et al. (2018) showed that meta-learners, models which try to *learn how to learn*, can aid rapid generalization to new concepts for few-shot RE. The best performing meta-learner for their new benchmark FewRel was the Prototypical Network by Snell et al. (2018): a few-shot classification model that tries to learn a prototypical representation for each class. We plan to investigate to what extent these various state-of-the-art systems can be employed, adapted and combined for RE in domain-specific patient forum data.

6.2 Assessing credibility

To assess credibility, we build upon extensive research into rumor verification on social media. Zubiaga et al. (2018) consider a rumor to be: "an item of circulating information whose veracity status is yet to be verified at time of posting". According to this definition, our unverified claims would qualify as rumors.

An important feature for verifying rumors is the aggregate stance of social media users towards the rumor (Enayet and El-Beltagy, 2017). This is based on the idea that social media users can collectively debunk inaccurate information (Procter et al., 2013), especially over a longer period of time (Zubiaga et al., 2016b). In employing a similar approach, we assume that collectively our users, namely patients and their close relatives, have sufficient expertise for judging a claim. Stances of posts are generally classified into supporting, denying, querying or commenting i.e. when a post is either unrelated to the rumor or to

its veracity (Qazvinian et al., 2011; Procter et al., 2013). We plan to combine the state-of-the-art LSTM approach by Kochkina et al. (2017) with the two-step decomposition of stance classification suggested by Wang et al. (2017): comments are first distinguished from non-comments to then classify non-comments into supporting, denying, or querying. We will take into account the entire conversation, as opposed to focusing on isolated messages, since this has been shown to improve stance classification (Zubiaga et al., 2016a). We may employ transfer learning by using a pre-trained language model tuned on domain-specific data as input. Additional features will be derived from previous studies into rumor stance classification e.g. Aker et al. (2017).

For determining credibility, we plan to experiment with the model-driven approach by Viviani and Pasi (2017b), which was used to assess the credibility of Yelp reviews. They argue that a model-driven MCDM (Multiple-Criteria Decision Analysis) grounded in domain knowledge can lead to better or comparable results to machine learning if the amount of criteria is manageable on top of allowing for better interpretability. According to Zubiaga et al. (2018), interpretability is essential to make a credibility assessment more reliable for users. Alternatively, we may use interpretable machine learning methods, such as Logistic Regression or Support Vector Machines, similar to the state-of-the-art rumor verification system (Enayet and El-Beltagy, 2017). Besides stance, other linguistic and temporal features for determining credibility could be derived from rumor veracity studies e.g. Kwon et al. (2013); Castillo et al. (2011). We also plan to conduct a survey amongst patients in order to include factors they indicate to be important for judging credibility of information on their forum.

A challenge we foresee is the absence of a ground truth for the credibility of claims. To solve this, we could make use of the ground truth of claims that match curated knowledge through distant supervised learning and extrapolate our method to the unknown instances, comparable to the work by Mukherjee et al. (2014). Likewise, we could mirror Mukherjee et al. (2014) in our evaluation of the credibility scores: we could ask experts to evaluate ten random claims and the ten most credible as determined by our method.

References

Alan Akbik, Duncan Blythe, and Roland Vollgraf. 2018. Contextual string embeddings for sequence labeling. In *Proceedings of the 27th International Conference on Computational Linguistics*, pages 1638–1649, Santa Fe, New Mexico, USA. Association for Computational Linguistics.

Ahmet Aker, Leon Derczynski, and Kalina Bontcheva. 2017. Simple open stance classification for rumour analysis. In *Proceedings of the International Conference Recent Advances in Natural Language Processing, RANLP 2017*, pages 31–39, Varna, Bulgaria. INCOMA Ltd.

Christoph Alt, Marc Hbner, and Leonhard Hennig. 2019. Improving Relation Extraction by Pre-trained Language Representations. In *Automated Knowledge Base Construction 2019*, pages 1–18.

Gabor Angeli, Melvin Johnson Premkumar, and Christopher D Manning. 2015. Leveraging Linguistic Structure For Open Domain Information Extraction. In *Proceedings of the 53rd Annual Meeting of the Association for Computational Linguistics and the 7th International Joint Conference on Natural Language Processing*, pages 344–354.

Sgolne Aymé, Anna Kole, and Stephen Groft. 2008. Empowerment of patients: lessons from the rare diseases community. *The Lancet*, 371(9629):2048–2051.

David G Bailey, George Dresser, and J Malcolm O Arnold. 2013. Grapefruit-medication interactions: forbidden fruit or avoidable consequences? *CMAJ : Canadian Medical Association journal = journal de l'Association medicale canadienne*, 185(4):309–16.

Adrian Benton, Lyle Ungar, Shawndra Hill, Sean Hennessy, Jun Mao, Annie Chung, Charles E Leonard, and John H Holmes. 2011. Identifying potential adverse effects using the web: a new approach to medical hypothesis generation HHS Public Access. *J Biomed Inform*, 44(6):989–996.

Laure Berti-Equille and Mouhamadou Lamine Ba. 2016. Veracity of Big Data: Challenges of Cross-Modal Truth Discovery. *ACM Journal of Data and Information Quality*, 7(3):12.

Marika H.F. Burda, Marjan Van Den Akker, Frans Van Der Horst, Paul Lemmens, and J. Andr Knottnerus. 2016. Collecting and validating experiential expertise is doable but poses methodological challenges. *Journal of Clinical Epidemiology*, 72:10–15.

Pam Carter, Roger Beech, Domenica Coxon, Martin J. Thomas, and Clare Jinks. 2013. Mobilising the experiential knowledge of clinicians, patients and carers for applied health-care research. *Contemporary Social Science*, 8(3):307–320.

Carlos Castillo, Marcelo Mendoza, and Barbara Poblete. 2011. Information credibility on twitter. In *Proceedings of the 20th International Conference on World Wide Web*, WWW '11, pages 675–684, New York, NY, USA. ACM.

Xiaoyi Chen, Carole Faviez, Stphane Schuck, Agns Lillo-Le-Louët, Nathalie Texier, Badisse Dahamna, Charles Huot, Pierre Foulquié, Suzanne Pereira, Vincent Leroux, Pierre Karapetiantz, Armelle Guenegou-Arnoux, Sandrine Katsahian, Cdric Bousquet, and Anita Burgun. 2018. Mining patients' narratives in social media for pharmacovigilance: Adverse effects and misuse of methylphenidate. *Frontiers in Pharmacology*, 9.

Kathryn P. Davison, James W. Pennebaker, and Sally S. Dickerson. 2000. Who talks? The social psychology of illness support groups. *American Psychologist*, 55(2):205–217.

Jacob Devlin, Ming-Wei Chang, Kenton Lee, and Kristina Toutanova. 2018. BERT: Pre-training of Deep Bidirectional Transformers for Language Understanding. *ArXiv*.

Anne Dirkson and Suzan Verberne. 2019. Transfer learning for health-related Twitter data. In *Proceedings of 2019 ACL workshop Social Media Mining 4 Health (SMM4H)*.

Anne Dirkson, Suzan Verberne, and Wessel Kraaij. 2019a. Narrative Detection in Online Patient Communities. In *Proceedings of the Text2StoryIR'19 Workshop at ECIR*, pages 21–28, Cologne, Germany. CEUR-WS.

Anne Dirkson, Suzan Verberne, Gerard van Oortmerssen, Hans van Gelderblom, and Wessel Kraaij. 2019b. Lexical Normalization of User-Generated Medical Forum Data. In *Proceedings of 2019 ACL workshop Social Media Mining 4 Health (SMM4H)*.

Anne Dirkson, Suzan Verberne, Gerard van Oortmerssen, and Wessel Kraaij. 2018. Lexical Normalization in User-Generated Data. In *Proceedings of the 17th Dutch-Belgian Information Retrieval Workshop*, pages 1–4.

Mark Dredze, David A Broniatowski, and Karen M Hilyard. 2016. Zika vaccine misconceptions: A social media analysis. *Vaccine*, 34(30):3441–2.

Omar Enayet and Samhaa R. El-Beltagy. 2017. Niletmrg at semeval-2017 task 8: Determining rumour and veracity support for rumours on twitter. In *Proceedings of the 11th International Workshop on Semantic Evaluation (SemEval-2017)*, pages 470–474, Vancouver, Canada. Association for Computational Linguistics.

Wilco W M Fleuren and Wynand Alkema. 2015. Application of text mining in the biomedical domain. *Methods*, 74:97–106.

Graciela Gonzalez-Hernandez, Abeed Sarker, Karen O 'Connor, and Guergana Savova. 2017. Capturing the Patient's Perspective: a Review of Advances in Natural Language Processing of Health-Related Text. *Yearbook of medical informatics*, pages 214–217.

Xu Han, Hao Zhu, Pengfei Yu, Ziyun Wang, Yuan Yao, Zhiyuan Liu, and Maosong Sun. 2018. Fewrel: A large-scale supervised few-shot relation classification dataset with state-of-the-art evaluation. In *Proceedings of the 2018 Conference on Empirical Methods in Natural Language Processing*, pages 4803–4809, Brussels, Belgium. Association for Computational Linguistics.

Andrea Hartzler and Wanda Pratt. 2011. Managing the personal side of health: how patient expertise differs from the expertise of clinicians. *Journal of medical Internet research*, 13(3):e62.

C. I. Hovland, I. L. Janis, and H. H. Kelley. 1953. *Communication and persuasion; psychological studies of opinion change*. Yale University Press, New Haven, CT, US.

Xiaolei Huang, Michael C. Smith, Michael Paul, Dmytro Ryzhkov, Sandra Quinn, David Broniatowski, and Mark Dredze. 2017. Examining Patterns of Influenza Vaccination in Social Media. In *AAAI Joint Workshop on Health Intelligence (W3PHIAI)*.

Alexander Kinsora, Kate Barron, Qiaozhu Mei, and V G Vinod Vydiswaran. 2017. Creating a Labeled Dataset for Medical Misinformation in Health Forums. In *IEEE International Conference on Healthcare Informatics*.

J. Andr Knottnerus and Peter Tugwell. 2012. The patients' perspective is key, also in research. *Journal of Clinical Epidemiology*, 65(6):581–583.

Elena Kochkina, Maria Liakata, and Isabelle Augenstein. 2017. Turing at SemEval-2017 task 8: Sequential approach to rumour stance classification with branch-LSTM. In *Proceedings of the 11th International Workshop on Semantic Evaluation (SemEval-2017)*, pages 475–480, Vancouver, Canada. Association for Computational Linguistics.

Sejeong Kwon, Meeyoung Cha, Kyomin Jung, Wei Chen, and Yajun Wang. 2013. Prominent features of rumor propagation in online social media. *2013 IEEE 13th International Conference on Data Mining*, pages 1103–1108.

Robert Leaman, Laura Wojtulewicz, Ryan Sullivan, Annie Skariah, Jian Yang, and Graciela Gonzalez. 2010. Towards internet-age pharmacovigilance: Extracting adverse drug reactions from user posts to health-related social networks. In *Proceedings of the 2010 Workshop on Biomedical Natural Language Processing*, BioNLP '10, pages 117–125, Stroudsburg, PA, USA. Association for Computational Linguistics.

Jing Liu, Songzheng Zhao, and Xiaodi Zhang. 2016. An ensemble method for extracting adverse drug events from social media. *Artificial Intelligence in Medicine*, 70:62–76.

Xiao Liu and Hsinchun Chen. 2013. AZDrugMiner: An Information Extraction System for Mining Patient-Reported Adverse Drug Events in Online Patient Forums. In *Smart Health. ICSH 2013. Lecture Notes in Computer Science*, pages 134–150. Springer, Berlin, Heidelberg.

Alejandro Metke-Jimenez and Sarvnaz Karimi. 2015. Concept Extraction to Identify Adverse Drug Reactions in Medical Forums: A Comparison of Algorithms. *CoRR ArXiv*.

Subhabrata Mukherjee, Gerhard Weikum, and Cristian Danescu-Niculescu-Mizil. 2014. People on Drugs: Credibility of User Statements in Health Communities. In *KDD'14*, pages 65–74.

National Library of Medicine. 2009. UMLS Reference Manual.

Azadeh Nikfarjam and Graciela H Gonzalez. 2011. Pattern mining for extraction of mentions of Adverse Drug Reactions from user comments. *AMIA Annual Symposium proceedings*, 2011:1019–26.

Azadeh Nikfarjam, Abeed Sarker, Karen O'Connor, Rachel Ginn, and Graciela Gonzalez. 2015. Pharmacovigilance from social media: mining adverse drug reaction mentions using sequence labeling with word embedding cluster features. *Journal of the American Medical Informatics Association: JAMIA*, 22(3):671–81.

Peter Norvig. 2009. Natural Language Corpus Data. In Jeff Hammerbacher Toby Segaran, editor, *Beautiful Data: The Stories Behind Elegant Data Solutions*, pages 219–242. O'Reilly Media.

Karen O'Connor, Pranoti Pimpalkhute, Azadeh Nikfarjam, Rachel Ginn, Karen L Smith, and Graciela Gonzalez. 2014. Pharmacovigilance on twitter? Mining tweets for adverse drug reactions. In *AMIA Annual Symposium proceedings*, volume 2014, pages 924–33. American Medical Informatics Association.

Albert Park, Andrea L Hartzler, Jina Huh, David W Mcdonald, and Wanda Pratt. 2015. Automatically Detecting Failures in Natural Language Processing Tools for Online Community Text. *J Med Internet Res*, 17(212).

Michael J Paul and Mark Dredze. 2009. A Model for Mining Public Health Topics from Twitter. Technical report, Johns Hopkins University.

Rob Procter, Farida Vis, and Alex Voss. 2013. Reading the riots on Twitter: methodological innovation for the analysis of big data. *International Journal of Social Research Methodology*, 16(3):197–214.

Vahed Qazvinian, Emily Rosengren, Dragomir R. Radev, and Qiaozhu Mei. 2011. Rumor has it: Identifying misinformation in microblogs. In *Proceedings of the 2011 Conference on Empirical Methods in Natural Language Processing*, pages 1589–1599, Edinburgh, Scotland, UK. Association for Computational Linguistics.

Lucia Sacchi and John H Holmes. 2016. Progress in Biomedical Knowledge Discovery: A 25-year Retrospective. *Yearbook of medical informatics*, pages 117–29.

Hariprasad Sampathkumar, Xue-Wen Chen, and Bo Luo. 2014. Mining Adverse Drug Reactions from online healthcare forums using Hidden Markov Model. *BMC Medical Informatics and Decision Making*, 14.

Abeed Sarker. 2017. A customizable pipeline for social media text normalization. *Social Network Analysis and Mining*, 7(1):45.

Abeed Sarker, Maksim Belousov, Jasper Friedrichs, Kai Hakala, Svetlana Kiritchenko, Farrokh Mehryary, Sifei Han, Tung Tran, Anthony Rios, Ramakanth Kavuluru, Berry de Bruijn, Filip Ginter, Debanjan Mahata, Saif M Mohammad, Goran Nenadic, and Graciela Gonzalez-Hernandez. 2018. Data and systems for medication-related text classification and concept normalization from Twitter: insights from the Social Media Mining for Health (SMM4H)-2017 shared task. *Journal of the American Medical Informatics Association*, 25(10):1274–1283.

Abeed Sarker, Rachel Ginn, Azadeh Nikfarjam, Karen O'Connor, Karen Smith, Swetha Jayaraman, Tejaswi Upadhaya, and Graciela Gonzalez. 2015. Utilizing social media data for pharmacovigilance: A review. *Journal of Biomedical Informatics*, 54:202–212.

Abeed Sarker, Azadeh Nikfarjam, and Graciela Gonzalez. 2016a. Social Media Mining Shared Task Workshop. In *Pacific Symposium Biocomputing*, pages 581–592.

Abeed Sarker, Karen O'Connor, Rachel Ginn, Matthew Scotch, Karen Smith, Dan Malone, and Graciela Gonzalez. 2016b. Social Media Mining for Toxicovigilance: Automatic Monitoring of Prescription Medication Abuse from Twitter. *Drug Safety*, 39(3):231–240.

Edin Smailhodzic, Wyanda Hooijsma, Albert Boonstra, and David J. Langley. 2016. Social media use in healthcare: A systematic review of effects on patients and on their relationship with healthcare professionals. *BMC Health Services Research*, 16(1):442.

Jake Snell, Kevin Swersky, and Richard S. Zemel. 2018. Prototypical networks for few-shot learning.

In *Proceedings of the 2018 Conference on Empirical Methods in Natural Language Processing*, pages 4803–4809.

Hongkui Tu, Zongyang Ma, Aixin Sun, and Xiaodong Wang. 2016. When MetaMap Meets Social Media in Healthcare: Are the Word Labels Correct? In *Information Retrieval Technology. AIRS 2016. Lecture Notes in Computer Science.*, pages 356–362. Springer, Cham.

Joseph M. Unger, Dawn L. Hershman, Mark E. Fleury, and Riha Vaidya. 2019. Association of Patient Comorbid Conditions With Cancer Clinical Trial Participation. *JAMA Oncology*, 5(3):326.

Shikhar Vashishth, Rishabh Joshi, Sai Suman Prayaga, Chiranjib Bhattacharyya, and Partha Talukdar. 2018. Reside: Improving distantly-supervised neural relation extraction using side information. In *Proceedings of the 2018 Conference on Empirical Methods in Natural Language Processing*, pages 1257–1266, Brussels, Belgium. Association for Computational Linguistics.

Suzan Verberne, Anika Batenburg, Remco Sanders, Mies van Eenbergen, Enny Das, and Mattijs S Lambooij. 2019. Analyzing empowerment processes among cancer patients in an online community: A text mining approach. *JMIR Cancer*, 5(1):e9887.

Marco Viviani and Gabriella Pasi. 2017a. Credibility in social media: opinions, news, and health informationa survey. *WIREs Data Mining Knowl Discov*, 7.

Marco Viviani and Gabriella Pasi. 2017b. Quantifier Guided Aggregation for the Veracity Assessment of Online Reviews. *International Journal of Intelligent Systems*, 32(5):481–501.

V G Vinod Vydiswaran, Chengxiang Zhai, and Dan Roth. 2011. Gauging the Internet Doctor: Ranking Medical Claims based on Community Knowledge. In *KDD-DMH*.

Feixiang Wang, Man Lan, and Yuanbin Wu. 2017. ECNU at SemEval-2017 task 8: Rumour evaluation using effective features and supervised ensemble models. In *Proceedings of the 11th International Workshop on Semantic Evaluation (SemEval-2017)*, pages 491–496, Vancouver, Canada. Association for Computational Linguistics.

SriJyothsna Yeleswarapu, Aditya Rao, Thomas Joseph, Vangala Govindakrishnan Saipradeep, and Rajgopal Srinivasan. 2014. A pipeline to extract drug-adverse event pairs from multiple data sources. *BMC medical informatics and decision making*, 14(13).

Yijia Zhang, Qingyu Chen, Zhihao Yang, Hongfei Lin, and Zhiyong Lu. 2019. BioWordVec,improving biomedical word embeddings with subword information and MeSH. *Scientific Data*, 6(1):52.

Arkaitz Zubiaga, Ahmet Aker, Kalina Bontcheva, Maria Liakata, and Rob Procter. 2018. Detection and resolution of rumours in social media: A survey. *ACM Comput. Surv.*, 51(2):32:1–32:36.

Arkaitz Zubiaga, Elena Kochkina, Maria Liakata, Rob Procter, and Michal Lukasik. 2016a. Stance classification in rumours as a sequential task exploiting the tree structure of social media conversations. In *COLING 2016, 26th International Conference on Computational Linguistics, Proceedings of the Conference: Technical Papers, December 11-16, 2016, Osaka, Japan*, pages 2438–2448.

Arkaitz Zubiaga, Maria Liakata, Rob Procter, Geraldine Wong Sak Hoi, and Peter Tolmie. 2016b. Analysing how people orient to and spread rumours in social media by looking at conversational threads. *PLOS ONE*, 11(3):1–29.

Automated Cross-language Intelligibility Analysis of Parkinson's Disease Patients Using Speech Recognition Technologies

Nina Hosseini-Kivanani [1], Juan Camilo Vásquez-Correa[2, 3], Manfred Stede[4], Elmar Nöth[2]

[1]International Experimental and Clinical Linguistics (IECL), University of Potsdam, Germany
[2] Pattern Recognition Lab, Friedrich-Alexander University Erlangen-Nüremberg, Germany
[3] Faculty of Engineering, University of Antioquia UdeA, Medellín, Colombia
[4]Applied Computational Linguistics, University of Potsdam, Germany

{hosseinikiva, stede}@uni-potsdam.de
jcamilo.vasquez@udea.edu.co
elmar.noeth@fau.de

Abstract

Speech deficits are common symptoms among Parkinson's Disease (PD) patients. The automatic assessment of speech signals is promising for the evaluation of the neurological state and the speech quality of the patients. Recently, progress has been made in applying machine learning and computational methods to automatically evaluate the speech of PD patients. In the present study, we plan to analyze the speech signals of PD patients and healthy control (HC) subjects in three different languages: German, Spanish, and Czech, with the aim to identify biomarkers to discriminate between PD patients and HC subjects and to evaluate the neurological state of the patients. Therefore, the main contribution of this study is the automatic classification of PD patients and HC subjects in different languages with focusing on phonation, articulation, and prosody. We will focus on an intelligibility analysis based on automatic speech recognition systems trained on these three languages. This is one of the first studies done that considers the evaluation of the speech of PD patients in different languages. The purpose of this research proposal is to build a model that can discriminate PD and HC subjects even when the language used for train and test is different.

1 Introduction

Parkinsons disease (PD) (i.e. Shaking palsy (Parkinson, 2002)) is the second most common neurodegenerative disorder after Alzheimers disease. PD displays a great prevalence in individuals of advanced age (Dexter and Jenner, 2013), especially, over the age of fifty (Fahn, 2003). The signs and symptoms of PD can significantly influence the quality of life of patients. They are grouped into two categories: motor and non-motor symptoms. Speech impairments are one of the earliest manifestations in PD patients.

Early diagnosis of PD is a vital challenge in this field. The first step in analyzing this disease is the development of markers of PD progression through collecting data from several cohorts. To reach this aim, different clinical rating scales have been developed, such as the Unified Parkinson's Disease Rating Scale (UPDRS), Movement Disorders Society - UPDRS (MDS-UPDRS) [1] (Goetz et al., 2008) and Hoehn & Yahr (H & Y) staging, (Visser et al., 2006).

The UPDRS is the most widely used rating tool for the clinical evaluation of PD patients. The examination requires observation and interview by a professional clinician. The scale is distributed into 4 sections: (i) Mentation, behavior and mood, (ii) Activities of daily living (ADL), (iii) Motor sections, and (iv) Motor complications.

One of the most common motor problems is related to speech impairments in PD (Jankovic, 2008). Most of the patients with PD show disabilities in speech production. The most common speech disturbances are monotonic speech, hypophonia (a speech weakness in the vocal musculature and vocal sounds) and hypokinetic dysarthria. These symptoms reduce the intelligibility of the patients, and affect different aspects of the speech production such as articulation, phonation, nasality, and prosody (Little et al., 2009; Goetz et al., 2008; Ramig et al., 2001). Therefore, there is a great interest to develop tools or methods to evaluate and improve the speech production of PD patients.

---

[1]MDS-UPDRS is the most updated version of the UPDRS.

74

Proceedings of the ACL 2019, Student Research Workshop, pages 74–80
Florence, Italy, July 28th-August 2nd, 2019. ©2019 Association for Computational Linguistics

Recently, there has been a proliferation of new speech recognition-based tools for the acoustic analysis of PD. The use of speech recognition software in clinical examinations could make a powerful supplement to the state-of-the-art subjective reports of experts and clinicians that are costly and time-consuming (e.g., Little et al., 2009; Hernandez-Espinosa et al., 2002). In the clinical field, the detection of PD is a complex task due to the fact that the symptoms of this disease are more related to clinicians' observations and perception of the way patients move and speak.

Recently, machine learning tools are used to develop speech recognition systems that make the whole process of objective evaluation and recognition faster and more accurate than analytical clinicians' methods (Yu and Deng, 2016; Hernandez-Espinosa et al., 2002). Using machine learning techniques to extract acoustic features for detecting the PD has become widely used in recent studies (e.g., Dahl et al., 2012; Little et al., 2009).

Automatic speech recognition (ASR) systems are used to decode and transcribe oral speech. In other words, the goal of ASR systems is to find and recognize the words that best represent the acoustic signal. For example, automatic speech recognition systems are used to evaluate how speech intelligibility is affected by the disease.

This study will seek to further investigate the speech patterns of HC and PD groups using recordings from patients speaking in German, Spanish, and Czech. Most of the previous studies only considered recordings in one language and focused on it for detecting PD, but in this study, we plan to evaluate the effect of the PD in three different languages.

2 Related work: ASR for detecting PD symptoms

Speech can be measured by acoustic tools simply using aperiodic vibrations in the voice. The field of speech recognition has been improved in recent years by research in computer-assisted speech training system for therapy (Beijer and Rietvel, 2012) machine learning techniques, which can lead to establish efficient biomarkers to discriminate HC from people with PD (e.g., Orozco-Arroyave et al., 2013).

There are a vast number of advanced techniques to design ASR systems: hybrid Deep Neural Networks-Hidden Markov Models (DNN [2]-HMM) (Hinton et al., 2012) and Convolutional Neural Networks (CNN) (Abdel-Hamid et al., 2014). Deep neural networks have recently received increasing attention in speech recognition (Canevari et al., 2013). Other studies have highlighted the strength of the DNN-HMM framework for speech recognition (e.g., Dahl et al., 2012).

On the other hand, regarding the assessment of PD from speech, Skodda et al. (2011) assessed the progression of speech impairments of PD from 2002 to 2012 in a longitudinal study by only using a statistical test to evaluate changes in aspects related to voice, articulation, prosody, and fluency of the recorded speech.

Orozco-Arroyave et al. (2016) considered more than one language for producing isolated words for discriminating PDs from HCs. The characterization and classification processes were based on a method on the systematic separation of voiced and unvoiced segments of speech in their study. Vásquez-Correa et al. (2017) analyzed the effect of acoustic conditions on different algorithms. The obtained detection accuracy of PD speech was reported and shown that the background noise affect the performance of the different algorithms. However, most of these systems are not yet capable of automatically detecting speech impairment of individual speech sounds, which are known to have an impact on speech intelligibility (Zhao et al., 2010; Ramaker et al., 2002).

Our goal is to develop robust ASR systems for pathological speech and incorporate the ASR technology to detect their speech intelligibility problems. A major interest is to investigate acoustic features in the mentioned languages (differences and similarities), including gender differences between subject (HC & PD) groups. The overall purpose of this project is to address the question of whether cross-lingual speech intelligibility among PDs and HCs can help the recognition system to detect the correct disease. The classification of PD from speech in different languages has to be carefully conducted to avoid bias towards the linguistic content present in each language. For instance, Czech and German languages are richer than Spanish language in terms of consonant production, which may cause that it is easier to produce consonant sounds by Czech PD patients than

---

[2]DNN is a feed-forward neural network that has more than one layer of hidden units between its inputs and its outputs (Hinton et al., 2012).

by Spanish PD patients. In addition, with the use of transfer learning strategies, a model trained with utterances from one language can be used as a base model to train a model in a different language.

After reviewing the aforementioned literature, the main contribution of our research for modeling speech signals in PD patients is twofold:

- This is one of the first cross-lingual studies done to evaluate speech of people with PD. This work requires a database consisting of recordings of different languages. There is currently a lack of cross-lingual research, which provides reliable classification methods for assessing PDs' speech available in the literature.

- Using speech data is expected to help the development of a diagnostic of PD patients.

This project seeks to bridge the gap in speech recognition for speech of PD, with the hope of moving towards a higher adoption rate of ASR-based technologies in the diagnosis of patients.

3 The set-up of the ASR system

In this work, we will build an ASR system to recognize the speech of patients of Parkinson's Disease. The task of ASR is to convert this raw audio into text. The ASR system is created based on three models: acoustic model (i.e. to recognize phonemes), pronunciation model (i.e. to map sequence of phonemes into word sequences), and language model (i.e. to estimate probabilities of word sequences). We place particular emphasis on the acoustic model portion of the system. We also provide some acoustic models output features that could be used in future speech recognition of PD severity in the clinical field. Ravanelli et al. (2019) stated that along with the improvement of ASR systems, several deep learning frameworks (e.g., TensorFlow (Abadi et al., 2016)) in machine learning are also widely used.

The next section describes the process for modeling the intelligibility of PD speech followed by the description of processes whether the speech signal is from PD patient or from HC subjects.

3.1 Training

The proposed ASR system will be developed using a standard state-of-the-art architecture hybrid DNN-HMM (see Nassif et al., 2019 for more information about the existing models in ASR), built using the Kaldi speech recognition toolkit [3]. The preprocessing (i.e. Feature extraction) of the acoustic signal into usable parameters (i.e. label computation) tries to remove any acoustic information that is not useful for the task; it will be done before beginning to train the acoustic model. In this study, we will use Mel-frequency Cepstral coefficients (MFCC) and Mel filter bank energies (e.g., compute-mfcc-feats and compute-fbank-feats) to train the acoustic models of the ASR systems. The task of calculating MFCCs from acoustic features is to characterize an underlying signal using spectrograms and represent the shape of the vocal tract including tongue, teeth etc.

It was observed that filter bank (fbank), one of the most popular speech recognition features, performs better than MFCCs when used with deep neural networks (Hinton et al., 2012). The purpose of using acoustic model is to help us to get boundaries of the phoneme labels. The acoustic models will be trained based on different acoustic features extracted in Kaldi "nnet3" recipes. The extracted acoustic features and the observation probabilities of our ASR system will be used to train the hybrid DNN-HMM acoustic model. The performance of an ASR system will be measured by Word Error Rate (WER) of the transcript produced by the system against the target transcript.

PyTorch: PyTorch is one of the most well known deep learning toolkit that facilitates the design of neural architectures. This tool will be used to design new DNN architectures to improve the performance of the ASR system. We will additionally use PyTorch-Kaldi (Ravanelli et al., 2019), to train[4] deep neural network based models (e.g., DNNs, CNNs, and Recurrent Neural Networks (RNNs) models) and traditional machine learning classifier. Ravanelli et al. (2019) stated that this PyTorch-Kaldi toolkit acts like an interface with different speech recognition features in it and can be used as a state-of-the-art in the field of ASR (See Figure 1). Figure 1 is shown the general methodology that will be applied in this research.

---

[3] Kaldi. http://kaldi-asr.org/doc/
[4] PyTorch-Kaldi:https://github.com/mravanelli/pytorch-kaldi

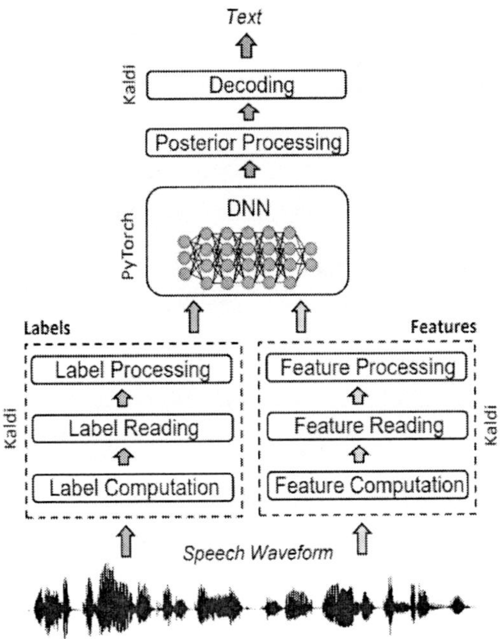

Figure 1: ASR system architecture that will be used in this study (Ravanelli et al., 2019).

4 Methods

4.1 Data

The data of this study comes from an extended version of PC-GITA database for Spanish (Orozco-Arroyave et al., 2014), German (Skodda et al., 2011), and Czech (Rusz et al., 2011) with more recordings from PDs and HCs. The database consists of both PD and HC subjects.

All subjects were asked to do multiple types of speaking tasks to understand how speech changes in different conditions, due to the fact that voice variation is difficult to identify without human experience (Jeancolas et al., 2017). The speech dimensions considered in this project are phonation, articulation and prosody (See Figure 2).

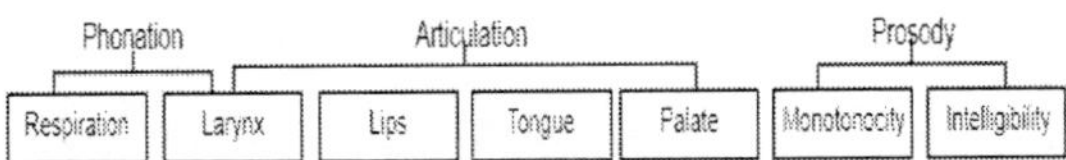

Figure 2: Speech dimensions: Phonation, Articulation and Prosody.

For each subject, speech material includes (i) sustained vowel phonation; participants were asked to phonate vowels for several seconds;, (ii) rapid syllable repetition (ideally Diadochokinetic (DDK)); participants were asked to produce such as /pa-ta-ka/, /pa-ka-ta/, /pe-ta-ka/, /pa/, /ta/,

and /ka/, (iii) connected speech, consisting of:, (iv) reading a specific text, and (v) spontaneous speech.

This dataset consists of speech samples recorded from 88 PD and 88 HC German speaking participants, 50 PD and 50 HC Spanish speaking participants (balanced in age and gender), and 20 PD and 16 HC Czech speaking participants. These speech samples were assessed by expert neurologists using UPDRS-III and H & Y scales. Their neurological labels were reported based on the UPDRS-III and H & Y scales ($mean \pm SD$) for each PD group:

- PD-German: UPDRS-III (22.7 $\pm$ 10.9), H&Y (2.4 $\pm$ 0.6)
- PD-Spanish: UPDRS-III (36.7 $\pm$ 18.7), H&Y (2.3 $\pm$ 0.8)
- PD-Czech: UPDRS-III (17.9 $\pm$ 7.3), H&Y (2.2 $\pm$ 0.5)

Further details are shown in Table 1:

Language	HC		PD	
	Female	Male	Female	Male
German	n= 44 (63.8 $\pm$ 12.7)	n= 44 (62.6 $\pm$ 15.2)	n= 41 (66.2 $\pm$ 9.7)	n= 47 (66.7 $\pm$ 8.4)
Spanish	n= 25 (61.4 $\pm$ 7.0)	n= 25 (60.3 $\pm$ 11.6)	n= 25 (60.7 $\pm$ 7.3)	n= 25 (61.6 $\pm$ 11.2)
Czech	—	n= 16 (61.8 $\pm$ 13.3)	—	n= 20 (61 $\pm$ 12)

Table 1: Age information of HC and PD subjects in the study (n = number of participant) & the mean and standard deviation are in the parenthesis ($Mean \pm SD$).

Although the size of the data is not big enough, the vocabulary that was used by the patients in the capture process of the speech was fixed. This aspect compensates the need to have a huge corpus to evaluate a vocabulary dependent task like the assessment of pathological speech (see Parra-Gallego et al., 2018).

4.2 Sample

Praat software (Boersma and Weenink, 2016) is used for segmenting speech, extracting acoustics features, removing silence from beginning and end of speech file and visualization of speech data. Generally, spoken words, represented as sound waves, have two axes: time on the x-axis and amplitude on the y-axis. Figure 3 illustrates the example of input feature maps extracted from the speech signal which shows the selected spectrograms (the audio waveform is encoded as a representation) of PD and HC subjects when they pronounce the syllable /pa-ta-ka/ that convey 3-dimensional information in 2 dimensions

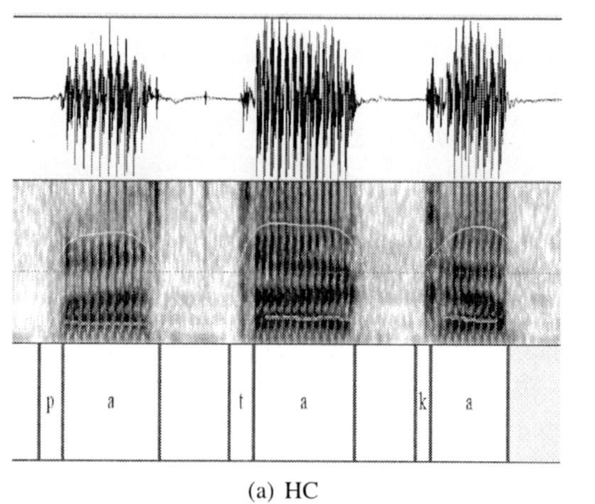
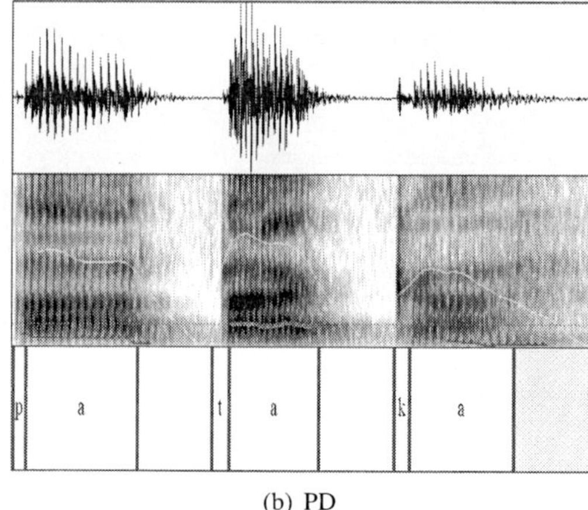

(a) HC   (b) PD

Figure 3: **Top:** Raw waveforms of /pa-ta-ka/ (x-axis: time; y-axis: amplitude). **Middle:** Spectrograms (x-axis: time; y-axis: frequency; shading: amplitude (energy), darker means higher). **Bottom:** the word-level annotation of the signal.

(i.e. Time: x-axis, Frequency: y-axis, and Amplitude: color intensity). The proposed model will be able to identify specific aspects in the speech related to the pronunciation of consonants, which are the most affected aspects of the speech of the patients due to the disease. The segmentation process will be performed using a trained model to detect phonological classes, like those ones used in the previous studies (Vásquez-Correa et al., 2019; Cernak et al., 2017). Figure 3 shows the possible differences in articulation and phonation in PD and HC subjects. By using Praat, the speech samples of syllable /pa-ta-ka/ will be segmented into vowel and consonant frames. The contour of HC sample is more stable than the obtained contour from PD sample. In each sample, silences will be removed from the beginning and the end of each token, using Praat.

5 Conclusion

In this research proposal, we introduced and described the background for speech recognition of PD patients. The focus is on Parkinsons disease speech recognition based on the acoustic analysis of their voice. A brief overview of clinical and machine learning research in this field was provided. The goal is to improve the ASR system to be able to model and detect PD patients independently from their language by taking speech as an input and using machine learning and natural language processing technologies to advance healthcare and provide an overview of the patients men-

tal health. All in all, the proposed method should be able to detect the patient with PD and discriminate them from HC subjects.

References

Martn Abadi, Paul Barham, Jianmin Chen, Zhifeng Chen, Andy Davis, Jeffrey Dean, Matthieu Devin, Sanjay Ghemawat, Geoffrey Irving, Michael Isard, Manjunath Kudlur, Josh Levenberg, Rajat Monga, Sherry Moore, Derek G Murray, Benoit Steiner, Paul Tucker, Vijay Vasudevan, Pete Warden, Martin Wicke, Yuan Yu, Xiaoqiang Zheng, and Google Brain. 2016. TensorFlow: A System for Large-Scale Machine Learning TensorFlow: A system for large-scale machine learning. In *In 12th {USENIX} Symposium on Operating Systems Design and Implementation ({OSDI} 16)*, pages 265–283.

Ossama Abdel-Hamid, Abdel Rahman Mohamed, Hui Jiang, Li Deng, Gerald Penn, and Dong Yu. 2014. Convolutional neural networks for speech recognition. *IEEE Transactions on Audio, Speech and Language Processing*, 22(10):1533–1545.

Lilian Beijer and Toni Rietvel. 2012. Potentials of Telehealth Devices for Speech Therapy in Parkinson's Disease. In *Diagnostics and Rehabilitation of Parkinson's Disease. InTech*, pages 379–402.

Paul Boersma and David Weenink. 2016. Praat: Doing phonetics by computer (Version 6.0. 14). *Retrieved from (last access: 29.04. 2018)*.

Claudia Canevari, Leonardo Badino, Luciano Fadiga, and Giorgio Metta Rbcs. 2013. Cross-corpus and cross-linguistic evaluation of a speaker-dependent DNN-HMM ASR system using EMA data In *In Speech Production in Automatic Speech Recognition (In SPASR-2013)*, pages 29–33.

Milos Cernak, Juan Rafael Orozco-Arroyave, Frank Rudzicz, Heidi Christensen, Juan Camilo Vásquez-Correa, and Elmar Nöth. 2017. Characterisation of voice quality of Parkinson's disease using differential phonological posterior features. *Computer Speech and Language*, 46(June):196–208.

George E. Dahl, Dong Yu, Li Deng, and Alex Acero. 2012. Context-dependent pre-trained deep neural networks for large-vocabulary speech recognition. *IEEE Transactions on Audio, Speech and Language Processing*, 20(1):30–42.

David T. Dexter and Peter Jenner. 2013. Parkinson disease: from pathology to molecular disease mechanisms. *Free Radical Biology and Medicine*, 62:132–144.

Stanley Fahn. 2003. Description of Parkinson's Disease as a Clinical Syndrome. *Annals of the New York Academy of Sciences*, 991(1):1–14.

Christopher G. Goetz, Barbara C. Tilley, Stephanie R. Shaftman, Glenn T. Stebbins, Stanley Fahn, Pablo Martinez-Martin, Werner Poewe, Cristina Sampaio, Matthew B. Stern, Richard Dodel, Bruno Dubois, Robert Holloway, Joseph Jankovic, Jaime Kulisevsky, Anthony E. Lang, Andrew Lees, Sue Leurgans, Peter A. LeWitt, David Nyenhuis, C. Warren Olanow, Olivier Rascol, Anette Schrag, Jeanne A. Teresi, Jacobus J. van Hilten, and Nancy LaPelle. 2008. Movement Disorder Society-sponsored revision of the Unified Parkinson's Disease Rating Scale (MDS-UPDRS): Scale presentation and clinimetric testing results. *Movement Disorders*, 23(15):2129–2170.

Carlos Hernandez-Espinosa, Pedro Gomez-Vilda, Juan I. Godino-Llorente, and Santiago Aguilera-Navarro. 2002. Diagnosis of vocal and voice disorders by the speech signal. In *Proceedings of the IEEE-INNS-ENNS International Joint Conference on Neural Networks. IJCNN 2000. Neural Computing: New Challenges and Perspectives for the New Millennium*, pages 253–258. IEEE.

Geoffrey Hinton, Li Deng, Dong Yu, George Dahl, Abdel Rahman Mohamed, Navdeep Jaitly, Andrew Senior, Vincent Vanhoucke, Patrick Nguyen, Tara Sainath, and Brian Kingsbury. 2012. Deep neural networks for acoustic modeling in speech recognition: The shared views of four research groups. *IEEE Signal Processing Magazine*, 29(6):82–97.

Joseph Jankovic. 2008. Parkinsons disease: clinical features and diagnosis. *Journal of Neurology, Neurosurgery & Psychiatry*, 79(4):368–376.

Laetitia Jeancolas, Habib Benali, Badr-Eddine Benkelfat, Graziella Mangone, Jean-Christophe Corvol, Marie Vidailhet, Stephane Lehericy, and Dijana Petrovska-Delacretaz. 2017. Automatic detection of early stages of Parkinson's disease through acoustic voice analysis with mel-frequency cepstral coefficients. In *International Conference on Advanced Technologies for Signal and Image Processing (ATSIP)*, pages 1–6. IEEE.

Max A Little, Patrick E McSharry, Eric J Hunter, Jennifer Spielman, and Lorraine O Ramig. 2009. Suitability of dysphonia measurements for telemonitoring of Parkinson's disease. *IEEE transactions on bio-medical engineering*, 56(4):1015.

Ali Bou Nassif, Ismail Shahin, Imtinan Attili, Mohammad Azzeh, and Khaled Shaalan. 2019. Speech Recognition Using Deep Neural Networks: A Systematic Review. *IEEE Access*, 7:19143–19165.

Juan R. Orozco-Arroyave, Julin D. Arias-Londoño, Jesus Francisco V. Bonilla, Mara C. Gonzalez-Rátiva, and Elmar Nöth. 2014. New Spanish speech corpus database for the analysis of people suffering from Parkinson's disease. In *Language Resources and Evaluation Conference, LREC*, pages 342–347.

Juan R. Orozco-Arroyave, Julin D. Arias-Londoño, Jess F. Vargas-Bonilla, and Elmar Nöth. 2013. Analysis of Speech from People with Parkinsons Disease through Nonlinear Dynamics. In *International conference on nonlinear speech processing*, pages 112–119. Springer, Berlin, Heidelberg.

Juan R. Orozco-Arroyave, Juan C. Vádsquez-Correa, Florian Honig, Julin D. Arias-Londono, Jess F. Vargas-Bonilla, Sabine Skodda, Jan Rusz, and Elmar Nöth. 2016. Towards an automatic monitoring of the neurological state of Parkinson's patients from speech. *ICASSP, IEEE International Conference on Acoustics, Speech and Signal Processing - Proceedings*, 2016-May(March):6490–6494.

James Parkinson. 2002. An Essay on the Shaking Palsy. *The Journal of Neuropsychiatry and Clinical Neurosciences*, 14(2):223–236.

Luis F. Parra-Gallego, Toms Arias-Vergara, Juan C. Vásquez-Correa, Nicanor Garcia-Ospina, Juan R. Orozco-Arroyave, and Elmar Nöth. 2018. Automatic Intelligibility Assessment of Parkinsons Disease with Diadochokinetic Exercises. pages 223–230. Springer, Cham.

Claudia Ramaker, Johan Marinus, Anne Margarethe Stiggelbout, and Bob Johannes van Hilten. 2002. Systematic evaluation of rating scales for impairment and disability in Parkinson's disease. *Movement Disorders*, 17(5):867–876.

Lorraine Olson Ramig, Steven Gray, Kristin Baker, Kim Corbin-Lewis, Eugene Buder, Erich Luschei, Hillary Coon, and Marshall Smith. 2001. The aging voice: A review, treatment data and familial and genetic perspectives. *Folia Phoniatrica et Logopaedica*, 53(5):252–265.

Mirco Ravanelli, Titouan Parcollet, and Yoshua Bengio. 2019. The PyTorch-Kaldi Speech Recognition Toolkit. *ICASSP 2019 - 2019 IEEE International Conference on Acoustics, Speech and Signal Processing (ICASSP)*, pages 6465–6469.

Jan Rusz, Roman Cmejla, Hana Ruzickova, and Evzen Ruzicka. 2011. Quantitative acoustic measurements for characterization of speech and voice disorders in early untreated Parkinsons disease. *The Journal of the Acoustical Society of America*, 129(1):350–367.

Sabine Skodda, Wenke Visser, and Uwe Schlegel. 2011. Vowel Articulation in Parkinson's Disease. *Journal of Voice*, 25(4):467–472.

Juan C. Vásquez-Correa, Philipp Klumpp, Juan R. Orozco-Arroyave, and Elmar Nöth. 2019. Phonet: a Tool Based on Gated Recurrent Neural Networks to Extract Phonological Posteriors from Speech. In *Proceedings of INTERSPEECH conference (Under review)*.

Juan C. Vásquez-Correa, Joan Serrà, Juan R. Orozco-Arroyave, Jess F. Vargas-Bonilla, and Elmar Nöth. 2017. Effect of acoustic conditions on algorithms to detect Parkinson's disease from speech. *ICASSP, IEEE International Conference on Acoustics, Speech and Signal Processing - Proceedings*, pages 5065–5069.

Martine Visser, Albert F.G. Leentjens, Johan Marinus, Anne M. Stiggelbout, and Jacobus J. van Hilten. 2006. Reliability and validity of the Beck depression inventory in patients with Parkinson's disease. *Movement Disorders*, 21(5):668–672.

Dong Yu and Li Deng. 2016. *Automatic Speech Recognition-A Deep Learning Approach*. Springer london limited.

Ying J. Zhao, Hwee L. Wee, Yiong H. Chan, Soo H. Seah, Wing L. Au, Puay Ngoh Lau, Emmanuel C. Pica, Shu Ch. Li, Nan Luo, and Louis C S Tan. 2010. Progression of Parkinson's disease as evaluated by Hoehn and Yahr stage transition times. *Movement Disorders*, 25(6):710–716.

Natural Language Generation: Recently Learned Lessons, Directions for Semantic Representation-based Approaches, and the case of Brazilian Portuguese Language

Marco Antonio Sobrevilla Cabezudo and Thiago Alexandre Salgueiro Pardo

Interinstitutional Center for Computational Linguistics (NILC)

Institute of Mathematical and Computer Sciences, University of São Paulo

São Carlos/SP, Brazil

`msobrevillac@usp.br, taspardo@icmc.usp.br`

Abstract

This paper presents a more recent literature review on Natural Language Generation. In particular, we highlight the efforts for Brazilian Portuguese in order to show the available resources and the existent approaches for this language. We also focus on the approaches for generation from semantic representations (emphasizing the Abstract Meaning Representation formalism) as well as their advantages and limitations, including possible future directions.

1 Introduction

Natural Language Generation (NLG) is a promising area in Natural Language Processing (NLP) community. NLG aims to build computer systems that may produce understandable texts in English or other human languages from some underlying non-linguistic representation of information (Reiter and Dale, 2000). Tools generated by this area are useful for other applications like Automatic Summarization, Question-Answering Systems, and others.

There are several efforts in NLG for English[1]. For example, one may see the works of Krahmer et al. (2003) and Li et al. (2018), which focused on referring expressions generation, and the work of (Gatt and Reiter, 2009), focused on developing a surface realisation tool called SimpleNLG. One may also easily find other works that tried to generate text from semantic representations (Flanigan et al., 2016; Ferreira et al., 2017; Puzikov and Gurevych, 2018b).

For Brazilian Portuguese, there are few works, some of them focused on representations like Universal Networking Language (UNL) (Nunes et al., 2002) or *Resource Description Framework* (RDF)

(Moussallem et al., 2018), and other ones that are very specific to the Referring Expression Generation (Pereira and Paraboni, 2008; Lucena et al., 2010) and Surface Realisation tasks (Oliveira and Sripada, 2014; Silva et al., 2013).

More recently, several representations have emerged in the NLP area (Gardent et al., 2017; Novikova et al., 2017; Mille et al., 2018). In particular, Abstract Meaning Representation (AMR) has gained interest from the research community (Banarescu et al., 2013). It is a semantic formalism that aims to encode the meaning of a sentence with a simple representation in the form of a directed rooted graph. This representation includes information about semantic roles, named entities, wiki entities, spatial-temporal information, and co-references, among other information.

AMR has gained attention mainly due to its simplicity to be read by humans and computers, its attempt to abstract away from syntactic idiosyncrasies (focusing only on semantic processing) and its wide use of other comprehensive linguistic resources, such as PropBank (Palmer et al., 2005) (Bos, 2016).

For English, there is a large AMR-annotated corpus that contains 39,260 AMR-annotated sentences[2], which allows deeper studies in NLG and experiments with different approaches (mainly statistical approaches). This may be evidenced in the SemEval-2017 shared-task 9 (May and Priyadarshi, 2017)[3].

For Brazilian Portuguese, Anchiêta and Pardo (2018) built the first corpus using sentences from the "The Little Prince" book. The authors took advantage of the alignment between the English and Brazilian Portuguese versions of the book to import the AMR structures from one language to

---

[1] Most of the works may be found in the main NLP publication portal at https://www.aclweb.org/anthology/

[2] Available at https://catalog.ldc.upenn.edu/LDC2017T10.

[3] Available at http://alt.qcri.org/semeval2017/task9/.

Proceedings of the ACL 2019, Student Research Workshop, pages 81–88

Florence, Italy, July 28th-August 2nd, 2019. ©2019 Association for Computational Linguistics

another (but also performing the necessary adaptations). They had to use the Verbo-Brasil repository (Duran et al., 2013; Duran and Aluísio, 2015), which is a PropBank-like resource for Portuguese. Nowadays, there is an effort to build a larger AMR-annotated corpus that is similar to the current one available for English.

In this context, this study presents a literature review on Natural Language Generation for Brazilian Portuguese in order to show the resources (in relation to semantic representations) that are available for Portuguese and the existent efforts in the area for this language. We focus on the NLG approaches based on semantic representations and discuss their advantages and limitations. Finally, we suggest some future directions to the area.

2 Literature Review

The literature review was based on the following research questions:

- What was the focus of the existent NLG efforts for Portuguese and which resources were used for this language?

- What challenges exist in the NLG approaches?

- What are the advantages and limitations in the approaches for NLG from semantic representations, specially Abstract Meaning Representation?

Such issues are discussed in what follows.

2.1 Natural Language Generation for Portuguese

In general, we could find few works for Portuguese (considering the existing works for English). These works focus mainly on the referring expression generation (Pereira and Paraboni, 2008; Lucena et al., 2010) and surface realization tasks (Silva et al., 2013; Oliveira and Sripada, 2014), usually restricted to specific domains and applications (like undergraduate test scoring). Nevertheless, there are some recent attempts focused on other tasks and in more general domains (Moussallem et al., 2018; Sobrevilla Cabezudo and Pardo, 2018).

Among the NLG approaches, we may highlight the use of templates (Pereira and Paraboni, 2008; Novais et al., 2010b), rules (Novais and Paraboni,

2013) and language models (LM) (Novais et al., 2010a). In general, these approaches were successful because they were focused on restricted domains. Specifically, template-based methods used basic templates to build sentences. Similarly, some basic rules involving noun and verbal phrases were defined to build sentences. Finally, LM-based methods applied a two-stage strategy to generate sentences. This strategy consisted in generating surface realization alternatives and selecting the best alternative according to the language model.

In the case of LM-based methods, we may point out that classical LMs (based on n-grams) were not suitable because it was necessary to use a large corpus to deal with sparsity of data. Sparsity is a big problem in morphologically marked languages like Portuguese. In order to solve the sparsity of the data, some works used Factored LMs, obtaining better results than the classical LMs (de Novais et al., 2011).

In relation to NLG from semantic representations for Portuguese, we may point out the work of Nunes et al. (2002) (focused on Universal Language Networking), and Moussallem et al. (2018) (focused on ontologies). Another representation was the one proposed by Mille et al. (2018) (based on Universal Dependencies), which is based on syntax instead of semantics.

In relation to NLG tools, we highlight PortNLG (Silva et al., 2013) and SimpleNLG-BP (Oliveira and Sripada, 2014) as surface realisers that were based on SimpleNLG initiative (Gatt and Reiter, 2009)[4]. Finally, other NLG works aimed to build NLP applications, e.g., for structured data visualization and human-computer interaction purposes (Pereira et al., 2012, 2015).

2.2 Natural Language Generation from Semantic Representations

Recently, the number of works on NLG from semantic representations has increased. This increase is reflected in the shared tasks WebNLG (Gardent et al., 2017), E2E Challenge (Novikova et al., 2017), Semeval Task-9 (May and Priyadarshi, 2017) and Surface Realization Shared-Task (Belz et al., 2011; Mille et al., 2018).

In general, there is a trend to apply methods based on neural networks. However, methods

---

[4]Specifically, SimpleNLG-BP was built using the French version of SimpleNLG due to the similarities between both languages.

based on templates, transformation to intermediate representations and language models have shown interesting results. It is also worthy noticing that most of these methods have been applied to English, except for the methods presented in the shared-task proposed by Mille et al. (2018).

In relation to the shared-tasks mentioned before, we point out that the one proposed by Belz et al. (2011) and Mille et al. (2018) (based on Universal Dependencies) used syntactic representations. Specifically, they presented two tracks, one focused on word reordering and inflection generation (superficial track), and other that focused on generating sentences from a deep syntactic representation that is similar to a semantic representation (deep track). Furthermore, these tasks focused on several languages in the superficial task (including Portuguese) and three languages in the deep track (English, Spanish, and French).

Among the methods used for the superficial track in these shared-tasks, we may highlight the use of rule-based methods and language models in the early years (Belz et al., 2011) and a wide application of neural models in recent years (Mille et al., 2018). In the case of the deep track, it is possible to notice that rule-based methods were applied in the first competition, and methods based on transformation to intermediate representations and based on neural models were applied in the last competition.

The results in these tasks showed that approaches based on transformation to intermediate representations obtained poor results in the automatic evaluation due to the great effort in building transformation rules for their own systems. However, they usually showed better results in human evaluations. This may be explained by the maturity of the original proposed systems. This way, although the coverage of the rules was not good, the results were good from a human point of view.

Differently from the approach mentioned before, methods based on neural models (deep learning) obtained the best results. However, some methods used data augmentation strategies to deal with data sparsity (Elder and Hokamp, 2018; Sobrevilla Cabezudo and Pardo, 2018).

One point to highlight is that the results for Portuguese were poor (compared to similar languages like Spanish). Two reasons to explain this issue are related to the amount of data for Portuguese in this task (less than English or Spanish) and the quality of the existing models for related tasks that were used. Another point to highlight is the division of the general task into two sub-tasks: linearisation and inflection generation. Puzikov and Gurevych (2018a) pointed out that there is a strong relation between the linearisation and the inflection generation, and, thus, both sub-tasks should be treated together.

In contrast to Puzikov and Gurevych (2018a), (Elder and Hokamp, 2018) showed that incorporating syntax and morphological information into neural models did not bring significant contribution in the generation process, but incorporated more difficulty in the task.

Finally, it is important to notice the proposal of Madsack et al. (2018), which trained linearisation models using the dataset for each language independently and in a joint way, using multilingual embeddings. Although the results of this work did not present a lot of variation when used for all languages together, this work suggests that it is possible to train systems with similar languages (for example, Spanish and French) in order to take advantage of the syntax similarities and to overcome the problems of lack of data.

In relation to other used representations (Gardent et al., 2017; Novikova et al., 2017), a large number of works based on deep learning strategies were proposed, obtaining good results. However, the use of pipeline-based methods yielded promising results regarding grammar and fluency criteria in a joint evaluation (for RDF representation), but these methods (which usually use rules) obtained the worst results in the E2E Challenge.

Methods based on Statistical Machine Translation kept a reasonable performance (ranking 2nd in RDF Shared-Task), obtaining good results when evaluating the grammar. The explanation for this result comes from the ability to learn complete phrases. Thus, these methods may generate grammatically correct phrases, but with poor general fluency and dissimilarity to the target output. Finally, methods based on template obtained promising results in restricted domains, like in the E2E Challenge.

2.3 Natural Language Generation from Abstract Meaning Representation

In relation to generation methods from Abstract Meaning Representation, it was possible to highlight approaches based on machine translation

(Pourdamghani et al., 2016; Ferreira et al., 2017), on transformation to intermediate representations (Lampouras and Vlachos, 2017; Mille et al., 2017), on deep learning models (Konstas et al., 2017; Song et al., 2018), and on rule extraction (from graphs and trees) (Song et al., 2016; Flanigan et al., 2016).

Methods based on transformation into intermediate representations focused on transforming AMR graphs into simpler representations (usually dependency trees) and then using an appropriate surface realization system. Authors usually took advantage of the similarity between dependency trees and AMR graphs to map some results. However, some problems in this approach were the need to manually build transformation rules (excepting for Lampouras and Vlachos (2017), who automatically perform this) and the need of alignments between the AMR graph and intermediate representations, which could bring noise into the generation process. Overall, this approach presented poor results (compared to other approaches) in automatic evaluations[5]

Methods based on rule extraction obtained better results than the approach mentioned previously. This approach tries to learn conversion rules from AMR graphs (or trees) to the final text. First methods of this approach tried to transform the AMR graph into a tree before learning rules. As (Song et al., 2017) mentioned, these methods suffer with the loss of information (by not using graphs and being restricted to trees), due to its projective nature. Likewise, (Song et al., 2016) and (Song et al., 2017) could suffer from the same problem (ability to deal with non-projective structures) due to their nature to extract and apply the learned rules. Furthermore, these methods used some manual rules to keep the text fluency. However, these rules did not produce a statistically significant increase in the performance, when compared to learned rules.

Some problems of this approach are related to: (1) the need of alignments between AMR graph and the target sentence, as the aligners could lead to more errors (depending of the performance) in the rule extraction process; (2) the argument realization modeling (Flanigan et al., 2016; Song et al., 2016); and (3) the data sparsity in the rules, as some rules are too specific and there is a need to generalize them.

Methods based on Machine Translation usually outperformed other methods. Specifically, methods based on Statistical Machines Translation (SMT) outperformed methods based on Neural Machine Translation (NMT), which use data augmentation strategies to improve their performance (Konstas et al., 2017). In general, both SMT and NMT-based methods explored some preprocessing strategies like delexicalisation[6], compression[7] and graph linearisation[8] (Ferreira et al., 2017)

In relation to the linearisation, the proposals of Pourdamghani et al. (2016) and Ferreira et al. (2017) depended on alignments to perform linearisation. Both works point out that the way linearisation is carried out affects performance, thus, linearisation is an important preprocessing strategy in NLG. However, Konstas et al. (2017) show that linearisation is not that important in NMT-based methods, as the authors propose a data augmentation strategy, decreasing the effect of the linearisation.

In relation to compression, the dependency of alignments also occurred. Moreover, it is necessary a deep analysis to determine the usefulness of compression. On the one hand, compression contributed positively in the SMT-based methods but, on the other hand, it was harmful in NMT-based methods (Ferreira et al., 2017). It is also important to point out that both compression and linearisation processes were executed in sequence in these works. This could be harmful, as the order of execution could lead to loss of information.

Finally, according to (Ferreira et al., 2017), delexicalisation produces an increase and decrease of performance in NMT-based and SMT-based methods, respectively. An alternative to deal with data sparsity is to use copy mechanisms, which have shown performance increase in NLG methods (Song et al., 2018).

Some limitations of these methods were the alignment dependency (similar to the previous approaches) and the linearisation of long sentences. NMT-based methods could not represent or capture information for long sentences, producing un-

---

[5]Except for the work of Gruzitis et al. (2017), who incorporated the system proposed by Flanigan et al. (2016) into their pipeline.

[6]Delexicalisation aims to decrease the data sparsity by replacing some common tokens by constants.

[7]Compression tries to keep important concepts and relations in the text generation process.

[8]Linearisation tries to transform the graph into a sequence of tokens.

satisfactory results.

In order to solve these problems, methods based on neural models proposed Graph-to-Sequence architectures to better capture information from AMR graphs. This architecture showed better results than its predecessors, requiring less training data (augmented data) (Beck et al., 2018).

The main difficulty associated to deep learning is the need of large corpora to get better results. Thus, this could be hard to get for languages like Portuguese, as there are no large available corpora as there are for English.

3 Conclusions and Future Directions

This work showed a more recent literature review on NLG, specially those based on semantic representations and for Brazilian Portuguese language. As it may be seen, NLG works for Portuguese were mainly focused on Referring Expression Generation and Surface Realisation. There were a few recent works about NLG from semantic representations like ontologies or Universal Dependencies (although this last one is of syntactic nature), producing poor results.

Some resources for Portuguese were found (additional to AMR-annotated corpus), as corpora for generation from RDF (Moussallem et al., 2018) and from Universal Dependencies (Mille et al., 2018). This opens the possibility to explore the use of other resources for similar tasks in order to improve the AMR-to-Text generation. There are also corpora for languages that are relatively similar to Portuguese. Considering the proposal of Madsack et al. (2018), to learn realisations from languages that share some characteristics with Portuguese (like French or Spanish) is a reasonable alternative.

Among other strategies to deal with lack of data, it is possible to consider Unsupervised Machine Translation and back-translation strategies. The first one tries to learn without parallel corpora (these would be a corpus of AMR graphs and a corpus of sentences). This strategy has proven to be useful in this context (Lample et al., 2018a,b; Freitag and Roy, 2018). In this case, it would be necessary to extend the corpus of AMR annotations, which could represent one of the challenges. The second one aims to generate corpus in a target language (Portuguese) from other languages (as English) in order to increase the corpus size and reduce the data sparseness. In this case, it is nec-

essary to evaluate the influence of the quality of translations and how this affects the performance of the text generator.

Additionally to the above issue, there are currently large corpora for Portuguese (for example, the corpus used by Hartmann et al. (2017)), which may allow to train robust language models.

The main challenges for Portuguese are its morphologically marked nature and its high syntactic variation[9]. These challenges contribute to data sparseness. Thus, two-stage strategies might not be useful, producing an explosion in the search for the best alternative. Moreover, to treat syntactic ordering and inflection generation together could lead to the introduction of more complexity into the models. Therefore, to tackle NLG for Portuguese as two separate tasks seems to be a good alternative, reducing the complexity of the syntactic ordering and treating inflection generation as a sequence labeling problem.

Among the challenges associated to the methods found in the literature, we may highlight two: (1) the alignment dependency, and (2) the need to better understand the semantic representations (in our case, the AMR graphs) to be able to deduce how they may be syntactically and morphologically realized.

Several approaches need alignments to learn rules and ways to linearise and compress data in AMR graphs. This is a problem because there is a need to manually align AMR graphs and target sentences in order to allow the tools to learn to align by themselves and, then, to introduce these tools into some existent NLG pipeline. Thus, limitations in the aligners may lead to errors in the NLG pipeline. This problem could be bigger in NLG for Portuguese as there is limited resources, and some of these do not present alignments. To solve this, it is possible to use approaches those are not constrained by explicit graph-to-text alignments (for example, graph-to-sequence architectures). Furthermore, this could help to join all the available resources for similar tasks (i. e., corpora for other semantic representations), with no need of alignments, in a easy way and train a semantic representation-independent text generation method. However, it is necessary to measure the usefulness of this approach, comparing it with traditional methods.

---

[9]The interested reader may find an overview of Portuguese characteristics at http://www.meta-net.eu/whitepapers/volumes/portuguese.

Finally, to better understand a semantic representation (and what it means) is very important, as one may better learn the possible syntactic realisations and, therefore, to give a better clue of how sentences may be morphologically constructed. For Portuguese, there is a challenge to deal with different semantic representations. Although the concepts may be shared among different semantic representations, relations are not the same, and the decision on how to code them could generate some problems in the NLG training.

Acknowledgments

The authors are grateful to CAPES and USP Research Office for supporting this work.

References

Rafael Anchiêta and Thiago Pardo. 2018. Towards AMR-BR: A SemBank for Brazilian Portuguese Language. In *Proceedings of the Eleventh International Conference on Language Resources and Evaluation (LREC 2018)*, Miyazaki, Japan. European Language Resources Association (ELRA).

Laura Banarescu, Claire Bonial, Shu Cai, Madalina Georgescu, Kira Griffitt, Ulf Hermjakob, Kevin Knight, Philipp Koehn, Martha Palmer, and Nathan Schneider. 2013. Abstract meaning representation for sembanking. In *Proceedings of the 7th Linguistic Annotation Workshop and Interoperability with Discourse*, pages 178–186, Sofia, Bulgaria. Association for Computational Linguistics.

Daniel Beck, Gholamreza Haffari, and Trevor Cohn. 2018. Graph-to-sequence learning using gated graph neural networks. In *Proceedings of the 56th Annual Meeting of the Association for Computational Linguistics (Volume 1: Long Papers)*, pages 273–283. Association for Computational Linguistics.

Anja Belz, Michael White, Dominic Espinosa, Eric Kow, Deirdre Hogan, and Amanda Stent. 2011. The first surface realisation shared task: Overview and evaluation results. In *Proceedings of the 13th European Workshop on Natural Language Generation*, ENLG '11, pages 217–226, Stroudsburg, PA, USA. Association for Computational Linguistics.

Johan Bos. 2016. Expressive power of abstract meaning representations. *Computational Linguistics*, 42(3):527–535.

Magali Sanches Duran and Sandra M. Aluísio. 2015. Automatic generation of a lexical resource to support semantic role labeling in portuguese. In *Proceedings of the Fourth Joint Conference on Lexical and Computational Semantics, *SEM 2015*, pages 216–221, Denver, Colorado, USA. Association for Computational Linguistics.

Magali Sanches Duran, Jhonata Pereira Martins, and Sandra Maria Aluísio. 2013. Um repositório de verbos para a anotação de papéis semânticos disponível na web (a verb repository for semantic role labeling available in the web) [in portuguese]. In *Proceedings of the 9th Brazilian Symposium in Information and Human Language Technology*.

Henry Elder and Chris Hokamp. 2018. Generating high-quality surface realizations using data augmentation and factored sequence models. In *Proceedings of the First Workshop on Multilingual Surface Realisation*, pages 49–53. Association for Computational Linguistics.

Thiago Castro Ferreira, Iacer Calixto, Sander Wubben, and Emiel Krahmer. 2017. Linguistic realisation as machine translation: Comparing different mt models for amr-to-text generation. In *Proceedings of the 10th International Conference on Natural Language Generation*, pages 1–10, Santiago de Compostela, Spain. Association for Computational Linguistics.

Jeffrey Flanigan, Chris Dyer, Noah A. Smith, and Jaime G. Carbonell. 2016. Generation from abstract meaning representation using tree transducers. In *Proceedings of the Conference of the North American Chapter of the Association for Computational Linguistics: Human Language Technologies*, pages 731–739, San Diego California, USA. Association for Computational Linguistics.

Markus Freitag and Scott Roy. 2018. Unsupervised natural language generation with denoising autoencoders. In *Proceedings of the 2018 Conference on Empirical Methods in Natural Language Processing*, pages 3922–3929, Brussels, Belgium. Association for Computational Linguistics.

Claire Gardent, Anastasia Shimorina, Shashi Narayan, and Laura Perez-Beltrachini. 2017. Creating training corpora for nlg micro-planning. In *Proceedings of the 55th Annual Meeting of the Association for Computational Linguistics (Volume 1: Long Papers)*, pages 179–188. Association for Computational Linguistics.

Albert Gatt and Ehud Reiter. 2009. Simplenlg: A realisation engine for practical applications. In *Proceedings of the 12th European Workshop on Natural Language Generation*, pages 90–93, Stroudsburg, PA, USA. Association for Computational Linguistics.

Normunds Gruzitis, Didzis Gosko, and Guntis Barzdins. 2017. Rigotrio at semeval-2017 task 9: Combining machine learning and grammar engineering for amr parsing and generation. In *Proceedings of the 11th International Workshop on Semantic Evaluation (SemEval-2017)*, pages 924–928. Association for Computational Linguistics.

Nathan Hartmann, Erick Fonseca, Christopher Shulby, Marcos Treviso, Jéssica Silva, and Sandra Aluísio. 2017. Portuguese word embeddings: Evaluating on word analogies and natural language tasks. In

Proceedings of the 11th Brazilian Symposium in Information and Human Language Technology, pages 122–131. Sociedade Brasileira de Computação.

Ioannis Konstas, Srinivasan Iyer, Mark Yatskar, Yejin Choi, and Luke Zettlemoyer. 2017. Neural amr: Sequence-to-sequence models for parsing and generation. In *Proceedings of the 55th Annual Meeting of the Association for Computational Linguistics (Volume 1: Long Papers)*, pages 146–157, Vancouver, Canada. Association for Computational Linguistics.

Emiel Krahmer, Sebastiaan Van Erk, and André Verleg. 2003. Graph-based generation of referring expressions. *Computational Linguistics*, 29(1):53–72.

Guillaume Lample, Alexis Conneau, Ludovic Denoyer, and Marc'Aurelio Ranzato. 2018a. Unsupervised machine translation using monolingual corpora only. In *International Conference on Learning Representations*.

Guillaume Lample, Myle Ott, Alexis Conneau, Ludovic Denoyer, and Marc'Aurelio Ranzato. 2018b. Phrase-based & neural unsupervised machine translation. In *Proceedings of the 2018 Conference on Empirical Methods in Natural Language Processing (EMNLP)*, pages 5039–5049, Brussels, Belgium. Association for Computational Linguistics.

Gerasimos Lampouras and Andreas Vlachos. 2017. Sheffield at semeval-2017 task 9: Transition-based language generation from amr. In *Proceedings of the 11th International Workshop on Semantic Evaluation (SemEval-2017)*, pages 586–591. Association for Computational Linguistics.

Xiao Li, Kees van Deemter, and Chenghua Lin. 2018. Statistical NLG for generating the content and form of referring expressions. In *Proceedings of the 11th International Conference on Natural Language Generation*, pages 482–491, Tilburg University, The Netherlands. Association for Computational Linguistics.

Diego Jesus De Lucena, Ivandré Paraboni, and Daniel Bastos Pereira. 2010. From semantic properties to surface text: the generation of domain object descriptions. *Inteligencia Artificial, Revista Iberoamericana de Inteligencia Artificial*, 14(45):48–58.

Andreas Madsack, Johanna Heininger, Nyamsuren Davaasambuu, Vitaliia Voronik, Michael Käufl, and Robert Weißgraeber. 2018. Ax semantics' submission to the surface realization shared task 2018. In *Proceedings of the First Workshop on Multilingual Surface Realisation*, pages 54–57. Association for Computational Linguistics.

Jonathan May and Jay Priyadarshi. 2017. Semeval-2017 task 9: Abstract meaning representation parsing and generation. In *Proceedings of the 11th International Workshop on Semantic Evaluation (SemEval-2017)*, pages 536–545. Association for Computational Linguistics.

Simon Mille, Anja Belz, Bernd Bohnet, Yvette Graham, Emily Pitler, and Leo Wanner. 2018. The first multilingual surface realisation shared task (sr'18): Overview and evaluation results. In *Proceedings of the First Workshop on Multilingual Surface Realisation*, pages 1–12. Association for Computational Linguistics.

Simon Mille, Roberto Carlini, Alicia Burga, and Leo Wanner. 2017. Forge at semeval-2017 task 9: Deep sentence generation based on a sequence of graph transducers. In *Proceedings of the 11th International Workshop on Semantic Evaluation (SemEval-2017)*, pages 920–923. Association for Computational Linguistics.

Diego Moussallem, Thiago Ferreira, Marcos Zampieri, Maria Cláudia Cavalcanti, Geraldo Xexéo, Mariana Neves, and Axel-Cyrille Ngonga Ngomo. 2018. Rdf2pt: Generating brazilian portuguese texts from rdf data. In *Proceedings of the Eleventh International Conference on Language Resources and Evaluation (LREC 2018)*. European Language Resources Association (ELRA).

Eder Miranda de Novais, Ivandré Paraboni, and Diogo Takaki Ferreira. 2011. Highly-inflected language generation using factored language models. In *Computational Linguistics and Intelligent Text Processing*, pages 429–438, Berlin, Heidelberg. Springer Berlin Heidelberg.

Eder Miranda De Novais, Thiago Dias Tadeu, and Ivandré Paraboni. 2010a. *Improved Text Generation Using N-gram Statistics*, pages 316–325. Springer Berlin Heidelberg, Berlin, Heidelberg.

Eder Miranda De Novais and Ivandré Paraboni. 2013. Portuguese text generation using factored language models. *Journal of the Brazilian Computer Society*, 19(2):135–146.

Eder Miranda De Novais, Thiago Dias Tadeu, and Ivandré Paraboni. 2010b. Text generation for brazilian portuguese: The surface realization task. In *Proceedings of the NAACL HLT 2010 Young Investigators Workshop on Computational Approaches to Languages of the Americas*, YIWCALA '10, pages 125–131, Stroudsburg, PA, USA. Association for Computational Linguistics.

Jekaterina Novikova, Ondřej Dušek, and Verena Rieser. 2017. The e2e dataset: New challenges for end-to-end generation. In *Proceedings of the 18th Annual SIGdial Meeting on Discourse and Dialogue*, pages 201–206. Association for Computational Linguistics.

Maria Nunes, Graças V Nunes, Ronaldo T Martins, Lucia Rino, and Osvaldo Oliveira. 2002. The decoding system for brazilian portuguese using the universal networking language (unl).

Rodrigo De Oliveira and Somayajulu Sripada. 2014. Adapting simplenlg for brazilian portuguese realisation. In *Proceedings of the Eighth International Natural Language Generation Conference, Including Proceedings of the INLG and SIGDIAL*, pages 93–94, Philadelphia, PA, USA. Association for Computational Linguistics.

Martha Palmer, Daniel Gildea, and Paul Kingsbury. 2005. The proposition bank: An annotated corpus of semantic roles. *Computational Linguistics.*, 31(1):71–106.

Daniel Bastos Pereira and Ivandré Paraboni. 2008. Statistical surface realisation of portuguese referring expressions. In *Proceedings of the 6th International Conference on Advances in Natural Language Processing*, pages 383–392, Gothenburg, Sweden.

JC Pereira, A Teixeira, and JS Pinto. 2015. Towards a Hybrid Nlg System for Data2Text in Portuguese. In *Proceedings of the 10th Iberian Conference on Information Systems and Technologies (CISTI)*, pages 1–6, Aveiro, Portugal. IEEE.

José Casimiro Pereira, António JS Teixeira, and Joaquim Sousa Pinto. 2012. Natural language generation in the context of multimodal interaction in portuguese. *Electrónica e Telecomunicações*, 5(4):400–409.

Nima Pourdamghani, Kevin Knight, and Ulf Hermjakob. 2016. Generating english from abstract meaning representations. In *Proceedings of the Ninth International Natural Language Generation Conference*, pages 21–25, Edinburgh, UK.

Yevgeniy Puzikov and Iryna Gurevych. 2018a. Binlin: A simple method of dependency tree linearization. In *Proceedings of the First Workshop on Multilingual Surface Realisation*, pages 13–28. Association for Computational Linguistics.

Yevgeniy Puzikov and Iryna Gurevych. 2018b. E2e nlg challenge: Neural models vs. templates. In *Proceedings of the 11th International Conference on Natural Language Generation*, pages 463–471. Association for Computational Linguistics.

Ehud Reiter and Robert Dale. 2000. *Building Natural Language Generation Systems*. Cambridge University Press, New York, NY, USA.

Douglas Fernandes Pereira Da Silva, Eder Miranda De Novais, and Ivandré Paraboni. 2013. Um sistema de realização superficial para geração de textos em português. *Revista de Informática Teórica e Aplicada*, 20(3):31–48.

Marco Antonio Sobrevilla Cabezudo and Thiago Pardo. 2018. Nilc-swornemo at the surface realization shared task: Exploring syntax-based word ordering using neural models. In *Proceedings of the First Workshop on Multilingual Surface Realisation*, pages 58–64. Association for Computational Linguistics.

Linfeng Song, Xiaochang Peng, Yue Zhang, Zhiguo Wang, and Daniel Gildea. 2017. Amr-to-text generation with synchronous node replacement grammar. In *Proceedings of the 55th Annual Meeting of the Association for Computational Linguistics*, pages 7–13. Association for Computational Linguistics.

Linfeng Song, Yue Zhang, Xiaochang Peng, Zhiguo Wang, and Daniel Gildea. 2016. Amr-to-text generation as a traveling salesman problem. In *Proceedings of the 2016 Conference on Empirical Methods in Natural Language Processing*, pages 2084–2089, Austin, Texas. Association for Computational Linguistics.

Linfeng Song, Yue Zhang, Zhiguo Wang, and Daniel Gildea. 2018. A graph-to-sequence model for amr-to-text generation. In *Proceedings of the 56th Annual Meeting of the Association for Computational Linguistics*, pages 1616–1626. Association for Computational Linguistics.

Long-Distance Dependencies don't have to be Long:
Simplifying through Provably (Approximately) Optimal Permutations

Rishi Bommasani
Department of Computer Science
Cornell University
rb724@cornell.edu

Abstract

Neural models at the sentence level often operate on the constituent words/tokens in a way that encodes the inductive bias of processing the input in a similar fashion to how humans do. However, there is no guarantee that the standard ordering of words is computationally efficient or optimal. To help mitigate this, we consider a dependency parse as a proxy for the inter-word dependencies in a sentence and simplify the sentence with respect to combinatorial objectives imposed on the sentence-parse pair. The associated optimization results in permuted sentences that are provably (approximately) optimal with respect to minimizing dependency parse lengths and that are demonstrably simpler. We evaluate our general-purpose permutations within a fine-tuning schema for the downstream task of subjectivity analysis. Our fine-tuned baselines reflect a new state of the art for the **SUBJ** dataset and the permutations we introduce lead to further improvements with a **2.0%** increase in classification accuracy (absolute) and a **45%** reduction in classification error (relative) over the previous state of the art.

1 Introduction

Natural language processing systems that operate at the sentence level often need to model the interaction between different words in a sentence. This kind of modelling has been shown to be necessary not only in explicit settings where we consider the relationships between words (GuoDong et al., 2005; Fundel et al., 2006) but also in opinion mining (Joshi and Penstein-Rosé, 2009), question answering (Cui et al., 2005), and semantic role labelling (Hacioglu, 2004). A standard roadblock in this process has been trying to model long-distance dependencies between words. Neural models for sentence-level tasks, for example, have leveraged recurrent neural networks (Sutskever et al., 2014) and attention mechanisms (Bahdanau et al., 2015; Luong et al., 2015) as improvements in addressing this challenge. LSTMs (Hochreiter and Schmidhuber, 1997) in particular have been touted as being well-suited for capturing these kinds of dependencies but recent work suggests that the modelling may be insufficient to various extents (Linzen et al., 2016; Liu et al., 2018; Dangovski et al., 2019). Fundamentally, these neural components do not restructure the challenge of learning long-distance dependencies but instead introduce computational expressiveness as a means to represent and retain inter-word relationships efficiently (Kuncoro et al., 2018).

Models that operate at the sentence level in natural language processing generally process sentences word-by-word in a left-to-right fashion. Some models, especially recurrent models, consider the right-to-left traversal (Sutskever et al., 2014) or a bidirectional traversal that combines both the left-to-right and right-to-left traversals (Schuster and Paliwal, 1997). Other models weaken the requirement of sequential processing by incorporating position embeddings to retain the sequential nature of the data and then use self-attentive mechanisms that don't explicitly model the sequential nature of the input (Vaswani et al., 2017). All such approaches encode the prior that computational processing of sentences should appeal to a cognitively plausible ordering of words.

Nevertheless in machine translation, re-orderings of both the input and output sequences have been considered for the purpose of improving *alignment* between the source and target languages. Specifically, *preorders*, or permuting the input sequence, and *postorders*, or permuting the output sequence, have been well-studied in statistical machine translation (Xia and McCord, 2004; Goto et al., 2012) and have been recently integrated towards fully neural machine translation

Proceedings of the ACL 2019, Student Research Workshop, pages 89–99
Florence, Italy, July 28th-August 2nd, 2019. ©2019 Association for Computational Linguistics

(De Gispert et al., 2015; Kawara et al., 2018). In general, these re-ordering methods assume some degree of supervision (Neubig et al., 2012) and have tried to implicitly maintain the original structure of the considered sequence despite modifying it to improve alignment. Similar approaches have also been considered for cross-lingual transfer in dependency parsing (Wang and Eisner, 2018) based on the same underlying idea of improving alignment.

In this work, we propose a general approach for permuting the words in an input sentence based on the notion of *simplification*, i.e. reducing the length of inter-word dependencies in the input. In particular, we appeal to graph-based combinatorial optimization as an unsupervised approach for producing permutations that are provably optimal, or provably approximately optimal, in minimizing inter-word dependency parse lengths.

Ultimately, we hypothesize that our simplification-based permutations over input sentences can be incorporated as a lightweight, drop-in preprocessing step for neural models to improve performance for a number of standard sentence-level NLP problems. As an initial case study, we consider the task of sentence-level subjectivity classification and using the **SUBJ** dataset (Pang and Lee, 2004), we first introduce baselines that achieve a state of the art **95.8%** accuracy and further improve on these baselines with our permutations to a new state of the art of **97.5%** accuracy.

2 Limitations

This work considers simplifying inter-word dependencies for neural models. However, we measure inter-word dependencies using dependency parses and therefore rely on an incomplete description of inter-word dependencies in general. Further, we assume the existence of a strong dependency parser, which is reasonably well-founded for English which is the language studied in this work. This assumption is required for providing theoretical guarantees regarding the optimality of sentence permutations with respect to the gold-standard dependency parse.[1] In spite of these assumptions, it is still possible for the subsequent neural models to recover from errors in the

initial sentence permutations.

Beyond this, we consider dependency parses which graph theoretically are edge-labelled directed trees. However, in constructing optimal sentence permutations, we simplify the graph structure by neglecting edge labels and edge directions. Both of these are crucial aspects of a dependency parse tree and in §6 we discuss possible future directions to help address these challenges.

Most concerningly, this approach alters the order of words in a sentence for the purpose of simplifying one class of dependencies — binary inter-word dependencies marked by dependency parses. However, in doing so, it is likely that other crucial aspects of the syntax and semantics of a sentence that are a function of word order are obscured. We believe the mechanism proposed in §3.3 helps to alleviate this by making use of powerful initial word representations that are made available through recent advances in pretrained contextual representations and transfer learning (Peters et al., 2018; Devlin et al., 2018; Liu et al., 2019).

3 Model

Our goal is to take a dependency parse of a sentence and use it is as scaffold for permuting the words in a sentence. We begin by describing two combinatorial measures on graphs that we can use to rank permutations of the words in a sentence by, and therefore optimize with respect to, in order to find the optimal permutation for each measure. Given the permutation, we then train a model end-to-end on a downstream task and exploit pretrained contextual word embeddings to initialize the word representations for our model.

3.1 Input Structure

Given a sentence as an input for some downstream task, we begin by computing a dependency parse for the sentence using an off-the-shelf dependency parser. This endows the sentence with a graph structure corresponding to an edge-labelled directed tree $\mathcal{G}^* = (\mathcal{V}^*, \mathcal{E}^*)$ where the vertices correspond to tokens in the sentence ($\mathcal{V}^* = \{w_1, w_2, \ldots, w_n\}$) and the edges correspond to dependency arcs. We then consider the undirected tree $\mathcal{G} = (\mathcal{V}, \mathcal{E})$ where $\mathcal{V} = \mathcal{V}^*$ and $\mathcal{E} = \mathcal{E}^*$ without the edge labels and edge directions.

---

[1] The generated permutations are always (approximately) optimal with respect to the system-generated dependency parse.

3.2 Combinatorial Objectives

We begin by defining a *linear layout* on $\mathcal{G}$ to be a bijective, i.e. one-to-one, ordering on the vertices $\pi : \mathcal{V} \to \{1, 2, \ldots, n\}$. For a graph associated with a sentence, we consider the *identity linear layout* π_I to be given by $\pi_I(w_i) = i$: the linear layout of vertices is based on the word order in the input sentence. For any given linear layout π we can further associate each edge $(u, v) \in \mathcal{E}$ with an *edge distance* $d_{u,v} = |\pi(u) - \pi(v)|$.[2]

By considering the modified dependency parse $\mathcal{G}$ alongside the sentence, we recognize that a computational model of the sentence may need to model any given dependency arc $(w_i, w_j) \in \mathcal{E}$. As a result, for a model that processes sentences word-by-word, information regarding this arc must be stored for a number of time-steps given by $d_{w_i, w_j} = |\pi_I(w_i) - \pi_I(w_j)| = |j - i|$. This implies that a model may need to store a dependency for a large number of time-steps (a long-distance dependency) and we instead consider finding an optimal linear layout π^* (that is likely not to be the identity) to minimize these edge distances with respect to two well-studied objectives on linear layouts.

Bandwidth Problem The *bandwidth* problem on graphs corresponds to finding an optimal linear layout π^* under the objective:

$$\operatorname*{argmin}_{\pi \in \Pi} \ \max_{(u,v) \in \mathcal{E}} d_{u,v} \tag{1}$$

The bandwidth problem is a well known problem dealing with linear layouts with applications in sparse matrix computation (Gibbs et al., 1976) and information retrieval (Botafogo, 1993) and has been posed in equivalent ways for graphs and matrices (Chinn et al., 1982). For dependency parses, it corresponds to finding a linear layout that minimizes the length of the longest dependency. Papadimitriou (1976) proved the problem was NP-hard and the problem was further shown to remain NP-hard for trees and even restricted classes of trees (Unger, 1998; Garey et al., 1978). In this work, we use the better linear layout of those produced by the guaranteed $\mathcal{O}(\log n)$ approximation of Haralambides and Makedon (1997) and the heuristic of Cuthill and McKee (1969) and refer to the resulting linear layout as π_b^*.

Minimum Linear Arrangement Problem Similar to the bandwidth problem, the *minimum linear arrangement* (minLA) problem considers finding a linear layout given by:

$$\operatorname*{argmin}_{\pi \in \Pi} \sum_{(u,v) \in \mathcal{E}} d_{u,v} \tag{2}$$

While less studied than the bandwidth problem, the minimum linear arrangement problem considers minimizing the sum of the edge lengths of the dependency arcs which may more closely resemble how models need to not only handle the longest dependency well, as in the bandwidth problem, but also need to handle the other dependencies. Although the problem is NP-hard for general graphs (Garey et al., 1974), it admits polynomial time exact solutions for trees (Shiloach, 1979). We use the algorithm of Chung (1984), which runs in $\mathcal{O}(n^{1.585})$, to find the optimal layout π_m^*.

3.3 Downstream Integration

Given a linear layout π, we can define the associated permuted sentence s' of the original sentence $s = w_1 \ w_2 \ \ldots \ w_n$ where the position of w_i in s' is given by $\pi(w_i)$. We can then train models end-to-end taking the permuted sentences as direct replacements for the original input sentences. However, this approach suffers from the facts that (a) the resulting sentences may have lost syntactic/semantic qualities of the original sentences due to the permutations and (b) existing pretrained embedding methods would need to be re-trained with these new word orders, which is computationally expensive, and pretraining objectives like language modelling may be less sensible given the problems noted in (a). To reconcile this, we leverage a recent three-step pattern for many NLP tasks (Peters et al., 2019):

1. **Pretrained Word Representations**: Represent each word in the sentence using a pretrained contextualizer (Peters et al., 2018; Devlin et al., 2018).

2. **Fine-tuned Sentence Representation**: Learn a task-specific encoding of the sentence using a task-specific encoder as a fine-tuning step on top of the pretrained word representations.

3. **Task Predictions**: Generate a prediction for the task using the fine-tuned representation.

---

[2]Refer to Díaz et al. (2002) for a survey of linear layouts, related problems, and their applications.

As a result, we can introduce the permutation between steps 1 and 2. What this means is the initial pretrained representations model the sentence using the standard ordering of words and therefore have access to the unchanged syntactic/semantic properties. These properties are diffused into the word-level representations and therefore the fine-tuning encoder may retrieve them even if they are not observable after the permutation. This allows the focus of the task-specific encoder to shift towards modelling useful dependencies specific to the task.

4 Experiments

Using our approach, we begin by studying how optimizing for these combinatorial objectives affects the complexity of the input sentence as measured using these objective functions. We then evaluate performance on the downstream task of subjectivity analysis and find our baseline model achieves a new state of the art for the dataset which is improved further by the permutations we introduce.

For all experiments, we use the spaCy dependency parser (Honnibal and Montani, 2017) to find the dependency parse. In studying properties of the bandwidth optimal permutation π_b^* and the minLA optimal permutation π_m^*, we compare to baselines where the sentence is not permuted/the identity permutation π_I as well as where the words in the sentence are ordered using a random permutation π_R. A complete description of experimental and implementation details is provided in Appendix A.

Our permutations do not introduce or change the size or runtime of existing models while providing models with dependency parse information implicitly. The entire preprocessing process, including the computation of permutations for both objectives, takes **21 minutes** in aggregate for the 10000 examples in the **SUBJ** dataset. A complete description of changes in model size, runtime, and convergence speed is provided in Appendix B.

Data and Evaluation To evaluate the direct effects of our permutations on input sentence simplification, we use 100000 sentences from Wikipedia; to evaluate the downstream impacts we consider the **SUBJ** dataset (Pang and Lee, 2004) for subjectivity analysis. The subjectivity analysis task requires deciding whether a given sentence is subjective or objective and the dataset is

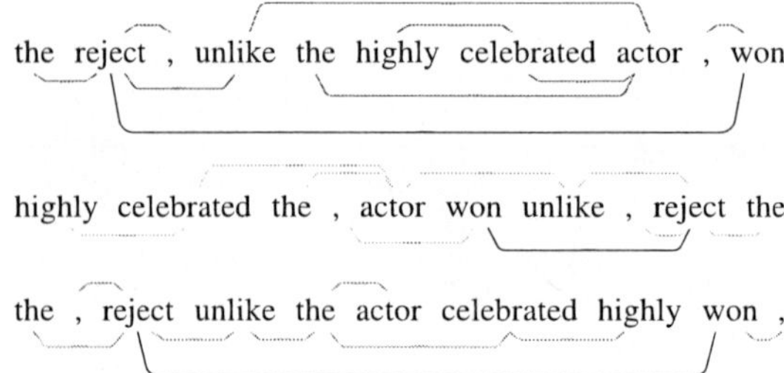

Figure 1: Example of the sentence permutation along with overlayed dependency parses. Blue indicates the standard ordering, green indicates the bandwidth optimal ordering, and red indicates the minLA optimal ordering. Black indicates the longest dependency arc in the original ordering.

balanced with 5000 subjective and 5000 objective examples. We consider this task as a starting point as it is well-studied and dependency features have been shown to be useful for similar opinion mining problems (Wu et al., 2009).

Examples In Figure 1, we present an example sentence and its permutations under π_I, π_b^* and π_m^*. Under the standard ordering, the sentence has bandwidth 8 and minLA score 22 and this is reduced by both the bandwidth optimal permutation to 3 and 17 respectively and similarly the minLA permutation also improves on both objectives with scores of 6 and 16 respectively. A model processing the sequence word-by-word may have struggled to retain the long dependency arc linking 'reject' and 'won' and therefore incorrectly deemed that 'actor' was the subject of the verb 'won' as it is the only other viable candidate and is closer to the verb. If this had occured, it would lead an incorrect interpretation (here the opposite meaning). While both of the introduced permutations still have 'actor' closer to the verb, the distance between 'reject' and 'won' shrinks (denoted by the black arcs) and similarly the distance between 'unlike' and 'actor' shrinks. These combined effects map help to mitigate this issue and allow for improved modelling. Across the Wikipedia data, we see a similar pattern for the minLA optimal permutations in that they yield improvements on both objectives but we find the bandwidth optimal permutations on average increase the minLA score as is shown in Table 1. We believe this is natural given the relationship of the objectives; the longest arc is accounted for in the minLA objective whereas the other arcs don't contribute to the

	Bandwidth	minLA
π_I (Standard)	17.64	82.39
π_R (Random)	20.94	294.43
π_b^* (Bandwidth)	6.75	101.23
π_m^* (minLA)	9.43	54.57

Table 1: Bandwidth and minimum linear arrangement scores for the specified permutation type averaged across 100000 Wikipedia sentences.

	Accuracy
π_I (Standard)	95.8
π_R (Random)	94.8
π_b^* (Bandwidth)	96.2
π_m^* (minLA)	**97.5**
AdaSent (Zhao et al., 2015)[†]	95.5
CNN+MCFA (Amplayo et al., 2018)[†]	94.8

Table 2: Accuracy on the **SUBJ** dataset using the specified ordering of pretrained representations for the fine-tuning LSTM. [†] indicates prior models that were evaluated using 10-fold cross validation instead of a held-out test set.

bandwidth cost. We also find the comparison of the standard and random orderings to be evidence that human orderings of words to form sentences (at least in English) are correlated with these objectives, as they are significantly better with respect to these objectives as compared to random orderings. Refer to Figure 3 for a larger example.

Downstream Performance In Table 2, we present the results on the downstream task. Despite the fact that the random permutation LSTM encoder cannot learn from the word order and implicitly is restrained to permutation-invariant features, the associated model performs comparably with previous state of the art systems, indicating the potency of current pretrained embeddings and specifically ELMo. When there is a deterministic ordering, we find that the standard ordering is the least helpful of the three orderings considered. We see a particularly significant spike in performance when using permutations that are minLA optimal and we conjecture that this may be because minLA permutations improve on both objectives on average and empirically we observe they better maintain the order of the original sentence (as can be seen in Figure 1).

5 Related Work

This work draws upon inspiration from the literature on psycholinguistics and cognitive science. Specifically, dependency lengths and the existing minimization in natural language has been studied under the dependency length minimization (DLM) hypothesis (Liu, 2008) which posits a bias in human languages towards constructions with shorter dependency lengths.[3]

In particular, the relationship described between random and natural language orderings of words to form sentences as in Table 1 has been studied more broadly across 37 natural languages in Futrell et al. (2015). This work, alongside Gildea and Temperley (2010); Liu et al. (2017); Futrell et al. (2017) helps to validate the extent and pervasiveness of DLM in natural languages. More generally, this literature body has proposed a number of reasons for this behavior, many of which center around the related notions of efficiency (Gibson et al., 2019) and memory constraints (Gulordava et al., 2015) for humans. Recent research at the intersection of psycholinguistics and NLP that has tried to probe for dependency-oriented understanding in neural networks (primarily RNNs) does indicate relationships with specific dependency-types and RNN understanding. This includes research considering specific dependency types (Wilcox et al., 2018, 2019a), word-order effects (Futrell and Levy, 2019), and structural supervision (Wilcox et al., 2019b).

Prompted by this, the permutations considered in this work can alternatively be seen as linearizations (Langkilde and Knight, 1998; Filippova and Strube, 2009; Futrell and Gibson, 2015; Puzikov and Gurevych, 2018) of a dependency parse in a minimal fashion which is closely related to Gildea and Temperley (2007); Temperley and Gildea (2018). While such linearizations have not been well-studied for downstream impacts, the usage of dependency lengths as a constraint has been studied for dependency parsing itself. Towards this end, Eisner and Smith (2010) showed that using dependency length can be a powerful heuristic tool in dependency parsing (by either enforcing a strict preference or favoring a soft preference for shorter dependencies).

---

[3]In this work, we partially deviate from this linguistic terminology, which primarily deals with the measure defined in Equation 2, and prefer algorithmic terminology to accommodate the measure defined in Equation 1 and disambiguate these related measures more clearly.

6 Future Directions

Graph Structure Motivated by recent work on graph convolutional networks that began with undirected unlabelled graphs (Kipf and Welling, 2016; Zhang et al., 2018) that was extended to include edge direction and edge labels (Marcheggiani and Titov, 2017), we consider whether these features of a dependency parse can also leveraged in computing an optimal permutation. We argue that bidirectionally traversing the permuted sequence may be sufficient to address edge direction. A natural approach to encode edge labels would be to define a mapping (either learned on an auxiliary objective or tuned as a hyperparameter) from categorical edge labels to numericals edge weights and then consider the weighted analogues of the objectives in Equation 1 and Equation 2.

Improved Objective The objectives introduced in Equation 1 and Equation 2 can be unified by considering the family of cost functions:

$$f_p(\pi) = \sum_{(u,v)\in\mathcal{E}} |\pi(u) - \pi(v)|^p \qquad (3)$$

Here, minLA correspond to $p = 1$ and the bandwidth problem corresponds to $p = \infty$. We can then propose a generalized objective that is the convex combination of the individual objectives, i.e. finding a permutation that minimizes:

$$f_{1,\infty}^{\alpha}(\pi) = \alpha f_1(\pi) + (1 - \alpha)f_\infty(\pi) \qquad (4)$$

Setting α to 0 or 1 reduces to the original objectives. This form of the new objective is reminiscent of Elastic Net regularization in statistical optimization (Zou and Hastie, 2005). Inspired by this parallel, a Lagrangian relaxation of one of the objectives as a constraint may be an approach towards (approximate) optimization.

Task-specific Permutations The permutations produced by these models are invariant with respect to the downstream task. However, different tasks may benefit from different sentence orders that go beyond task-agnostic simplification. A natural way to model this in neural models is to learn the permutation in a differentiable fashion and train the permutation model end-to-end within the overarching model for the task. Refer to Appendix C for further discussion.

7 Conclusion

In this work, we propose approaches that permute the words in a sentence to provably minimize combinatorial objectives related to the length of dependency arcs. We find that this is a lightweight procedure that helps to simplify input sentences for downstream models and that it leads to improved performance and state of the art results (**97.5%** classification accuracy) for subjectivity analysis using the **SUBJ** dataset.

Acknowledgements

I thank Bobby Kleinberg for his tremendous insight into the present and future algorithmic challenges of layout-based optimization problems, Tianze Shi for his pointers towards the dependency length minimization literature in psycholinguistics and cognitive science, and Arzoo Katiyar for her advice on comparing against random sequence orderings and considering future work towards soft/differentiable analogues. I also thank the anonymous reviewers for their perceptive and constructive feedback. Finally, I thank Claire Cardie for her articulate concerns and actionable suggestions with regards to this work and, more broadly, for her overarching guidance and warm mentoring as an adviser.

References

Reinald Kim Amplayo, Kyungjae Lee, Jinyoung Yeo, and Seung won Hwang. 2018. Translations as additional contexts for sentence classification. In *IJCAI*.

Dzmitry Bahdanau, Kyunghyun Cho, and Yoshua Bengio. 2015. Neural machine translation by jointly learning to align and translate. In *3rd International Conference on Learning Representations, ICLR 2015, San Diego, CA, USA, May 7-9, 2015, Conference Track Proceedings*.

Rodrigo A Botafogo. 1993. Cluster analysis for hypertext systems. In *Proceedings of the 16th annual international ACM SIGIR conference on Research and development in information retrieval*, pages 116–125. ACM.

P. Z. Chinn, J. Chvtalov, A. K. Dewdney, and N. E. Gibbs. 1982. The bandwidth problem for graphs and matricesa survey. *Journal of Graph Theory*, 6(3):223–254.

FRK Chung. 1984. On optimal linear arrangements of trees. *Computers & mathematics with applications*, 10(1):43–60.

Hang Cui, Renxu Sun, Keya Li, Min-Yen Kan, and Tat-Seng Chua. 2005. Question answering passage retrieval using dependency relations. In *Proceedings of the 28th annual international ACM SIGIR conference on Research and development in information retrieval*, pages 400–407. ACM.

E. Cuthill and J. McKee. 1969. Reducing the bandwidth of sparse symmetric matrices. In *Proceedings of the 1969 24th National Conference*, ACM '69, pages 157–172, New York, NY, USA. ACM.

Rumen Dangovski, Li Jing, Preslav Nakov, Mico Tatalovic, and Marin Soljacic. 2019. Rotational unit of memory: A novel representation unit for rnns with scalable applications. *Transactions of the Association for Computational Linguistics*, 7:121–138.

Adrià De Gispert, Gonzalo Iglesias, and Bill Byrne. 2015. Fast and accurate preordering for smt using neural networks. In *Proceedings of the 2015 Conference of the North American Chapter of the Association for Computational Linguistics: Human Language Technologies*, pages 1012–1017.

Jacob Devlin, Ming-Wei Chang, Kenton Lee, and Kristina Toutanova. 2018. Bert: Pre-training of deep bidirectional transformers for language understanding. *arXiv preprint arXiv:1810.04805*.

Josep Díaz, Jordi Petit, and Maria Serna. 2002. A survey of graph layout problems. *ACM Computing Surveys (CSUR)*, 34(3):313–356.

Jason Eisner and Noah A Smith. 2010. Favor short dependencies: Parsing with soft and hard constraints on dependency length. In *Trends in Parsing Technology*, pages 121–150. Springer.

Katja Filippova and Michael Strube. 2009. Tree linearization in english: Improving language model based approaches. In *Proceedings of Human Language Technologies: The 2009 Annual Conference of the North American Chapter of the Association for Computational Linguistics, Companion Volume: Short Papers*, NAACL-Short '09, pages 225–228, Stroudsburg, PA, USA. Association for Computational Linguistics.

Katrin Fundel, Robert Küffner, and Ralf Zimmer. 2006. Relexrelation extraction using dependency parse trees. *Bioinformatics*, 23(3):365–371.

Richard Futrell and Edward Gibson. 2015. Experiments with generative models for dependency tree linearization. In *Proceedings of the 2015 Conference on Empirical Methods in Natural Language Processing*, pages 1978–1983.

Richard Futrell, Roger Levy, and Edward Gibson. 2017. Generalizing dependency distance: Comment on dependency distance: A new perspective on syntactic patterns in natural languages by haitao liu et al. *Physics of life reviews*, 21:197–199.

Richard Futrell and Roger P. Levy. 2019. Do RNNs learn human-like abstract word order preferences? In *Proceedings of the Society for Computation in Linguistics (SCiL) 2019*, pages 50–59.

Richard Futrell, Kyle Mahowald, and Edward Gibson. 2015. Large-scale evidence of dependency length minimization in 37 languages. *Proceedings of the National Academy of Sciences*, 112(33):10336–10341.

Michael R Garey, Ronald L Graham, David S Johnson, and Donald Ervin Knuth. 1978. Complexity results for bandwidth minimization. *SIAM Journal on Applied Mathematics*, 34(3):477–495.

Michael R Garey, David S Johnson, and Larry Stockmeyer. 1974. Some simplified np-complete problems. In *Proceedings of the sixth annual ACM symposium on Theory of computing*, pages 47–63. ACM.

Norman E. Gibbs, William G. Poole, and Paul K. Stockmeyer. 1976. An algorithm for reducing the bandwidth and profile of a sparse matrix. *SIAM Journal on Numerical Analysis*, 13(2):236–250.

Edward Gibson, Richard Futrell, Steven T Piandadosi, Isabelle Dautriche, Kyle Mahowald, Leon Bergen, and Roger Levy. 2019. How efficiency shapes human language. *Trends in cognitive sciences*.

Daniel Gildea and David Temperley. 2007. Optimizing grammars for minimum dependency length. In *Proceedings of the 45th Annual Meeting of the Association of Computational Linguistics*, pages 184–191.

Daniel Gildea and David Temperley. 2010. Do grammars minimize dependency length? *Cognitive Science*, 34(2):286–310.

Isao Goto, Masao Utiyama, and Eiichiro Sumita. 2012. Post-ordering by parsing for japanese-english statistical machine translation. In *50th Annual Meeting of the Association for Computational Linguistics*, page 311.

Kristina Gulordava, Paola Merlo, and Benoit Crabbé. 2015. Dependency length minimisation effects in short spans: a large-scale analysis of adjective placement in complex noun phrases. In *Proceedings of the 53rd Annual Meeting of the Association for Computational Linguistics and the 7th International Joint Conference on Natural Language Processing (Volume 2: Short Papers)*, volume 2, pages 477–482.

Zhou GuoDong, Su Jian, Zhang Jie, and Zhang Min. 2005. Exploring various knowledge in relation extraction. In *Proceedings of the 43rd Annual Meeting on Association for Computational Linguistics*, ACL '05, pages 427–434, Stroudsburg, PA, USA. Association for Computational Linguistics.

Kadri Hacioglu. 2004. Semantic role labeling using dependency trees. In *Proceedings of the 20th international conference on Computational Linguistics*, page 1273. Association for Computational Linguistics.

J. Haralambides and F. Makedon. 1997. Approximation algorithms for the bandwidth minimization problem for a large class of trees. *Theory of Computing Systems*, 30(1):67–90.

Sepp Hochreiter and Jürgen Schmidhuber. 1997. Long short-term memory. *Neural computation*, 9(8):1735–1780.

Matthew Honnibal and Ines Montani. 2017. spacy 2: Natural language understanding with bloom embeddings, convolutional neural networks and incremental parsing. *To appear*.

Jeremy Howard and Sebastian Ruder. 2018. Universal language model fine-tuning for text classification. In *Proceedings of the 56th Annual Meeting of the Association for Computational Linguistics (Volume 1: Long Papers)*, pages 328–339.

Mahesh Joshi and Carolyn Penstein-Rosé. 2009. Generalizing dependency features for opinion mining. In *Proceedings of the ACL-IJCNLP 2009 conference short papers*, pages 313–316.

Yuki Kawara, Chenhui Chu, and Yuki Arase. 2018. Recursive neural network based preordering for english-to-japanese machine translation. In *Proceedings of ACL 2018, Student Research Workshop*, pages 21–27, Melbourne, Australia. Association for Computational Linguistics.

Diederik P. Kingma and Jimmy Ba. 2014. Adam: A method for stochastic optimization. *CoRR*, abs/1412.6980.

Thomas N Kipf and Max Welling. 2016. Semi-supervised classification with graph convolutional networks. *arXiv preprint arXiv:1609.02907*.

Adhiguna Kuncoro, Chris Dyer, John Hale, Dani Yogatama, Stephen Clark, and Phil Blunsom. 2018. Lstms can learn syntax-sensitive dependencies well, but modeling structure makes them better. In *Proceedings of the 56th Annual Meeting of the Association for Computational Linguistics (Volume 1: Long Papers)*, pages 1426–1436.

Irene Langkilde and Kevin Knight. 1998. Generation that exploits corpus-based statistical knowledge. In *Proceedings of the 36th Annual Meeting of the Association for Computational Linguistics and 17th International Conference on Computational Linguistics-Volume 1*, pages 704–710. Association for Computational Linguistics.

Tal Linzen, Emmanuel Dupoux, and Yoav Goldberg. 2016. Assessing the ability of lstms to learn syntax-sensitive dependencies. *Transactions of the Association for Computational Linguistics*, 4:521–535.

Haitao Liu. 2008. Dependency distance as a metric of language comprehension difficulty. *Journal of Cognitive Science*, 9(2):159–191.

Haitao Liu, Chunshan Xu, and Junying Liang. 2017. Dependency distance: a new perspective on syntactic patterns in natural languages. *Physics of life reviews*, 21:171–193.

Nelson F. Liu, Matt Gardner, Yonatan Belinkov, Matthew Peters, and Noah A. Smith. 2019. Linguistic knowledge and transferability of contextual representations. *CoRR*, abs/1903.08855.

Nelson F Liu, Omer Levy, Roy Schwartz, Chenhao Tan, and Noah A Smith. 2018. Lstms exploit linguistic attributes of data. In *Proceedings of The Third Workshop on Representation Learning for NLP*, pages 180–186.

Thang Luong, Hieu Pham, and Christopher D Manning. 2015. Effective approaches to attention-based neural machine translation. In *Proceedings of the 2015 Conference on Empirical Methods in Natural Language Processing*, pages 1412–1421.

Diego Marcheggiani and Ivan Titov. 2017. Encoding sentences with graph convolutional networks for semantic role labeling. In *Proceedings of the 2017 Conference on Empirical Methods in Natural Language Processing*, pages 1506–1515.

Graham Neubig, Taro Watanabe, and Shinsuke Mori. 2012. Inducing a discriminative parser to optimize machine translation reordering. In *Proceedings of the 2012 Joint Conference on Empirical Methods in Natural Language Processing and Computational Natural Language Learning*, pages 843–853, Jeju Island, Korea. Association for Computational Linguistics.

Bo Pang and Lillian Lee. 2004. A sentimental education: Sentiment analysis using subjectivity summarization based on minimum cuts. In *Proceedings of the 42nd annual meeting on Association for Computational Linguistics*, page 271. Association for Computational Linguistics.

Christos H. Papadimitriou. 1976. The np-completeness of the bandwidth minimization problem. *Computing*, 16:263–270.

Adam Paszke, Sam Gross, Soumith Chintala, Gregory Chanan, Edward Yang, Zachary DeVito, Zeming Lin, Alban Desmaison, Luca Antiga, and Adam Lerer. 2017. Automatic differentiation in pytorch.

Matthew Peters, Mark Neumann, Mohit Iyyer, Matt Gardner, Christopher Clark, Kenton Lee, and Luke Zettlemoyer. 2018. Deep contextualized word representations. In *Proceedings of the 2018 Conference of the North American Chapter of the Association for Computational Linguistics: Human Language Technologies, Volume 1 (Long Papers)*, pages 2227–2237.

Matthew Peters, Sebastian Ruder, and Noah A. Smith. 2019. To tune or not to tune? adapting pretrained representations to diverse tasks.

Yevgeniy Puzikov and Iryna Gurevych. 2018. BinLin: A simple method of dependency tree linearization. In *Proceedings of the First Workshop on Multilingual Surface Realisation*, pages 13–28, Melbourne, Australia. Association for Computational Linguistics.

Rodrigo Santa Cruz, Basura Fernando, Anoop Cherian, and Stephen Gould. 2017. Deeppermnet: Visual permutation learning. In *Proceedings of the IEEE Conference on Computer Vision and Pattern Recognition*, pages 3949–3957.

Mike Schuster and Kuldip K Paliwal. 1997. Bidirectional recurrent neural networks. *IEEE Transactions on Signal Processing*, 45(11):2673–2681.

Yossi Shiloach. 1979. A minimum linear arrangement algorithm for undirected trees. *SIAM Journal on Computing*, 8(1):15–32.

Ilya Sutskever, Oriol Vinyals, and Quoc V Le. 2014. Sequence to sequence learning with neural networks. In *Advances in neural information processing systems*, pages 3104–3112.

David Temperley and Daniel Gildea. 2018. Minimizing syntactic dependency lengths: Typological/cognitive universal? *Annual Reviews of Linguistics*.

Walter Unger. 1998. The complexity of the approximation of the bandwidth problem. In *Proceedings 39th Annual Symposium on Foundations of Computer Science (Cat. No. 98CB36280)*, pages 82–91. IEEE.

Ashish Vaswani, Noam Shazeer, Niki Parmar, Jakob Uszkoreit, Llion Jones, Aidan N Gomez, Łukasz Kaiser, and Illia Polosukhin. 2017. Attention is all you need. In *Advances in neural information processing systems*, pages 5998–6008.

Dingquan Wang and Jason Eisner. 2018. Synthetic data made to order: The case of parsing. In *Proceedings of the 2018 Conference on Empirical Methods in Natural Language Processing*, pages 1325–1337, Brussels, Belgium. Association for Computational Linguistics.

Ethan Wilcox, Roger Levy, Takashi Morita, and Richard Futrell. 2018. What do rnn language models learn about filler–gap dependencies? In *Proceedings of the 2018 EMNLP Workshop BlackboxNLP: Analyzing and Interpreting Neural Networks for NLP*, pages 211–221.

Ethan Wilcox, Roger P. Levy, and Richard Futrell. 2019a. What syntactic structures block dependencies in rnn language models? In *Proceedings of the 41st Annual Meeting of the Cognitive Science Society*.

Ethan Wilcox, Peng Qian, Richard Futrell, Miguel Ballesteros, and Roger Levy. 2019b. Structural supervision improves learning of non-local grammatical dependencies. In *Proceedings of the 18th Annual Conference of the North American Chapter of the Association for Computational Linguistics: Human Language Technologies*.

Yuanbin Wu, Qi Zhang, Xuanjing Huang, and Lide Wu. 2009. Phrase dependency parsing for opinion mining. In *Proceedings of the 2009 Conference on Empirical Methods in Natural Language Processing: Volume 3-Volume 3*, pages 1533–1541. Association for Computational Linguistics.

Fei Xia and Michael McCord. 2004. Improving a statistical mt system with automatically learned rewrite patterns. In *Proceedings of the 20th international conference on Computational Linguistics*, page 508. Association for Computational Linguistics.

Yuhao Zhang, Peng Qi, and Christopher D Manning. 2018. Graph convolution over pruned dependency trees improves relation extraction. In *Proceedings of the 2018 Conference on Empirical Methods in Natural Language Processing*, pages 2205–2215.

Han Zhao, Zhengdong Lu, and Pascal Poupart. 2015. Self-adaptive hierarchical sentence model. In *Twenty-Fourth International Joint Conference on Artificial Intelligence*.

Hui Zou and Trevor Hastie. 2005. Regularization and variable selection via the elastic net. *Journal of the royal statistical society: series B (statistical methodology)*, 67(2):301–320.

A   Implementation Details

We implement our models in PyTorch (Paszke et al., 2017) using the Adam optimizer (Kingma and Ba, 2014) with its default parameters in PyTorch. We split the dataset using a 80/10/10 split and the results in Table 2 are on the test set whereas those in Figure 2 are on the development set. We use ELMo embeddings (Peters et al., 2018)[4], for the initial pretrained word representations by concatenating the two 1024 dimensional pretrained vectors, yielding a 2048 dimensional initial pretrained representation for each token. These representations are frozen based on the results of Peters et al. (2019) and passed through a single-layer bidirectional LSTM with output dimensionality 256. The outputs of the forward and backward LSTMs at position i are concatenated and a sentence representation is produced by max-pooling as was found to be effective in Howard and Ruder (2018) and Peters et al. (2019). The sentence representation is passed through a linear classifier $M \in \mathbb{R}^{512 \times 2}$ and the entire model is trained to minimize cross entropy loss. All models are trained for 13 epochs with a batch size of

---

[4]Specifically, we use embeddings available at:
```
https://s3-us-west-2.amazonaws.com/
allennlp/models/elmo/2x4096_512_2048cnn_
2xhighway/elmo_2x4096_512_2048cnn_
2xhighway_options.json
```

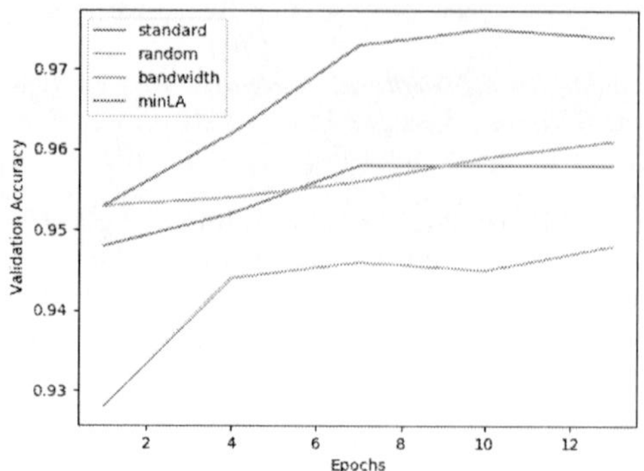

Figure 2: Development set performance for each ordering. Values are reported beginning at epoch 1 in intervals of 3 epochs.

16 with the test set results reported being from the model checkpoint after epoch 13. We also experimented with changing the LSTM task-specific encoder to be unidirectional but found the results were strictly worse.

B   Efficiency Analysis

Model Size   The changes we introduce only impact the initial preprocessing and ordering of the pretrained representations for the model. As a result, we make no changes to the number of model parameters and the only contribution to the model footprint is we need to store the permutation on a per example basis. This can actually be avoided in the case where we have frozen pretrained embeddings as the permutation can be computed in advance. Therefore, for the results in this paper, the model size is entirely unchanged.

Runtime   The wall-clock training time, i.e. the wall-clock time for a fixed number of epochs, and inference time are unchanged as we do not change the underlying model in any way and the permutations can be precomputed. As noted in the paper, on a single CPU it takes **21** minutes to complete the entire preprocessing process and 25% of this time is a result of computing bandwidth optimal permutations and 70% of this time is a result of computing minLA optimal permutations. The preprocessing time scales linearly in the number of examples and we verify this as it takes **10** minutes to process only the subjective examples (and the dataset is balanced). Figure 2 shows the development set performance for each of the permutation types over the course of the fine-tuning process.

C   End-to-End Permutations

In order to approach differentiable optimization for permutations, we must specify a representation. A standard choice that is well-suited for linear algebraic manipulation is a permutation matrix, i.e $P_\pi \in \mathbb{R}^{n \times n}$, where $P_\pi[i,j] = 1$ if $\pi(i) = j$ and 0 otherwise. As a result, permutation matrices are discrete, and therefore sparse, in the space of real matrices. As such they are poorly suited for the gradient-based optimization that supports most neural models. A recent approach from vision has considered a generalization of permutation matrices to the associated class of *doubly stochastic matrices* and then considered optimization with respect to the manifold they define (the *Sinkhorn Manifold*) to find a discrete permutation (Santa Cruz et al., 2017). This approach cannot be immediately applied for neural models for sentences since the algorithms exploits that images, and therefore permutations of the pixels in an image, are of fixed size between examples. That being said we ultimately see this as being an important direction of study given the shift from discrete optimization to soft/differentiable alternatives for similar problems in areas such as structured prediction.

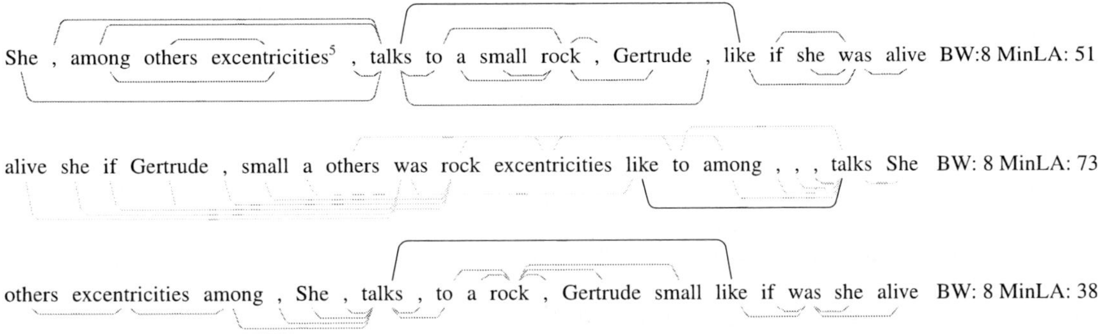

Figure 3: Addition example sentence with sentence permutations and overlayed dependency parses. Blue indicates the standard ordering, green indicates the bandwidth optimal ordering, and red indicates the minLA optimal ordering. Black indicates the longest dependency arc in the original ordering.

Predicting the Outcome of Deliberative Democracy: A Research Proposal

Conor McKillop
School of Science and Engineering
University of Dundee
Dundee, United Kingdom
c.z.mckillop@dundee.ac.uk

Abstract

As liberal states across the world face a decline in political participation by citizens, deliberative democracy is a promising solution for the publics decreasing confidence and apathy towards the democratic process (Dahl et al., 2017). Deliberative dialogue is method of public interaction that is fundamental to the concept of deliberative democracy. The ability to identify and predict consensus in the dialogues could bring greater accessibility and transparency to the face-to-face participatory process. The paper sets out a research plan for the first steps at automatically identifying and predicting consensus in a corpus of German language debates on hydraulic fracking. It proposes the use of a unique combination of lexical, sentiment, durational and further derivative features of adjacency pairs to train traditional classification models. In addition to this, the use of deep learning techniques to improve the accuracy of the classification and prediction tasks is also discussed. Preliminary results at the classification of utterances are also presented, with an F1 between 0.61 and 0.64 demonstrating that the task of recognising agreement is demanding but possible.

1 Introduction

Liberal states across the world are facing a significant decline in political participation by citizens. The global voter turnout rate has dropped by more than 10% over the last 25 years (Groupe de la Banque mondiale, 2017), and this trend does not appear to be slowing down. The public have reported decreasing confidence and apathy towards the democratic process (Dahl et al., 2017). Deliberative Democracy represents a potential solution to these problems. Through the evaluation of different policy proposals using a process of truthful and rational discussion between citizens and authority, Deliberative democracy can enable consensual, well-justified, decision making. It can improve the political competence of citizens by; facilitating the exchange of arguments and sharing of ideas on proposals from authority (Estlund et al., 1989); reconfiguring democracy as a process of 'public reasoning' and connecting citizens with each other and with their governing institutions (Parkinson and Mansbridge, 2012; Dryzek, 2012).

Deliberative Dialogue is a structured, face-to-face method of public interaction. As a form of participatory process, it is fundamental to the concept of Deliberative Democracy (McCoy and Scully, 2002). There are many different forms of deliberative dialogue, including, but not limited to: citizens' assemblies, citizens' juries and planning cells. The European Commission's 'Future of Europe debates' (Directorate-General for Communication, 2017b) are an exemplar of hosting deliberative dialogue successfully at large scale.

The 'Future of Europe debates' are due to come to their natural conclusion after a two year long process that started with the release of the 'White paper on the future of Europe' in March of 2017 (ibid.). This white paper set out the main challanges and opportunities facing the 27 European Union (EU) member states for the next decade. To encourage citizens' participation, the Commission hosted a series of debates across cities and regions within Europe (Directorate-General for Communication, 2017a). At the debates, all members of the Commission engaged in dialogue with citizens and listened to their views and expectations concerning the future of Europe. The debates were well received, with 129 debates in more than 80 towns, attended by over 21,000 citizens (ibid.).

In the deliberative democratic process, one of the main aims is for informed agreement to be reached among all involved parties. However, in dialogues with larger citizenry, it is less likely that consensus is reached between all participants (Peter, 2016). As can be seen with the 'Future of Europe debates', numbers in attendance can be high. Therefore, the ability to automatically identify, or even predict, consensus between participants in these dialogues can make the participatory process even more transparent and accessible. In the future, it could even provide authority with a tool for deciding when to move to an aggregative mechanism for deciding the outcome, such as majority voting.

2 Related Work

Previous work has reported some levels of success in the automatic classification of agreement and no agreement using machine learning techniques.

Galley et al. (2004) used a statistical approach, with Bayesian networks to model agreements and disagreements in conversational interaction. Simple Bayesian networks were trained with contextual features of adjacency pairs identified in an annotated corpus of meetings. With the recent advances in deep learning techniques, there is an opportunity to apply the techniques from this paper to multi-speaker debates

On the use of sentiment analysis to aid in the detection of agreement, as employed in this paper, a number of previous works have successfully applied the technique. For example, Thomas et al. (2006) used sentiment property for classifying support or opposition of proposed legislative speeches in transcripts from United States' Congress debates. Further work by Balasubramanyan et al. (2011) investigated classifying sentiment polarity of comments on a blog post, towards the topics in the blog.

Abbott et al. (2011) reported on automatically recognising disagreement between online posts. The paper presented the ARGUE corpus, containing thousands of quote and response pairs posted to an online debate forum. Abbott et al. proposed the use of simple classifiers to label a quote and response pair as in either agreement or disagreement. An improvement over baseline was achieved by the authors, though this was limited to informal, online political arguments.

The majority of research into the classification of agreement and disagreement has been heavily focused on postings in online forums and social networks. There has been very little work on the classification of agreement in face-to-face participatory process; the research area of this paper.

3 Data Set

The data set for the task is drawn from a total of 34 German language dialogues which all took place in an experimentally controlled environment. In each of the dialogues, there are four participants who were recorded discussing the topic of hydraulic fracking in Germany. The participants are tasked with coming to consensus around allowing or disallowing fracking within a time period of 60 minutes. Whole dialogues within the data set are annotated with either agreement or no agreement, by trusted annotators. These annotators also explicitly mark the utterance at which consensus occurs. All utterances are plain text, with a limited number of attributes, including the utterance identifier and speaker name.

This data set is composed of 20 dialogues where consensus is reached by the participants, 9 dialogues where no consensus took place and 5 dialogues where the session 'timed out' before any consensus was reached. By extracting single utterances from each dialogue, this is broken down into 1,376 utterances of agreement, 458 with no agreement and 240 with timeout. A manual investigation into the dialogues revealed that there was no clear difference in text between the dialogues of time out and no agreement.

For training and testing of the classifier, the data set was split into multiple subsets, with cross validation (Mosteller and Tukey, 1968) used to evaluate performance. The risk of overfitting by the classifier is minimised through the use of a 5-fold cross validation method.

4 Methodology

4.1 Tasks

There are two main goals of research which provide the body of work proposed in this paper. These two goals are:

- To identify where consensus has occurred between participants

- Prediction of whether it is likely that consensus between participants is going to occur

Of note is that these tasks are performed on a corpus of lower resource language.

4.2 Features

Work has already begun on the extraction of features from the data set in its current form without any further embellishment, such as the identification of *argumentation structure*, discussed in further detail in section 5 of this paper.

Three distinct feature sets have been created from the data for use in machine learning techniques, these are termed:

- *Base Features* – Attributes connected to a single utterance

- *Derivative Features* – The change of Base Features across a pair of utterances

- *Second Derivative Features* – The change of Derivative Features between pairs of utterance pairs.

Base Features

A number of attributes from each singular utterance were extracted for input into the classifier responsible for identifying agreement and disagreement of utterances.

Lexical In order to capture basic lexical information, unigram and bigram features are extracted from each utterance. Text of an utterance is first processed before tokenisation and occurrence counting. In the text pre-processing: speaker names and punctuation are removed from the text, unicode characters normalised, German diacritics and ligatures translated[1], and finally words lemmatised.

Sentiment Prior work has shown that sentiment features can provide some value in the prediction of speakers' position on a topic, such as what the speaker supports or opposes (Pang and Lee, 2008). To access this information, an analysis of speaker sentiment within each utterance is undertaken. The SentimentWortschatz (SentiWS) (Remus et al., 2010) resource for German-language is used. The latest version[2] of the resource contains over 1,600 positive words and 1,800 negative words, or over 16,000 positive and 17,500 negative words when calculated to include inflections of every word. For each word in the resource, a polarity score, weighted between [-1; 1] is provided. It should be noted, that in cases where a word cannot be found in the resource, a 'neutral' score of 0 is used. For this work, a method was developed using SentiWS to give a score for each utterance in the corpus. By summing up the sentiment score for each word in the utterance, a total score for the utterance can be calculated. This total is then used as a feature for the classification model.

Durational Durational features for each utterance are also calculated. This includes, word count and character count, average word length and number of stop words.

Derivative Features

Adjacency Pairs Adjacency pairs, composed of two utterances from two speakers in succession are extracted from the dialogues and similarity measures are calculated for the features of each utterance in a pair.

Durational The change in Durational features between utterances in an adjacency pair.

Sentiment The change in Sentiment features between utterances in an adjacency pair to capture any possible shift in sentiment between speaker turns.

Similarity Measures To test the hypothesis that utterance pairs in agreement, are higher in similarity, this paper proposes using a similarity measure calculated between utterance pairs as a feature variable. An example of term based similarity, cosine similarity uses the cosine angle between the two vectors as a similarity measure. The spaCy[3] open-source software library for Natural Language Processing (NLP) will be used to calculate the similarity between the utterance text of two adjacency pairs.

Further Adjacency Pairs

Collection of Adjacency Pairs Similarity measures are calculated between a collection of two or more adjacency pairs.

4.3 Techniques

To classify an utterance as either agreement or no agreement, some work has already been undertaken using traditional machine learning models.

Traditional Classification Models

Support Vector Machine A *Support Vector Machine* (SVM) is a classifier that can be used to

---

[1] Translation as per the DIN 5007-2 standard.
[2] SentiWS v2.0 at the time of writing.

[3] Git repository for the library is hosted at: `https://github.com/explosion/spaCy/`.

perform identification of agreement on each utterance. SVMs are a versatile, supervised learning method that are well-suited to classification and regression tasks. The method produces non-linear boundaries using a linear boundary in a transformed version of the input feature space (Hastie et al., 2009). For the work in this paper, an SVM from the Scikit-learn open-source project (Pedregosa et al., 2011) was used. The input features to the classifier are from the aforementioned set, whilst the output is the binary label of agreement or no agreement.

Random Decision Forest The *Random Decision Forest* is a machine learning algorithm that is particularly suited for problems of both classification and regression. They operate by constructing and then average the results of a large collection of de-correlated decision trees (Hastie et al., 2009). The algorithm is particularly attractive for its high speed of classification and straight-forward training (Ho, 1995). A Random Decision Forest classifier from the Scikit-learn project (Pedregosa et al., 2011) is used for this work.

Naïve Bayes Another family of machine learning algorithms that remain popular and receives continuous levels of high usage, are *Naïve Bayes*. This is a method of classification that simplifies estimation by assuming that every attribute or feature contributes independently to the probability of a class (McCallum and Nigam, 1998). The family can often outperform more sophisticated alternatives (Hastie et al., 2009). However, when classifying text there is the potential for the model to adversely affect results if some adjustments are not made (Rennie et al., 2003).

Naïve Bayes Another family of machine learning algorithms that remain popular and receives continuous levels of high usage, are *Naïve Bayes*. This is a method of classification that simplifies estimation by assuming that every attribute or feature contributes independently to the probability of a class (McCallum and Nigam, 1998). The family can often outperform more sophisticated alternatives (Hastie et al., 2009). However, when classifying text there is the potential for the model to adversely affect results if some adjustments are not made (Rennie et al., 2003).

Deep Learning Models

For the second task discussed in this paper – predicting the point at which consensus between speakers is likely to occur – the use of a supervised, deep structured learning technique could possibly offer an advantage over the more traditional machine learning algorithms discussed previously.

RNN The *Recurrent Neural Network* (RNN) overcomes the shortcomings of traditional neural networks when dealing with sequential data, such as text. A class of artificial neural network, it uses connections between nodes to form a direct graph along a sequence (Graves, 2012). RNNs are limited to a short-term memory due to the 'vanishing gradient problem' (Bengio et al., 1994).

LSTM A class of RNN, *Long Short Term Memory* (LSTM) networks are capable of learning long-term dependencies. The repeating module of an LSTM has four neural network layers which interact to enable an RNN to remember inputs over a longer period of time (Graves, 2012). LSTMs reduce the problem of vanishing gradient (Chung et al., 2014). This will prove particularly important, due to the sequential nature of the adjacency pairs in the dialogues.

5 Proposed Work

Whilst work has been done using traditional machine learning algorithms to classify utterances, as per the first task described in section 4.1 of this paper, there remains work to be done in the use of deep learning models as a means for improved accuracy and performance in classification.

At present, the data set is mostly represented as plain text, with no further dimension to the utterances. One opportunity that could bring another dimension and realise unknown relationships in this data, is through the identification of argument structure within the discourse.

Argument structures are associated with, and constructed from, basic 'building blocks', and these components could also be identified. The blocks can come in the form of a *premise, conclusion* or *argumentation scheme*. There also exists a further opportunity for diversification of data through the analysis of relationships between argument pairs and their components. By modelling these structures, there arises the ability to gather a deeper understanding of what is being uttered by a speaker (Lawrence et al., 2015). So, not only can the views expressed by a speaker be drawn from the argument structure, but it can also expose why these particular views are held.

Automatic identification or 'mining' of such argument structures would provide a significant time saving, allowing almost immediate use of the extracted model as features in a machine learning algorithm. However, despite the enormous growth in the field of Argument Mining, it is still difficult to identify argument structures with accuracy and reliability (Stede and Schneider, 2018). As a consequence of this, before the aforementioned advantages can be applied to this data set, it must be manually annotated by a human.

Manual annotation of the dialogues in this data set is not an insignificant cost, with regards to time and funding. As to guarantee the accuracy of the modelled arguments, annotation must follow predefined schemes, such as those set out by Reed and Budzynska (2011). The annotators carrying out the analysis must be trained to a sufficient level on the necessary schemes and also trusted. This work must be undertaken before the data can be put through the process responsible for identification and prediction of consensus. The manual annotation process of dialogues in the corpus is still ongoing.

Once the dialogues have been annotated, extraction of argumentative structure showing 'conflict' between two propositions should take place. The presence, count and exact arrangement of the propositions in conflict can then be used as an additional feature for training of the classifiers.

6 Preliminary Results

Classifier	Precision	Recall	F-measure
Naïve Bayes	0.63	0.66	0.61
SVM (Linear)	0.64	0.67	0.61
Random Forest	0.66	0.69	0.64

Table 1: Results of classification using traditional classifiers

Preliminary results related to the identification of agreement and no agreement in utterances can be seen in Table 1. This was a classification process using only the *Base Features* set and with traditional machine learning algorithms. These results suggest that the task as framed is feasible, though there is still significant opportunity for improvement.

7 Conclusion

The potential benefits resulting from the automatic identification and prediction of consensus between participants can be of significant advantage to government around the world. With only the preliminary results from classification of utterances into agreement and disagreement, it can be seen that the accuracy is nearing useable values. With the addition of advanced neural network models, such as LSTM, there is the possibility to increase the accuracy even further. The immediate goal after successfully classifying agreement and no agreement will be to predict where it is likely that agreement between participants is likely to occur.

Acknowledgements

The work reported in this paper has been supported, in part, by The Volkswagen Foundation (VolkswagenStiftung) under grant 92-182.

References

Rob Abbott, Marilyn Walker, Pranav Anand, Jean E. Fox Tree, Robeson Bowmani, and Joseph King. 2011. How can you say such things?!?: Recognizing disagreement in informal political argument. In *Proceedings of the Workshop on Languages in Social Media*, LSM '11, pages 2–11, Stroudsburg, PA, USA. Association for Computational Linguistics.

Ramnath Balasubramanyan, William W. Cohen, Doug Pierce, and David P. Redlawsk. 2011. What pushes their buttons?: Predicting comment polarity from the content of political blog posts. In *Proceedings of the Workshop on Languages in Social Media*, LSM '11, pages 12–19, Stroudsburg, PA, USA. Association for Computational Linguistics.

Y. Bengio, P. Simard, and P. Frasconi. 1994. Learning long-term dependencies with gradient descent is difficult. *IEEE Transactions on Neural Networks*, 5(2):157–166.

Junyoung Chung, Çaglar Gülçehre, KyungHyun Cho, and Yoshua Bengio. 2014. Empirical evaluation of gated recurrent neural networks on sequence modeling. *CoRR*, abs/1412.3555.

Viktor Dahl, Erik Amnå, Shakuntala Banaji, Monique Landberg, Jan Šerek, Norberto Ribeiro, Mai Beilmann, Vassilis Pavlopoulos, and Bruna Zani. 2017.

Apathy or alienation? political passivity among youths across eight european union countries. *European Journal of Developmental Psychology*, 15(3):284–301.

Directorate-General for Communication. 2017a. Citizens' dialogues on the future of europe. White Paper NA-01-17-787-EN-N, European Union, Brussels.

Directorate-General for Communication. 2017b. White paper on the future of europe. White Paper NA-02-17-345-EN-N, European Union, Brussels.

John S Dryzek. 2012. *Foundations and frontiers of deliberative governance*. Oxford University Press.

David M. Estlund, Jeremy Waldron, Bernard Grofman, and Scott L. Feld. 1989. Democratic theory and the public interest: Condorcet and rousseau revisited. *American Political Science Review*, 83(4):13171340.

Michel Galley, Kathleen McKeown, Julia Hirschberg, and Elizabeth Shriberg. 2004. Identifying agreement and disagreement in conversational speech: Use of bayesian networks to model pragmatic dependencies. In *Proceedings of the 42nd Annual Meeting on Association for Computational Linguistics*, page 669. Association for Computational Linguistics.

Alex Graves. 2012. *Supervised Sequence Labelling with Recurrent Neural Networks*, volume 385 of *Studies in Computational Intelligence*. Springer.

Groupe de la Banque mondiale. 2017. *World development report 2017: Governance and the law*. World Bank Group.

Trevor Hastie, Robert Tibshirani, and Jerome H. Friedman. 2009. *The Elements of Statistical Learning*, second edition. Springer Series in Statistics. Springer-Verlag, New York.

Tin Kam Ho. 1995. Random decision forests. In *Proceedings of 3rd International Conference on Document Analysis and Recognition*, volume 1, pages 278–282 vol.1.

J. Lawrence, M. Janier, and C. Reed. 2015. Working with open argument corpora. In *Proceedings of the 1st European Conference on Argumentation (ECA 2015)*, Lisbon. College Publications.

Andrew McCallum and Kamal Nigam. 1998. A comparison of event models for naive bayes text classification. In *Proceedings of the AAAI-98 Workshop on Learning for Text Categorization*, pages 41–48. AAAI Press.

Martha L. McCoy and Patrick L. Scully. 2002. Deliberative dialogue to expand civic engagement: What kind of talk does democracy need? *National Civic Review*, 91(2):117–135.

F. Mosteller and J Tukey. 1968. Data analysis, including statistics. In G. Lindzey and E. Aronson, editors, *Revised Handbook of Social Psychology*, volume 2, pages 80–203. Addison Wesley.

Bo Pang and Lillian Lee. 2008. Opinion mining and sentiment analysis. *Foundations and Trends in Information Retrieval*, 2(12):1–135.

John Parkinson and Jane Mansbridge. 2012. *Deliberative systems: Deliberative democracy at the large scale*. Cambridge University Press.

F. Pedregosa, G. Varoquaux, A. Gramfort, V. Michel, B. Thirion, O. Grisel, M. Blondel, P. Prettenhofer, R. Weiss, V. Dubourg, J. Vanderplas, A. Passos, D. Cournapeau, M. Brucher, M. Perrot, and E. Duchesnay. 2011. Scikit-learn: Machine learning in Python. *Journal of Machine Learning Research*, 12:2825–2830.

Fabienne Peter. 2016. *The Epistemology of Deliberative Democracy*, chapter 6. John Wiley & Sons, Ltd.

Chris Reed and Katarzyna Budzynska. 2011. How dialogues create arguments. In *Proceedings of the 7th Conference of the International Society for the Study of Argumentation (ISSA)*, pages 1633–1645. SicSat.

Robert Remus, Uwe Quasthoff, and Gerhard Heyer. 2010. Sentiws - a publicly available germanlanguage resource for sentiment analysis. In *Proceedings of the Seventh International Conference on Language Resources and Evaluation (LREC'10)*, Valletta, Malta. European Language Resources Association (ELRA).

Jason D. M. Rennie, Lawrence Shih, Jaime Teevan, and David R. Karger. 2003. Tackling the poor assumptions of naive bayes text classifiers. In *Proceedings of the Twentieth International Conference on International Conference on Machine Learning*, ICML'03, pages 616–623, Washington, D.C. AAAI Press.

Manfred Stede and Jodi Schneider. 2018. Argumentation mining. *Synthesis Lectures on Human Language Technologies*, 11(2):1–191.

Matt Thomas, Bo Pang, and Lillian Lee. 2006. Get out the vote: Determining support or opposition from Congressional floor-debate transcripts. In *Proceedings of EMNLP*, pages 327–335.

Active Reading Comprehension: A dataset for learning the Question-Answer Relationship strategy

Diana Galvan
Tohoku University
Graduate School of Information Sciences
Sendai, Japan
dianags@ecei.tohoku.ac.jp

Abstract

Reading comprehension (RC) through question answering is a useful method for evaluating if a reader understands a text. Standard accuracy metrics are used for evaluation, where a high accuracy is taken as indicative of a good understanding. However, literature in quality learning suggests that task performance should also be evaluated on the undergone process to answer. The Question-Answer Relationship (QAR) is one of the strategies for evaluating a reader's understanding based on their ability to select different sources of information depending on the question type. We propose the creation of a dataset to learn the QAR strategy with weak supervision. We expect to complement current work on reading comprehension by introducing a new setup for evaluation.

1 Introduction

Computer system researchers have long been trying to imitate human cognitive skills like memory (Hochreiter and Schmidhuber, 1997; Chung et al., 2014) and attention (Vaswani et al., 2017). These skills are essential for a number of Natural Language Processing (NLP) tasks including reading comprehension (RC). Until now, the method for evaluating a system's understanding imitated the common classroom setting where students are evaluated based on their number of correct answers. In the educational assessment literature this is known as *product-based* evaluation and is one of the performance-based assessments types (McTighe and Ferrara, 1994). However, there is an alternative form: *process-based* evaluation. Process-based evaluation does not emphasize the output of the activity. This assessment aims to know the step-by-step procedure followed to resolve a given task.

When a reading comprehension system is not able to identify the correct answer, product-based evaluation can result in the false impression of weak understanding (i.e., misunderstanding of the text, the question, or both) or the absence of required knowledge. However, the system could have failed to arrive at the correct answer for some other reasons. For example, consider the reading comprehension task shown in Figure 1. For the question *"What were the consequences of Elizabeth Choy's parents and grandparents being 'more advanced for their times'?"* the correct answer is in the text but it is located in different sentences. If the system only identifies *"They wanted their daughters to be educated"* as an answer, it would be judged to be incorrect when it did not fail at finding the answer, it failed at connecting it with the fact *"we were sent to schools away from home"* (linking problem). Similarly, any answer the system infers from the text for the question *"What do you think are the qualities of a war heroine?"* would be wrong because the answer is not in the text, it relies exclusively on background knowledge (wrong choice of information source). We propose to adopt the thesis that reading is not a passive process by which readers soak up words and information from the text, but an active process[1] by which they predict, sample, and confirm or correct their hypotheses about the text (Weaver, 1988). One of these hypotheses is which source of information the question requires. The reader might think it is necessary to look in the text to then realize she could have answered without even reading or, on the contrary, try to think of an answer even though it is directly in the text. For this reason, Raphael (1982) devised the Question-Answer Relation (QAR) strategy, a technique to help the reader decide the most suitable source of information as well as the level of reasoning

---

[1]Not to be confused with *active learning*, a machine learning concept for a series of methods that actively participate in the collection of training examples. (Thompson et al., 1999)

Proceedings of the ACL 2019, Student Research Workshop, pages 106–112
Florence, Italy, July 28th-August 2nd, 2019. ©2019 Association for Computational Linguistics

Figure 1 content (reproduced interview and QAR categories):

Interviewer: Mrs. Choy, would you like to tell us something about your background before the Japanese invasion?

Elizabeth Choy: 1. Oh, it will go back quite a long way, you know, because I came to Singapore in December 1929 for higher education. 2. I was born in North Borneo which is Sabah now. 3. My ancestors were from China. 4. They went to Hong Kong, and from Hong Kong, they came to Malaysia. 5. They started plantations, coconut plantations, rubber plantations. 6. My parents and grandparents were more advanced for their times and when they could get on a bit, they wanted their daughters to be educated too.

7. So, we were sent to schools away from home. 8. First, we went to Jesselton which is Kota Kinabalu now. 9. There was a girls' school run by English missionaries. 10. My aunt and I were there for half a year. 11. And then we heard there was another better school – bigger school in Sandakan also run by English missionaries. 12. So we went to Sandakan as boarders.

13. When we reached the limit, that is, we couldn't study anymore in Malaysia, we had to come to Singapore for higher education. And I was very lucky to be able to get into the Convent of the Holy Infant Jesus where my aunt had been for a year already.

In the text

Right there question: When did Elizabeth Choy come to Singapore for higher education?
Answer: December 1929

Think and search: What were the consequences of Elizabeth Choy's parents and grandparents being 'more advanced for their times'?
Answer: They wanted their daughters to be educated so they sent them to schools away from home.

In my head

Author and me: What do you think of Elizabeth Choy's character from the interview?

On my own: What do you think are the qualities of a war heroine?

Figure 1: Example of reading comprehension applying the Question-Answer Relationship strategy to categorize the questions.

needed based on the question type.

In this work, we introduce a new evaluation setting for reading comprehension systems. We overview the QAR strategy as an option to move beyond a scenario where only the product of comprehension is evaluated and not the process. We discuss our proposed approach to create a new dataset for learning the QAR strategy using existing reading comprehension datasets.

2 Related work

Reading comprehension is an active research area in NLP. It is composed of two main components: text and questions. This task can be found in many possible variations: setups where no options are given and the machine has to come up with an answer (Yang et al., 2015; Weston et al., 2015; Nguyen et al., 2016; Rajpurkar et al., 2016) and setups where the question has multiple choices and the machine needs to choose one of them (Richardson et al., 2013; Hill et al., 2015; Onishi et al., 2016; Mihaylov et al., 2018). In either case, standard accuracy metrics are used to evaluate systems based on the number of correct answers retrieved; a product-based evaluation. In addition to this evaluation criteria, the current reading comprehension setting constrains systems to be trained on a particular domain for a specific

type of reasoning. As a result, the good performance of a model drops when it is tested on a different domain. For example, the knowledgeable reader of Mihaylov and Frank (2018) was trained to solve questions from children narrative texts that require commonsense knowledge, achieving competitive results. However, it did not perform equally well when tested on basic science questions that also required commonsense knowledge (Mihaylov et al., 2018). Systems have been able to match human performance but it has also been proven by Jia and Liang (2017) that they can be easily fooled with adversarial distracting sentences that would not change the correct answer or mislead humans.

The motivation behind introducing adversarial examples for evaluating reading comprehension is to discern to what extent systems truly understand language. Mudrakarta et al. (2018) followed the steps of Jia and Liang (2017) proposing a technique to analyze the sensitivity of a model to question words, with the aim to empower investigation of reading models' performance. With the same goal in mind, we propose a process-based evaluation that will favor a closer examination of the process taken by current systems to solve a reading comprehension task. In the educational assessment literature, this approach is recommended to identify the weaknesses of a student. If we transfer this concept to computers, we would be able to focus on the comprehension tasks a computer is weak in, regardless of the data in which the system has been trained.

3 Question-answer relationship

Raphael (1982) devised the Question-Answer Relationship as a way of improving children reading performance across grades and subject areas. This approach reflects the current concept of reading as an active process influenced by characteristics of the reader, the text, and the context within which the reading happens (McIntosh and Draper, 1995). Since its publication, several studies have explored its positive effects (Benito et al., 1993; McIntosh and Draper, 1995; Ezell et al., 1996; Thuy and Huan, 2018; Apriani, 2019).

QAR states that an answer and its source of information are directly related to the type of question being asked. It emphasizes the importance of being able to locate this source to then identify the level of reasoning the question requires. QAR defines four type of questions categorized in two broad sources of information:

In the text

- **Right There questions:** The answer can be literally found in the text.

- **Think and Search questions:** The answer can be found in several sentences in the text that need to be pieced together.

In my head

- **Author and Me questions:** The answer is not directly stated in the text. It is necessary to fit text information with background knowledge.

- **On My Own questions:** The answer can be given without reading the text. The answer relies solely on background knowledge.

Each one of the QAR categories requires a different level of reasoning. For *Right there* questions, the reader only needs to match the question with one of the sentences within the text. *Think and search* requires simple inference to relate pieces of information contained in different parts of the text. *In my head* questions introduce the use of background knowledge. Thus, deeper thinking is required to relate the information provided in the text with background information. Finally, *On my own* questions ask the reader to only use their background knowledge to come up with an answer. Figure 1 shows how QAR is applied to a reading comprehension task. Note that for both *In the text* questions, one can easily match the words in the question with the words in the text. However, *Think and search* goes beyond matching ability; the reader should be able to conclude that the information in sentences 6 and 7 are equally required to answer the question being asked. Thus, the correct answer is a combination of these two. For the *Author and me* question, the readers need to merge the information given in the text with their own background knowledge since the question explicitly asks for an opinion *"from the interview."* Without this statement, the question could be considered as *On my own* if the reader is already familiar with Elizabeth Choy. This is not the case in the last question, where even though the topic of the interview is related, the qualities of a war heroine are not in the text. The readers need to use their own background knowledge about heroes.

In the case of computers, *In my head* questions can be understood as *In a knowledge base*. We hypothesize that once the system establishes that the source of information is not in the text, it could trigger a connection to a knowledge base. For the time being, the type of knowledge needed is fixed for RC datasets by design (e.g., general domain, commonsense, elementary science) and the source is chosen accordingly in advance by the author (e.g., Wikipedia, ConceptNet). Automatically selecting the appropriate external resource for a reading comprehension task is a problem that we would like to explore in the future.

3.1 QAR use cases

As a process-based evaluation strategy, QAR can be used to understand a reader's ability in terms of the reasoning level applied and the elected source of information to answer a given question. In the case of humans, this outcome is later used as feedback to improve performance on a particular process. The incorporation of general reading strategies to a RC system has been recently proven effective by Sun et al. (2018) and we aim to explore QAR in the same way. However, our short-term objective is to test the QAR strategy as a complementary evaluation method for existing machine

Figure 2 (top-left):

Sentence	Answer	Sentence needed
1 Mary moved to the bathroom.		
2 John went to the hallway		
3 Where is Mary?	bathroom	1
4 Daniel went back to the hallway.		
5 Sandra moved to the garden.		
6 Where is Daniel?	hallway	4
7 John moved to the office.		
8 Sandra journeyed to the bathroom.		
9 Where is Daniel?	hallway	4

Figure 2 (top-right):

Sentence	Answer	Sentence needed
1 Mary moved to the bathroom.		
2 Sandra journeyed to the bedroom.		
3 John went to the kitchen.		
4 Mary took the football there.		
5 How many objects is Mary carrying?	one	4
6 Sandra went back to the office.		
7 How many objects is Mary carrying?	one	4
8 Mary dropped the football.		
9 How many objects is Mary carrying?	none	4 8

Figure 2 (bottom-left):

Sentence	Answer	QAR category
1 Mary moved to the bathroom.		
2 John went to the hallway		
3 Where is Mary?	bathroom	1
4 Daniel went back to the hallway.		
5 Sandra moved to the garden.		
6 Where is Daniel?	hallway	1
7 John moved to the office.		
8 Sandra journeyed to the bathroom.		
9 Where is Daniel?	hallway	1

Figure 2 (bottom-right):

Sentence	Answer	QAR category
1 Mary moved to the bathroom.		
2 Sandra journeyed to the bedroom.		
3 John went to the kitchen.		
4 Mary took the football there.		
5 How many objects is Mary carrying?	one	1
6 Sandra went back to the office.		
7 How many objects is Mary carrying?	one	1
8 Mary dropped the football.		
9 How many objects is Mary carrying?	none	2

Figure 2: Example of bAbI annotations for the *single supportive fact* task (left) and the *counting* task (right). Below, our proposed annotations with QAR category.

reading comprehension models, somewhat similar to PROTEST (Guillou and Hardmeier, 2016), a test suite for the evaluation of pronoun translation by Machine Translation systems.

In the next section, we discuss how the QAR strategy can be imported from the educational literature to the NLP domain by using existing reading comprehension datasets to create a new resource for active reading comprehension evaluation.

4 Research plan

4.1 Dataset

We propose to model QAR learning as a multiclass classification task with weak supervision. The dataset would contain labels corresponding to each one of the QAR categories and the annotation process will depend on the two sources of information Raphael (1982) defined.

In recent years, we have seen a lot of effort from the NLP community in creating datasets to test different aspects of RC, like bAbI (Weston et al., 2015), SQuAD (Rajpurkar et al., 2016), NarrativeQA (Kočiskỳ et al., 2018), QAngaroo (Welbl et al., 2018), HotpotQA (Yang et al., 2018), MCScript (Ostermann et al., 2018), MultiRC (Khashabi et al., 2018) and CommonsenseQA (Talmor et al., 2018). In the following sections, we will briefly overview these datasets and explain how they can be adapted for our proposed task.

4.1.1 In the text questions

For this type of questions, we can rely on the bAbI dataset (Weston et al., 2015), a set of synthetically

generated, simple narratives for testing text understanding. The dataset has several tasks with 1000 questions each for training and 1000 for testing. For our purposes, we will focus on the annotations of Task 8 and 7. Task 8 is a "single supporting fact" task that shows a small passage in which each sentence describes the location of a character (e.g. *"Mary moved to the bathroom. John went to the hallway."*). After some sentences, there is a question asking where the character is (e.g. *"Where is Mary?"*) and the goal is to give a single word answer to it (e.g. *"bathroom"*). Task 7 is a "counting" task describing the same situation, but it aggregates a sentence where one of the characters either takes (e.g. *"Mary took the football there."*) or drops (e.g. *"Mary dropped the football."*) an object. This time, the question asks how many objects is the character carrying and the answer is also a single word (e.g. *"none"*). As shown in Figure 2, bAbI annotations enumerate each one of the sentences. The number next to the single word answer is the number of the sentence needed to answer the question. Instead of the number of the sentence, we will use as label the number of the QAR category. This can be done following this rule:

$$QARcategory = \left\{ \begin{array}{ll} 1, & \text{for } n = 1 \\ 2, & \text{for } n > 1 \end{array} \right\}$$

Where n is the number of sentences and the categories *1, 2* correspond to *Right there* and *Think and Search*, respectively. The bottom of Figure 2 shows how the new annotations will look like. This annotations can be generated automatically

Figure 3: MCScript annotations for *text-based questions* (left) and *common sense questions* (right). In blue, key words and phrases necessary to arrive at the correct answer.

using a script that implements the aforementioned rule.

The same approach can be applied to HotpotQA and MultiRC. HotpotQA is a dataset with 113k Wikipedia-based question-answer pairs for which reasoning over multiple documents is needed to answer. Its annotations already identify the sentence-level supporting facts required for reasoning, making this dataset a perfect match for our subset of *Think and search* questions. SQuAD (100,000+ questions) has a very similar design and format, although questions are designed to be answered by a single paragraph. Since the correct answer is literally contained in one part of the text, questions will fall under the *Right there* category. The annotations only include the start-offset of the answer in the text, but we can easily use this information to identify the answer's position at a sentence level. In the same line of multiple-sentence reasoning, MultiRC presents $\sim 6k$ multiple-choice questions from paragraphs across 7 different domains. The additional challenge of this dataset is that multiple correct answers are allowed. Since the supporting sentences are already annotated, this dataset can be used entirely as a *Think and search* instance.

The multi-hop nature of QAngaroo and NarrativeQA questions also match the *Think and search* category. However, no span or sentence-level annotation is provided, making this datasets unsuitable for our approach.

4.1.2   In my head questions

For these questions we will use the MCScript dataset (Ostermann et al., 2018). This dataset is intended to be used in a machine reading comprehension task that requires reasoning over *script knowledge*, sequences of events describing stereotypical human activities. MCScript contains 2,100 narrative texts annotated with two types of ques-

tions: *Text-based* questions and *commonsense* questions with 10,160 and 3,827 questions each. *Text-based* questions match *Author and me* category since the answer is not directly contained within the text; it is necessary to combine the text information with background knowledge (script knowledge). *Commonsense* questions, on the other hand, depend only on background knowledge. Thus, there is no need to read the text to answer if the script activity is known.

Consider the example annotations shown in Figure 3. For the text on the left, the reader cannot give an answer even if it has knowledge of types of foods. It is necessary to read the text to identify the types of food the characters in the text packed. In contrast, the questions for the text on the right can be answered if the reader is familiar with the scenario of planting a tree.

The MCScript training annotations identify the correct answer and whether this can be found in the text or if commonsense knowledge is needed. All questions where commonsense is required can be assumed to be *On my own* questions. However, there are some *Text-based* questions in which the answer is explicitly contained in the text. It would be necessary to review these questions to manually annotate the *Author and me* QAR type. This could be achieved in a crowd-sourcing process, instructing the annotators on script knowledge and asking them to label a question as *Author and me* if they first are not able to answer without reading the text.

With a major focus on background knowledge, CommonsenseQA shifts from the common text-question-answer candidates setting to only question-answer candidates. This dataset could in principle complement the *On my own* questions type, but the absence of a passage makes CommonsenseQA inconsistent for a RC task.

To ensure the integrity of our resulting dataset, we will take a subset for manual inspection.

5 Summary

We introduced process-based evaluation as a new setting to evaluate systems in reading comprehension. We propose to model QAR learning as a weak supervision classification task and discussed how existing RC datasets can be used to generate new data for this purpose. Our work is inspired by the findings of the educational assessment field and we expect it to complement current work in reading comprehension. We will leave the details on how to use the QAR classification task for a RC model's evaluation performance to future work.

Acknowledgements

I would like to thank my supervisors Jun Suzuki, Koji Matsuda and Kentaro Inui for their feedback, support and helpful discussions. I am also thankful to Benjamin Heinzerling, Kyosuke Nishida and the anonymous reviewers for their insightful comments. This work was supported by JST CREST Grant Number JPMJCR1513, Japan.

References

Luthfiyah Apriani. 2019. The use of question-answer relationship to improve students' reading comprehension. In *International Seminar and Annual Meeting BKS-PTN Wilayah Barat*, volume 1.

Yolande M Benito, Christy L Foley, Craig D Lewis, and Perry Prescott. 1993. The effect of instruction in question-answer relationships and metacognition on social studies comprehension. *Journal of Research in Reading*, 16(1):20–29.

Junyoung Chung, Caglar Gulcehre, KyungHyun Cho, and Yoshua Bengio. 2014. Empirical evaluation of gated recurrent neural networks on sequence modeling. *arXiv preprint arXiv:1412.3555*.

Helen K Ezell, Stacie A Hunsicker, Maria M Quinque, and Elizabeth Randolph. 1996. Maintenance and generalization of qar reading comprehension strategies. *Literacy Research and Instruction*, 36(1):64–81.

Liane Guillou and Christian Hardmeier. 2016. Protest: A test suite for evaluating pronouns in machine translation. In *LREC*.

Felix Hill, Antoine Bordes, Sumit Chopra, and Jason Weston. 2015. The goldilocks principle: Reading children's books with explicit memory representations. *arXiv preprint arXiv:1511.02301*.

Sepp Hochreiter and Jürgen Schmidhuber. 1997. Long short-term memory. *Neural computation*, 9(8):1735–1780.

Robin Jia and Percy Liang. 2017. Adversarial examples for evaluating reading comprehension systems. *arXiv preprint arXiv:1707.07328*.

Daniel Khashabi, Snigdha Chaturvedi, Michael Roth, Shyam Upadhyay, and Dan Roth. 2018. Looking beyond the surface: A challenge set for reading comprehension over multiple sentences. In *Proceedings of the 2018 Conference of the North American Chapter of the Association for Computational Linguistics: Human Language Technologies, Volume 1 (Long Papers)*, pages 252–262.

Tomáš Kočiskỳ, Jonathan Schwarz, Phil Blunsom, Chris Dyer, Karl Moritz Hermann, Gáabor Melis, and Edward Grefenstette. 2018. The narrativeqa reading comprehension challenge. *Transactions of the Association of Computational Linguistics*, 6:317–328.

Margaret E McIntosh and Roni Jo Draper. 1995. Applying the question-answer relationship strategy in mathematics. *Journal of Adolescent & Adult Literacy*, 39(2):120–131.

Jay McTighe and Steven Ferrara. 1994. Performance-based assessment in the classroom. *Pennsylvania Educational Leadership*, pages 4–16.

Todor Mihaylov, Peter Clark, Tushar Khot, and Ashish Sabharwal. 2018. Can a suit of armor conduct electricity? a new dataset for open book question answering. In *Proceedings of the 2018 Conference on Empirical Methods in Natural Language Processing*, pages 2381–2391, Brussels, Belgium. Association for Computational Linguistics.

Todor Mihaylov and Anette Frank. 2018. Knowledgeable reader: Enhancing cloze-style reading comprehension with external commonsense knowledge. *arXiv preprint arXiv:1805.07858*.

Pramod Kaushik Mudrakarta, Ankur Taly, Mukund Sundararajan, and Kedar Dhamdhere. 2018. Did the model understand the question? *arXiv preprint arXiv:1805.05492*.

Tri Nguyen, Mir Rosenberg, Xia Song, Jianfeng Gao, Saurabh Tiwary, Rangan Majumder, and Li Deng. 2016. Ms marco: A human generated machine reading comprehension dataset. *arXiv preprint arXiv:1611.09268*.

Takeshi Onishi, Hai Wang, Mohit Bansal, Kevin Gimpel, and David McAllester. 2016. Who did what: A large-scale person-centered cloze dataset. *arXiv preprint arXiv:1608.05457*.

Simon Ostermann, Ashutosh Modi, Michael Roth, Stefan Thater, and Manfred Pinkal. 2018. Mcscript: a novel dataset for assessing machine comprehension using script knowledge. *arXiv preprint arXiv:1803.05223*.

Pranav Rajpurkar, Jian Zhang, Konstantin Lopyrev, and Percy Liang. 2016. Squad: 100,000+ questions for machine comprehension of text. *arXiv preprint arXiv:1606.05250*.

Taffy E Raphael. 1982. Question-answering strategies for children. *Reading Teacher*.

Matthew Richardson, Christopher JC Burges, and Erin Renshaw. 2013. Mctest: A challenge dataset for the open-domain machine comprehension of text. In *Proceedings of the 2013 Conference on Empirical Methods in Natural Language Processing*, pages 193–203.

Kai Sun, Dian Yu, Dong Yu, and Claire Cardie. 2018. Improving machine reading comprehension with general reading strategies. *arXiv preprint arXiv:1810.13441*.

Alon Talmor, Jonathan Herzig, Nicholas Lourie, and Jonathan Berant. 2018. Commonsenseqa: A question answering challenge targeting commonsense knowledge. *arXiv preprint arXiv:1811.00937*.

Cynthia A Thompson, Mary Elaine Califf, and Raymond J Mooney. 1999. Active learning for natural language parsing and information extraction. In *ICML*, pages 406–414. Citeseer.

Nguyen Thi Bich Thuy and Nguyen Buu Huan. 2018. The effects of question-answer relationship strategy on efl high school studentsreading comprehension. *European Journal of English Language Teaching*.

Ashish Vaswani, Noam Shazeer, Niki Parmar, Jakob Uszkoreit, Llion Jones, Aidan N Gomez, Łukasz Kaiser, and Illia Polosukhin. 2017. Attention is all you need. In *Advances in neural information processing systems*, pages 5998–6008.

Constance Weaver. 1988. *Reading process and practice: From socio-psycholinguistics to whole language*. ERIC.

Johannes Welbl, Pontus Stenetorp, and Sebastian Riedel. 2018. Constructing datasets for multi-hop reading comprehension across documents. *Transactions of the Association of Computational Linguistics*, 6:287–302.

Jason Weston, Antoine Bordes, Sumit Chopra, Alexander M Rush, Bart van Merriënboer, Armand Joulin, and Tomas Mikolov. 2015. Towards ai-complete question answering: A set of prerequisite toy tasks. *arXiv preprint arXiv:1502.05698*.

Yi Yang, Wen-tau Yih, and Christopher Meek. 2015. Wikiqa: A challenge dataset for open-domain question answering. In *Proceedings of the 2015 Conference on Empirical Methods in Natural Language Processing*, pages 2013–2018.

Zhilin Yang, Peng Qi, Saizheng Zhang, Yoshua Bengio, William Cohen, Ruslan Salakhutdinov, and Christopher D. Manning. 2018. HotpotQA: A dataset for diverse, explainable multi-hop question answering. In *Proceedings of the 2018 Conference on Empirical Methods in Natural Language Processing*, pages 2369–2380, Brussels, Belgium. Association for Computational Linguistics.

Paraphrases as Foreign Languages
in Multilingual Neural Machine Translation

Zhong Zhou
Carnegie Mellon University
zhongzhou@cmu.edu

Matthias Sperber
Karlsruhe Institute of Technology
matthias.sperber@kit.edu

Alex Waibel
Carnegie Mellon University
Karlsruhe Institute of Technology
alex@waibel.com

Abstract

Paraphrases, the rewordings of the same semantic meaning, are useful for improving generalization and translation. However, prior works only explore paraphrases at the word or phrase level , not at the sentence or corpus level. Unlike previous works that only explore paraphrases at the word or phrase level, we use different translations of the whole training data that are consistent in structure as paraphrases at the corpus level. We train on parallel paraphrases in multiple languages from various sources. We treat paraphrases as foreign languages, tag source sentences with paraphrase labels, and train on parallel paraphrases in the style of multilingual Neural Machine Translation (NMT). Our multi-paraphrase NMT that trains only on two languages outperforms the multilingual baselines. Adding paraphrases improves the rare word translation and increases entropy and diversity in lexical choice. Adding the source paraphrases boosts performance better than adding the target ones. Combining both the source and the target paraphrases lifts performance further; combining paraphrases with multilingual data helps but has mixed performance. We achieve a BLEU score of 57.2 for French-to-English translation using 24 corpus-level paraphrases of the Bible, which outperforms the multilingual baselines and is +34.7 above the single-source single-target NMT baseline.

1 Introduction

Paraphrases, rewordings of texts with preserved semantics, are often used to improve generalization and the sparsity issue in translation (Callison-Burch et al., 2006; Fader et al., 2013; Ganitkevitch et al., 2013; Narayan et al., 2017; Sekizawa et al., 2017). Unlike previous works that use paraphrases at the word/phrase level, we research on different translations of the whole corpus that are consistent in structure as paraphrases at the corpus level;

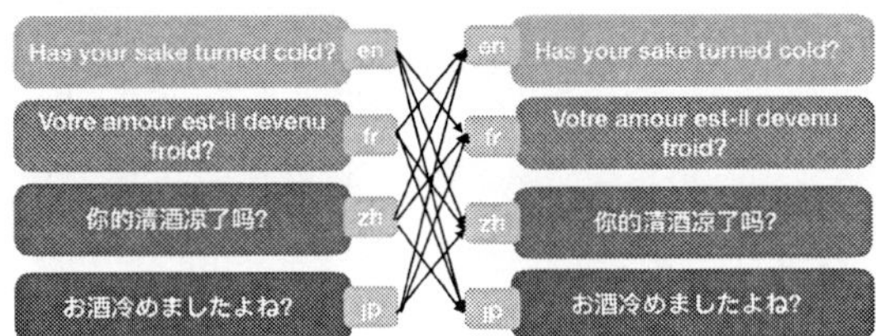

(a) multilingual NMT

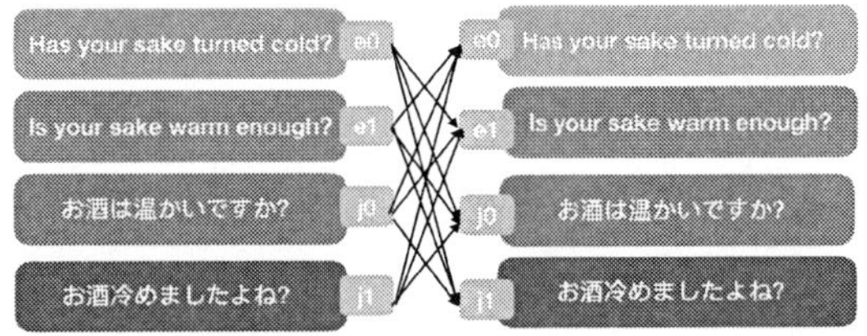

(b) multi-paraphrase NMT

Figure 1: Translation Paths in (a) multilingual NMT (b) multi-paraphrase NMT. Both form almost a complete bipartite graph.

we refer to paraphrases as the different translation versions of the same corpus. We train paraphrases in the style of multilingual NMT (Johnson et al., 2017; Ha et al., 2016) . Implicit parameter sharing enables multilingual NMT to learn across languages and achieve better generalization (Johnson et al., 2017). Training on closely related languages are shown to improve translation (Zhou et al., 2018). We view paraphrases as an extreme case of closely related languages and view multilingual data as paraphrases in different languages. Paraphrases can differ randomly or systematically as each carries the translator's unique style.

We treat paraphrases as foreign languages, and train a unified NMT model on paraphrase-labeled data with a shared attention in the style of multilingual NMT. Similar to multilingual NMT's objective of translating from any of the N input languages to any of the M output languages (Firat et al., 2016), multi-paraphrase NMT aims to translate from any of the N input paraphrases to any

Proceedings of the ACL 2019, Student Research Workshop, pages 113–122
Florence, Italy, July 28th-August 2nd, 2019. ©2019 Association for Computational Linguistics

of the M output paraphrases in Figure 1. In Figure 1, we see different expressions of a host showing courtesy to a guest to ask whether sake (a type of alcohol drink that is normally served warm in Asia) needs to be warmed. In Table 6, we show a few examples of parallel paraphrasing data in the Bible corpus. Different translators' styles give rise to rich parallel paraphrasing data, covering wide range of domains. In Table 7, we also show some paraphrasing examples from the modern poetry dataset, which we are considering for future research.

Indeed, we go beyond the traditional NMT learning of one-to-one mapping between the source and the target text; instead, we exploit the many-to-many mappings between the source and target text through training on paraphrases that are consistent to each other at the corpus level. Our method achieves high translation performance and gives interesting findings. The differences between our work and the prior works are mainly the following.

Unlike previous works that use paraphrases at the word or phrase level, we use paraphrases at the entire corpus level to improve translation performance. We use different translations of the whole training data consistent in structure as paraphrases of the full training data. Unlike most of the multilingual NMT works that uses data from multiple languages, we use paraphrases as foreign languages in a single-source single-target NMT system training only on data from the source and the target languages.

Our main findings in harnessing paraphrases in NMT are the following.

1. Our multi-paraphrase NMT results show significant improvements in BLEU scores over all baselines.

2. Our paraphrase-exploiting NMT uses only two languages, the source and the target languages, and achieves higher BLEUs than the multi-source and multi-target NMT that incorporates more languages.

3. We find that adding the source paraphrases helps better than adding the target paraphrases.

4. We find that adding paraphrases at both the source and the target sides is better than adding at either side.

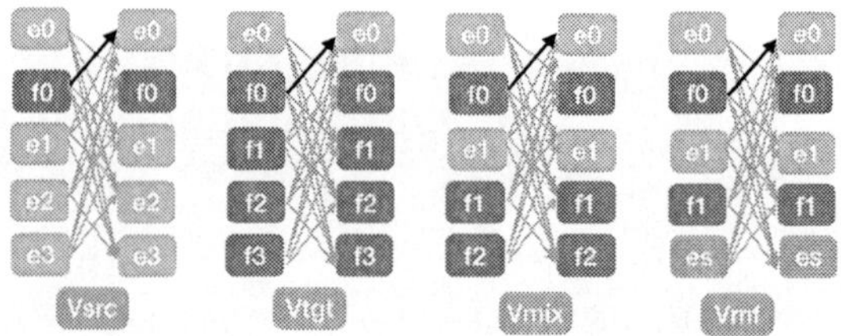

Figure 2: Examples of different ways of adding 5 paraphrases. e[?n] and f[?n] refers to different English and French paraphrases, es refers to the Spanish (an example member of Romance family) data. We always evaluate the translation path from f0 to e0.

5. We also find that adding paraphrases with additional multilingual data yields mixed performance; its performance is better than training on language families alone, but is worse than training on both the source and target paraphrases without language families.

6. Adding paraphrases improves the sparsity issue of rare word translation and diversity in lexical choice.

In this paper, we begin with introduction and related work in Section 1 and 2. We introduce our models in Section 3. Finally, we present our results in Section 4 and conclude in Section 5.

2   Related Work

2.1   Paraphrasing

Many works generate and harness paraphrases (Barzilay and McKeown, 2001; Pang et al., 2003; Callison-Burch et al., 2005; Mallinson et al., 2017; Ganitkevitch et al., 2013; Brad and Rebedea, 2017; Quirk et al., 2004; Madnani et al., 2012; Suzuki et al., 2017; Hasan et al., 2016). Some are on question and answer (Fader et al., 2013; Dong et al., 2017), evaluation of translation (Zhou et al., 2006) and more recently NMT (Narayan et al., 2017; Sekizawa et al., 2017). Past research includes paraphrasing unknown words/phrases/sub-sentences (Callison-Burch et al., 2006; Narayan et al., 2017; Sekizawa et al., 2017; Fadaee et al., 2017). These approaches are similar in transforming the difficult sparsity problem of rare words prediction and long sentence translation into a simpler problem with known words and short sentence translation. It is worthwhile to contrast paraphrasing that diversifies data, with knowledge distillation that benefits from making data more consistent (Gu et al., 2017).

Our work is different in that we exploit paraphrases at the corpus level, rather than at the word

Data	1	6	11	13
Vsrc	22.5	41.4	48.9	48.8
Vtgt	22.5	40.5	47.0	47.4

Table 1: Comparison of adding source paraphrases and adding target paraphrases. All acronyms including data are explained in Section 4.3.

data	1	6	11	16	22	24
WMT	22.5	30.8	29.8	30.8	29.3	-
Family	22.5	39.3	45.4	49.2	46.6	-
Vmix	22.5	44.8	50.8	53.3	55.4	57.2
Vmf	-	-	49.3	-	-	-

Table 2: Comparison of adding a mix of the source paraphrases and the target paraphrases against the baselines. All acronyms including data are explained in Section 4.3.

or phrase level.

2.2 Multilingual Attentional NMT

Machine polyglotism which trains machines to translate any of the N input languages to any of the M output languages from many languages to many languages, many languages is a new paradigm in multilingual NMT (Firat et al., 2016; Zoph and Knight, 2016; Dong et al., 2015; Gillick et al., 2016; Al-Rfou et al., 2013; Tsvetkov et al., 2016). The objective is to translate from any of the N input languages to any of the M output languages (Firat et al., 2016).

Many multilingual NMT systems involve multiple encoders and decoders (Ha et al., 2016), and it is hard to combine attention for quadratic language pairs bypassing quadratic attention mechanisms (Firat et al., 2016). An interesting work is training a universal model with a shared attention mechanism with the source and target language labels and Byte-Pair Encoding (BPE) (Johnson et al., 2017; Ha et al., 2016). This method is elegant in its simplicity and its advancement in low-resource language translation and zero-shot translation using pivot-based translation mechanism (Johnson et al., 2017; Firat et al., 2016).

Unlike previous works, our parallelism is across paraphrases, not across languages. In other words, we achieve higher translation performance in the single-source single-target paraphrase-exploiting NMT than that of the multilingual NMT.

3 Models

We have four baseline models. Two are single-source single-target attentional NMT models, the other two are multilingual NMT models with a shared attention (Johnson et al., 2017; Ha et al., 2016). In Figure 1, we show an example of multilingual attentional NMT. Translating from

all 4 languages to each other, we have 12 translation paths. For each translation path, we label the source sentence with the source and target language tags. Translating from "你的清酒凉了吗?" to "Has your sake turned cold?", we label the source sentence with `__opt_src_zh __opt_tgt_en`. More details are in Section 4.

In multi-paraphrase model, all source sentences are labeled with the paraphrase tags. For example, in French-to-English translation, a source sentence may be tagged with `__opt_src_f1 __opt_tgt_e0`, denoting that it is translating from version "f1" of French data to version "e0" of English data. In Figure 1, we show 2 Japanese and 2 English paraphrases. Translating from all 4 paraphrases to each other ($N = M = 4$), we have 12 translation paths as $N \times (N - 1) = 12$. For each translation path, we label the source sentence with the source and target paraphrase tags. For the translation path from "お酒冷めましたよね?" to "Has your sake turned cold?", we label the source sentence with `__opt_src_j1 __opt_tgt_e0` in Figure 1. Paraphrases of the same translation path carry the same labels. Our paraphrasing data is at the corpus level, and we train a unified NMT model with a shared attention. Unlike the paraphrasing sentences in Figure 1, We show this example with only one sentence, it is similar when the training data contains many sentences. All sentences in the same paraphrase path share the same labels.

4 Experiments and Results

4.1 Data

Our main data is the French-to-English Bible corpus (Mayer and Cysouw, 2014), containing 12 versions of the English Bible and 12 versions of the French Bible [1]. We translate from French to English. Since these 24 translation versions are consistent in structure, we refer to them as paraphrases at corpus level. In our paper, each paraphrase refers to each translation version of whole Bible corpus. To understand our setup, if we use all 12 French paraphrases and all 12 English paraphrases so there are 24 paraphrases in total, i.e., $N = M = 24$, we have 552 translation paths be-

---

[1] We considered the open subtitles with different scripts of the same movie in the same language; they covers many topics, but they are noisy and only differ in interjections. We also considered the poetry dataset where a poem like "If" by Rudyard Kipling is translated many times, by various people into the same language, but the data is small.

Source Sentence	Machine Translation	Correct Target Translation
Comme de l'eau fraîche pour une personne fatigué, Ainsi est une bonne nouvelle venant d'une terre lointaine.·	As cold waters to a thirsty soul, so is good news from a distant land.	Like cold waters to a weary soul, so is a good report from a far country.
Lorsque tu seras invité par quelqu'un à des noces, ne te mets pas à la première place, de peur qu'il n'y ait parmi les invités une personne plus considérable que toi,	When you are invited to one to the wedding, do not be to the first place, lest any one be called greater than you.	When you are invited by anyone to wedding feasts, do not recline at the chief seat lest one more honorable than you be invited by him,
Car chaque arbre se connaît à son fruit. On ne cueille pas des figues sur des épines, et l'on ne vendange pas des raisins sur des ronces.	For each tree is known by its own fruit. For from thorns they do not gather figs, nor do they gather grapes from a bramble bush.	For each tree is known from its own fruit. For they do not gather figs from thorns, nor do they gather grapes from a bramble bush.
Vous tous qui avez soif, venez aux eaux, Même celui qui n'a pas d'argent! Venez, achetez et mangez, Venez, achetez du vin et du lait, sans argent, sans rien payer!	Come, all you thirsty ones, come to the waters; come, buy and eat. Come, buy for wine, and for nothing, for without money.	Ho, everyone who thirsts, come to the water; and he who has no silver, come buy grain and eat. Yes, come buy grain, wine and milk without silver and with no price.
Oui , vous sortirez avec joie , Et vous serez conduits en paix ; Les montagnes et les collines éclateront d'allégresse devant vous , Et tous les arbres de la campagne battront des mains .	When you go out with joy , you shall go in peace ; the mountains shall rejoice before you , and the trees of the field shall strike all the trees of the field .	For you shall go out with joy and be led out with peace . The mountains and the hills shall break out into song before you , and all the trees of the field shall clap the palm .

Table 3: Examples of French-to-English translation trained using 12 French paraphrases and 12 English paraphrases.

cause $N \times (N - 1) = 552$. The original corpus contains missing or extra verses for different paraphrases; we clean and align 24 paraphrases of the Bible corpus and randomly sample the training, validation and test sets according to the 0.75, 0.15, 0.10 ratio. Our training set contains only 23K verses, but is massively parallel across paraphrases.

For all experiments, we choose a specific English corpus as e0 and a specific French corpus as f0 which we evaluate across all experiments to ensure consistency in comparison, and we evaluate all translation performance from f0 to e0.

4.2 Training Parameters

In all our experiments, we use a minibatch size of 64, dropout rate of 0.3, 4 RNN layers of size 1000, a word vector size of 600, number of epochs of 13, a learning rate of 0.8 that decays at the rate of 0.7 if the validation score is not improving or it is past epoch 9 across all LSTM-based experiments. Byte-Pair Encoding (BPE) is used at preprocessing stage (Ha et al., 2016). Our code is built on OpenNMT (Klein et al., 2017) and we evaluate our models using BLEU scores (Papineni et al., 2002), entropy (Shannon, 1951), F-measure and qualitative evaluation.

4.3 Baselines

We introduce a few acronyms for our four baselines to describe the experiments in Table 1, Table 2 and Figure 3. Firstly, we have two single-source single-target attentional NMT models, *Single* and *WMT*. *Single* trains on f0 and e0 and gives a BLEU of 22.5, the starting point for all curves in Figure 3. *WMT* adds the out-domain WMT'14 French-to-English data on top of f0 and e0; it serves as a weak baseline that helps us to evaluate all experiments' performance discounting the effect of increasing data.

Moreover, we have two multilingual baselines[2] built on multilingual attentional NMT, *Family* and *Span* (Zhou et al., 2018). *Family* refers to the multilingual baseline by adding one language family at a time, where on top of the French corpus f0 and the English corpus e0, we add up to 20 other European languages. *Span* refers to the multilingual baseline by adding one *span* at a time, where a span is a set of languages that contains at least one language from all the families in the data; in other words, span is a sparse representation of all the families. Both *Family* and *Span* trains on the Bible in 22 Europeans languages trained using multilingual NMT. Since *Span* is always suboptimal to *Family* in our results, we only show numerical results for *Family* in Table 1 and 2, and we plot both *Family* and *Span* in Figure 3. The two multilingual baselines are strong baselines while the f*WMT* baseline is a weak baseline that helps us to evaluate all experiments' performance discounting the effect of increasing data. All baseline results are taken from

---

[2] For multilingual baselines, we use the additional Bible corpus in 22 European languages that are cleaned and aligned to each other.

data	6	11	16	22	24
Entropy	5.6569	5.6973	5.6980	5.7341	5.7130
Bootstr.	5.6564	5.6967	5.6975	5.7336	5.7125
95% CI	5.6574	5.6979	5.6986	5.7346	5.7135
WMT	-	5.7412	5.5746	5.6351	-

Table 4: Entropy increases with the number of paraphrase corpora in $Vmix$. The 95% confidence interval is calculated via bootstrap resampling with replacement.

data	6	11	16	22	24
F1(freq1)	0.43	0.54	0.57	0.58	0.62
WMT	-	0.00	0.01	0.01	-

Table 5: F1 score of frequency 1 bucket increases with the number of paraphrase corpora in $Vmix$, showing training on paraphrases improves the sparsity at tail and the rare word problem.

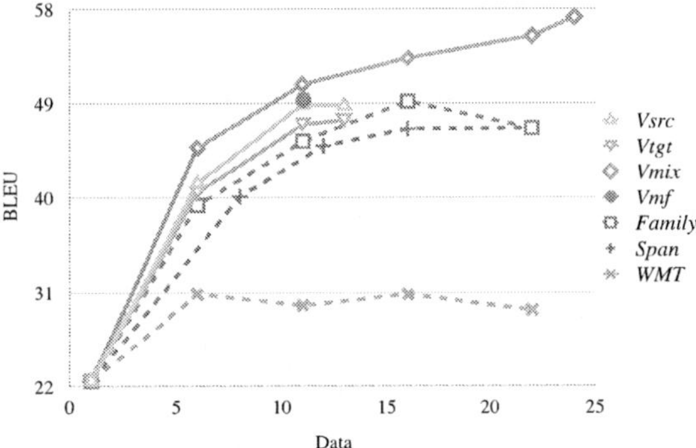

Figure 3: BLEU plots showing the effects of different ways of adding training data in French-to-English Translation. All acronyms including data are explained in Section 4.3.

a research work which uses the grid of (1, 6, 11, 16, 22) for the number of languages or equivalent number of unique sentences and we follow the same in Figure 3 (Zhou et al., 2018). All experiments for each grid point carry the same number of unique sentences.

Furthermore, $Vsrc$ refers to adding more source (English) paraphrases, and $Vtgt$ refers to adding more target (French) paraphrases. $Vmix$ refers to adding both the source and the target paraphrases. Vmf refers to combining $Vmix$ with additional multilingual data; note that only Vmf, $Family$ and $Span$ use languages other than French and English, all other experiments use only English and French. For the x-axis, data refers to the number of paraphrase corpora for $Vsrc$, $Vtgt$, $Vmix$; data refers to the number of languages for $Family$; data refers to and the equivalent number of unique training sentences compared to other training curves for *WMT* and Vmf.

4.4 Results

Training on paraphrases gives better performance than all baselines: The translation performance of training on 22 paraphrases, i.e., 11 English paraphrases and 11 French paraphrases, achieves a BLEU score of 55.4, which is +32.9 above the $Single$ baseline, +8.8 above the $Family$ baseline, and +26.1 above the *WMT* baseline. Note that the $Family$ baseline uses the grid of (1, 6, 11, 16, 22) for number of languages, we continue to use this grid for our results on number of paraphrases, which explains why we pick 22 as an example here. The highest BLEU 57.2 is achieved when we train on 24 paraphrases, i.e., 12 English paraphrases and 12 French paraphrases.

Adding the source paraphrases boosts translation performance more than adding the target get paraphrases: The translation performance of adding the source paraphrases is higher than that of adding the target paraphrases. Adding the source paraphrases diversifies the data, exposes the model to more rare words, and enables better generalization. Take the experiments training on 13 paraphrases for example, training on the source (i.e., 12 French paraphrases and the English paraphrase e0) gives a BLEU score of 48.8, which has a gain of +1.4 over 47.4, the BLEU score of training on the target (i.e., 12 English paraphrases and the French paraphrase f0). This suggests that adding the source paraphrases is more effective than adding the target paraphrases.

Adding paraphrases from both sides is better than adding paraphrases from either side: The curve of adding paraphrases from both the source and the target sides is higher than both the curve of adding the target paraphrases and the curve of adding the source paraphrases. Training on 11 paraphrases from both sides, i.e., a total of 22 paraphrases achieves a BLEU score of 50.8, which is +3.8 higher than that of training on the target side only and +1.9 higher than that of training on the source side only. The advantage of combining both sides is that we can combine paraphrases from both the source and the target to reach 24 paraphrases in total to achieve a BLEU score of 57.2.

Adding both paraphrases and language families yields mixed performance: We conduct one more experiment combining the source and target paraphrases together with additional multilingual data. This is the only experiment on paraphrases where we use multilingual data other than only French and English data. The BLEU score is 49.3, higher than training on families alone, in fact, it is higher than training on eight European families altogether. However, it is lower than training on English and French paraphrases alone. Indeed, adding paraphrases as foreign languages is effective, however, when there is a lack of data, mixing the paraphrases with multilingual data is helpful.

Adding paraphrases increases entropy and diversity in lexical choice, and improves the sparsity issue of rare words: We use bootstrap resampling and construct 95% confidence intervals for entropies (Shannon, 1951) of all models of $Vmix$, i.e., models adding paraphrases at both the source and the target sides. We find that the more paraphrases, the higher the entropy, the more diversity in lexical choice as shown in Table 4. From the word F-measure shown in Table 5, we find that the more paraphrases, the better the model handles the sparsity of rare words issue. Adding paraphrases not only achieves much higher BLEU score than the WMT baseline, but also handles the sparsity issue much better than the WMT baseline.

Adding paraphrases helps rhetoric translation and increases expressiveness: Qualitative evaluation shows many cases where rhetoric translation is improved by training on diverse sets of paraphrases. In Table 3, Paraphrases help NMT to use a more contemporary synonym of "silver", "money", which is more direct and easier to understand. Paraphrases simplifies the rhetorical or subtle expressions, for example, our model uses "rejoice" to replace "break out into song", a personification device of mountains to describe joy, which captures the essence of the meaning being conveyed. However, we also observe that NMT wrongly translates "clap the palm" to "strike". We find the quality of rhetorical translation ties closely with the diversity of parallel paraphrases data. Indeed, the use of paraphrases to improve rhetoric translation is a good future research question. Please refer to the Table 3 for more qualitative examples.

5 Conclusion

We train on paraphrases as foreign languages in the style of multilingual NMT. Adding paraphrases improves translation quality, the rare word issue, and diversity in lexical choice. Adding the source paraphrases helps more than adding the target ones, while combining both boosts performance further. Adding multilingual data to paraphrases yields mixed performance. We would like to explore the common structure and terminology consistency across different paraphrases. Since structure and terminology are shared across paraphrases, we are interested in a building an explicit representation of the paraphrases and extend our work for better translation, or translation with more explicit and more explainable hidden states, which is very important in all neural systems.

We are interested in broadening our dataset in our future experiments. We hope to use other parallel paraphrasing corpora like the poetry dataset as shown in Table 7. There are very few poems that are translated multiple times into the same language, we therefore need to train on extremely small dataset. Rhetoric in paraphrasing is important in poetry dataset, which again depends on the training paraphrases. The limited data issue is also relevant to the low-resource setting.

We would like to effectively train on extremely small low-resource paraphrasing data. As discussed above about the potential research poetry dataset, dataset with multiple paraphrases is typically small and yet valuable. If we can train using extremely small amount of data, especially in the low-resource scenario, we would exploit the power of multi-paraphrase NMT further.

Cultural-aware paraphrasing and subtle expressions are vital (Levin et al., 1998; Larson, 1984). Rhetoric in paraphrasing is a very important too. In Figure 1, "is your sake warm enough?" in Asian culture is an implicit way of saying "would you like me to warm the sake for you?". We would like to model the culture-specific subtlety through multi-paraphrase training.

References

Rami Al-Rfou, Bryan Perozzi, and Steven Skiena. 2013. Polyglot: Distributed word representations for multilingual nlp. In *Proceedings of the 17th Conference on Computational Natural Language Learning*, pages 183–192, Sofia, Bulgaria. Association for Computational Linguistics.

Regina Barzilay and Kathleen R McKeown. 2001. Extracting paraphrases from a parallel corpus. In *Proceedings of the 39th Annual Meeting on Association for Computational Linguistics*, pages 50–57. Association for Computational Linguistics.

Florin Brad and Traian Rebedea. 2017. Neural paraphrase generation using transfer learning. In *Proceedings of the 10th International Conference on Natural Language Generation*, pages 257–261.

Chris Callison-Burch, Colin Bannard, and Josh Schroeder. 2005. Scaling phrase-based statistical machine translation to larger corpora and longer phrases. In *Proceedings of the 43rd Annual Meeting on Association for Computational Linguistics*, pages 255–262. Association for Computational Linguistics.

Chris Callison-Burch, Philipp Koehn, and Miles Osborne. 2006. Improved statistical machine translation using paraphrases. In *Proceedings of North American Chapter of the Association for Computational Linguistics on Human Language Technologies*, pages 17–24. Association for Computational Linguistics.

Daxiang Dong, Hua Wu, Wei He, Dianhai Yu, and Haifeng Wang. 2015. Multi-task learning for multiple language translation. In *Proceedings of the 53rd Annual Meeting of the Association for Computational Linguistics*, pages 1723–1732.

Li Dong, Jonathan Mallinson, Siva Reddy, and Mirella Lapata. 2017. Learning to paraphrase for question answering. In *Proceedings of the 22nd Conference on Empirical Methods in Natural Language Processing*, pages 875–886.

Marzieh Fadaee, Arianna Bisazza, and Christof Monz. 2017. Data augmentation for low-resource neural machine translation. *arXiv preprint arXiv:1705.00440*.

Anthony Fader, Luke Zettlemoyer, and Oren Etzioni. 2013. Paraphrase-driven learning for open question answering. In *Proceedings of the 51st Annual Meeting of the Association for Computational Linguistics*, pages 1608–1618.

Orhan Firat, Kyunghyun Cho, and Yoshua Bengio. 2016. Multi-way, multilingual neural machine translation with a shared attention mechanism. In *Proceedings of the 15th Conference of the North American Chapter of the Association for Computational Linguistics on Human Language Technologies*, pages 866–875.

Juri Ganitkevitch, Benjamin Van Durme, and Chris Callison-Burch. 2013. Ppdb: The paraphrase database. In *Proceedings of the 12th Conference of the North American Chapter of the Association for Computational Linguistics on Human Language Technologies*, pages 758–764.

Dan Gillick, Cliff Brunk, Oriol Vinyals, and Amarnag Subramanya. 2016. Multilingual language processing from bytes. In *Proceedings of the 15th Conference of the North American Chapter of the Association for Computational Linguistics on Human Language Technologies*, pages 1296–1306.

Jiatao Gu, James Bradbury, Caiming Xiong, Victor OK Li, and Richard Socher. 2017. Non-autoregressive neural machine translation. *arXiv preprint arXiv:1711.02281*.

Thanh-Le Ha, Jan Niehues, and Alexander Waibel. 2016. Toward multilingual neural machine translation with universal encoder and decoder. *arXiv preprint arXiv:1611.04798*.

Sadid A Hasan, Bo Liu, Joey Liu, Ashequl Qadir, Kathy Lee, Vivek Datla, Aaditya Prakash, and Oladimeji Farri. 2016. Neural clinical paraphrase generation with attention. In *Proceedings of the Clinical Natural Language Processing Workshop*, pages 42–53.

Melvin Johnson, Mike Schuster, Quoc V Le, Maxim Krikun, Yonghui Wu, Zhifeng Chen, Nikhil Thorat, Fernanda Viégas, Martin Wattenberg, Greg Corrado, et al. 2017. Google's multilingual neural machine translation system: Enabling zero-shot translation. *Transactions of the Association for Computational Linguistics*, 5:339–351.

Guillaume Klein, Yoon Kim, Yuntian Deng, Jean Senellart, and Alexander Rush. 2017. Opennmt: Open-source toolkit for neural machine translation. *Proceedings of the 55th annual meeting of the Association for Computational Linguistics, System Demonstrations*, pages 67–72.

Mildred L Larson. 1984. *Meaning-based translation: A guide to cross-language equivalence*. University press of America Lanham.

Lori Levin, Donna Gates, Alon Lavie, and Alex Waibel. 1998. An interlingua based on domain actions for machine translation of task-oriented dialogues. In *Proceedings of the 5th International Conference on Spoken Language Processing*.

Nitin Madnani, Joel Tetreault, and Martin Chodorow. 2012. Re-examining machine translation metrics for paraphrase identification. In *Proceedings of the 11th Conference of the North American Chapter of the Association for Computational Linguistics on Human Language Technologies*, pages 182–190. Association for Computational Linguistics.

Jonathan Mallinson, Rico Sennrich, and Mirella Lapata. 2017. Paraphrasing revisited with neural machine translation. In *Proceedings of the 15th Conference of the European Chapter of the Association for Computational Linguistics*, pages 881–893.

Thomas Mayer and Michael Cysouw. 2014. Creating a massively parallel bible corpus. *Oceania*, 135(273):40.

Shashi Narayan, Claire Gardent, Shay Cohen, and Anastasia Shimorina. 2017. Split and rephrase. In *Proceedings of the 22nd Conference on Empirical Methods in Natural Language Processing*, pages 617–627.

Bo Pang, Kevin Knight, and Daniel Marcu. 2003. Syntax-based alignment of multiple translations: Extracting paraphrases and generating new sentences. In *Proceedings of North American Chapter of the Association for Computational Linguistics on Human Language Technologies*.

Kishore Papineni, Salim Roukos, Todd Ward, and Wei-Jing Zhu. 2002. Bleu: a method for automatic evaluation of machine translation. In *Proceedings of the 40th annual meeting on association for computational linguistics*, pages 311–318. Association for Computational Linguistics.

Chris Quirk, Chris Brockett, and William Dolan. 2004. Monolingual machine translation for paraphrase generation. In *Proceedings of the 9th Conference on Empirical Methods in Natural Language Processing*.

Yuuki Sekizawa, Tomoyuki Kajiwara, and Mamoru Komachi. 2017. Improving japanese-to-english neural machine translation by paraphrasing the target language. In *Proceedings of the 4th Workshop on Asian Translation*, pages 64–69.

Claude E Shannon. 1951. Prediction and entropy of printed english. *Bell Labs Technical Journal*, 30(1):50–64.

Yui Suzuki, Tomoyuki Kajiwara, and Mamoru Komachi. 2017. Building a non-trivial paraphrase corpus using multiple machine translation systems. In *Proceedings of ACL 2017, Student Research Workshop*, pages 36–42.

Yulia Tsvetkov, Sunayana Sitaram, Manaal Faruqui, Guillaume Lample, Patrick Littell, David Mortensen, Alan W Black, Lori Levin, and Chris Dyer. 2016. Polyglot neural language models: A case study in cross-lingual phonetic representation learning. In *Proceedings of the 15th Conference of the North American Chapter of the Association for Computational Linguistics on Human Language Technologies*, pages 1357–1366.

Liang Zhou, Chin-Yew Lin, and Eduard Hovy. 2006. Re-evaluating machine translation results with paraphrase support. In *Proceedings of the 11th Conference on Empirical Methods in Natural Language Processing*, pages 77–84. Association for Computational Linguistics.

Zhong Zhou, Matthias Sperber, and Alex Waibel. 2018. Massively parallel cross-lingual learning in low-resource target language translation. *2018 Third Conference on Machine Translation (WMT18)*, pages 232—-243.

Barret Zoph and Kevin Knight. 2016. Multi-source neural translation. In *Proceedings of the 15th Conference of the North American Chapter of the Association for Computational Linguistics on Human Language Technologies*, pages 30–34.

Appendix A   Supplemental Materials

We show a few examples of parallel paraphrasing data in the Bible corpus. We also show some paraphrasing examples from the modern poetry dataset, which we are considering for future research.

English Paraphrases	Consider the lilies, how they grow: they neither toil nor spin, yet I tell you, even Solomon in all his glory was not arrayed like one of these. *English Standard Version.*
	Look how the wild flowers grow! They don't work hard to make their clothes. But I tell you Solomon with all his wealth wasn't as well clothed as one of these flowers. *Contemporary English Version.*
	Consider how the wild flowers grow. They do not labor or spin. Yet I tell you, not even Solomon in all his splendor was dressed like one of these. *New International Version.*
French Paraphrases	Considérez les lis! Ils poussent sans se fatiguer à tisser des vêtements. Et pourtant, je vous l'assure, le roi Salomon lui-même, dans toute sa gloire, n'a jamais été aussi bien vêtu que l'un d'eux! *La Bible du Semeur.*
	Considérez comment croissent les lis: ils ne travaillent ni ne filent; cependant je vous dis que Salomon même, dans toute sa gloire, n'a pas été vêtu comme l'un d'eux. *Louis Segond.*
	Observez comment poussent les plus belles fleurs: elles ne travaillent pas et ne tissent pas; cependant je vous dis que Salomon lui-même, dans toute sa gloire, n'a pas eu d'aussi belles tenues que l'une d'elles. *Segond 21.*
Tagalog Paraphrases	Wariin ninyo ang mga lirio, kung paano silang nagsisilaki: hindi nangagpapagal, o nangag-susulid man; gayon ma'y sinasabi ko sa inyo, Kahit si Salomon man, sa buong kaluwalhatian niya, ay hindi nakapaggayak na gaya ng isa sa mga ito. *Ang Biblia 1978.*
	Isipin ninyo ang mga liryo kung papaano sila lumalaki. Hindi sila nagpapapagal o nag-iikid. Gayunman, sinasabi ko sa inyo: Maging si Solomon, sa kaniyang buong kaluwalhatian ay hindi nadamitan ng tulad sa isa sa mga ito. *Ang Salita ng Diyos.*
	Tingnan ninyo ang mga bulaklak sa parang kung paano sila lumalago. Hindi sila nagtatrabaho ni humahabi man. Ngunit sinasabi ko sa inyo, kahit si Solomon sa kanyang karangyaan ay hindi nakapagdamit ng singganda ng isa sa mga bulaklak na ito. *Magandang Balita Biblia.*
Spanish Paraphrases	Considerad los lirios, cómo crecen; no trabajan ni hilan; pero os digo que ni Salomón en toda su gloria se vistió como uno de éstos. *La Biblia de las Américas.*
	Fíjense cómo crecen los lirios. No trabajan ni hilan; sin embargo, les digo que ni siquiera Salomón, con todo su esplendor, se vestía como uno de ellos. *Nueva Biblia al Día.*
	Aprendan de las flores del campo: no trabajan para hacerse sus vestidos y, sin embargo, les aseguro que ni el rey Salomón, con todas sus riquezas, se vistió tan bien como ellas. *Traducción en lenguaje actual.*

Table 6: Examples of parallel paraphrasing data with English, French, Tagalog and Spanish paraphrases in Bible translation.

English Original	If you can fill the unforgiving minute with sixty seconds' worth of distance run, yours is the Earth and everything that's in it, and—which is more—you'll be a Man, my son! "if", *Rudyard Kipling.*
German Translations	Wenn du in unverzeihlicher Minute Sechzig Minuten lang verzeihen kannst: Dein ist die Welt—und alles was darin ist— Und was noch mehr ist—dann bist du ein Mensch! Translation by *Anja Hauptmann.*
	Wenn du erfüllst die herzlose Minute Mit tiefstem Sinn, empfange deinen Lohn: Dein ist die Welt mit jedem Attribute, Und mehr noch: dann bist du ein Mensch, mein Sohn! Translation by *Izzy Cartwell.*
	Füllst jede unerbittliche Minute Mit sechzig sinnvollen Sekunden an; Dein ist die Erde dann mit allem Gute, Und was noch mehr, mein Sohn: Du bist ein Mann! Translation by *Lothar Sauer.*
Chinese Translations	若胸有激雷，而能面如平湖，则山川丘壑，天地万物皆与尔共，吾儿终成人也！ Translation by *Anonymous.*
	如果你能惜时如金利用每一分钟不可追回的光阴；那么，你的修为就会如天地般博大，并拥有了属于自己的世界，更重要的是：孩子，你成为了真正顶天立地之人！ Translation by *Anonymous.*
	假如你能把每一分宝贵的光阴，化作六十秒的奋斗——你就拥有了整个世界，最重要的是——你就成了一个真正的人，我的孩子！ Translation by *Shan Li.*
Portuguese Translations	Se você puder preencher o valor do inclemente minuto perdido com os sessenta segundos ganhos numa longa corrida, sua será a Terra, junto com tudo que nela existe, e—mais importante—você será um Homem, meu filho! Translation by *Dascomb Barddal.*
	Pairando numa esfera acima deste plano, Sem receares jamais que os erros te retomem, Quando já nada houver em ti que seja humano, Alegra-te, meu filho, então serás um homem!... Translation by *Féliz Bermudes.*
	Se és capaz de dar, segundo por segundo, ao minuto fatal todo valor e brilho. Tua é a Terra com tudo o que existe no mundo, e—o que ainda é muito mais—és um Homem, meu filho! Translation by *Guilherme de Almeida.*

Table 7: Examples of parallel paraphrasing data with German, Chinese, and Portuguese paraphrases of the English poem "If" by Rudyard Kipling.

Improving Mongolian-Chinese Neural Machine Translation with Morphological Noise

Yatu JI* **Hongxu HOU*†** **Nier WU*** **Junjie CHEN***

`jiyatu0@126.com cshhx@imu.edu.cn wunier04@126.comchenjj@imau.edu.cn`

*Computer Science dept, Inner Mongolia University / Hohhot, China

Abstract

For the translation of agglutinative language such as typical Mongolian, unknown (UNK) words not only come from the quite restricted vocabulary, but also mostly from misunderstanding of the translation model to the morphological changes. In this study, we introduce a new adversarial training model to alleviate the UNK problem in Mongolian→Chinese machine translation. The training process can be described as three adversarial sub models (generator, value screener and discriminator), playing a win−win game. In this game, the added screener plays the role of emphasizing that the discriminator pays attention to the added Mongolian morphological noise[1] in the form of pseudo-data and improving the training efficiency. The experimental results show that the newly emerged Mongolian→Chinese task is state-of-the-art. Under this premise, the training time is greatly shortened.

1 Introduction

The dominant neural machine translation (NMT) (Sutskever et al., 2014) models are based on recurrent (RNN, (Mikolov et al., 2011)), convolutional neural networks (CNN, (Gehring et al., 2017)) or entirely eliminates recurrent connections and relies instead on a repeated attention mechanism (Transformer, (Vaswani et al., 2017)) which are achieved by an attention mechanism (Bahdanau et al., 2014). A considerable weakness in these NMT systems is their inability to correctly translate very rare words: end-to-end NMTs tend to have relatively small vocabularies with a single $< unk >$ symbol that represents every possible

out-of-vocabulary (OOV) word. The problem is more prominent in agglutinative language tasks, because the varied morphology brings great confusion to model decoding. The change of suffix and component case[2] in Mongolian largely deceives the translation model directly resulting in a large amount of OOV during decoding. This OOV is then crudely considered the same as an $< unk >$ symbol.

Generally, there are three ways to solve this problem. A usual practice is to speed up training (Morin and Bengio, 2005; Jean et al., 2015; Mnih et al., 2013), these approaches can maintain a very large vocabulary. However, it works well when there are only a few unknown words in the target sentence. These approaches have been observed that the translation performance degrades rapidly as the number of unknown words increases. Another aspect is the information in context (Luong et al., 2015; Hermann et al., 2015; Gulcehre et al., 2016), they motivate their work from a psychological evidence that humans naturally have a tendency to point towards objects in the context. The last aspect is the input/output change, these approaches change to a smaller resolution, such as characters (Graves, 2013a) and bytecodes (Sennrich et al., 2016). However, it is worth thinking that the training process usually becomes much harder because of the length of sequences considerable increases.

For NLP tasks, generative adversarial network (GAN) is immature. Some studies, such as (Chen et al., 2016; Zhang et al., 2017), used GAN for semantic analysis and domain adaptation. (Yu et al., 2016; Zhen et al., 2018; Wu et al., 2018) successfully applied GAN to sequence generation tasks. (Zhang Y, 2017) propose matching the high-dimensional latent feature distributions of re-

---

[1] These morphological noises exist in most agglutinative languages in the form of appended stem, which are used to determine the presentation or tense of words. Some typical noises, such as suffixes and cases in Mongolian, Korean and Japanese.

[2] Mongolian-case is a special suffix used to determine its relationship to other words in a sentence.

Proceedings of the ACL 2019, Student Research Workshop, pages 123–129
Florence, Italy, July 28th-August 2nd, 2019. ©2019 Association for Computational Linguistics

al and synthetic sentences, via a kernelized discrepancy metric. This eases adversarial training by alleviating the mode-collapsing problem.

In the present study, GAN is used for UNK problem. The motivation for this is GAN's advantage in approaching real data effectively based on noise in a game training. To obtain generalizable adversarial training, we propose a noise-added strategy to add noise samples into the training set in the form of pseudo data. The noise is the main cause of UNK, such as the segmentation of suffixes and the handling of case components in Mongolian. A representative example is used to illustrate the decoding search process of Mongolian sentences in adversarial training (Fig. 1). During decoding, decoder usually can not solve the problem of morphological variability of words (caused by morphological noise) through vocabulary, which leads to OOV. Therefore, we introduce GAN mod-

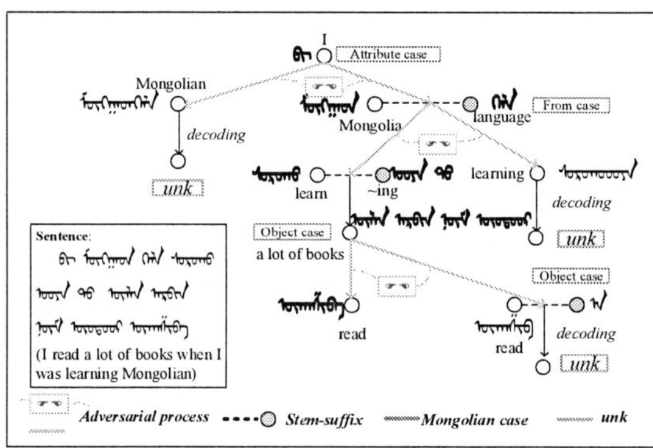

Figure 1: Given a sentence, Mongolian words face different suffix and case noises in each decoding process of the adversarial training, which are the main reasons for $< unk >$. For instance, the verb '*(learn)*' and '*(read)*' need to add the verb-suffixes and tense-cases in order to associate with nouns in Mongolian. Conversely, (*"learning"*) and (*read+' '*), which are confused by suffixes and cases, do not appear in the vocabulary. This will directly cause $<unk>$ appear in the decoding process. The proposed model aims to improve the generalization ability of noise through adversarial training.

el with a value screener (VS-GAN), a generalization of GAN, which makes the adversarial training specific to the noise. The model also improves the efficiency of GAN training by value iteration network (VIN) (Tamar et al., 2016) and addresses the problem of optimal parameter updating in Reinforcement Learning(RL) training. These are our two contributions. The third contribution is a thorough empirical evaluation on four differen-

t noises. We compare several strong baselines, including MIXER (Ranzato et al., 2015), Transformer (Vaswani et al., 2017), and BR-CSGAN (Zhen et al., 2018). The experimental results show that VS-GAN achieves much better time efficiency and the newly emerged state-of-the-art result on Mongolian-Chinese MT.

2 GAN with the Value Screener

In this section, we describe the architecture of VS-GAN in detail. VS-GAN consists of the following components: generator G, value screener, and discriminator D. Given the source language sequence $\{x_1, ..., x_{N_x}\}$ with length N, G aims to generate sentences $\{y'_1, ..., y'_{N_y}\}$, which are indistinguishable by D. D attempts to discriminate between $\{y'_1, ..., y'_{N_y}\}$ and human translated ones $\{y_1, ..., y_{N_y}\}$. The value screener uses the reward information generated by G to convert the decoding cost into a simple value, and determines whether the predictions of current state need to be passed to D.

2.1 Generator G

The selection of G is individualized and targeted. In this work, we focus on long short term memory (LSTM(Graves, 2013b)) with attention mechanism and Transformer (Vaswani et al., 2017). The temporal structure of LSTM enables it to capture dependency semantics in agglutinative language. Transformer has refreshed state-of-the-art performance on several languages pairs. For the necessary policy optimization in GAN training, we focus our problem on the RL framework (Mnih et al., 2013). The approach can solve the long-term reward problem because a standard model for sequential decision making and planning is the markov decision process (MDP) (Dayan and Abbott, 2003) in RL training. G can be viewed as an agent which interacts with the external environment (the words and the context vector at every timestep). The parameters of agent define a policy θ, whose execution results in the agent is selecting an action $a \epsilon A$. In NMT, an action represents the prediction of the next word y'_t in the sequence at t-th timestep. After taking an action, the agent will update its internal state $s \epsilon S$ (i.e., the hidden units). RL will observe a reward $R(s, a)$ once the end of a sequence (or the maximum sequence length) is reached. We can choose any reward function, and in this case, we choose BLEU because it is the metric we used at the test time.

2.2 Value Screener

So far, the constructed G is still confused by noise because the effect of noise has not been fully utilized due to the lack of attention from D. To solve this problem, we add a VIN implemented value screener between G and D to enhance the generalization ability of G to the noise. In VIN, the $< unk >$ symbol corresponds to a low training reward, whereas the low training reward corresponds to a low value. This is what the screener wants to emphasize.

To achieve VIN, we introduce an interpretation of an approximate VI algorithm as a particular form of a standard CNN. Specifically, VI in this form, which makes learning the MDP (R., 1957; Bertsekas., 2012) parameters and reward function natural by backpropagation through the network. We can train the entire policy end-to-end on the basis of its simplification by backpropagation. For the training process, each iteration of VI algorithm can be seen as passing the previous value of V_{t-1} and reward R by a convolution layer and max-pooling layer. In this analogy, the active function in the convolution layer corresponds to the Q function. We can formulate the value iteration as:

$$y_t = max_a Q(s, a)$$
$$= max \left[R(s, a) + \sum_{t=1}^{N} P(s|s_{t-1}, a) V_{t-1} \right] \quad (1)$$

where $Q(s,a)$ indicates the value of action a under state s at t-th timestep, the reward $R(s, a)$ and discounted transition probabilities $P(s|s_{t-1}, a)$ are obtained from G which mentioned in Section 2.1. N denotes the length of the sequence. Thus, the value of sequence V_n will be produced by applying the convolution layer recurrently several times according to the length of the sentence, and for a batch, n is valued between 1 and $batchsize$ of training. The optimal value $V_{update} = Average(V_1, ..., V_{batchsize})$ is the average long-term return possible from a state. The value of current predictions represents the cost of decoding at current state. We select the value of optimal pre-training model as the initial V^* and compare it with V_{update}. Subsequently, we observe the decoding effect of the current batch; thus, we can decide the necessity of taking the negative example as an input of D. The conditions of

screening are as follows:

$$\begin{cases} \quad direct\ input\ to\ D & if\ V_{update} < V^* \\ screening\ and\ V^* = V_{update} & if\ V_{update} > V^* \end{cases} \quad (2)$$

Since VIN is simply a form of CNN, once a VIN design is selected, implementing the screener is straightforward. The networks in the experiments all require only several lines of Tensor code.

2.3 Discriminator D

We implement D on the basis of CNN. The reason for this is that CNN has advantages in dealing with variable length sequences. The CNN padding is used to transform the sentences to sequences with fixed length. A source matrix $X_{1:N}$ and a target matrix $Y_{1:N}$ are created to represent $\{x_1, ..., x_{N_x}\}$ and $\{y'_1, ..., y'_{N_y}\}$. We concatenate every k dimensional word embedding into the final matrix $x_{1:N}$ and $y_{1:N}$ respectively. A kernel $w_j \epsilon R_{l \times k}$ applies a convolutional operation to a window size of l words to produce a series of feature maps:

$$c_{ji} = a(w_j \oplus X_{i:i+l-1} + b), \quad (3)$$

where b is a bias term and $\oplus$ is the summation of element production. We use $Relu$ as the function to implement the nonlinear activation function a. Then a max-pooling operation is leveraged over the feature maps:

$$c_{j \sim max} = max(c_{j_1}, ..., c_{j_{N-l+1}}). \quad (4)$$

For different window sizes, we set the corresponding kernel to extract the valid features, and then we concatenate them to form the source sentence representation c_x for D. And the target sentence representation c_y can be extracted from the target matrix $Y_{1:N}$. Then given the source sentence, the probability that the target sentence is being real can be computed as:

$$p_D = sigmoid(T[c_x; c_y]), \quad (5)$$

where T is the transform matrix which transforms the concatenation of c_x and c_y into a 2-dimension embedding. We can get the final probability if we use the matrix of 2-dimensional mapping as the input of the sigmoid function.

2.4 Training Process

We present a standard VS-GAN training process in the form of data flow directions (Fig. 2):

• *Pre-training G with RL algorithm.* Note that we pre-train G to ensure that an optimal parameter is directly involved in training, and provides a good search space for beam search.

- *Observe the reinforcement reward.* Once the end of sentence (or the maximum sequence length) is reached, a cumulative reward matrix R is generated. The observed reward can measure the cumulative value of agent (G) in the prediction process (action) of a set of sequences.

- *Value screening.* The reward R is fed into a convolutional layer and a linear activation function. This layer corresponds to a particular action Q. The next-iteration value is then stacked with the reward and fed back into the convolutional layer N times, where N depends on the length of the sequence. Subsequently, a long-term value V_{update} is generated by decoding a sentence. The batch is screened by the set conditions, as shown in Eq.(2).

- *Stay awake.* D is dedicated to differentiating the screened negative result with the human-translated sentences, which provide the probability p_D.

- *Adversarial game.* When a win-win situation is achieved, adversarial training will converge to an optimal state. That is, G can generate confusing negative samples, and D has an efficient discrimination ability for negative and human translations. Thus, the training objective is as follows:

$$J_\theta = E_{(x,y)}[log p_D(x,y)] + E_{(x,y')}[log(1-p_D(x,y'))], \quad (6)$$

where (x,y) is the ground truth sentence pair, (x,y') is the sampled translation pair, as positive and negative training data respectively. $p_D(.,.)$ represents a probability which mentioned in D about the similarity. J_θ can be regard as a game process between maximum and minimum expectations. That is, the maximum expectation for the generation G, and the minimum expectation for D.

A common shortcoming of adversarial training in NLP applications is that it is non-trivial to design the training process, i.e., texts (Huszr, 2015). Given that the discretely sampled y' makes it difficult to back-propagate the *error signals* from D to G directly, making J_θ nondifferentiable w.r.t. $G's$ model parameters θ. To solve this problem, the Monte Carlo search under the policy of G is applied to sample the unknown tokens for the estimation of the *signals*. The objective of training G can be described as minimizing the following loss:

$$Loss = E_{(x,y')}[log(1-p_D(x,y'))]. \quad (7)$$

We use $log(1-p_D(x,y')$ as a Monte-Carlo estimation of the *signals*. By simple derivation, we can get the corresponding gradient of θ:

$$\frac{\partial Loss}{\partial \theta \sim G} = E_{y'}[log(1-p_D(x,y'))\frac{\partial}{\partial \theta \sim G}log G(y'|x)], \quad (8)$$

where $\frac{\partial}{\partial \theta \sim G}log G(y'|x)$ represents the gradients specified with parameters of the translation model based on RL. Therefore, the gradient update of parameters can be described as:

$$\theta_{\sim G} \leftarrow \theta_{\sim G} + l\frac{\partial}{\partial \theta_{\sim G}}, \quad (9)$$

where l is the learning rate, and we back propagate the gradient along negative direction. Note that we have not observed a high variance is accompanied by such a computation.

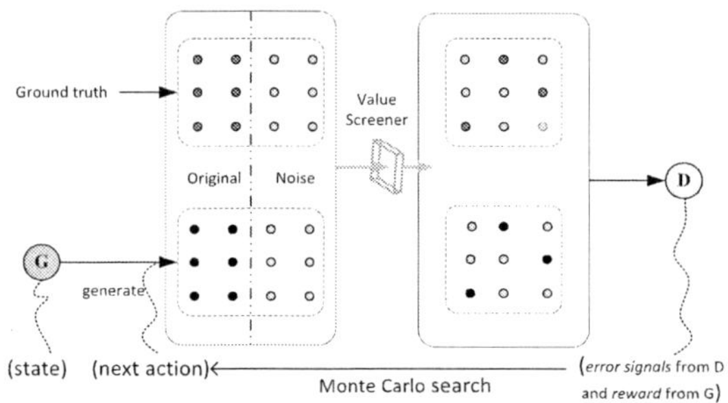

Figure 2: Presentation of VS-GAN model, in which different colors represent each component in VS-GAN.

3 Experiment and Analysis

3.1 Dataset and Noise Addition

We verify the effectiveness of our model on a language pair where one of the languages involved is agglutinative: Mongolian-Chinese(M-C). We use the data from CLDC and CWMT2017 evaluation campaign. To avoid allocating excessive training time on long sentences, all sentence pairs longer than 50 words either on the source or target side are discarded. Finally, by adding noise, we divide the training data of Mongolian into five categories[3]:{Original, BPE[4], Original&Suffixes, Original&Case, Original&Suffixes&Case}. For the target Chinese besides BPE processing, we adopt character granularity to provide a smaller unit corresponding to the morphological noise. Some effective work on morphological segmentation (Ataman D, 2017; ThuyLinh Nguyen, 2010) can be ap-

---

[3](Original&*) represents a mixed sample of the original data and the * segmentation of the original data.

[4]Note that BPE can only represent an open vocabulary through the variable-length character sequence, it is *insensitive* to morphological noise.

plied to agglutinative language. However, in order to be more specific and accurately, we perform independent-developed Mongolian segmenter. The final training corpus consists of about 230K original sentences (including 1000 validation and 1000 test) and corresponding pseudo-data sentences. We tried several num-operands of BPE[5] on the data set, and the final selection is: Mongolian: 35,000, Chinese: 15,000.

3.2 Experimental Setup

We select three strong baselines. Transformer presents an outstanding approach to most MT tasks. MIXER addresses exposure bias problem in traditional NMT well through RL, and BR-CSGAN is among the best endeavors to introduce the generative adversarial training into NMT.

The screening conditions mentioned in Section 2 enable the model to be trained efficiently. One problem is that under such conditions, V will gradually increase. Therefore, in the screening process, one situation should be considered, e.g., in $batch_1$ $\{V_1 = 1, ..., V_n = 10\}$, $V_{update} = 5.5$, in $batch_2$ $\{V_1 = 4, ..., V_n = 6\}$, $V_{update} = 5$. We have observed that $batch_1$ has worse sentences worth noting by D. However, because of the higher average value, the $batch_1$ will be screened out. In fact, we insist that such an operation is still reasonable, because the higher value batches occur only at the end of the training, and the n-gram natural of BLEU calculation indicates that the $batch_2$ needs more attention.

For the LSTM and MIXER, we set the dimension of word embedding as 512 and dropout rate as 0.1/0.1/0.3. We use a beam search with a beam size of 4 and length penalty of 0.6. For the Transformer, the Transformer_base configuration in (Vaswani et al., 2017) is an effective experience setting for our experiments. We set the G to generate 500 negative examples per iteration, and the number for Monte Carlo search is set as 20.

3.3 Main Results and Analysis

We mainly analyze the experimental results in three aspects: BLEU evaluation, the number of $< unk >$ symbols in the translations, and the time efficiency of model training.

• **BLEU** We use BLEU (Papineni et al., 2002) score as an evaluation metric to measure the sim-

ilarity degree between the generation and the human translation.

For G, we select the model with 50 epochs of pre-training as the initial state, and 80 adversarial training epochs is used to joint train G and D. The results (Table 1) show that the GAN-based model is obviously superior to baseline systems in any kind of noisy corpus, and VS-GAN performs better than each baseline with average 2-3 BLEU. For the same model, the added noise provides the excellent generalization ability in testing, a notable result shows that VS-GAN improves 3.8 BLEU on the basis of the original corpus by adding both two kinds of noise. We notice that in the training of adding case noise only, the effect of VS-GAN is not outstanding. The reason for this is that the individual Mongolian-case is not obviously 'helpful' to the production of $< unk >$ symbol in Mongolian, so the screener is insensitive to it.

• **UNK** We count the number of $< unk >$ symbols in each system with 50 epochs of training to

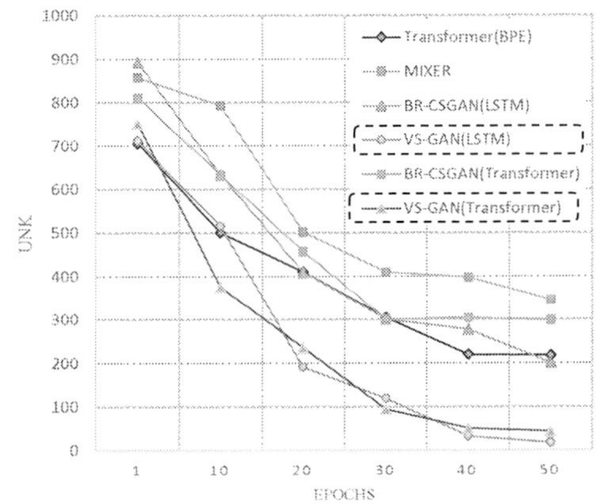

Figure 3: Number of $< unk >$ symbols in the translations of different models in each epoch.

translate the source sentences (Fig. 3). For BR-CSGAN and VS-GAN, we directly count the number of $< unk >$ symbols in the negative example.

In comparison with Transformer, MIXER optimizes BLEU through RL training, which can directly enhance the BLEU score of the translation. However, in terms of UNK, it is inefficient. The optimal initial state cannot be effectively maintained in the rest of the training (orange lines). We can see that the change of BLEU coincides with the change of UNK number in combination with Table 1 and Fig. 3. Furthermore, we note that UNK not only affects the accuracy of source word decoding, but also affects the semantic prediction of

---

[5]https://github.com/rsennrich/subword-nmt

Table 1: Training time consuming and BLEU score of systems under different noise modes. We stop the pre-training of G (including Transformer and LSTM) until the validation accuracy achieves at δ which is set to 0.6 in BR-CSGAN and VS-GAN. For the pre-training of D, we consider the threshold of classification accuracy and set it to 0.7.

	Original	BPE	Original&suffixes	Original&Case	Original&Suffixes&Case
MIXER(Ranzato et al., 2015)	29.7	26	30.4	28.6	31.3
BR-CSGAN (G:LSTM)(Zhen et al., 2018)	$29.9\|(15+17)h$	$30.8\|(21+30)h$	$31.7\|(22+25)h$	$31.1\|(15+19)h$	$32.3\|(27+32)h$
VS-GAN (*G:LSTM*)	$29.6\|(15+\underline{11})h$	$31.5\|(21+\underline{18})h$	$32.5\|(22+\underline{19})h$	$30.8\|(15+\underline{15})h$	$\star\textbf{\textit{35.4}}\|(27+\underline{21})h$
Transformer(Vaswani et al., 2017)	30.5	31.5	30.2	29.8	30.5
BR-CSGAN (G:Transformer)(Zhen et al., 2018)	$27.4\|(22+29)h$	$28\|(27+34)h$	$28.9\|(23+25)h$	$28.1\|(22+30)h$	$32.1\|(38+36)h$
VS-GAN (*G:Transformer*)	$28.8\|(22+\underline{18})h$	$31.1\|(27+\underline{26})h$	$32\|(23+\underline{18})h$	$29.4\|(22+\underline{18})h$	$\textbf{\textit{33.2}}\|(38+\underline{22})h$

the entire sentence in translation.

• **Training Efficiency** In terms of training efficiency, we compared the two GAN-based models by counting the time of pre-training and adversarial training(italics in Table 1), (e.g., 15 + 17 indicates 15 h of pre-training and 17 h of adversarial training). Reinforcement pre-training is the same for BR-CSGAN and VS-GAN. In adversarial training, VS-GAN has a remarkable time reduction in each noise training strategy. This result depends on the screener for negative generations, so that D can regulate G, following UNK directly. Such combination of structures can converge to an optimal state rapidly. From the results in Table1, in the case of the two GANs the training time for the LSTM is shorter than for the Transformer. We attribute this to two reasons: i) the time consumed by LSTM is mainly used to explore long-distance dependencies in sequences. However, most of our corpus consists of short sentences (<50 words), which bridges the gap between LSTM and Transformer and even exceeds Transformer (when it achieves the same accuracy of validation set). i-i) in fact, according to our extensive experimental results on Mongolian-based NMT(including Mongolian-Chinese and Mongolian-Cyrillic Mongolian), Transformer usually converges slower than LSTM when the corpus size exceeds *0.2M*.

4 Conclusion

We propose a GAN model with an additional VIN approximation of value screener to solve the UNK problem in Mongolian→Chinese MT, which is caused by the change of suffixes or component cases in Mongolian and the limited vocabulary. In our experiment, we adopt the pretreatment method on the basis of noise addition to enhance the generalization ability of the model for UNK problem. Experimental results show that our approach surpasses the state-of-the-art results in a variety of noise-based training strategies and significantly saves training time. In future research, we will focus more on the combination of GAN and language features to enhance other agglutinative language NMT tasks, such as the guidance of syntax tree for GAN training. On the contrary, it is also a worthwhile attempt to modify the grammar tree constructed by adversarial training.

5 Acknowledgments

This study is supported by the Natural Science Foundation of Inner Mongolia (No.2018MS06005), and Mongolian Language Information Special Support Project of Inner Mongolia (No.MW-2018-MGYWXXH-302).

References

Turchi M et al. Ataman D, Negri M. 2017. Linguistically motivated vocabulary reduction for neural machine translation from turkish to english. *The Prague Bulletin of Mathematical Linguistics*, 108(1):331–342.

Dzmitry Bahdanau, Kyunghyun Cho, and Yoshua Bengio. 2014. Neural machine translation by jointly learning to align and translate. *arXiv*, 1409(0473).

D Bertsekas. 2012. Dynamic programming and optimal control. *Athena Scientific*, (04).

Xilun Chen, Yu Sun, and et al. 2016. Adversarial deep averaging networks for cross-lingual sentiment classification. In *Association for Computational Linguistics (ACL)*, pages 557–570.

P. Dayan and L F Abbott. 2003. Theoretical neuroscience: Computational and mathematical modelling of neural systems. *Journal of Cognitive Neuroscience*, 15(1):154–155.

Jonas Gehring, Michael Auli, David Grangier, and et al. 2017. Convolutional sequence to sequence learning. In *International conference on machine learning(ICML)*, pages 1243–1252.

Alex Graves. 2013a. Generating sequences with recurrent neural networks. *arXiv preprint arXiv*, 1308(0850).

Alex Graves. 2013b. Generating sequences with recurrent neural networks. *arXiv preprint arXiv*, 1308(0850).

Caglar Gulcehre, Sungjin Ahn, and et al. 2016. Pointing the unknown words. In *Association for computational linguistics (ACL)*, pages 140–149.

Karl Moritz Hermann, Tom Kocisk, and et al. 2015. Teaching machines to read and comprehend. In *Neural Information Processing Systems (NIPS)*, pages 1693–1701.

Ferenc Huszr. 2015. How (not) to train your generative model: Scheduled sampling, likelihood, adversary? *Computer Science*, 1511(05101).

Sbastien Jean, Kyunghyun Cho, Roland Memisevic, and Yoshua Bengio. 2015. On using very large target vocabulary for neural machine translation. In *International joint conference on natural language processing (IJCNLP)*, pages 1–10.

Minh-Thang Luong, Ilya Sutskever, and et al. 2015. Addressing the rare word problem in neural machine translation. In *International joint conference on natural language processing (IJCNLP)*, pages 11–19.

Tom Mikolov, Stefan Kombrink, Luk Burget, and et al. 2011. Extensions of recurrent neural network language model. In *International conference on acoustics, speech, and signal processing*, pages 5528–5531.

Volodymyr Mnih, Koray Kavukcuoglu, David Silver, and et al. 2013. Playing atari with deep reinforcement learning. *arXiv*, 1312(5602).

Frederic Morin and Yoshua Bengio. 2005. Hierarchical probabilistic neural network language model. In *International conference on artificial intelligence and statistics (Aistats)*, volume 5, pages 246–252.

Kishore Papineni, Salim Roukos, Todd Ward, and Wei-Jing Zhu. 2002. Bleu: a method for automatic evaluation of machine translation. In *Proceedings of the 40th annual meeting on association for computational linguistics(ACL)*, pages 311–318.

Bellman R. 1957. Terminal control, time lags, and dynamic programming. *National Academy of Sciences of the United States of America*, 43(10):927–930.

Marc'Aurelio Ranzato, Sumit Chopra, and et al. 2015. Sequence level training with recurrent neural networks. *arXiv*, 1511(06732).

Rico Sennrich, Barry Haddow, and Alexandra Birch. 2016. Neural machine translation of rare words with subword units. In *Association for computational linguistics (ACL)*, pages 1715–1725.

Ilya Sutskever, Oriol Vinyals, and Quoc V. Le. 2014. Sequence to sequence learning with neural networks. In *Conference and Workshop on Neural Information Processing Systems (NIPS)*, pages 3104–3112.

A Tamar, Y Wu, G Thomas, and et al. 2016. Value iteration networks. In *Neural Information Processing Systems (NIPS)*, pages 2154–2162.

Noah A.Smith. ThuyLinh Nguyen, Stephan Vogel. 2010. Nonparametric word segmentation for machine translation. In *Proceedings of the International Conference on Computational Linguistics, (COLING10)*, pages 815–823.

Ashish Vaswani, Noam Shazeer, and et al. 2017. Attention is all you need. In *Conference and Workshop on Neural Information Processing Systems (NIPS)*, pages 5998–6008.

L Wu, Y Xia, L Zhao, and et al. 2018. Adversarial neural machine translation. In *Asian Conference on Machine Learning (ACML)*, pages 374–385.

Lantao Yu, Weinan Zhang, Jun Wang, and Yong Yu. 2016. Seqgan: Sequence generative adversarial nets with policy gradient. In *The Association for the Advancement of Artificial Intelligence (AAAI)*, pages 2852–2858.

Yuan Zhang, Regina Barzilay, and Tommi Jaakkola. 2017. Aspect-augmented adversarial networks for domain adaptation. *Transactions of the Association for Computational Linguistics*, 5(1):515–528.

Fan K et al. Zhang Y, Gan Z. 2017. Adversarial feature matching for text generation. In *Proceedings of the International conference on machine learning, (ICML17)*, pages 4006–4015.

Yang Zhen, Chen Wei, Wang Feng, and Xu Bo. 2018. Improving neural machine translation with conditional sequence generative adversarial nets. In *The North American Chapter of the Association for Computational Linguistics (NAACL)*, pages 1346–1355.

Unsupervised Pretraining for Neural Machine Translation
Using Elastic Weight Consolidation

Dušan Variš
Charles University,
Faculty of Mathematics and Physics
Malostranské náměstí 25
118 00 Prague, Czech Republic
`varis@ufal.mff.cuni.cz`

Ondřej Bojar
Charles University,
Faculty of Mathematics and Physics
Malostranské náměstí 25
118 00 Prague, Czech Republic
`bojar@ufal.mff.cuni.cz`

Abstract

This work presents our ongoing research of unsupervised pretraining in neural machine translation (NMT). In our method, we initialize the weights of the encoder and decoder with two language models that are trained with monolingual data and then fine-tune the model on parallel data using Elastic Weight Consolidation (EWC) to avoid forgetting of the original language modeling tasks. We compare the regularization by EWC with the previous work that focuses on regularization by language modeling objectives.

The positive result is that using EWC with the decoder achieves BLEU scores similar to the previous work. However, the model converges 2-3 times faster and does not require the original unlabeled training data during the fine-tuning stage.

In contrast, the regularization using EWC is less effective if the original and new tasks are not closely related. We show that initializing the bidirectional NMT encoder with a left-to-right language model and forcing the model to remember the original left-to-right language modeling task limits the learning capacity of the encoder for the whole bidirectional context.

1 Introduction

Neural machine translation (NMT) using sequence to sequence architectures (Sutskever et al., 2014; Bahdanau et al., 2014; Vaswani et al., 2017) has become the dominant approach to automatic machine translation. While being able to approach human-level performance (Popel, 2018), it still requires a huge amount of parallel data, otherwise it can easily overfit. Such data, however, might not always be available. At the same time, it is generally much easier to gather large amounts of monolingual data, and therefore, it is interesting to find ways of making use of such data. The simplest

strategy is to use backtranslation (Sennrich et al., 2016), but it can be rather costly since it requires training a model in the opposite translation direction and then translating the monolingual corpus.

It was suggested by Lake et al. (2017) that during the development of a general human-like AI system, one of the desired characteristics of such a system is the ability to learn in a continuous manner using previously learned tasks as building blocks for mastering new, more complex tasks. Until recently, continuous learning of neural networks was problematic, among others, due to the catastrophic forgetting (McCloskey and Cohen, 1989). Several methods were proposed (Li and Hoiem, 2016; Aljundi et al., 2017; Zenke et al., 2017), however, they mainly focus only on adapting the whole network (not just its parts) to new tasks while maintaining good performance on the previously learned tasks.

In this work, we present an unsupervised pretraining method for NMT models using Elastic Weight Consolidation (Kirkpatrick et al., 2017). First, we initialize both encoder and decoder with source and target language models respectively. Then, we fine-tune the NMT model using the parallel data. To prevent the encoder and decoder from forgetting the original language modeling (LM) task, we regularize their weights individually using Elastic Weight Consolidation based on their importance to that task. Our hypothesis is the following: by forcing the network to remember the original LM tasks we can reduce overfitting of the NMT model on the limited parallel data.

We also provide a comparison of our approach with the method proposed by Ramachandran et al. (2017). They also suggest initialization of the encoder and decoder with a language model. However, during the fine-tuning phase they use the original language modeling objectives as an additional training loss in place of model regular-

Proceedings of the ACL 2019, Student Research Workshop, pages 130–135
Florence, Italy, July 28th-August 2nd, 2019. ©2019 Association for Computational Linguistics

ization. Their approach has two main drawbacks: first, during the fine-tuning phase, they still require the original monolingual data which might not be available anymore in a life-long learning scenario. Second, they need to compute both machine translation and language modeling losses which increases the number of operations performed during the update slowing down the fine-tuning process. Our proposed method addresses both problems: it requires only a small held-out set to estimate the EWC regularization term and converges 2-3 times faster than the previous method.[1]

2   Related Work

Several other approaches towards exploiting the available monolingual data for NMT have been previously proposed.

Currently, the most common method is creating synthetic parallel data by backtranslating the target language monolingual corpora using machine translation (Sennrich et al., 2016). While being consistently beneficial, this method requires a pretrained model to prepare the backtranslations. Additionally, Ramachandran et al. (2017) showed that the unsupervised pretraining approach reaches at least similar performance to the backtranslation approach.

Recently, Lample and Conneau (2019) suggested using a single cross-lingual language model trained on multiple monolingual corpora as an initialization for various NLP tasks, including machine translation. While our work focuses strictly on a monolingual language model pretraining, we believe that our work can further benefit from using cross-lingual language models.

Another possible approach is to introduce an additional reordering (Zhang and Zong, 2016) or de-noising objectives, the latter being recently employed in the unsupervised NMT scenarios (Artetxe et al., 2018; Lample et al., 2017). These approaches try to force the NMT model to learn useful features by presenting it with either shuffled or noisy sentences teaching it to reconstruct the original input.

Furthermore, Khayrallah et al. (2018) show how to prevent catastrophic forgeting during domain adaptation scenarios. They fine-tune the general-domain NMT model using in-domain data adding

---

[1]The speedup is with regard to the wall-clock time. In our experiments both EWC and the LM-objective methods require similar number of training examples to converge.

an additional cross-entropy objective to restrict the distribution of the fine-tuned model to be similar to the distribution of the original general-domain model.

3   Elastic Weight Consolidation

Elastic Weight Consolidation (Kirkpatrick et al., 2017) is a simple, statistically motivated method for selective regularization of neural network parameters. It was proposed to counteract catastrophic forgetting in neural networks during a life-long continuous training. The previous work described the method in the context of adapting the whole network for each new task. In this section, we show that EWC can be also used to preserve only parts of the network that were relevant for the previous task, thus being potentially useful for compositional learning.

To justify the choice of the parameter constraints, Kirkpatrick et al. (2017) approach the neural network training as a Bayesian inference problem. To put it into the context of NMT, we would like to find the most probable network parameters θ, given a parallel data D_{mt} and monolingual data D_{src} and D_{tgt} for source and target languages, respectively:

$$p(\theta|D_{mt} \cup D_{src} \cup D_{tgt}) = \frac{p(D_{mt}|\theta)p(\theta|D_{src} \cup D_{tgt})}{p(D_{mt})} \tag{1}$$

Equation 1 holds, assuming datasets D_{mt}, D_{src} and D_{tgt} being mutually exclusive. The probability $p(D_{mt}|\theta)$ is the negative of the MT loss function and $p(\theta|D_{src} \cup D_{tgt})$ is the result of the unsupervised pretraining. We can assume that during the unsupervised pretraining, the parameters θ_{src} of the encoder are independent of the parameters θ_{tgt} of the decoder. Furthermore, we assume that the parameters of the encoder are independent of the target-side monolingual data and the parameters of the decoder are independent of the source-side monolingual data. Given these assumptions, we can express the posterior probability $p(\theta|D_{src} \cup D_{tgt})$ in the following way:

$$p(\theta|D_{src} \cup D_{tgt}) = p(\theta_{src}|D_{src})p(\theta_{tgt}|D_{tgt}) \tag{2}$$

Probabilities $p(\theta_{src}|D_{src})$ and $p(\theta_{tgt}|D_{tgt})$ are given by the pretrained source and target language models respectively. The true posterior probabilities given by the language models are intractable during fine-tuning, however, similarly to the work of Kirkpatrick et al. (2017), we can estimate $p(\theta_{src}|D_{src})$ as Gaussian distribution using Laplace approximation (MacKay, 1992), with mean given by the pretrained parameters θ_{src} and variance given by a diagonal of the Fisher information matrix F_{src}. Then, we can add the following regularization term to our loss function:

$$L_{ewc-src}(\theta) = \sum_{i, \theta_i \subset \theta_{src}} \frac{\lambda}{2} F_{src,i}(\theta_i - \theta^{\star}_{src,i})^2 \quad (3)$$

The model parameters not present during the language model pretraining are ignored by the regularization term. Analogically, the same can be applied for the target-side posterior probability $p(\theta_{tgt}|D_{tgt})$ giving a target-side regularization term $L_{ewc-tgt}$.

In the following section, we show that these regularization terms can be useful in a low-resource machine translation scenario. Since we do not necessarily need to preserve the knowledge of the original language modeling tasks, we focus on using them only as prior knowledge to prevent overfitting during the fine-tuning.

4 Experiments

In this section, we present the results of our experiments with EWC regularization and compare them with the previously proposed regularization by language modeling objectives.

4.1 Model Description

In all experiments, we use the self-attentive Transformer network (Vaswani et al., 2017) because it is the current state-of-the-art NMT architecture, providing us with a strong baseline. In general, it follows the standard encoder-decoder paradigm, with encoder creating hidden representations of the input tokens based on their surrounding context and decoder generating the output tokens autoregressively while attending to the source sentence token representations and tokens it generated in the previous decoding steps.[2]

We use Transformer with 6 layers in both encoder and decoder. We set the dimension of the hidden states to 512 and the dimension of the feedforward layer to 2048. We use multi-head attention with 16 attention heads. To simplify the pretraining process, we use a separate vocabulary for source and target languages, each containing around 32k subwords. We use separate embeddings in the encoder and decoder. In the decoder, we tie the embeddings with the output softmax layer (Press and Wolf, 2017). During both pretraining and fine tuning, we use Adam optimizer (Kingma and Ba, 2014) and gradient clipping. We set the initial learning rate to 3.1, use a linear warm-up for 33500 training steps and then decay the learning rate exponentially. We set the training batch size to a maximum of 2048 tokens per batch together with sentence bucketing for more efficient training. We set dropout to 0.1. During the final evaluation, we use beam search decoding with beam size of 8 and length normalization set to 1.0.

When pretraining the encoder and decoder, we use identical network parameters. We train each language model to maximize the probability of each word in a sentence using its leftward context. To pretrain the decoder, we use the decoder architecture from Transformer with encoder-attention sub-layer removed due to the lack of source sentences. Later, we initialize the NMT decoder with the language model weights and the encoder-attention weights by a normal distribution. We reset all training-related variables (learning rate, Adam moments) during the NMT initialization.

For simplicity, we apply the same approach for the encoder pretraining. In Section 4.2, we discuss the drawbacks of our encoder pretraining and suggest possible improvements. In all experiments, we set the weight λ of each EWC regularization term to 0.02.

The model implementation is available in Neural Monkey[3] (Helcl and Libovický, 2017) framework for sequence-to-sequence modeling.

4.2 Dataset and Evaluation

In our experiments, we focused on the low-resource Basque-to-English machine translation task featured in IWSLT 2018.[4] We used the parallel data provided by IWSLT organizers, consisting of 5,600 in-domain sentence pairs (TED Talks) and around 940,000 general-domain sentence pairs. During pretraining, we used Basque Wikipedia for source language model and News-

---

[2]For more details about the architecture, see the original paper.

[3]https://github.com/ufal/neuralmonkey
[4]https://sites.google.com/site/iwsltevaluation2018/TED-tasks

		SRC	TGT	ALL
Baseline	15.68	–	–	–
Backtrans.	19.65	–	–	–
LM best	–	13.96	15.56	16.83
EWC best	–	10.77	**15.91**	14.10
LM ens.	–	15.16	16.60	17.14
EWC ens.	–	10.73	**16.63**	14.66

Table 1: Comparison of the previous work (LM) with the proposed method (EWC). We compared models with only pretrained encoder (SRC), pretrained decoder (TGT) and both (ALL). All pretrained language models contained 3 layers. We compared both single best models and ensemble (using checkpoint averaging) of 4 best checkpoints. Results where the proposed method outperformed the previous work are in bold.

Commentary 2015 provided by WMT[5] for target language model. Both corpora contain close to 3 million sentences. We used UDPipe[6] (Straka and Straková, 2017) to split the monolingual data to sentences and SentencePiece[7] to prepare the subword tokenization. We used the subword models trained on the monolingual data to preprocess the parallel data.

During training, we used development data provided by IWSLT 2018 organizers which contains 1,140 parallel sentences. To approximate the Fisher Information Matrix diagonal of the pretrained Basque and English language models, we used the respective parts of the IWSLT validation set. For final evaluation, we used the IWSLT 2018 test data consisting of 1051 sentence pairs.

Table 1 compares the performance of the models fine-tuned using the LM objective regularization and the EWC regularization. First, we can see that using EWC when only the decoder was pretrained slightly outperforms the previous work. On the other hand, our method fails when used in combination with the encoder initialization by the source language model. The reason might be a difference between the original LM task that is trained in a left-to-right autoregressive fashion while the strength of the Transformer encoder is in modelling of the whole left-and-right context for each source token. The learning capacity of

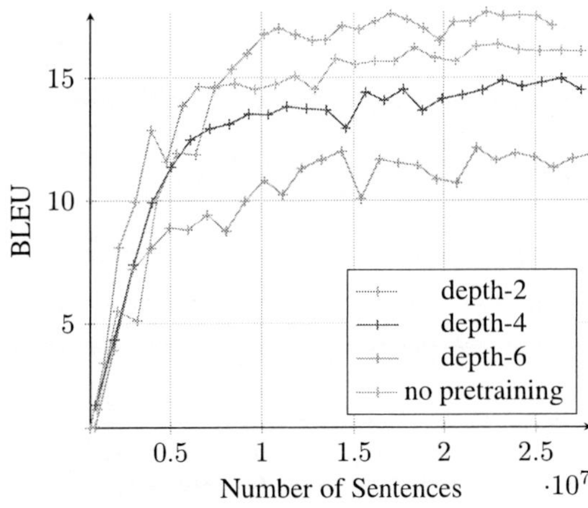

Figure 1: Performance of MT models where only the encoder was initialized by the language model of varying depths and then regularized by EWC. We include the performance of the MT system that was not pretrained for comparison.

the encoder is therefore restricted by forcing it to remember a task that is not so closely related to the sentence encoding in Transformer NMT. Figure 1 supports our claim: the deeper the pretrained language model and therefore more layers regularized by EWC, the lower the performance of the fine-tuned NMT system. We think that this behaviour can be mitigated by initializing the encoder with a language model that considers the whole bidirectional context, e.g. a recently introduced BERT encoder (Devlin et al., 2018). We leave this for our future work.

In addition to improving model performance, EWC converges much faster than the previously introduced LM regularizer. Figure 2 shows that the model fine-tuned without LM regularization converged in about 10 hours, while it took around 20-30 hours to converge when LM regularization was in place. Note, that all models converged after seeing a similar number of training examples, however, computing the LM loss for regularization introduces an additional computation overhead. The main benefit of both EWC and LM-based regularization is apparent here, too. The non-regularized model quickly overfits.

As the comparison to the model trained on the backtranslated monolingual corpus shows, none of our regularization methods can match this simple but much more computationally demanding benchmark.

133

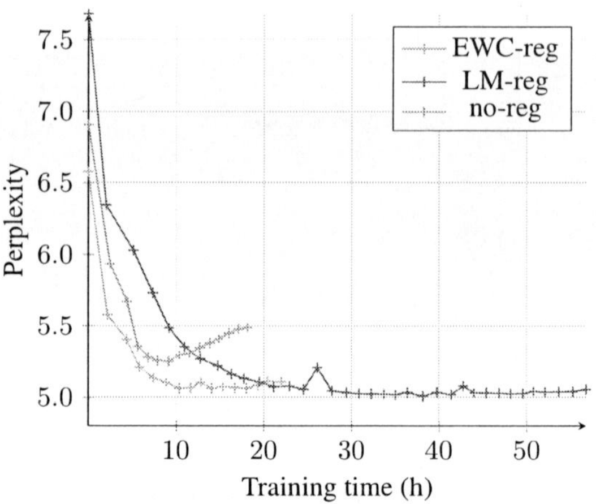

Figure 2: Comparison of relative convergence times (measured by perplexity) of models where only the decoder was pretrained. The models were regularized using EWC, LM objective or were not using any regularization (no reg.). All models were trained on the same number of training examples ($\sim$27M sentences). All used a pretrained LM with 3 Transformer layers.

5 Conclusion

We introduced our work in progress, and exploration of model regularization of NMT encoder and decoder parameters based on their importance for previously learned tasks and its application in the unsupervised pretraining scenario. We documented that our method slightly improves the NMT performance (compared to the baseline as well as the previous work of LM-based regularization) when combined with a pretrained target language model. We achieve this improvement at a reduced training time.

We also showed that the method is less effective if the original language modeling task used to pretrain the NMT encoder is too different from the task learned during the fine-tuning. We plan to further investigate whether we can gain improvements by using a different pretraining method for the encoder and how much this task mismatch relates to the learning capacity of the encoder.

Acknowledgments

This work has been in part supported by the project no. 19-26934X (NEUREM3) of the Czech Science Foundation, by the Charles University SVV project number 260 453 and by the grant no. 1140218 of the Grant Agency of the Charles University.

References

R. Aljundi, P. Chakravarty, and T. Tuytelaars. 2017. Expert gate: Lifelong learning with a network of experts. In *2017 IEEE Conference on Computer Vision and Pattern Recognition (CVPR)*, volume 00, pages 7120–7129.

Mikel Artetxe, Gorka Labaka, Eneko Agirre, and Kyunghyun Cho. 2018. Unsupervised neural machine translation. In *Proceedings of the Sixth International Conference on Learning Representations*.

Dzmitry Bahdanau, Kyunghyun Cho, and Yoshua Bengio. 2014. Neural machine translation by jointly learning to align and translate. *CoRR*, abs/1409.0473.

Jacob Devlin, Ming-Wei Chang, Kenton Lee, and Kristina Toutanova. 2018. Bert: Pre-training of deep bidirectional transformers for language understanding.

Jindřich Helcl and Jindřich Libovický. 2017. Neural Monkey: An Open-source Tool for Sequence Learning. *The Prague Bulletin of Mathematical Linguistics*, (107):5–17.

Huda Khayrallah, Brian Thompson, Kevin Duh, and Philipp Koehn. 2018. Regularized training objective for continued training for domain adaptation in neural machine translation. In *Proceedings of the 2nd Workshop on Neural Machine Translation and Generation*, pages 36–44, Melbourne, Australia. Association for Computational Linguistics.

Diederik P. Kingma and Jimmy Ba. 2014. Adam: A Method for Stochastic Optimization. *CoRR*, abs/1412.6980.

James Kirkpatrick, Razvan Pascanu, Neil C. Rabinowitz, Joel Veness, Guillaume Desjardins, Andrei A. Rusu, Kieran Milan, John Quan, Tiago Ramalho, Agnieszka Grabska-Barwinska, Demis Hassabis, Claudia Clopath, Dharshan Kumaran, and Raia Hadsell. 2017. Overcoming catastrophic forgetting in neural networks. *Proceedings of the National Academy of Sciences of the United States of America*, 114 13:3521–3526.

Brenden M. Lake, Tomer D. Ullman, Joshua B. Tenenbaum, and Samuel J. Gershman. 2017. Building machines that learn and think like people. *Behavioral and Brain Sciences*, 40:e253.

Guillaume Lample and Alexis Conneau. 2019. Cross-lingual language model pretraining. *arXiv preprint arXiv:1901.07291*.

Guillaume Lample, Ludovic Denoyer, and Marc'Aurelio Ranzato. 2017. Unsupervised machine translation using monolingual corpora only. *CoRR*, abs/1711.00043.

Zhizhong Li and Derek Hoiem. 2016. Learning without forgetting. In *European Conference on Computer Vision*, pages 614–629. Springer.

David J. C. MacKay. 1992. A practical bayesian framework for backpropagation networks. *Neural Computation*, 4(3):448–472.

Michael McCloskey and Neil J. Cohen. 1989. Catastrophic interference in connectionist networks: The sequential learning problem. *The Psychology of Learning and Motivation*, 24:104–169.

Martin Popel. 2018. CUNI transformer neural MT system for WMT18. In *Proceedings of the Third Conference on Machine Translation, Volume 2: Shared Tasks*, volume 2, pages 486–491, Stroudsburg, PA, USA. Association for Computational Linguistics, Association for Computational Linguistics.

Ofir Press and Lior Wolf. 2017. Using the output embedding to improve language models. In *Proceedings of the 15th Conference of the European Chapter of the Association for Computational Linguistics: Volume 2, Short Papers*, pages 157–163, Valencia, Spain. Association for Computational Linguistics.

Prajit Ramachandran, Peter J. Liu, and Quoc V. Le. 2017. Unsupervised pretraining for sequence to sequence learning. In *Proceedings of the 2017 Conference on Empirical Methods in Natural Language Processing, EMNLP 2017, Copenhagen, Denmark, September 9-11, 2017*, pages 383–391.

Rico Sennrich, Barry Haddow, and Alexandra Birch. 2016. Improving neural machine translation models with monolingual data. In *Proceedings of the 54th Annual Meeting of the Association for Computational Linguistics (Volume 1: Long Papers)*, pages 86–96, Berlin, Germany. Association for Computational Linguistics.

Milan Straka and Jana Straková. 2017. Tokenizing, pos tagging, lemmatizing and parsing ud 2.0 with udpipe. In *Proceedings of the CoNLL 2017 Shared Task: Multilingual Parsing from Raw Text to Universal Dependencies*, pages 88–99, Vancouver, Canada. Association for Computational Linguistics.

Ilya Sutskever, Oriol Vinyals, and Quoc V Le. 2014. Sequence to sequence learning with neural networks. In *Advances in neural information processing systems*, pages 3104–3112.

Ashish Vaswani, Noam Shazeer, Niki Parmar, Jakob Uszkoreit, Llion Jones, Aidan N Gomez, Lukasz Kaiser, and Illia Polosukhin. 2017. Attention is all you need. In I. Guyon, U. V. Luxburg, S. Bengio, H. Wallach, R. Fergus, S. Vishwanathan, and R. Garnett, editors, *Advances in Neural Information Processing Systems 30*, pages 6000–6010. Curran Associates, Inc.

Friedemann Zenke, Ben Poole, and Surya Ganguli. 2017. Continual learning through synaptic intelligence. In *Proceedings of the 34th International Conference on Machine Learning, ICML 2017, Sydney, NSW, Australia, 6-11 August 2017*, pages 3987–3995.

Jiajun Zhang and Chengqing Zong. 2016. Exploiting source-side monolingual data in neural machine translation. In *Proceedings of the 2016 Conference on Empirical Methods in Natural Language Processing*, pages 1535–1545. Association for Computational Linguistics.

Māori Loanwords: A Corpus of New Zealand English Tweets

David Trye
Computing and Mathematical Sciences
University of Waikato, New Zealand
dgt12@students.waikato.ac.nz

Andreea S. Calude
School of General and Applied Linguistics
University of Waikato, New Zealand
andreea.calude@waikato.ac.nz

Felipe Bravo-Marquez
Department of Computer Science
University of Chile & IMFD
fbravo@dcc.uchile.cl

Te Taka Keegan
Computing and Mathematical Sciences
University of Waikato, New Zealand
tetaka.keegan@waikato.ac.nz

Abstract

Māori loanwords are widely used in New Zealand English for various social functions by New Zealanders within and outside of the Māori community. Motivated by the lack of linguistic resources for studying how Māori loanwords are used in social media, we present a new corpus of New Zealand English tweets. We collected tweets containing selected Māori words that are likely to be known by New Zealanders who do not speak Māori. Since over 30% of these words turned out to be irrelevant (e.g., *mana* is a popular gaming term, *Moana* is a character from a Disney movie), we manually annotated a sample of our tweets into relevant and irrelevant categories. This data was used to train machine learning models to automatically filter out irrelevant tweets.

1 Introduction

One of the most salient features of New Zealand English (NZE) is the widespread use of Māori words (loanwords), such as *aroha* (love), *kai* (food) and *Aotearoa* (New Zealand). See ex. (1) specifically from Twitter (note the informal, conversational style and the Māori loanwords emphasised in bold).

(1) Led the **waiata** for the **manuhiri** at the **pōwhiri** for new staff for induction week. Was told by the **kaumātua** I did it with **mana** and integrity.

The use of Māori words has been studied intensively over the past thirty years, offering a comprehensive insight into the evolution of one of the youngest dialects of English – New Zealand English (Calude et al., 2017; Daly, 2007, 2016; Davies and Maclagan, 2006; De Bres, 2006; Degani and Onysko, 2010; Kennedy and Yamazaki, 1999; Macalister, 2009, 2006a; Onysko and Calude, 2013). One aspect which is missing in

this body of work is the online discourse presence of the loanwords - almost all studies come from (collaborative) written language (highly edited, revised and scrutinised newspaper language, Davies and Maclagan 2006; Macalister 2009, 2006a,b; Onysko and Calude 2013, and picture-books, Daly 2007, 2016), or from spoken language collected in the late 1990s (Kennedy and Yamazaki, 1999).

In this paper, we build a corpus of New Zealand English tweets containing Māori loanwords. Building such a corpus has its challenges (as discussed in Section 3.1). Before we discuss these, it is important to highlight the uniqueness of the language contact situation between Māori and (NZ) English.

The language contact situation in New Zealand provides a unique case-study for loanwords because of a number of factors. We list three particularly relevant here. First, the direction of lexical transfer is highly unusual, namely, from an endangered indigenous language (Māori) into a dominant lingua franca (English). The large-scale lexical transfer of this type has virtually never been documented elsewhere, to the best of our knowledge (see summary of current language contact situations in Stammers and Deuchar 2012, particularly Table 1, p. 634).

Secondly, because Māori loanwords are "New Zealand's and New Zealand's alone" (Deverson, 1991, p. 18-19), and above speakers' consciousness, their ardent study over the years provides a fruitful comparison of the use of loanwords across genres, contexts and time.

Finally, the aforementioned body of previous research on the topic is rich and detailed, and still rapidly changing, with loanword use being an increasing trend (Macalister, 2006a; Kennedy and Yamazaki, 1999). However, the jury is still out regarding the reasons for the loanword use (some hypotheses have been put forward), and the pat-

Proceedings of the ACL 2019, Student Research Workshop, pages 136–142
Florence, Italy, July 28th-August 2nd, 2019. ©2019 Association for Computational Linguistics

terns of use across different genres (it is unclear how language formality influences loanword use).

We find that Twitter data complements the growing body of work on Māori loanwords in NZE, by adding a combination of institutional and individual linguistic exchanges, in a non-editable online platform. Social media language shares properties with both spoken and written language, but is not exactly like either. More specifically, Twitter allows for creative expression and lexical innovation (Grieve et al., 2017).

Our Twitter corpus was created by following three main steps: collecting tweets over a ten-year period using "query words" (Section 3.1), manually labelling thousands of randomly-sampled tweets as "relevant" or "irrelevant" (Section 3.2), and then training a classifier to obtain automatic predictions for the relevance of each tweet and deploying this model on our target tweets, in a bid to filter out all those which are "irrelevant" (Section 3.3). As will be discussed in Section 2, our corpus is not the first of its kind but is the first corpus of New Zealand English tweets and the first collection of online discourse built specifically to analyse the use of Māori loanwords in NZE. Section 4 outlines some preliminary findings from our corpus and Section 5 lays out plans for future work.

2   Related Work

It is uncontroversial that Māori loanwords are both productively used in NZE and increasing in popularity (Macalister, 2006a). The corpora analysed previously indicate that loanword use is highly skewed, with some language users leading the way – specifically Māori women (Calude et al., 2017; Kennedy and Yamazaki, 1999), and with certain topics of discourse drawing significantly higher counts of loanwords than others – specifically those related to Māori people and Māori affairs, *Māoritanga* (Degani, 2010). The type of loanwords being borrowed from Māori is also changing. During the first wave of borrowing, some two-hundred years ago, many flora and fauna words were being borrowed; today, it is social culture terms that are increasingly adopted, e.g., *aroha* (love), *whaea* (woman, teacher), and *tangi* (Māori funeral), see Macalister (2006a). However, the data available for loanword analysis is either outdated (Calude et al., 2017; Kennedy and Yamazaki, 1999), or exclusively formal and highly edited (mainly newspaper language, Macalister 2006a; Davies and Maclagan 2006; Degani 2010), so little is known about Māori loanwords in recent informal NZE interactions – a gap we hope to address here.

With the availability of vast amounts of data, building Twitter corpora has been a fruitful endeavour in various languages, including Turkish (Şimşek and Özdemir, 2012; Çetinoglu, 2016), Greek (Sifianou, 2015), German (Scheffler, 2014; Cieliebak et al., 2017), and (American) English (Huang et al., 2016) (though notably, not New Zealand English, while a modest corpus of te reo Māori tweets does exist, Keegan et al. 2015). Twitter corpora of mixed languages are tougher to collect because it is not straightforward to detect mixed language data automatically. Geolocations can help to some extent, but they have limitations (most users do not use them to begin with). Recent work on Arabic has leveraged the presence of distinct scripts – the Roman and Arabic alphabet – to create a mixed language corpus (Voss et al., 2014), but this option is not available to us. Māori has traditionally been a spoken (only) language, and was first written down in the early 1800s by European missionaries in conjunction with Māori language scholars, using the Roman alphabet (Smyth, 1946). Our task is more similar to studies such as Das and Gambäck (2014) and Çetinoglu (2016), who aim to find a mix of two languages which share the same script (in their case, Hindi and English, and Turkish and German, respectively), but our method for collecting tweets is not user-based; instead we use a set of target query words, as detailed in Section 3.1.

3   The Corpus

In this section, we describe the process of building the Māori Loanword Twitter Corpus (hereafter, the *MLT Corpus*)[1]. This process consists of three main steps, as depicted in Figure 1.

3.1   Step 1: Collecting Tweets

In order to facilitate the collection of relevant data for the *MLT Corpus*, we compiled a list of 116 target loanwords, which we will call "query words".

---

[1]The corpus is available online at `https://kiwiwords.cms.waikato.ac.nz/corpus/`. Note that we have only released the tweet IDs, together with a download script, in accordance with Twitter's terms and conditions. We have also released the list of query words used.

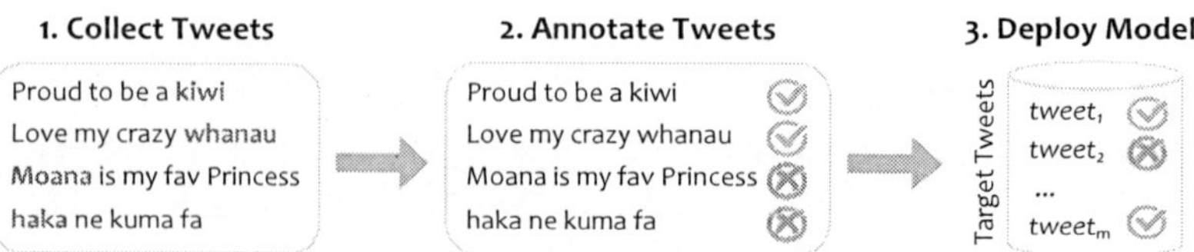

Figure 1: The corpus-building process.

Most of these are individual words but some are short phrasal units (*tangata whenua*, people of the land; *kapa haka*, cultural performance). The list is largely derived from Hay (2018) but was modified to exclude function words (such as numerals) and most proper nouns, except five that have native English counterparts: *Aotearoa* (New Zealand), *Kiwi(s)* (New Zealander(s)), *Māori* (indigenous New Zealander), *Pākehā* (European New Zealander), *non-Māori* (non-indigenous New Zealander). We also added three further loanwords which we deemed useful for increasing our data, namely *haurangi* (drunk), *wairangi* (drugged, confused), and *pōrangi* (crazy).

Using the Twitter Search API, we harvested 8 million tweets containing at least one query word (after converting all characters to lowercase). The tweets were collected diachronically over an eleven year period, between 2007-2018. We ensured that tweets were (mostly) written in English by using the *lang:en* parameter.

A number of exclusions and further adjustments were made. With the aim of avoiding redundancy and uninformative data, retweets and tweets with URLs were discarded. Tweets in which the query word was used as part of a username or mention (e.g., @*happy_kiwi*) were also discarded. For those query words which contained macrons, we found that users were inconsistent in their macron use. Consequently, we consolidated the data by adjusting our search to include both the macron and the non-macron version (e.g., both *Māori* and *Maori*). We also removed all tweets containing fewer than five tokens (words), due to insufficient context of analysis.

Owing to relaxed spelling conventions on Twitter (and also the use of hashtags), certain query words comprising multiple lexical items were stripped of spaces in order to harvest all variants of the phrasal units (e.g., *kai moana* and *kaimoana*). As *kai* was itself a query word (in its own right), we excluded tweets containing *kai moana* when searching for tweets containing *kai* (and repeated this process with similar items).

After inspecting these tweets, it was clear that a large number of our query words were polysemous (or otherwise unrelated to NZE), and had introduced a significant amount of noise into the data. The four main challenges we encountered are described below.

First, because Twitter contains many different varieties of English, NZE being just one of these, it is not always straightforward to disentangle the dialect of English spoken in New Zealand from other dialects of English. This could be a problem when, for instance, a Māori word like *Moana* (sea) is used in American English tweets to denote the Disney movie (or its main character).

Secondly, Māori words have cognate forms with other Austronesian languages, such as Hawaiian, Samoan and Tongan, and many speakers of these languages live and work (and tweet) in New Zealand. For instance, the word *wahine* (woman) has the same written form in Māori and in Hawaiian. But cognates are not the only problematic words. Homographs with other, genealogically-unrelated languages can also pose problems. For instance, the Māori word *hui* (meeting) is sometimes used as a proper noun in Chinese, as can be seen in the following tweet: "Yo is Tay Peng Hui okay with the tip of his finger?".

Proper nouns constitute a third problematic aspect in our data. As is typical for many language contact situations where an indigenous language shares the same geographical space as an incoming language, Māori has contributed many place names and personal names to NZE, such as *Timaru*, *Aoraki*, *Titirangi*, *Hēmi*, *Mere* and so on. While these proper nouns theoretically count as loanwords, we are less interested in them than in content words because the use of the former does not constitute a choice, whereas the use of the latter does (in many cases). The "choice" of whether to use a loanword or whether to use a native English word (or sometimes a native English phrase) is interesting to study because it provides insights into idiolectal lexical preferences (which words different speakers or writers prefer in given contexts) and relative borrowing success rates (Calude et al., 2017; Zenner et al., 2012).

Finally, given the impromptu and spontaneous nature of Twitter in general, we found that certain Māori words coincided with misspelled versions of intended native English words, e.g., *whare* (house) instead of *where*.

The resulting collection of tweets, termed the *Original Dataset*, was used to create the *Raw Corpus*, as explained below.

3.2 Step 2: Manually Annotating Tweets

We decided to address the "noisy" tweets in our data using supervised machine learning. Two coders manually inspected a random sample of 30 tweets for each query word, by checking the word's context of use, and labelled each tweet as "relevant" or "irrelevant". For example, a tweet like that in example (1) would be coded as relevant and one like " awesome!! Congrats to Tangi :)", would be coded as irrelevant (because the query word *tangi* is used as a proper noun). Since 39 of the query words consistently yielded irrelevant tweets (at least 90% of the time), these (and the tweets they occurred in) were removed altogether from the data. Our annotators produced a total of $3,685$ labelled tweets for the remaining 77 query words, which comprise the *Labelled Corpus* (see Tables 1 and 4; note that irrelevant tweets have been removed from the latter for linguistic analysis).

Assuming our coded samples are representative of the real distribution of relevant/irrelevant tweets that occur with each query word, it makes sense to also discard the 39 "noisy" query words from our *Original Dataset*. In this way, we created the (unlabelled) *Raw Corpus*, which is a fifth of the size (see Table 4).

We computed an inter-rater reliability score for our two coders, based on a random sample of 200 tweets. Using Cohen's Kappa, we calculated this value to be 0.87 ("strong"). In light of the strong agreement between the initial coders, no further coders were enlisted for the task.

3.3 Step 3: Automatically Extracting Relevant Tweets

The next step was to train a classifier using the *Labelled Corpus* as training data, so that the resulting model could be deployed on the *Raw Corpus*. Our goal is to obtain automatic predictions for the relevance of each tweet in this corpus, according to probabilities given by our model.

We created (stratified) test and training sets that maintain the same proportion of relevant and irrelevant tweets associated with each query word in the *Labelled Corpus*. We chose to include 80% of these tweets in the training set and 20% in the test set (see Table 1 for a break-down of relevant and irrelevant instances).

	Train	Test	Total
Relevant	$1,995$	500	$2,495$
Irrelevant	954	236	$1,190$
Total	$2,949$	736	$3,685$

Table 1: Dataset statistics for our labelled tweets. This Table shows the relevant, irrelevant and total number of instances (i.e., tweets) in the independent training and test sets.

Using the *AffectiveTweets* package (Bravo-Marquez et al., 2019), our labelled tweets were transformed into feature vectors based on the word n-grams they contain. We then trained various classification models on this transformed data in Weka (Hall et al., 2009). The models we tested were 1) Multinomial Naive Bayes (McCallum et al., 1998) with unigram attributes and 2) L2-regularised logistic regression models with different word n-gram features, as implemented in LIB-LINEAR[2]. We selected Multinomial Naive Bayes as the best model because it produced the highest AUC, Kappa and weighted average F-Score (see Table 2 for a summary of results). Overall, logistic regression with unigrams performed the worst, yielding (slightly) lower values for all three measures.

After deploying the Multinomial Naive Bayes model on the *Raw Corpus*, we found that 1,179,390 tweets were classified as relevant and 448,652 as irrelevant (with probability threshold = 0.5).

Table 3 shows examples from our corpus of each type of classification. Some tweets were falsely classified as "irrelevant" and some were falsely classified as "relevant". A short explanation why the irrelevant tweets were coded as such is given in brackets at the end of each tweet.

We removed all tweets classified as irrelevant,

---

[2]https://www.csie.ntu.edu.tw/~cjlin/liblinear/

	AUC	Kappa	F-Score
Multinomial Naive Bayes			
$n = 1$	**0.872**	**0.570**	**0.817**
Logistic Regression			
$n = 1$	0.863	0.534	0.801
$n = 1, 2$	0.868	**0.570**	0.816
$n = 1, 2, 3$	0.869	0.560	0.811
$n = 1, 2, 3, 4$	0.869	0.563	0.813
$n = 1, 2, 3, 4, 5$	0.869	0.556	0.810

Table 2: Classification results on the test set. The best results for each column are shown in **bold**. The value of n corresponds to the type of word n-grams included in the feature space.

thereby producing the *Processed Corpus*. A summary of all three corpora is given in Table 4.

4 Preliminary Findings

As we are only just beginning to sift through the *MLT Corpus*, we note two particular sets of preliminary findings.

First, even though our corpus was primarily geared up to investigate loanword use, we are finding that, unlike other NZE genres analysed, the Twitter data exhibits use of Māori which is more in line with code-switching than with loanword use, see ex. (2-3). This is particularly interesting in light of the reported increase in te reo Māori language tweets (Keegan et al., 2015).

(2) **Mōrena e hoa!** We must really meet IRL when I get back to Tāmaki Makaurau! You have a fab day too!

(3) Heh! **He porangi toku ngeru** - especially at 5 in the morning!! **Ata marie e hoa ma**. I am well thank you.

Secondly, we also report the use of hybrid hashtags, that is, hashtags which contain a Māori part and an English part, for example *#mycrazywhanau, #reostories, #Matarikistar, #bringitonmana, #growingupkiwi, #kaitoputinmyfridge*. To our knowledge, these hybrid hashtags have never been analysed in the current literature. Hybrid hashtags parallel the phenomenon of hybrid compounds discussed by Degani and Onysko (2010). Degani and Onysko report that hybrid compounds are both productive and semantically novel, showing that the borrowed words take on reconceptualised meanings in their adoptive language (2010, p.231).

	Irrelevant tweets	Relevant tweets
f(x)<0.5 Classified irrelevant	**Haka ne!** And i know even the good guys get blood for body (0.282, foreign language)	son didnt get my chop ciggies 2day so stopped talking 2 him. he just walked past and gave me the **maori** eyebrow lift and a smile. were friends (0.337)
	Whare has the year gone (0.36, misspelling)	Shorts and bare feet in this **whare** (0.41)
	chegar na **morena** e falar can i be your girlfriend can i (0.384, foreign language)	**Tangata whenua** charged for killing 6 #kererū for **Kai** meanwhile forestry corps kill off widespread habitat for millions #efficiency #doc (0.306)
f(x)≥0.5 Classified relevant	**Te Wanganga o Aotearoa's** moving to a new campus in Palmy, but their media person has refused to talk to us about it. #whatajoke (0.998, proper noun)	Our whole worldview as Maori is **whanau** based. **Pakeha** call it nepotism, tribalism, gangsterism, LinkedInism blah de blah. It's our way of doing stuff and it's not going to change to suit another point of view. (0.995)
	I cant commit to anything but if I were to commit to one song, it would be **kiwi** - harry styles (0.791, proper noun)	**Kia ora koutou** - does anyone know the **te reo** word for Cornwall? (1.0)
	Why am I getting headaches out of no **whero** never get them :(I guess its all the stress (0.542, spelling mistake)	The New Zealand team do another energetic **haka** though (0.956)

Table 3: A selection of tweets and their classification types. The first three irrelevant tweets were classified correctly (i.e. true negatives), as were the last three relevant tweets (i.e. true positives). Function $f(x)$ corresponds to the posterior probability of the "relevant" class. The entries in brackets for the irrelevant examples correspond to the values of $f(x)$ and the reason why the target word was coded as irrelevant.

	Raw	Labelled	Processed
Tokens (words)	28,804,640	49,477	21,810,637
Tweets	1,628,042	2,495	1,179,390
Tweeters (authors)	604,006	1,866	426,280

Table 4: A description of the *MLT Corpus'* three components (namely, the *Raw Corpus*, *Labelled Corpus* and *Processed Corpus*), which were harvested using the same 77 query words.

5 Conclusions and Future Work

This paper introduced the first purpose-built corpus of Māori loanwords on Twitter, as well as a methodology for automatically filtering out irrelevant data via machine learning. The *MLT Corpus* opens up a myriad of opportunities for future work.

Since our corpus is a diachronic one (i.e., all tweets are time-stamped), we are planning to use it for testing hypotheses about language change. This is especially desirable in the context of New Zealand English, which has recently undergone considerable change as it comes into the final stage of dialect formation (Schneider, 2003).

Another avenue of future research is to automatically identify other Māori loanwords that are not part of our initial list of query words. This could be achieved by deploying a language detector tool on every unique word in the corpus (Martins and Silva, 2005). The "discovered" words could be used as new query words to further expand our corpus.

In addition, we intend to explore the meaning of our Māori loanwords using distributional semantic models. We will train popular word embeddings algorithms on the *MLT Corpus*, such as *Word2Vec* (Mikolov et al., 2013) and *FastText* (Bojanowski et al., 2017), and identify words that are close to our loanwords in the semantic space. We predict that these neighbouring words will enable us to understand the semantic make-up of our loanwords according to their usage.

Finally, we hope to extrapolate these findings by deploying our trained classifier on other online discourse sources, such as *Reddit* posts. This has great potential for enriching our understanding of how Māori loanwords are used in social media.

6 Acknowledgements

The authors would like to thank former Honours student Nicole Chan for a preliminary study on Māori Loanwords in Twitter. Felipe Bravo-Marquez was funded by Millennium Institute for Foundational Research on Data. Andreea S. Calude acknowledges the support of the NZ Royal Society Marsden Grant. David Trye acknowledges the generous support of the Computing and Mathematical Sciences group at the University of Waikato.

References

Piotr Bojanowski, Edouard Grave, Armand Joulin, and Tomas Mikolov. 2017. Enriching word vectors with subword information. *Transactions of the Association for Computational Linguistics*, 5:135–146.

Felipe Bravo-Marquez, Eibe Frank, Bernhard Pfahringer, and Saif M. Mohammad. 2019. AffectiveTweets: a Weka package for analyzing affect in tweets. *Journal of Machine Learning Research*, 20:1–6.

Andreea Simona Calude, Steven Miller, and Mark Pagel. 2017. Modelling loanword success–a sociolinguistic quantitative study of Māori loanwords in New Zealand English. *Corpus Linguistics and Linguistic Theory*.

Özlem Çetinoglu. 2016. A Turkish-German code-switching corpus. In *International Conference on Language Resources and Evaluation*.

Mark Cieliebak, Jan Milan Deriu, Dominic Egger, and Fatih Uzdilli. 2017. A twitter corpus and benchmark resources for German sentiment analysis. In *5th International Workshop on Natural Language Processing for Social Media, Boston, MA, USA, December 11, 2017*, pages 45–51. Association for Computational Linguistics.

Nicola Daly. 2007. Kūkupa, koro, and kai: The use of Māori vocabulary items in New Zealand English children's picture books.

Nicola Daly. 2016. Dual language picturebooks in English and Māori. *Bookbird: A Journal of International Children's Literature*, 54(3):10–17.

Amitava Das and Björn Gambäck. 2014. Identifying languages at the word level in code-mixed Indian social media text.

Carolyn Davies and Margaret Maclagan. 2006. Māori words–read all about it: Testing the presence of 13 māori words in four New Zealand newspapers from 1997 to 2004. *Te Reo*, 49.

Julia De Bres. 2006. Maori lexical items in the mainstream television news in New Zealand. *New Zealand English Journal*, 20:17.

Marta Degani. 2010. The Pakeha myth of one New Zealand/Aotearoa: An exploration in the use of Maori loanwords in New Zealand English. *From international to local English–and back again*, pages 165–196.

Marta Degani and Alexander Onysko. 2010. Hybrid compounding in New Zealand English. *World Englishes*, 29(2):209–233.

Tony Deverson. 1991. New Zealand English lexis: the Maori dimension. *English Today*, 7(2):18–25.

Jack Grieve, Andrea Nini, and Diansheng Guo. 2017. Analyzing lexical emergence in Modern American English online. *English Language & Linguistics*, 21(1):99–127.

Mark Hall, Eibe Frank, Geoffrey Holmes, Bernhard Pfahringer, Peter Reutemann, and Ian H Witten. 2009. The WEKA data mining software: an update. *ACM SIGKDD explorations newsletter*, 11(1):10–18.

Jennifer Hay. 2018. What does it mean to "know a word?". In *Language and Society Conference of NZ in November 2018 in Wellington, NZ*, Wellington, NZ.

Yuan Huang, Diansheng Guo, Alice Kasakoff, and Jack Grieve. 2016. Understanding US regional linguistic variation with twitter data analysis. *Computers, Environment and Urban Systems*, 59:244–255.

Te Taka Keegan, Paora Mato, and Stacey Ruru. 2015. Using Twitter in an indigenous language: An analysis of Te Reo Māori tweets. *AlterNative: An International Journal of Indigenous Peoples*, 11(1):59–75.

Graeme Kennedy and Shunji Yamazaki. 1999. The influence of Maori on the Nw Zealand English lexicon. *LANGUAGE AND COMPUTERS*, 30:33–44.

John Macalister. 2006a. The Maori lexical presence in New Zealand English: Constructing a corpus for diachronic change. *Corpora*, 1(1):85–98.

John Macalister. 2006b. the Maori presence in the New Zealand English lexicon, 1850–2000: Evidence from a corpus-based study. *English World-Wide*, 27(1):1–24.

John Macalister. 2009. Investigating the changing use of Te Reo. *NZ Words*, 13:3–4.

Bruno Martins and Mário J Silva. 2005. Language identification in web pages. In *Proceedings of the 2005 ACM symposium on Applied computing*, pages 764–768. ACM.

Andrew McCallum, Kamal Nigam, et al. 1998. A comparison of event models for naive Bayes text classification. In *AAAI-98 workshop on learning for text categorization*, volume 752, pages 41–48. Citeseer.

Tomas Mikolov, Ilya Sutskever, Kai Chen, Greg S Corrado, and Jeff Dean. 2013. Distributed representations of words and phrases and their compositionality. In *Advances in neural information processing systems*, pages 3111–3119.

Alexander Onysko and Andreea Calude. 2013. Comparing the usage of Māori loans in spoken and written New Zealand English: A case study of Māori, Pākehā, and Kiwi. *New perspectives on lexical borrowing: Onomasiological, methodological, and phraseological innovations*, pages 143–170.

Tatjana Scheffler. 2014. A German twitter snapshot. In *LREC*, pages 2284–2289. Citeseer.

Edgar W Schneider. 2003. The dynamics of New Englishes: From identity construction to dialect birth. *Language*, 79(2):233–281.

Maria Sifianou. 2015. Conceptualizing politeness in Greek: Evidence from twitter corpora. *Journal of Pragmatics*, 86:25–30.

Mehmet Ulvi Şimşek and Suat Özdemir. 2012. Analysis of the relation between Turkish twitter messages and stock market index. In *2012 6th International Conference on Application of Information and Communication Technologies (AICT)*, pages 1–4. IEEE.

Patrick Smyth. 1946. *Maori Pronunciation and the Evolution of Written Maori*. Whitcombe & Tombs Limited.

Jonathan R Stammers and Margaret Deuchar. 2012. Testing the nonce borrowing hypothesis: Counter evidence from English-origin verbs in Welsh. *Bilingualism: Language and Cognition*, 15(3):630–643.

Clare R Voss, Stephen Tratz, Jamal Laoudi, and Douglas M Briesch. 2014. Finding Romanized Arabic dialect in code-mixed tweets. In *LREC*, pages 2249–2253.

Eline Zenner, Dirk Speelman, and Dirk Geeraerts. 2012. Cognitive Sociolinguistics meets loanword research: Measuring variation in the success of anglicisms in Dutch. *Cognitive Linguistics*, 23(4):749–792.

Ranking of Potential Questions

Luise Schricker
Department of Linguistics
University of Potsdam
Germany
luise.schricker@uni-potsdam.de

Tatjana Scheffler
Department of Linguistics
University of Potsdam
Germany
tatjana.scheffler@uni-potsdam.de

Abstract

Questions are an integral part of discourse. They provide structure and support the exchange of information. One linguistic theory, the Questions Under Discussion model, takes question structures as integral to the functioning of a coherent discourse. This theory has not been tested on the count of its validity for predicting observations in real dialogue data though. In the present study, a system for ranking explicit and implicit questions by their appropriateness in a dialogue is presented. This system implements constraints and principles put forward in the linguistic literature.

1 Introduction

Questions are important for keeping a dialogue flowing. Some linguistic theories of discourse structure, such as the Questions under Discussion model (Roberts, 2012, and others), view questions and their answers as the main structuring element in discourse. As not all questions are explicitly stated, the complete analysis of a discourse in this framework involves selecting adequate implicit questions from the set of questions that could potentially be asked at any given time. Correspondingly, a theory of discourse must provide constraints and principles by which these potential questions can be generated and ranked at each step in the progression of a discourse.

As a first move towards putting this linguistic model of discourse structure into practice, we implemented a ranking system for potential questions. Such a system might be used to investigate the validity of theoretic claims and to analyze data in order to enrich the theory with further insights.

The given task is also relevant for practical considerations. A system for ranking potential questions, i.e. questions that are triggered by some assertion and could be asked in a felicitous discourse, is a useful component for applications that

Q0: *What is the way things are?*
- Q1: **What did you eat for lunch?**
– A1: **I ate fries,**
– Q1.1: *How did you like the fries?*
— A1.1: **but I didn't like them at all!**
— Q1.1.1: **Why?**
—- A1.1.1: **They were too salty.**
— Q1.1.2: *What did you do?*
—- A1.1.1: **So I threw them away.**

Figure 1: Constructed example of a QUD annotated discourse. Explicit questions and answers are marked in bold typeface. Implicit questions are set in italic type.

generate dialogue, such as chatbots. At some point in a dialogue, several questions could be asked next and the most appropriate one has to be determined, for example by using a question ranker.

2 Background

2.1 The Questions-Under-Discussion Model

In 1996[1], Roberts (2012) published a seminal paper describing a framework that models discourse as a game. This game allows two kinds of moves, questions and assertions. The questions that have been accepted by the participants, also referred to as *questions under discussion* (QUDs), provide the structure of a discourse. An example discourse annotated with a question-structure is shown in Figure 1. The overall goal of the game is to answer the big question of *how things are*. The question structure is given by explicit questions that are proffered and accepted by the participants and implicit questions that can be accommodated.

We follow the variant by Riester (2019), who developed the QUD framework further and formalized the model. Riester models the question

---

[1]Here, we cite the reissued 2012 version.

Proceedings of the ACL 2019, Student Research Workshop, pages 143–148
Florence, Italy, July 28th-August 2nd, 2019. ©2019 Association for Computational Linguistics

structures as *QUD trees* and introduces the notion of assertions that trigger subsequent questions. Following Van Kuppevelt (1995), he refers to such assertions as *feeders*. Furthermore, Riester introduces three constraints on the formulation of implicit QUDs in coherent discourse. These constraints ensure that modeled discourses are well-formed. The first constraint, **Q-A-Congruence**, states that the assertions that are immediately dominated by a QUD must provide an answer for it. The second constraint, **Q-Givenness**, specifies that implicit QUDs can only consist of given or highly salient material. Finally, the third constraint, **Maximize-Q-Anaphoricity**, prescribes that as much given or salient material as possible should be used in the formulation of an implicit QUD. Implicit questions are therefore constrained by both the previous discourse and the following answer.

The notion of questions triggered by feeders was strengthened by Onea (2013) who introduces the concept of *potential questions* within a QUD discourse structure. This concept refers to questions that are licensed by some preceding discourse move. That move can be a question, but also an assertion. Depending on the context, some potential questions are more appropriate than others. In chapter 8, Onea addresses this observation by describing a number of generation and ordering principles, which are listed below. In this paper, we implement Riester's Q-Anaphoricity constraint and Onea's potential question principles as features for a question ranker, allowing us to test them on naturally occurring dialog.

2.2   Generation Principles

Follow formal hints Certain linguistic markers trigger the generation of potential questions, e.g. appositives, indefinite determiners and overanswers.

Unarticulated constituents Whenever constituents in an assertion are not articulated, questions about these constituents are generated.

Indexicals For every assertion, questions about unspecified indexicals are generated.

Rhetorical relations Any assertion licenses typical questions related to rhetorical relations, e.g. questions about the result, justification, elaboration, and explanation.

Parallelism and contrast For any question in the discourse, parallel or contrastive questions that are triggered by a following assertion should be generated as potential questions.

Animacy hierarchy Every time a human individual is introduced into the discourse, questions about this individual should be generated.

Mystery Questions about surprising objects or events that enter the discourse should be generated.

2.3   Ordering Principles

Strength Rule The Strength Rule states that more specific questions are generally better (i.e., more coherent) than less specific ones.

Normality Rule The Normality Rule predicts that a question triggered by a normal or common context is better than a question triggered by an unusual context.

2.4   Question Ranking

While the described work by Roberts, Riester, and Onea is purely theoretical, other research is practically concerned with the ranking of questions. This research does not consider the notion of potential questions though and can therefore not offer a direct point of comparison for the present study. Heilman and Smith (2010), for example, present a system for automatically generating questions from a given answering paragraph. The system overgenerates questions, which are subsequently ranked regarding the questions' acceptability given the answering text. In contrast to this, the system described in the present paper considers the assertion *preceding* the question, rather than the answer, when determining a question's felicity in discourse.

3   System

In order to investigate which role the linguistic constraints and principles play in practice, we implemented a ranking system based on the theoretical insights. The system takes an assertion and a set of potential questions triggered by this assertion as input and ranks the set of potential questions by appropriateness, given the preceding assertion.

3.1   Data

The task of implementing a system for ranking potential questions is difficult, as no datasets exist that fulfils the requirements of the input. To circumvent this problem, the required data was approximated by different data extraction schemes. We used two corpora: the test set was extracted from a small manually annotated corpus of interview fragments. The training set was mined from the Switchboard Dialog Act corpus.

The test corpus consists of eight short texts. The texts are copies of a segment of an interview with Edward Snowden[2] that was annotated with a QUD structure like the one in Figure 1 by students of the class *Questions and Models of Discourse*, held at the University of Potsdam in 2018.[3] Some preprocessing, manual and automatic, had to be done in order to ensure a consistent structure amongst the texts. The interviews were segmented into assertions and explicit and implicit questions. Assertions are often not complete sentences and the segmentation differs between the individual texts.

We extracted every assertion that was followed by a question, explicit or implicit, together with the following question. The three preceding and three next questions were saved as an approximation of the set of alternative potential questions.[4] We deemed this acceptable because it is likely that the immediately surrounding questions will be about similar topics as the assertion. The question immediately following the assertion was regarded as the correct label, i.e. the question that should be ranked highest by the system. Items that contained the same assertions were merged, which resulted in several correct labels, and a larger set of alternative potential questions per assertion.

As the test set was not sufficiently big to use for training in a machine learning setting, a second dataset was extracted from the Switchboard Dialog Act corpus (SWDA)[5] (Stolcke et al., 2000). The SWDA corpus contains spontaneous telephone conversations that are annotated with dialog acts. The reasoning behind using this corpus was that a question following an assertion in a dialog can be interpreted as the highest ranked potential question available at that point.

Similar to the extraction of the test set, assertions directly followed by a question were extracted along with the question. We considered only prototypical types of assertions and questions[6], excluding for example rhetorical questions, to avoid inconsistent items. For each item, three questions were randomly picked from the set of all questions in the corpus to arrive at a set of approximate alternative potential questions. The individual questions and assertions were cleaned from disfluency annotation. The resulting training set consists of 2777 items.

3.2 Feature Extraction

In this work, we implemented a subset of Onea's (2013) generation and ordering principles and Riester's (2019) QUD constraints as features for ranking a question following a preceding assertion. For linguistic processing spaCy (Honnibal and Montani, 2019) (e.g. dependency parsing, named entity recognition and POS tagging), NLTK (Bird et al., 2009) (wordnet, stopwords) and neuralcoref[7] (coreference resolution) were used. For features using word embeddings, a pretrained Word2vec model[8] (Mikolov et al., 2013a,b) was used, the model was handled via the gensim package (Řehůřek and Sojka, 2010). Below, the implemented features are described.

Indefinite Determiners This feature detects indefinite noun phrases in the assertion that are coreferent to some mention in the question.

Indexicals This feature analyzes whether the question is about a time or a place by searching for question phrases that inquire about a time or a place (e.g. *when*, *where* etc.).

Explanation Following Onea (2019), who draws parallels between certain patterns in discourse trees with question structures and rhetorical relations, the rhetorical relation *Explanation* is detected by searching for *why*-questions.

Elaboration The rhetorical relation *Elaboration* is linked by Onea (2019) to questions that ask

---

[2]https://edwardsnowden.com/2014/01/27/video-ard-interview-with-edward-snowden/

[3]The raw annotated files can be accessed under: https://github.com/QUD-comp/analysis-of-QUD-structures/tree/master/Snowden

[4]Incomplete datapoints from the start and end of a document, which were followed or preceded by fewer than three questions, were excluded.

[5]The version distributed by Christopher Potts (https://github.com/cgpotts/swda) was used, as well as the code he provided for better accessibility of the corpus.

[6]List of considered assertion tags: ['s', 'sd', 'sv'] (statements with or without opinions); list of considered question tags: ['qy', 'qw', '^d', 'qo', 'qr', 'qw^d'] (different syntactic sub-types of questions).

[7]https://github.com/huggingface/neuralcoref

[8]https://code.google.com/archive/p/word2vec/

about an explicit or unarticulated constituent in an assertion with a *wh*-question phrase. This is implemented by checking the question for *wh*-question phrases that enquire about properties of some NP (e.g. *which, what kind* etc.) and that are used in a non-embedded sentence.

Animacy This feature detects mentions of persons, i.e. named entities or words that belong to the Wordnet synset *person*, in the assertion and checks whether any of these are coreferent to mentions in the question.

Strength Rule I This method approximates the specificity of the question as the relation between the length of assertion and question. A question much shorter than the assertion is likely unspecific, a question much longer might talk about something else and therefore also lose specificity.

Strength Rule II Questions specific to an assertion are likely to be semantically similar to the assertion. Following this observation, the feature approximates specificity as the cosine similarity of the word vector representation of the assertion to the representation of the question. These representations are computed by adding the word vectors for the individual words.

Normality Rule This feature checks the normality of a context by first computing separately the average cosine similarities of the words within the question and within the assertion. Unexpected words in a sentence should have a lower similarity score than expected words when compared to the rest of the sentence. For example, the words *sandwich* and *ham* should have a higher similarity score than the words *sandwich* and *screws*, giving the phrase *a sandwich with ham* a higher normality score than the phrase *a sandwich with screws*. In a second step, a ratio of the normality scores of the assertion and the question is computed. If the assertion talks about an unnormal context it is normal for the question to relate to this.[9] Overall, the closer the score is to 1.0, the more normal the context of the question is, given the assertion.

Maximize Anaphoricity This method counts mentions in the question that are coreferent to something in the assertion and string matches between question and assertion that were not already counted as coreference mentions.

---

[9]Imagine the following conversation: A: *"I had a sandwich with screws yesterday."* B: *"A sandwich with screws??"* (example adapted from (Onea, 2013)). In this context, it would be rather unnormal if B did not ask about the screws.

Assertion: "It was the right thing to do."
Potential questions:
"When was this your greatest fear?"
"But isn't there anything you're afraid of?"
"Why don't you lose sleep?"
"Was it the right thing to do?"
"But are you afraid?"
"Mr. Snowden, did you sleep well the last couple of nights?"
"Is this quote still accurate?"

Figure 2: Example input for the potential question ranker from the test set. The correct following question is marked in italic.

3.3 Ranking Component

The ranking component takes an assertion and a list of potential questions as input (see Figure 2 for an example input), transforms every assertion-question pair into a feature representation, and ranks the questions based on this representation. Three modes of ranking are possible. The *Baseline* mode shuffles the questions randomly and returns them in this order.

The *Uniform* mode transforms every assertion-question pair into a scalar representation by adding up the individual features. All features based on Onea's generation principles return either 0 or 1, depending on whether the feature is present or not. Strength Rule I and the Normality Rule should return a value as close to 1.0 as possible for a high ranking question. Therefore, the absolute distance of the return value from 1.0 is subtracted from the representation. Strength Rule II and the Maximize Anaphoricity feature return continuous values. These are also added to the scalar representation. The questions are sorted by the value of the feature representation.

The *ML* (short for machine learning) mode accumulates features for an assertion-question pair into vector representations which are fed into a Random Forest classifier. The choice of using a Random Forest classifier was motivated by the amount of available training data and by considerations about transparency. Decision Trees are usually a good option for small training datasets and it's easy to analyze the patterns they learn by inspecting feature importance. Scikit-learn's (Pedregosa et al., 2011) Random Forest implementation was used. A grid search was performed on a small set of parameters to arrive at an optimal con-

Mode	Top-1	Top-3	Top-5
Baseline	19.23	46.15	65.38
Uniform	38.46	61.54	**88.46**
ML	**50.00**	**73.08**	80.77

Table 1: Results on test set. *Top-N* signifies the stage of evaluation.

Type	Utterance
Assertion	*There are significant threats*
Question	*Are there significant threats?*
Assertion	*"The greatest fear I have," and I quote you, "regarding these disclosures is nothing will change."*
Question	*But isn't there anything you're afraid of?*

Table 2: Examples of questions incorrectly ranked in top place that the assertion already answers

figuration, results for the best configuration[10] are detailed in Table 1.

4 Evaluation

The different ranking modes and classifier configs were evaluated on the test set extracted from the annotated Snowden interview. In order to get a more detailed insight into the performance of the ranking system, evaluations were done in three stages. To this end, the *Top-N accuracy* measure was used. As a result of the merging of items described in section 3.1, the average number of questions that are correct if ranked in first place is three per item, and the average number of potential questions available for ranking is 21 per item. Results are listed in Table 1.

Interestingly, the uniform mode works quite well, providing the best result in the easiest evaluation setting with an accuracy score of almost 90%. The overall best ranking system (ML mode) achieves an accuracy of 50% for ranking a correct label highest and a score of 73% for placing a correct label amongst the top three ranks. These numbers show improvements of over 30 and over 25 points compared to the random baseline.

It should be noted that the data in the training and test sets have different properties. While the training data is built from spontaneous dialogue, the test set contains QUD annotations that were added in hindsight and that are sometimes not phrased like natural speech. Training and test sets that are more similar might therefore provide better results. This experiment should be repeated in the future if a reasonably sized QUD-annotated corpus becomes available.

Furthermore, the random baseline is quite simple and might be too easy to beat. An anonymous reviewer suggested implementing a deep learning model trained for next sentence prediction as an additional baseline. While we agree that this would be worthwhile, we have to leave it for future work due to time constraints.

An additional inspection of the best performing Random Forest model's features by importance showed the three ordering constraint features, Strength Rule II, the Normality Rule and Strength Rule I in top position. This confirms the theoretic background: the ordering principles should be more important for ranking potential questions than the generation principles.

4.1 Error Analysis

In order to better understand the failings of the ranking system, the best configuration was inspected more closely in an error analysis. The most prominent error by far is ranking a question that the assertion already answers highest, instead of one that is triggered by the assertion. Some examples of this type of error are listed in Table 2.

This can be explained by the nature of the training data. As alternative potential questions were sampled randomly from the data during training, they are more likely to be about a different topic than the assertion compared to the correct question, which would enhance the importance of similarity features like Strength Rule II. An answer to a question can be as similar to the question as the assertion directly preceding a question. In a real application, questions that are answered by the preceding assertion should not be part of the set of potential questions that are fed into the system, though.

5 Conclusion

Potential questions are a concept stemming from theories that organize discourse around questions. A ranking system[11] based on these theories was

---

[10]The best configuration has *min_samples_leaf* = 5, *max_depth* = 10, and *class_weight* = {0:0.5, 1:1}.

[11]The code and data presented here have been made available for public use under a GPL-3.0 license: https://github.com/QUD-comp/ranking-potential-questions.

able to improve rankings of a small test dataset by
up to 30 percentage points compared to a random
Baseline. This system is a first step towards an implementation of the until now theoretic but influen-
tial QUD discourse model. It might be of help for
further evaluation and enrichment of these linguistic theories, but might also be useful in dialogue
generation applications, e.g. for machine dialogue
systems and chatbots.

Acknowledgements

We would like to thank the participants of the 2018
University of Potsdam class *Questions and Models of Discourse* for annotating the interview segments that were used as test data. Furthermore,
we would like to thank Bonnie Webber for the detailed and extremely valuable mentoring feedback.
Finally, we are grateful to the anonymous reviewers for their helpful comments.

References

Steven Bird, Edward Loper, and Ewan Klein.
2009. *Natural Language Processing with Python*.
O'Reilly Media Inc., Sebastopol, CA.

Michael Heilman and Noah A. Smith. 2010. Good
question! statistical ranking for question generation. In *Human Language Technologies: The 2010
Annual Conference of the North American Chapter of the Association for Computational Linguistics*,
pages 609–617. Association for Computational Linguistics.

Matthew Honnibal and Ines Montani. 2019. spacy 2:
Natural language understanding with bloom embeddings, convolutional neural networks and incremental parsing. *To appear*.

Tomas Mikolov, Kai Chen, Greg Corrado, and Jeffrey
Dean. 2013a. Efficient estimation of word representations in vector space. *CoRR*, abs/1301.3781.

Tomas Mikolov, Ilya Sutskever, Kai Chen, Greg Corrado, and Jeffrey Dean. 2013b. Distributed representations of words and phrases and their compositionality. *CoRR*, abs/1310.4546.

Edgar Onea. 2013. *Potential questions in discourse
and grammar*. Habilitation thesis, University of
Göttingen.

Edgar Onea. 2019. Underneath rhetorical relations. the
case of result. In K. v. Heusinger, E. Onea, and
M. Zimmermann, editors, *Questions in Discourse*,
volume 2. Brill, Leiden.

F. Pedregosa, G. Varoquaux, A. Gramfort, V. Michel,
B. Thirion, O. Grisel, M. Blondel, P. Prettenhofer, R. Weiss, V. Dubourg, J. Vanderplas, A. Passos, D. Cournapeau, M. Brucher, M. Perrot, and
E. Duchesnay. 2011. Scikit-learn: Machine learning
in Python. *Journal of Machine Learning Research*,
12:2825–2830.

Radim Řehůřek and Petr Sojka. 2010. Software Framework for Topic Modelling with Large Corpora. In
*Proceedings of the LREC 2010 Workshop on New
Challenges for NLP Frameworks*, pages 45–50, Valletta, Malta. ELRA.

Arndt Riester. 2019. Constructing QUD trees. In
Klaus v. Heusinger, Edgar Onea, and Malte Zimmer-
mann, editors, *Questions in Discourse*, volume 2.
Brill, Leiden.

Craige Roberts. 2012. Information structure in discourse: Towards an integrated formal theory of pragmatics. *Semantics and Pragmatics*, 5(6):1–69.

Andreas Stolcke, Klaus Ries, Noah Coccaro, Elizabeth Shriberg, Rebecca Bates, Daniel Jurafsky, Paul
Taylor, Rachel Martin, Carol Van Ess-Dykema, and
Marie Meteer. 2000. Dialogue act modeling for automatic tagging and recognition of conversational
speech. *Computational linguistics*, 26(3):339–373.

Jan Van Kuppevelt. 1995. Discourse structure, top-
icality and questioning. *Journal of linguistics*,
31(1):109–147.

Controlling Grammatical Error Correction Using Word Edit Rate

Kengo Hotate, Masahiro Kaneko, Satoru Katsumata and **Mamoru Komachi**
Tokyo Metropolitan University
`{hotate-kengo, kaneko-masahiro, satoru-katsumata}@ed.tmu.ac.jp`
`komachi@tmu.ac.jp`

Abstract

When professional English teachers correct grammatically erroneous sentences written by English learners, they use various methods. The correction method depends on how much corrections a learner requires. In this paper, we propose a method for neural grammar error correction (GEC) that can control the degree of correction. We show that it is possible to actually control the degree of GEC by using new training data annotated with word edit rate. Thereby, diverse corrected sentences is obtained from a single erroneous sentence. Moreover, compared to a GEC model that does not use information on the degree of correction, the proposed method improves correction accuracy.

1 Introduction

The number and types of corrections in a sentence containing grammatical errors written by an English learner vary from annotator to annotator (Bryant and Ng, 2015). For example, it is known that the JFLEG dataset (Napoles et al., 2017) has a higher *degree of correction* in terms of the amount of corrections per sentence than that in the CoNLL-2014 dataset (Ng et al., 2014). This is because CoNLL-2014 contains only minimal edits, whereas JFLEG contains corrections with fluency edits (Napoles et al., 2017). Similarly, the degree of correction depends on the learners because it should be personalized to the level of learners. In this study, we used *word edit rate (WER)* as an index of the degree of correction. As WER is an index that shows the number of rewritten words in sentences, the WER between an erroneous sentence and a corrected sentence can represent the degree of correction of the sentence. Figure 1 shows that the WER of the JFLEG test set is higher than that of the CoNLL-2014 test set; thus, the WER shows the degree of correction.

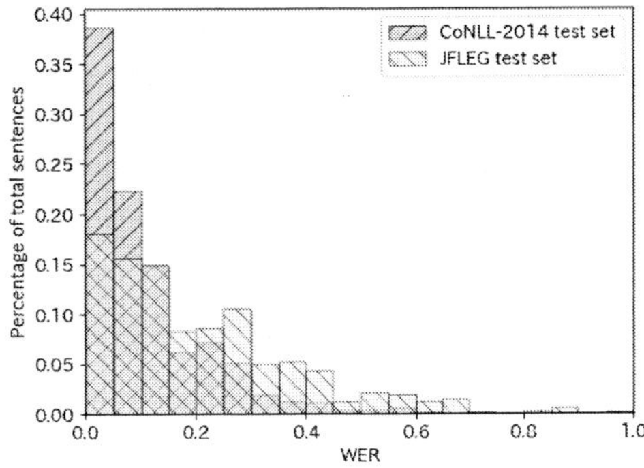

Figure 1: Histogram of the WER in one sentence.

However, existing GEC models consider only the single degree of correction suited for training corpus. Recently, neural network-based models have been actively studied for use in grammatical error correction (GEC) tasks (Chollampatt and Ng, 2018). These models outperform conventional models using phrase-based statistical machine translation (SMT) (Junczys-Dowmunt and Grundkiewicz, 2016). Nonetheless, controlling the amount of correction required to obtain an error-free sentence is not possible.

Therefore, we propose a method for neural GEC that can control the degree of correction. In the training data, in which grammatical errors are corrected, we add information about the degree of correction to erroneous sentences as WER tokens to create new training data. Then, we train the neural network model using the new training data annotated with the degree of correction. At the time of inference, this model can control the degree of correction by adding a WER token to the input. In addition, we propose a method to select and estimate the degree of correction required for each input sequence.

Proceedings of the ACL 2019, Student Research Workshop, pages 149–154
Florence, Italy, July 28th-August 2nd, 2019. ©2019 Association for Computational Linguistics

Corpus	Sent.
Lang-8	1.3M
NUCLE	16K
Extra Data (NYT 2007)	0.4M

Table 1: Summary of training data.[1]

WER Token	Min	Max	Sent.
$\langle 1 \rangle$	0.01	0.12	350K
$\langle 2 \rangle$	0.12	0.20	350K
$\langle 3 \rangle$	0.20	0.31	350K
$\langle 4 \rangle$	0.31	0.53	350K
$\langle 5 \rangle$	0.53	38.00 [2]	350K

Table 2: Thresholds of WER and number of sentences corresponding to WER tokens in the training data.

In the experiments, we controlled the degree of correction of the model for the CoNLL and JF-LEG. As a result, we confirmed that the degree of correction of the model can actually be controlled, and consequently diverse corrected sentences can be generated. Moreover, we calculated the correction accuracies of both the CoNLL-2014 test set and JFLEG test set and demonstrated that the proposed method improved the scores of both $F_{0.5}$ using the softmax score and GLEU using the language model (LM) score more than the baseline model.

The main contributions of this work are summarized as follows:

- The degree of correction of the neural GEC model can be controlled using the WER.

- The proposed method increases correction accuracy and produces diverse corrected sentences to further improve GEC.

2   Controlling the degree of correction by using WER

We propose a method to control the degree of correction of the GEC model by adding tokens based on the WER, which is calculated for all sentences in the training data. The method of calculating WER and adding WER tokens is described as follows.

First, the Levenshtein distance is calculated from the erroneous sentence and the corresponding corrected sentence in the training data. Then, WER is calculated by normalizing this distance with respect to the source length.

Second, appropriate cutoffs are selected to divide the sentences into five equal-sized subsets. Different WER tokens are defined for each subset and added to the beginning of the source sentences.

Finally, the following parallel corpus is obtained: error-containing sentences annotated with the WER token representing the correction degree at the beginning of sentences and the corresponding sentences in which errors are corrected. The GEC model is trained using this newly created training data.

At the time of inference, five kinds of output sentences are obtained for each input sentence through the WER token. Therefore, we propose two simple ranking methods to automatically decide the optimal degree of correction for each input sentence.

Softmax.   Ranking the 5 single best candidates $\mathbf{Y}$ using the sum of log probabilities of softmax score normalized by the hypothesis sentence length $|y|$. The softmax score shows whether the hypothesis sentence y is appropriate for source sentence x.

$$\hat{y} = \arg\max_{y \in \mathbf{Y}} \frac{1}{|y|} \sum_{i=1}^{|y|} \log P(y_i | y_1, \cdots, y_{i-1}, x)$$

Language model (LM).   Ranking the 5 single best candidates $\mathbf{Y}$ using the score of an n-gram LM. This score is normalized by the sentence length of the GEC model, and shows the fluency of hypothesis sentence y.

$$\hat{y} = \arg\max_{y \in \mathbf{Y}} \frac{1}{|y|} \sum_{i=1}^{|y|} \log P(y_i | y_{i-(n-1)}, \cdots, y_{i-1})$$

3   Experiments

3.1   Datasets

Table 1 summarizes the training data. We used Lang-8 (Mizumoto et al., 2012) and NUCLE (Dahlmeier et al., 2013) as the training data. The accuracy of the GEC task is known to be improved by increasing the amount of the training data (Xie et al., 2018). Therefore, we added more

---

[1]Only sentences with corrections are used, and the sentence length limit is 80 words.

[2]WER may exceed the one in which the Levenshtein distance is larger than the number of words in the target sentence.

Model	CoNLL-2013 (Dev)			CoNLL-2014 (Test)			JFLEG (Dev)	JFLEG (Test)	
	P	R	$F_{0.5}$	P	R	$F_{0.5}$	GLEU		WER
Baseline	42.19	15.28	31.20	53.20	25.18	43.52	47.92	51.77	0.10
WER Token									
$\langle 1 \rangle$	**52.45**	13.60	33.39	**60.07**	23.52	*45.83	44.85	*48.45	0.06
$\langle 2 \rangle$	47.55	17.94	**35.75**	54.64	28.41	***46.12**	47.96	*52.01	0.09
$\langle 3 \rangle$	43.38	20.05	35.19	50.48	31.45	*45.03	**49.45**	***53.59**	0.12
$\langle 4 \rangle$	40.91	**21.32**	34.56	47.43	**32.68**	43.50	49.16	*53.47	0.17
$\langle 5 \rangle$	29.48	13.98	24.13	33.77	22.95	*30.86	37.52	*42.21	0.43

Table 3: Results of GEC experiments with controlled degree of correction.

Method	CoNLL-2014 (Test)			JFLEG (Test)
	P	R	$F_{0.5}$	GLEU
Softmax	60.15	24.03	*46.25	49.07
LM	44.34	20.20	35.79	*53.87
Oracle WER	72.57	34.40	59.39	58.49
Gold WER	55.25	28.38	46.45	54.48

Table 4: Results of GEC experiments with ranking of the 5 single best candidates. The oracle WER shows the scores when selecting a corrected sentence for each erroneous sentence that maximizes the $F_{0.5}$ on CoNLL-2014 test set and GLEU on JFLEG test set. The gold WER shows the scores when using the WER token calculated from the reference in evaluation datasets.

data by introducing synthetic grammatical errors to the 2007 New York Times Annotated Corpus (LDC2008T19)[3] to the original training data in the same manner as the random noising method done by Xie et al. (2018). We used the CoNLL-2014 test set and JFLEG test set as the test sets and CoNLL-2013 dataset (Ng et al., 2013) and JFLEG dev set as the development sets, respectively.

3.2 Model

We used a multilayer convolutional encoder-decoder neural network without pre-trained word embeddings and re-scoring using the edit operation and language model features (Chollampatt and Ng, 2018) as the GEC model with the same hyperparameters. We conducted the following two experiments. First, we trained the GEC model (baseline) by using the training data as is. Second, we created new training data by adding WER tokens defined by WER to the beginning of sentences in the original training data, and used it to train a GEC model. We added five types of WER tokens to the training data,

as shown in Table 2, defined according to the WER score: $\langle 1 \rangle$ (the sentence set with the highest WER), $\langle 2 \rangle$, $\langle 3 \rangle$, $\langle 4 \rangle$, and $\langle 5 \rangle$ (the sentence set with the lowest WER).

In the ranking experiment, we used a 5-gram KenLM (Heafield, 2011) with Kneser-Ney smoothing trained on the web-scale Common Crawl corpus (Junczys-Dowmunt and Grundkiewicz, 2016).

As an evaluation method, we computed the $F_{0.5}$ score by using the MaxMatch (M^2) scorer (Dahlmeier and Ng, 2012) for the CoNLL-2013 dataset and CoNLL-2014 test set and computed the GLEU score for the JFLEG dev and test sets. In addition, we calculated the average WER of the JFLEG test set.

3.3 Controlling experiment

Table 3 shows the experimental result of controlling the degree of correction using WER. The "WER Token" models are all the same model except for each WER token added to the beginning of the all of input sentences at the time of inference.

The WER in Table 3 show that the average WER is proportional to the WER tokens added to the input sentences. Hence, the WER of the GEC model can be controlled by the WER tokens defined by WER.

The precision is the highest for the WER token $\langle 1 \rangle$ and the recall is low. In contrast, the precision is the lowest for the WER token $\langle 4 \rangle$, while the recall is the highest. Therefore, the recall is in proportional to the WER, while the precision is inversely proportion to the WER.

However, even with the WER of model $\langle 5 \rangle$ being the highest, both its precision and recall are low. In addition, the GLEU and $F_{0.5}$ scores of

---

[3]https://catalog.ldc.upenn.edu/LDC2008T19

*A statistically significant difference can be observed from the baseline ($p < 0.05$).

Source	Disadvantage is parking their car is very difficult .	WER
Reference	**The disadvantage** is **that** parking their car is very difficult .	0.33
Baseline	Disadvantage is parking their car is very difficult .	0.00
WER Token		
$\langle 1 \rangle$	Disadvantage is parking **;** their car is very difficult .	0.11
$\langle 2 \rangle$	**Disadvantages are** parking their car is very difficult .	0.22
$\langle 3 \rangle$	**The disadvantage** is parking their car is very difficult .	0.22
$\langle 4 \rangle$	**The disadvantage** is **that** parking their car is very difficult .	0.33
$\langle 5 \rangle$	**The disadvantage** is **that** their car **parking lot** is very difficult .	0.56

Table 5: Example of outputs on the JFLEG test set.

model $\langle 5 \rangle$ are the lowest. Table 2 shows the WER of the training data with WER token $\langle 5 \rangle$ is more than 0.5. The manual inspection of this training data revealed that it includes noisy data, for example, very short source sentences or very long target sentences with inserted comments not related to corrections. Consequently, the score is considered to decrease because the training fails.

The degree of correction differs between the CoNLL and JFLEG sets, as described in Section 1. In this result, the WER token with the highest score differs in CoNLL and JFLEG. Moreover, these scores are higher than the baseline scores.

The correction accuracies of both the CoNLL and JFLEG differ for each WER token. Hence, the proposed model can generate diverse corrected sentences by using the WER token.

3.4 Ranking experiment

In the controlling experiment, we obtained the 5 single best candidates with different degrees of correction. Table 4 shows the experimental results of GEC with the ranking of the 5 single best candidates. As shown, these simple ranking methods can decide the best WER token.

The row of softmax in Table 4 shows the result of the ranking of the 5 single best using the softmax score for each sentence. The result shows that the $F_{0.5}$ score of CoNLL-2014 test set is higher than the scores of the baseline. In contrast, the GLEU score of JFLEG test set is low. The WER in Table 3 shows that the GEC model does not correct much. Hence, the softmax score of the GEC model tends to be high when there are few corrections.

The result of ranking the 5 single best sentences using the LM score is shown in the LM row of Table 4. The GLEU score of JFLEG containing fluency corrections is higher than the scores of the baseline model; however, the $F_{0.5}$ score of

CoNLL-2014 test set containing minimal corrections is low. This outcome is plausible because LM prefers fluency in a sentence regardless of the input.

Table 4 shows the scores of "Oracle WER" when selecting the corrected sentence, which has a higher evaluation score than any other corrected sentences for each input sentence. As a result, $F_{0.5}$ achieves a score of 59.39 on the CoNLL-2014 test set and GLEU achieves a score of 58.49 on the JFLEG test set. These scores significantly outperform the baseline scores. This could be because the proposed model can generate diverse sentences by controlling the degree of correction. These results imply that the proposed model can be improved by selecting the best corrected sentences.

3.5 Example

Table 5 illustrates outputs of the GEC model with the addition of different WER tokens to the input sentences. This example is obtained from the outputs on the JFLEG test set for each WER token. The bold words represent the parts changed from the source sentence.

This example shows several gold edits to correct grammatical errors in the source sentence. Model $\langle 3 \rangle$ corrects only two of these errors, whereas model $\langle 4 \rangle$ covers all the parts to be corrected. Model $\langle 5 \rangle$ makes further changes although these edits are termed as erroneous corrections. This example confirms that the proposed method corrects errors with different degrees of correction. Although the output of the baseline is not corrected, the proposed method could be used to correct all the errors by performing substantial corrections by using the WER token.

3.6 Analysis

Effect of the WER token. We confirmed how accurately the WER token could control the de-

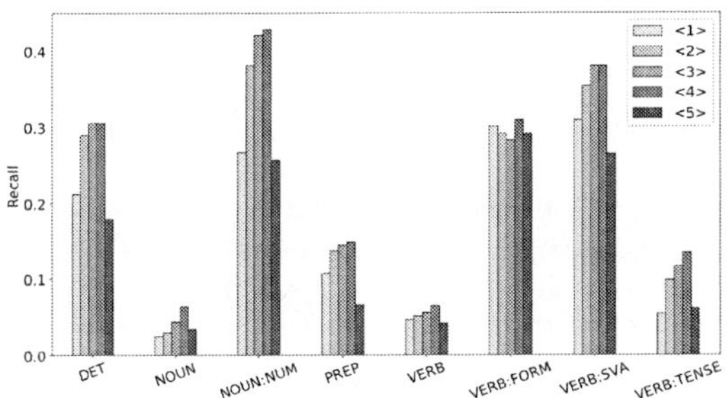

Figure 2: Comparison of the recall of each WER token per error type breakdown , which occurs more than 100 times in the CoNLL-2013 dataset.

gree of correction of model. Therefore, we determined the gold WER tokens for each sentence from the WERs calculated from erroneous and corrected sentences in the CoNLL-2014 test set and JFLEG test set, as shown in Table 2. Then, we calculated the average of the M^2 score, GLEU, and the controlling accuracy because the CoNLL-2014 test set and JFLEG test set have multiple references. The controlling accuracy is the concordance rate of the gold and system WER tokens determined from system output sentences using the gold WER token and erroneous sentences of the CoNLL-2014 test set and JFLEG test set.

The scores of $F_{0.5}$ and GLEU shown in the "Gold WER" row in Table 4 are higher than the baseline scores. However, the scores of $F_{0.5}$ and GLEU are not higher than the oracle WER. Moreover, the controlling accuracy is 62.16 for the CoNLL-2014 test set and 53.18 for the JFLEG test set. This could be because the proposed model corrects less than the degree of correction corresponding to the gold WER token. Specifically, the average number of output sentences below the degree of the correction of the gold WER token is 459.5 within 1,312 sentences in the CoNLL-2014 test set and 64 within 747 sentences in the JFLEG test set. This result shows that it is difficult to estimate of the WER from erroneous sentences. In other words, to improve the correction accuracy, considering GEC methods without relying on WER is necessary.

Error types. We calculated recall to analyze whether the degree of correction can be controlled in more detail for each error type by using ER-RANT[4] (Bryant et al., 2017) on the CoNLL-2013 dataset. Figure 2 shows the result of compari-

son of each WER token and each error type. As the WER increases, the recall increases for almost all error types except for model $\langle 5 \rangle$. Among them, the recall of DET and NOUN:NUM especially increases compared to the recall of VERB and VERB:FORM. This result also shows that the degree of correction can be controlled by using the WER.

4 Related work

Junczys-Dowmunt and Grundkiewicz (2016) used an SMT model with task-specific features, which outperformed previously published results. However, the SMT model can only correct few words or phrases based on a local context, resulting in unnatural sentences. Therefore, several methods using a neural network were proposed to ensure fluent corrections, considering the context and meaning between words. Among them, the method by Chollampatt and Ng (2018) uses a multilayer convolutional encoder-decoder neural network (Gehring et al., 2017). This model is one of the state-of-the-art models in GEC, and its implementation is currently being published[5]. However, these models cannot be controlled in terms of the degree of correction.

Kikuchi et al. (2016) proposed to control the output length by hinting about the output length to the encoder-decoder model in the text summarization task. Sennrich et al. (2016) controlled the politeness of output sentences by adding politeness information to the training data as WER tokens in machine translation. In this research, similar to Sennrich et al. (2016), we added WER indicating the degree of correction as WER tokens to the training data to control the degree of correction for the input sentences.

Similar to our method, Junczys-Dowmunt et al. (2018) and Schmaltz et al. (2017) trained a GEC model with corrective edits information to control the tendency of generating corrections.

5 Conclusion

This study showed that it is possible to control the degree of correction of a neural GEC model by creating training data with WER tokens based on the WER to train a GEC model. Therefore, diverse corrected sentences can be generated from one erroneous sentence. We also showed that the proposed method improved correction accuracy.

[4]https://github.com/chrisjbryant/errant

[5]https://github.com/nusnlp/mlconvgec2018

In the future, we would like to work on selecting the best sentence from a wide variety of corrected sentences generated by a model varying the degree of correction.

Acknowledgments

We thank Yangyang Xi of Lang-8, Inc. for kindly allowing us to use the Lang-8 learner corpus.

References

Christopher Bryant, Mariano Felice, and Ted Briscoe. 2017. Automatic annotation and evaluation of error types for grammatical error correction. In *Proc. of ACL*.

Christopher Bryant and Hwee Tou Ng. 2015. How far are we from fully automatic high quality grammatical error correction? In *Proc. of ACL*.

Shamil Chollampatt and Hwee Tou Ng. 2018. A multi-layer convolutional encoder-decoder neural network for grammatical error correction. In *Proc. of AAAI*.

Daniel Dahlmeier and Hwee Tou Ng. 2012. Better evaluation for grammatical error correction. In *Proc. of NAACL-HLT*.

Daniel Dahlmeier, Hwee Tou Ng, and Siew Mei Wu. 2013. Building a large annotated corpus of learner English: The NUS corpus of learner English. In *Proc. of BEA*.

Jonas Gehring, Michael Auli, David Grangier, Denis Yarats, and Yann N. Dauphin. 2017. Convolutional sequence to sequence learning. In *Proc. of ICML*.

Kenneth Heafield. 2011. Kenlm: Faster and smaller language model queries. In *Proc. of WMT*.

Marcin Junczys-Dowmunt and Roman Grundkiewicz. 2016. Phrase-based machine translation is state-of-the-art for automatic grammatical error correction. In *Proc. of EMNLP*.

Marcin Junczys-Dowmunt, Roman Grundkiewicz, Shubha Guha, and Kenneth Heafield. 2018. Approaching neural grammatical error correction as a low-resource machine translation task. In *Proc. of NAACL-HLT*.

Yuta Kikuchi, Graham Neubig, Ryohei Sasano, Hiroya Takamura, and Manabu Okumura. 2016. Controlling output length in neural encoder-decoders. In *Proc. of EMNLP*.

Tomoya Mizumoto, Yuta Hayashibe, Mamoru Komachi, Masaaki Nagata, and Yuji Matsumoto. 2012. The effect of learner corpus size in grammatical error correction of ESL writings. In *Proc. of COLING*.

Courtney Napoles, Keisuke Sakaguchi, and Joel Tetreault. 2017. JFLEG: A fluency corpus and benchmark for grammatical error correction. In *Proc. of EACL*.

Hwee Tou Ng, Siew Mei Wu, Ted Briscoe, Christian Hadiwinoto, Raymond Hendy Susanto, and Christopher Bryant. 2014. The CoNLL-2014 shared task on grammatical error correction. In *Proc. of CoNLL*.

Hwee Tou Ng, Siew Mei Wu, Yuanbin Wu, Christian Hadiwinoto, and Joel Tetreault. 2013. The CoNLL-2013 shared task on grammatical error correction. In *Proc. of CoNLL*.

Allen Schmaltz, Yoon Kim, Alexander Rush, and Stuart Shieber. 2017. Adapting sequence models for sentence correction. In *Proc. of EMNLP*.

Rico Sennrich, Barry Haddow, and Alexandra Birch. 2016. Controlling politeness in neural machine translation via side constraints. In *Proc. of NAACL-HLT*.

Ziang Xie, Guillaume Genthial, Stanley Xie, Andrew Ng, and Dan Jurafsky. 2018. Noising and denoising natural language: Diverse backtranslation for grammar correction. In *Proc. of NAACL-HLT*.

From brain space to distributional space:
the perilous journeys of fMRI decoding

Gosse Minnema and Aurélie Herbelot
Center for Mind/Brain Sciences
University of Trento
`gosseminnema@gmail.com`
`aurelie.herbelot@unitn.it`

Abstract

Recent work in cognitive neuroscience has introduced models for predicting distributional word meaning representations from brain imaging data. Such models have great potential, but the quality of their predictions has not yet been thoroughly evaluated from a computational linguistics point of view. Due to the limited size of available brain imaging datasets, standard quality metrics (e.g. similarity judgments and analogies) cannot be used. Instead, we investigate the use of several alternative measures for evaluating the predicted distributional space against a corpus-derived distributional space. We show that a state-of-the-art decoder, while performing impressively on metrics that are commonly used in cognitive neuroscience, performs unexpectedly poorly on our metrics. To address this, we propose strategies for improving the model's performance. Despite returning promising results, our experiments also demonstrate that much work remains to be done before distributional representations can reliably be predicted from brain data.

1 Introduction

Over the last decade, there has been a growing body of research on the relationship between neural and distributional representations of semantics (e.g., Mitchell et al., 2008; Anderson et al., 2013; Xu et al., 2016). This type of research is relevant for cognitive neuroscientists interested in how semantic information is represented in the brain, as well as to computational linguists interested in the cognitive plausibility of distributional models (Murphy et al., 2012). So far, most studies investigated the correlation between neural and distributional representations either by predicting brain activity patterns from distributional representations (Mitchell et al., 2008; Abnar et al., 2018), or by using more direct correlation analyses

like Representational Similarity Analysis (RSA; introduced in Kriegeskorte et al. 2008) or similar techniques (Anderson et al., 2013; Xu et al., 2016). Recently, however, a new model has been proposed (Pereira et al., 2018) for decoding distributional representations *from* brain images.

This new approach is different from the earlier approaches in a number of interesting ways. First of all, whereas predicting brain images from distributional vectors tells us something about how much neurally relevant information is present in distributional representations, doing the prediction in the opposite way could tell us something about how much of the textual co-occurrence information that distributional models are based on is present in the brain. Brain decoding is also interesting from an NLP point of view: the output of the model is a word embedding that could, at least in principle, be used in downstream tasks. Ultimately, a sufficiently accurate model for predicting distributional representations would amount to a sophisticated 'mind reading' device with numerous theoretical and practical applications.

Interestingly, despite being an early model and being trained on a (for NLP standards) very small dataset, Pereira et al. (2018) already report impressively high accuracy scores for their decoder. However, despite these positive results, there are reasons to doubt whether it is really possible to decode distributional representations from brain images. Given the high-dimensional nature of both neural and distributional representations, it is reasonable to expect that the mapping function between the two spaces, if it indeed exists, is potentially very complicated, and, given the inherent noisiness of fMRI data, could be very hard to learn, especially from a small dataset.

Moreover, we believe that the evaluation metrics used in Pereira et al. (2018) are too limited. Both of these metrics, *pairwise accuracy* and *rank*

155

Proceedings of the ACL 2019, Student Research Workshop, pages 155–161
Florence, Italy, July 28th-August 2nd, 2019. ©2019 Association for Computational Linguistics

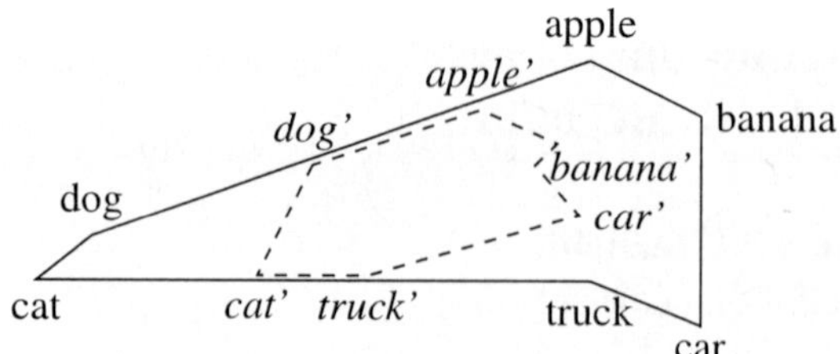

Figure 1: Hypothetical example where the predicted word embeddings (*cat'*, *apple'*, ...) are relatively close to their corresponding target word embeddings (cat, apple, ...), but are far from their correct position in absolute terms and have the wrong nearest neighbours.

accuracy, measure a predicted word embeddings's distance to its corresponding target word embedding, relative to its distance to other target word embeddings; for example, the prediction for *cat* is 'good' if it is closer to the target word embedding of *cat* than to the target word embedding of *truck* (see 3.1 for more details). Such metrics are useful for evaluating how well the original word labels can be reconstructed from the model's predictions, but do not say much about the overall quality of the predicted space. As shown in Figure 1, a bad mapping that fails to capture the similarity structure of the gold space could still get a high accuracy score. Scenarios like this are quite plausible given that cross-space mappings are known to be prone to over-fitting (and hence, poor generalization) and often suffer from 'hubness', a distortion of similarity structure caused by a lack of variability in the predicted space (Lazaridou et al., 2015).

In this paper, we fill a gap in the literature by proposing a thorough evaluation of Pereira et al. (2018), using previously untried evaluation metrics. Based on our findings, we identify possible weaknesses in the model and propose several strategies for overcoming these.

2   Related work

Our work is largely built on top of Pereira et al. (2018), which to date is the most extensive attempt at decoding meaning representations from brain imaging data. In this study (Experiment 1), fMRI images of 180 different content words were collected for 16 participants. The stimulus words were presented in three different ways: the written word plus an image representing the word, the word in a word cloud, and the word in a sentence. Thus, the dataset consists of $180 \times 3 = 540$ images

per participant. Additionally, a combined representation was created for each word by averaging the images from the three stimulus presentation paradigms. Note that data for different participants cannot be directly combined due to differences in brain organization;[1] decoders are always trained for each participant individually.

The vocabulary was selected by clustering a pre-trained GloVe space (Pennington et al., 2014)[2] consisting of 30,000 words into regions, and then manually selecting a word from each region, yielding a set of 180 content words that include nouns (both concrete and abstract), verbs, and adjectives. Next, for every participant, a vector space was created whose dimensions are voxel activation values in that participant's brain scan.[3] This (approximately) 200,000-dimensional space can be optionally reduced to 5,000 dimensions using a complex feature selection process. Finally, for every participant, a ridge regression model was trained for mapping this brain space to the GloVe space. Crucially, this model predicts each of the 300 GloVe dimensions separately, the authors' hypothesis being that variation in each dimension of semantic space corresponds to specific brain activation patterns.

The literature relating distributional semantics to neural data started with Mitchell et al. (2008), who predicted fMRI brain activity patterns from distributional representations for 60 hand-picked nouns from 12 different semantic categories (e.g. 'animals', 'vegetables', etc.). Many later studies built on top of this; for example, Sudre et al. (2012) was a similar experiment using MEG, another neuroimaging technique. Other studies (e.g., Xu et al. 2016) reused Mitchell et al. (2008)'s original dataset but experimented with different word embedding models, including distributional models such as word2vec (Mikolov et al., 2013) or GloVe, perceptual models (Anderson et al., 2013; Abnar et al., 2018) and dependency-based models (Abnar et al., 2018). Similarly, Gauthier and Ivanova (2018) reused Pereira et al. (2018)'s data and regression model but tested it on alternative sentence embedding models.

---

[1]Techniques like *hyperalignment* do allow for this, but they require very large datasets (Van Uden et al., 2018).

[2]Version 42B.300d, obtained from https://nlp.stanford.edu/projects/glove/.

[3]A voxel is a 3D pixel representing the blood oxygenation level of a small part of the brain.

3 Methods

Our work builds on top of Experiment 1 in Pereira et al. (2018) (described above) and uses the same datasets and experimental pipeline. In this section, we introduce our evaluation experiments (3.1) and our model improvement experiments (3.2).[4] Unless indicated otherwise, our models were trained on averaged fMRI images, which Pereira et al. showed to work better than using images from any of the individual stimulus presentation paradigms.

3.1 Evaluation experiments

Our evaluation experiments consist of two parts: a re-implementation of the pairwise and rank-based accuracy scores methods used in Pereira et al. (2018) and the introduction of additional evaluation metrics.

Pairwise accuracy is calculated by considering all possible pairs of words (u, v) in the vocabulary and computing the similarity between the predictions $(p_u,\ p_v)$ for these words and their corresponding target word embeddings (g_u, g_v). Accuracy is then defined as the fraction of pairs where 'the highest correlation was between a decoded vector and the corresponding text semantic vector' (Pereira et al., 2018, p. 11). Unfortunately, the original code for computing the scores was not published, but we interpret this as meaning that a pair is considered to be 'correct' iff $\max(r(p_u, g_u), r(p_v, g_v)) > \max(r(p_u, p_v), r(p_v, p_u))$, where $r(x, y)$ is the Pearson correlation between two vectors. That is, for each pair of words, all four possible combinations of the two predictions and the two golds should be considered, and the highest of the four correlations should be either between p_u and g_u or between p_v and g_v.

Rank accuracy is calculated by calculating the correlation, for every word in the vocabulary, between the predicted word embedding for that word and all of the target word embeddings, and then ranking the target word embeddings accordingly. The accuracy score for that word is then defined as $1 - \frac{\text{rank}-1}{|V|-1}$, where *rank* is the rank of the correct target word embedding (Pereira et al., 2018, p. 11). This accuracy score is then averaged over all words in the vocabulary. Rank accuracy is very similar to pairwise accuracy but is slightly stricter.

Under pairwise evaluation, it is sufficient if, for any word pair under consideration (say, *cat* and *dog*), only one of the predicted vectors is 'good': as long as the correlation between p_{cat} and g_{cat} is higher than the other correlations, the pair counts as 'correct', even if the prediction for *dog* is far off. Suppose that *dog* were the only badly predicted word in the dataset, then one could theoretically still get a pairwise accuracy score of 100%. By contrast, under rank evaluation a bad prediction for *dog* would not be 'forgiven' and the low rank of *dog* would affect the overall accuracy score, no matter how good the other predictions were.

In order to evaluate the quality of the predicted word embeddings more thoroughly, one would ideally use standard metrics such as semantic relatedness judgement tasks, analogy tasks, etc. (Baroni et al., 2014). However, this is not possible due to the limited vocabulary sizes of the available brain datasets. Instead, we test under four additional metrics that are based on well-established analysis tools in distributional semantics and elsewhere but have not yet been applied to our problem. The first two of these measure directly how close the predicted vectors are in semantic space relative to there expected location, whereas the last two measure how well the similarity structure of the semantic space is preserved.

Cosine (Cos) scores are a direct way of measuring how far each prediction is from 'where it should be', using cosine similarity as this is a standard metric in distributional semantics. Given a vocabulary V and predicted word embeddings (p_w) and target word embeddings (g_w) for every word $w \in V$, we define the cosine score for a given model as $\frac{\sum_{w \in V} \text{sim}(p_w, g_w)}{|V|}$ (i.e., the cosine similarity between each prediction and its corresponding target word embedding, averaged over the entire vocabulary).

$\mathbf{R^2}$ **scores** are a standard metric for evaluating regression models, and are useful for testing how well the value of each individual dimensions is predicted (recall that the ridge regression model predicts every dimension separately) and how much of their variation is explain by the model. We use the definition of R^2 scores from the `scikit-learn` Python package (Pedregosa et al., 2011), which defines it as the total squared distance between the predicted values and the true values relative to the total squared distance of each

---

[4]A software toolkit for reproducing all of our experiments can be found at `https://gitlab.com/gosseminnema/ds-brain-decoding`.

prediction to the mean true value:

$$R^2(y, \hat{y}) = 1 - \frac{\sum_{i=0}^{n-1}(y_i - \hat{y}_i)^2}{\sum_{i=0}^{n-1}(y_i - \bar{y})^2}$$

where y is an array of true values and $\hat{y}$ is an array of predicted values. Note that R^2 is defined over single dimensions; in order to obtain a score for the whole prediction matrix, we take the average R^2 score over all dimensions. Scores normally lie between 0 and 1 but can be negative if the model does worse than a constant model that always predicts the same value regardless of input data.

Nearest neighbour (NN) scores evaluate how well the similarity structure of the predicted semantic space matches that of the original GloVe space. For each word in V, we take its predicted and target word embeddings, and then compare the ten nearest neighbours of these vectors in their respective spaces. The final score is the mean Jaccard distance computed over all pairs of neighbour lists: $\frac{\sum_{w \in V} J(P_{10}(p_w), T_{10}(t_w))}{|V|}$, where $J(S, T) = \frac{|S \cap T|}{|S \cup T|}$ is the Jaccard distance between two sets (Lescovec et al., 2014) and $P_n(v)$ and $T_n(v)$ denote the set of n nearest neighbours (computed using cosine similarity) of a vector in the prediction space and in the original GloVe space, respectively.

Representational Similarity Analysis (RSA) is a common method in neuroscience for comparing the similarity structures of two (neural or stimulus) representations by computing the Pearson correlation between their respective similarity matrices (Kriegeskorte et al., 2008). We use it as an additional metric for evaluating how well the model captures the similarity structure of the GloVe space. This involves computing two similarity matrices of size $V \times V$, one for the predicted space and one for the target space, whose entries are defined as $P_{i,j} = r(p_i, p_j)$ and $T_{i,j} = r(t_i, t_j)$, respectively. Then, the representational similarity score can be defined as the Pearson correlation between the two upper halves of each similarity matrix: $r(\text{upper}(P), \text{upper}(T))$, where $\text{upper}(M) = [M_{2,1}, M_{3,1}, \dots, M_{n,m-1}]$ is the concatenation of all entries $M_{i,j}$ such that $i > j$.

3.2 Model improvement experiments

The second part of our work tries to improve on the results of Pereira et al. (2018)'s model, using three different strategies: (1) alternative regression models, (2) data augmentation techniques, and (3) combining predictions from different participants.

Ridge is the original ridge regression model proposed in Pereira et al. (2018). Ridge regression is a variant on linear regression that tries to avoid large weights (by minimizing the squared sum of the parameters), which is similar to applying weight decay when training neural networks; this is useful for data (like fMRI data) with a high degree of correlation between many of the input variables (Hastie et al., 2009). However, an important limitation is that, when there are multiple output dimensions, the weights for each of these dimensions are trained independently. This seems inappropriate for predicting distributional representations because values for individual dimensions in such representations do not have much inherent meaning; instead, it is the interplay between dimensions that encodes semantic information, which we would like to capture this in our regression model.

Perceptron is a simple single-layer, linear perceptron model that is conceptually very similar to Ridge, but uses gradient descent for finding the weight matrix. A possible advantage of this approach is that the weights for all dimensions are learned at the same time, which means that the model should be able to capture relationships between dimensions. The choice for a linear model is also in line with earlier work on cross-space mapping functions (Lazaridou et al., 2015). Like Ridge, Perceptron takes a flattened representation of the 5000 'best' voxels as input (see section 2). Best results were found using a model using cosine similarity as the loss function, Adam for optimization (Kingma and Ba, 2014), with a learning rate and weight decay set to 0.001, trained for 10 epochs.

CNN is a convolutional model that takes as input a 3D representation of the full fMRI image. Our hypothesis is that brain images, like ordinary photographs, contain strong correlations between spatially close pixels (or 'voxels', as they are called in the MRI literature) and could thus benefit from a convolutional approach. We kept the CNN model as simple as possible and included only a single sequence of a convolutional layer, a max-pool layer, and a fully-connected layer (with a ReLU activation function). Best results were found with the same settings as for Perceptron, and a convolutional kernel size of 3 and a pooling ker-

Model	Pair			Rank			Cos			R2			NN			RSA		
	I_B	I_A	A	I_B	I_A	A	I_B	I_A	A	I_B	I_A	A	I_B	I_A	A	I_B	I_A	A
Random	0.54	0.50	0.49	0.54	0.50	0.51	-0.04	-0.05	-0.05	-3.16	-3.19	-2.48	0.04	0.03	0.03	0.01	-0.00	-0.01
Ridge	0.86	0.76	0.93	0.84	0.73	0.91	0.14	0.09	0.22	-0.30	-0.46	-0.06	0.07	0.05	0.11	0.14	0.08	0.25
Ridge+exp2	0.89*	**0.81***	**0.94***	0.86*	**0.79***	**0.92***	0.16*	**0.11***	0.23*	-0.12*	-0.25*	-0.06*	**0.09***	**0.06***	**0.12***	0.18*	**0.13***	0.25*
Ridge+para	**0.90**	0.78	**0.94**	**0.88**	0.75	**0.92**	**0.18**	0.10	**0.24**	**-0.16**	**-0.24**	**-0.05**	**0.09**	0.05	**0.12**	**0.20**	0.11	**0.26**
Ridge+aug	0.87	0.77	0.94	0.86	0.75	0.91	0.16	0.10	**0.24**	-0.18	-0.26	-0.05	0.07	0.05	0.11	0.16	0.09	0.25
Perceptron	0.81	0.70	0.87	0.78	0.68	0.83	0.09	0.05	0.11	-0.75	-41.89	-2.64	0.05	0.04	0.07	0.09	0.05	0.16
CNN	0.72	0.59	0.76	0.70	0.60	0.76	0.07	0.04	0.12	-0.40	-1.02	-0.13	0.05	0.03	0.05	0.08	0.03	0.13

Table 1: Decoding performance of all models. I_B: score of the best individual participant; I_A: average score for individual participants; A: score for the combined (averaged) predictions from all participants. '*' indicates that the model was tested on a subset of participants due to missing data.

nel size of 10.

We also propose several strategies for making better use of available data. **+exp2** adds completely new data points from Experiment 2 in Pereira et al. (2018)'s study: fMRI scans of 8 participants (who also participated in Experiment 1) reading 284 sentences, and distributional vectors for these sentences, obtained by summing the GloVe vectors for the content words in each sentence. By contrast, **+para** and **+aug** add extra data for every word in the existing vocabulary, in order to force the model to learn a mapping between regions in the brain space and regions in the target space, rather than between single points. In **+para**, the model is trained on four fMRI images per word: one from each stimulus presentation paradigm (i.e., the word plus a picture, the word plus a word cloud or the word in a sentence, and the average of these). By contrast, under the standard approach, the model is trained on only one brain image for each word (either the image from one of the three paradigms or the average image). Finally, **+aug** adds data on the distributional side: rather than mapping each brain image to just its 'own' GloVe vector (e.g. the image for *dog* to the GloVe vector of *dog*), we map it to its own vector plus the six nearest neighbours of that vector in the full GloVe space (e.g. not only *dog* but also *dogs, puppy, pet, cat, cats,* and *puppies*).

A final experiment does not aim at enhancing the models' training data, but rather changes how the model's predictions are processed. In the brain decoding literature, models are usually trained and evaluated for individual participants. However, to make maximal use of limited training data, one would like to combine brain images from different participants, but as noted, this is not feasible for our dataset. Instead, we propose a simple alternative method for obtaining group-level predictions: we average the predictions from all of the models for individual participants to pro-

duce a single prediction for each stimulus word. We hypothesize that this can help 'smooth out' flaws in individual participants' models. To compare individual-level and group-level predictions, we calculate three different scores for each model: the highest score for the predictions of any individual participant (I_B), the average score for the predictions of all individual participants (I_A), and the score for the averaged predictions (A).

4 Results

The results of all models are summarized in Table 1.[5] All models beat a simple baseline model that predicts vectors of random numbers (except on the R^2 metric, where Perceptron performs below baseline). Performance on the Pair and Rank scores is generally good, but performance on the other metrics is much worse: Cos is very low and R^2 scores are negative, meaning that the predicted word embeddings are very far in semantic space from where they should be. Moreover, the low NN and RSA scores indicate that the model captures the similarity structure of the GloVe space only to a very limited extent. On the model improvement side, the alternative models Perceptron and CNN fail to outperform Ridge, while the data augmentation experiments do achieve slightly higher performance. Finally, combining predictions seems to be quite effective: the scores for the averaged predictions are better than those for any individual participant, reaching Pair and Rank scores of more than 0.90 and Cos, NN, and RSA scores of up to two times the averaged score for individual participants.

5 Discussion and conclusion

Our results show that none of our tested models learns a good cross-space mapping: the predicted

---

[5]MLP and Ridge were run with and without feature selection; table lists best results (MLP: with, Ridge: without).

semantic vectors are far from their expected location and fail to capture the target space's similarity structure. Meanwhile, excellent performance is achieved on pairwise and rank-based classification tasks, which implies that the predictions contain sufficient information for reconstructing stimulus word labels. These contradictory results suggest a situation not unlike the one sketched in Fig. 1. This means that from a linguistic point of view, early claims about the success of brain decoding techniques should be taken cautiously.

Two obvious questions are how such a situation can arise and how it can be prevented. First of all, it seems likely that there is simply not enough training data to learn a precise mapping; the results of our experiments with adding 'extra' data are in line with this hypothesis. Moreover, the fact that all vocabulary words are relatively far from each other could make the mapping problem harder. For example, the 'correct' nearest neighbours of *dog* are *pig*, *toy*, and *bear*; the model might predict *fish*, *play* and *bird*, which are 'wrong' but intuitively do not seem much worse. We speculate that using a dataset with a more diverse similarity structure (i.e. where each word is very close to some words and further from others) could help the model learn a better mapping. Yet another issue is contextuality: standard GloVe embeddings are context-independent (i.e. a given word always has the same representation regardless of its word sense and syntactic position in the sentence), whereas the brain images are not because they were obtained using contextualized stimuli (e.g. a word in a sentence). Hence, an interesting question is whether trying to predict contextualized word embeddings, obtained using more traditional distributional approaches (e.g. Erk and Padó, 2010; Thater et al., 2011) or deep neural language models (e.g. Devlin et al., 2018), would be an easier task. Finally, the success of our experiment with combining participants suggests that using group-level data can help overcome the challenges inherent in predicting corpus-based (GloVe) representations from individual-level (brain) representations.

Acknowledgments

The first author of this paper (GM) was enrolled in the European Master Program in Language and Communication Technologies (LCT) while writing the paper, and was supported by the European Union Erasmus Mundus program.

References

Samira Abnar, Rasyan Ahmed, Max Mijnheer, and Willem Zuidema. 2018. Experiential, distributional and dependency-based word embeddings have complementary roles in decoding brain activity. In *Proceedings of the 8th Workshop on Cognitive Modeling and Computational Linguistics (CMCL 2018)*, pages 57–66.

Andrew J. Anderson, Elia Bruni, Ulisse Bordignon, Massimo Poesio, and Marco Baroni. 2013. Of words, eyes and brains: Correlating image-based distributional semantic models with neural representations of concepts. In *Proceedings of the 2013 Conference on Empirical Methods in Natural Language Processing*, pages 1960–1970.

Marco Baroni, Georgiana Dinu, and Germán Kruszewski. 2014. Don't count, predict! a systematic comparison of context-counting vs. context-predicting semantic vectors. In *Proceedings of the 52nd Annual Meeting of the Association for Computational Linguistics (Volume 1: Long Papers)*, volume 1, pages 238–247.

Jacob Devlin, Ming-Wei Chang, Kenton Lee, and Kristina Toutanova. 2018. BERT: pre-training of deep bidirectional transformers for language understanding. *CoRR*, abs/1810.04805.

Katrin Erk and Sebastian Padó. 2010. Examplar-based models for word meaning in context. In *Proceedings of the ACL 2010 Conference Short Papers*, pages 92–97.

Jon Gauthier and Anna Ivanova. 2018. Does the brain represent words? an evaluation of brain decoding studies of language understanding. *CoRR*, abs/1806.00591. ArXiv preprint, http://arxiv.org/abs/1806.00591.

Trevor Hastie, Robert Tibshirani, and J. H. Friedman. 2009. *The Elements of Statistical Learning: Data Mining, Inference, and Prediction.*, second edition, corrected 7th printing edition. Springer Series in Statistics. Springer.

Diederik P. Kingma and Jimmy Lei Ba. 2014. Adam: A method for stochastic optimization. *CoRR*, abs/1412.6980. ArXiv preprint, http://arxiv.org/abs/1412.6980.

Nikolaus Kriegeskorte, Marieke Mur, and Peter Bandettini. 2008. Representational similarity analysis: connecting the branches of systems neuroscience. *Frontiers in Systems Neuroscience*, 2.

Angeliki Lazaridou, Georgina Dinu, and Marco Baroni. 2015. Hubness and polution: Delving into cross-space mapping for zero-shot learning. In *Proceedings of the 53rd Annual Meeting of the Association for Computational Linguistics and the 7th International Joint Conference on Natural Language Processing*, pages 270–280.

Jure Lescovec, Anand Rajaraman, and Jeffrey David Ullman. 2014. *Mining of Massive Datasets*, 2nd edition. Cambridge University Press. Online version, `http://www.mmds.org/#ver21`.

Tomas Mikolov, Kai Chen, Greg Corrado, and Jeffrey Dean. 2013. Efficient estimation of word representations in vector space. *CoRR*, abs/1301.3781. `http://arxiv.org/abs/1301.3781`.

Tom M. Mitchell, Svetlana V. Shinkareva, Andrew Carlson, Kai-Min Chang, Vicente L. Malave, Robert A. Mason, and Marcel Adam Just. 2008. Predicting human brain activity associated with the meanings of nouns. *Science*, 320(5880):1191–1195.

Brian Murphy, Partha Talukdar, and Tom Mitchell. 2012. Selecting corpus-semantic models for neurolinguistic decoding. In *Proceedings of the First Joint Conference on Lexical and Computational Semantics-Volume 1: Proceedings of the main conference and the shared task, and Volume 2: Proceedings of the Sixth International Workshop on Semantic Evaluation*, pages 114–123. Association for Computational Linguistics.

Fabian Pedregosa, Gaël Varoquaux, Alexandre Gramfort, Vincent Michel, Bertrand Thirion, Olivier Grisel, Mathieu Blondel, Peter Prettenhofer, Ron Weiss, Vincent Dubourg, Jake Vanderplas, Alexandre Passos, David Cournapeau, Matthieu Brucher, Matthieu Perrot, and Édouard Duchesnay. 2011. Scikit-learn: Machine learning in Python. *Journal of Machine Learning Research*, 12:2825–2830.

Jeffrey Pennington, Richard Socher, and Christopher D. Manning. 2014. Glove: Global vectors for word representation. In *Proceedings of the 2014 Conference on Empirical Methods in Natural Language Processing (EMNLP)*, pages 1532–1543.

Francisco Pereira, Bin Lou, Brianna Pritchett, Samuel Ritter, Samuel J. Gershman, Nancy Kanwisher, Matthew Botvinick, and Evelina Fedorenko. 2018. Toward a universal decoder of linguistic meaning from brain activation. *Nature Communications*, 9(963).

Gustavo Sudre, Dean Pomerleau, Palatucci Mark, Leila Wehbe, Alona Fyshe, Riita Salmelin, and Tom Mitchell. 2012. Tracking neural coding of perceptual and semantic features of concrete nouns. *NeuroImage*, 62:451–463.

Stefan Thater, Hagen Fürstenau, and Manfred Pinkel. 2011. Word meaning in context: A simple and effective vector model. In *Proceedings of the 5th International Joint Conference on Natural Language Processing*, pages 1134–1143.

Cara E. Van Uden, Samuel A. Nastase, Andrew C. Connolly, Ma Feilong, Isabella Hansen, M. Ida Gobbini, and James V. Haxby. 2018. Modeling semantic encoding in a common neural representational space. *Frontiers in Neuroscience*, 12.

Haoyan Xu, Brian Murphy, and Alona Fyshe. 2016. Brainbench: A brain-image test suite for distributional semantic models. In *Proceedings of the 2016 Conference on Empirical Methods in Natural Language Processing*, pages 2017–2021.

Towards incremental learning of word embeddings using context informativeness

Alexandre Kabbach
Dept. of Linguistics
University of Geneva
Center for Mind/Brain Sciences
University of Trento

Kristina Gulordava
Dept. of Translation
and Language Sciences
Universitat Pompeu Fabra

Aurélie Herbelot
Center for Mind/Brain Sciences,
Dept. of Information Engineering
and Computer Science
University of Trento

{firstname.lastname}@{unige.ch;upf.edu;unitn.it}

Abstract

In this paper, we investigate the task of learning word embeddings from very sparse data in an incremental, cognitively-plausible way. We focus on the notion of *informativeness*, that is, the idea that some content is more valuable to the learning process than other. We further highlight the challenges of online learning and argue that previous systems fall short of implementing incrementality. Concretely, we incorporate informativeness in a previously proposed model of nonce learning, using it for context selection and learning rate modulation. We test our system on the task of learning new words from definitions, as well as on the task of learning new words from potentially uninformative contexts. We demonstrate that informativeness is crucial to obtaining state-of-the-art performance in a truly incremental setup.

1 Introduction

Distributional semantics models such as word embeddings (Bengio et al., 2003; Collobert et al., 2011; Huang et al., 2012; Mikolov et al., 2013b) notoriously require exposure to a large amount of contextual data in order to generate *high quality* vector representations of words. This poses practical challenges when the available training data is scarce, or when distributional models are intended to mimic humans' word learning abilities by constructing reasonable word representations from limited observations (Lazaridou et al., 2017). In recent work, various approaches have been proposed to tackle these problems, ranging from task-specific auto-encoders generating word embeddings from dictionary definitions only (Bosc and Vincent, 2017, 2018), to Bayesian models used for acquiring definitional properties of words via one-shot learning (Wang et al., 2017), or recursive neural network models making use of morphological structure (Luong et al., 2013).

Arguing that the ideal model should rely on an all-purpose architecture able to learn from *any* amount of data, Herbelot and Baroni (2017) proposed a model called Nonce2Vec (N2V), designed as a modification of Word2Vec (W2V; Mikolov et al., 2013b), refactored to allow incremental learning. The model was tested on two datasets: a) the newly introduced *definitional* dataset, where the task is to learn a nonce word from its Wikipedia definition; and b) the *chimera* dataset of Lazaridou et al. (2017), where the task is to reproduce human similarity judgements related to a novel word observed in 2-6 randomly extracted sentences. The N2V model performed much better than W2V on both datasets but failed to outperform a basic additive model on the chimera dataset, leading the authors to hypothesise that their system would need to perform content selection to deal with the potentially uninformative chimera sentences.

There are two motivations to the present work. The first is to provide a formal definition of the notion of *informativeness* applied to both sentential context (as a whole) and context words (taken individually). To do so, we rely on the intuition that an *informative* context is a context that is more *specific* to a given target, and that this notion of *context specificity* can be quantified by computing the entropy of the probability distribution generated by a language model over a set of vocabulary words, given the context.

The secondary motivation of this work lays in considerations over incrementality. We show that N2V itself did not fully implement its ideal of 'online' concept learning. We also point out that architectures that have outperformed N2V since its inception actually move even further from this ideal. In contrast, we attempt to make our architecture as close as possible to a realistic belief update system, and we demonstrate that informativeness

Proceedings of the ACL 2019, Student Research Workshop, pages 162–168
Florence, Italy, July 28th-August 2nd, 2019. ©2019 Association for Computational Linguistics

is an essential part of retaining acceptable performance in such a challenging setting.

2 Related work

The original Nonce2Vec (N2V) model is designed to simulate new word acquisition by an adult speaker who already masters a substantial vocabulary. The system uses some 'background' lexical knowledge in the shape of a distributional space acquired over a large text corpus. A novel word is then learnt by using information present in its context sentence. To achieve its goal, N2V proposes some modifications to the original Word2Vec architecture to make it suitable for novel word learning. Three main changes are suggested: a) the learning rate should be greatly heightened to allow for learning via backpropagation using only the limited amount of data; b) random subsampling should be reduced to a minimum so that all available data is used; and c) embeddings in the background should be 'frozen' so that the high learning rate is prevented from 'unlearning' old lexical knowledge in favour of the scarce, and potentially uninformative, new context information.

Recent work outperforms N2V on the chimera (Khodak et al., 2018; Schick and Schütze, 2019a) and the definitional (Schick and Schütze, 2018) datasets (see §1 for a description of the datasets). However, they both deviate from the original motivation of N2V which is to learn word representations *incrementally* from *any* amount of data. Instead, those state-of-the-art models rely—at least in part—on a learned linear regression matrix which is fixed for a given corpus and thus does not lend itself well to incremental learning.

Our work follows the philosophy of N2V but pushes the notion of incrementality further by identifying aspects of the original system that in fact do not play well with true online learning. For a start, the original model is not fully incremental as it adopts a *one-shot* evaluation setup where each test instance is considered individually and where the background model is reloaded from scratch at each test iteration. This does not test how the system would react to learning *multiple* nonces one after the other (as humans do in the course of their lives). Related to this, whilst 'freezing' background vectors makes sense as a safety net when using very high learning rates, it similarly goes against the notion of incrementality. In any re-alistic setup, indeed, we would like newly learnt words to inform our background lexical knowledge and become part of that background themselves, being refined over time and contributing to acquiring the next nonce. Following this philosophy, the system we present in this paper does away with freezing previously learnt embeddings and does not reload the background model at each test iteration.

We should further note that our work on informativeness echoes recent research on the use of *attention* mechanisms. Vaswani et al. (2017), followed by Devlin et al. (2018) and Schick and Schütze (2019b), have shown that such mechanisms can provide very powerful tools to build sentence and contextualised word embeddings which are amenable to transfer learning tasks. However, we note that from our point of view, these systems suffer from the same problem as the previously mentioned architectures: the underlying model consists of a large set of parameters which can be used to learn a task-specific regression. It is not designed to be updated with each new encountered experience.

3 Model

Let us consider *context* to be defined as a window of $\pm n$ words around a given *target*. We define two specific functions: *context informativeness* (CI) which characterises how informative an entire context is with respect to its corresponding target; and *context word informativeness* (CWI) which characterises how informative a *particular context item* is with respect to the target. For instance, if target *chases* is seen in context $c = \{the, cat, the, mouse\}$, the context informativeness is the informativeness of c, and the context word informativeness can be computed for each element in c, with the expectation, in this case, that *the* might be less informative than *cat* or *mouse*. The CWI measure is dependent on CI, as we proceed to show.

3.1 Context informativeness

Let us consider a sequence c of n context items $c = c_1 \ldots c_n$. We define the *context informativeness* of a context sequence c as:

$$CI(c) = 1 + \frac{1}{\ln(|\mathcal{V}|)} \sum_{w \in \mathcal{V}} p(w|c) \ln p(w|c) \quad (1)$$

CI is a slight modification of the Shannon entropy $H = -\sum_{w \in \mathcal{V}} p(w|c) \ln p(w|c)$, normalised over the cardinality of the vocabulary $|\mathcal{V}|$ to output values in $[0, 1]$. In this work, we use a CBOW model (Mikolov et al., 2013a) to obtain the probability distribution $p(w|c)$. We use CBOW because it is the simplest word-generation model which takes the relation between context words into account, i.e., in contrast to skipgram.

A context will be considered maximally informative ($CI = 1$) if only a single vocabulary item is predicted to occur in context c with a non-null probability. Conversely, a context will be considered minimally informative ($CI = 0$) if all vocabulary items are predicted to occur in context c with equal probability. CI should therefore quantify how *specific* a given context is regarding a given target.

3.2 Context word informativeness

Let us consider $c_{\neq i} = c_1 \ldots c_{i-1}, c_{i+1} \ldots c_n$ to be the sequence of context items taken from c to which the ith item has been removed. We define the *context word informativeness* of a context item c_i in a context sequence c as:

$$CWI(c_i) = CI(c) - CI(c_{\neq i}) \qquad (2)$$

CWI outputs values in $[-1, 1]$: a context word c_i will be considered maximally informative ($CWI = 1$) if removing it from a maximally informative context leads to a minimally informative one. Conversely, a context word c_i will be considered minimally informative ($CWI = -1$) if removing it from a minimally informative context leads to a maximally informative one.

3.3 CWI-augmented Nonce2Vec

As explained in §2, N2V introduces several high-level changes to the W2V architecture to achieve learning from very sparse data. In practice, this translates into the following design choices: a) nonces are initialised by summing context word embeddings (after subsampling); and b) nonces are trained with an adapted skipgram function incorporating decaying window size, sampling and learning rates at each iteration, while all other vectors remain frozen. The learning rate is computed via $\alpha = \alpha_0 e^{-\lambda t}$ with a high α_0.

The modifications we propose are as follows: i) we incorporate informativeness into the initialisation phase by summing over the set of context words with positive CWI only; ii) we train on the entire context without subsampling and window

decay; and iii) we remove freezing and compute the learning rate as a function of CWI for each context item c_i via:

$$\alpha(c_i) = \alpha_{max} \frac{e^{\tanh(\beta * CWI(c_i)) + 1} - 1}{e^2 - 1} \qquad (3)$$

The purpose of equation 3 is to modulate the learning rate depending on the context word informativeness for a context–target pair: α should be maximal ($\alpha = \alpha_{max}$, where α_{max} is a hyperparameter) when context is maximally informative ($CWI = 1$) and minimal ($\alpha = 0$) when context is minimally informative ($CWI = -1$). The function $x \mapsto \frac{e^{x+1} - 1}{e^2 - 1}$ is therefore designed as a logistic "S-shape" function with domain $[-1, 1] \rightarrow [0, 1]$. In practice, CWI values are highly dependant on the language model used and may end up all being close to 0 (± 0.01 with our CBOW model for instance). The $tanh$ function and the β parameter are therefore added to compensate for this effect that would otherwise produce identical learning rates for all target-context pairs, regardless of CWI values.

4 Experimental setup and evaluation

To test the robustness of the results of Herbelot and Baroni (2017), we retrain a skipgram background model with the same hyperparameters but from the more recent Wikipedia snapshot of January 2019, and obtain a similar correlation ratio on the MEN similarity dataset (Bruni et al., 2014): $\rho = 0.74$ vs $\rho = 0.75$ for Herbelot and Baroni (2017). Probability distributions used for computing CI and CWI are generated with a CBOW model trained with gensim (Řehůřek and Sojka, 2010) on the same Wikipedia snapshot as our skipgram background model, and with the same hyperparameters. For the CWI-based learning rate computation, we set $\alpha_{max} = 1$, chosen according to α_0 in the original N2V for fair comparison; and $\beta = 1000$, chosen given min and max CWI values output by CBOW to produce $tanh(\beta * x)$ values distributed across $[-1, 1]$ and apply a learning rate $\alpha_{max} = 1$ to maximally informative context words.

We report results on the *definitional* and the *chimera* datasets (see §1). The definitional dataset contains first sentences from Wikipedia for 1000 words: e.g. *Insulin is a peptide hormone produced by beta cells of the pancreatic islets*, where the task is to learn the nonce *insulin*. Evaluation is performed on 300 test instances in terms of Median Rank (MR) and Mean Reciprocal Rank (MRR). That is, for each instance, the Reciprocal Rank of the *gold* vector (the one that would be obtained by training standard W2V over the entire corpus) is computed over the sorted list of neighbours of the *predicted* representation.

The chimera dataset simulates a nonce situation where speaker encounters words for the first time in naturally-occurring (and not necessarily informative) sentences. Each *nonce* instance in the data is associated with 2 (L2), 4 (L4) or 6 (L6) sentences showing the nonce in context, and a set of six word *probes* human-annotated for similarity to the nonce. For instance, the nonce *VALTUOR* is shown in *Canned sardines and VALTUOR between two slices of wholemeal bread and thinly spread Flora Original [...]*, and its similarity assessed with respect to *rhubarb, onion, pear, strawberry, limousine* and *cushion*. Evaluation is performed on 110 test instances by computing the Spearman correlation between the similarities output by the system for each nonce-probe pair and the similarities from the human subjects.

We evaluate both datasets using a *one-shot* setup, as per the original N2V paper: each nonce word in considered individually and the background model is reloaded at each test iteration. We further propose an *incremental* evaluation setup where the background model is loaded only once at the beginning of testing, keeping its word vectors modifiable during subsequent learning, and where each newly learned nonce representation is added to the background model. As performance in the incremental setup proved to be dependent on the order of the test items, we report average and standard deviation scores computed from 10 test runs where the test set is shuffled each time.

5 Results

5.1 Improving additive models

Herbelot and Baroni (2017) show that a simple additive model provides an extremely strong baseline for nonce learning. So we first measure the contribution of our notion of informativeness to the context filtering module of a sum model. Comparison takes place across four settings: a) *no filter*, where all words are retained; b) *random*, which applies standard subsampling with a sample rate of 10,000, following the original N2V approach; c) *self*, where all items found in training with a frequency above a given threshold are discarded;[1] and d) *CWI*, which only retains context items with a positive CWI value.

Our results on the definitional dataset, displayed in Table 1, show a consistent hierarchy of filters with the SUM CWI model outperforming all other SUM models, in both one-shot and incremental evaluation setups. Results on the chimera dataset, displayed in Table 2, are not as clear-cut, although they do exhibit a similar trend on both L4 and L6 test sets, with the notable result of achieving state-of-the-art performances with our SUM CWI model on the L4 and L6 test sets in incremental setup, and near state-of-the-art performance on the L6 test set in one-shot setup. This confirms once again that additive models can provide very robust baselines.

Qualitatively, the contribution of each filter on the definitional dataset can be exemplified on the following sentence, with nonce word *Honeywell*: *"Honeywell International Inc is an American multinational conglomerate company that produces [...] aerospace systems for a wide variety of customers from private consumers to major corporations and governments."*. The *no-filter* additive model outputs a rank of 383 (the gold vector for *honeywell* is found to be the 383th closest neighbour of the predicted vector). The *random* model randomly removes most (but not all) high frequency words before summing, outputting a rank of 192 (filtered-out words include also content words like *international* or *company*). The *self*-information model reduces the size of the context words set even further by removing all high-frequency words left over by the random process (rank 170). Finally, the *CWI* model outputs the best rank at 85, removing all function words while keeping some useful high-frequency words such as *international* or *company*.

5.2 Improving neural models in one-shot settings

Our results for neural models are also displayed in Table 1 and Table 2: *as-is* refers to the original N2V system; *CWI init* is N2V as-is with CWI-based context filtering instead of subsampling; and *CWI alpha* is a model with a CWI-based

---

[1] We take the log of the *sample_int* values computed by gensim for each word during training, keeping only items with log values above 22, which gave us the best performances overall.

| | one-shot | | incremental | |
Model	MR	MRR	MR	MRR
SOTA	**49**	**.1754**	–	–
SUM no-filter	5,969	.0087	6,461± 225	.0014±.0002
SUM random	3,047	.0221	3,113± 179	.0071±.0012
SUM self	1,769	.0242	2,095±125	.0121±.0008
SUM CWI	935	.0374	**961**±**24**	**.0322**±**.0011**
N2V as-is	955	.0477	81,705±14,076	.0096±.0038
N2V CWI init	540	.0493	70,992±17,312	.0079±.0025
N2V CWI alpha	763	.0404	**983**±**175**	**.0341**±**.0021**

Table 1: Performance of various additive (SUM) and neural (N2V) models on the definitional dataset, measured in terms of Median Rank (MR) and Mean Reciprocal Rank (MRR). SOTA in *one-shot* evaluation setup is reported by the *Form-Context* model of Schick and Schütze (2018).

sum initialisation (as in SUM CWI), and a CWI-based learning rate computed on unfiltered context words, as detailed in §3.3.

When informativeness is incorporated to N2V in the original one-shot evaluation setup, we also observe near-systematic improvements. On the definitional dataset in Table 1, CWI init improves over the standard N2V as-is model (MR 540 vs 955; MRR .0493 vs .0477) or over the SUM CWI baseline (MR 540 vs 935; MRR .0493 vs .0374). In comparison to CWI init, our CWI alpha model provides robust performances across evaluation setups and datasets, often reaching similar if not better results than our best baseline model (SUM CWI) showing that a neural model fully based on informativeness is a more robust alternative than its counterparts. See for example Table 1 on the definitional dataset where the N2V CWI alpha model performs better than the SUM CWI model in one-shot setup (MR 763 vs. 935; MRR .0404 vs .0374) or Table 2 on the chimera dataset where it also performs better than the SUM CWI model on both the L2 (ρ .3129 vs .3074) and the L4 (ρ .3928 vs .3739) test sets and achieves state-of-the-art performance on the L4 test set.

5.3 Improving incremental learning

As stated in §2, recent approaches to nonce learning have deviated from the original philosophy of N2V and in fact, N2V itself did not fully implement an incremental setting. We now show that the original N2V performance decreases significantly on both datasets in an incremental evaluation setup, without freezing of background vec-tors. Compare the results of the N2V as-is model in both *one-shot* and *incremental* evaluation setups on the definitional dataset in Table 1: MR 955 vs 81,705±14,076 and MRR .0477 vs .0096±.0038; and on the chimera dataset in Table 2: ρ .3412 vs .1650±.0384 on L2; ρ .3514 vs .1144±.0620 on L4 and ρ .4077 vs .1391±.0694 on L6. We find this drastic decrease in performance to be related to two distinct phenomena: 1) a *sum* effect which leads vector representations for nonces to be close to each other due to the sum initialisation creating very similar vectors in a 'special' portion of the vector space; and 2) a *snowball* effect related to the 'unfreezing' of the background space which leads background vectors to be updated by backpropagation at a very high learning rate at every test iteration, moving their original meaning towards the semantics of the new context they are encountered in. This includes vectors for very frequent words, which are encountered again in their now shifted version when a new nonce is presented to the system. This snowball effect ends up significantly altering the quality of the background model and its generated representations.

The *sum effect* is best illustrated by the decrease in performance of SUM models between *one-shot* and *incremental* setups on the definitional dataset in Table 1, as this effect has the property of specifically changing the nature and order of the nearest neighbours of the predicted nonce vectors, which is directly reflected in the MR and MRR evaluation metrics on the definitional dataset given the evaluation task. On the chimera dataset in Table 2 however, this effect does not appear to neg-

Model	one-shot			incremental		
	L2	L4	L6	L2	L4	L6
SOTA	**.3634**	.3844	**.4360**	–	–	–
SUM no-filter	.3047	.3288	.3063	.3047±.0000	.3288±.0000	.3063±.0000
SUM random	.3358	.3717	.3584	.3358±.0002	.3717±.0004	.3584±.0003
SUM self	.3455	.3638	.3651	**.3455±.0000**	.3638±.0000	.3651±.0000
SUM CWI	.3074	.3739	.4243	.3074±.0000	**.3739±.0000**	**.4243±.0000**
N2V as-is	.3412	.3514	.4077	.1650±.0384	.1144±.0620	.1391±.0694
N2V CWI init	.3002	.3482	.4218	.1451±.0265	.1522±.0396	.1225±.0544
N2V CWI alpha	.3129	**.3928**	.4181	.2970±.0262	.3000±.0268	.2678±.0408

Table 2: Performance of various additive (SUM) and neural (N2V) models on the chimera dataset, measured in terms of Spearman correlation. SOTA in *one-shot* evaluation setup on the L2 and L4 test sets are reported by the *A la carte* model of Khodak et al. (2018), while SOTA on the L6 test set is reported by the *attentive mimicking* model of Schick and Schütze (2019a).

atively impact performance given that evaluation compares correlations between gold and predicted similarity rankings of nonces with a prefixed set of probes. The *snowball* effect however is visible on both datasets in Table 1 and Table 2 when comparing performances of N2V models between *one-shot* and *incremental* setups. It proves particularly salient for neural models which do not make use of informativeness-based adaptative learning rate (all N2V models but N2V CWI alpha).

Our notion of informativeness proves even more useful in the context of incremental nonce learning: on the definitional dataset in Table 1, our informativeness-based models, be it SUM CWI or N2V CWI alpha, achieve best (and comparable) performances (MR 961±24 vs 983±175; MRR .0322±.0011 vs .0341±.0021). Moreover, we observe that those models are able to mitigate the undesirable effects mentioned above, almost totally for the sum effect (compare the performance of the SUM CWI model in Table 1 between the incremental and one-shot setups, versus the other SUM models), and partially for the snowballing interference of the high learning rate (compare the performance of the N2V CWI alpha model in Table 1 between the incremental and one-shot setups, versus the other N2V models). Performances of our SUM CWI and N2V CWI alpha models in incremental setup approach those of the one-shot setting. On the chimera dataset in Table 2, which proves only sensitive to the snowball effect, we also observe that our N2V CWI alpha model is able to mitigate this effect, although performances of the model in

incremental setup remain below those of the one-shot setup, as well as those of the additive models in incremental setup.

6 Conclusion

We have proposed an improvement of the original N2V model which incorporates a notion of informativeness in the nonce learning process. We showed that our informativeness function was very beneficial to a vector addition baseline, and could be usefully integrated into the original N2V approach, both at initialisation stage and during learning, achieving state-of-the-art results on the chimera dataset and on the definitional dataset in an incremental evaluation setup. Although our proposed notion of informativeness proved to be mostly beneficial to incremental learning, nothing prevents it from being incorporated to other non-incremental models of nonce learning, provided that those models make use of contextual information. On top of the performance improvements observed, our proposed definition of informativeness benefits from being intuitive, debuggable at each step of the learning process, and of relying on no external resource. We make our code freely available at `https://github.com/minimalparts/nonce2vec`.

Acknowledgements

We are grateful to our two anonymous reviewers for their helpful comments.

References

Yoshua Bengio, Réjean Ducharme, Pascal Vincent, and Christian Janvin. 2003. A neural probabilistic language model. *Journal of Machine Learning Research*, 3:1137–1155.

Tom Bosc and Pascal Vincent. 2017. Learning word embeddings from dictionary definitions only. In *Proceedings of the NIPS 2017 Workshop on Meta-Learning*.

Tom Bosc and Pascal Vincent. 2018. Auto-encoding dictionary definitions into consistent word embeddings. In *Proceedings of the 2018 Conference on Empirical Methods in Natural Language Processing*, pages 1522–1532, Brussels, Belgium. Association for Computational Linguistics.

Elia Bruni, Nam-Khanh Tran, and Marco Baroni. 2014. Multimodal distributional semantics. *Journal of Artificial Intelligence Research*, 49:1–47.

Ronan Collobert, Jason Weston, Léon Bottou, Michael Karlen, Koray Kavukcuoglu, and Pavel Kuksa. 2011. Natural language processing (almost) from scratch. *Journal of Machine Learning Research*, 12:2493–2537.

Jacob Devlin, Ming-Wei Chang, Kenton Lee, and Kristina Toutanova. 2018. BERT: pre-training of deep bidirectional transformers for language understanding. *CoRR*, abs/1810.04805.

Aurélie Herbelot and Marco Baroni. 2017. High-risk learning: acquiring new word vectors from tiny data. In *Proceedings of the 2017 Conference on Empirical Methods in Natural Language Processing*, pages 304–309, Copenhagen, Denmark. Association for Computational Linguistics.

Eric Huang, Richard Socher, Christopher Manning, and Andrew Ng. 2012. Improving word representations via global context and multiple word prototypes. In *Proceedings of the 50th Annual Meeting of the Association for Computational Linguistics (Volume 1: Long Papers)*, pages 873–882, Jeju Island, Korea. Association for Computational Linguistics.

Mikhail Khodak, Nikunj Saunshi, Yingyu Liang, Tengyu Ma, Brandon Stewart, and Sanjeev Arora. 2018. A la carte embedding: Cheap but effective induction of semantic feature vectors. In *Proceedings of the 56th Annual Meeting of the Association for Computational Linguistics (Volume 1: Long Papers)*, pages 12–22, Melbourne, Australia. Association for Computational Linguistics.

Angeliki Lazaridou, Marco Marelli, and Marco Baroni. 2017. Multimodal word meaning induction from minimal exposure to natural text. *Cognitive Science*, 41(S4):677–705.

Thang Luong, Richard Socher, and Christopher Manning. 2013. Better word representations with recursive neural networks for morphology. In *Proceedings of the Seventeenth Conference on Computational Natural Language Learning*, pages 104–113, Sofia, Bulgaria. Association for Computational Linguistics.

Tomas Mikolov, Kai Chen, Greg Corrado, and Jeffrey Dean. 2013a. Efficient estimation of word representations in vector space. *CoRR*, abs/1301.3781.

Tomas Mikolov, Ilya Sutskever, Kai Chen, Greg Corrado, and Jeffrey Dean. 2013b. Distributed representations of words and phrases and their compositionality. In *Proceedings of the 26th International Conference on Neural Information Processing Systems - Volume 2*, NIPS'13, pages 3111–3119, USA. Curran Associates Inc.

Radim Řehůřek and Petr Sojka. 2010. Software Framework for Topic Modelling with Large Corpora. In *Proceedings of the LREC 2010 Workshop on New Challenges for NLP Frameworks*, pages 45–50, Valletta, Malta. ELRA.

Timo Schick and Hinrich Schütze. 2018. Learning semantic representations for novel words: Leveraging both form and context. *CoRR*, abs/1811.03866.

Timo Schick and Hinrich Schütze. 2019a. Attentive mimicking: Better word embeddings by attending to informative contexts. *CoRR*, abs/1904.01617.

Timo Schick and Hinrich Schütze. 2019b. Rare words: A major problem for contextualized embeddings and how to fix it by attentive mimicking. *CoRR*, abs/1904.06707.

Ashish Vaswani, Noam Shazeer, Niki Parmar, Jakob Uszkoreit, Llion Jones, Aidan N. Gomez, Łukasz Kaiser, and Illia Polosukhin. 2017. Attention is all you need. In *Advances in neural information processing systems*, pages 5998–6008.

Su Wang, Stephen Roller, and Katrin Erk. 2017. Distributional Modeling on a Diet: One-shot Word Learning from Text Only. In *Proceedings of the Eighth International Joint Conference on Natural Language Processing (Volume 1: Long Papers)*, pages 204–213. Asian Federation of Natural Language Processing.

A Strong and Robust Baseline for Text-Image Matching

Fangyu Liu
University of Waterloo
`fangyu.liu@uwaterloo.ca`

Rongtian Ye
Aalto University
`rongtian7@gmail.com`

Abstract

We review the current schemes of text-image matching models and propose improvements for both training and inference. First, we empirically show limitations of two popular loss (sum and max-margin loss) widely used in training text-image embeddings and propose a trade-off: a kNN-margin loss which 1) utilizes information from hard negatives and 2) is robust to noise as all K-most hardest samples are taken into account, tolerating *pseudo* negatives and outliers. Second, we advocate the use of Inverted Softmax (IS) and Cross-modal Local Scaling (CSLS) during inference to mitigate the so-called hubness problem in high-dimensional embedding space, enhancing scores of all metrics by a large margin.

1 Introduction

In recent years, deep eural models have gained a significant edge over *shallow*[1] models in cross-modal matching tasks. Text-image matching has been one of the most popular ones among them. Most methods involve two phases: 1) training: two neural networks (one image encoder and one text encoder) are learned end-to-end, mapping texts and images into a joint space, where vectors (either texts or images) with similar meanings are close to each other; 2) inference: for a query in modality A, after being encoded into a vector, a nearest neighbor search is performed to match the vector against all vector representations of items[2] in modality B. As the embedding space is learned through jointly modeling vision and language, it is often referred to as *Visual Semantic Embeddings* (VSE).

While the state-of-the-art architectures being consistently advanced (Nam et al., 2017; You et al., 2018; Wehrmann et al., 2018; Wu et al., 2019), few works have focused on the more fundamental problem of text-image matching - that is, the optimization objectives during training and inference. And that is what this paper focuses on. In the following of the paper, we will discuss 1) the optimization objective during training, i.e., loss function, and 2) the objective used in inference (how should a text-image correspondence graph be predicted).

Loss function. Faghri et al. (2018) brought the most notable improvement on loss function used for training VSE. They proposed a max-margin triplet ranking loss that emphasizes on the hardest negative sample within a min-batch. The max-margin loss has gained significant popularity and is used by a big set of recent works (Engilberge et al., 2018; Faghri et al., 2018; Lee et al., 2018; Wu et al., 2019). We, however, point out that the max-margin loss is very sensitive to label noise and encoder performance, and also easily overfits. Through experiments, we show that it only achieves the best performance under a careful selection of model architecture and dataset. Before Faghri et al. (2018), a pairwise ranking loss has been usually adopted for text-image model training. The only difference is that, instead of only using the hardest negative sample, it sums over all negative samples (we thus refer to it as the sum-margin loss). Though sum-margin loss yields stable and consistent performance under all dataset and architecture conditions, it does not make use information from hard samples but treats all samples equally by summing the margins up. Both Faghri et al. (2018) and our own experiments point to a clear trend that, more and cleaner data there is, the higher quality the encoders have, the better performance the max-margin loss has; while the smaller and less clean the data is, the less powerful the encoders are, the better sum-margin loss

---

[1] *shallow* means non-neural methods.
[2] In this paper, we refer to vectors used for searching as "queries" and vectors in the searched space as "items".

Proceedings of the ACL 2019, Student Research Workshop, pages 169–176
Florence, Italy, July 28th-August 2nd, 2019. ©2019 Association for Computational Linguistics

would perform (and max-margin would fail).

In this paper, we propose the use of a trade-off: a kNN-margin loss that sums over the k hardest sample within a mini-batch. It 1) makes sufficient use of hard samples and also 2) is robust across different model architectures and datasets. In experiments, the kNN-margin loss prevails in (almost) all data and model configurations.

Inference. During text-image matching inference, a nearest-neighbor search is usually performed to obtain a ranking for each of the queries. It has been pointed out by previous works (Radovanović et al., 2010; Dinu et al., 2015; Zhang et al., 2017) that *hubs* will emerge in such high-dimensional space and nearest neighbor search can be problematic for this need. Qualitatively, the hubness problem means a small portion of queries becoming "popular" nearest neighbor in the search space. Hubs harm model's performance as we already know that the predicted text-image correspondence should be a *bipartite matching*[3]. In experiments, we show that the hubness problem is the primary source of error for inference. Though has not attracted enough attention in text-image matching, hubness problem has been extensively studied in Bilingual Lexicon Induction (BLI) which aims to find a matching between two sets of bilingual word vectors. We thus propose to use similar tools during the inference phase of text-image matching. Specifically, we experiment with Inverted Softmax (IS) (Smith et al., 2017) and Cross-modal Local Scaling (CSLS) (Lample et al., 2018) to mitigate the hubness problem in text-image embeddings.

Contributions. The major contributions of this work are

- analyzing the shortcomings of sum and max-margin loss, proposing a kNN-margin loss as a trade-off (for training);

- proposing the use of Inverted Softmax and Cross-modal Local Scaling to replace naive nearest neighbor search (for inference).

2 Method

We first introduce the basic formulation of text-image matching model and sum/max-margin loss in 2.1. Then we propose our intended kNN-margin

---

[3]In Graph Theory, a set of edges is said to be a **matching** if none of the edges share a common endpoint.

loss in Section 2.2 and the use of IS and CSLS for inference in Section 2.3.

2.1 Basic Formulation

The bidirectional text-image retrieval framework consists of a text encoder and an image encoder. The text encoder is composed of word embeddings, a GRU (Chung et al., 2014) or LSTM (Hochreiter and Schmidhuber, 1997) layer and a temporal pooling layer. The image encoder is a VGG19 (Simonyan and Zisserman, 2014) or ResNet152 (He et al., 2016) pre-trained on ImageNet (Deng et al., 2009) and a linear layer. We denote them as functions f and g which map text and image to two vectors of size d respectively.

For a text-image pair (t, i), the similarity of t and i is measured by cosine similarity of their normalized encodings:

$$s(i, t) = \left\langle \frac{f(t)}{\|f(t)\|_2}, \frac{g(i)}{\|g(i)\|_2} \right\rangle : \mathbb{R}^d \times \mathbb{R}^d \to \mathbb{R}. \tag{1}$$

During training, a margin based triplet ranking loss is adopted to cluster positive pairs and push negative pairs away from each other. We list the both the sum-margin loss used in Frome et al. (2013); Kiros et al. (2015); Nam et al. (2017); You et al. (2018); Wehrmann et al. (2018):

$$\min_\theta \sum_{i \in I} \sum_{\bar{t} \in T \setminus \{t\}} [\alpha - s(i, t) + s(i, \bar{t})]_+ \\ + \sum_{t \in T} \sum_{\bar{i} \in I \setminus \{i\}} [\alpha - s(t, i) + s(t, \bar{i})]_+; \tag{2}$$

and the max-margin loss used by Engilberge et al. (2018); Faghri et al. (2018); Lee et al. (2018); Wu et al. (2019):

$$\min_\theta \sum_{i \in I} \max_{\bar{t} \in T \setminus \{t\}} [\alpha - s(i, t) + s(i, \bar{t})]_+ \\ + \sum_{t \in T} \max_{\bar{i} \in I \setminus \{i\}} [\alpha - s(t, i) + s(t, \bar{i})]_+, \tag{3}$$

where $[\cdot]_+ = \max(0, \cdot)$; α is a preset margin (we use $\alpha = 0.2$); T and I are all text and image encodings in a mini-batch; t is the descriptive text for image i and vice versa; $\bar{t}$ denotes non-descriptive texts for i while $\bar{i}$ denotes non-descriptive images for t.

2.2 kNN-margin Loss

We propose a simple yet robust strategy for selecting negative samples: instead of counting all

(Eq. 2) or hardest (Eq. 3) sample in a mini-batch, we take the k-hardest samples. We first define a function $\mathrm{kNN}(x, M, k)$ to return the k closest points in point set M to x. Then the kNN-margin loss is formulated as:

$$\min_\theta \sum_{i \in I} \sum_{\bar{t} \in K_1} [\alpha - s(i,t) + s(i,\bar{t}))]_+ \\ + \sum_{t \in T} \sum_{\bar{i} \in K_2} [\alpha - s(t,i) + s(t,\bar{i}))]_+ \quad (4)$$

where

$$K_1 = \mathrm{kNN}(i, T\backslash\{t\}, k),\, K_2 = \mathrm{kNN}(t, I\backslash\{i\}, k).$$

In max-margin loss, when the hardest sample is misleading or incorrectly labeled, the wrong gradient would be imposed on the network. We call it a *pseudo* hard negative. In kNN-margin loss, though some *pseudo* hard negatives might still generate false gradients, they are likely to be canceled out by the negative samples with correct information. As only the k hardest negatives are considered, the selected samples are still hard enough to provide meaningful supervision to the model. In experiments, we show that kNN-margin loss indeed demonstrates such characteristics.

2.3 Hubness Problem During Inference

The standard procedure for inference is performing a naive nearest neighbor search. This, however, leads to the hubness problem which is the primary source or error as we will show in Section 3.5. We thus leverage the prior that "one query should not be the nearest neighbor for multiple items" to improve the text-image matching. Specifically, we use two tools introduced in BLI: Inverted Softmax (Is) (Smith et al., 2017) and Cross-modal Local Scaling (CSLS) (Lample et al., 2018).

2.3.1 Inverted Softmax (Is)

The main idea of Is is to estimate the confidence of a prediction $i \rightarrow t$ not merely by similarity score $s(i,t)$, but the score reweighted by t's similarity with other queries:

$$s'(i,t) = \frac{e^{\beta s(i,t)}}{\sum_{\bar{i} \in I\backslash\{i\}} e^{\beta s(\bar{i},t)}} \quad (5)$$

where β is a temperature (we use $\beta = 30$). Intuitively, it scales down the similarity if t is also very close to other queries.

2.3.2 Cross-modal Local Scaling (CSLS)

CSLS aims to decrease a query vector's similarity to item vectors lying in *dense* areas while increase similarity to *isolated*[4] item vectors. It punishes the occurrences of an item being the nearest neighbor to multiple queries. Specifically, we update the similarity scores with the formula:

$$s'(i,t) = 2s(i,t) - \frac{1}{k} \sum_{i_t \in K_1} s(i_t, t) \\ - \frac{1}{k} \sum_{t_i \in K_2} s(i, t_i) \quad (6)$$

where $K_1 = \mathrm{kNN}(t, I, k)$ and $K_2 = \mathrm{kNN}(i, T, k)$ (we use $k = 10$).

3 Experiments

In this section we introduce our experimental setups (Section 3.1, 3.2, 3.3) and quantitative results (Section 3.4, 3.5).

3.1 Dataset

dataset	# train	# validation	# test
Flickr30k	$30,000$	$1,000$	$1,000$
MS-COCO 1k	$113,287$	$5,000$	$1,000$
MS-COCO 5k	$113,287$	$5,000$	$5,000$

Table 3: Train-validation-test splits of used datasets.

We use Flickr30k (Young et al., 2014) and MS-COCO (Lin et al., 2014) as our experimental datasets. We list their splitting protocols in Table 3. For MS-COCO, there has been several different splits used by the research community. In convenience of comparing to a wide range of results reported by other works, we use two protocols and they are referred as MS-COCO 1k and 5k where 1k and 5k differs only in the test set used (1k's test set is a subset of 5k's). Notice that MS-COCO 5k computes the average of 5 folds of 1k images. Also, in both Flickr30k and MS-COCO, 1 image has 5 captions - so 5 (text,image) pairs are used for every image.

3.2 Evaluation Metrics

We use R@Ks (recall at K), Med r and Mean r to evaluate the results:

---

[4]*Dense* and *isolated* are in terms of query.

#	architecture	loss	image→text					text→image				
			R@1	R@5	R@10	Med r	Mean r	R@1	R@5	R@10	Med r	Mean r
1.1		sum-margin	30.2	58.7	70.4	4.0	33.0	22.9	50.6	61.4	**5.0**	49.5
1.2		max-margin	30.7	58.7	69.6	4.0	30.3	22.4	48.4	59.3	6.0	39.0
1.3	GRU+VGG19	kNN-margin ($k = 3$)	**34.1**	**61.7**	69.9	**3.0**	**24.7**	**25.1**	**52.5**	64.6	**5.0**	34.3
1.4		kNN-margin ($k = 5$)	33.4	61.6	**71.1**	**3.0**	26.7	24.2	51.8	**64.8**	**5.0**	**32.7**
1.5		kNN-margin ($k = 10$)	33.3	59.4	69.4	**3.0**	28.4	23.4	50.6	63.5	**5.0**	33.8

Table 1: Quantitative results on Flickr30k (Young et al., 2014).

#	architecture	loss	image→text					text→image				
			R@1	R@5	R@10	Med r	Mean r	R@1	R@5	R@10	Med r	Mean r
2.1		sum-margin	48.9	79.9	89.0	1.8	5.6	38.3	73.5	85.3	**2.0**	**8.4**
2.2	GRU+VGG19	max-margin	**51.8**	**81.1**	90.5	**1.0**	5.5	**39.0**	73.9	84.7	**2.0**	12.0
2.3		kNN-margin	50.6	**81.1**	**90.6**	1.4	5.5	38.7	**74.0**	**85.5**	**2.0**	11.8
2.4		sum-margin	53.2	85.0	93.0	**1.0**	3.9	41.9	77.2	88.0	**2.0**	8.7
2.5	GRU+ResNet152	max-margin	**58.7**	**88.2**	94.0	**1.0**	**3.2**	**45.0**	78.9	88.6	**2.0**	8.6
2.6		kNN-margin	57.8	87.6	**94.4**	**1.0**	3.4	43.9	**79.0**	**88.8**	**2.0**	**8.1**

Table 2: Quantitative results on MS-COCO (Lin et al., 2014). Using the 5k test set.

- $R@K$: the ratio of "# of queries that the ground-truth item is ranked in top K" to "total # of queries" (we use $K = \{1, 5, 10\}$; the higher the better);
- Med r: the median of the ground-truth ranking (the lower the better);
- Mean r: the mean of the ground-truth ranking (the lower the better).

We compute all metrics for both text→image retrieval and image→text matching. We follow the convention of taking the model with maximum $R@K$s sum (both text→image and image→text) on the validation set as the best model for testing.

3.3 Hyperparameters

Training. For max-margin models, we follow the configuration specified in Faghri et al. (2018). For all other models, we start with a learning rate of 0.001 and decay it by 10 times after every 10 epochs. We train all models for 30 epochs with a batch size of 128. All models are optimized using an Adam optimizer (Kingma and Ba, 2015).

Model. We use 300-d word embeddings and 1024 internal states for GRU text encoders (all randomly initialized with Xavier init. (Glorot and Bengio, 2010); $d = 1024$ for both text and image embeddings. All image encoders are fixed (with no finetuning) for fair comparison.

3.4 Loss Function Performance

Table 1 and 2 show quantitative results on Flickr30k and MS-COCO respectively.

Flickr30k. kNN-margin loss achieves significantly better performance on all metrics than all other loss. It is worth noticing that max-margin loss fails on this dataset (even much worse than sum-margin). kNN-margin loss with $k = \{3, 5\}$ get the highest scores. We use $k = 3$ for the following experiments unless explicitly specified.

MS-COCO. Max-margin loss performs much better on MS-COCO, especially on R@1 - it has the best R@1 across both configurations. kNN-margin is comparable to max-margin. Specifically, it produces slightly worse R@1s, almost identical R@5s, and slightly better R@10s. Sum-margin, however, performs poorly on MS-COCO. It is worth noting that here we are using the 5k test set, which is a superset of the widely adopted 1k test set. We will compare with quantitative results reported on the 1k test set in the next section.

3.5 Hubs during Inference

To show hubness is indeed a major source of error, we select one of the text-image embeddings to do statistics. We use the model on Table 2 line 2.1 to generate embeddings on MS-COCO's test set. Among the $25,000$ (query, item) pairs, only $1,027$ (4.1%) items are the nearest neighbor (NN) of solely 1 query; there are, however, $19,805$ (79.2%) items that are NN to 0 query and $3,007$ (12.0%) items that are NN to ≥ 5 queries, indicating wide existence of hubs. Moreover, the most "popular" item is NN to 51 queries. We know that one item ought to be NN to only one query

#	dataset	model	inference	image→text					text→image				
				R@1	R@5	R@10	Med r	Mean r	R@1	R@5	R@10	Med r	Mean r
3.1	Flickr30k	GRU+VGG19 kNN-margin	naive	34.1	61.7	69.9	**3.0**	24.7	25.1	52.5	64.6	5.0	34.3
3.2			Is	**36.0**	**64.5**	**72.9**	**3.0**	**20.1**	25.2	52.6	64.4	5.0	31.1
3.3			CSLS	**36.0**	64.4	72.5	**3.0**	20.3	**26.7**	**54.3**	**65.7**	**4.0**	**30.8**
3.4	MS-COCO 5k	GRU+ResNet152 kNN-margin	naive	57.8	87.6	94.4	**1.0**	3.4	43.9	79.0	88.8	**2.0**	8.1
3.5			Is	**64.2**	**89.4**	95.0	**1.0**	3.2	46.7	80.1	89.3	**2.0**	7.8
3.6			CSLS	62.4	89.3	**95.4**	**1.0**	**3.0**	**47.2**	**80.7**	**89.9**	**2.0**	**7.7**
3.7	MS-COCO 1k	(Kiros et al., 2015) (ours[5])		49.9	79.4	90.1	2.0	5.2	37.3	74.3	85.9	**2.0**	10.8
3.8		(Vendrov et al., 2016)		46.7	-	88.9	2.0	5.7	37.9	-	85.9	**2.0**	8.1
3.9		(Huang et al., 2017)		53.2	83.1	91.5	**1.0**	-	40.7	75.8	87.4	**2.0**	-
3.10		(Liu et al., 2017)		56.4	85.3	91.5	-	-	43.9	78.1	88.6	-	-
3.11		(You et al., 2018)		56.3	84.4	92.2	**1.0**	-	45.7	81.2	90.6	**2.0**	-
3.12		(Faghri et al., 2018)		58.3	86.1	93.3	**1.0**	-	43.6	77.6	87.8	**2.0**	
3.13		(Faghri et al., 2018) (ours)		60.5	89.6	94.9	**1.0**	3.1	46.1	79.5	88.7	**2.0**	8.5
3.14		(Wu et al., 2019)		64.3	89.2	94.8	**1.0**	-	48.3	81.7	**91.2**	**2.0**	-
3.15		GRU+ResNet152 kNN-margin	naive	58.3	89.2	95.4	**1.0**	3.1	45.0	80.4	89.6	**2.0**	7.2
3.16			Is	**66.4**	91.8	96.1	**1.0**	2.7	48.6	81.5	90.3	**2.0**	7.3
3.17			CSLS	65.4	**91.9**	**97.1**	**1.0**	**2.5**	**49.6**	**82.7**	**91.2**	**2.0**	**6.5**

Table 4: Quantitative results of different inference methods across different datasets and models. Line 3.1-3.3 are using the model from Table 1 line 1.3 and line 3.4-3.6, 3.15-3.17 are using the model from Table 2 line 2.9. Line 3.7-3.14 are results reported by previous works which all adopted naive nearest neighbor search for inference.

in the ground-truth query-item matching. So, we can spot errors even before ground-truth labels are revealed - for instance, the most "popular" item with 51 NNs must be the *false* NN for at least 50 queries. Table 5 shows the brief statistics.

	$k=0$	$k=1$	$k \geq 2$	$k \geq 5$	$k \geq 10$
#	19,805	1,026	4,169	3,007	500
percentage	79.2%	4.1%	16.7%	12.0%	2.0%

Table 5: Statistics of # items being NN to k queries in the embeddings of Table 2, line 2.1, text→image. There are in total 25,000 (text,image) paris in this embedding.

Both Is and CSLS demonstrate compelling empirical performance in mitigating the hubness problem. Table 4 shows the quantitative results. R@Ks and also Med r, Mean r are improved by a large margin with both methods. In most configurations, CSLS is slightly better than Is on improving text→image inference while Is is better at image→text. The best results (line 3.8, 3.9) are even better than the recently reported state-of-the-art (Wu et al., 2019) (Table 4 line 3.14), which performs a naive nearest neighbor search. This suggests that the hubness problem deserves much more attention and careful selection of inference methods is vital for text-image matching.

4 Limitations and Future Work

This paper brings up a baseline with excellent empirical performance. We plan to contribute more theoretical and technical novelty in follow up works for both the training and inference phase of text-image matching models.

Loss function. Though the kNN-margin loss has superior empirical performance, it is leveraging the prior knowledge we hardcoded in it - it relies on a suitable k to maximize its power. Flickr30k and MS-COCO are relatively clean and high-quality datasets while the real world data is usually not. With the kNN-margin loss being a strong baseline, we plan to bring a certain form of self-adaptiveness into the loss function to help it automatically decide what to learn based on the distribution of data points.

Also, to further validate the robustness of loss functions, we plan to experiment models on more *noisy* data. The reason for max-margin's failure on Flikr30k is more likely that the training set is too small - so the model easily overfits. However, the dataset (Flikr30k) itself is rather clean and accurate. It makes more sense to experiment with a noisy dataset with *weak* text-image correspondence or even false labels. We have two types of candidates for this need: 1) academic datasets that contain "foil" (Shekhar et al., 2017) or adversarial samples (Shi et al., 2018); 2) a real-world text-image dataset such as a news article-image dataset (Elliott and Kleppe, 2016; Biten et al., 2019).

Inference. Both IS and CSLS are *soft* criteria. If we do have the strong prior that the final text-image correspondence is a bipartite matching, we might as well make use of that information and impose a *hard* constraint on it. The task of text-image matching, after all, is also a form of assignment problem in Combinatorial Optimization (CO). We thus plan to investigate tools from the CO literature such as the Hungarian Algorithm (Kuhn, 1955), which is the best-known algorithm for producing a maximum weight bipartite matching; the Murty's Algorithm (Murty, 1968), which generalizes the Hungarian Algorithm into producing the K-best matching - so that rankings are available for computing R@K scores.

5   Related Work

In this section, we introduce works from two fields which are highly-related to our work: 1) text-image matching and VSE; 2) Bilingual Lexicon Induction (BLI) in the context of cross-modal matching.

5.1   Text-image Matching

Since the dawn of deep learning, works have emerged using a two-branch structure to connect both language and vision. Frome et al. (2013) brought up the idea of VSE, which is to embed pairs of (text, image) data and compare them in a joint space. Later works extended VSE for the task of text-image matching (Hodosh et al., 2013; Kiros et al., 2015; Gong et al., 2014; Vendrov et al., 2016; Hubert Tsai et al., 2017; Faghri et al., 2018; Wang et al., 2019), which is also our task of interest. It is worth noting that there are other lines of works which also jointly model language and vision. The closest one might be image captioning (Lebret et al., 2015; Karpathy and Fei-Fei, 2015). But image captioning aims to generate novel captions while text-image matching retrieves existing descriptive texts or images in a database.

5.2   Bilingual Lexicon Induction (BLI)

We specifically talk about BLI as the tools we used to improve inference performance come from this literature. BLI is the task of inducing word translations from monolingual corpora in two languages (Irvine and Callison-Burch, 2017). Words are usually represented by vectors trained from Distributional Semantics, eg.   Mikolov et al. (2013). So, the word translation problem converts to finding the appropriate matching among two sets of vectors which makes it similar to our task of interest. Smith et al. (2017); Lample et al. (2018) proposed to first conduct a direct Procrustes Analysis (Schönemann, 1966) between two sets of vectors, then use criteria that heavily punish hubs during inference to avoid the hubness problem. We experimented with both methods in our task.

6   Conclusion

We discuss the pros and cons of prevalent loss functions used in text-image matching and propose a kNN-margin loss as a trade-off which yields strong and robust performance across different model architectures and datasets. Instead of using naive nearest neighbor search, we advocate to adopt more polished inference strategies such as Inverted Softmax (IS) and Cross-modal Local Scaling (CSLS), which can significantly improve scores of all metrics.

We also analyze the limitations of this work and indicate the next step for improving both the loss function and the inference method.

7   Acknowledgement

We thank the reviewers for their careful and insightful comments. We thank our family members who have both spiritually and financially supported our independent research. The author Fangyu Liu thanks Rémi Lebret for introducing him this interesting problem and many of the related works.

References

Ali Furkan Biten, Lluis Gomez, Marçal Rusiñol, and Dimosthenis Karatzas. 2019. Good news, everyone! context driven entity-aware captioning for news images. *CVPR*.

Junyoung Chung, Caglar Gulcehre, KyungHyun Cho, and Yoshua Bengio. 2014. Empirical evaluation of gated recurrent neural networks on sequence modeling. *arXiv preprint arXiv:1412.3555*.

J. Deng, W. Dong, R. Socher, L.-J. Li, K. Li, and L. Fei-Fei. 2009. Imagenet: A large-scale hierarchical image database. In *Proceedings of the IEEE conference on computer vision and pattern recognition (CVPR)*, pages 248–255. IEEE.

Georgiana Dinu, Angeliki Lazaridou, and Marco Baroni. 2015. Improving zero-shot learning by mitigating the hubness problem. *ICLR worshop*.

Desmond Elliott and Martijn Kleppe. 2016. 1 million captioned dutch newspaper images.

Martin Engilberge, Louis Chevallier, Patrick Pérez, and Matthieu Cord. 2018. Finding beans in burgers: Deep semantic-visual embedding with localization. In *Proceedings of the IEEE Conference on Computer Vision and Pattern Recognition*, pages 3984–3993.

F. Faghri, D. J. Fleet, J. R. Kiros, and S. Fidler. 2018. Vse++: Improving visual-semantic embeddings with hard negatives.

A. Frome, G. S. Corrado, J. Shlens, S. Bengio, J. Dean, and T. Mikolov. 2013. Devise: A deep visual-semantic embedding model. In *NIPS*, pages 2121–2129.

Xavier Glorot and Yoshua Bengio. 2010. Understanding the difficulty of training deep feedforward neural networks. In *Proceedings of the thirteenth international conference on artificial intelligence and statistics*, pages 249–256.

Yunchao Gong, Liwei Wang, Micah Hodosh, Julia Hockenmaier, and Svetlana Lazebnik. 2014. Improving image-sentence embeddings using large weakly annotated photo collections. In *European Conference on Computer Vision (ECCV)*, pages 529–545. Springer.

Kaiming He, Xiangyu Zhang, Shaoqing Ren, and Jian Sun. 2016. Deep residual learning for image recognition. In *Proceedings of the IEEE conference on computer vision and pattern recognition*, pages 770–778.

S. Hochreiter and J. Schmidhuber. 1997. Long short-term memory. *Neural computation*, 9(8):1735–1780.

Micah Hodosh, Peter Young, and Julia Hockenmaier. 2013. Framing image description as a ranking task: Data, models and evaluation metrics. *Journal of Artificial Intelligence Research*, 47:853–899.

Yan Huang, Wei Wang, and Liang Wang. 2017. Instance-aware image and sentence matching with selective multimodal lstm. In *Proceedings of the IEEE Conference on Computer Vision and Pattern Recognition*, pages 2310–2318.

Yao-Hung Hubert Tsai, Liang-Kang Huang, and Ruslan Salakhutdinov. 2017. Learning robust visual-semantic embeddings. In *Proceedings of the IEEE International Conference on Computer Vision (ICCV)*, pages 3571–3580.

Ann Irvine and Chris Callison-Burch. 2017. A comprehensive analysis of bilingual lexicon induction. *Computational Linguistics*, 43(2):273–310.

Andrej Karpathy and Li Fei-Fei. 2015. Deep visual-semantic alignments for generating image descriptions. In *Proceedings of the IEEE conference on computer vision and pattern recognition*, pages 3128–3137.

Diederik P Kingma and Jimmy Ba. 2015. Adam: A method for stochastic optimization. *ICLR*.

R. Kiros, R. Salakhutdinov, and R. S. Zemel. 2015. Unifying visual-semantic embeddings with multimodal neural language models. *Transactions of the Association for Computational Linguistics (TACL)*.

Harold W Kuhn. 1955. The hungarian method for the assignment problem. *Naval research logistics quarterly*, 2(1-2):83–97.

Guillaume Lample, Alexis Conneau, Marc'Aurelio Ranzato, Ludovic Denoyer, and Herv Jgou. 2018. Word translation without parallel data. In *International Conference on Learning Representations*.

Rémi Lebret, Pedro O Pinheiro, and Ronan Collobert. 2015. Phrase-based image captioning. In *Proceedings of the 32nd International Conference on International Conference on Machine Learning-Volume 37 (ICML)*, pages 2085–2094. JMLR. org.

Kuang-Huei Lee, Xi Chen, Gang Hua, Houdong Hu, and Xiaodong He. 2018. Stacked cross attention for image-text matching. In *Proceedings of the European Conference on Computer Vision (ECCV)*, pages 201–216.

T.-Y. Lin, M. Maire, S. Belongie, J. Hays, P. Perona, D. Ramanan, P. Dollár, and L. Zitnick. 2014. Microsoft coco: Common objects in context. In *European conference on computer vision (ECCV)*, pages 740–755. Springer.

Yu Liu, Yanming Guo, Erwin M Bakker, and Michael S Lew. 2017. Learning a recurrent residual fusion network for multimodal matching. In *Proceedings of the IEEE International Conference on Computer Vision*, pages 4107–4116.

Tomas Mikolov, Ilya Sutskever, Kai Chen, Greg S Corrado, and Jeff Dean. 2013. Distributed representations of words and phrases and their compositionality. In *Advances in neural information processing systems*, pages 3111–3119.

Katta G Murty. 1968. Letter to the editoran algorithm for ranking all the assignments in order of increasing cost. *Operations research*, 16(3):682–687.

Hyeonseob Nam, Jung-Woo Ha, and Jeonghee Kim. 2017. Dual attention networks for multimodal reasoning and matching. In *Proceedings of the IEEE Conference on Computer Vision and Pattern Recognition*, pages 299–307.

Miloš Radovanović, Alexandros Nanopoulos, and Mirjana Ivanović. 2010. Hubs in space: Popular nearest neighbors in high-dimensional data. *Journal of Machine Learning Research*, 11(Sep):2487–2531.

Peter H Schönemann. 1966. A generalized solution of the orthogonal procrustes problem. *Psychometrika*, 31(1):1–10.

Ravi Shekhar, Sandro Pezzelle, Yauhen Klimovich, Aurelie Herbelot, Moin Nabi, Enver Sangineto, and Raffaella Bernardi. 2017. "foil it! find one mismatch between image and language caption". In *Proceedings of the 55th Annual Meeting of the Association for Computational Linguistics (ACL) (Volume 1: Long Papers)*, pages 255–265.

Haoyue Shi, Jiayuan Mao, Tete Xiao, Yuning Jiang, and Jian Sun. 2018. Learning visually-grounded semantics from contrastive adversarial samples. In *Proceedings of the 27th International Conference on Computational Linguistics*, pages 3715–3727.

K. Simonyan and A. Zisserman. 2014. Very deep convolutional networks for large-scale image recognition. *CoRR*, abs/1409.1556.

Samuel L Smith, David HP Turban, Steven Hamblin, and Nils Y Hammerla. 2017. Offline bilingual word vectors, orthogonal transformations and the inverted softmax. *ICLR*.

I. Vendrov, R. Kiros, S. Fidler, and R/ Urtasun. 2016. Order-embeddings of images and language. *ICLR*.

Liwei Wang, Yin Li, Jing Huang, and Svetlana Lazebnik. 2019. Learning two-branch neural networks for image-text matching tasks. *IEEE Transactions on Pattern Analysis and Machine Intelligence*, 41(2):394–407.

Jônatas Wehrmann et al. 2018. Bidirectional retrieval made simple. In *Proceedings of the IEEE Conference on Computer Vision and Pattern Recognition*, pages 7718–7726.

Hao Wu, Jiayuan Mao, Yufeng Zhang, Yuning Jiang, Lei Li, Weiwei Sun, and Wei-Ying Ma. 2019. Unified visual-semantic embeddings: Bridging vision and language with structured meaning representations. In *The IEEE Conference on Computer Vision and Pattern Recognition (CVPR)*.

Quanzeng You, Zhengyou Zhang, and Jiebo Luo. 2018. End-to-end convolutional semantic embeddings. In *The IEEE Conference on Computer Vision and Pattern Recognition (CVPR)*.

Peter Young, Alice Lai, Micah Hodosh, and Julia Hockenmaier. 2014. From image descriptions to visual denotations: New similarity metrics for semantic inference over event descriptions. *Transactions of the Association for Computational Linguistics*, 2:67–78.

Li Zhang, Tao Xiang, and Shaogang Gong. 2017. Learning a deep embedding model for zero-shot learning. In *Proceedings of the IEEE Conference on Computer Vision and Pattern Recognition*, pages 2021–2030.

Incorporating Textual Information on User Behavior
for Personality Prediction

Kosuke Yamada   **Ryohei Sasano**   **Koichi Takeda**

Graduate School of Informatics, Nagoya University

yamada.kosuke@c.mbox.nagoya-u.ac.jp,
{sasano,takedasu}@i.nagoya-u.ac.jp

Abstract

Several recent studies have shown that textual information of user posts and user behaviors such as *liking* and *sharing* the specific posts are useful for predicting the personality of social media users. However, less attention has been paid to the textual information derived from the user behaviors. In this paper, we investigate the effect of textual information on user behaviors for personality prediction. Our experiments on the personality prediction of Twitter users show that the textual information of user behaviors is more useful than the co-occurrence information of the user behaviors. They also show that taking user behaviors into account is crucial for predicting the personality of users who do not post frequently.

1 Introduction

Personality information of social media users can be used for various situations such as analyzing crowd behaviors (Guy et al., 2011) and building recommender systems (Wu et al., 2013). Many researchers have focused on developing techniques for predicting personalities and reported that models that use the textual information of target user's posts achieved relatively high performance (Luyckx and Daelemans, 2008; Iacobelli et al., 2011; Liu et al., 2017; Arnoux et al., 2017). However, some social media users frequently read others' posts but rarely post their own messages. Predicting the personalities of such users is generally difficult, but a substantial portion of them often express their opinion or preference through social media activities such as *liking* and *sharing*.

Figure 1 shows tweet examples related to Halloween. The upper tweet was posted by a user who is hosting a Halloween party and thus this user is considered to be extraverted. In contrast, the lower tweet is a post consisting of Halloween illustrations, which is considered to be posted by

Figure 1: Tweet examples. The upper tweet is about a Halloween party and the lower tweet is about Halloween illustrations.

an introverted user. In this way, user personalities can be predicted from their posts. Moreover, users who like or share such tweets are expected to have a similar personality to the user who posted the tweet. Henceforth, we collectively refer to *likes* and *shares* as **behaviors**.

Several studies have leveraged the information derived from the user behaviors for personality prediction (Azucar et al., 2018). For example, Kosinski et al. (2013) and Youyou et al. (2015) proposed personality prediction models for Facebook users that leveraged a user-like matrix, the entries of which were set to 1 if there existed an association between a user and a like and 0 otherwise. Shen et al. (2015) considered the types of the posts (e.g., photos, videos, or status updates) that a target user likes or shares. However, these studies do not take into account the textual information related to user behaviors. We consider that the textual information of tweets that target users have liked/retweeted (shared) contains useful information for predicting their personalities. Therefore, in this paper, we investigate the effect of the textual information of the tweets that target users liked/retweeted.

Proceedings of the ACL 2019, Student Research Workshop, pages 177–182
Florence, Italy, July 28th-August 2nd, 2019. ©2019 Association for Computational Linguistics

2   Related Work

Many studies on personality prediction for social media users utilize the textual information derived from the user's posts. Luyckx and Daelemans (2008) extract syntactic features like part-of-speech n-grams to predict personality of essay authors. Iacobelli et al. (2011) test different extraction settings with stop words and inverse document frequency for predicting personality in a large corpus of blogs using support vector machines (SVM) as a classifier. Liu et al. (2017) use Twitter user posts and propose a deep-learning-based model utilizing a character-level bi-directional recurrent neural network. Arnoux et al. (2017) build a personality prediction model for Twitter users that utilizes word embedding with Gaussian processes (Rasmussen and Williams, 2005). Reasonably good performance can be achieved by taking only 25 tweets into consideration.

Several studies have shown that user behaviors such as likes and shares are also useful to predict user personalities. Kosinski et al. (2013) and Youyou et al. (2015) used page likes on Facebook to create a user-like matrix and proposed personality prediction models based on the matrix. While Kosinski et al. (2013) and Youyou et al. (2015) only use the binary information related to user behaviors, Shen et al. (2015) proposed a personality prediction model that considers the number of likes and shares. Farnadi et al. (2013) focus on network properties such as network size, density, and transitivity, and time factors such as the frequency of status updates per day and the number of tweets per hour in addition to user posts.

For tasks other than personality prediction, several studies leverage the textual information derived from user behaviors in social media. Ding et al. (2017) applied texts that users liked and posted to predict substance users such as people who drink alcohol. They showed that the distributed bag-of-words (DBOW) models (Le and Mikolov, 2014) achieve good performance. Perdana and Pinandito (2018) used texts that users liked, shared, and posted for sentiment analysis. They convert them into weighted features using tf-idf and applied Naïve Bayes. They reported that texts posted by a user lead to a better performance than texts that the user liked/shared, but that the best performance can be realized by combining them.

Figure 2: An example tweet including MBTI analysis by 16Personalities.

3   Dataset

In this study, we predict the personalities of Twitter users. As the personality model, we use the Myers-Briggs Type Indicator (MBTI) (Myers et al., 1990), one of the most widely used personality models, as well as the Big Five (Goldberg, 1990).

3.1   Myers-Briggs Type Indicator

The MBTI recognizes 16 personality types spanned by four dimensions. **E**xtraverted and **I**ntroverted (**E/I**) describe the preference of approaching the outer world of people and things vs. the inner world of ideas; i**N**tuition and **S**ensing (**N/S**) describe the preference of the intuition and the possibilities in the future vs. the perception of things of the present moment; **T**hinking and **F**eeling (**T/F**) describe the preference of rational decision making based on logic vs. subjective values; and **J**udging and **P**erceiving (**J/P**) describe the preference for the control of external events vs. the observation of these events.

The MBTI is often identified through a personality analysis test that consists of selective questions. Several Web sites offer such personality analysis tests, such as 16Personalities[1] is one of such websites, where users can determine their MBTI type by answering 60 questions. The results are represented by 16 *roles*, such as Mediator for INFP and Executive for ESTJ—one for each combination of the four MBTI dimensions (e.g., I, N, F, and P). The Web site has a function that lets users post their results to Twitter with the hashtag #16Personalities. Figure 2 shows an example of such tweets. In this example, the user is analyzed to be "Protagonist", which corresponds to ENFJ in the MBTI. We collected the tweets that contain the hashtag #16Personalities and use them in the experiments.

---

[1]https://www.16personalities.com/

	Users
E / I	4,483 / 15,881
N / S	13,733 / 6,631
T / F	6,498 / 13,866
J / P	7,008 / 13,356
Total	20,364

Table 1: The number of users in each dimension.

No. of collected tweets	Likes	Retweets
0	157	162
1–255	2,076	6,836
256–511	1,331	4,903
512–1,023	2,065	5,326
1,024	14,735	3,137

Table 2: Distribution of users based on number of likes or retweets.

3.2 Data Collection from Twitter

We collected tweets written in Japanese. Twitter Premium search APIs[2] were used to find the tweets containing the hashtag #16personalities and listed 72,847 users who posted such tweets in 2017 and 2018. We refer to a tweet with #16personalities as the gold standard tweet. Next, we collected the latest 3,200 tweets for each user and then discarded the tweets that were posted after the gold standard tweet. Only the users with 1,024 or more tweets were used in this study. The number of such users was 20,364. Table 1 lists the statistics of users for each personality dimension. We can confirm that there are biases in the number of users for all dimensions and that the bias for the E/I dimension is particularly noticeable.

To build a model based on the text related to user behaviors such as *like* and *retweet*, we collected up to 1,024 liked tweets and 1,024 retweeted tweets for each user. Table 2 shows the distribution of users based on the number of likes or retweets. 14,735 out of 20,364 users liked more than 1,023 tweets and 157 users liked no tweets. Only 3,137 users retweeted more than 1,023 tweets and 162 users retweeted no tweets.

4 Personality Prediction Models

We treat personality prediction as a set of binary classification tasks and build four binary classifiers independently for each dimension of the MBTI. We regard the personality of the users shown in

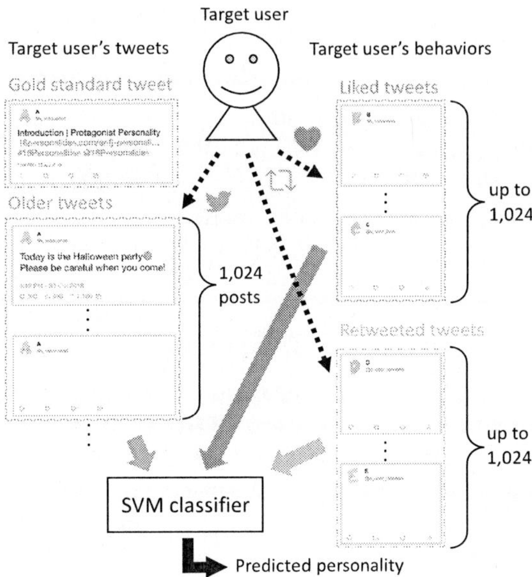

Figure 3: Overview of the personality prediction model.

the tweets with #16personalities as the gold standard personality and attempt to predict it using the SVM classifier. Figure 3 shows an overview of the model. Specifically, we use linear SVM for classification with two types of features: those derived from the tweets that the target user likes or retweets and those derived from the tweets that the target user posts.

4.1 Features derived from User Behaviors

Use of co-occurrence information We build a model similar to Kosinski et al. (2013). They leveraged a co-occurrence matrix of users and likes, the entries of which were set to 1 if there existed an association between a user and a like and 0 otherwise. Similarly, we create the binary matrix of users and behaviors, the entries of which were set to 1 if the user liked/retweeted a tweet, 0 otherwise. For the sake of computational efficiency, we consider tweets that are liked or retweeted by at least ten users. Then, we apply singular value decomposition (SVD) to the matrix and use the dimension-reduced vectors as the features of the SVM classifier.

Use of textual information We propose three models that consider the textual information on user behavior. All three models use MeCab[3] with the IPA dictionary[4] to perform morpholog-

---

[2]https://developer.twitter.com/en/docs/tweets/search/api-reference/premium-search.html

[3]http://taku910.github.io/mecab/
[4]mecab-ipadic-2.7.0-20070801

ical analysis. The first and second models use the 10,000 most frequent words. The first model uses them as BOW features of the SVM classifier and the second model further applies SVD. The third model is a model using DBOW proposed by Ding et al. (2017). This model uses words that have appeared ten or more times. Henceforth, we refer to these models as BOW, BOW w/ SVD, and DBOW, respectively.

4.2 Features derived from User Posts

We apply a similar procedure to generate features derived from user's posts as BOW w/ SVD. We first extract the 10,000 most frequent words and make a user-word matrix. We then apply SVD to the matrix and use the dimension-reduced vectors as the features of SVM.

5 Experiments

5.1 Experimental Settings

We randomly split the users in our Twitter dataset into three parts: training, development, and test sets. Specifically, we used 5,000 users as the test set, 5,000 users as the development set, and the other 10,364 users as the training set. We adopted the area under the curve (AUC) of the receiver operating characteristic (ROC) to evaluate each model.

5.2 Textual vs. Co-occurrence Information of User Behaviors

We first compared the performance of the models using the textual information of user behaviors and the performance of the models using the co-occurrence information of the user behaviors. We built the BOW models, BOW w/ SVD, and DBOW as the models using the textual information. We report results on three settings: 1) considering only likes, 2) considering only retweets, and 3) considering both likes and retweets for each model. We varied the number of dimensions in the reduced space of SVD with 50, 100, 200, 300, and 500, and the vector sizes for DBOW with 50, 100, 200, 300, and 500 and tuned them on the development set. We also optimized SVM parameter C on the development set.

Table 3 shows the experimental results. We found that the models using the textual information of user behaviors performed better than the models using the co-occurrence information of

Models	Likes	Retweets	L & R
BOW	0.6366	0.6348	0.6478
BOW w/ SVD	**0.6453**	**0.6442**	**0.6576**
DBOW	0.6412	0.6433	0.6534
Co-occurrence	0.5950	0.5956	0.6137

Table 3: Average AUC scores of user behavior-based models.

user behaviors. Among the textual information-based models, BOW w/ SVD achieved the best AUC scores. We thus adopt the BOW w/ SVD model as the textual information model in the following subsections.

As for the types of behavior, the models based on likes and the models based on retweets achieved almost the same performance, and the models that combine both of the features achieved the best performance.

5.3 Effect of the Number of User Behaviors

We are interested in the relation between the performance of the personality prediction and the number of behaviors that the model takes into account. Thus, we performed experiments with various sizes of user behaviors. We used the BOW w/ SVD model for this experiment.

Table 4 shows the experimental results for each dimension. We can see that there is a strong correlation between the performance and the number of user behaviors taken into account. However, because the performance improvement between 256 and 1,024 was considerably small, we assume that the performance of the models will not be largely improved even if the models consider more behaviors. For each feature, as in the previous experiment, the models of likes and the models of retweets had almost the same performance, and the models that combine both features achieved the best performance.

5.4 Incorporating Textual Information of User Posts and Behaviors

We compare the performance of the models based only on the textual information of user posts and the models that also leverage the textual information of user behaviors. Specifically, we examined the effect of the textual information derived from user behaviors by changing the number of user posts. The number of texts varied from 1 to 1,024 in multiples of four. We selected the same SVD dimension for posts, likes, and retweets from 50,

		1	4	16	64	256	1024
	EI	0.5491	0.5655	0.6167	0.6401	0.6512	0.6649
	NS	0.5186	0.5353	0.5816	0.6334	0.6715	0.6786
Likes	TF	0.5208	0.5379	0.5750	0.6324	0.6561	0.6626
	JP	0.5084	0.5288	0.5316	0.5473	0.5713	0.5752
	Avg.	0.5242	0.5419	0.5762	0.6133	0.6375	0.6453
	EI	0.5188	0.5432	0.6085	0.6365	0.6590	0.6661
	NS	0.5182	0.5211	0.5717	0.6235	0.6543	0.6600
Retweets	TF	0.5307	0.5467	0.6090	0.6413	0.6650	0.6678
	JP	0.5236	0.5122	0.5321	0.5595	0.5779	0.5830
	Avg.	0.5228	0.5308	0.5803	0.6152	0.6391	0.6442
	EI	0.5506	0.5774	0.6336	0.6449	0.6702	0.6797
	NS	0.5174	0.5372	0.5938	0.6462	0.6782	0.6849
Likes & Retweets	TF	0.5362	0.5588	0.6187	0.6655	0.6732	0.6797
	JP	0.5231	0.5257	0.5397	0.5656	0.5836	0.5859
	Avg.	0.5318	0.5498	0.5965	0.6281	0.6513	0.6576

Table 4: AUC scores of user behavior-based model (BOW w/ SVD) for different number of user behaviors.

		1	4	16	64	256	1024
	EI	0.5666	0.5931	0.6188	0.6678	0.7090	0.7318
	NS	0.5261	0.5641	0.6039	0.6400	0.6765	0.6989
Posts	TF	0.5430	0.5848	0.6344	0.6662	0.6959	0.7096
	JP	0.5243	0.5374	0.5680	0.5878	0.6032	0.6210
	Avg.	0.5400	0.5699	0.6063	0.6405	0.6712	0.6903
	EI	0.6829	0.6880	0.6894	0.6995	0.7126	0.7272
	NS	0.6801	0.6779	0.6840	0.6894	0.6930	0.7042
+ Likes & Retweets	TF	0.6760	0.6800	0.6850	0.6898	0.7048	0.7082
	JP	0.5863	0.5909	0.5906	0.5998	0.6111	0.6176
	Avg.	0.6563	0.6592	0.6623	0.6696	0.6804	0.6893

Table 5: AUC scores of models with features derived from user posts with different number of user posts with/without behavior-based features.

100, 200, 300, and 500 and tuned the vector dimensions and SVM parameter C on the development set. Note that we used all 1,024 behaviors to make the features derived from user behaviors in this experiment.

Table 5 shows the experimental results. We can confirm that there is a strong correlation between performance and the number of user posts taken into account. When we used only a small amount of a user's posts, the performance was significantly improved by taking the user behaviors into account. However, when we used 1,024 of user's posts, we could not confirm any improvement by taking the user behaviors into account. Therefore, we conclude that utilizing user behavior is crucial for predicting the personality of users who do not post frequently—say, users who posted fewer than 256 tweets—but it is not useful when we can collect a large number of tweets posted by the target user.

When we focus on the performance of each dimension, we can find that the importance of the information derived from user behaviors, especially likes, is relatively large for the N/S dimension. For example, in the case of the N/S dimension, the AUC score taking 1,024 liked tweets into account (0.6786) was higher than that achieved by taking 256 user tweets into account (0.6765), unlike the other dimensions.

6 Conclusion and Future Work

In this paper, we investigated the effects of considering user behaviors such as likes and retweets for personality prediction. Through experiments using Twitter data, we found that the textual information of user behaviors is beneficial to predict the user's personality and that utilizing user behaviors is crucial for predicting the personality of users who do not post many tweets, e.g., less than 256, but that the effect of taking user behaviors into account is very limited when we can collect many tweets posted by the target user.

In the future, we plan to explore other useful textual information for personality prediction, such as text in a web page to which the target user linked and public comments directed to the user (as reported by Jurgens et al. (2017)). We can also include replies to the target user's tweets to see if we can improve personality prediction.

Acknowledgements

This work was partly supported by JSPS KAKENHI Grant Number 16K16110.

References

Pierre Arnoux, Anbang Xu, Neil Boyette, Jalal Mahmud, Rama Akkiraju, and Vibha Sinha. 2017. 25 tweets to know you: A new model to predict personality with social media. In *Proceedings of the 11th International AAAI Conference on Web and Social Media (ICWSM'17)*, pages 472–475.

Danny Azucar, Davide Marengo, and Michele Settanni. 2018. Predicting the big 5 personality traits from digital footprints on social media: A meta-analysis. *Personality and Individual Differences*, 124:150–159.

Tao Ding, Warren K. Bickel, and Shimei Pan. 2017. Multi-view unsupervised user feature embedding for social media-based substance use prediction. In *Proceedings of the 2017 Conference on Empirical Methods in Natural Language Processing (EMNLP'17)*, pages 2275–2284.

Golnoosh Farnadi, Susana Zoghbi, Marie-Francine Moens, and Martine De Cock. 2013. Recognising personality traits using facebook status updates. In *Proceedings of the Workshop on Computational Personality Recognition (WCPR'13) at the 7th International AAAI Conference on Weblogs and Social Media (ICWSM'13)*, pages 14–18.

Lewis R Goldberg. 1990. An alternative "description of personality": the big-five factor structure. *Journal of personality and social psychology*, 59(6):1216–1229.

Stephen J Guy, Sujeong Kim, Ming C Lin, and Dinesh Manocha. 2011. Simulating heterogeneous crowd behaviors using personality trait theory. In *Proceedings of the 2011 ACM SIGGRAPH/Eurographics Symposium on Computer Animation (SCA'11)*, pages 43–52.

Francisco Iacobelli, Alastair J Gill, Scott Nowson, and Jon Oberlander. 2011. Large scale personality classification of bloggers. In *Proceedings of the 4th international conference on Affective Computing and Intelligent Interaction (ACII'11)*, pages 568–577.

David Jurgens, Yulia Tsvetkov, and Dan Jurafsky. 2017. Writer profiling without the writer's text. In *Proceedings of the 9th International Conference on Social Informatics (SocInfo'17)*, pages 537–558.

Michal Kosinski, David Stillwell, and Thore Graepel. 2013. Private traits and attributes are predictable from digital records of human behavior. *Proceedings of the National Academy of Sciences*, 110(15):5802–5805.

Quoc Le and Tomas Mikolov. 2014. Distributed representations of sentences and documents. In *Proceedings of the 31st International Conference on Machine Learning (ICML'14)*, pages 1188–1196.

Fei Liu, Julien Perez, and Scott Nowson. 2017. A language-independent and compositional model for personality trait recognition from short texts. In *Proceedings of the 15th Conference of the European Chapter of the Association for Computational Linguistics (EACL'17)*, pages 754–764.

Kim Luyckx and Walter Daelemans. 2008. Personae: a corpus for author and personality prediction from text. In *Proceedings of the 6th International Conference on Language Resources and Evaluation (LREC'08)*, pages 2981–2987.

Isabel Briggs Myers, Mary H McCaulley, and Allen L Hammer. 1990. *Introduction to Type: A description of the theory and applications of the Myers-Briggs type indicator*. Consulting Psychologists Press.

Rizal Setya Perdana and Aryo Pinandito. 2018. Combining likes-retweet analysis and naive bayes classifier within twitter for sentiment analysis. *Journal of Telecommunication, Electronic and Computer Engineering (JTEC)*, 10(1-8):41–46.

Carl Edward Rasmussen and Christopher KI Williams. 2005. *Gaussian processes for machine learning*. The MIT Press.

Jianqiang Shen, Oliver Brdiczka, and Juan Liu. 2015. A study of facebook behavior: What does it tell about your neuroticism and extraversion? *Computers in Human Behavior*, 45:32–38.

Wen Wu, Li Chen, and Liang He. 2013. Using personality to adjust diversity in recommender systems. In *Proceedings of the 24th ACM Conference on Hypertext and Social Media (HT'13)*, pages 225–229.

Wu Youyou, Michal Kosinski, and David Stillwell. 2015. Computer-based personality judgments are more accurate than those made by humans. *Proceedings of the National Academy of Sciences*, 112(4):1036–1040.

Corpus Creation and Analysis for Named Entity Recognition in Telugu-English Code-Mixed Social Media Data

Vamshi Krishna Srirangam, Appidi Abhinav Reddy, Vinay Singh, Manish Shrivastava
Language Technologies Research Centre (LTRC)
Kohli Centre on Intelligent Systems(KCIS)
International Institute of Information Technology, Hyderabad, India.
{v.srirangam, abhinav.appidi, vinay.singh}@research.iiit.ac.in
m.shrivastava@iiit.ac.in

Abstract

Named Entity Recognition(NER) is one of the important tasks in Natural Language Processing(NLP) and also is a sub task of Information Extraction. In this paper we present our work on NER in Telugu-English code-mixed social media data. Code-Mixing, a progeny of multilingualism is a way in which multilingual people express themselves on social media by using linguistics units from different languages within a sentence or speech context. Entity Extraction from social media data such as tweets(twitter)[1] is in general difficult due to its informal nature, code-mixed data further complicates the problem due to its informal, unstructured and incomplete information. We present a Telugu-English code-mixed corpus with the corresponding named entity tags. The named entities used to tag data are Person('Per'), Organization('Org') and Location('Loc'). We experimented with the machine learning models Conditional Random Fields(CRFs), Decision Trees and Bidirectional LSTMs on our corpus which resulted in a F1-score of 0.96, 0.94 and 0.95 respectively.

1 Introduction

People from Multilingual societies often tend to switch between languages while speaking or writing. This phenomenon of interchanging languages is commonly described by two terms "code-mixing" and "code-switching". Code-Mixing refers to the placing or mixing of various linguistic units such as affixes, words, phrases and clauses from two different grammatical systems within the same sentence and speech context. Code-Switching refers to the placing or mixing of units such as words, phrases and sentences from two codes within the same speech context. The structural difference between code-mixing and code-switching can be understood in terms of the position of altered elements. Intersentential modification of codes occurs in code-switching where as the modification of codes is intrasentential in code-mixing. Bokamba (1988). Both code-mixing and code-switching can be observed in social media platforms like Twitter and Facebook, In this paper, we focus on the code-mixing aspect between Telugu and English Languages. Telugu is a Dravidian language spoken majorly in the Indian states of Andhra Pradesh and Telangana. A significant amount of linguistic minorities are present in the neighbouring states. It is one of six languages designated as a classical language of India by the Indian government

The following is an instance taken from Twitter depicting Telugu-English code-mixing, each word in the example is annotated with its respective Named Entity and Language Tags ('Eng' for English and 'Tel' for Telugu).

T1 : *"Sir/other/Eng Rajanna/Person/Tel Siricilla/Location/Tel district/other/Eng loni/other/Tel ee/other/Tel government/other/Eng school/other/Eng ki/other/Tel computers/other/Eng fans/other/Eng vochi/other/Tel samvastharam/other/Tel avthunna/other/Tel Inka/other/Tel permanent/other/Eng electricity/other/Eng raledu/other/Tel Could/other/Eng you/other/Eng please/other/Eng respond/other/Eng @KTRTRS/person/Tel @Collector_RSL/other/Eng"*

Translation: *"Sir it has been a year that this government school in Rajanna Siricilla district has got computers and fans still there is no permanent electricity, Could you please respond @KTRTRS @Collector_RSL "*

---

[1] https://twitter.com/

Proceedings of the ACL 2019, Student Research Workshop, pages 183–189
Florence, Italy, July 28th-August 2nd, 2019. ©2019 Association for Computational Linguistics

2 Background and Related work

There has been a significant amount of research done in Named Entity Recognition(NER) of resource rich languages Finkel et al. (2005), English Sarkar (2015), German Tjong Kim Sang and De Meulder (2003), French Azpeitia et al. (2014) and Spanish Zea et al. (2016) while the same is not true for code-mixed Indian languages. The FIRE(Forum for Information Retrieval and Extraction)[2] tasks have shed light on NER in Indian languages as well as code-mixed data. The following are some works in code-mixed Indian languages. Bhargava et al. (2016) proposed an algorithm which uses a hybrid approach of a dictionary cum supervised classification approach for identifying entities in Code Mixed Text of Indian Languages such as Hindi- English and Tamil-English.

Nelakuditi et al. (2016) reported work on annotating code mixed English-Telugu data collected from social media site Facebook and creating automatic POS Taggers for this corpus, Singh et al. (2018a) presented an exploration of automatic NER of Hindi-English code-mixed data, Singh et al. (2018b) presented a corpus for NER in Hindi-English Code-Mixed along with experiments on their machine learning models. To the best of our knowledge the corpus we created is the first Telugu-English code-mixed corpus with named entity tags.

3 Corpus and Annotation

The corpus created consists of code-mixed Telugu-English tweets from Twitter. The tweets were scrapped from Twitter using the Twitter Python API[3] which uses the advanced search option of Twitter. The mined tweets are from the past 2 years and belong to topics such as politics, movies, sports, social events etc.. The Hashtags used for tweet mining are shown in the appendicies section. Extensive Pre-processing of tweets is done. The tweets which are noisy and useless i.e contain only URL's and hash-tags are removed. Tokenization of tweets is done using Tweet Tokenizer. Tweets which are written only in English or in Telugu Script are removed too. Finally the tweets which contain linguistic units from both Telugu and English language are considered. This way we made sure that the tweets are Telugu-English code-mixed. We have retrieved a total of

[2]http://fire.irsi.res.in/fire/2018/home

[3]https://pypi.python.org/pypi/twitterscraper/0.2.7

2,16,800 tweets using the python twitter API and after the extensive cleaning we are left with 3968 code-mixed Telugu-English Tweets. The corpus will be made available online soon. The following explains the mapping of tokens with their respective tags.

3.1 Annotation: Named Entity Tagging

We used the following three Named Entities(NE) tags "Person", "Organization" and "Location" to tag the data. The Annotation of the corpus for Named Entity tags was manually done by two persons with linguistic background who are well proficient in both Telugu and English. Each of three tags("Person", "Organization" and "Location") is divided into B-tag (Beginner tag) and I-tag (Intermediate tag) according to the BIO standard. Thus we have now a total of six tags and an 'Other' tag to indicate if it does not belong to any of the six tags. The B-tag is used to tag a word which is the Beginning word of a Named Entity. I-tag is used if a Named Entity is split into multiple continuous and I-tag is assigned to the words which follow the Beginning word. The following explains each of the six tags used for annotation.

The 'Per' tag refers to the 'Person' entity which is the name of the Person, twitter handles and nicknames of people. The 'B-Per' tag is given to the Beginning word of a Person name and 'I-Per' tag is given to the Intermediate word if the Person name is split into multiple continuous.

The 'Org' tag refers to 'Organization' entity which is the name of the social and political organizations like 'Hindus', 'Muslims', 'Bharatiya Janatha Party', 'BJP', 'TRS' and government institutions like 'Reserve Bank of India'. Social media organizations and companies like 'Twitter', 'facebook', 'Google'. The 'B-Org' tag is given to the beginning word of a Organization name and the 'I-Org' tag is given to the Intermediate word of the Organization name, if the Organization name is split into multiple continuous.

The 'Loc' tag refers to 'Location' entity which is the name of the places like 'Hyderabad', 'USA', 'Telangana', 'India'. The 'B-Loc' tag is given to the Beginning word of the Location name and 'I-Loc' tag is given to the Intermediate word of a

	Cohen Kappa
B-Loc	0.97
B-Org	0.95
B-Per	0.94
I-Loc	0.97
I-Org	0.92
I-Per	0.93

Table 1: Inter Annotator Agreement.

Tag	**Count of Tokens**
B-Loc	5429
B-Org	2257
B-Per	4888
I-Loc	352
I-Org	201
I-Per	782
Total NE tokens	13909

Table 2: Tags and their Count in Corpus

Location name, if the Location name is split into multiple continuous.

The following is an instance of annotation.

T2 : *"repu/other Hyderabad/B-Loc velli/other canara/B-Org bank/I-Org main/other office/other lo/other mahesh/B-Per babu/I-per ni/other meet/other avudham/other "*

Translation: "we will meet mahesh babu tomorrow at the canara bank main office in Hyderabad"

3.2 Inter Annotator Agreement

The Annotation of the corpus for NE tags was done by two persons with linguistic background who are well proficient in both Telugu and English. The quality of the annotation is validated using inter annotator agreement(IAA) between two annotation sets of 3968 tweets and 115772 tokens using Cohen's Kappa coefficient Hallgren (2012). The agreement is significantly high. The agreement between the 'Location' tokens is high while that of 'Organization' and 'Person' tokens is comparatively low due to unclear context and the presence of uncommon or confusing person and organization names. Table 1 shows the Inter annotator agreement.

4 Data statistics

We have retrieved 2,16,800 tweets using the python twitter API. we are left with 3968 code-mixed Telugu-English Tweets after the extensive cleaning. As part of the annotation using six named entity tags and 'other' tag we tagged 115772 tokens. The average length of each tweet is about 29 words. Table 9 shows the distribution of tags.

5 Experiments

In this section we present the experiments using different combinations of features and systems. In order to determine the effect of each feature and parameters of the model we performed several experiments using some set of features at once and all at a time simultaneously changing the parameters of the model, like criterion ('Information gain', 'gini') and maximum depth of the tree for decision tree model, regularization parameters and algorithms of optimization like 'L2 regularization'[4], 'Avg. Perceptron' and 'Passive Aggressive' for CRF. Optimization algorithms and loss functions in LSTM. We used 5 fold cross validation in order to validate our classification models. We used 'scikit-learn' and 'keras' libraries for the implementation of the above algorithms.

Conditional Random Field (CRF) : Conditional Random Fields (CRF's) are a class of statistical modelling methods applied in machine learning and often used for structured prediction tasks. In sequence labelling tasks like POS Tagging, adjective is more likely to be followed by a noun than a verb. In NER using the BIO standard annotation, I-ORG cannot follow I-PER. We wish to look at sentence level rather than just word level as looking at the correlations between the labels in sentence is beneficial, so we chose to work with CRF's in this problem of named entity tagging. We have experimented with regularization parameters and algorithms of optimization like 'L2 regularization', 'Avg. Perceptron' and 'Passive Aggressive' for CRF.

Decision Tree : Decision Trees use tree like structure to solve classification problems where the leaf nodes represent the class labels and the internal nodes of the tree represent attributes. We

---

[4]https://towardsdatascience.com/l1-and-l2-regularization-methods-ce25e7fc831c

have experimented with parameters like criterion ('Information gain', 'gini') and maximum depth of the tree. Pedregosa et al. (2011)

BiLSTMs : Long short term memory is a Recurrent Neural Network architecture used in the field of deep learning. LSTM networks were first introduced by Hochreiter and Schmidhuber (1997) and then they were popularized by significant amount of work done by many other authors. LSTMs are capable of learning the long term dependencies which help us in getting better results by capturing the previous context. We have BiLSTMs in our experiments, a BiLSTM is a Bi-directional LSTM in which the signal propagates both backward as well as forward in time. We have experimented with Optimization algorithms and loss functions in LSTM.

5.1 Features

The features to our machine learning models consists of character, lexical and word level features such as char N-Grams of size 2 and 3 in order to capture the information from suffixes, emoticons, social special mentions like '#', '@' patterns of punctuation, numbers, numbers in the string and also previous tag information, the same all features from previous and next tokens are used as contextual features.

1. **Character N-Grams:** N-gram is a contiguous sequence of n items from a given sample of text or speech, here the items are characters. N-Grams are simple and scalable and can help capture the contextual information. Character N-Grams are language independent Majumder et al. (2002) and have proven to be efficient in the task of text classification. They are helpful when the text suffers from problems such as misspellings Cavnar et al. (1994); Huffman (1995); Lodhi et al. (2002). Group of chars can help in capturing the semantic information and especially helpful in cases like ours of code-mixed language where there is an informal use of words, which vary significantly from the standard Telugu-English words.

2. **Word N-Grams:** We use word N-Grams, where we used the previous and the next word as a feature vector to train our model which serve as contextual features. Jahangir et al. (2012)

3. **Capitalization:** In social media people tend to use capital letters to refer to the names of the persons, locations and orgs, at times they write the entire name in capitals von Däniken and Cieliebak (2017) to give special importance or to denote aggression. This gives rise to a couple of binary features. One feature is to indicate if the beginning letter of a word is capital and the other to indicate if the entire word is capitalized.

4. **Mentions and Hashtags:** In social media organizations like twitter, people use '@' mentions to refer to persons or organizations, they use '#' hash tags in order to make something notable or to make a topic trending. Thus the presence of these two gives a good probability for the word being a named entity.

5. **Numbers in String:** In social media, we can see people using alphanumeric characters, generally to save the typing effort, shorten the message length or to showcase their style. When observed in our corpus, words containing alphanumeric are generally not named entities. Thus the presence of alphanumeric in words helps us in identifying the negative samples.

6. **Previous Word Tag:** Contextual features play an important role in predicting the tag for the current word. Thus the tag of the previous word is also taken into account while predicting the tag of the current word. All the I-tags come after the B-tags.

7. **Common Symbols:** It is observed that currency symbols, brackets like '(', '[', etc and other symbols are followed by numeric or some mention not of much importance. Hence the presence of these symbols is a good indicator for the words before or after them for not to be a named entity.

5.2 Results and Discussion

Table 3 shows the results of the CRF model with 'l2sgd'(Stochastic Gradient Descent with L2 regularization term) algorithm for 100 iterations. The c2 value corresponds to the 'L2 regression' which is used to restrict our estimation of w*. Experiments using the algorithms 'ap'(Averaged Perceptron) and 'pa'(Passive Aggressive) yielded almost similar F1-scores of 0.96. Table 5 shows

Tag	Precision	Recall	F1-score
B-Loc	0.958	0.890	0.922
I-Loc	0.867	0.619	0.722
B-Org	0.802	0.600	0.687
I-Org	0.385	0.100	0.159
B-Per	0.908	0.832	0.869
I-Per	0.715	0.617	0.663
OTHER	0.974	0.992	0.983
weighted avg	0.963	0.966	0.964

Table 3: CRF Model with 'c2=0.1' and 'l2sgd' algo.

Tag	Precision	Recall	F1-score
B-Org	0.55	0.61	0.58
I-Per	0.43	0.50	0.47
B-Per	0.76	0.76	0.76
I-Loc	0.50	0.59	0.54
OTHER	0.98	0.97	0.97
B-Loc	0.83	0.84	0.84
I-Org	0.09	0.13	0.11
weighted avg	0.94	0.94	0.94

Table 4: Decision Tree Model with 'max-depth=32'

Feature	Precision	Recall	F1-score
Char N-Grams	0.73	0.56	0.62
Word N-Grams	0.88	0.59	0.70
Capitalization	0.15	0.02	0.03
Mentions, Hashtags	0.36	0.14	0.19
Numbers in String	0.01	0.01	0.01
Previous Word tag	0.78	0.19	0.15
Common Symbols	0.21	0.06	0.09

Table 5: Feature Specific Results for CRF

Feature	Precision	Recall	F1-score
Char N-Grams	0.42	0.72	0.51
Word N-Grams	0.57	0.59	0.58
Capitalization	0.19	0.31	0.23
Mentions, Hashtags	0.29	0.20	0.22
Numbers in String	0.06	0.16	0.07
Previous Word tag	0.14	0.20	0.16
Common Symbols	0.16	0.20	0.16

Table 6: Feature Specific Results for Decision tree

Tag	Precision	Recall	F1-score
BL	0.94	0.86	0.89
BO	0.76	0.56	0.64
BP	0.80	0.70	0.74
IL	0.41	0.55	0.47
IO	0.04	0.09	0.056
IP	0.33	0.52	0.40
OTHER	0.97	0.98	0.97

Table 7: Bi-LSTM model with optimizer = 'adam' and has a weighted f1-score of 0.95

the weighted average feature specific results for the CRF model where the results are calculated excluding the 'OTHER' tag. Table 4 shows the results for the decision tree model. The maximum depth of the model is 32. The F1-score is 0.94. Figure 1 shows the results of a Decision tree with max depth = 32. Table 6 shows the weighted average feature specific results for the Decision tree model where the results are calculated excluding the 'OTHER' tag. In the experiments with BiLSTM we experimented with the optimizer, activation functions, no of units and no of epochs. After several experiment, the best result we came through was using 'softmax' as activation function, 'adam' as optimizer and 'categorical cross entropy' as our loss function. The table 7 shows the results of BiLSTM on our corpus using a dropout of 0.3, 15 epochs and random initialization of embedding vectors. The F1-score is 0.95. Figure 2 shows the BiLSTM model architecture.

Table 8 shows an example prediction by our CRF model. This is a good example which shows the areas in which the model suffers to learn. The model predicted the tag of '@Thirumalagiri' as 'B-Per' instead of 'B-Loc' because their are person names which are lexically similar to it. The tag of the word 'Telangana' is predicted as 'B-Loc' instead of 'B-Org' this is because 'Telangana' is a 'Location' in most of the examples and it is an 'Organization' in very few cases. We can

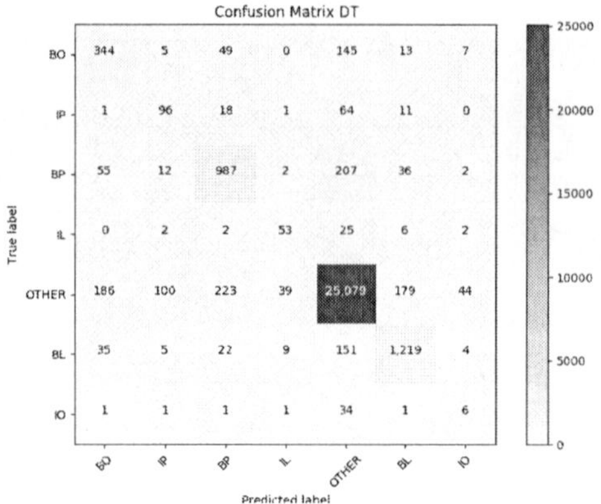

Figure 1: Results from a Decision Tree

Word	Truth	Predicted
Today	OTHER	OTHER
paper	OTHER	OTHER
clippings	OTHER	OTHER
manam	B-Org	OTHER
vartha	I-Org	OTHER
@Thirumalagiri	B-Loc	B-Per
@Nagaram	B-Loc	B-Per
Telangana	B-Org	B-Loc
Jagruthi	I-Org	OTHER
Thungathurthy	B-Loc	B-Loc
Niyojakavargam	OTHER	OTHER
@MedayRajeev	B-Per	B-Org
@JagruthiFans	B-Org	B-Org

Table 8: An Example Prediction of our CRF Model

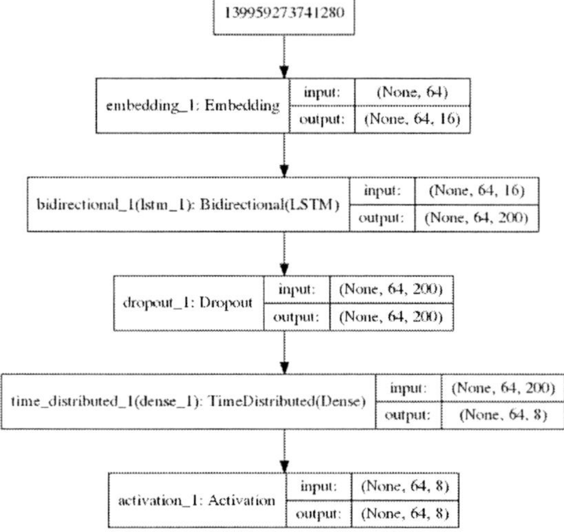

Figure 2: BiLSTM model architecture

also see '@MedayRajeev' is predicted as 'B-Org' instead of 'B-Per'. The model performs well for 'OTHER' and 'Location' tags. Lexically similar words having different tags and insufficient data makes it difficult for the model to train at times as a result of which we can see some incorrect predictions of tags.

6 Conclusion and future work

The following are our contributions in this paper.

1. Presented an annotated code-mixed Telugu-English corpus for named entity recognition which is to the best of our knowledge is the first corpus. The corpus will be made available online soon.

2. Experimented with the machine learning models Conditional Random Fields(CRF), Decision tree, BiLSTM on our corpus, the F1-score for which is 0.96, 0.94 and 0.95 respectively. Which is looking good considering the amount of research done in this new domain.

3. Introducing and addressing named entity recognition of Telugu-English code-mixed corpus as a research problem.

As part of the future work, the corpus can be enriched by also giving the respective POS tags for each token. The size of the corpus can be increased with more NE tags.The problem can be extended for NER identification in code-mixed text containing more than two languages from multilingual societies.

References

Andoni Azpeitia, Montse Cuadros, Seán Gaines, and German Rigau. 2014. Nerc-fr: supervised named entity recognition for french. In *International Conference on Text, Speech, and Dialogue*, pages 158–165. Springer.

Rupal Bhargava, Bapiraju Vamsi, and Yashvardhan Sharma. 2016. Named entity recognition for code mixing in indian languages using hybrid approach. *Facilities*, 23(10).

Eyamba G Bokamba. 1988. Code-mixing, language variation, and linguistic theory:: Evidence from bantu languages. *Lingua*, 76(1):21–62.

William B Cavnar, John M Trenkle, et al. 1994. N-gram-based text categorization. *Ann arbor mi*, 48113(2):161–175.

Pius von Däniken and Mark Cieliebak. 2017. Transfer learning and sentence level features for named entity recognition on tweets. In *Proceedings of the 3rd Workshop on Noisy User-generated Text*, pages 166–171.

Jenny Rose Finkel, Trond Grenager, and Christopher Manning. 2005. Incorporating non-local information into information extraction systems by gibbs sampling. In *Proceedings of the 43rd annual meeting on association for computational linguistics*, pages 363–370. Association for Computational Linguistics.

Kevin A Hallgren. 2012. Computing inter-rater reliability for observational data: an overview and tutorial. *Tutorials in quantitative methods for psychology*, 8(1):23.

Sepp Hochreiter and Jürgen Schmidhuber. 1997. Long short-term memory. *Neural computation*, 9(8):1735–1780.

Stephen Huffman. 1995. Acquaintance: Language-independent document categorization by n-grams. Technical report, DEPARTMENT OF DEFENSE FORT GEORGE G MEADE MD.

Faryal Jahangir, Waqas Anwar, Usama Ijaz Bajwa, and Xuan Wang. 2012. N-gram and gazetteer list based named entity recognition for urdu: A scarce resourced language. In *24th International Conference on Computational Linguistics*, page 95.

Huma Lodhi, Craig Saunders, John Shawe-Taylor, Nello Cristianini, and Chris Watkins. 2002. Text classification using string kernels. *Journal of Machine Learning Research*, 2(Feb):419–444.

P Majumder, M Mitra, and BB Chaudhuri. 2002. N-gram: a language independent approach to ir and nlp. In *International conference on universal knowledge and language*.

Kovida Nelakuditi, Divya Sai Jitta, and Radhika Mamidi. 2016. Part-of-speech tagging for code mixed english-telugu social media data. In *International Conference on Intelligent Text Processing and Computational Linguistics*, pages 332–342. Springer.

F. Pedregosa, G. Varoquaux, A. Gramfort, V. Michel, B. Thirion, O. Grisel, M. Blondel, P. Prettenhofer, R. Weiss, V. Dubourg, J. Vanderplas, A. Passos, D. Cournapeau, M. Brucher, M. Perrot, and E. Duchesnay. 2011. Scikit-learn: Machine learning in Python. *Journal of Machine Learning Research*, 12:2825–2830.

Kamal Sarkar. 2015. A hidden markov model based system for entity extraction from social media english text at fire 2015. *arXiv preprint arXiv:1512.03950*.

Kushagra Singh, Indira Sen, and Ponnurangam Kumaraguru. 2018a. Language identification and named entity recognition in hinglish code mixed tweets. In *Proceedings of ACL 2018, Student Research Workshop*, pages 52–58.

Vinay Singh, Deepanshu Vijay, Syed Sarfaraz Akhtar, and Manish Shrivastava. 2018b. Named entity recognition for hindi-english code-mixed social media text. In *Proceedings of the Seventh Named Entities Workshop*, pages 27–35.

Erik F Tjong Kim Sang and Fien De Meulder. 2003. Introduction to the conll-2003 shared task: Language-independent named entity recognition. In *Proceedings of the seventh conference on Natural language learning at HLT-NAACL 2003-Volume 4*, pages 142–147. Association for Computational Linguistics.

Jenny Linet Copara Zea, Jose Eduardo Ochoa Luna, Camilo Thorne, and Goran Glavaš. 2016. Spanish ner with word representations and conditional random fields. In *Proceedings of the Sixth Named Entity Workshop*, pages 34–40.

A Appendices

Category	Hash Tags
Politics	#jagan, #CBN, #pk, #ysjagan, #kcr
Sports	#kohli, #Dhoni, #IPL #srh
Social Events	#holi, #Baahubali #bathukamma,
Others	#hyderabad #Telangana #maheshbabu

Table 9: Hashtags used for tweet mining

Joint Learning of Named Entity Recognition and Entity Linking

Pedro Henrique Martins[Ψ]   **Zita Marinho**[Ɔ][ɱ] and **André F.T. Martins**[Ψ][♭]

[Ψ]Instituto de Telecomunicações [Ɔ]Priberam Labs [ɱ]Institute of Systems and Robotics [♭]Unbabel
pedrohenriqueamartins@gmail.com,   zita.marinho@priberam.pt,
andre.martins@unbabel.com.

Abstract

Named entity recognition (NER) and entity
linking (EL) are two fundamentally related
tasks, since in order to perform EL, first the
mentions to entities have to be detected. However, most entity linking approaches disregard the mention detection part, assuming that
the correct mentions have been previously detected. In this paper, we perform joint learning of NER and EL to leverage their relatedness and obtain a more robust and generalisable system. For that, we introduce a model
inspired by the Stack-LSTM approach (Dyer
et al., 2015). We observe that, in fact, doing
multi-task learning of NER and EL improves
the performance in both tasks when comparing with models trained with individual objectives. Furthermore, we achieve results competitive with the state-of-the-art in both NER
and EL.

1   Introduction

In order to build high quality systems for complex natural language processing (NLP) tasks, it
is useful to leverage the output information of
lower level tasks, such as named entity recognition
(NER) and entity linking (EL). Therefore NER
and EL are two fundamental NLP tasks.

NER corresponds to the process of detecting
mentions of named entities in a text and classifying them with predefined types such as person, location and organisation. However, the majority of
the detected mentions can refer to different entities
as in the example of Table 1, in which the mention
"Leeds" can refer to "Leeds", the city, and "Leeds
United A.F.C.", the football club. To solve this ambiguity EL is performed. It consists in determining to which entity a particular mention refers to,
by assigning a knowledge base entity id.

In this example, the knowledge base id of the
entity "Leeds United A.F.C." should be selected.

Leeds' Bowyer fined for part in fast-food fracas.		
	NER	EL
Separate	Leeds-ORG	Leeds
Joint	Leeds-ORG	Leeds_United_A.F.C.

Table 1: Example showing benefits of doing joint learning. Wrong entity in red and correct in green.

In real world applications, EL systems have to
perform two tasks: mention detection or NER and
entity disambiguation. However, most approaches
have only focused on the latter, being the mentions
that have to be disambiguated given.

In this work we do joint learning of NER and
EL in order to leverage the information of both
tasks at every decision. Furthermore, by having
a flow of information between the computation of
the representations used for NER and EL we are
able to improve the model.

One example of the advantage of doing joint
learning is showed in Table 1, in which the joint
model is able to predict the correct entity, by
knowing that the type predicted by NER is Organisation.

This paper introduces two main contributions:

- A system that jointly performs NER and EL,
  with competitive results in both tasks.

- A empirical qualitative analysis of the advantage of doing joint learning vs using separate
  models and of the influence of the different
  components to the result obtained.

2   Related work

The majority of NER systems treat the task has
sequence labelling and model it using conditional
random fields (CRFs) on top of hand-engineered
features (Finkel et al., 2005) or bi-directional Long
Short Term Memory Networks (LSTMs) (Lample

Proceedings of the ACL 2019, Student Research Workshop, pages 190–196
Florence, Italy, July 28th-August 2nd, 2019. ©2019 Association for Computational Linguistics

Action	Buffer	Stack	Output	Entity
	[Obama, met, Donald, Trump]	[]	[]	
Shift	[met, Donald, Trump]	[Obama]	[]	
Reduce-PER	[met, Donald, Trump]	[]	[(Obama)-PER]	Barack_Obama
Out	[Donald, Trump]	[]	[(Obama)-PER, met]	Barack_Obama
Shift	[Trump]	[Donald]	[(Obama)-PER, met]	Barack_Obama
Shift	[]	[Donald, Trump]	[(Obama)-PER, met]	Barack_Obama
Reduce-PER	[]	[]	[(Obama)-PER, met, (Donald Trump)-PER]	Barack_Obama, Donald_Trump

Table 2: Actions and stack states when processing sentence "Obama met Donald Trump". The predicted types and detected mentions are contained in the Output and the entities the mentions refer to in the Entity.

et al., 2016; Chiu and Nichols, 2016). Recently, NER systems have been achieving state-of-the-art results by using word contextual embeddings, obtained with language models (Peters et al., 2018; Devlin et al., 2018; Akbik et al., 2018).

Most EL systems discard mention detection, performing only entity disambiguation of previously detected mentions. Thus, in these cases the dependency between the two tasks is ignored. EL state-of-the-art methods often correspond to local methods which use as main features a candidate entity representation, a mention representation, and a representation of the mention's context (Sun et al., 2015; Yamada et al., 2016, 2017; Ganea and Hofmann, 2017). Recently, there has also been an increasing interest in attempting to improve EL performance by leveraging knowledge base information (Radhakrishnan et al., 2018) or by allying local and global features, using information about the neighbouring mentions and respective entities (Le and Titov, 2018; Cao et al., 2018; Yang et al., 2018). However, these approaches involve knowing the surrounding mentions which can be impractical in a real case because we might not have information about the following sentences. It also adds extraneous complexity that might implicate a longer time to process.

Some works, as in this paper, perform end-to-end EL trying to leverage the relatedness of mention detection or NER and EL, and obtained promising results. Kolitsas et al. (2018) proposed a model that performs mention detection instead of NER, not identifying the type of the detected mentions, as in our approach. Sil and Yates (2013), Luo et al. (2015), and Nguyen et al. (2016) introduced models that do joint learning of NER and EL using hand-engineered features. (Durrett and Klein, 2014) performed joint learning of en-

tity typing, EL, and coreference using a structured CRF, also with hand-engineered features. In contrast, in our model we perform multi-task learning (Caruana, 1997; Evgeniou and Pontil, 2004), using learned features.

3 Model Description

In this section firstly, we briefly explain the Stack-LSTM (Dyer et al., 2015; Lample et al., 2016), model that inspired our system. Then we will give a detailed explanation of our modifications and of how we extended it to also perform EL, as showed in the diagram of Figure 1. An example of how the model processes a sentence can be viewed in Table 2.

3.1 Stack-LSTM

The Stack-LSTM corresponds to an action-based system which is composed by LSTMs augmented with a stack pointer. In contrast to the most common approaches which detect the entity mentions for a whole sequence, with Stack-LSTMs the entity mentions are detected and classified on the fly. This is a fundamental property to our model, since we perform EL when a mention is detected.

This model is composed by four stacks: the *Stack*, that contains the words that are being processed, the *Output*, that is filled with the completed chunks, the *Action* stack, which contains the previous actions performed during the processing of the current document, and the *Buffer*, that contains the words to be processed.

For NER, in the Stack-LSTM there are three possible types of actions:

- *Shift*, that pops a word off the *Buffer* and pushes it into the *Stack*. It means that the last word of the *Buffer* is part of a named entity.

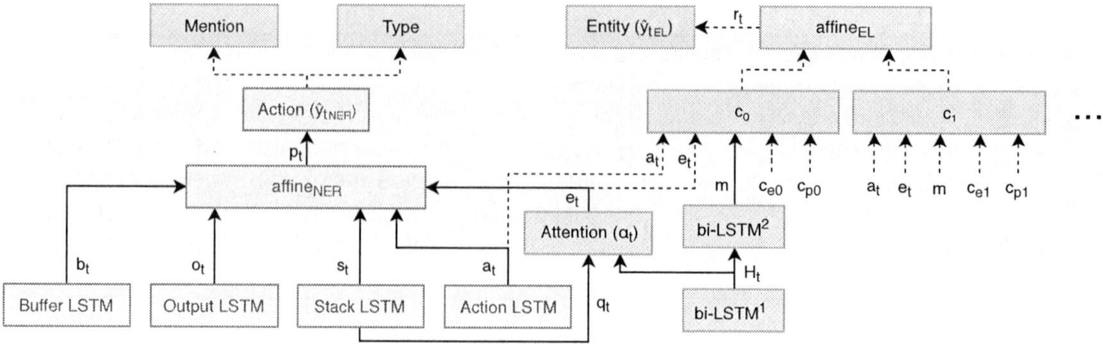

Figure 1: Simplified diagram of our model. The dashed arrows only occur when the action is *Reduce*. The blocks in blue correspond to our extensions to the Stack-LSTM and the green blocks correspond to the model's predictions. The grey blocks correspond to the stack-LSTM, the blue blocks to our extensions, and the green ones to the outputs.

- *Out*, that pops a word off the *buffer* and inserts it into the *Output*. It means that the last word of the *Buffer* is not part of a named entity.

- *Reduce*, that pops all the words in the *Stack* and pushes them into the *Output*. There is one action *Reduce* for each possible type of named entities, e.g. *Reduce-PER* and *Reduce-LOC*.

Moreover, the actions that can be performed at each step are controlled: the action *Out* can only occur if the stack is empty and the actions *Reduce* are only available when the *Stack* is not empty.

3.2 Our model

NER. To better capture the context, we complement the Stack-LSTM with a representation v_t of the sentence being processed, for each action step t. For that the sentence $x_1, \ldots, x_{|w|}$ is passed through a bi-directional LSTM, being h_w^1 the hidden state of its 1st layer (bi-LSTM^1 in Figure 1), that corresponds to the word with index w:

$$\{h_1^1, \ldots, h_{|w|}^1\} = \text{BiLSTM}^1(x_1, \ldots, x_{|w|}).$$

We compute a representation of the words contained in the *Stack*, q_t, by doing the mean of the hidden states of the 1st layer of the bi-LSTM that correspond to the words contained in the stack at action step t, set $\mathcal{S}_{t,}$:

$$q_t = \frac{\sum_{k \in \mathcal{S}_t} h_k^1}{|\mathcal{S}_t|}.$$

This is used to compute the attention scores α_t:

$$z_{tw} = u^\top (W_1 h_w^1 + W_2 q_t)$$
$$\alpha_t = \text{softmax}(z_t),$$

where W_1, W_2, and u are trainable parameters. The representation v_t is then obtained by doing the weighted average of the bi-LSTM 1st layer's hidden states:

$$v_t = \sum_{w=1}^{|w|} h_w^1 \, \alpha_{tw}.$$

To predict the action to be performed, we implement an affine transformation (affine$_{NER}$ in Figure 1) whose input is the concatenation of the last hidden states of the *Buffer* LSTM b_t, *Stack* LSTM s_t, *Action* LSTM a_t, and *Output* LSTM o_t, as well as the sentence representation v_t.

$$d_t = [b_t; \ s_t; \ a_t; \ o_t; \ v_t]$$

Then, for each step t, we use these representations to compute the probability distribution p_t over the set of possible actions $\mathcal{A}$, and select the action $\hat{y}_{t_{\text{NER}}}$ with the highest probability:

$$p_t = \text{softmax}(\text{affine}(d_t))$$
$$\hat{y}_{t_{\text{NER}}} = \arg\max_{a \subset \mathcal{A}} (p_t(a)).$$

The NER loss function is the cross entropy, with the gold action for step t being represented by the one-hot vector $y_{t_{\mathrm{NER}}}$:

$$\mathcal{L}_{NER} = -\sum_{t=1}^{T} y_{t_{\mathrm{NER}}}^{\top} \log(p_t).$$

where T is the total number of action steps for the current document.

EL. When the action predicted is *Reduce*, a mention is detected and classified. This mention is then disambiguated by selecting its respective entity knowledge base id. The disambiguation step is performed by ranking the mention's candidate entities.

The candidate entities $c \in C$ for the present mention are represented by their entity embedding c_e and their prior probability c_p. The prior probabilities were previously computed based on the co-occurrences between mentions and candidates in Wikipedia.

To represent the mention detected the 2nd layer of the sentence bi-LSTM (bi-LSTM^2 in Figure 1), is used, being the representation m obtained by averaging the hidden states h_w^2 that correspond to the words contained in the mention, set $\mathcal{M}$:

$$\{h_1^2, \ldots, h_{|w|}^2\} = \mathrm{BiLSTM}^2(h_1^1, \ldots, h_{|w|}^1)$$
$$m = \frac{\sum_{w \in \mathcal{M}} h_w^2}{|\mathcal{M}|}.$$

These features are concatenated with the representation of the sentence v_t, and the last hidden state of the *Action* stack-LSTM a_t:

$$c_i = [c_{ei};\ c_{pi};\ m;\ v_t;\ a_t].$$

We compute a score for each candidate with affine transformations (affine$_{\mathrm{EL}}$ in Figure 1) that have c as input, and select the candidate entity with the highest score, $\widehat{y}_{t_{\mathrm{EL}}}$:

$$l_t = \mathrm{affine}(\tanh(\mathrm{affine}(c_i, \ldots, c_n)))$$
$$r_t = \mathrm{softmax}(l_t)$$
$$\widehat{y}_{t_{\mathrm{EL}}} = \arg\max_{c \in C} (r_t(c)).$$

The EL loss function is the cross entropy, with the gold entity for step t being represented by the one-hot vector $y_{t_{\mathrm{EL}}}$:

$$\mathcal{L}_{EL} = -\sum_{t=1}^{T} y_{t_{\mathrm{EL}}}^{\top} \log(r_t)).$$

where T is the total number of mention that correspond to entities in the knowledge base.

Due to the fact that not every mention detected has a corresponding entity in the knowledge base, we first classify whether this mention contains an entry in the knowledge base using an affine transformation followed by a sigmoid. The affine's input is the stack LSTM last hidden state s_t:

$$d = \mathrm{sigmoid}(\mathrm{affine}(s_t)).$$

The NIL loss function, binary cross-entropy, is given by:

$$\mathcal{L}_{NIL} = -(y_{NIL} \log(d) + (1 - y_{NIL}) \log(1 - d)),$$

where y_{NIL} corresponds to the gold label, 1 if mention should be linked and 0 otherwise.

During training we perform teacher forcing, i.e. we use the gold labels for NER and the NIL classification, only performing EL when the gold action is *Reduce* and the mention has a corresponding id in the knowledge base. The multi-task learning loss is then obtained by summing the individual losses:

$$\mathcal{L} = \mathcal{L}_{NER} + \mathcal{L}_{EL} + \mathcal{L}_{NIL}.$$

4 Experiments

4.1 Datasets and metrics

We trained and evaluated our model on the biggest NER-EL English dataset, the AIDA/CoNLL dataset (Hoffart et al., 2011). It is a collection of news wire articles from Reuters, composed by a training set of 18,448 linked mentions in 946 documents, a validation set of 4,791 mentions in 216 documents, and a test set of 4,485 mentions in 231 documents. In this dataset, the entity mentions are classified as person, location, organisation and miscellaneous. It also contains the knowledge base id of the respective entities in Wikipedia.

For the NER experiments we report the F1 score while for the EL we report the micro and macro F1 scores. The EL scores were obtained with the Gerbil benchmarking platform, which offers a reliable evaluation and comparison with the state-of-the-art models (Röder et al.). The results were obtained using strong matching settings, which requires exactly predicting the gold mention boundaries and their corresponding entity.

4.2 Training details and settings

In our work, we used 100 dimensional word embeddings pre-trained with structured skip-gram on the Gigaword corpus (Ling et al., 2015). These were concatenated with 50 dimensional character embeddings obtained using a bi-LSTM over the sentences. In addition, we use contextual embeddings obtained using a character bi-LSTM language model by Akbik et al. (2018). The entity embeddings are 300 dimensional and were trained by Yamada et al. (2017) on Wikipedia. To get the set of candidate entities to be ranked for each mention, we use a pre-built dictionary (Pershina et al., 2015).

The LSTM used to extract the sentence and mention representations, v_t and m is composed by 2 hidden layers with a size of 100 and the ones used in the Stack-LSTM have 1 hidden layer of size 100. The feedforward layer used to determine the entity id has a size of 5000. The affine layer used to predict whether the mention is NIL has a size of 100. A dropout ratio of 0.3 was used throughout the model.

The model was trained using the ADAM optimiser (Kingma and Ba, 2014) with a decreasing learning rate of 0.001 and a decay of 0.8 and 0.999 for the first and second momentum, respectively.

4.3 Results

Comparison with state of the art models. We compared the results obtained using our joint learning approach with state-of-the-art NER models, in Table 3, and state-of-the-art end-to-end EL models, in Table 4. In the comparisons, it can be observed that our model scores are competitive in both tasks.

System	Test F1
Flair (Akbik et al., 2018)	**93.09**
BERT Large (Devlin et al., 2018)	92.80
CVT + Multi (Clark et al., 2018)	92.60
BERT Base (Devlin et al., 2018)	92.40
BiLSTM-CRF+ELMo (Peters et al., 2018)	92.22
Our model	92.43

Table 3: NER results in CoNLL 2003 test set.

System	Validation F1		Test F1	
	Macro	Micro	Macro	Micro
Kolitsas et al. (2018)	**86.6**	**89.4**	**82.6**	**82.4**
Cao et al. (2018)	77.0	79.0	80.0	80.0
Nguyen et al. (2016)	-	-	-	78.7
Our model	82.8	85.2	81.2	81.9

Table 4: End-to-end EL results on validation and test sets in AIDA/CoNLL.

Comparison with individual models. To understand whether the multi-task learning approach is advantageous for NER and EL we compare the results obtained when using a multi-task learning objective with the results obtained by the same models when training with separate objectives. In the EL case, in order to perform a fair comparison, the mentions that are linked by the individual system correspond to the ones detected by the multi-task approach NER.

These comparisons results can be found in Tables 5 and 6, for NER and EL, respectively. They show that, as expected, doing joint learning improves both NER and EL results consistently. This indicates that by leveraging the relatedness of the tasks, we can achieve better models.

System	Validation F1	Test F1
Only NER	95.46	92.34
NER + EL	**95.72**	**92.52**

Table 5: Comparison of Named Entity Recognition multi-task results with single model results.

System	Validation F1		Test F1	
	Macro	Micro	Macro	Micro
Only EL	81.3	83.5	79.9	80.2
NER + EL	**82.6**	**85.2**	**81.1**	**81.8**

Table 6: Comparison of Entity Linking results multi-task results with single model results.

Ablation tests. In order to comprehend which components had the greatest contribution to the obtained scores, we performed an ablation test for each task, which can be seen in Tables 7 and 8, for NER and EL, respectively. These experiments show that the use of contextual embeddings (Flair) is responsible for a big boost in the NER performance and, consequently, in EL due to the better detection of mentions. We can also see that the addition of the sentence representation (sent rep v_t) improves the NER performance slightly. Interestingly, the use of a mention representation (ment rep m) for EL that is computed by the sentence LSTM, not only yields a big improvement on the EL task but also contributes to the improvement of the NER scores. The results also indicate that having a simple affine transformation selecting whether the mention should be linked, improves the EL results.

System	Validation F1	Test F1
Stack-LSTM	93.54	90.47
+ Flair	95.40	92.16
+ sent rep	95.55	92.22
+ ment rep	**95.72**	**92.52**
+ NIL	95.68	92.43

Table 7: Ablation test for Named Entity Recognition.

System	Validation F1		Test F1	
	Macro	Micro	Macro	Micro
Stack-LSTM	81.95	84.76	80.37	80.12
+ Flair	82.59	85.75	80.86	81.05
+ sent rep	82.31	85.43	80.49	80.62
+ ment rep	82.64	85.17	81.07	81.76
+ NIL	**82.78**	**85.23**	**81.19**	**81.94**

Table 8: Ablation test for Entity Linking.

5 Conclusions and Future Work

We proposed doing joint learning of NER and EL, in order to improve their performance. Results show that our model achieves results competitive with the state-of-the-art. Moreover, we verified that the models trained with the multi-task objective have a better performance than individual ones. There is, however, further work that can be done to improve our system, such as training entity contextual embeddings and extending it to be cross-lingual.

Acknowledgements

This work was supported by the European Research Council (ERC StG DeepSPIN 758969), and by the Fundação para a Ciência e Tecnologia through contracts UID/EEA/50008/2019 and CMUPERI/TIC/0046/2014 (GoLocal). We thank Afonso Mendes, David Nogueira, Pedro Balage, Sebastião Miranda, Gonçalo Correia, Erick Fonseca, Vlad Niculae, Tsvetomila Mihaylova, Marcos Treviso, and the anonymous reviewers for helpful discussion and feedback.

References

Alan Akbik, Duncan Blythe, and Roland Vollgraf. 2018. Contextual string embeddings for sequence labeling. In *Proceedings of the 27th International Conference on Computational Linguistics*, pages 1638–1649. Association for Computational Linguistics.

Yixin Cao, Lei Hou, Juanzi Li, and Zhiyuan Liu. 2018. Neural collective entity linking. In *Proceedings of the 27th International Conference on Computational Linguistics*, pages 675–686. Association for Computational Linguistics.

Rich Caruana. 1997. Multitask learning. *Machine learning*, 28(1):41–75.

Jason PC Chiu and Eric Nichols. 2016. Named entity recognition with bidirectional lstm-cnns. *Transactions of the Association for Computational Linguistics*, 4:357–370.

Kevin Clark, Minh-Thang Luong, Christopher D. Manning, and Quoc Le. 2018. Semi-supervised sequence modeling with cross-view training. In *Proceedings of the 2018 Conference on Empirical Methods in Natural Language Processing*, pages 1914–1925. Association for Computational Linguistics.

Jacob Devlin, Ming-Wei Chang, Kenton Lee, and Kristina Toutanova. 2018. Bert: Pre-training of deep bidirectional transformers for language understanding. *arXiv preprint arXiv:1810.04805*.

Greg Durrett and Dan Klein. 2014. A joint model for entity analysis: Coreference, typing, and linking. *Transactions of the association for computational linguistics*, 2:477–490.

Chris Dyer, Miguel Ballesteros, Wang Ling, Austin Matthews, and Noah A. Smith. 2015. Transition-based dependency parsing with stack long short-term memory. In *Proceedings of the 53rd Annual Meeting of the Association for Computational Linguistics and the 7th International Joint Conference on Natural Language Processing (Volume 1: Long Papers)*, pages 334–343. Association for Computational Linguistics.

Theodoros Evgeniou and Massimiliano Pontil. 2004. Regularized multi–task learning. In *Proceedings of the tenth ACM SIGKDD international conference on Knowledge discovery and data mining*, pages 109–117. ACM.

Jenny Rose Finkel, Trond Grenager, and Christopher Manning. 2005. Incorporating non-local information into information extraction systems by gibbs sampling. In *Proceedings of the 43rd annual meeting on association for computational linguistics*, pages 363–370. Association for Computational Linguistics.

Octavian-Eugen Ganea and Thomas Hofmann. 2017. Deep joint entity disambiguation with local neural attention. In *Proceedings of the 2017 Conference on Empirical Methods in Natural Language Processing*, pages 2619–2629.

Johannes Hoffart, Mohamed Amir Yosef, Ilaria Bordino, Hagen Fürstenau, Manfred Pinkal, Marc Spaniol, Bilyana Taneva, Stefan Thater, and Gerhard Weikum. 2011. Robust disambiguation of named entities in text. In *Proceedings of the Conference on Empirical Methods in Natural Language Processing*, pages 782–792. Association for Computational Linguistics.

Diederik Kingma and Jimmy Ba. 2014. Adam: A method for stochastic optimization. *arXiv:1412.6980 [cs.LG]*, pages 1–13.

Nikolaos Kolitsas, Octavian-Eugen Ganea, and Thomas Hofmann. 2018. End-to-end neural entity linking. In *Proceedings of the 22nd Conference on Computational Natural Language Learning*, pages 519–529. Association for Computational Linguistics.

Guillaume Lample, Miguel Ballesteros, Sandeep Subramanian, Kazuya Kawakami, and Chris Dyer. 2016. Neural architectures for named entity recognition. *arXiv preprint arXiv:1603.01360*.

Phong Le and Ivan Titov. 2018. Improving entity linking by modeling latent relations between mentions. In *Proceedings of the 56th Annual Meeting of the Association for Computational Linguistics (Volume 1: Long Papers)*, pages 1595–1604.

Wang Ling, Chris Dyer, Alan W Black, and Isabel Trancoso. 2015. Two/too simple adaptations of word2vec for syntax problems. In *Proceedings of the 2015 Conference of the North American Chapter of the Association for Computational Linguistics: Human Language Technologies*, pages 1299–1304. Association for Computational Linguistics.

Gang Luo, Xiaojiang Huang, Chin-Yew Lin, and Zaiqing Nie. 2015. Joint entity recognition and disambiguation. In *Proceedings of the 2015 Conference on Empirical Methods in Natural Language Processing*, pages 879–888.

Dat Ba Nguyen, Martin Theobald, and Gerhard Weikum. 2016. J-nerd: joint named entity recognition and disambiguation with rich linguistic features. *Transactions of the Association for Computational Linguistics*, 4:215–229.

Maria Pershina, Yifan He, and Ralph Grishman. 2015. Personalized page rank for named entity disambiguation. In *Proceedings of the 2015 Conference of the North American Chapter of the Association for Computational Linguistics: Human Language Technologies*, pages 238–243.

Matthew E Peters, Mark Neumann, Mohit Iyyer, Matt Gardner, Christopher Clark, Kenton Lee, and Luke Zettlemoyer. 2018. Deep contextualized word representations. In *Proceedings of NAACL-HLT*, pages 2227–2237, New Orleans, Louisiana.

Priya Radhakrishnan, Partha Talukdar, and Vasudeva Varma. 2018. Elden: Improved entity linking using densified knowledge graphs. In *Proceedings of the 2018 Conference of the North American Chapter of the Association for Computational Linguistics: Human Language Technologies, Volume 1 (Long Papers)*, pages 1844–1853.

Michael Röder, Ricardo Usbeck, and Axel-Cyrille Ngonga Ngomo. Gerbil–benchmarking named entity recognition and linking consistently. *Semantic Web*, (Preprint):1–21.

Avirup Sil and Alexander Yates. 2013. Re-ranking for joint named-entity recognition and linking. In *Proceedings of the 22nd ACM international conference on Information & Knowledge Management*, pages 2369–2374. ACM.

Yaming Sun, Lei Lin, Duyu Tang, Nan Yang, Zhenzhou Ji, and Xiaolong Wang. 2015. Modeling mention, context and entity with neural networks for entity disambiguation. In *Twenty-Fourth International Joint Conference on Artificial Intelligence*.

Ikuya Yamada, Hiroyuki Shindo, Hideaki Takeda, and Yoshiyasu Takefuji. 2016. Joint learning of the embedding of words and entities for named entity disambiguation. In *Proceedings of The 20th SIGNLL Conference on Computational Natural Language Learning*, pages 250–259.

Ikuya Yamada, Hiroyuki Shindo, Hideaki Takeda, and Yoshiyasu Takefuji. 2017. Learning distributed representations of texts and entities from knowledge base. *TACL*, 5:397–411.

Yi Yang, Ozan Irsoy, and Kazi Shefaet Rahman. 2018. Collective entity disambiguation with structured gradient tree boosting. In *Proceedings of the 2018 Conference of the North American Chapter of the Association for Computational Linguistics: Human Language Technologies, Volume 1 (Long Papers)*, pages 777–786.

Dialogue-Act Prediction of Future Responses based on Conversation History

Koji Tanaka[†], Junya Takayama[†], Yuki Arase[†‡]
[†]Graduate School of Information Science and Technology, Osaka University
[‡]Artificial Intelligence Research Center (AIRC), AIST
{tanaka.koji, takayama.junya, arase}@ist.osaka-u.ac.jp

Abstract

Sequence-to-sequence models are a common approach to develop a chatbot. They can train a conversational model in an end-to-end manner. One significant drawback of such a neural network based approach is that the response generation process is a black-box, and how a specific response is generated is unclear. To tackle this problem, an interpretable response generation mechanism is desired. As a step toward this direction, we focus on dialogue-acts (DAs) that may provide insight to understand the response generation process. In particular, we propose a method to predict a DA of the next response based on the history of previous utterances and their DAs. Experiments using a Switch Board Dialogue Act corpus show that compared to the baseline considering only a single utterance, our model achieves 10.8% higher F1-score and 3.0% higher accuracy on DA prediction.

1 Introduction

Dialogue systems adopt neural networks (NNs) (Vinyals and Le, 2015) because they allow a model to be developed in an end-to-end manner without manually designed rules and patterns for response generation. However, in a NN-based approach, the response generation process is hidden in the model, which makes it difficult to understand why the model generates a specific response. This is a significant problem in commercially produced chatbots because the model outputs cannot be controlled. To tackle this problem, Zhao et al. (2018) argued that interpretable response generation models are important. As the first step toward this direction, we focus on dialogue-acts (DAs) as clues to understand the response generation process. We speculate that the predicted DAs indicates which types of response the model tries to generate.

	Utterance (DA)
1	Oh, I've only, I've only skied in Utah once. (Statement)
2	Oh, really? (Question)
3	I only skied once my whole life. (Statement)
4	Uh-huh. (Uninterpretable)
5	But, do you do a lot of skiing there? (Question)

Table 1: Example of utterances and their DAs (in parenthesis) sampled from the SwDA corpus.

Specifically, we propose a method to predict the DA of the next response. This problem was proposed by Reithinger et al. (1996). A conversation consists of a sequence of utterances and responses, where the next response depends on the history of utterances and responses. Table 1 shows an example of a conversation with utterances and their DAs sampled from the Switch Board Dialogue Act (SwDA) corpus. The DA of the last response, "But, do you do a lot of skiing there? (Question)" is not predictable using the previous utterance of "Uh-huh." nor using its DA of "Uninterpretable". To correctly predict the DA, we need to refer to the entire sequence starting from first utterance of "Oh, I've only skied in Utah once." when the speaker is talking about skiing experience.

Our model considers the conversation history for DA prediction. It independently encodes sequences of text surfaces and DAs of utterances using a recurrent neural network (RNN). Then it predicts the most likely DA of the next response based on the outputs of RNNs. Cervone et al. (2018) showed that a DA is useful to improve the coherency of response. The predicted DAs can be used to generate a future response, which adds controllability and interpretability into a neural di-

197

Proceedings of the ACL 2019, Student Research Workshop, pages 197–202
Florence, Italy, July 28th-August 2nd, 2019. ©2019 Association for Computational Linguistics

alogue system.

We used a SwDA corpus for the evaluation, in which telephone conversations are transcribed and annotated with DAs. The macro Precision, Recall, F1, and overall Accuracy measure the performance compared the baseline. The results show that our model, which considers the history of utterances and their DAs, outperforms the baseline, which only considers the input utterance by 10.8% F1 and 3.0% Accuracy.

2   Related Works

Previous studies on DA prediction aimed to predict the current DA from the corresponding utterance text. Kalchbrenner and Blunsom (2013) proposed a method using Convolutional Neural Network (CNN) to obtain a representation capturing the local features of utterance and RNN to obtain the context representation of the utterance. Experiments using the SwDA corpus showed that their method outperformed previous methods for DA prediction using non-neural machine learning models. Khanpour et al. (2016) proposed a method based on multi-layer RNN that uses an utterance as an input. Their method achieved an 80.1% prediction accuracy of the SwDA corpus, and is the current state-of-the-art method.

Unlike these previous studies, we focus on DA prediction of the next (*i.e.*, unseen) response. Reithinger et al. (1996) proposed a statistical method using a Markov chain. Using their original corpus, their method achieved of the 76.1% top_3 accuracy. We tackled the problem of DA prediction of the next utterance considering the history of utterances and previous DAs using a NN. We anticipate that the predicted DA is useful for understanding the response generation process and improving the quality of the response generation.

3   Proposed Model

Figure 1 illustrates the design of our model, which consists of three encoders with different purposes. The Utterance Encoder encodes the utterance text into a vector, which is then inputted into the Context Encoder that handles the history of utterance texts. The Dialogue-act (DA) Encoder encodes and handles the sequence of DAs. Finally, outputs of the Context and DA Encoders are concatenated and input to a classifier that predicts the DA of the next response. Note that our model does not peek into the text of next response to predict the DA.

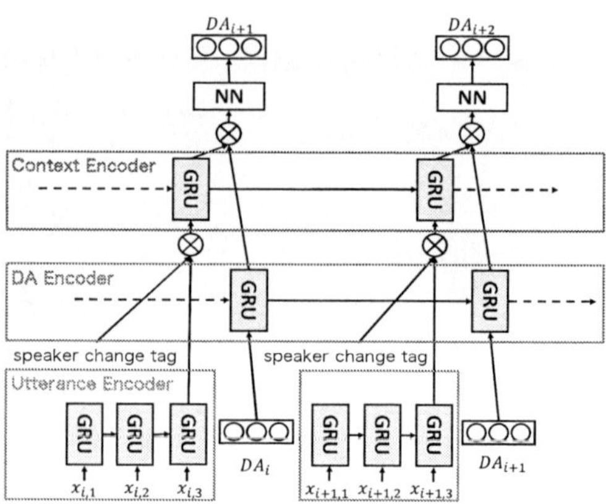

Figure 1: Design of our model consisting of three encoders that encode 1) text surfaces, 2) DAs, and 3) utterance history. ($\otimes$ concatenates vectors)

Consequently, the predicted DA is used to generate the response text in the future.

3.1   Utterance Encoder & Context Encoder

The Utterance Encoder vectorizes an input utterance. It is an RNN that takes each word in the utterance in a forward direction by applying padding in order to realize a uniform input size. Then, the Context Encoder, which is another RNN, takes the final output of the Utterance Encoder to generate a context vector that handles the history of utterances. While our model takes a single sentence as an input to the Utterance Encoder, the speakers do not necessarily change at every single sentence in a natural conversation. Hence, our model allows cases where the same speaker continuously speaks. Specifically, a speaker change tag, which is inputted into the Context Encoder, is used to indicate when the speaker changes.

3.2   Dialogue-act (DA) Encoder

The DA Encoder plays the role of handling the history of DAs. A DA is represented as a one-hot vector and encoded by RNN. During the training, we use teacher forcing to avoid error propagation. That is, the gold DA of the current utterance is inputted into the model instead of the predicted one.

3.3   Dialogue-act Prediction

Finally, the classifier determines the DA of the next response. It is a single fully-connected layer culminating in the soft-max layer. Given a concatenation of outputs from the Context Encoder

Tag	# of tags in the corpus
Statement	$576,005$
Uninterpretable	$93,238$
Understanding	$241,008$
Agreement	$55,375$
Directive	$3,685$
Greeting	$6,618$
Question	$54,498$
Apology	$11,446$
Other	$19,882$

Table 2: Distribution of DA tags in the preprocessed SwDA corpus.

and DA Encoder, the classifier conducts a multi-class classification and identifies the most likely DA of the next response.

4 Experiment

4.1 Switch Board Dialogue Act Corpus (SwDA)

We evaluate the accuracy of our model to predict the DA of the next response using the SwDA corpus, which transcribes telephone conversation and annotates DAs of utterances. The SwDA corpus conforms to the damsl tag schema.[1] We assembled the tag sets referring to easy damsl (Isomura et al., 2009) into 9 tags (Table 2) in order to consolidate tags with a significantly low frequency. The SwDA corpus provides transcriptions of $1,155$ conversations with $219,297$ utterances. One conversation contains 189 utterances on average. Because the average length of utterance sequences is large, we use a sliding window with a size of 5 to cut a sequence into several conversations.

The number of conversations increases to $212,367$ with $1,061,835$ utterances. Table 2 shows the distribution of DAs in the processed corpus. We randomly divide the conversations in the corpus into 80%, 10%, and 10% for training, development, and testing, respectively.

4.2 Model Settings

We apply a Gated Recurrent Unit (GRU) (Cho et al., 2014) to each RNN in our model. We set the dimensions of word embedding to 300 and those of the DA embedding to 100. The dimensions of the GRU hidden unit of the Utterance Encoder are

[1] https://web.stanford.edu/~jurafsky/ws97/manual.august1.html

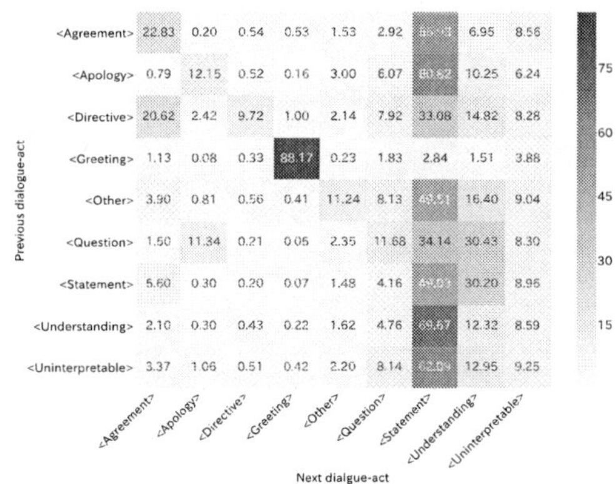

Figure 2: Conditional Probabilities of DA transitions. "Greeting" has a clear pattern, which is followed by a "Greeting". Other DAs tend to be followed by a "Statement".

set to 512, while those the Context Encoder are set to 513 (one element is for the speaker change tag) and those of the DA Encoder are set to 128. Hence, the dimensions of an input into the classifier are 641. The dimensions of the hidden unit of the fully-connected layer are set to 100. The cross-entropy error is used for the loss function, and the Adam (Kingma and Ba, 2014) optimizer with a learning rate of $5e - 5$ is used for optimization. The number of epochs is set to 30. We use the model with the lowest development loss for testing.

We use teacher forcing for training and similar setting for testing by inputting the gold DA of the previous time step into the DA Encoder. This means that the evaluation results here show the performance when the predictions of the previous time steps are all correct.

As Table 2 shows, the numbers of DAs are highly diverse. To avoid frequent tags dominating the results, we measure the macro averages of precision, recall, and F1-score of each DA. We also measure the overall accuracy.

4.3 Baselines

To investigate the effects of each encoder in our model, we compare our model to the baseline (Table 3). The second and third rows are simple methods. Max-Probability is another non-neural baseline that outputs the DA with highest conditional probability from the input DA. Figure 2 shows the conditional probability of DA transitions computed in our training set. "Greeting" has a no-

	Utterance Encoder	Context Encoder	DA Encoder	Precision	Recall	F1-score	Accuracy
Proposed model	✓	✓	✓	52.7	**32.5**	**32.4**	**69.7**
Max-Probability				15.9	19.6	16.9	54.8
Utterance-only	✓			24.4	21.6	21.6	66.7
Utterance-seq	✓	✓		30.9	25.1	23.8	68.5
DA+Utterance-seq	✓	✓	✓ (single-turn)	**53.1**	29.9	30.3	68.7
DAseq-only			✓	44.7	28.7	27.9	67.1
DAseq+Utterance	✓		✓	45.8	29.0	29.3	68.2

Table 3: Macro averages of precision, recall, F1-score, and overall accuracy

ticeable pattern in which it is followed by "Greeting". This is natural considering human communication. On the other hand, other DAs are mostly followed by "Statement". This implies that only a previous DA is insufficient to predict the next DA.

The rest of Table 3 shows NN-based baselines. The Utterance-only is the model that only has the Utterance Encoder (*i.e.*, it predicts the DA of the next response based only on the input utterance). The Utterance-seq, which has the Utterance Encoder and Context Encoder, predicts the DA based on a sequence of utterances. On the other hand, the DAseq-only has only the DA Encoder and predicts the DA of the next response based on the sequence of previous DAs. The DAseq+Utterance has the Utterance Encoder and DA Encoder, which considers the sequence of DAs and the single utterance. The DA+Utterance-seq contains the Utterance Encoder and Context Encoder. It considers only the DA of the input utterance and not the sequence.

4.4 Results

Table 3 shows the macro averages of the precision, recall, and F1-score, as well as overall accuracies for each model. For all evaluation model, our model exhibits the best performances; recall, F1, and accuracy 32.5%, 32.4%, and 69.7%, respectively. As discussed in Section 1, Khanpour et al. (2016) achieved 80.1% prediction accuracy for the same SwDA corpus. Their method predicts the DAs of the current utterance given in text. Although their accuracy is not directly comparable to ours due to differences in data splits, 80.1% can be regarded as the upper-bounds of our task. Our method achieves 87.0% of this upper-bound. Below we investigate which encoders contribute to prediction.

Max-Probability performs quite poorly rather than other neural network based model. This may be because of the imbalanced transition patterns of DAs as shown in Figure 2, which shows that

Tag	# of tags in the corpus	Proposed model	Utterance-seq
Statement	576,005	80.8	80.4
Uninterpretable	93,238	4.7	2.6
Understanding	241,008	69.5	67.6
Agreement	55,375	23.1	15.3
Directive	3,685	2.7	0.0
Greeting	6,618	81.3	46.7
Question	54,498	8.1	2.0
Apology	11,446	22.7	11.3
Other	19,882	3.6	0.0

Table 4: F1-score per DA

the next DA prediction requires more features to achieve precise prediction.

Utterance-seq achieves 1.8% higher accuracy than Utterance-only, demonstrating the effectiveness of considering the history of utterances rather than a single utterance.

The DA+Utterance-seq outperforms Utterance-seq on F1 by 6.5%. This result implies that a previous DA is an effective hint for DA prediction of next responses. In addition, the sequence of DAs is also effective for the next DA prediction, which is shown by the superior performance of the DAseq-only to the Utterance-seq. Specifically, DAseq-only performs 4.1% higher macro-F1 than Utterance-seq, but has 1.4% lower accuracy than Utterance-seq. Similarly, DAseq+Utterance achieves 5.5% higher F1 than Utterance-seq. Overall, DAs of either single-turn or a sequence largely boost precision, recall, and F1. On the other hand, a sequence of utterances contributes to accuracy. These results imply that the sequence of DAs is effective to predict infrequent DAs and the sequence of utterances is effective to predict common DAs. This may be because the DA Encoder is more robust against the data sparseness issue due to its much smaller vocabulary size compared to that of the Utterance Encoder. These analyses show that our model achieves the best performance considering both sequence of utterances and DAs.

Table 4 shows the F1-scores per DA of the

	Utterance (DA)	Gold DA	Proposed model	Utterance-seq
1	What are they , (Uninterpretable)	Statement	Statement	Statement
2	the , (Statement)	Statement	Statement	Statement
3	I know , (Statement)	Statement	Statement	Statement
4	a Rabbit 's one , diesel (Statement)	Agreement	Understanding	Understanding
5	Uh-huh , (Agreement)	**Agreement**	**Agreement**	**Statement**
1	I hope so too . (Statement)	Statement	Statement	Statement
2	You know . Right now there 's a lot on the market for sale because of people having lost Yes . (Statement)	Understanding	Understanding	Understanding
3	Yes . (Understanding)	Statement	Statement	Statement
4	and everything (Statement)	Statement	Statement	Statement
5	so that 's , you know , that keeps prices down (Statement)	**Understanding**	**Understanding**	**Understanding**
1	It does n't seem like , (Statement)	Statement	Statement	Statement
2	but I guess when you think of it everybody has some sort of aerosol in their home (Statement)	Understanding	Understanding	Understanding
3	Yeah . (Understanding)	Statement	Statement	Statement
4	You know , (Statement)	Statement	Statement	Statement
5	and it 's kind of dangerous . (Statement)	**Agreement**	**Understanding**	**Understanding**

Table 5: Examples of predicted DAs by the proposed model and Utterance-seq. DA in a parenthesis shows that of the input utterance, while "Gold DA" shows the DAs of the next responses. The column of "Proposed Model" column shows the predicted DAs of the next responses by the proposed model, and the column of "Utterance-seq" shows the predicted DAs of the next responses by Utterance-seq.

proposed model and Utterance-seq. The proposed model outperforms Utterance-seq on all the DAs. In particular, infrequent tags of "Agreement", "Greeting", "Question" and "Apology" show significant improvements between 6.1% and 34.6%. Furthermore, the proposed model correctly predicts "Directive" and "Other" even though Utterance-seq does not predict any of these correctly.

4.5 Examples of Predicted DAs

Table 5 shows examples of the predicted DAs by the proposed model and Utterance-seq. The first example shows that the proposed model correctly predicts "Agreement", which only has 5.2% occurrence in the training set, whereas Utterance-seq most frequently predicts it as "Statement".

The second and third examples demonstrate the difficulty of DA prediction of the next response. The input utterances of these examples have the same DA sequences, but the DAs of the final responses differ ("Understanding" and "Agreement"). While both the proposed model and Utterance-seq correctly predict the final DA of the second example, both fail in the third example.

The third conversation is about an aerosol, and the response to the final utterance of "and it's kind of dangerous." depends on if one of the speakers understands the danger of the aerosol. To correctly predict DAs in such a case, a much longer conversation sequence and/or personalize the prediction model must be considered based on profiles or knowledge of speakers. This is the direction of our future work.

5 Conclusion

We propose a method to predict a DA of the next response considering the sequences of utterances and DAs. The evaluation results using the SwDA corpus show that the proposed model achieves 69.7% accuracy and 32.4% macro-F1. Additionally, the results show that the sequence of DAs significantly helps the prediction of infrequent DAs.

In the future, we plan to develop a response generation model using the predicted DAs.

Acknowledgements

This project is funded by Microsoft Research Asia, Microsoft Japan Co., Ltd., and JSPS KAKENHI Grant Number JP18K11435.

References

Alessandra Cervone, Evgeny Stepanov, and Giuseppe Riccardi. 2018. Coherence models for dialogue. In *Proceedings of the Interspeech*, pages 1011–1015.

Kyunghyun Cho, Bart Van Merriënboer, Caglar Gulcehre, Dzmitry Bahdanau, Fethi Bougares, Holger Schwenk, and Yoshua Bengio. 2014. Learning Phrase Representations using RNN Encoder-Decoder for Statistical Machine Translation. In *Proceedings of the EMNLP*, pages 1724–1734.

Naoki Isomura, Fujio Toriumi, and Kenichiro Ishii. 2009. Evaluation method of non-task-oriented dialogue system by HMM. *The IEICE transactions on information and systems (Japanese edition)*, 92(4):542–551.

Nal Kalchbrenner and Phil Blunsom. 2013. Recurrent convolutional neural networks for discourse compositionality. In *Proceedings of the Workshop on CVSC*, pages 119–126.

Hamed Khanpour, Nishitha Guntakandla, and Rodney Nielsen. 2016. Dialogue act classification in domain-independent conversations using a deep recurrent neural network. In *Proceedings of the COLING*, pages 2012–2021.

Diederik Kingma and Jimmy Ba. 2014. Adam: A method for stochastic optimization. In *Proceedings of the ICLR*.

Norbert Reithinger, Ralf Engel, Michael Kipp, and Martin Klesen. 1996. Predicting dialogue acts for a speech-to-speech translation system. In *Proceeding of the ICSLP*, pages 654–657 vol.2.

Oriol Vinyals and Quoc V Le. 2015. A Neural Conversational Model. In *Proceedings of the ICML*.

Tiancheng Zhao, Kyusong Lee, and Maxine Eskenazi. 2018. Unsupervised discrete sentence representation learning for interpretable neural dialog generation. In *Proceedings of the ACL*, pages 1098–1107.

Computational ad hominem detection

Pieter Delobelle, Murilo Cunha, Eric Massip Cano,
Jeroen Peperkamp and **Bettina Berendt**
KU Leuven, Department of Computer Science
Celestijnenlaan 200A, 3000 Leuven, Belgium
{pieter.delobelle,murilo.cunha, eric.massipcano}@student.kuleuven.be
and {jeroen.peperkamp, bettina.berendt}@kuleuven.be

Abstract

Fallacies like the personal attack—also known as the ad hominem attack—are introduced in debates as an easy win, even though they provide no rhetorical contribution. Although their importance in argumentation mining is acknowledged, automated mining and analysis is still lacking. We show TF-IDF approaches are insufficient to detect the ad hominem attack. Therefore we present a machine learning approach for information extraction, which has a recall of 80% for a social media data source. We also demonstrate our approach with an application that uses online learning.

1 Introduction

Debates are shaping our world, with them happening online more than ever. But for these debates—and their offline variants as well—to be valuable, their argumentation needs to be solid. As Stede and Schneider (2018, Sec. 1.3) recognize, studying fallacies is crucial for the understanding of arguments and their validity. The ad hominem fallacy, the personal attack, is one of the more prevalent fallacies. Despite its common occurrence, a personal attack can be quite effective and might shape the course of debates.

In online discussion fora, these attacks are often unwanted for their low rhetorical quality. These debates are watched by dedicated members of those fora, so-called moderators. They follow entire discussion threads and flag any unwanted posts; which can take up a lot of their time and the discussion might have already panned out. Automated flagging could significantly improve the quality of debates and save moderators a lot of time.

When developing such an automated system, the variety and ambiguity of ad hominem attacks can be difficult to cope with. These attacks range from simple name calling (*i.e.* *"You're stupid"*), abusive attacks (*i.e.* *"He's dishonest"*) to more complex circumstantial attacks (*i.e.* *"You smoke yourself!"*) (Walton, 1998). Detecting all these varieties is quite challenging, since there can even be discussion about some of those labels amongst humans.

We hereby focus in this paper on detecting mainly two variants of the ad hominem fallacy: name calling and abusive attacks. To realize this automated system, we present a recurrent neural model to detect ad hominem attack in a paragraph, and we experiment with various other models to compare them. Finally, we look into the issues related to crowd sourcing of additional labeled paragraphs through an application as a web demo.

This article is structured as follows: Section 2 covers related work on ad hominem fallacies, detecting those fallacies, and crowd sourcing data sets. Section 3 will then review the components used in our approach, which is then further discussed in Section 4. Section 5 outlines the used data set, the training setup, and baseline models; afterwards the results are discussed in Subsection 5.3. Finally, Section 6 concludes this work and discusses future improvements.

2 Related work

The study of argumentations has a long history, with *Rethoric* by Aristotle being one of the more traditional works. In the second book, he discussed the concept of *Logos*, the argument or reasoning pattern in a debate. More recently, reasoning and argumentations are studied in the field of natural language processing (NLP). The subfield of argumentation mining focusses on extracting arguments and their relations (i.e. graphs) from texts (Stede and Schneider, 2018).

Ad hominem attacks The work of Walton (1998) describes at the structure of ad hominem attacks in great depth, from a non-computational view. In addition to this, the work also analyzes

203

Proceedings of the ACL 2019, Student Research Workshop, pages 203–209
Florence, Italy, July 28th-August 2nd, 2019. ©2019 Association for Computational Linguistics

different subtypes of ad hominem attacks. The simplest form is the direct ad hominem, and an example of a more complex attack is guilt by association. Similarly, programmer and venture capitalist Paul Graham introduces a hierarchical view of discussions, with name-calling and ad hominem attacks as the lowest layers (Graham, 2008). Although both discussions of ad hominem fallacies and debating in general are an important aspect to keep in mind, neither of them discuss automated detection of ad hominem fallacies.

Mining ad hominem fallacies Habernal et al. (2018) discusses methods to detect name calling, a subset of ad hominem attacks. Their work is focussed on how and where these fallacies occur in so-called discussion trees, of which online fora and social media are examples. But they also look into two models for identifying these fallacies: firstly, a two-stacked bi-directional LSTM network, and secondly, a convolutional neural network. Their analysis on the occurrence of those fallacies is an important contribution, and their brief attempt at classifying the fallacies is an important baseline for our work.

Sourcing data Sourcing data from public fora, such as Reddit, is used by other works in the field of NLP, like for hateful speech detection (Saleem et al., 2017) or agreement amongst participants in a discussion on a community on Reddit called *ChangeMyView* (Musi, 2018). Habernal et al. (2018) also collect their data from this community, since each post is expected to be relevant to the discussion. Moderators dedicate their time to flag and remove those posts. One of those flags is that a post attacks another person, which is included in the data set assembled by Habernal et al. (2018).

Crowdsourcing the labeling is another option; either by paying the participants (Hube and Fetahu, 2018) or by providing a service in return, like a game (Habernal et al., 2017).

3   Components of the classifier

This section will review current techniques for sentence representation in Subsection 3.1. Recurrent neural networks, which are used for the classifier in this paper, are covered in Subsection 3.2.

3.1   Sentence representation

Word2vec Word2Vec (Mikolov et al., 2013; Goldberg and Levy, 2014) offers a way to vector-ize words whilst also encoding meaning into the vectors. The vector representation of the word "cats" would be similar—measured for example by the cosine similarity—to the vector representation of the word "dogs" but different than the vector representation of the word "knowledge". This also allows arithmetic operations to take place (Mikolov et al., 2013). For example:

$$\vec{w}\,(\text{``king''}) - \vec{w}\,(\text{``man''}) \\ + \vec{w}\,(\text{``woman''}) \approx \vec{w}\,(\text{``queen''}) \tag{1}$$

The vectors are obtained by maximizing the likelihood of predicting a determined word (or term), given other surrounding ones. Thus, a vectorized paragraph yields a matrix of $l \times w$, where l is the length of each vector for a particular word (arbitrarily chosen) and w are the number of words for that paragraph. The first input of our model is a vectorized version of each paragraph from our dataset, where every element of the vector represents each word on that paragraph. This vector is mapped to a pre-trained Word2Vec model from GoogleNews, which has vector representations of 300 values for 3 million words, names, slang and bi-grams. Even though the paragraphs do not have the same length, the amount of words is equal for all of them and the empty values of shorter paragraphs are masked.

Par2vec Doc2vec or par2vec is extremely similar to Word2Vec. The difference is that a sentence or paragraph is represented as a vector, instead of a single word. The vector values are adjusted by maximizing the likelihood of a word (or term), given the surrounding words (or terms) with an adjustment for the discrepancy between the likelihood and actual value. Doc2Vec generates a vector of size l, which can be arbitrarily chosen. The second input of our model generates a vector representation of the paragraph itself (Le and Mikolov, 2014)

POS tagging Part-Of-Speech (POS) tagging applies a tag to each word in a particular sentence. For example, words can be tagged as "noun", "adjective", or "verb". For verbs, the tags can also encode the tense, and further information can be contained. These labels have been used successfully in NLP tasks (Hube and Fetahu, 2018). In this work, the POS tagging is done by the Python

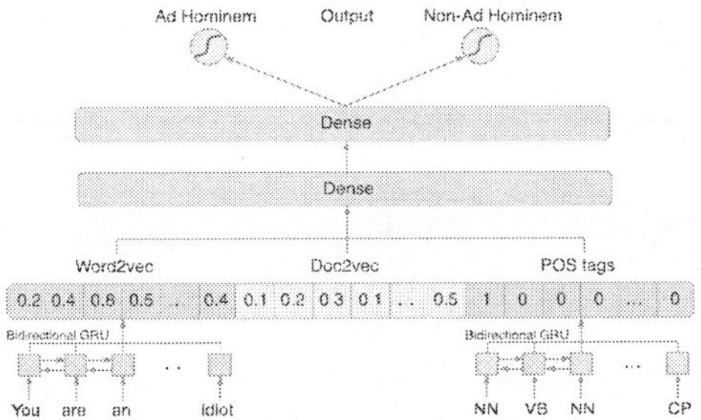

Figure 1: Graph of the combined neural network which gave the best results.

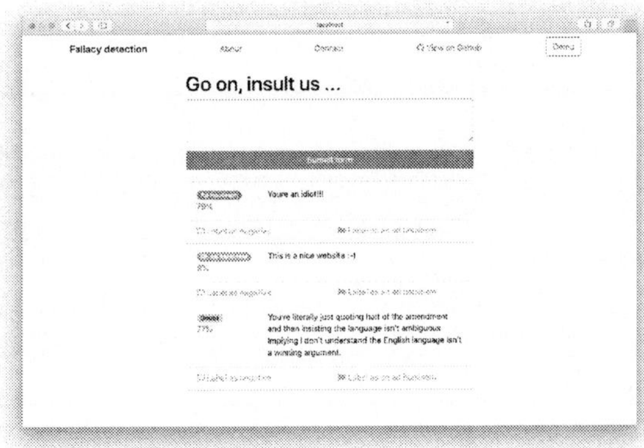

Figure 2: Screenshot of the web app with some example sentences.

library NLTK (Bird et al., 2009), which uses the Penn Treebank tagset.

3.2 RNN sentence encoding

Recurrent neural networks (RNNs) have successfully been used in sequence learning problems (Lipton et al., 2015), for example machine translation (Sutskever et al., 2014; Luong et al., 2015), and language modeling (Kim et al., 2015). RNNs extend feedforward neural networks by introducing a connection to adjacent time steps. So recurrent nodes are not only dependent on the current input $\mathbf{x}^{(t)}$, but also on the previous hidden states $\mathbf{h}^{(t-1)}$ at a time t.

$$\mathbf{h}^{(t)} = \sigma \left(W \mathbf{x}^{(t)} + W' \mathbf{h}^{(t-1)} + b \right) \quad (2)$$

Some applications, for instance sentence modeling, can benefit not only from past, but from future input as well. For this reason, bidirectional recurrent neural networks were developed (Schuster and Paliwal, 1997).

The recurrent nodes can also be adapted by introducing memory cells. This forms the foundation for long short-term memory (LSTM) nodes (Hochreiter and Schmidhuber, 1997). By leaving out the memory cell, but maintaining the introduced gating mechanism, a gated recurrent unit (GRU) is created.

4 Model architecture

In this section, our approach will be discussed in detail. Subsection 4.1 will go in depth about our approach and its architecture. Finally, Subsection 4.2 illustrates how the classifier can be used in a web demo with online training.

4.1 Approach

Our approach is based on an RNN, as is illustrated in Figure 1. The Word2Vec vectorization is sent into a Bidirectional GRU. The POS tagging vectorization is also sent into a Bidirectional GRU. Both GRU layers consist of 100 recurrent cells each, with a ReLU activation. Lastly, the Doc2Vec vectorization output is already a vector, so we don't need to manipulate it to concatenate it with the other 2 vectors. Consequently, we concatenate the 3 previously mentioned output vectors in one single vector.

This vector is fed into 2 consecutive fully connected layers with a ReLU activation function. The last layer is also a fully connected layer but with a sigmoid activation that represents the probability that the input paragraph includes an ad hominem attack.

Even though the network uses masking on the inputs, an upper word limit L is introduced. Paragraphs with more words are restrained to the this limit L. The following section will also analyze how different limits affect the performance. These networks are then trained with the AdaDelta optimizer (Zeiler, 2012) with the default learning rate $l_r = 1.0$ and binary cross entropy as the loss function. Each of them was trained on a NVIDIA K80 GPU in one hour. In addition, class weights were used to tackle the imbalanced data.

4.2 Web demo

To demonstrate the classifier, a web application is built. It uses the same implementation of the classifier in Keras (Chollet and others, 2015), which is made available through a REST API with Flask. The front end is a Vue.js application.

Table 1: Illustration of how fallacies in the middle of a paragraph are contributing less to the overall output of the model, even though the attack itself is the same.

Sentence	Confidence
Augmented recurrent neural networks, and the underlying technique of attention, are incredibly exciting. You're so wrong and a f*cking idiot! We look forward to seeing what happens next.	0.39
You're so wrong and a f*cking idiot! Augmented recurrent neural networks, and the underlying technique of attention, are incredibly exciting. We look forward to seeing what happens next.	0.79

The web application also supports online learning and labeling of paragraphs. Each queried paragraph has two buttons to label the input, after which the backend saves the feedback and optionally retrains the network. However, as will be discussed in Section 5.3, this approach can actually worsen the accuracy of the classifier.

5 Evaluation

To correctly compare different models, the data set is split into a training and test set. All models are evaluated on a withheld test set (Flach, 2012). In this case, the test set contains over 8k labeled paragraphs. In two instances, memory issues forced us to train and evaluate on a smaller data set. These issues can be mitigated by streaming smaller batches of data, but this was made less of a priority since the provisional results were in favor of the RNN network. A further breakdown of the data collection and processing is discussed in Subsection 5.1.

Our model is compared to different baselines, which are reviewed in Subsection 5.2.

5.1 Data set

Our models were trained on a data set that was initially collected by Habernal et al. (2018). This data set is in essence a database dump of a Reddit community called *Change My View*, which focusses on online debating. In this context, ad hominem attacks are unwelcome and thus removed by moderators. The data set contains these labels amongst other things. The authors analyzed this data set extensively to make sure the labels were correct, in part by relabeling a subset by crowd-sourced workers.

However, our goal is different than that of Habernal et al. (2018): we classify each post individually, without taking any context about the discussion into account. Habernal et al. (2018) focusses on what this context—which they call a discussion tree—means for the occurrence of an attack. For this reason, we decided to not use the filtered dataset with only discussing trees that end up in ad hominem attacks. Instead we used the database dump and applied our own data cleaning.

Reddit allows the use of text formatting with Markdown (i.e. *bold* or _italics_). These were filtered, and more complex tags like links were removed, while still preserving the text associated with the link. Finally, the Markdown format also allows citations, which were commonly used to quote sentences of other posts. Since these citations could contain ad hominem attacks, they are removed as well.

5.2 Baselines

We compare our approach to multiple baselines. One of them is a CNN approach by Habernal et al. (2018), whilst the others are baselines we consider without recurrent layers.

1. **SVM$_a$**: our first model is based on a TF-IDF vectorizer and an SVM classifier (Flach, 2012). The TF-IDF vectorizer uses the top 3000 words from the test set. The SVM classifier is a linear SVM.

2. **SVM$_b$**: this model also uses a linear classifier, but the features are based on word representations. Instead of the TF-IDF vectors for a paragraph, the 300 most occurring words from the training set are used. For each of these 300 words, the TF-IDF value is replaced by a weighted word embedding. So for words that don't occur in a sentence or paragraph, all elements of this vector are zero. Otherwise the word representation is scaled by the TF-IDF value of that word. In total, this yields an array of 300 words by 300

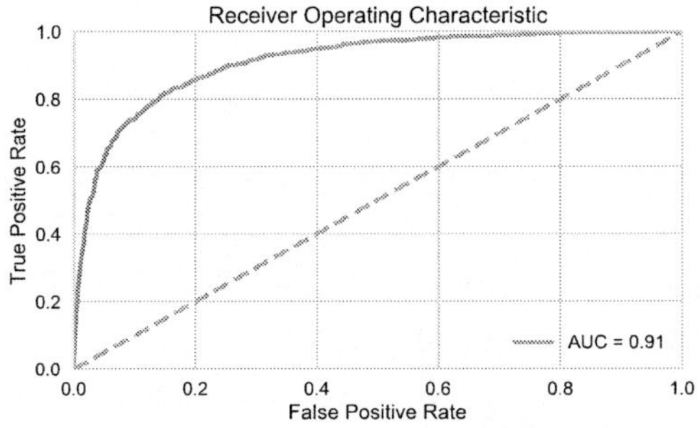

Figure 3: ROC curve of the best performing model, based on the test set.

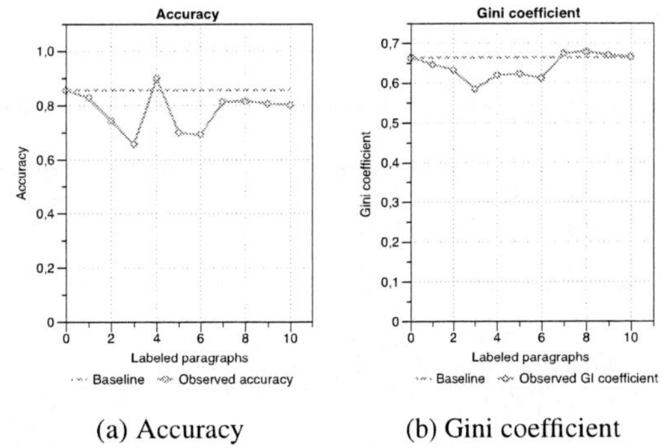

(a) Accuracy   (b) Gini coefficient

Figure 4: Influence of online training on three metrics. The dashed line is the best performing model before any additional online learning.

vector values. This approach is an extension of Kenter et al. (2016), which used a bag-of-words approach.

Other approaches—like as averaging all vectors—don't perform as well (Le and Mikolov, 2014).

3. **NN**: the NN approach continues with the above described vectorizing and uses a neural network for classification instead of an SVM. The output is formed by two sigmoid-activated neurons after one fully connected layer.

5.3   Results

Table 2 compares the models discussed in Section 3. The models are compared based on several metrics on a test set of 8531 paragraphs with 726 ad homimems. (Haghighi et al., 2018). Figure 3 show the ROC curve for the RNN model.

The best performing model is the RNN with word2vec, doc2vec, and POS tag features. This model scored best on recall R, the Gini coefficient GI, and the F1 score. The accuracy is slightly higher for the SVM model with word2vec features, due to the class imbalance.

These results—and in particular the difference between the our RNN model and both SVM_a and SVM_b—show that a TF-IDF approach is insufficient to distinguish most ad hominems from neutral comments, as the Gini coefficients indicate. The recurrent neural network incorporates sequential information, which has a positive effect on all metrics. Using longer input lengths L might allow to classify longer paragraphs at once, but this has a negative impact on the classification results. A possible reason of this is discussed in Subsecion 5.4.

5.4   Limitations

An issue is that the output of the model, which can be interpreted as a confidence scale between 0 and 1, is strongly influenced by the position of an ad hominem attack. This is illustrated in Table 1.

The web demo features a feedback button to label the input, and also allows to train the model directly with this new input. Since only the input sentence is used, this can cause an issue, namely *catastrophic forgetting* (McCloskey and Cohen, 1989). In this case, the model forgets all previously learned weights and instead of the intended increase in accuracy, it decreases.

Figure 4 illustrates how the online training of 10 paragraphs affects three metrics. This experiment is executed on the same test set and the baseline—the original model—is indicated as well. This clearly illustrates that when all parameters are taken into account, the model slowly degenerates, so it clearly highlights an issue with online learning.

6   Conclusion and further work

In this paper, we presented a machine learning approach to classify ad hominem fallacies. This model is based on two sequence models: a bidirectional GRU neural network for a sequence of word representations and another similar network for POS tags. The outputs of these two networks are combined with an additional feature, a paragraph representation, and fed into a fully connected neural network. This approach yields better results than a TF-IDF approach, which doesn't take any sequence information into account.

During the writing of this paper, a novel representation model based on transformers is

Table 2: Comparison of different models. All models are trained on 70% of the dataset and evaluated on the remaining 30%, unless annotated with an asterisk (*). In this case, 3k paragraphs of the dataset were used.

Model	L	ACC	R	GI	F1
CNN (Habernal et al., 2018)		0.810			
SVM$_a$		0.88819	0.29967	0.28208	0.42519
SVM$_b$		**0.90044**	0.34519	0.29812	0.37455
NN (word2vec)*		0.81667	0.52066	0.38331	0.43299
NN (word2vec and doc2vec)*		0.71222	0.69421	0.40923	0.39344
	150	0.83523	0.72853	0.57371	0.43006
	200	0.85647	**0.80256**	**0.66406**	**0.48854**
RNN (word2vec, doc2vec, POS tags)	300	0.81755	0.74614	0.57034	0.41049
	400	0.84480	0.69284	0.55177	0.35214

published (Devlin et al., 2018). This multilingual model could be used as an alternative for Word2vec, which has been critiqued for gender bias (Bolukbasi et al., 2016). Another posibility is ELMo (Peters et al., 2018), which takes the entire sentence into account before assigning an embedding to each word.

Finally we also discussed the issue of how the position of an attack changes the output. A possible solution would be to add attention to the RNN layer. This attention mechanism grants the network access to historical hidden states, so not all information has to be encoded in a single fixed-length vector (Bahdanau et al., 2014; Hermann et al., 2015). Continuing in this direction, it would also be possible to use hierarchical attention on both the word and sentence level (Yang et al., 2016).

References

Dzmitry Bahdanau, Kyunghyun Cho, and Yoshua Bengio. 2014. Neural machine translation by jointly learning to align and translate.

Steven Bird, Ewan Klein, and Edward Loper. 2009. *Natural language processing with Python: analyzing text with the natural language toolkit.* " O'Reilly Media, Inc.".

Tolga Bolukbasi, Kai-Wei Chang, James Zou, Venkatesh Saligrama, and Adam Kalai. 2016. Man is to computer programmer as woman is to homemaker? debiasing word embeddings.

François Chollet and others. 2015. *Keras.*

Jacob Devlin, Ming-Wei Chang, Kenton Lee, and Kristina Toutanova. 2018. Bert: Pre-training of deep bidirectional transformers for language understanding. *arXiv preprint arXiv:1810.04805.*

Peter Flach. 2012. *Machine learning: the art and science of algorithms that make sense of data.* Cambridge University Press.

Yoav Goldberg and Omer Levy. 2014. word2vec Explained: deriving Mikolov et al.'s negative-sampling word-embedding method. *arXiv:1402.3722 [cs, stat].* ArXiv: 1402.3722.

Paul Graham. 2008. How to Disagree.

Ivan Habernal, Raffael Hannemann, Christian Pollak, Christopher Klamm, Patrick Pauli, and Iryna Gurevych. 2017. Argotario: Computational Argumentation Meets Serious Games. In *Proceedings of the 2017 Conference on Empirical Methods in Natural Language Processing: System Demonstrations,* pages 7–12, Copenhagen, Denmark. Association for Computational Linguistics.

Ivan Habernal, Henning Wachsmuth, Iryna Gurevych, and Benno Stein. 2018. Before Name-Calling: Dynamics and Triggers of Ad Hominem Fallacies in Web Argumentation. In *Proceedings of the 2018 Conference of the North American Chapter of the Association for Computational Linguistics: Human Language Technologies, Volume 1 (Long Papers),* pages 386–396, New Orleans, Louisiana. Association for Computational Linguistics.

Sepand Haghighi, Masoomeh Jasemi, Shaahin Hessabi, and Alireza Zolanvari. 2018. PyCM: Multiclass confusion matrix library in Python. *Journal of Open Source Software,* 3(25):729.

Karl Moritz Hermann, Tomáš Kočiský, Edward Grefenstette, Lasse Espeholt, Will Kay, Mustafa Suleyman, and Phil Blunsom. 2015. Teaching Machines to Read and Comprehend.

Sepp Hochreiter and Jürgen Schmidhuber. 1997. Long short-term memory. *Neural computation,* 9(8):1735–1780.

Christoph Hube and Besnik Fetahu. 2018. Neural Based Statement Classification for Biased Language. *CoRR,* abs/1811.05740.

Tom Kenter, Alexey Borisov, and Maarten de Rijke. 2016. Siamese cbow: Optimizing word embeddings for sentence representations. *arXiv preprint arXiv:1606.04640*.

Yoon Kim, Yacine Jernite, David Sontag, and Alexander M. Rush. 2015. Character-Aware Neural Language Models. *arXiv:1508.06615 [cs, stat]*. ArXiv: 1508.06615.

Quoc Le and Tomas Mikolov. 2014. Distributed representations of sentences and documents. In *International Conference on Machine Learning*, pages 1188–1196.

Zachary C. Lipton, John Berkowitz, and Charles Elkan. 2015. A Critical Review of Recurrent Neural Networks for Sequence Learning. *arXiv:1506.00019 [cs]*. ArXiv: 1506.00019.

Minh-Thang Luong, Hieu Pham, and Christopher D. Manning. 2015. Effective Approaches to Attention-based Neural Machine Translation. *arXiv:1508.04025 [cs]*. ArXiv: 1508.04025.

Michael McCloskey and Neal J Cohen. 1989. Catastrophic interference in connectionist networks: The sequential learning problem. In *Psychology of learning and motivation*, volume 24, pages 109–165. Elsevier.

Tomas Mikolov, Kai Chen, Greg Corrado, and Jeffrey Dean. 2013. Efficient estimation of word representations in vector space. *arXiv preprint arXiv:1301.3781*.

Elena Musi. 2018. How did you change my view? A corpus-based study of concessions' argumentative role. *Discourse Studies*, 20(2):270–288.

Matthew E. Peters, Mark Neumann, Mohit Iyyer, Matt Gardner, Christopher Clark, Kenton Lee, and Luke Zettlemoyer. 2018. Deep contextualized word representations. In *Proc. of NAACL*.

Haji Mohammad Saleem, Kelly P. Dillon, Susan Benesch, and Derek Ruths. 2017. A Web of Hate: Tackling Hateful Speech in Online Social Spaces. *arXiv:1709.10159 [cs]*. ArXiv: 1709.10159.

M. Schuster and K.K. Paliwal. 1997. Bidirectional recurrent neural networks. *IEEE Transactions on Signal Processing*, 45(11):2673–2681.

Manfeld Stede and Jodi Schneider. 2018. *Argumentation Mining*. Morgan & Claypool Publishers, San Rafael, United States.

Ilya Sutskever, Oriol Vinyals, and Quoc V. Le. 2014. Sequence to Sequence Learning with Neural Networks. *arXiv:1409.3215 [cs]*. ArXiv: 1409.3215.

Douglas Walton. 1998. *Ad Hominem Arguments (Studies in Rhetoric & Communication)*. The University of Alabama Press, Alabama.

Zichao Yang, Diyi Yang, Chris Dyer, Xiaodong He, Alex Smola, and Eduard Hovy. 2016. Hierarchical attention networks for document classification. In *Proceedings of the 2016 Conference of the North American Chapter of the Association for Computational Linguistics: Human Language Technologies*, pages 1480–1489.

Matthew D Zeiler. 2012. Adadelta: an adaptive learning rate method. *arXiv preprint arXiv:1212.5701*.

Multiple Character Embeddings for Chinese Word Segmentation

Jingkang Wang[*] **Jianing Zhou**[*] **Jie Zhou** **Gongshen Liu**[†]

The Lab of Information Content Intelligent Analysis, Shanghai, China
School of Cyber Science and Engineering, Shanghai Jiao Tong University
{wangjksjtu,zhjjn1919}@gmail.com, {sanny02,lgshen}@sjtu.edu.cn

Abstract

Chinese word segmentation (CWS) is often regarded as a character-based sequence labeling task in most current works which have achieved great success with the help of powerful neural networks. However, these works neglect an important clue: *Chinese characters incorporate both semantic and phonetic meanings*. In this paper, we introduce multiple character embeddings including *Pinyin Romanization* and *Wubi Input*, both of which are easily accessible and effective in depicting semantics of characters. We propose a novel *shared Bi-LSTM-CRF* model to fuse linguistic features efficiently by sharing the LSTM network during the training procedure. Extensive experiments on five corpora show that extra embeddings help obtain a significant improvement in labeling accuracy. Specifically, we achieve the state-of-the-art performance in AS and CityU corpora with F1 scores of 96.9 and 97.3, respectively without leveraging any external lexical resources.

1 Introduction

Chinese is written without explicit word delimiters so word segmentation (CWS) is a preliminary and essential pre-processing step for most natural language processing (NLP) tasks in Chinese, such as part-of-speech tagging (POS) and named-entity recognition (NER). The representative approaches are treating CWS as a character-based sequence labeling task following Xu (2003) and Peng et al. (2004).

Although not relying on hand-crafted features, most of the neural network models rely heavily on the embeddings of characters. Since Mikolov et al. (2013) proposed word2vec technique, the vector representation of words or characters has become

a prerequisite for neural networks to solve NLP tasks in different languages.

However, existing approaches neglect an important fact that Chinese characters contain both semantic and phonetic meanings - there are various representations of characters designed for capturing these features. The most intuitive one is *Pinyin Romanization* (拼音) that keeps many-to-one relationship with Chinese characters - for one character, different meanings in specific context may lead to different pronunciations. This phenomenon called *Polyphony* (and *Polysemy*) in linguistics is very common and crucial to word segmentation task. Apart from Pinyin Romanization, *Wubi Input* (五笔) is another effective representation which absorbs semantic meanings of Chinese characters. Compared to Radical (偏旁) (Sun et al., 2014; Dong et al., 2016; Shao et al., 2017), Wubi includes more comprehensive graphical and structural information that is highly relevant to the semantic meanings and word boundaries, due to plentiful pictographic characters in Chinese and effectiveness of Wubi in embedding the structures.

This paper will thoroughly study how important the extra embeddings are and what scholars can achieve by combining extra embeddings with representative models. To leverage extra phonetic and semantic information efficiently, we propose a shared Bi-LSTMs-CRF model, which feeds embeddings into three stacked LSTM layers with shared parameters and finally scores with CRF layer. We evaluate the proposed approach on five corpora and demonstrate that our method produces state-of-the-art results and is highly efficient as previous single-embedding scheme.

Our contributions are summarized as follows: 1) We firstly propose to leverage both semantic and phonetic features of Chinese characters in NLP tasks by introducing Pinyin Romanization and Wubi Input embeddings, which are easily

---

[*] Equal contribution (alphabetical order).
[†] Corresponding author.

Proceedings of the ACL 2019, Student Research Workshop, pages 210–216
Florence, Italy, July 28th-August 2nd, 2019. ©2019 Association for Computational Linguistics

(a)   (b)   (c)

Figure 1: Examples of phono-semantic compound characters and polyphone characters.

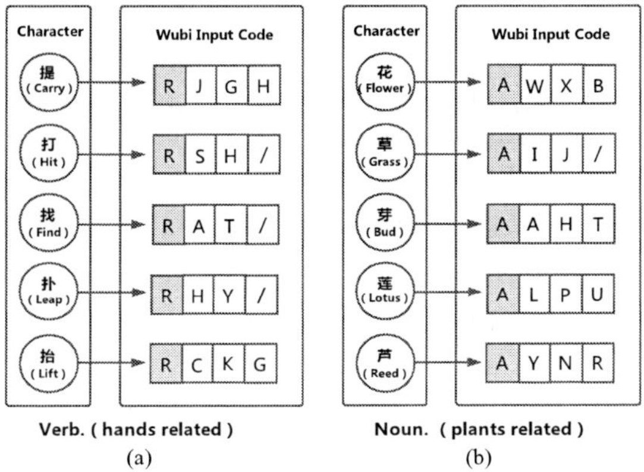

Figure 2: Potential semantic relationships between Chinese characters and Wubi Input. Gray area indicates that these characters have the same first letter in the Wubi Input representation.

accessible and effective in representing semantic and phonetic features; 2) We put forward a *shared Bi-LSTM-CRF* model for efficiently integrating multiple embeddings and sharing useful linguistic features; 3) We evaluate the proposed multi-embedding scheme on Bakeoff2005 and CTB6 corpora. Extensive experiments show that auxiliary embeddings help achieve state-of-the-art performance without external lexical resources.

2 Multiple Embeddings

To fully leverage various properties of Chinese characters, we propose to split the character-level embeddings into three parts: character embeddings for textual features, Pinyin Romanization embeddings for phonetic features and Wubi Input embeddings for structure-level features.

2.1 Chinese Characters

CWS is often regarded as a character-based sequence labeling task, which aims to label every character with $\{B, M, E, S\}$ tagging scheme. Recent studies show that character embeddings are the most fundamental inputs for neural networks (Chen et al., 2015; Cai and Zhao, 2016; Cai

et al., 2017). However, Chinese characters are developed to absorb and fuse phonetics, semantics, and hieroglyphology. In this paper, we would like to explore other linguistic features so the characters are the basic inputs with two other presentations (*Pinyin* and *Wubi*) introduced as auxiliary.

2.2 Pinyin Romanization

Pinyin Romanization (拼音) is the official romanization system for standard Chinese characters (ISO 7098:2015, E), representing the pronunciation of Chinese characters like phonogram in English. Moreover, Pinyin is highly relevant to semantics - one character may correspond varied Pinyin code that indicates different semantic meanings. This phenomenon is very common in Asian languages and termed as polyphone.

Figure 1 shows several examples of polyphone characters. For instance, the character '乐' in Figure 1 (a) has two different pronunciations (Pinyin code). When pronounced as 'yue', it means 'music', as a noun. However, with the pronunciation of 'le', it refers to 'happiness'. Similarly, the character '和' in Figure 1 (b) even has four meanings with three varied Pinyin code.

Through Pinyin code, a natural bridge is constructed between the words and their semantics. Now that human could understand the different meanings of characters according to varied pronunciations, the neural networks are also likely to learn the mappings between semantic meanings and Pinyin code automatically.

Obviously, Pinyin provides extra phonetic and semantic information required by some basic tasks such as CWS. It is worthy to notice that Pinyin is a dominant computer input method of Chinese characters, and it is easy to represent characters with Pinyin code as supplementary inputs.

2.3 Wubi Input

Wubi Input (五笔) is based on the structure of characters rather than the pronunciation. Since plentiful Chinese characters are hieroglyphic, Wubi Input can be used to find out the potential semantic relationships as well as the word boundaries. It is beneficial to CWS task mainly in two aspects: 1) Wubi encodes high-level semantic meanings of characters; 2) characters with similar structures (e.g., radicals) are more likely to make up a word, which effects the word boundaries.

To understand its effectiveness in structure description, one has to go through the rules of Wubi

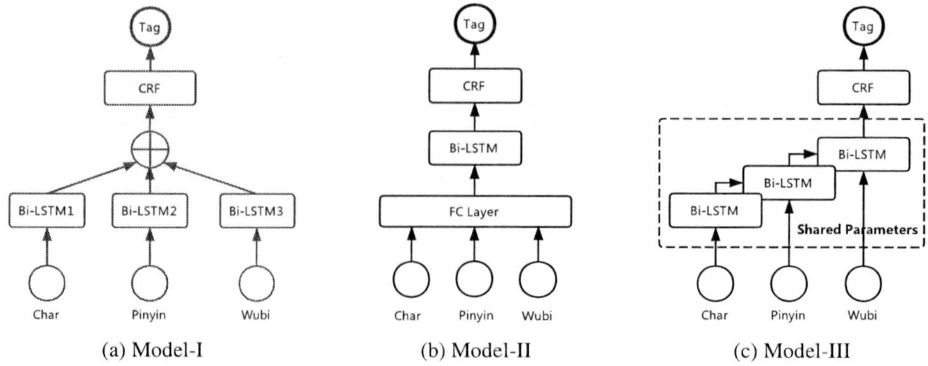

Figure 3: Network architecture of three multi-embedding models. (a) Model-I: Multi-Bi-LSTMs-CRF Model. (b) Model-II: FC-Layer Bi-LSTMs-CRF Model. (c) Model-III: Shared Bi-LSTMs-CRF Model.

Input method. It is an efficient encoding system which represents each Chinese character with at most four English letters. Specifically, these letters are divided into five regions, each of which represents a type of structure (stroke, 笔画) in Chinese characters.

Figure 2 provides some examples of Chinese characters and their corresponding Wubi code (four letters). For instance, '提' (carry), '打' (hit) and '抬' (lift) in Figure 2 (a) are all verbs related to hands and correspond different spellings in English. On the contrary, in Chinese, these characters are all left-right symbols and have the same radical ('R' in Wubi code). That is to say, Chinese characters that are highly semantically relevant usually have similar structures which could be perfectly captured by Wubi. Besides, characters with similar structures are more likely to make up a word. For example, '花' (flower), '草' (grass) and '芽' (bud) in Figure 2 (b) are nouns and represent different plants. Whereas, they are all up-down symbols and have the same radical ('A' in Wubi code). These words usually make up new words such as '花草' (flowers and grasses) and '花芽' (the buds of flowers).

In addition, the sequence in Wubi code is one approach to interpret the relationships between Chinese characters. In Figure 2, it is easy to find some interesting component rules. For instance, we can conclude: 1) the sequence order implies the order of character components (e.g., 'IA' vs 'AI' and 'IY' vs 'YI'); 2) some code has practical meanings (e.g., 'I' denotes water). Consequently, Wubi is an efficient encoding of Chinese characters so incorporated as a supplementary input like Pinyin in our multi-embedding model.

2.4 Multiple Embeddings

To fully utilize various properties of Chinese characters, we construct the Pinyin and Wubi embeddings as two supplementary character-level features. We firstly pre-process the characters and obtain the basic character embedding following the strategy in Lample et al. (2016); Shao et al. (2017). Then we use the Pypinyin Library[1] to annotate Pinyin code, and an official transformation table[2] to translate characters to Wubi code. Finally, we retrieve multiple embeddings using word2vec tool (Mikolov et al., 2013).

For simplicity, we treat Pinyin and Wubi code as units like characters processed by canonical word2vec, which may discard some semantic affinities. It is worth noticing that the sequence order in Wubi code is an intriguing property considering the fact that structures of characters are encoded by the order of letters (see Sec 2.3). This point merits further study. Finally, we remark that generating Pinyin code relies on the external resources (statistics prior). Nontheless, Wubi code is converted under a transformation table so does not introduce any external resources.

3 Multi-Embedding Model Architecture

We adopt the popular Bi-LSTMs-CRF as our baseline model (Figure 4 without Pinyin and Wubi input), similar to the architectures proposed by Lample et al. (2016) and Dong et al. (2016). To obtain an efficient fusion and sharing mechanism for multiple features, we design three varied architectures (see Figure 3). In what follows, we will provide detailed explanations and analysis.

[1] https://pypi.python.org/pypi/pypinyin
[2] http://wubi.free.fr/index_en.html

212

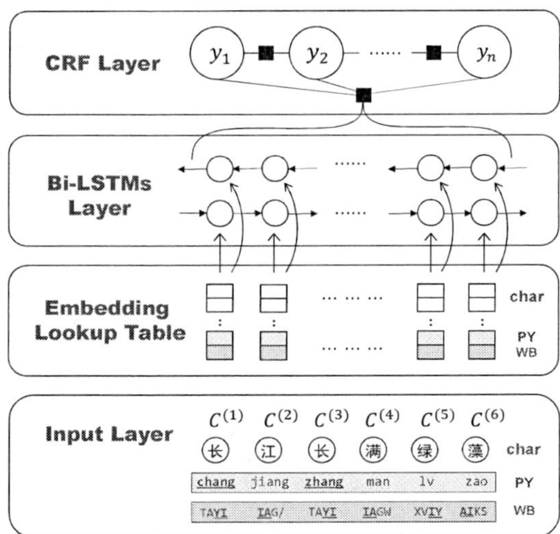

Figure 4: The architecture of Bi-LSTM-CRF network. PY and WB represent *Pinyin Romanization* and *Wubi Input* introduced in this paper.

3.1 Model-I: Multi-Bi-LSTMs-CRF Model

In Model-I (Figure 3a), the input vectors of character, pinyin and wubi embeddings are fed into three independent stacked Bi-LSTMs networks and the output high-level features are fused via addition:

$$
\begin{aligned}
\mathbf{h}_{3,c}^{(t)} &= \text{Bi-LSTMs}_1(\mathbf{x}_c^{(t)}, \theta_c), \\
\mathbf{h}_{3,p}^{(t)} &= \text{Bi-LSTMs}_2(\mathbf{x}_p^{(t)}, \theta_p), \\
\mathbf{h}_{3,w}^{(t)} &= \text{Bi-LSTMs}_3(\mathbf{x}_w^{(t)}, \theta_w), \\
\mathbf{h}^{(t)} &= \mathbf{h}_{3,c}^{(t)} + \mathbf{h}_{3,p}^{(t)} + \mathbf{h}_{3,w}^{(t)},
\end{aligned}
\tag{1}
$$

where θ_c, θ_p and θ_w denote parameters in three Bi-LSTMs networks respectively. The outputs of three-layer Bi-LSTMs are $\mathbf{h}_{3,c}^{(t)}$, $\mathbf{h}_{3,p}^{(t)}$ and $\mathbf{h}_{3,w}^{(t)}$, which form the input of the CRF layer $\mathbf{h}_{(t)}$. Here three LSTM networks maintain independent parameters for multiple features thus leading to a large computation cost during training.

3.2 Model-II: FC-Layer Bi-LSTMs-CRF Model

On the contrary, Model-II (Figure 3b) incorporates multiple raw features directly by inserting one fully-connected (FC) layer to learn a mapping between fused linguistic features and concatenated raw input embeddings. Then the output of this FC layer is fed into the LSTM network:

$$
\begin{aligned}
\mathbf{x}_{in}^{(t)} &= [\mathbf{x}_c^{(t)}; \mathbf{x}_p^{(t)}; \mathbf{x}_w^{(t)}], \\
\mathbf{x}^{(t)} &= \sigma(\mathbf{W}_{fc}\mathbf{x}_{in}^{(t)} + \mathbf{b}_{fc}),
\end{aligned}
\tag{2}
$$

where σ is the logistic sigmoid function; $\mathbf{W}_{fc}$ and $\mathbf{b}_{fc}$ are trainable parameters of fully connected layer; $\mathbf{x}_c^{(t)}$, $\mathbf{x}_p^{(t)}$ and $\mathbf{x}_w^{(t)}$ are the input vectors of character, pinyin and wubi embeddings. The output of the fully connected layer $\mathbf{x}^{(t)}$ forms the input sequence of the Bi-LSTMs-CRF. This architecture benefits from its low computation cost but suffers from insufficient extraction from raw code. Meanwhile, Model-I and Model-II ignore the interactions between different embeddings.

3.3 Model-III: Shared Bi-LSTMs-CRF Model

To address feature dependency while maintaining training efficiency, Model-III (Figure 3c) introduces a sharing mechanism - rather than employing independent Bi-LSTMs networks for Pinyin and Wubi, we let them share the same LSTMs with character embeddings.

In Model-III, we feed character, Pinyin and Wubi embeddings sequentially into a stacked Bi-LSTMs network shared with the same parameters:

$$
\begin{bmatrix} \mathbf{h}_{3,c}^{(t)} \\ \mathbf{h}_{3,p}^{(t)} \\ \mathbf{h}_{3,w}^{(t)} \end{bmatrix} = \text{Bi-LSTMs}(\begin{bmatrix} \mathbf{w}_c^{(t)} \\ \mathbf{w}_p^{(t)} \\ \mathbf{w}_w^{(t)} \end{bmatrix}, \theta),
\tag{3}
$$

$$
\mathbf{h}^t = \mathbf{h}_{3,c}^{(t)} + \mathbf{h}_{3,p}^{(t)} + \mathbf{h}_{3,w}^{(t)},
$$

where θ denotes the shared parameters of Bi-LSTMs. Different from Eqn (1), there is only one shared Bi-LSTMs rather than three independent LSTM networks with more trainable parameters. In consequence, the shared Bi-LSTMs-CRF model can be trained more efficiently compared to Model-I and Model-II (extra FC-Layer expense).

Specifically, at each epoch, the parameters of three networks are updated based on unified sequential character, Pinyin and Wubi embeddings. The second LSTM network will share (or synchronize) the parameters with the first network before it begins the training procedure with Pinyin as inputs. In this way, the second network will take fewer efforts in refining the parameters based on the former correlated embeddings. So does the third network (taking Wubi embedding as inputs).

4 Experimental Evaluations

In this section, we provide empirical results to verify the effectiveness of multiple embeddings for CWS. Besides, our proposed Model-III can be

Models	CTB6			PKU			MSR			AS			CityU		
	P	R	F	P	R	F	P	R	F	P	R	F	P	R	F
baseline	94.1	94.0	94.1	95.8	95.9	95.8	95.3	95.7	95.5	95.6	95.5	95.6	95.9	96.0	96.0
Model-I	94.9	95.0	94.9	95.7	95.7	95.7	96.8	96.6	96.7	96.6	96.5	96.5	96.7	96.5	96.6
Model-II	**95.4**	**95.3**	**95.4**	**96.3**	95.7	96.0	96.6	96.5	96.6	96.8	96.5	96.7	**97.2**	**97.0**	**97.1**
Model-III	**95.4**	95.0	95.2	**96.3**	**96.1**	**96.2**	**97.0**	**96.9**	**97.0**	**96.9**	**96.8**	**96.9**	97.1	**97.0**	**97.1**

Table 1: Comparison of different architectures on five corpora. Bold font signifies the best performance in all given models. Our proposed multiple-embedding models result in a significant improvement compared to vanilla character-embedding baseline model.

trained efficiently (slightly costly than baseline) and obtain the state-of-the-art performance.

4.1 Experimental Setup

To make the results comparable and convincing, we evaluate our models on SIGHAN 2005 (Emerson, 2005) and Chinese Treebank 6.0 (CTB6) (Xue et al., 2005) datasets, which are widely used in previous works. We leverage standard word2vec tool to train multiple embeddings. In experiments, we tuned the embedding size following Yao and Huang (2016) and assigned equal size (256) for three types of embedding. The number of Bi-LSTM layers is set as 3.

4.2 Experimental Results

Performance under Different Architectures

We comprehensively conduct the analysis of three architecture proposed in Section 3. As illustrated in Table 1, considerable improvements are obtained by three multi-embedding models compared with our baseline model which only takes character embeddings as inputs. Overall, Model-III (shared Bi-LSTMs-CRF) achieves better performance even with fewer trainable parameters.

Competitive Performance

To demonstrate the effectiveness of supplementary embeddings for CWS, we compare our models with previous state-of-the-art models.

Table 2 shows the comprehensive comparison of performance on all Bakeoff2005 corpora. To the best of our knowledge, we have achieved the best performance on AS and CityU datasets (with F1 score 96.9 and 97.3 respectively) and competitive performance on PKU and MSR even if not leveraging external resources (e.g. pre-trained char/word embeddings, extra dictionaries, labeled or unlabeled corpora). It is worthy to notice that AS and CityU datasets are considered more difficult by researchers due to its larger capacity and

Model	PKU	MSR	AS	CityU
(Sun and Wan, 2012)	95.4	97.4	-	-
(Chen et al., 2015)	94.8	95.6	-	-
(Chen et al., 2017)	94.3	96.0	-	94.8
(Ma et al., 2018)	96.1	**97.4**	96.2	97.2
(Zhang et al., 2013)*	96.1	97.4	-	-
(Chen et al., 2015)*	96.5	97.4	-	-
(Cai et al., 2017)*	95.8	97.1	95.6	95.3
(Wang and Xu, 2017)*	96.5	98.0	-	-
(Sun et al., 2017)*	96.0	97.9	96.1	96.9
baseline	95.8	95.5	95.6	96.0
ours (+PY)*	96.0	96.8	96.7	97.0
ours (+WB)	**96.3**	97.2	96.5	**97.3**
ours (+PY+WB)*	96.2	97.0	**96.9**	97.1

Table 2: Comparison with previous state-of-the-art models on all four Bakeoff2005 datasets. The second block (*) represents allowing the use of external resources such as lexicon dictionary or trained embeddings on large-scale external corpora. Note that our WB approach **does not** leverage any external resources.

higher out of vocabulary rate. It again verifies that Pinyin and Wubi embeddings are capable of decreasing mis-segmentation rate in large-scale data.

Embedding Ablation

We conduct embedding ablation experiments on CTB6 and CityU to explore the effectiveness of Pinyin and Wubi embeddings individually. As shown in Table 3, Pinyin and Wubi result in a considerable improvement on F1-score compared to vanilla single character-embedding model (baseline). Moreover, Wubi-aided model usually leads to a larger improvement than Pinyin-aided one.

Convergence Speed

To further study the additional expense after incorporating Pinyin and Wubi, we record the training time (batch time and convergence time in Table 4) of proposed models on MSR. Compared to

Models	CTB6			CityU		
	P	R	F	P	R	F
baseline	94.1	94.0	94.1	95.9	96.0	96.0
IO + PY	94.6	94.9	94.8	96.8	96.4	96.6
IO + WB	95.3	**95.4**	95.3	**97.3**	**97.3**	**97.3**
Model-II	**95.4**	95.3	**95.4**	97.2	97.0	97.1

Table 3: Feature ablation on CTB6 and CityU. IO + PY and IO + WB denote injecting Pinyin and Wubi embeddings separately under Model-II.

Model	Time (batch)	Time (P-95%)
baseline	1 ×	1 ×
Model-I	2.61 ×	2.51 ×
Model-II	1.03 ×	1.50 ×
Model-III	**1.07 ×**	**1.04 ×**

Table 4: Relative training time on MSR. (a) averaged training time per batch; (b) convergence time, where above 95% precision is considered as convergence.

the baseline model, it almost takes the same training time (1.07×) per batch and convergence time (1.04×) for Model-III. By contrast, Model-II leads to slower convergence (1.50×) in spite of its lower batch-training cost. In consequence, we recommend Model-III in practice for its high efficiency.

5 Related Work

Since Xu (2003), researchers have mostly treated CWS as a sequence labeling problem. Following this idea, great achievements have been reached in the past few years with the effective embeddings introduced and powerful neural networks armed.

In recent years, there are plentiful works exploiting different neural network architectures in CWS. Among these architectures, there are several models most similar to our model: Bi-LSTM-CRF (Huang et al., 2015), Bi-LSTM-CRF (Lample et al., 2016; Dong et al., 2016), and Bi-LSTM-CNNs-CRF (Ma and Hovy, 2016).

Huang et al. (2015) was the first to adopt Bi-LSTM network for character representations and CRF for label decoding. Lample et al. (2016) and Dong et al. (2016) exploited the Bi-LSTM-CRF model for named entity recognition in western languages and Chinese, respectively. Moreover, Dong et al. (2016) introduced radical-level information that can be regarded as a special case of Wubi code in our model.

Ma and Hovy (2016) proposed to combine Bi-LSTM, CNN and CRF, which results in faster convergence speed and better performance on POS and NER tasks. In addition, their model leverages both the character-level and word-level information.

Our work distinguishes itself by utilizing multiple dimensions of features in Chinese characters. With phonetic and semantic meanings taken into consideration, three proposed models achieve better performance on CWS and can be also adapted to POS and NER tasks. In particular, compared to radical-level information in (Dong et al., 2016), Wubi Input encodes richer structure details and potentially semantic relationships.

Recently, researchers propose to treat CWS as a word-based sequence labeling problem, which also achieves competitive performance (Zhang et al., 2016; Cai and Zhao, 2016; Cai et al., 2017; Yang et al., 2017). Other works try to introduce very deep networks (Wang and Xu, 2017) or treat CWS as a gap-filling problem (Sun et al., 2017). We believe that proposed linguistic features can also be transferred into word-level sequence labeling and correct the error. In a nutshell, multiple embeddings are generic and easily accessible, which can be applied and studied further in these works.

6 Conclusion

In this paper, we firstly propose to leverage phonetic, structured and semantic features of Chinese characters by introducing multiple character embeddings (*Pinyin* and *Wubi*). We conduct a comprehensive analysis on why Pinyin and Wubi embeddings are so essential in CWS task and could be translated to other NLP tasks such as POS and NER. Besides, we design three generic models to fuse the multi-embedding and produce the start-of-the-art performance in five public corpora. In particular, the shared Bi-LSTM-CRF models (Model III in Figure 3) could be trained efficiently and produce the best performance on AS and CityU corpora. In future, the effective ways of leveraging hierarchical linguistic features to other languages, NLP tasks (e.g., POS and NER) and refining mis-labeled sentences merit further study.

Acknowledgement

This research work has been partially funded by the National Natural Science Foundation of China (Grant No.61772337, U1736207), and the National Key Research and Development Program of China NO.2016QY03D0604.

References

Deng Cai and Hai Zhao. 2016. Neural word segmentation learning for chinese. In *ACL (1)*, Berlin, Germany. The Association for Computer Linguistics.

Deng Cai, Hai Zhao, Zhisong Zhang, Yuan Xin, Yongjian Wu, and Feiyue Huang. 2017. Fast and accurate neural word segmentation for chinese. In *ACL (2)*, pages 608–615. Association for Computational Linguistics.

Xinchi Chen, Xipeng Qiu, Chenxi Zhu, Pengfei Liu, and Xuanjing Huang. 2015. Long short-term memory neural networks for chinese word segmentation. In *EMNLP*, pages 1197–1206. The Association for Computational Linguistics.

Xinchi Chen, Zhan Shi, Xipeng Qiu, and Xuanjing Huang. 2017. Adversarial multi-criteria learning for chinese word segmentation. In *ACL (1)*, pages 1193–1203. Association for Computational Linguistics.

Chuanhai Dong, Jiajun Zhang, Chengqing Zong, Masanori Hattori, and Hui Di. 2016. Character-based LSTM-CRF with radical-level features for chinese named entity recognition. In *NLPCC/ICCPOL*, volume 10102 of *Lecture Notes in Computer Science*, pages 239–250. Springer.

Thomas Emerson. 2005. The second international chinese word segmentation bakeoff. In *Proceedings of the Fourth SIGHAN Workshop on Chinese Language Processing, SIGHAN@IJCNLP 2005, Jeju Island, Korea, 14-15, 2005*.

Zhiheng Huang, Wei Xu, and Kai Yu. 2015. Bidirectional LSTM-CRF models for sequence tagging. *CoRR*, abs/1508.01991.

ISO 7098:2015(E). 2015. Information and documentation – Romanization of Chinese. Standard, International Organization for Standardization, Geneva, CH.

Guillaume Lample, Miguel Ballesteros, Sandeep Subramanian, Kazuya Kawakami, and Chris Dyer. 2016. Neural architectures for named entity recognition. In *HLT-NAACL*, pages 260–270. The Association for Computational Linguistics.

Ji Ma, Kuzman Ganchev, and David Weiss. 2018. State-of-the-art chinese word segmentation with bi-lstms. In *EMNLP*, pages 4902–4908. Association for Computational Linguistics.

Xuezhe Ma and Eduard H. Hovy. 2016. End-to-end sequence labeling via bi-directional lstm-cnns-crf. In *ACL (1)*. The Association for Computer Linguistics.

Tomas Mikolov, Ilya Sutskever, Kai Chen, Greg Corrado, and Jeffrey Dean. 2013. Distributed representations of words and phrases and their compositionality. *CoRR*, abs/1310.4546.

Fuchun Peng, Fangfang Feng, and Andrew McCallum. 2004. Chinese segmentation and new word detection using conditional random fields. In *Proceedings of the 20th International Conference on Computational Linguistics*, COLING '04, Stroudsburg, PA, USA. Association for Computational Linguistics.

Yan Shao, Christian Hardmeier, Jörg Tiedemann, and Joakim Nivre. 2017. Character-based joint segmentation and POS tagging for chinese using bidirectional RNN-CRF. In *IJCNLP(1)*, pages 173–183. Asian Federation of Natural Language Processing.

Weiwei Sun and Xiaojun Wan. 2012. Reducing approximation and estimation errors for chinese lexical processing with heterogeneous annotations. In *ACL (1)*, pages 232–241. The Association for Computer Linguistics.

Yaming Sun, Lei Lin, Nan Yang, Zhenzhou Ji, and Xiaolong Wang. 2014. Radical-enhanced chinese character embedding. In *ICONIP (2)*, volume 8835 of *Lecture Notes in Computer Science*, pages 279–286. Springer.

Zhiqing Sun, Gehui Shen, and Zhi-Hong Deng. 2017. A gap-based framework for chinese word segmentation via very deep convolutional networks. *CoRR*, abs/1712.09509.

Chunqi Wang and Bo Xu. 2017. Convolutional neural network with word embeddings for chinese word segmentation. In *IJCNLP(1)*, pages 163–172. Asian Federation of Natural Language Processing.

Nianwen Xu. 2003. Chinese word segmentation as character tagging. *Computational Linguistics and Chinese Language Processing*, 8(1):29–48.

Naiwen Xue, Fei Xia, Fu-Dong Chiou, and Martha Palmer. 2005. The penn chinese treebank: Phrase structure annotation of a large corpus. *Natural Language Engineering*, 11(2):207–238.

Jie Yang, Yue Zhang, and Fei Dong. 2017. Neural word segmentation with rich pretraining. In *ACL (1)*, pages 839–849. Association for Computational Linguistics.

Yushi Yao and Zheng Huang. 2016. Bi-directional LSTM recurrent neural network for chinese word segmentation. In *ICONIP (4)*, volume 9950 of *Lecture Notes in Computer Science*, pages 345–353.

Longkai Zhang, Houfeng Wang, Xu Sun, and Mairgup Mansur. 2013. Exploring representations from unlabeled data with co-training for chinese word segmentation. In *EMNLP*, pages 311–321. ACL.

Meishan Zhang, Yue Zhang, and Guohong Fu. 2016. Transition-based neural word segmentation. In *Proceedings of the 54th Annual Meeting of the Association for Computational Linguistics, ACL 2016, August 7-12, 2016, Berlin, Germany, Volume 1: Long Papers*.

Attention over Heads:
A Multi-Hop Attention for Neural Machine Translation

Shohei Iida[†], Ryuichiro Kimura[†], Hongyi Cui[†], Po-Hsuan Hung[†],
Takehito Utsuro[†] and Masaaki Nagata[‡]

[†]Graduate School of Systems and Information Engineering, University of Tsukuba, Japan
[‡]NTT Communication Science Laboratories, NTT Corporation, Japan

Abstract

In this paper, we propose a multi-hop attention for the Transformer. It refines the attention for an output symbol by integrating that of each head, and consists of two hops. The first hop attention is the scaled dot-product attention which is the same attention mechanism used in the original Transformer. The second hop attention is a combination of multi-layer perceptron (MLP) attention and head gate, which efficiently increases the complexity of the model by adding dependencies between heads. We demonstrate that the translation accuracy of the proposed multi-hop attention outperforms the baseline Transformer significantly, +0.85 BLEU point for the IWSLT-2017 German-to-English task and +2.58 BLEU point for the WMT-2017 German-to-English task. We also find that the number of parameters required for a multi-hop attention is smaller than that for stacking another self-attention layer and the proposed model converges significantly faster than the original Transformer.

1 Introduction

Multi-hop attention was first proposed in end-to-end memory networks (Sukhbaatar et al., 2015) for machine comprehension. In this paper, we define a hop as a computational step which could be performed for an output symbol many times. By "multi-hop attention", we mean that some kind of attention is calculated many times for generating an output symbol. Previous multi-hop attention can be classified into "recurrent attention" (Sukhbaatar et al., 2015) and "hierarchical attention" (Libovický and Helcl, 2017). The former repeats the calculation of attention many times to refine the attention itself while the latter integrates attentions for multiple input information sources. The proposed multi-hop attention for the Transformer is different from previous recurrent attentions because the mechanism for the first hop attention and that for the second hop attention is different. It is also different from previous hierarchical attention because it is designed to integrate attentions from different heads for the same information source.

In neural machine translation, hierarchical attention (Bawden et al., 2018; Libovický and Helcl, 2017) can be thought of a multi-hop attention because it repeats attention calculation to integrate the information from multiple source encoders. On the other hand, in the Transformer (Vaswani et al., 2017), the state-of-the-art model for neural machine translation, feed-forward neural network (FFNN) integrates information from multiple heads. In this paper, we propose a multi-hop attention mechanism as a possible alternative to integrate information from multi-head attention in the Transformer.

We find that the proposed Transformer with multi-hop attention converges faster than the original Transformer. This is likely because all heads learn to influence each other, through a head gate mechanism, in the second hop attention (Figure 1). Recently, many Transformer-based pre-trained language models such as BERT have been proposed and take about a month for training. The speed at which the proposed model converges may be even more important than the fact that its accuracy is slightly better.

2 Multi-Hop Multi-Head Attention for the Transformer

2.1 Multi-Head Attention

One of the Transformer's major successes is multi-head attention, which allows each head to capture different features and achieve better results compared to a single-head case.

$$a^{(h)} \quad = \quad softmax(\frac{Q^{(h)}K^{(h)\mathrm{T}}}{\sqrt{d}})V^{(h)} \quad (1)$$

$$m \quad = \quad Concat(a^{(1)}, ..., a^{(h)})W_O \quad (2)$$

Proceedings of the ACL 2019, Student Research Workshop, pages 217–222
Florence, Italy, July 28th-August 2nd, 2019. ©2019 Association for Computational Linguistics

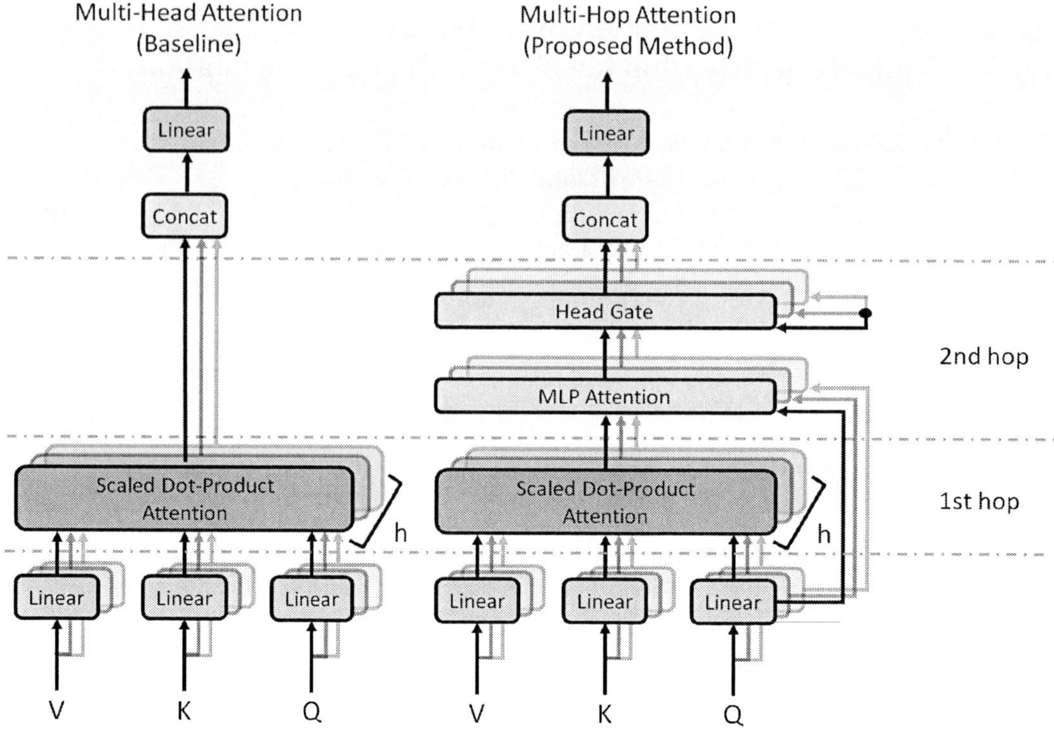

Figure 1: Multi-hop attention

Given the query Q, the key K, and the value V, they are divided into each head. Here, h (= $1, \ldots, H$) denotes the index of the head, where a is the output of scaled dot-product attention, W_O is a parameter for a linear transformation, and d is a scaling factor. Finally, the output of multi-head attention, m, is input to the next layer. The calculation of attention using scaled dot-product attention is defined as the first hop (Figure 1).

2.2 Multi-Hop Attention

In the original Transformer (Vaswani et al., 2017), information from each head is integrated by simple concatenation followed by a linear transformation. Attention is refined by stacking the combination of self-attention sub-layer and position-wise feed-forward neural network sub-layer. However, as layers are stacked, convergence becomes unstable. Consequently, there is a limit to the iterative approach by layering. Therefore, we propose a mechanism to repeat the calculation of attention based on a mechanism other than stacking layers.

The original Transformer is considered to consist of six single-hop attention layers. On the contrary, in the proposed method, some layers have

| | | IWSLT2017 | |
Model	2nd hop	de→en	en→de
Baseline	-	33.46	27.21
Multi-hop	1	33.52	27.75†
Multi-hop	2	33.86†	27.98†
Multi-hop	3	33.74‡	27.98†
Multi-hop	4	**34.31†**	**28.08†**
Multi-hop	5	33.81†	27.81†
Multi-hop	6	33.83†	27.96†
Multi-hop	1,2	33.77‡	27.73†
Multi-hop	1,2,3	33.71‡	27.90†
Multi-hop	1,2,3,4	33.58	27.88†
Multi-hop	1,2,3,4,5	33.30	27.60†
Multi-hop	1,2,3,4,5,6	32.53	27.30
Multi-hop	2,3,4,5,6	32.80	27.54‡
Multi-hop	3,4,5,6	33.22	27.75†
Multi-hop	4,5,6	33.40	27.74†
Multi-hop	5,6	33.60	27.92†

†($p \leq 0.01$) and ‡($p \leq 0.05$) indicate that the proposed methods significantly outperform the Transformer baseline.

The encoder and the decoder each had six layers, respectively.

Table 1: Best position for multi-hop

a multi-hop (two-hop) attention. By experiments, we have established the appropriate position of the proposed multi-hop attention in the neural machine translation system. If the number of layers for encoders and decoders are six, then there are

Model	IWSLT2017		WMT17	
	de→en	en→de	de→en	en→de
Baseline	33.46	27.21	21.33	18.15
Multi-hop	**34.31**†	**28.08**†	**23.91**†	**19.88**†

†($p \leq 0.01$) indicates that the proposed methods significantly outperform the Transformer baseline.

Table 2: Evaluation Result

Model	Layers	IWSLT2017	
		de→en	en→de
Vanilla	4	30.02	27.60
Multi-hop	4	30.09	27.63
Vanilla	5	33.80	28.00
Multi-hop	5	33.78	**28.15**
Vanilla	6	33.46	27.21
Multi-hop	6	**34.31**†	28.08†
Vanilla	7	31.80	26.58
Multi-hop	7	32.55†	27.36†

Table 3: Difference between 6-layer Transformer with multi-hop and 7-layer stacked vanilla Transformer

Model	Layers	IWSLT2017	
		de→en	en→de
Vanilla	4	40,747K	41,882K
Multi-hop	4	40,763K	41,898K
Vanilla	5	48,103K	49,238K
Multi-hop	5	48,120K	49,254K
Vanilla	6	55,459K	56,594K
Multi-hop	6	55,492K	56,627K
Vanilla	7	62,816K	63,951K
Multi-hop	7	62,833K	63,967K

Table 4: Model Parameters

six self-attention layers in both the encoder and the decoder, respectively, and six source-to-target attention layers in the decoder.

The first hop attention of the multi-hop attention is equivalent to the calculation of scaled dot-product attention (Equation 1) in the original Transformer. The second hop attention consists of multi-layer perceptron (MLP) attention and head gate, as shown in Figure 1 and the following equations.

$$e_i^{(h)} = v_b^{\mathrm{T}} \tanh(W_b Q^{(h)} + U_b^{(h)} a_i^{(h)}) \quad (3)$$

$$\beta_i^{(h)} = \frac{\exp(e_i^{(h)})}{\sum_{n=1}^{N} \exp(e_i^{(h)})} \quad (4)$$

$$a_i'^{(h)} = \beta_i^{(h)} U_c^{(h)} a_i^{(h)} \quad (5)$$

First, MLP attention between the output of the first hop, $a_i^{(h)}$, and the query, Q, is calculated. Attention is considered as the calculation of a relationship between the query and the key/value. Therefore, in the second hop, attention is calculated again by using the output of the first hop, rather than the key/value.

Equations 4 and 5 are head gate in Figure 1. The head gate normalizes the attention score of each head to $\beta_i^{(h)}$, using the softmax function, where h ranges over all heads. In hierarchical attention (Bawden et al., 2018), the softmax function is used to select a single source from multiple sources. Here, the proposed head gate uses the softmax function to select a head from multi-

ple heads. Finally, the head gate calculates new attention, $a_i'^{(h)}$, using the learnable parameters $U_c^{(h)}$, $\beta_i^{(h)}$, and $a_i^{(h)}$. The second hop MLP attention learns the optimal parameters for integration under the influence of the head gate. Although Vaswani et al. (2017) reported that dot-product attention is superior to MLP attention, we used MLP attention in the second hop of the proposed multi-hop attention because it can learn the dependence between heads by appropriately tuning the MLP parameters. We conclude that we can increase the expressive power of the network more efficiently by adding the second hop attention layer, rather than by stacking another single-hop multi-head attention layer.

3 Experiment

3.1 Data

We used German-English parallel data obtained from the IWSLT2017[1] and the WMT17[2] shared tasks.

The IWSLT2017 training, validation, and test sets contain approximately 160K, 7.3K, and 6.7K sentence pairs, respectively. There are approximately 5.9M sentence pairs in the WMT17 training dataset. For the WMT17 corpus, we used newstest2013 as the validation set and newstest2014 and newstest2017 as the test sets.

For tokenization, we used the subword-nmt tool (Sennrich et al., 2016) to set a vocabulary size of 32,000 for both German and English.

3.2 Experimental Setup

In our experiments, the baseline was the Transformer (Vaswani et al., 2017) model. We used

---

[1] https://sites.google.com/site/iwsltevaluation2017/
[2] http://www.statmt.org/wmt17/translation-task.html

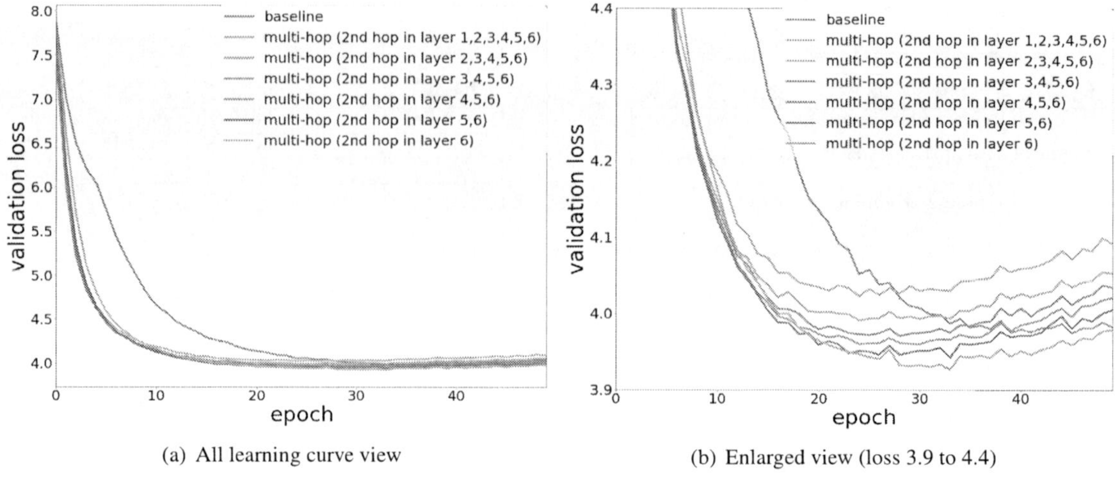

(a) All learning curve view
(b) Enlarged view (loss 3.9 to 4.4)

Figure 2: Validation loss by each epoch for IWSLT2017 de-en - second hop in layer n to 6

fairseq (Gehring et al., 2017) [3] toolkit and the source code will be available at our github repository [4]. For training, we used the Adam optimizer with a learning rate of 0.0003. The embedding size was 512, the hidden size was 2048, and the number of heads was 8. The encoder and the decoder each had six layers. The number of tokens per batch was 2,000. The number of training epochs for IWSLT2017 and WMT17 were 50 and 10, respectively. In all experiments using the IWSLT2017, models were trained on an Nvidia GeForce RTX 2080 Ti GPU, while in all experiments using the WMT17, models were trained on an Nvidia Tesla P100 GPU.

3.3 Results

Results of the evaluation are presented in Tables 1 and 2. In Table 2, the proposed multi-hop attention is used only at the fourth layer in the encoder. In the evaluation of German-to-English translation for IWSLT2017, the proposed method achieved a BLEU score of 34.31, which indicates that it significantly outperforms the Transformer baseline, which returned a BLEU score of 33.46. For WMT17, the proposed method achieved a BLEU score of 23.91, indicating that it also significantly outperformed the Transformer baseline, which returned a BLEU score of 21.33.

In IWSLT2017 German-to-English and English-to-German translation tasks, various conditions were investigated, as shown in Table 1.

[3]https://github.com/pytorch/fairseq
[4]https://github.com/siida36/
   fairseq_mhda

The best models are shown in Figure 2.

The baseline training time was 1143.2s per epoch in IWSLT2017 German-to-English translation, and the training time for the proposed method is 1145.6s per epoch. We found that increasing the number of parameters did not affect training time.

4 Analysis

4.1 Difference between Multi-Hop and 7-layer Stacked Transformer

We compared the proposed method with the original Transformer. Table 3 shows the translation accuracies when the number of layers was changed from 4 to 7, encoder and decoder, respectively. Here, "Vanilla" refers to the original Transformer and "Multi-hop" refers to the proposed method where the multi-hop attention layer is used at the fourth layer in the encoder. As shown in Table 3, the 7-layer model BLEU score is lower than that of the 6-layer model. In the experiments, the number of parameters required by the 6- and 7-layer models was 55,459K, and 62,816K, respectively, and the number of parameters for the multi-hop method was 55,492K. The proposed method only increases the number of parameters by one percent compared to simply stacking one multi-head layer. Thus, it is evident that simply increasing the number of parameters and repeating the attention calculation doesn't necessarily improve performance. On the other hand, the proposed method does not improve the BLEU score when the number of layers is four and five. This is probably because the parameters of each head in the baseline Trans-

Epoch	Baseline	Second hop					
		Layer 1,2,3,4,5,6	Layer 2,3,4,5,6	Layer 3,4,5,6	Layer 4,5,6	Layer 5,6	Layer 6
1	7.87	**7.49**	**7.49**	7.53	7.56	7.70	7.82
10	4.80	4.21	4.18	**4.17**	**4.17**	**4.17**	4.21
20	4.15	4.04	4.00	3.99	3.98	**3.97**	**3.97**
30	4.01	4.04	4.00	3.97	3.96	3.95	**3.93**
40	3.97	4.05	4.02	4.00	3.98	3.97	**3.94**
50	**3.98**	4.09	4.05	4.03	4.02	4.00	**3.98**

Table 5: Validation loss by epoch for IWSLT2017 de-en

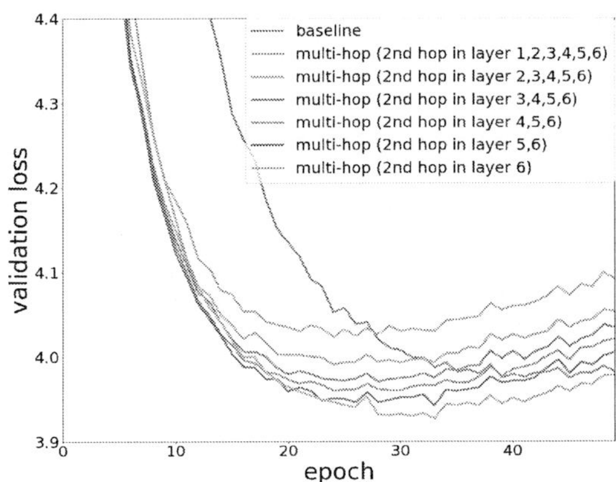

Figure 3: Validation loss by each epoch for IWSLT2017 de-en - second hop in only n layer

former are likely to converge properly when there are relatively few parameters. Another interpretation is that the normalization among heads forced by the proposed method works as noise.

As a conclusion, the proposed method demonstrates that appropriate connection can be obtained by recalculating attention in the layer where the head has a dependency.

Table 1 shows the effect of introducing second hop attention to various positions in the encoder. The second column shows the positions where the second hop attention is used. The best result was obtained when the second hop attention was used only for the fourth layer in the encoder. Performance decreased as the second hop attention was introduced to more layers, i.e., the worst result was obtained when using the second hop in all layers (second hop in layer 1,2,3,4,5,6). Further studies are needed to elucidate the relationship between performance and position of the second hop attention.

4.2 Effect on Learning Speed

Table 5 shows the validation loss of models for the IWSLT2017 German-to-English translation task with the second hop layers whose dropout rate is 30%. All models have 6 layers and the positions of the second hop layers have narrowed from all 6 layers to only 6th layers. It should be noted that, in the first epoch (row 1, Table 5), the model with the second hop in all layers has the lowest validation loss, while the baseline model has the highest validation loss.

Figure 2(a) shows the learning curve based on the same data shown in Table 5, It is apparent that the models with the second hop converge faster than the baseline model. Figure 2(b) is an enlarged view of Figure 2(a), focused on the lowest validation loss for different models. We find that the validation loss is lower when there are fewer second hop attentions.

Figure 3 shows the learning curves for the models with multi-hop attention used only once anywhere in layer 1 to 6. We find the model with second hop attention in layer 6 converges fastest. In terms of convergence, as opposed to accuracy, it seems appropriate to use second hop attention only in the last (6th) layer in the encoder.

5 Related Work

The mechanism of the proposed multi-hop attention for the Transformer was inspired by the hierarchical attention in multi-source sequence-to-sequence model (Libovický and Helcl, 2017). The term "multi-hop" is borrowed from the end-to-end memory network (Sukhbaatar et al., 2015) and the title "attention over heads" is inspired by Attention-over-Attention neural network (Cui et al., 2017), respectively.

Ahmed et al. (2018) proposed Weighted Transformer which replaces multi-head attention by multiple self-attention branches that learn to combine during the training process. They reported that it slightly outperformed the baseline Transformer (0.5 BLEU points on the WMT 2014 English-to-German translation task) and converges 15-40% faster. They linearly combined the multiple sources of attention, while we combined multiple attention non-linearly using softmax function in the second hop.

It is well known that the Transformer is difficult to train (Popel and Bojar, 2018). As it has a large number of parameters, it takes time to converge and sometimes it does not do so at all without appropriate hyper parameter tuning. Considering the experimental results of our multi-hop attention experiments, and that of the Weight Transformer, an appropriate design of the network to combine multi-head attention could result in faster and more stable convergence of the Transformer. As the Transformer is used as a building block for the recently proposed pre-trained language models such as BERT (Devlin et al., 2019) which takes about a month for training, we think it is worthwhile to pursue this line of research including the proposed multi-hop attention.

Universal Transformer (Dehghani et al., 2019) can be thought of variable-depth recurrent attention. It obtained Turing-complete expressive power in exchange for a vast increase in the number of parameters and training time. As shown in Table 4, we have proposed an efficient method to increase the depth of recurrence in terms of the number of parameters and training time. Recently, Voita et al. (2019) and Michel et al. (2019) independently reported that only a certain subset of the heads plays an important role in the Transformer. They performed analyses by pruning heads from an already trained model, while we have proposed a method to assign weights to heads automatically. We assume our method (multi-hop attention or attention-over-heads) selects important heads in the early stage of training, which results in faster convergence than the original Transformer.

6 Conclusion

In this paper, we have proposed a multi-hop attention mechanism for a Transformer model in which all heads depend on each other repeatedly. We found that the proposed method significantly outperforms the original Transformer in accuracy and converges faster with little increase in the number of parameters. In future work, we would like to implement a multi-hop attention mechanism to the decoder side and investigate other language pairs.

References

K. Ahmed, N. S. Keskar, and R.Socher. 2018. Weighted transformer network for machine translation. *arXiv preprint arXiv:1711.02132*.

R. Bawden, R. Sennrich, A. Birch, and B. Haddow. 2018. Evaluating discourse phenomena in neural machine translation. In *Proc. NAACL-HLT*, pages 1304–1313.

Y. Cui, Z. Chen, S. Wei, S. Wang, T. Liu, and G. Hu. 2017. Attention-over-attention neural networks for reading comprehension. In *Proc. 55th ACL*, pages 593–602.

M. Dehghani, S. Gouws, O. Vinyals, J. Uszkoreit, and Ł. Kaiser. 2019. Universal transformers. In *Proc. 7th ICLR*.

J. Devlin, M.-W. Chang, K. Lee, and K. Toutanova. 2019. BERT: Pre-training of deep bidirectional transformers for language understanding. In *Proc. NAACL-HLT*, volume abs/1810.04805.

J. Gehring, M. Auli, D. Grangier, D. Yarats, and Y. N. Dauphin. 2017. Convolutional Sequence to Sequence Learning. In *Proc. 34th ICML*.

J. Libovický and J. Helcl. 2017. Attention strategies for multi-source sequence-to-sequence learning. In *Proc. 55th ACL*, pages 196–202.

P. Michel, O. Levy, and G. Neubig. 2019. Are sixteen heads really better than one? *arXiv preprint arXiv:1905.10650*.

M. Popel and O. Bojar. 2018. Training tips for the transformer model. *The Prague Bulletin of Mathematical Linguistics*, 110(1):43–70.

R. Sennrich, B. Haddow, and A. Birch. 2016. Neural machine translation of rare words with subword units. In *Proc. 54th ACL*, pages 1715–1725.

S. Sukhbaatar, A. Szlam, J. Weston, and R. Fergus. 2015. End-to-end memory networks. In *Proc. 28th NIPS*, pages 2440–2448.

A. Vaswani, N. Shazeer, N. Parmar, J. Uszkoreit, L. Jones, A. Gomez, L. Kaiser, and I. Polosukhin. 2017. Attention is all you need. In *Proc. 30th NIPS*, pages 5998–6008.

E. Voita, D. Talbot, F. Moiseev, R. Sennrich, and I. Titov. 2019. Analyzing multi-head self-attention: Specialized heads do the heavy lifting, the rest can be pruned. *arXiv preprint arXiv:1905.09418*.

Reducing Gender Bias in Word-Level Language Models with a Gender-Equalizing Loss Function

Yusu Qian[*]
Tandon School
of Engineering
New York University
6 MetroTech Center
Brooklyn, NY, 11201
yq729@nyu.edu

Urwa Muaz[*]
Tandon School
of Engineering
New York University
6 MetroTech Center
Brooklyn, NY, 11201
um367@nyu.edu

Ben Zhang
Center for
Data Science
New York University
60 Fifth Avenue
New York, NY, 10012
bz957@nyu.edu

Jae Won Hyun
Department of
Computer Science
New York University
251 Mercer St
New York, NY, 10012
jaewhyun@nyu.edu

Abstract

Gender bias exists in natural language datasets which neural language models tend to learn, resulting in biased text generation. In this research, we propose a debiasing approach based on the loss function modification. We introduce a new term to the loss function which attempts to equalize the probabilities of male and female words in the output. Using an array of bias evaluation metrics, we provide empirical evidence that our approach successfully mitigates gender bias in language models without increasing perplexity by much. In comparison to existing debiasing strategies, data augmentation, and word embedding debiasing, our method performs better in several aspects, especially in reducing gender bias in occupation words. Finally, we introduce a combination of data augmentation and our approach, and show that it outperforms existing strategies in all bias evaluation metrics.

1 Introduction

Natural Language Processing (NLP) models are shown to capture unwanted biases and stereotypes found in the training data which raise concerns about socioeconomic, ethnic and gender discrimination when these models are deployed for public use (Lu et al., 2018; Zhao et al., 2018).

There are numerous studies that identify algorithmic bias in NLP applications. Lapowsky (2018) showed ethnic bias in Google autocomplete suggestions whereas Lambrecht and Tucker (2018) found gender bias in advertisement delivery systems. Additionally, Zhao et al. (2018) demonstrated that coreference resolution systems exhibit gender bias.

Language modelling is a pivotal task in NLP with important downstream applications such as text generation (Sutskever et al., 2011). Recent studies by Lu et al. (2018) and Bordia and Bowman (2019) have shown that this task is vulnerable to gender bias in the training corpus. Two prior works focused on reducing bias in language modelling by data preprocessing (Lu et al., 2018) and word embedding debiasing (Bordia and Bowman, 2019). In this study, we investigate the efficacy of bias reduction during training by introducing a new loss function which encourages the language model to equalize the probabilities of predicting gendered word pairs like *he* and *she*. Although we recognize that gender is non-binary, for the purpose of this study, we focus on female and male words.

Our main contributions are summarized as follows: i) to our best knowledge, this study is the first one to investigate bias alleviation in text generation by direct modification of the loss function; ii) our new loss function effectively reduces gender bias in the language models during training by equalizing the probabilities of male and female words in the output; iii) we show that end-to-end debiasing of the language model can achieve word embedding debiasing; iv) we provide an interpretation of our results and draw a comparison to other existing debiasing methods. We show that our method, combined with an existing method, counterfactual data augmentation, achieves the best result and outperforms all existing methods.

2 Related Work

Recently, the study of bias in NLP applications has received increasing attention from researchers. Most relevant work in this domain can be broadly divided into two categories: word embedding debiasing and data debiasing by preprocessing.

Word Embedding Debiasing Bolukbasi et al. (2016) introduced the idea of gender subspace as low dimensional space in an embedding that cap-

---

[*]Yusu Qian and Urwa Muaz contributed equally to the paper.

Proceedings of the ACL 2019, Student Research Workshop, pages 223–228
Florence, Italy, July 28th-August 2nd, 2019. ©2019 Association for Computational Linguistics

tures the gender information. Bolukbasi et al. (2016) and Zhao et al. (2017) defined gender bias as a projection of gender-neutral words on a gender subspace and removed bias by minimizing this projection. Gonen and Goldberg (2019) proved that bias removal techniques based on minimizing projection onto the gender space are insufficient. They showed that male and female stereotyped words cluster together even after such debiasing treatments. Thus, gender bias still remains in the embeddings and is easily recoverable.

Bordia and Bowman (2019) introduced a co-occurrence based metric to measure gender bias in texts and showed that the standard datasets used for language model training exhibit strong gender bias. They also showed that the models trained on these datasets amplify bias measured on the model-generated texts. Using the same definition of embedding gender bias as Bolukbasi et al. (2016), Bordia and Bowman (2019) introduced a regularization term that aims to minimize the projection of neutral words onto the gender subspace. Throughout this paper,we refer to this approach as REG. They found that REG reduces bias in the generated texts for some regularization coefficient values. But, this bias definition is shown to be incomplete by Gonen and Goldberg (2019). Instead of explicit geometric debiasing of the word embedding, we implement a loss function that minimizes bias in the output and thus adjust the whole network accordingly. For each model, we analyze the generated word embedding to understand how it is affected by output debiasing.

Data Debiasing Lu et al. (2018) showed that gender bias in coreference resolution and language modelling can be mitigated through a data augmentation technique that expands the corpus by swapping the gender pairs like *he* and *she*, or *father* and *mother*. They called this Counterfactual Data Augmentation (CDA) and concluded that it outperforms the word embedding debiasing strategy proposed by Bolukbasi et al. (2016). CDA doubles the size of the training data and increases time needed to train language models. In this study, we intend to reduce bias during training without requiring an additional data preprocessing step.

3 Methodology

3.1 Dataset

For the training data, we use Daily Mail news articles released by Hermann et al. (2015). This dataset is composed of 219,506 articles covering a diverse range of topics including business, sports, travel, etc., and is claimed to be biased and sensational (Bordia and Bowman, 2019). For manageability, we randomly subsample 5% of the text. The subsample has around 8.25 million tokens in total.

3.2 Language Model

We use a pre-trained 300-dimensional word embedding, GloVe, by Pennington et al. (2014). We apply random search to the hyperparameter tuning of the LSTM language model. The best hyperparameters are as follows: 2 hidden layers each with 300 units, a sequence length of 35, a learning rate of 20 with an annealing schedule of decay starting from 0.25 to 0.95, a dropout rate of 0.25 and a gradient clip of 0.25. We train our models for 150 epochs, use a batch size of 48, and set early stopping with a patience of 5.

3.3 Loss Function

Language models are usually trained using cross-entropy loss. Cross-entropy loss at time step t is

$$L^{CE}(t) = -\sum_{w \in V} y_{w,t} \log\left(\hat{y}_{w,t}\right),$$

where V is the vocabulary, y is the one hot vector of ground truth and $\hat{y}$ indicates the output softmax probability of the model.

We introduce a loss term L^B, which aims to equalize the predicted probabilities of gender pairs such as *woman* and *man*.

$$L^B(t) = \frac{1}{G} \sum_{i}^{G} \left| \log \frac{\hat{y}_{f_i,t}}{\hat{y}_{m_i,t}} \right|$$

f and m are a set of corresponding gender pairs, G is the size of the gender pairs set, and $\hat{y}$ indicates the output softmax probability. We use gender pairs provided by Zhao et al. (2017). By considering only gender pairs we ensure that only gender information is neutralized and distribution over semantic concepts is not altered. For example, it will try to equalize the probabilities of *congressman* with *congresswoman* and *actor* with *actress* but distribution of *congressman, congresswoman* versus *actor, actress* will not be affected. Overall loss can be written as

$$L = \frac{1}{T} \sum_{t=1}^{T} L^{CE}(t) + \lambda L^{B}(t),$$

where λ is a hyperparameter and T is the corpus size. We observe that among the similar minima of the loss function, L^B encourages the model to converge towards a minimum that exhibits the lowest gender bias.

3.4 Model Evaluation

Language models are evaluated using perplexity, which is a standard measure of performance for unseen data. For bias evaluation, we use an array of metrics to provide a holistic diagnosis of the model behavior under debiasing treatment. These metrics are discussed in detail below. In all the evaluation metrics requiring gender pairs, we use gender pairs provided by Zhao et al. (2017). This list contains 223 pairs, all other words are considered gender-neutral.

3.4.1 Co-occurrence Bias

Co-occurrence bias is computed from the model-generated texts by comparing the occurrences of all gender-neutral words with female and male words. A word is considered to be biased towards a certain gender if it occurs more frequently with words of that gender. This definition was first used by Zhao et al. (2017) and later adapted by Bordia and Bowman (2019). Using the definition of gender bias similar to the one used by Bordia and Bowman (2019), we define gender bias as

$$B^N = \frac{1}{N} \sum_{w \in N} \left| \log \frac{c(w, m)}{c(w, f)} \right|,$$

where N is a set of gender-neutral words, and $c(w, g)$ is the occurrences of a word w with words of gender g in the same window. This score is designed to capture unequal co-occurrences of neutral words with male and female words. Co-occurrences are computed using a sliding window of size 10 extending equally in both directions. Furthermore, we only consider words that occur more than 20 times with gendered words to exclude random effects.

We also evaluate a normalized version of B^N which we denote by conditional co-occurrence bias, B_c^N. This is defined as

$$B_c^N = \frac{1}{N} \sum_{w \in N} \left| \log \frac{P(w|m)}{P(w|f)} \right|,$$

where

$$P(w|g) = \frac{c(w, g)}{c(g)}.$$

B_c^N is less affected by the disparity in the general distribution of male and female words in the text. The disparity between the occurrences of the two genders means that text is more inclined to mention one over the other, so it can also be considered a form of bias. We report the ratio of occurrence of male and female words in the model generated text, GR, as

$$GR = \frac{c(m)}{c(f)}.$$

3.4.2 Causal Bias

Another way of quantifying bias in NLP models is based on the idea of causal testing. The model is exposed to paired samples which differ only in one attribute (e.g. gender) and the disparity in the output is interpreted as bias related to that attribute. Zhao et al. (2018) and Lu et al. (2018) applied this method to measure bias in coreference resolution and Lu et al. (2018) also used it for evaluating gender bias in language modelling.

Following the approach similar to Lu et al. (2018), we limit this bias evaluation to a set of gender-neutral occupations. We create a list of sentences based on a set of templates. There are two sets of templates used for evaluating causal occupation bias (Table 1). The first set of templates is designed to measure how the probabilities of occupation words depend on the gender information in the seed. Below is an example of the first set of templates:

$$[Gendered\,word]\,is\,a\,|\,[occupation].$$

Here, the vertical bar separates the seed sequence that is fed into the language models from the target occupation, for which we observe the output softmax probability. We measure causal occupation bias conditioned on gender as

$$CB|g = \frac{1}{|O|} \frac{1}{G} \sum_{o \in O} \sum_{i}^{G} \left| \log \frac{p(o|f_i)}{p(o|m_i)} \right|,$$

where O is a set of gender-neutral occupations and G is the size of the gender pairs set. For example, $P(doctor|he)$ is the softmax probability of

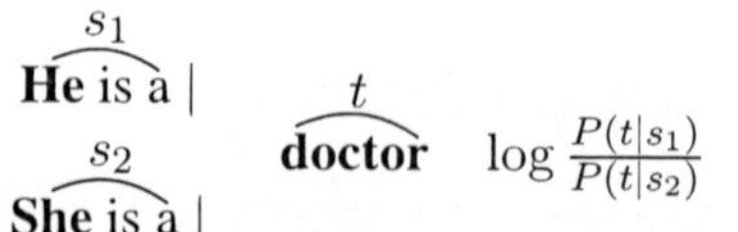

(a) Occupation bias conditioned on gendered words

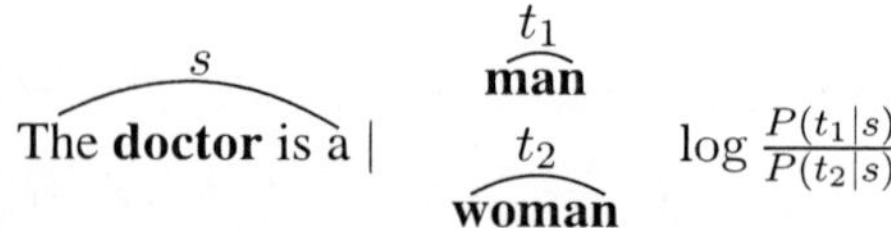

(b) Occupation bias conditioned on occupations

Table 1: Example templates of two types of occupation bias

the word *doctor* where the seed sequence is *He is a*. The second set of templates like below, aims to capture how the probabilities of gendered words depend on the occupation words in the seed.

$$The\ [occupation]\ is\ a\ |\ [gendered\ word]\,.$$

Causal occupation bias conditioned on occupation is represented as

$$CB|o = \frac{1}{|O|} \frac{1}{G} \sum_{o \in O} \sum_{i}^{G} \left| \log \frac{p(f_i|o)}{p(m_i|o)} \right|,$$

where O is a set of gender-neutral occupations and G is the size of the gender pairs set. For example, $P(man|doctor)$ is the softmax probability of *man* where the seed sequence is *The doctor is a*.

We believe that both $CB|g$ and $CB|o$ contribute to gender bias in the model-generated texts. We also note that $CB|o$ is more easily influenced by the general disparity in male and female word probabilities.

3.4.3 Word Embedding Bias

Our debiasing approach does not explicitly address the bias in the embedding layer. Therefore, we use gender-neutral occupations to measure the embedding bias to observe if debiasing the output layer also decreases the bias in the embedding. We define the embedding bias, EB_d, as the difference between the Euclidean distance of an occupation word to male words and the distance of the occupation word to the female counterparts. This definition is equivalent to bias by projection described by Bolukbasi et al. (2016). We define EB_d as

$$EB_d = \sum_{o \in O} \sum_{i}^{G} \Big| \|E(o) - E(m_i)\|_2$$
$$- \|E(o) - E(f_i)\|_2 \Big|,$$

where O is a set of gender-neutral occupations, G is the size of the gender pairs set and E is the word-to-vector dictionary.

3.5 Existing Approaches

We apply CDA where we swap all the gendered words using a bidirectional dictionary of gender pairs described by Lu et al. (2018). This creates a dataset twice the size of the original data, with exactly the same contextual distributions for both genders and we use it to train the language models.

We also implement the bias regularization method of Bordia and Bowman (2019) which debiases the word embedding during language model training by minimizing the projection of neutral words on the gender axis. We use hyperparameter tuning to find the best regularization coefficient and report results from the model trained with this coefficient. We later refer to this strategy as REG.

4 Experiments

Initially, we measure the co-occurrence bias in the training data. After training the baseline model, we implement our loss function and tune for the λ hyperparameter. We test the existing debiasing approaches, CDA and REG, as well but since Bordia and Bowman (2019) reported that results fluctuate substantially with different REG regularization coefficients, we perform hyperparameter tuning and report the best results in Table 2. Additionally, we implement a combination of our loss function and CDA and tune for λ. Finally, bias evaluation is performed for all the trained models. Causal occupation bias is measured directly from the models using template datasets discussed above and co-occurrence bias is measured from the model-generated texts, which consist of 10,000 documents of 500 words each.

4.1 Results

Results for the experiments are listed in Table 2. It is interesting to observe that the baseline model amplifies the bias in the training data set as measured by B^N and B_c^N. From measurements using the described bias metrics, our method effectively mitigates bias in language modelling with-

Model	B^N	B_c^N	GR	$Ppl.$	$CB\|o$	$CB\|g$	EB_d
Dataset	0.340	0.213		-	-	-	-
Baseline	0.531	0.282	1.415	117.845	1.447	97.762	0.528
REG	0.381	0.329	1.028	**114.438**	1.861	108.740	0.373
CDA	0.208	0.149	1.037	117.976	0.703	56.82	0.268
$\lambda_{0.01}$	0.492	0.245	1.445	118.585	0.111	9.306	0.077
$\lambda_{0.1}$	0.459	0.208	1.463	118.713	0.013	2.326	0.018
$\lambda_{0.5}$	0.312	0.173	1.252	120.344	**0.000**	1.159	0.006
$\lambda_{0.8}$	0.226	0.151	1.096	119.792	0.001	1.448	0.002
λ_1	0.218	0.153	1.049	120.973	**0.000**	0.999	0.002
λ_2	0.221	0.157	1.020	123.248	**0.000**	0.471	**0.000**
$\lambda_{0.5}$ + CDA	**0.205**	**0.145**	**1.012**	117.971	**0.000**	**0.153**	**0.000**

Table 2: Evaluation results for models trained on Daily Mail and their generated texts

out a significant increase in perplexity. At λ value of 1, it reduces B^N by 58.95%, B_c^N by 45.74%, $CB|o$ by 100%, $CB|g$ by 98.52% and EB_d by 98.98%. Compared to the results of CDA and REG, it achieves the best results in both occupation biases, $CB|g$ and $CB|o$, and EB_d. We notice that all methods result in GR around 1, indicating that there are near equal amounts of female and male words in the generated texts. In our experiments we note that with increasing λ, the bias steadily decreases and perplexity tends to slightly increase. This indicates that there is a trade-off between bias and perplexity.

REG is not very effective in mitigating bias when compared to other methods, and fails to achieve the best result in any of the bias metrics that we used. But REG results in the best perplexity and even does better than the baseline model in this respect. This indicates that REG has a slight regularization effect. Additionally, it is interesting to note that our loss function outperforms REG in EB_d even though REG explicitly aims to reduce gender bias in the embeddings. Although our method does not explicitly attempt geometric debiasing of the word embedding, the results show that it results in the most debiased embedding as compared to other methods. Furthermore, Gonen and Goldberg (2019) emphasizes that geometric gender bias in word embeddings is not completely understood and existing word embedding debiasing strategies are insufficient. Our approach provides an appealing end-to-end solution for model debiasing without relying on any measure of bias in the word embedding. We believe this concept is generalizable to other NLP applications.

Our method outperforms CDA in $CB|g$, $CB|o$, and EB_d. While CDA achieves slightly better results for co-occurrence biases, B^N and B_c^N, and results in a better perplexity. With a marginal differences, our results are comparable to those of CDA and both models seem to have similar bias mitigation effects. However, our method does not require a data augmentation step and allows training of an unbiased model directly from biased datasets. For this reason, it also requires less time to train than CDA since its training data has a smaller size without data augmentation. Furthermore, CDA fails to effectively mitigate occupation bias when compared to our approach. Although the training data for CDA does not contain gender bias, the model still exhibits some gender bias when measured with our causal occupation bias metrics. This reinforces the concept that some model-level constraints are essential to debiasing a model and dataset debiasing alone cannot be trusted.

Finally, we note that the combination of CDA and our loss function outperforms all the methods in all measures of biases without compromising perplexity. Therefore, it can be argued that a cascade of these approaches can be used to optimally debias the language models.

5 Conclusion and Discussion

In this research, we propose a new approach for mitigating gender bias in neural language models and empirically show its effectiveness in reducing bias as measured with different evaluation metrics. Our research also highlights the fact that debiasing the model with bias penalties in the loss function is an effective method. We emphasize that loss function based debiasing is powerful and generalizable to other downstream NLP applications. The research also reinforces the idea that geometric debiasing of the word embedding is not a complete solution for debiasing the downstream applications but encourages end-to-end approaches to debiasing.

All the debiasing techniques experimented in this paper rely on a predefined set of gender pairs in some way. CDA used gender pairs for flipping, REG uses it for gender space definition and our technique uses them for computing loss. This reliance on pre-defined set of gender pairs can be considered a limitation of these methods. It also results in another concern. There are gender associated words which do not have pairs, like pregnant. These words are not treated properly by techniques relying on gender pairs.

Future work includes designing a context-aware version of our loss function which can distinguish between the unbiased and biased mentions of the gendered words and only penalize the biased version. Another interesting direction is exploring the application of this method in mitigating racial bias which brings more challenges.

6   Acknowledgment

We are grateful to Sam Bowman for helpful advice, Shikha Bordia, Cuiying Yang, Gang Qian, Xiyu Miao, Qianyi Fan, Tian Liu, and Stanislav Sobolevsky for discussions, and reviewers for detailed feedback.

References

Tolga Bolukbasi, Kai-Wei Chang, James Zou, Venkatesh Saligrama, and Adam Kalai. 2016. Man is to computer programmer as woman is to homemaker? debiasing word embeddings. In *NIPS'16 Proceedings of the 30th International Conference on Neural Information Processing Systems*, pages 4356–4364.

Shikha Bordia and Samuel R. Bowman. 2019. Identifying and reducing gender bias in word-level language models. ArXiv:1904.03035.

Hila Gonen and Yoav Goldberg. 2019. Lipstick on a pig: Debiasing methods cover up systematic gender biases in word embeddings but do not remove them. ArXiv:1903.03862.

Karl Hermann, Tom Koisk, Edward Grefenstette, Lasse Espeholt, Will Kay, Mustafa Suleyman, and Phil Blunsom. 2015. Teaching machines to read and comprehend. In *NIPS'15 Proceedings of the 28th International Conference on Neural Information Processing Systems*, pages 1693–1701.

Anja Lambrecht and Catherine E. Tucker. 2018. Algorithmic bias? an empirical study into apparent gender-based discrimination in the display of stem career ads.

Issie Lapowsky. 2018. Google autocomplete still makes vile suggestions.

Kaiji Lu, Piotr Mardziel, Fangjing Wu, Preetam Amancharla, and Anupam Datta. 2018. Gender bias in neural natural language processing. ArXiv:1807.11714v1.

Jeffrey Pennington, Richard Socher, and Christopher Manning. 2014. Glove: Global vectors for word representation. In *Proceedings of the 2014 Conference on Empirical Methods in Natural Language Processing*, pages 1532–1543. Association for Computational Linguistics.

Ilya Sutskever, James Martens, and Geoffrey Hinton. 2011. Generating text with recurrent neural networks. In *ICML'11 Proceedings of the 28th International Conference on International Conference on Machine Learning*, pages 1017–1024.

Jieyu Zhao, Tianlu Wang, Mark Yatskar, Vicente Ordonez, and Kai-Wei Chag. 2017. Men also like shopping: Reducing gender bias amplification using corpus-level constraints. In *Conference on Empirical Methods in Natural Language Processing*.

Jieyu Zhao, Yichao Zhou, Zeyu Li, Wei Wang, and Chang Kaiwei. 2018. Learning gender-neutral word embeddings. In *Proceedings of the 2018 Conference on Empirical Methods in Natural Language Processing*, pages 4847–4853. Association for Computational Linguistics.

Automatic Generation of Personalized Comment Based on User Profile

Wenhuan Zeng[1]*, **Abulikemu Abuduweili[2]***, **Lei Li[3]**, **Pengcheng Yang[4]**

[1]School of Mathematical Sciences, Peking University
[2]State Key Lab of Advanced Optical Communication System and Networks,
School of EECS, Peking University
[3]School of Computer Science and Technology, Xidian University
[4]MOE Key Lab of Computational Linguistics, School of EECS, Peking University
`{zengwenhuan, abduwali}@pku.edu.cn`
`tobiaslee@foxmail.com, yang_pc@pku.edu.cn`

Abstract

Comments on social media are very diverse, in terms of content, style and vocabulary, which make generating comments much more challenging than other existing natural language generation (NLG) tasks. Besides, since different user has different expression habits, it is necessary to take the user's profile into consideration when generating comments. In this paper, we introduce the task of automatic generation of personalized comment (AGPC) for social media. Based on tens of thousands of users' real comments and corresponding user profiles on weibo, we propose Personalized Comment Generation Network (PCGN) for AGPC. The model utilizes user feature embedding with a gated memory and attends to user description to model personality of users. In addition, external user representation is taken into consideration during the decoding to enhance the comments generation. Experimental results show that our model can generate natural, human-like and personalized comments.[1]

1 Introduction

Nowadays, social media is gradually becoming a mainstream communication tool. People tend to share their ideas with others by commenting, reposting or clicking *like* on posts in social media. Among these behaviors, *comment* plays a significant role in the communication between posters and readers. Automatically generate personalized comments (AGPC) can be useful due to the following reasons. First, AGPC helps readers express their ideas more easily, thus make them engage more actively in the platform. Second, bloggers can capture different attitudes to the event from multiple users with diverse backgrounds. Lastly,

the platform can also benefit from the increasing interactive rate.

Despite its great applicability, the AGPC task faces two important problems: whether can we achieve it and how to implement it? The *Social Differentiation Theory* proposed by Riley and Riley (1959) proved the feasibility of building a universal model to automatically generate personalized comments based on part of users' data. The *Individual Differences Theory* pointed by Hovland et al. (1953) answers the second question by introducing the significance of users' background, which inspires us to incorporating user profile into comments generation process. More specifically, the user profile consists of demographic features (for example, where does the user live), individual description and the common word dictionary extracted from user's comment history. There are few works exploring the comments generation problem. Zheng et al. (2017) first paid attention to generating comments for news articles by proposing a gated attention neural network model (GANN) to address the contextual relevance and the diversity of comments. Similarly, Qin et al. (2018) introduced the task of automatic news article commenting and released a large scale Chinese corpus. Nevertheless, AGPC is a more challenging task, since it not only requires generating relevant comments given the blog text, but also needs the consideration of the diverse users' background.

In this paper, we propose a novel task, automatically generating personalized comment based on user profile. We build the bridge between user profiles and social media comments based on a large-scale and high-quality Chinese dataset. We elaborately design a generative model based on sequence-to-sequence (Seq2Seq) framework. A gated memory module is utilized to model the user personality. Besides, during the decoding process,

---

*Equal Contribution.

[1]Source codes of this paper are available at https://github.com/Walleclipse/AGPC

Proceedings of the ACL 2019, Student Research Workshop, pages 229–235
Florence, Italy, July 28th-August 2nd, 2019. ©2019 Association for Computational Linguistics

the model attends to user description to enhance the comments generation process. In addition, the vocabulary distribution of generated word is adapted by considering the external user representation.

Our main contributions are as follows:

- We propose the task of automatic generating personalized comment with exploiting user profile.

- We design a novel model to incorporate the personalized style in large-scale comment generation. The model has three novel mechanisms: user feature embedding with gated memory, blog-user co-attention, and an external personality expression.

- Experimental results show that the proposed method outperforms various competitive baselines by a large margin. With novel mechanisms to exploit user information, the generated comments are more diverse and informative. We believe that our work can benefit future work on developing personalized and human-like NLG model.

2 Personalized Comments Dataset

We introduce the dataset as follows:

Data Preparation We collect short text posts from Weibo, one of the most popular social media platform in China, which has hundreds of millions of active users. Each instance in the dataset has province, city, gender, age, marital status, individual description of user's, comment added by user and homologous blog content. Figure 1 visually shows a sample instance. We tokenized all text like individual description, comment and blog content into words, using a popular python library Jieba[2]. To facilitate the model to learn valid information from the dataset, we removed @, url, expressions in the text, and unified Chinese into simplified characters. Discrete variables such as province, city, gender and marital status were treated uniformly by one-hot coding. To ensure the quality of text, we filtered out samples with less than two words in the variable of comment and blog content. Besides, in order to learn user-specific expression habits, we retain users with 50 or more records. The resulting dataset contains

---

[2]https://github.com/fxsjy/jieba

UID: 215803	Age: 24	Birthday: 1994-01-21
Gender: 女 Female	Province: 上海 Shanghai	City: 未知 NULL
Individual Description: 笨鸟一直飞 Practice makes prefect		
Blog: 医生开了新药，吃了胃会不舒服。。要是所有的事情都是梦就好了 The doctor prescribed the new medicine which let my stomach uncomfortable. If only everything were a dream.		
Comment: 一切都会好起来的 Everything will be ok.		

Figure 1: A data example in personalized comment dataset. Corresponding English translation is provided.

Statistic	User	Comment	Microblog
Train	32,719	2,659,870	1,450,948
Dev	24,739	69,659	27,822
Test	20,157	43,866	17,052
Total	32,719	4,463,767	1,495,822

Table 1: Sample size of three datasets

4,463,767 comments on 1,495,822 blog posts by 32,719 users.

Data Statistics We split the corpus into training, validation and testing set according to the microblog. To avoid overfitting, the records of the same microblog will not appear in the above three sets simultaneously. Table 1 displays the detail sample size of user, comment and blog about training set, validation set and testing set. Each user in the resulting dataset has an average of 56 samples. The average lengths of blog post, comment and individual description are 50, 11 and 9 words, respectively. The particular statistics of each experimental dataset are shown in Table 2.

Average length	Train	Dev	Test	Total
ID	8.84	9.04	8.83	8.85
Comment	11.28	11.32	11.86	11.28
Microblog	49.67	47.95	50.30	49.65

Table 2: Statistics of text variables. Individual description, abbreviated ID.

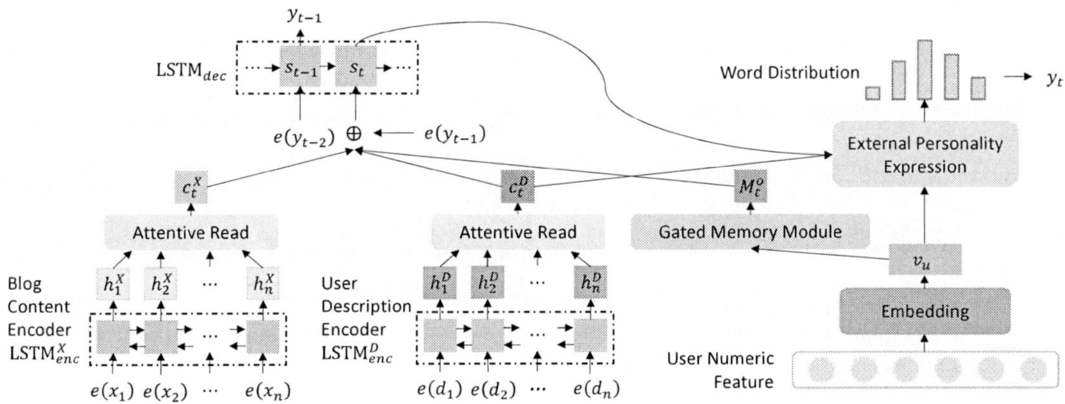

Figure 2: Personalized comment generation network

3 Personalized Comment Generation Network

Given a blog $X = (x_1, x_2, \cdots, x_n)$ and a user profile $U = \{F, D\}$, where $F = (f_1, f_2, \cdots, f_k)$ denotes the user's numeric feature (for example, age, city, gender) and $D = (d_1, d_2, \cdots, d_l)$ denotes the user's individual description, the AGPC aims at generating comment $Y = (y_1, y_2, \cdots, y_m)$ that is coherent with blog X and user U. Figure 2 presents an overview of our proposed model, which is elaborated on in detail as follows.

3.1 Encoder-Decoder Framework

Our model is based on the encoder-decoder framework of the general sequence-to-sequence (Seq2Seq) model (Sutskever et al., 2014). The encoder converts the blog sequence $X = (x_1, x_2, \cdots, x_n)$ to hidden representations $h^X = (h_1^X, h_2^X, \cdots, h_n^X)$ by a bi-directional Long Short-Term Memory (LSTM) cell (Hochreiter and Schmidhuber, 1997):

$$h_t^X = \text{LSTM}_{\text{enc}}^X(h_{t-1}^X, x_t) \tag{1}$$

The decoder takes the embedding of a previously decoded word $e(y_{t-1})$ and a blog context vector c_t^X as input to update its state s_t:

$$s_t = \text{LSTM}_{\text{dec}}(s_{t-1}, [c_t^X; e(y_{t-1})]) \tag{2}$$

where $[\cdot; \cdot]$ denotes vector concatenation. The context vector c_t^X is a weighted sum of encoder's hidden states, which carries key information of the input post (Bahdanau et al., 2014). Finally, the decoder samples a word y_t from the output probability distribution as follows

$$y_t \sim \text{softmax}(\mathbf{W_o} s_t) \tag{3}$$

where W_o is a weight matrix to be learned. The model is trained via maximizing the log-likelihood of ground-truth $Y^* = (y_1^*, \cdots, y_n^*)$ and the objective function is defined as

$$\mathcal{L} = -\sum_{t=1}^{n} \log\left(p(y_t^*|y_{<t}^*, X, U)\right) \tag{4}$$

3.2 User Feature Embedding with Gated Memory

To encode the information in user profile, we map user's numeric feature F to a dense vector v_u through a fully-connected layer. Intuitively, v_u can be treated as a user feature embedding denotes the character of the user. However, if the user feature embedding is static during decoding, the grammatical correctness of sentences generated may be sacrificed as argued in Ghosh et al. (2017). To tackle this problem, we design an gated memory module to dynamically express personality during decoding, inspired by Zhou et al. (2018). Specifically, we maintain a internal personality state during the generation process. At each time step, the personality state decays by a certain amount. Once the decoding process is completed, the personality state is supposed to decay to zero, which indicates that the personality is completely expressed. Formally, at each time step t, the model computes an update gate $g^u{}_t$ according to the current state of the decoder s_t. The initial personality state M_0 is set as user feature embedding v_u. Hence, the personality state M_t is erased by a certain amount (by g_t^u) at each step. This process is described as

$$g_t^u = \text{sigmoid}(\mathbf{W_g^u} s_t) \tag{5}$$
$$M_0 = v_u \tag{6}$$
$$M_t = g_t^u \otimes M_{t-1}, \quad t > 0 \tag{7}$$

where $\otimes$ denotes element-wise multiplication. Besides, the model should decide how much attention should be paid to the personality state at each time step. Thus, output gate g_t^o is introduced to control the information flow by considering the previous decoder state s_{t-1}, previous target word $e(y_{t-1})$ and the current context vector c_t^X

$$g_t^o = \text{sigmoid}(\mathbf{W_g^o}[s_{t-1}; e(y_{t-1}); c_t^X]). \quad (8)$$

By an element-wise multiplication of g_t^o and M_t, we can obtain adequate personality information M_t^o for current decoding step

$$M_t^o = g_t^o \otimes M_t. \quad (9)$$

3.3 Blog-User Co-Attention

Individual description is another important information source when generating personalized comments. For example, a user with individual description "只爱朱一龙" (I only love Yilong Zhu[3]), tends to writes a positive and adoring comments on the microblog related to Zhu. Motivated by this, we propose Blog-user co-attention to model the interactions between user description and blog content. More specifically, we encode the user's individual description $D = (d_1, d_2, \cdots, d_l)$ to hidden states $(h_1^D, h_2^D, \cdots, h_l^D)$ via another LSTM

$$h_t^D = \text{LSTM}_{\text{enc}}^D(h_{t-1}^D, d_t) \quad (10)$$

We can obtain a description context vector c_t^D by attentively reading the hidden states of user description,

$$
\begin{aligned}
c_t^D &= \sum_j \alpha_{tj} h_j^D & (11) \\
\alpha_{tj} &= \text{softmax}(e_{tj}) & (12) \\
e_{tj} &= s_{t-1} \mathbf{W_a} h_j^D & (13)
\end{aligned}
$$

where e_{tj} is a alignment score (Bahdanau et al., 2014). Similarly, we can get the blog content vector c_t^X. Finally, the context vector c_t is a concatenation of c_t^X and c_t^D, in order provide more comprehensive information of user's personality

$$c_t = [c_t^X; c_t^D] \quad (14)$$

Therefore, the state update mechanism in Eq.(2) is modified to

$$s_t = \text{LSTM}_{\text{dec}}(s_{t-1}, [c_t; c(y_{t-1}); M_t^o]) \quad (15)$$

---

[3] A famous Chinese star.

3.4 External Personality Expression

In the gated memory module, the correlation between the change of the internal personality state and selection of a word is implicit. To fully exploit the user information when selecting words for generation, we first compute a user representation r_t^u with user feature embedding and user description context.

$$r_t^u = \mathbf{W_r}[v_u; c_t^D] \quad (16)$$

where $\mathbf{W_r}$ is a weight matrix to align user representation dimention.

The final word is then sampled from output distribution based on the concatenation of decoder state s_t and r_t^u as

$$\tilde{y}_t \sim \text{softmax}(\mathbf{W_{\tilde{o}_t}}[\text{s}_t; \text{r}_t^u]) \quad (17)$$

where $\mathbf{W_{\tilde{o}_t}}$ is a learnable weight matrix.

4 Experiments

4.1 Implementation

The blog content encoder and comment decoder are both 2-layer bi-LSTM with 512 hidden units for each layer. The user's personality description encoder is a single layer bi-LSTM with 200 hidden units. The word embedding size is set to 300 and vocabulary size is set to 40,000. The embedding size of user's numeric feature is set to 100.

We adopted beam search and set beam size to 10 to promote diversity of generated comments. We used SGD optimizer with batch size set to 128 and the learning rate is 0.001.

To further enrich the information provided by user description, we collected most common k words in user historical comments ($k = 20$ in our experiment). We concatenate the common words with the user individual description. Therefore, we can obtain more information about users' expression style. The model using concatenated user description is named PCGN with common words (PCGN+ComWord).

4.2 Baseline

We implemented a general Seq2Seq model (Sutskever et al., 2014) and a user embedding model (Seq2Seq+Emb) proposed by Li et al. (2016) as our baselines. The latter model embeds user numeric features into a dense vector and feeds it as extra input into decoder at every time step.

Method	PPL	B-2	METEOR
Seq2Seq	32.47	0.071	0.070
Seq2Seq+Emb	31.13	0.084	0.079
PCGN	27.94	0.162	0.132
PCGN+ComWord	**24.48**	**0.193**	**0.151**

Table 3: Automatic evaluation results of different methods. **PPL** denotes perplexity and **B-2** denotes BLEU-2. Best results are shown in bold.

Method	PPL	B-2
Seq2Seq	32.47	0.071
+ Mem	30.73 (-1.74)	0.099 (+0.028)
+ CoAtt	27.12 (-3.61)	0.147 (+0.078)
+ External	27.94 (+0.82)	0.162 (+0.015)

Table 4: Incremental experiment results of proposed model. Performance on METEOR is similar to B-2. **Mem** denotes gated memory, **CoAtt** denotes blog-user co-attention and **External** denotes external personality expression

4.3 Evaluation Result

Metrics: We use BLEU-2 (Papineni et al., 2002) and METEOR (Banerjee and Lavie, 2005) to evaluate overlap between outputs and references. Besides, perplexity is also provided.

Results: The results are shown in Table 3. As can be seen, PCGN model with common words obtains the best performance on perplexity, BLEU-2 and METEOR. Note that the performance of Seq2Seq is extremely low, since the user profile is not taken into consideration during the generation, resulting repetitive responses. In contrast, with the help of three proposed mechanism (gated memory, blog-user co-attention and external personality expression), our model can utilize user information effectively, thus is capable of generating diverse and relevant comments for the same blog. Further, we conducted incremental experiments to study the effect of proposed mechanisms by adding them incrementally, as shown in Table 4. It can be found that all three mechanism help generate more diverse comments, while blog-user co-attention mechanism contributes most improvements. An interesting finding is that external personality expression mechanism causes the decay on perplexity. We speculate that the modification on word distribution by personality influence the fluency of generated comments.

5 Related Work

This paper focuses on comments generation task, which can be further divided into generating a comment according to the structure data (Mei et al., 2015), text data (Qin et al., 2018), image (Vinyal et al., 2015) and video (Ma et al., 2018a), separately.

There are many works exploring the problem of text-based comment generation. Qin et al. (2018) contributed a high-quality corpus for article comment generation problem. Zheng et al. (2017) proposed a gated attention neural network model (GANN) to generate comments for news article, which addressed the contextual relevance and the diversity of comments. To alleviate the dependence on large parallel corpus, Ma et al. (2018b) designed an unsupervised neural topic model based on retrieval technique. However, these works focus on generating comments on news text, while comments on social media are much more diverse and personal-specific.

In terms of the technique for modeling user character, the existing works on machine commenting only utilized part of users' information. Ni and McAuley (2018) proposed to learn a latent representation of users by utilizing history information. Lin et al. (2018) acquired readers' general attitude to event mentioned by article through its upvote count. Compared to the indirection information obtained from history or indicator, user features in user profile, like demographic factors, can provide more comprehensive and specific information, and thus should be paid more attention to when generating comments. Sharing the same idea that user personality counts, Luo et al. (2018) proposed personalized MemN2N to explore personalized goal-oriented dialog systems. Equipped with a profile model to learn user representation and a preference model learning user preferences, the model is capable of generating high quality responses. In this paper, we focus on modeling personality in a different scenario, where the generated comments is supposed to be general and diverse.

6 Conclusion

In this paper, we introduce the task of automatic generating personalized comment. We also propose Personality Comment Generation Network (PCGN) to model the personality influence in comment generation. The PCGN model utilized gated memory for user feature embedding, blog-user co-attention, and external personality representation to generate comments in personalized style. Evaluation results show that PCGN outperforms baseline models by a large margin. With the help of three proposed mechanisms, the generated comments are more fluent and diverse.

References

Dzmitry Bahdanau, Kyunghyun Cho, and Yoshua Bengio. 2014. Neural machine translation by jointly learning to align and translate. *arXiv preprint arXiv:1409.0473*.

Satanjeev Banerjee and Alon Lavie. 2005. Meteor: An automatic metric for mt evaluation with improved correlation with human judgments. In *Proceedings of the acl workshop on intrinsic and extrinsic evaluation measures for machine translation and/or summarization*, pages 65–72.

Sayan Ghosh, Mathieu Chollet, Eugene Laksana, Louis-Philippe Morency, and Stefan Scherer. 2017. Affect-lm: A neural language model for customizable affective text generation. *arXiv preprint arXiv:1704.06851*.

Sepp Hochreiter and Jürgen Schmidhuber. 1997. Long short-term memory. *Neural computation*, 9(8):1735–1780.

Carl I. Hovland, Irving L. Janis, and Harold H. Kelley. 1953. *Communication and Persuasion:Psychological Studies of Opinion Change*. Yale University Press.

Jiwei Li, Michel Galley, Chris Brockett, Georgios P Spithourakis, Jianfeng Gao, and Bill Dolan. 2016. A persona-based neural conversation model. *arXiv preprint arXiv:1603.06155*.

Zhaojiang Lin, Genta Indra Winata, and Pascale Fung. 2018. Learning comment generation by leveraging user-generated data. *CoRR*, abs/1810.12264.

Liangchen Luo, Wenhao Huang, Qi Zeng, Zaiqing Nie, and Xu Sun. 2018. Learning personalized end-to-end goal-oriented dialog.

Shuming Ma, Lei Cui, Damai Dai, Furu Wei, and Xu Sun. 2018a. Livebot: Generating live video comments based on visual and textual contexts. *CoRR*, abs/1809.04938.

Shuming Ma, Lei Cui, Furu Wei, and Xu Sun. 2018b. Unsupervised machine commenting with neural variational topic model. *arXiv preprint arXiv:1809.04960*.

Hongyuan Mei, Mohit Bansal, and Matthew R. Walter. 2015. What to talk about and how? selective generation using lstms with coarse-to-fine alignment. *arXiv preprint arXiv:1509.00838*.

Jianmo Ni and Julian McAuley. 2018. Personalized review generation by expanding phrases and attending on aspect-aware representations. In *In Proceedings of the 56th Annual Meeting of the Association for Computational Linguistics*, pages 706–711.

Kishore Papineni, Salim Roukos, Todd Ward, and Wei-Jing Zhu. 2002. Bleu: a method for automatic evaluation of machine translation. In *Proceedings of the 40th annual meeting on association for computational linguistics*, pages 311–318. Association for Computational Linguistics.

Lianhui Qin, Lemao Liu, Wei Bi, Yan Wang, Xiaojiang Liu, Zhiting Hu, Hai Zhao, and Shuming Shi. 2018. Automatic article commenting: the task and dataset. In *Proceedings of the 56th Annual Meeting of the Association for Computational Linguistics, ACL 2018, Melbourne, Australia, July 15-20, 2018, Volume 2: Short Papers*, pages 151–156.

J. W. Riley and Matilda White Riley. 1959. Mass communication and the social system.

Ilya Sutskever, Oriol Vinyals, and Quoc V Le. 2014. Sequence to sequence learning with neural networks. In *Advances in neural information processing systems*, pages 3104–3112.

Oriol Vinyal, Alexander Toshev, Samy Bengio, and Dumitru Erhan. 2015. Show and tell: A neural image caption generator. In *Proceedings of the IEEE conference on computer vision and pattern recognition*, pages 3156–3164.

Hai-Tao Zheng, Wei Wang, Wang Chen, and Arun Kumar Sangaiah. 2017. Automatic generation of news comments based on gated attention neural networks. 6.

Hao Zhou, Minlie Huang, Tianyang Zhang, Xiaoyan Zhu, and Bing Liu. 2018. Emotional chatting machine: Emotional conversation generation with internal and external memory. In *Thirty-Second AAAI Conference on Artificial Intelligence*.

A   Case Study

We present some generated cases in Figure 4, 5. There are multiple users (corresponding profiles are shown in Figure 3) that are suitable for generating comments. Seq2Seq generates same comments for the same blog, while PCGN can generate personalized comment conditioned on given user. According to the user profile, U1 adores Yilong Zhu very much. Therefore, U1 tends to express her affection in comments when responses to blogs related to Yilong Zhu. For users whose individual descriptions can not offer helpful information or there is missing value for individual description, the PCGN model pays more attention to numeric features and learns representation from similar seen users.

User	Age	Gender	Province	City	Individual Description
U1	24	女 Female	其他 Others	NULL	只爱朱一龙 I only love Yilong Zhu
U2	23	女 Female	黑龙江 Heilong Jiang	NULL	努力成为更好的自己 Become a better me
U3	20	女 Female	浙江 Zhejiang	宁波 Ningbo	NULL

Figure 3: Part of user profile of case study users. In order to protect user privacy, the birthday variable is not shown here.

Blog
#朱一龙 温柔的力量 [超话]#[小仙女]#朱一龙并肩前行#遇见你，是旷野的风闯进心房，是眉间的闯进眼眶。想把一切与你分享，清晨的暖阳、浩瀚的夜空、过去的美好、未来的相伴。「朱一龙」 Yilong Zhu Gentle power [super topic]# walking side by side with Yilong Zhu#The moment I met you seems like the wind of the wilderness, breaking into my heart. The moment I met you seems like the snow between the eyebrows, blending into the eyes. I want to share everything with you, the warm sun in the morning, the vast night sky, the beauty of the past and the companion in the future.

Comments
Seq2Seq: #朱一龙温柔的力量 [超话]##朱一龙并肩前行# #Yilong Zhu Gentle power [super topic]# #Yilong Zhu, move forward together#
PCGN U1: 『朱一龙』甜有 100 种方式，吃糖，还有每天 99 次的想你。 There is one hunderd ways of sweetness, have a candy and miss you 99 times a day.
PCGN U2: #朱一龙温柔的力量 [超话]# #朱一龙 并肩前行# 朱一龙	ZYL #Yilong Zhu Gentle power [super topic]# #Yilong Zhu, move forward together# Yilong Zhu| ZYL
PCGN U3: 『 朱一龙 』愿你一直如少年，干净纯粹心安，看透不美好却相信美好 I hope that you are always young, with a clean and pure heart, always believing something beautiful

Figure 4: Generated comments based on blog of different users. Since Seq2Seq model does not take user profile into consideration, it generates same comments for the same blog.

Blog
#我的真朋友#运用日剧和漫画的镜头切割，芭莎特别策划打造视觉大片，将三位主演的剧中人物关系呈现在视觉大片里，让你在放映前先睹为快! Angelababy 发型/刘雪亮 Angelababy 化妆/春楠 邓伦妆发/李健成 朱一龙妆发/李鹏坤 #My true friend # Using the lens of Japanese TV dramas and comics, Bazaar specially plans to create visual blockbusters, and present the relationship among the three main characters in the photo, which will give you a sneak of the movie before its showing! Angelababy Hairstyle / Liu Xueliang Angelababy Makeup / Chun Nan Lun Deng makeup hair / Jiancheng Li Yilong Zhu makeup hair / Pengkun Li

Comments
Seq2Seq: #angelababy [超话]# # angelababy [super topic] #
PCGN U1: #朱一龙[超话]##朱一 龙井然#期待井然哥哥 Yilong Zhu[super topic]# #朱一龙井然# Looking forward to Jingan brother
PCGN U2: 期待 期待 looking forward to
PCGN U3: 期待邓伦 looking forward to Lun Deng

Figure 5: Generated comments based on blog of different users.

From Bilingual to Multilingual Neural Machine Translation by Incremental Training

Carlos Escolano, Marta R. Costa-jussà, José A. R. Fonollosa,
`{carlos.escolano,marta.ruiz,jose.fonollosa}@upc.edu`
TALP Research Center
Universitat Politècnica de Catalunya, Barcelona

Abstract

Multilingual Neural Machine Translation approaches are based on the use of task-specific models and the addition of one more language can only be done by retraining the whole system. In this work, we propose a new training schedule that allows the system to scale to more languages without modification of the previous components based on joint training and language-independent encoder/decoder modules allowing for zero-shot translation. This work in progress shows close results to the state-of-the-art in the WMT task.

1 Introduction

In recent years, neural machine translation (NMT) has had an important improvement in performance. Among the different neural architectures, most approaches are based in an encoder-decoder structure and the use of attention-based mechanisms (Cho et al., 2014; Bahdanau et al., 2014; Vaswani et al., 2017). The main objective is computing a representation of the source sentence that is weighted with attention-based mechanisms to compute the conditional probability of the tokens of the target sentence and the previously decoded target tokens. Same principles have been successfully applied to multilingual NMT, where the system is able to translate to and from several different languages.

Two main approaches have been proposed for this task, language independent or shared encoder-decoders. Language independent architectures(Firat et al., 2016a,b; Schwenk and Douze, 2017) in which each language has its own encoder and some additional mechanism is added to produce shared representations, as averaging of the context vectors or sharing the attention mechanism. These architectures have the flexibility that each language can be trained with its own vocab-

ulary all languages are trained in parallel. Recent work (Lu et al., 2018) show how to perform many to many translations with independent encoders and decoders just by sharing additional language-specific layers that transformed the language-specific representations into a shared one without the need of a pivot language,

On the other hand, architectures that share parameters between all languages (Johnson et al., 2017) by using a single encoder and decoder trained to be able to translate from and to any of the languages of the system. This approach presents the advantage that no further mechanisms are required to produced shared representation of the languages as they all share the same vocabulary and parameters, and by training all languages without distinction they allow low resources languages to take benefit of other languages in the system improving their performance. Even though by sharing vocabulary between all languages the number of required tokens grows as more languages are included in the system, especially when languages employ different scripts in the system, such as Chinese or Russian. Recent work proposes a new approach to add new languages to a system by adapting the vocabulary (Lakew et al., 2018), relying on the shared tokens between the languages to share model parameters, showing that the amount of shared tokens between the languages had an impact in the model performance. This could limit the capability of the system to adapt to languages with a different script.

These approaches can be further explored into unsupervised machine translation where the system learns to translate between languages without parallel data just by enforcing the generation and representation of the tokens to be similar (Artetxe et al., 2017; Lample et al., 2018).

Also related to our method, recent work has explored transfer learning for NMT (Zoph et al.,

Proceedings of the ACL 2019, Student Research Workshop, pages 236–242
Florence, Italy, July 28th-August 2nd, 2019. ©2019 Association for Computational Linguistics

2016; Kim et al., 2019) to improve the performance of new translation directions by taking benefit of the information of a previous model. These approaches are particularly useful in low resources scenarios when a previous model trained with orders of magnitude more examples is available.

This paper proposes a proof of concept of a new multilingual NMT approach. The current approach is based on joint training without parameter or vocabulary sharing by enforcing a compatible representation between the jointly trained languages and using multitask learning (Dong et al., 2015). This approach is shown to offer a scalable strategy to new languages without retraining any of the previous languages in the system and enabling zero-shot translation. Also it sets up a flexible framework to future work on the usage of pretrained compatible modules for different tasks.

2 Definitions

Before explaining our proposed model we introduce the annotation and background that will be assumed through the paper. Languages will be referred as capital letters X, Y, Z while sentences will be referred in lower case x, y, z given that $x \in X, y \in Y$ and $z \in Z$.

We consider as an encoder (e_x, e_y, e_z) the layers of the network that given an input sentence produce a sentence representation $(h(x), h(y), h(z))$ in a space. Analogously, a decoder (d_x, d_y, d_z) is the layers of the network that given the sentence representation of the source sentence is able to produce the tokens of the target sentence. Encoders and decoders will be always considered as independent modules that can be arranged and combined individually as no parameter is shared between them. Each language and module has its own weights independent from all the others present in the system.

3 Joint Training

In this section, we are going to describe the training schedule of our language independent decoder-encoder system. The motivation to choose this architecture is the flexibility to add new languages to the system without modification of shared components and the possibility to add new modalities in the future as the only requirement of the architecture is that encodings are projected in the same space. Sharing network parameters may seem a more efficient approach to the task, but it would not support modality specific modules while

Given two languages X and Y, our objective is to train independent encoders and decoders for each language, e_x, d_x and e_y, d_y that produce compatible sentence representations $h(x), h(y)$. For instance, given a sentence x in language X, we can obtain a representation $h(x)$ from that the encoder e_x that can be used to either generate a sentence reconstruction using decoder d_x or a translation using decoder d_y. With this objective in mind, we propose a training schedule that combines two tasks (auto-encoding and translation) and the two translation directions simultaneously by optimizing the following loss:

$$L = L_{XX} + L_{YY} + L_{XY} + L_{YX} + d \qquad (1)$$

where L_{XX} and L_{YY} correspond to the reconstruction losses of both language X and Y (defined as the cross-entropy of the generated tokens and the source sentence for each language); L_{XY} and L_{YX} correspond to the translation terms of the loss measuring token generation of each decoder given a sentence representation generated by the other language encoder (using the cross-entropy between the generated tokens and the translation reference); and d corresponds to the distance metric between the representation computed by the encoders. This last term forces the representations to be similar without sharing parameters while providing a measure of similarity between the generated spaces. We have tested different distance metrics such as L1, L2 or the discriminator addition (that tried to predict from which language the representation was generated). For all these alternatives, we experienced a space collapse in which all sentences tend to be located in the same spatial region. This closeness between the sentences of the same languages makes them non-informative for decoding. As a consequence, the decoder performs as a language model, producing an output only based on the information provided by the previously decoded tokens. Weighting the distance loss term in the loss did not improve the performance due to the fact that for the small values required to prevent the collapse the architecture did not learn a useful representation of both languages to work with both decoders. To prevent this collapse, we propose a less restrictive measure based on correlation distance (Chandar et al., 2016) computed as in equations 2 and 3. The rationale behind this loss is maximizing the correlation between the representations produced by each language while not enforcing the distance over the individual values of the representations.

$$d = 1 - c(h(X), h(Y)) \qquad (2)$$

$$c(h(X), h(Y)) =$$
$$\frac{\sum_{i=1}^{n}(h(x_i - \overline{h(X)}))(h(y_i - \overline{h(Y)}))}{\sqrt{\sum_{i}^{n}(h(x_i) - \overline{h(X)})^2 \sum_{i}^{n}(h(y_i) - \overline{h(Y)})^2}} \qquad (3)$$

where X and Y correspond to the data sources we are trying to represent; $h(x_i)$ and $h(y_i)$ correspond to the intermediate representations learned by the network for a given observation; and $\overline{h(X)}$ and $\overline{h(Y)}$ are, for a given batch, the intermediate representation mean of X and Y, respectively.

4 Incremental training

Given the jointly trained model between languages X and Y, the following step is to add new languages in order to use our architecture as a multilingual system. Since parameters are not shared between the independent encoders and decoders, our architecture enables to add new languages without the need to retrain the current languages in the system. Let's say we want to add language Z. To do so, we require to have parallel data between Z and any language in the system. So, assuming that we have trained X and Y, we need to have either $Z - X$ or $Z - Y$ parallel data. For illustration, let's fix that we have $Z - X$ parallel data. Then, we can set up a new bilingual system with language Z as source and language X as target. To ensure that the representation produced by this new pair is compatible with the previously jointly trained system, we use the previous X decoder (d_x) as the decoder of the new ZX system and we freeze it. During training, we optimize the cross-entropy between the generated tokens and the language X reference data but only updating the layers belonging to the language Z encoder (e_z). Doing this, we train e_z not only to produce good quality translations but also to produce similar representations to the already trained languages. No additional distance is added during this step. The language Z sentence representation $h(z)$ is only enforced by the loss of the translation to work with the already trained module as it would be trained in a bilingual NMT system.

Our training schedule enforces the generation of a compatible representation, which means that the

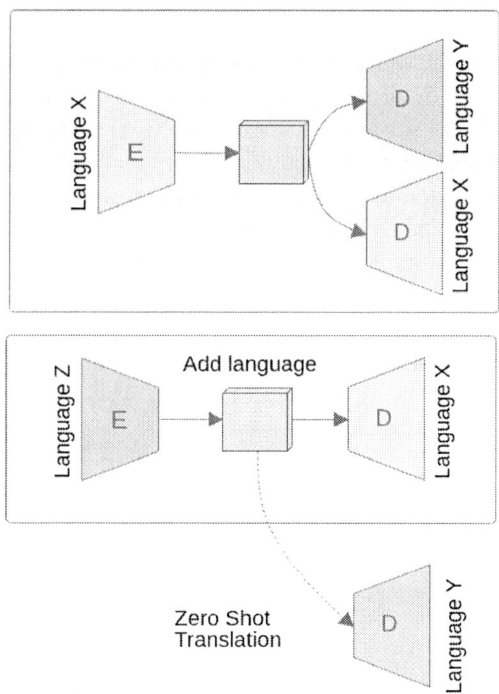

Figure 1: Language addition and zero shoot training scheme

newly trained encoder e_z can be used as input of the decoder d_y from the jointly trained system to produce zero-shot Z to Y translations. See Figure 1 for illustration.

The fact that the system enables zero-shot translation shows that the representations produced by our training schedule contain useful information and that this can be preserved and shared to new languages just by enforcing the new modules to train with the previous one, without any modification of the architecture. Another important aspect is that no pivot language is required to perform the translation, once the added modules are trained the zero-shot translation is performed without generating the language used for training as the sentence representations in the shared space are compatible with all the modules in the system.

A current limitation is the need to use the same vocabulary for the shared language (X) in both training steps. The use of subwords (Sennrich et al., 2015) mitigates the impact of this constraint.

5 Data and Implementation

Experiments are conducted using data extracted from the UN (Ziemski et al., 2016) and EPPS datasets (Koehn, 2005) that provide 15 million parallel sentences between English and Spanish, German and French. *newstest2012* and *new-*

System	ES-EN	EN-ES	FR-EN	DE-EN
Baseline	32.60	32.90	31.81	28.96
Joint	29.70	30.74	-	-
Added lang	-	-	30.93	27.63

Table 1: Experiment results measured in BLEU score. All blank positions are not tested or not viable combinations with our data.

System	FR-ES	DE-ES
Pivot	29.09	21.74
Zero-shot	19.10	10.92

Table 2: Zero-shot results measured in BLEU score

stest2013 were used as validation and test sets, respectively. These sets provide parallel data between the four languages that allow for zero-shot evaluation. Preprocessing consisted of a pipeline of punctuation normalization, tokenization, corpus filtering of longer sentences than 80 words and true-casing. These steps were performed using the scripts available from Moses (Koehn et al., 2007). Preprocessed data is later tokenized into BPE subwords (Sennrich et al., 2015) with a vocabulary size of 32000 tokens. We ensure that the vocabularies are independent and reusable when new languages were added by creating vocabularies monolingually, i.e. without having access to other languages during the code generation.

6 Experiments

Our first experiment consists in comparing the performance of the jointly trained system to the standard Transformer. As explained in previous sections, this joint model is trained to perform two different tasks, auto-encoding and translation in both directions. In our experiments, these directions are Spanish-English and English-Spanish. In auto-encoding, both languages provide good results at 98.21 and 97.44 BLEU points for English and Spanish, respectively. In translation, we observe a decrease in performance. Table 1 shows that for both directions the new training performs more than 2 BLEU points below the baseline system. This difference suggests that even though the encoders and decoders of the system are compatible they still present some differences in the internal representation.

Note that the languages chosen for the joint training seem relevant to the final system performance because they are used to define the representations of additional languages. Further experimentation is required to understand such impact.

Our second experiment consists of incrementally adding different languages to the system, in this case, German and French. Note that, since we freeze the weights while adding the new language, the order in which we add new languages does not have any impact on performance. Table 1 shows that French-English performs 0.9 BLEU points below the baseline and German-English performs 1.33 points below the baseline. French-English is closer to the baseline performance and this may be due to its similarity to Spanish, one of the languages of the initial system languages.

The added languages have better performance than the jointly trained languages (Spanish-English from the previous section). This may be to the fact that the auto-encoding task may have a negative impact on the translation task.

Finally, another relevant aspect of the proposed architecture is enabling zero-shot translation. To evaluate it, we compare the performance of each of the added languages compared to a pivot system based on cascade. Such a system consists of translating from French (German) to English and from English to Spanish with the standard Transformer. Results show that the zero shot translation provides a consistent decrease in performance for both cases of zero-shot translation.

7 Visualization

Our training schedule is based on training modules to produce compatible representations, in this section we want to analyze this similarity at the last attention block of encoders, where we are forcing the similarity. In order to graphically show the presentation a UMAP (McInnes et al., 2018) model was trained to combine the representations of all languages. Figures show 130 sentences extracted from the test set. These sentences have been selected to have a similar length to minimize the amount of padding required.

Figure 2 (A) shows the representations of all languages created by their encoders. Languages are represented in clusters and no overlapping between languages occurs, similarly to what (Lu et al., 2018) reported in their multilingual approach, the language dependent features of the sentences have a great impact in their representations.

However, since our encoder/decoders are compatible and produce competitive translations, we decided to explore the representations generated

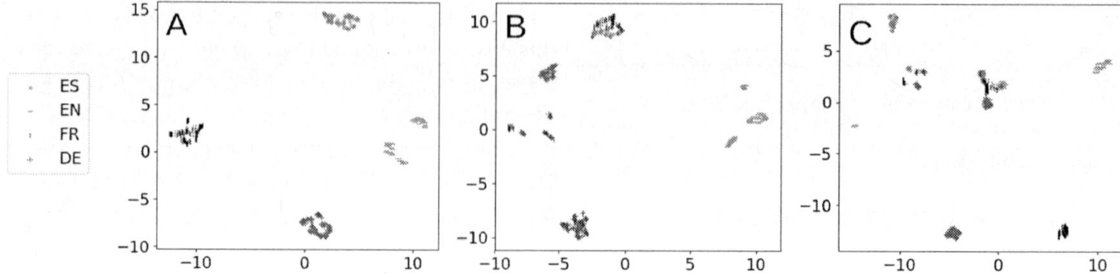

Figure 2: Plot A shows the source sentence representation of each of the encoder modules(ES,EN,DE,FR). Plots B and C show the representation of the target sentence generated by English(B) and Spanish(C) decoders given the sentence encodings of parallel sentences generated for all four language encoder modules.

at the last attention block of the English decoder, and are shown in Figure 2 (B). We can observe much more similarity between English, French, and German, (except for a small German cluster) and separated clusters for Spanish. The reason behind these different behaviors may be due to the fact that French and German have directly been trained with the frozen English decoder and being adjusted to produce representations for this decoder. Finally, figure 2 (C) shows the representations of the Spanish decoder. Some sentences have the same representation for all languages, whereas others no. Looking at the specific sentences that are plotted, we found that close representations do not correlate with better translations or better BLEU. Sentence examples are shown in the appendix. More research is required to analyze which layer in the decoder is responsible for approaching languages in a common space. This information could be used in the future to train encoders of new languages by wisely sharing parameters with the decoder as in previous works (He et al., 2018).

8 Conclusions

This work proposes a proof of concept of a bilingual system NMT which can be extended to a multilingual NMT system by incremental training. We have analyzed how the model performs for different languages. Even though the model does not outperform current bilingual systems, we show first steps towards achieving competitive translations with a flexible architecture that enables scaling to new languages (achieving multilingual and zero-shot translation) without retraining languages in the system.

Acknowledgments

This work is supported in part by a Google Faculty Research Award. This work is also supported in part by the Spanish Ministerio de Economa y Competitividad, the European Regional Development Fund and the Agencia Estatal de Investigacin, through the postdoctoral senior grant Ramn y Cajal, contract TEC2015-69266-P (MINECO/FEDER,EU) and contract PCIN-2017-079 (AEI/MINECO).

References

Mikel Artetxe, Gorka Labaka, Eneko Agirre, and Kyunghyun Cho. 2017. Unsupervised neural machine translation. *arXiv preprint arXiv:1710.11041*.

Dzmitry Bahdanau, Kyunghyun Cho, and Yoshua Bengio. 2014. Neural machine translation by jointly learning to align and translate. *arXiv preprint arXiv:1409.0473*.

Sarath Chandar, Mitesh M Khapra, Hugo Larochelle, and Balaraman Ravindran. 2016. Correlational neural networks. *Neural computation*, 28(2):257–285.

Kyunghyun Cho, Bart van Merrienboer, Caglar Gulcehre, Dzmitry Bahdanau, Fethi Bougares, Holger Schwenk, and Yoshua Bengio. 2014. Learning phrase representations using RNN encoder–decoder for statistical machine translation. In *Proceedings of the 2014 Conference on Empirical Methods in Natural Language Processing (EMNLP)*, pages 1724–1734, Doha, Qatar. Association for Computational Linguistics.

Daxiang Dong, Hua Wu, Wei He, Dianhai Yu, and Haifeng Wang. 2015. Multi-task learning for multiple language translation. In *Proceedings of the 53rd Annual Meeting of the Association for Computational Linguistics and the 7th International Joint Conference on Natural Language Processing (Volume 1: Long Papers)*, volume 1, pages 1723–1732.

Orhan Firat, Kyunghyun Cho, and Yoshua Bengio. 2016a. Multi-way, multilingual neural machine translation with a shared attention mechanism. In *Proceedings of the 2016 Conference of the North American Chapter of the Association for Computational Linguistics: Human Language Technologies*, pages 866–875, San Diego, California. Association for Computational Linguistics.

Orhan Firat, Baskaran Sankaran, Yaser Al-Onaizan, Fatos T. Yarman Vural, and Kyunghyun Cho. 2016b. Zero-resource translation with multi-lingual neural machine translation. In *Proceedings of the 2016 Conference on Empirical Methods in Natural Language Processing*, pages 268–277, Austin, Texas. Association for Computational Linguistics.

Tianyu He, Xu Tan, Yingce Xia, Di He, Tao Qin, Zhibo Chen, and Tie-Yan Liu. 2018. Layer-wise coordination between encoder and decoder for neural machine translation. In S. Bengio, H. Wallach, H. Larochelle, K. Grauman, N. Cesa-Bianchi, and R. Garnett, editors, *Advances in Neural Information Processing Systems 31*, pages 7955–7965. Curran Associates, Inc.

Melvin Johnson, Mike Schuster, Quoc V Le, Maxim Krikun, Yonghui Wu, Zhifeng Chen, Nikhil Thorat, Fernanda Viégas, Martin Wattenberg, Greg Corrado, et al. 2017. Googles multilingual neural machine translation system: Enabling zero-shot translation. *Transactions of the Association for Computational Linguistics*, 5:339–351.

Yunsu Kim, Yingbo Gao, and Hermann Ney. 2019. Effective cross-lingual transfer of neural machine translation models without shared vocabularies. *arXiv preprint arXiv:1905.05475*.

Philipp Koehn. 2005. Europarl: A parallel corpus for statistical machine translation. In *MT summit*, volume 5, pages 79–86.

Philipp Koehn, Hieu Hoang, Alexandra Birch, Chris Callison-Burch, Marcello Federico, Nicola Bertoldi, Brooke Cowan, Wade Shen, Christine Moran, Richard Zens, et al. 2007. Moses: Open source toolkit for statistical machine translation. In *Proceedings of the 45th annual meeting of the association for computational linguistics companion volume proceedings of the demo and poster sessions*, pages 177–180.

Surafel M. Lakew, Aliia Erofeeva, Matteo Negri, Marcello Federico, and Marco Turchi. 2018. Transfer learning in multilingual neural machine translation with dynamic vocabulary. In *Proceedings of the 15th International Workshop on Spoken Language Translation*, pages 54–61, Belgium, Bruges.

Guillaume Lample, Alexis Conneau, Ludovic Denoyer, and Marc'Aurelio Ranzato. 2018. Unsupervised machine translation using monolingual corpora only. In *International Conference on Learning Representations*.

Yichao Lu, Phillip Keung, Faisal Ladhak, Vikas Bhardwaj, Shaonan Zhang, and Jason Sun. 2018. A neural interlingua for multilingual machine translation. In *Proceedings of the Third Conference on Machine Translation: Research Papers*, pages 84–92, Belgium, Brussels. Association for Computational Linguistics.

Leland McInnes, John Healy, Nathaniel Saul, and Lukas Grossberger. 2018. Umap: Uniform manifold approximation and projection. *The Journal of Open Source Software*, 3(29):861.

Holger Schwenk and Matthijs Douze. 2017. Learning joint multilingual sentence representations with neural machine translation. *arXiv preprint arXiv:1704.04154*.

Rico Sennrich, Barry Haddow, and Alexandra Birch. 2015. Neural machine translation of rare words with subword units. *arXiv preprint arXiv:1508.07909*.

Ashish Vaswani, Noam Shazeer, Niki Parmar, Jakob Uszkoreit, Llion Jones, Aidan N Gomez, Łukasz Kaiser, and Illia Polosukhin. 2017. Attention is all you need. In *Advances in Neural Information Processing Systems*, pages 5998–6008.

Michal Ziemski, Marcin Junczys-Dowmunt, and Bruno Pouliquen. 2016. The united nations parallel corpus v1. 0. In *Lrec*.

Barret Zoph, Deniz Yuret, Jonathan May, and Kevin Knight. 2016. Transfer learning for low-resource neural machine translation. In *Proceedings of the 2016 Conference on Empirical Methods in Natural Language Processing*, pages 1568–1575, Austin, Texas. Association for Computational Linguistics.

A Examples

This appendix shows some examples of sentences visualized in Figure 2 in order to further analyse the visualization. Table 1 reports outputs produced by the Spanish decoder given encoding representations produced by the Spanish, English, French and German encoder. The first two sentences have similar representations between the languages in Figure 2 (right) (in the Spanish decoder visualization). While the first one keeps the meaning of the sentence, the second one produces meaningless translations. The third sentence produces disjoint representations but the meaning is preserved in the translations. Therefore, since close representations may imply different translation performance, further research is required to understand the correlation between representations and translation quality.

Table 2 shows outputs produced by the English decoder given encoding representations produced

System	Sentence
Reference	ponemos todo nuestro empeo en participar en este proyecto .
ES	ponemos todo nuestro empeo en participar en este proyecto .
EN	participamos con esfuerzo en estos proyctos .
FR	nos esfuerzos por lograr que los participantes intensivamente en estos proyectos.
DE	nuestro objetivo es incorporar estas personas de manera intensiva en nuestro proyecto.
Reference	Caja Libre!
ES	Caja Libre—
EN	Free chash points!
FR	librecorrespondinte.
DE	cisiguinente
Reference	Cómo aplica esta definición en su vida cotidiana y en las redes sociales?
ES	Cómo aplica esta definición en su vida cotidiana y en las redes sociales?
EN	Cómo se aplica esta definición a su vida diaria?
FR	Cómo aplicar esta definición en la vida diaria y sobre los red sociales?
DE	Qué es aplicar este definición a su dadadato y las redes sociales?

Table 3: Outputs produced by the Spanish decoder given encoding representations produced by the Spanish, English, French and German encoder.

System	Sentence
Reference	it was a terrific season.
ES	we had a strong season .
EN	it was a terrific season.
FR	we made a very big season .
DE	we have finished the season with a very strong performance.
Reference	in London and Madrid it is completely natural for people with serious handicaps to be independently out in public, and they can use the toilets, go to the museum, or wherever ...
ES	in London and Madrid , it is very normal for people with severe disability to be left to the public and be able to serve , to the museum , where ...
EN	in London and Madrid it is completely natural for people with serious handicaps to be independently out in public, and they can use the toilets, go to the museum, or wherever ...
FR	in London and Madrid, it is quite common for people with a heavy disability to travel on their own in public spaces; they can go to the toilets, to the museum, anywhere ...
DE	in London and Madrid, it is absolutely common for people with severe disabilities to be able to move freely in public spaces, go to the museum, use lets, etc.
Reference	from the Czech viewpoint, it seems they tend to put me to the left.
ES	from a Czech point of view, I have the impression that people see me more than on the left.
EN	from the Czech viewpoint, it seems they tend to put me to the left.
FR	from a Czech point of view , I have the impression that people are putting me on the left .
DE	from a Czech point of view, it seems to me that people see me rather on the left.

Table 4: Outputs produced by the English decoder given encoding representations produced by the Spanish, English, French and German encoder.

by the Spanish, English, French and German encoder. All examples appear to be close in Figure 2 (center) between German, French and English. We see that the German and French outputs preserve the general meaning of the sentence. Also and differently from previous Table 1, the outputs do not present errors in the attention, repeating several times tokens or non unintelligible translations. There are no sentences from French that appear distant in the visualization, so again, we need further exploration to understand the information of this representation.

STRASS: A Light and Effective Method for Extractive Summarization Based on Sentence Embeddings

Léo Bouscarrat, Antoine Bonnefoy, Thomas Peel, Cécile Pereira
EURA NOVA
Marseille, France
{leo.bouscarrat,antoine.bonnefoy,
thomas.peel,cecile.pereira}@euranova.eu

Abstract

This paper introduces STRASS: Summarization by TRAnsformation Selection and Scoring. It is an extractive text summarization method which leverages the semantic information in existing sentence embedding spaces. Our method creates an extractive summary by selecting the sentences with the closest embeddings to the document embedding. The model learns a transformation of the document embedding to minimize the similarity between the extractive summary and the ground truth summary. As the transformation is only composed of a dense layer, the training can be done on CPU, therefore, inexpensive. Moreover, inference time is short and linear according to the number of sentences. As a second contribution, we introduce the French CASS dataset, composed of judgments from the French Court of cassation and their corresponding summaries. On this dataset, our results show that our method performs similarly to the state of the art extractive methods with effective training and inferring time.

1 Introduction

Summarization remains a field of interest as numerous industries are faced with a growing amount of textual data that they need to process. Creating summary by hand is a costly and time-demanding task, thus automatic methods to generate them are necessary. There are two ways of summarizing a document: abstractive and extractive summarization.

In abstractive summarization, the goal is to create new textual elements to summarize the text. Summarization can be modeled as a sequence-to-sequence problem. For instance, Rush et al. (2015) tried to generate a headline from an article. However, when the system generates longer summaries, redundancy can be a problem. See et al.

(2017) introduce a pointer-generator model (PGN) that generates summaries by copying words from the text or generating new words. Moreover, they added a coverage loss as they noticed that other models made repetitions on long summaries. Even if it provides state of the art results, the PGN is slow to learn and generate. Paulus et al. (2017) added a layer of reinforcement learning on an encoder-decoder architecture but their results can present fluency issues.

In extractive summarization, the goal is to extract part of the text to create a summary. There are two standard ways to do that: a sequence labeling task, where the goal is to select the sentences labeled as being part of the summary, and a ranking task, where the most salient sentences are ranked first. It is hard to find datasets for these tasks as most summaries written by humans are abstractive.Nallapati et al. (2016a) introduce a way to train an extractive summarization model without labels by applying a Recurrent Neural Network (RNN) and using a greedy matching approach based on ROUGE. Recently, Narayan et al. (2018b) combined reinforcement learning (to extract sentences) and an encoder-decoder architecture (to select the sentences).

Some models combine extractive and abstractive summarization, using an extractor to select sentences and then an abstractor to rewrite them (Chen and Bansal, 2018; Cao et al., 2018; Hsu et al., 2018). They are generally faster than models using only abstractors as they filter the input while maintaining or even improving the quality of the summaries.

This paper presents two main contributions. First, we propose an inexpensive, scalable, CPU-trainable and efficient method of extractive text summarization based on the use of sentence embeddings. Our idea is that similar embeddings are semantically similar, and so by looking at the

Proceedings of the ACL 2019, Student Research Workshop, pages 243–252
Florence, Italy, July 28th-August 2nd, 2019. ©2019 Association for Computational Linguistics

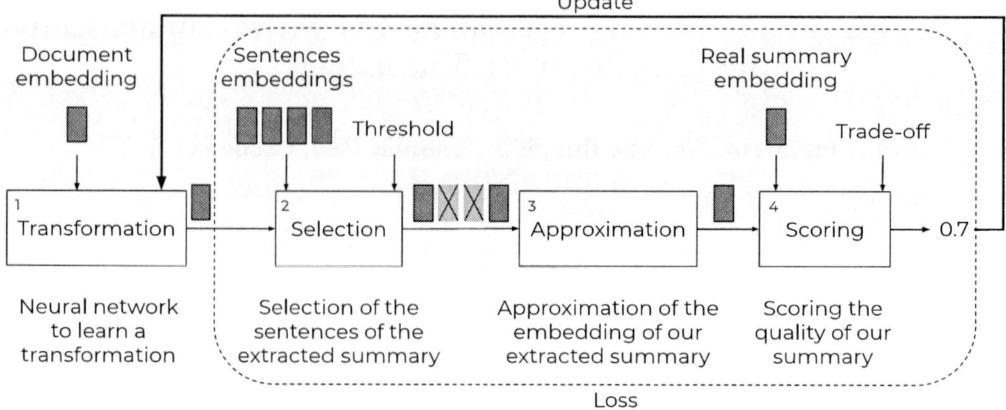

Figure 1: Training of the model. The blocks present steps of the analysis. All the elements above the blocks are inputs (document embedding, sentences embeddings, threshold, real summary embedding, trade-off).

proximity of the embeddings it is possible to rank the sentences. Secondly, we introduce the French CASS dataset (section 4.1), composed of 129,445 judgments with their corresponding summaries.

2　Related Work

In our model, STRASS, it is possible to use an embedding function [1] trained with state of the art methods.

Word2vec is a classical method used to transform a word into a vector (Mikolov et al., 2013a). Methods like word2vec keep information about semantics (Mikolov et al., 2013b). Sent2vec (Pagliardini et al., 2017) create embedding of sentences. It has state-of-the-art results on datasets for unsupervised sentence similarity evaluation.

EmbedRank (Bennani-Smires et al., 2018) applies sent2vec to extract keyphrases from a document in an unsupervised fashion. It hypothesizes that keyphrases that have an embedding close to the embedding of the entire document should represent this document well.

We adapt this idea to select sentences for summaries (section 4.2). We suppose that sentences close to the document share some meaning with the document and are sentences that summarize well the text. We go further by proposing a supervised method where we learn a transformation of the document embedding to an embedding of the same dimension, but closer to sentences that summarize the text.

3　Model

The aim is to construct an extractive summary. Our approach, STRASS, uses embeddings to select a subset of sentences from a document.

We apply sent2vec to the document, to the sentences of the document, and to the summary. We suppose that, if we have a document with an embedding[2] $\mathbf{d}$ and a set S with all the embeddings of the sentences of the document, and a reference summary with an embedding $\mathbf{ref\_sum}$, there is a subset of sentences $E_S \subset S$ forming the reference summary. Our target is to find an affine function $f(\cdot): \mathbb{R}^n \longrightarrow \mathbb{R}^n$, such that:

$$\begin{cases} sim(\mathbf{s}, f(\mathbf{d})) \geq t & \text{if } \mathbf{s} \in E_S \\ sim(\mathbf{s}, f(\mathbf{d})) < t, & \text{otherwise} \end{cases}$$

Where t is a threshold, and sim is a similarity function between two embeddings.

The training of the model is based on four main steps (shown in Figure 1):

- (1) Transform the document embedding by applying an affine function learned by a neural network (section 3.1);

- (2) Extract a subset of sentences to form a summary (section 3.2);

- (3) Approximate the embedding of the extractive summary formed by the selected sentences (section 3.3);

---

[1] In this paper, 'embedding function', 'embedding space' and 'embedding' will refer to the function that takes a textual element as input and outputs a vector, the vector space, and the vectors.

[2] Scalars are lowercased, vectors/embeddings are lowercased and in bold, sets are uppercased and matrices are uppercased and in bold.

- (4) Score the embedding of the resulting summary approximation with respect to the embedding of the real summary (section 3.4).

To generate the summary, only the first two steps are used. The selected sentences are the output. Approximation and scoring are only necessary during the training phase when computing loss function.

3.1 Transformation

To learn an affine function in the embedding space, the model uses a simple neural network. A single fully-connected feed-forward layer. $f(\cdot)$: $\mathbb{R}^n \longrightarrow \mathbb{R}^n$:

$$f(\mathbf{d}) = \mathbf{W} \times \mathbf{d} + \mathbf{b}$$

with $\mathbf{W}$ the weight matrix of the hidden layer and $\mathbf{b}$ the bias vector. Optimization is only conducted on these two elements.

3.2 Sentence Extraction

Inspired by EmbedRank (Bennani-Smires et al., 2018) our proposed approach is based on embeddings similarities. Instead of selecting the top n elements, our approach uses a threshold. All the sentences with a score above this threshold are selected. As in Pagliardini et al. (2017), our similarity score is the cosine similarity. Selection of sentences is the first element:

$$sel(\mathbf{s}, \mathbf{d}, S, t) =$$
$$sigmoid(ncos^+(\mathbf{s}, f(\mathbf{d}), S) - t)$$

with $sigmoid$ the sigmoid function and $ncos^+$ a normalized cosine similarity explained in section 3.5. A sigmoid function is used instead of a hard threshold as all the functions need to be differentiable to make the back-propagation. Sel outputs a number between 0 and 1. 1 indicates that a sentence should be selected and 0 that it should not. With this function, we select a subset of sentences from the text that forms our generated summary.

3.3 Approximation

As we want to compare the embedding of our generated extractive summary and the embedding of the reference summary, the model approximates the embedding of the proposed summary. As the system uses sent2vec, the approximation is the average of the sentences weighted by the number of words in each sentence. We have to apply this approximation to the sentences extracted with sel, which compose our generated summary. The approximation is:

$$app(\mathbf{d}, S, t) = \sum_{\mathbf{s} \in S} \mathbf{s} \times nb\_w(\mathbf{s}) \times sel(\mathbf{s}, \mathbf{d}, S, t)$$

where, $nb\_w(\mathbf{s})$ is the number of words in the sentence corresponding to the embedding $\mathbf{s}$.

3.4 Scoring

The quality of our generated summary is scored by comparing its embedding with the reference summary embedding. Here, the compression ratio is added to the score in order to force the model to output shorter summaries. The compression ratio is the number of words in the summary divided by the number of words in the document.

$$loss = \lambda \times \frac{nb\_w(\mathbf{gen\_sum})}{nb\_w(\mathbf{d})} +$$
$$(1 - \lambda) \times cos\_sim(\mathbf{gen\_sum}, \mathbf{ref\_sum})$$

with λ a trade-off between the similarity and the compression ratio, $cos\_sim(\mathbf{x}, \mathbf{y})$, $\mathbf{x}, \mathbf{y} \in \mathbb{R}^n$ the cosine similarity and $\mathbf{gen\_sum} = app(\mathbf{d}, S, t)$. The user should note that λ is also useful to change the trade-off between the proximity of the summaries and the length of the generated one. A higher λ results in a shorter summary.

3.5 Normalization

To use a single selection threshold on all our documents, a normalization is applied on the similarities to have the same distribution for the similarities on all the documents. First, we transform the cosine similarity from $(\mathbb{R}^n, \mathbb{R}^n) \longrightarrow [-1, 1]$ to $(\mathbb{R}^n, \mathbb{R}^n) \longrightarrow [0, 1]$:

$$cos^+(\mathbf{x}, \mathbf{y}) = \frac{cos\_sim(\mathbf{x}, \mathbf{y}) + 1}{2}$$

Then as in Mori and Sasaki (2002) the function is reduced and centered in 0.5:

$$rcos^+(\mathbf{x}, \mathbf{y}, X) =$$
$$0.5 + \frac{cos^+(\mathbf{x}, \mathbf{y}) - \mu_{\mathbf{x_k} \in X}\left(cos^+(\mathbf{x_k}, \mathbf{y})\right)}{\sigma_{\mathbf{x_k} \in X}\left(cos^+(\mathbf{x_k}, \mathbf{y})\right)}$$

where $\mathbf{y}$ is an embedding, X is a set of embeddings, $\mathbf{x} \in X$, μ and σ are the mean and standard deviation.

A threshold is applied to select the closest sentences on this normalized cosine similarity. In order to always select at least one sentence, we restricted our similarity measure in $(-\infty, 1]$, where, for each document, the closest sentence has a similarity of 1:

$$ncos^+(\mathbf{x}, \mathbf{y}, X) = \frac{rcos^+(\mathbf{x}, \mathbf{y}, X)}{\max\limits_{\mathbf{x_k} \in X}(rcos^+(\mathbf{x_k}, \mathbf{y}, X))}$$

4 Experiments

4.1 Datasets

To evaluate our approach, two datasets were used with different intrinsic document and summary structures which are presented in this section. More detailed information is available in the appendices (table 3, figure 3 and figure 4).

We introduce a new dataset for text summarization, the CASS dataset[3]. This dataset is composed of 129,445 judgments given by the French Court of cassation between 1842 and 2016 and their summaries (one summary by original document). Those summaries are written by lawyers and explain in a short way the main points of the judgments. As multiple lawyers have written summaries, there are different types of summary ranging from purely extractive to purely abstractive. This dataset is maintained up-to-date by the French Government and new data are regularly added. Our version of the dataset is composed of 129,445 judgements.

The CNN/DailyMail dataset (Hermann et al., 2015; Nallapati et al., 2016b) is composed of 312,084 couples containing a news article and its highlights. The highlights show the key points of an article. We use the split created by Nallapati et al. (2016b) and refined by See et al. (2017).

4.2 Baseline

An unsupervised version of our approach is to use the document embedding as an approximation for the position in the embedding space used to select the sentences of the summary. It is the application of EmbedRank (Bennani-Smires et al., 2018) on the extractive summarization task. This approach is used as a baseline for our model

---

[3]The dataset is available here: `https://github.com/euranova/CASS-dataset`

4.3 Oracles

We introduce two oracles. Even if these models do not output the best possible results for extractive summarization, they show good results.

The first model, called $Oracle$, is the same as the baseline, but instead of taking the document embedding, the model takes the embedding of the summary and then extracts the closest sentences.

The second model, called $Oracle_{sent}$, extracts the closest sentence to each sentence of the summary. This is an adaptation of the idea that Nallapati et al. (2016a) and Chen and Bansal (2018) used to create their reference extractive summaries.

4.4 Evaluation details

ROUGE (Lin, 2004) is a widely used set of metrics to evaluate summaries. The three main metrics in this set are ROUGE-1 and ROUGE-2, which compare the 1-grams and 2-grams of the generated and reference summaries, and ROUGE-L, which measures the longest sub-sequence between the two summaries. ROUGE is the standard measure for summarization, especially because more sophisticated ones like METEOR (Denkowski and Lavie, 2014) require resources not available for many languages.

Our results are compared with the unsupervised system TextRank (Mihalcea and Tarau, 2004; Barrios et al., 2016) and with the supervised systems Pointer-Generator Network (See et al., 2017) and $rnn - ext$ (Chen and Bansal, 2018). The Pointer-Generator Network is an abstractive model and $rnn - ext$ is extractive.

For all datasets, a sent2vec embedding of dimension 700 was trained on the training split. To choose the hyperparameters, a grid search was computed on the validation set. Then the set of hyperparameters with the highest ROUGE-L were used on the test set. The selected hyperparameters are available in appendix A.3.

5 Results

Tables 1 and 2 present the results for the CASS and the CNN/DailyMail datasets. As expected, the supervised model performs better than the unsupervised one. On the three datasets, the supervision has improved the score in terms of ROUGE-2 and ROUGE-L. In the same way, our oracles are always better than the learned models, proving that there is still room for improvements. Information concerning the length of the generated summaries

	R1 F1	R2 F1	RL F1
Baseline	39.57	22.11	29.71
TextRank	39.30	23.49	31.45
PGN	**53.25**	**40.25**	**45.58**
rnn-ext	**53.05**	38.21	44.62
STRASS	52.68	38.87	44.72
Oracle	62.79	50.10	55.03
Oracle sent	63.90	50.56	55.75

Table 1: Results of different models on the French CASS dataset using ROUGE with 95% confidence. The models of the first block are unsupervised, the models of the second block are supervised and the models of the last block are the oracles. F1 is the F-measure. R1, R2 and RL stand for ROUGE1, ROUGE2, and ROUGE-L.

	R1 F1	R2 F1	RL F1
Baseline	34.02	12.48	28.27
TextRank	30.83	13.02	27.39
PGN*	39.53	17.28	**36.38**
rnn-ext*	**40.17**	**18.11**	**36.41**
STRASS	33.99	14.18	30.04
Oracle	43.55	22.43	38.47
Oracle sent	46.21	25.81	42.47
Lead3	40.00	17.56	36.33
Lead3 - PGN*	40.34	17.70	36.57

Table 2: Results of different models on the CNN/DailyMail. The Lead3 - PGN is the lead 3 score as reported in (See et al., 2017). The scores with * are taken from the corresponding publications. F1 is the F-measure. R1, R2 and RL stand for ROUGE1, ROUGE2, and ROUGE-L.

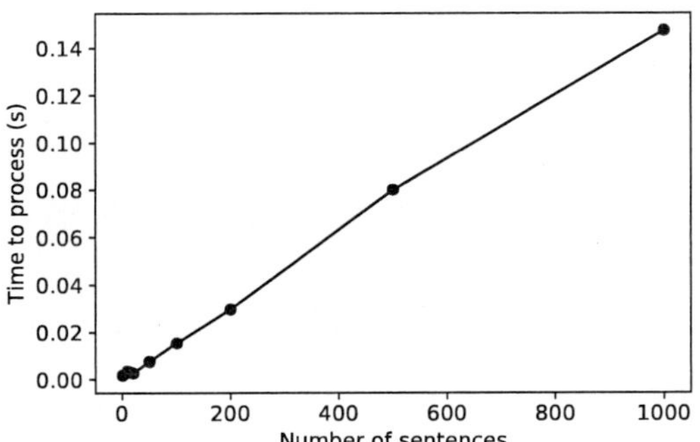

Figure 2: Processing time of the summarization function (y-axis) by the number of lines of the text as input (x-axis). Results computed on an i7-8550U.

and the position of the sentences taken are available in the appendices A.4.2.

On the French CASS dataset, our method performs similarly to the $rnn - ext$. The PGN performs a bit better (+0.13 ROUGE-1, +0.38 ROUGE-2, + 0.81 ROUGE-L compared to the other models), which could be linked to the fact that it can select elements smaller than sentences.

On the CNN/DailyMail dataset, our supervised model performs poorly. We observe a significant difference (+2.66 ROUGE-1, +3.38 ROUGE-2, and +4.00 ROUGE-L) between the two oracles. It could be explained by the fact that the summaries are multi-topic and our models do not handle such case. Therefore, as our loss doesn't look at the diversity, STRASS may miss some topics in the generated summary.

A second limitation of our approach is that our model doesn't consider the position of the sentences in the summary, information which presents a high relevance in the CNN-Dailymail dataset.

STRASS has some advantages. First, it is trainable on CPU and thus light to train and run. Indeed, the neural network in our model is only composed of one dense layer. The most recent advances in text summarization with neural networks are all based on deep neural networks requiring GPU to be learned efficiently. Second, the method is scalable. The processing time is linear with the number of lines of the documents (Figure 2). The model is fast at inference time as sent2vec embeddings are fast to generate. Our model generated the 13,095 summaries of the CASS dataset in less than 3 minutes on an i7-8550U CPU.

6 Conclusion and Perspectives

To conclude, we proposed here a simple, cost-effective and scalable extractive summarization method. STRASS creates an extractive summary by selecting the sentences with the closest embeddings to the projected document embedding. The model learns a transformation of the document embedding to maximize the similarity between the extractive summary and the ground truth summary. We showed that our approach obtains similar results than other extractive methods in an effective way.

There are several perspectives to our work. First, we would like to use the sentence embeddings as an input of our model, as this should increase the accuracy. Additionally, we want to investigate the effect of using other sent2vec embedding spaces (especially more generalist ones) or other embedding functions like doc2vec (Le and Mikolov, 2014) or BERT (Devlin et al., 2019).

For now, we have only worked on sentences but this model can use any embeddings, so we could try to build summaries with smaller textual elements than sentences such as key-phrases, noun phrases... Likewise, to apply our model on multitopic texts, we could try to create clusters of sentences, where each cluster is a topic, and then extract one sentence by cluster.

Moreover, currently, the loss of the system is only composed of the proximity and the compression ratio. Other meaningful metrics for document summarization such as diversity and representativity could be added into the loss. Especially, submodular functions could (1) allow to obtain near-optimal results and (2) allow to include elements like diversity (Lin and Bilmes, 2011). Another information we could add is the position of the sentences in the documents like Narayan et al. (2018a).

Finally, the approach could be extended to query-based summarization (V.V.MuraliKrishna et al., 2013). One could use the embedding function on the query and take the sentences that are the closest to the embedding of the query.

Acknowledgement

We thank Cécile Capponi, Carlos Ramisch, Guillaume Stempfel, Jakey Blue and our anonymous reviewer for their helpful comments.

References

Federico Barrios, Federico López, Luis Argerich, and Rosa Wachenchauzer. 2016. Variations of the similarity function of textrank for automated summarization. *CoRR*, abs/1602.03606.

Kamil Bennani-Smires, Claudiu Musat, Andreea Hossmann, Michael Baeriswyl, and Martin Jaggi. 2018. Simple unsupervised keyphrase extraction using sentence embeddings. In *Proceedings of the 22nd Conference on Computational Natural Language Learning*, pages 221–229. Association for Computational Linguistics.

Ziqiang Cao, Wenjie Li, Sujian Li, and Furu Wei. 2018. Retrieve, rerank and rewrite: Soft template based neural summarization. In *Proceedings of the 56th Annual Meeting of the Association for Computational Linguistics (Volume 1: Long Papers)*, pages 152–161. Association for Computational Linguistics.

Yen-Chun Chen and Mohit Bansal. 2018. Fast abstractive summarization with reinforce-selected sentence rewriting. In *Proceedings of the 56th Annual Meeting of the Association for Computational Linguistics (Volume 1: Long Papers)*, pages 675–686. Association for Computational Linguistics.

Michael Denkowski and Alon Lavie. 2014. Meteor universal: Language specific translation evaluation for any target language. In *Proceedings of the Ninth Workshop on Statistical Machine Translation*, pages 376–380. Association for Computational Linguistics.

Jacob Devlin, Ming-Wei Chang, Kenton Lee, and Kristina Toutanova. 2019. BERT: Pre-training of deep bidirectional transformers for language understanding. In *Proceedings of the 2019 Conference of the North American Chapter of the Association for Computational Linguistics: Human Language Technologies, Volume 1 (Long and Short Papers)*, pages 4171–4186, Minneapolis, Minnesota. Association for Computational Linguistics.

Karl Moritz Hermann, Tomáš Kočiský, Edward Grefenstette, Lasse Espeholt, Will Kay, Mustafa Suleyman, and Phil Blunsom. 2015. Teaching machines to read and comprehend. In *Proceedings of the 28th International Conference on Neural Information Processing Systems - Volume 1*, NIPS'15, pages 1693–1701, Cambridge, MA, USA. MIT Press.

Wan-Ting Hsu, Chieh-Kai Lin, Ming-Ying Lee, Kerui Min, Jing Tang, and Min Sun. 2018. A unified model for extractive and abstractive summarization using inconsistency loss. In *Proceedings of the 56th Annual Meeting of the Association for Computational Linguistics (Volume 1: Long Papers)*, pages 132–141. Association for Computational Linguistics.

Quoc Le and Tomas Mikolov. 2014. Distributed representations of sentences and documents. In *Proceedings of the 31st International Conference on Machine Learning*, volume 32 of *Proceedings of Machine Learning Research*, pages 1188–1196, Bejing, China. PMLR.

Chin-Yew Lin. 2004. Rouge: A package for automatic evaluation of summaries. In *Text Summarization Branches Out: Proceedings of the ACL-04 Workshop*, pages 74–81, Barcelona, Spain. Association for Computational Linguistics.

Hui Lin and Jeff Bilmes. 2011. A class of submodular functions for document summarization. In *Proceedings of the 49th Annual Meeting of the Association for Computational Linguistics: Human Language Technologies - Volume 1*, HLT '11, pages 510–520, Stroudsburg, PA, USA. Association for Computational Linguistics.

Rada Mihalcea and Paul Tarau. 2004. TextRank: Bringing order into text. In *Proceedings of EMNLP*

2004, pages 404–411, Barcelona, Spain. Association for Computational Linguistics.

Tomas Mikolov, Kai Chen, Greg Corrado, and Jeffrey Dean. 2013a. Efficient estimation of word representations in vector space. *CoRR*, abs/1301.3781.

Tomas Mikolov, Wen-tau Yih, and Geoffrey Zweig. 2013b. Linguistic regularities in continuous space word representations. In *Proceedings of the 2013 Conference of the North American Chapter of the Association for Computational Linguistics: Human Language Technologies*, pages 746–751, Atlanta, Georgia. Association for Computational Linguistics.

Tatsunori Mori and Takuro Sasaki. 2002. Information gain ratio meets maximal marginal relevance - a method of summarization for multiple documents. In *NTCIR*.

Ramesh Nallapati, Feifei Zhai, and Bowen Zhou. 2016a. Summarunner: A recurrent neural network based sequence model for extractive summarization of documents. *CoRR*, abs/1611.04230.

Ramesh Nallapati, Bowen Zhou, Cicero dos Santos, Caglar Gulcehre, and Bing Xiang. 2016b. Abstractive text summarization using sequence-to-sequence rnns and beyond. In *Proceedings of The 20th SIGNLL Conference on Computational Natural Language Learning*, pages 280–290, Berlin, Germany. Association for Computational Linguistics.

Shashi Narayan, Shay B. Cohen, and Mirella Lapata. 2018a. Don't give me the details, just the summary! topic-aware convolutional neural networks for extreme summarization. In *Proceedings of the 2018 Conference on Empirical Methods in Natural Language Processing*, pages 1797–1807, Brussels, Belgium. Association for Computational Linguistics.

Shashi Narayan, Shay B. Cohen, and Mirella Lapata. 2018b. Ranking sentences for extractive summarization with reinforcement learning. In *Proceedings of the 2018 Conference of the North American Chapter of the Association for Computational Linguistics: Human Language Technologies, Volume 1 (Long Papers)*, pages 1747–1759. Association for Computational Linguistics.

Matteo Pagliardini, Prakhar Gupta, and Martin Jaggi. 2017. Unsupervised learning of sentence embeddings using compositional n-gram features. *CoRR*, abs/1703.02507.

Romain Paulus, Caiming Xiong, and Richard Socher. 2017. A deep reinforced model for abstractive summarization. *CoRR*, abs/1705.04304.

Alexander M. Rush, Sumit Chopra, and Jason Weston. 2015. A neural attention model for abstractive sentence summarization. In *Proceedings of the 2015 Conference on Empirical Methods in Natural Language Processing*, pages 379–389. Association for Computational Linguistics.

Abigail See, Peter J. Liu, and Christopher D. Manning. 2017. Get to the point: Summarization with pointer-generator networks. In *Proceedings of the 55th Annual Meeting of the Association for Computational Linguistics (Volume 1: Long Papers)*, pages 1073–1083. Association for Computational Linguistics.

R V.V.MuraliKrishna, S Y. Pavan Kumar, and Ch Reddy. 2013. A hybrid method for query based automatic summarization system. *International Journal of Computer Applications*, 68:39–43.

A   Appendices

A.1   Datasets

The composition of the datasets and the splits are available in table 3.

A.2   Preprocessing

On the French CASS dataset, we have deleted all the accents of the texts and we have lower-cased all the texts as some of them where entirely upper-cased without any accent. To create the summaries, all the ANA parts of the XML files provided in the original dataset where taken and concatenate to form a single summary for each document. These summaries explain different key points of the judgment. On the CNN/DailyMail, the preprocessing of See et al. (2017) was used. As an extra cleaning step, we deleted the documents that had an empty story.

A.3   Hyperparameters

To obtain the embeddings functions for both datasets we trained a sent2vec model of dimension 700 with unigrams on the train splits.

For the CASS dataset, the baseline model has a threshold at 0.8, the oracle at 0.8 and STRASS has a threshold at 0.8 and a λ at 0.3. TextRank was used with a ratio of 0.2. The PGN For the CNN/DailyMail dataset, the baseline model has a threshold at 1.0, the oracle at 0.9 and STRASS has a threshold at 0.8 and a λ at 0.4. TextRank was used with a ratio of 0.15.

A.4   Results

A.4.1   ROUGE Score

More detailed results are available in tables 4 and 5. High recall with low precision is generally synonym of long summary.

Dataset	s_d	s_s	t_d	t_s	train	val	test
CASS	19.4	1.6	894	114	103,434	12,916	13,095
CNN/DailyMail	28.9	3.8	786	53	287,112	13,367	11,489

Table 3: Size information for the datasets, s_d and s_s are respectively the average number of sentences in the document and in the summary, t_d and t_t are respectively the number of tokens in the document and in the summary. train, val and test are respectively the number of documents in the train, validation and test sets.

	R1 P	R1 R	R1 F1	R2 P	R2 R	R2 F1	RL P	RL R	RL F1
Baseline	32.27	65.81	39.55	17.98	36.88	22.09	24.13	50.11	29.69
TextRank	32.62	68.58	39.30	19.47	41.95	23.49	25.98	56.16	31.45
PGN	69.70	49.01	53.25	53.46	36.67	40.25	60.31	41.65	45.58
rnn-ext	49.54	69.62	53.12	35.94	50.00	38.30	42.03	58.43	44.77
STRASS	56.23	62.55	52.68	41.97	45.71	38.87	48.05	52.93	44.72
Oracle	66.40	68.41	62.79	53.80	53.40	50.10	58.73	59.20	55.03
Oracle sent	69.50	64.82	63.90	55.36	50.91	50.56	60.77	56.34	55.75

Table 4: Full results of different models on the French CASS dataset using ROUGE with 95% confidence. The models in the first part are unsupervised models, then supervised models and the last part is the oracle. P is precision, R is recall and F1 is the F-measure. R1, R2 and RL stand for ROUGE1, ROUGE2, and ROUGE-L.

	R1 P	R1 R	R1 F1	R2 P	R2 R	R2 F1	RL P	RL R	RL F1
Baseline	32.67	40.09	34.02	12.07	14.65	12.48	27.29	33.14	28.27
TextRank	23.44	59.29	30.83	9.95	25.02	13.02	20.77	53.02	27.39
PGN*			39.53			17.28			36.38
rnn-ext*			40.17			18.11			36.41
STRASS	28.56	53.53	33.99	11.89	22.62	14.18	25.21	47.46	30.04
Oracle	44.92	50.93	43.55	24.14	25.47	22.43	39.98	44.75	38.47
Oracle sent	35.17	74.30	46.21	19.84	40.83	25.81	32.37	68.12	42.47
Lead3	33.89	53.35	40.00	14.84	23.59	17.56	30.80	48.43	36.33
Lead - PGN*			40.34			17.70			36.57

Table 5: Full results of different models on the CNN/DailyMail. The Lead3 - PGN is the lead 3 score as reported in (See et al., 2017). The scores with * are taken from the corresponding publications. P is precision, R is recall and F1 is the F-measure. R1, R2 and RL stand for ROUGE1, ROUGE2, and ROUGE-L.

Model	s	w	w/s
Reference	1.6	117	73.1
STRASS	2.0	151	75.5
Oracle	1.7	138	81.2
Oracle sent	1.5	112	74.7

(a) Size information for the generated summary on the test split of the CASS dataset, s, w, w/s are respectively the average number of sentences, the average number of words and the average number of words per sentences.

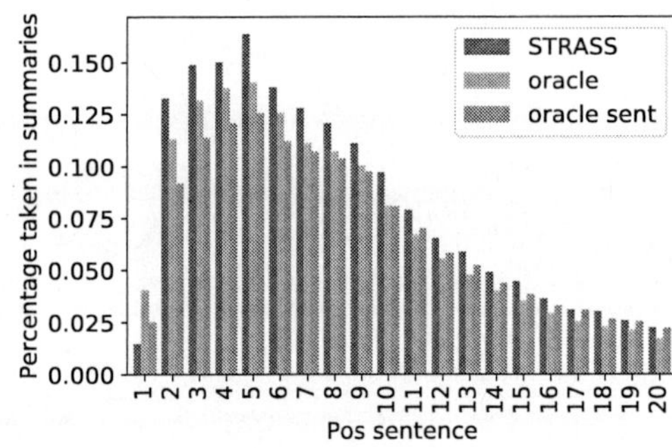

(b) Percentage of times that a sentence is taken in a generated summary in function of their position in the document on the CASS dataset.

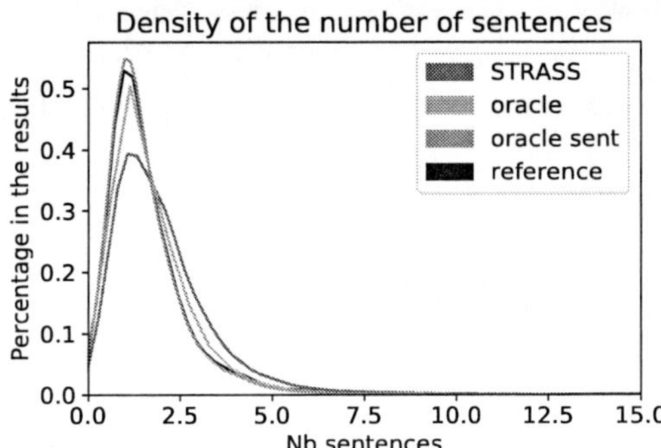

(c) Density of the number of sentences in the generated summaries for several models and the reference on the CASS dataset.

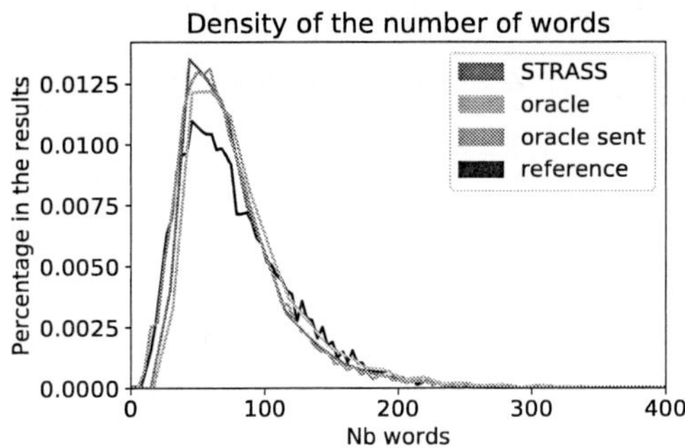

(d) Density of the number of words in the generated summaries for several models and the reference on the CASS dataset.

Figure 3: Information about the length of the generated summaries for the CASS dataset.

A.4.2 Words and sentences

On the French CASS dataset the summaries generated by the models are generally close in terms of length (number of words, number of sentences and number of words per sentences (figure 3a, 3c, 3d)). All the tested extractive methods tend to select sentences at the beginning of the documents. The first sentence make an exception to that rule (figure 3b). We observe that this sentence can have the list of the lawyers and judges that were present at the case. STRASS tends to generate longer summaries with more sentences. The discrepancy in the average number of sentences between the reference and $Oraclesent$ is due to sentences that are extracted multiple times.

On the CNN/DailyMail dataset, STRASS tends to extract less sentences but longer ones comparing to the $Oraclesent$ (figure 4a, 4c, 4d). On the figure 4b we can see that the three models tend to extract different sentences. $Oraclesent$ which is the best performing model tends to extract the 4 first sentences, $Oracle$ extracts more of-ten the fourth sentences than the first three and still have better results than the $Lead3$, which means that the fourth sentences could have some interest. With STRASS the first three sentences have a different tendency than the rest of the text, showing that the first three sentences may have a different structure than the rest. Then, the farther a sentence is in the text, the lower the probability to take it.

Model	s	w	w/s
Reference	3.9	55	14.1
STRASS	2.7	135	50
Oracle	1.5	84	56
Oracle sent	3.5	137	39.1

(a) Size information for the generated summary on the test split of the CNN/DM dataset, s, w, w/s are respectively the average number of sentences, the average number of words and the average number of words per sentences.

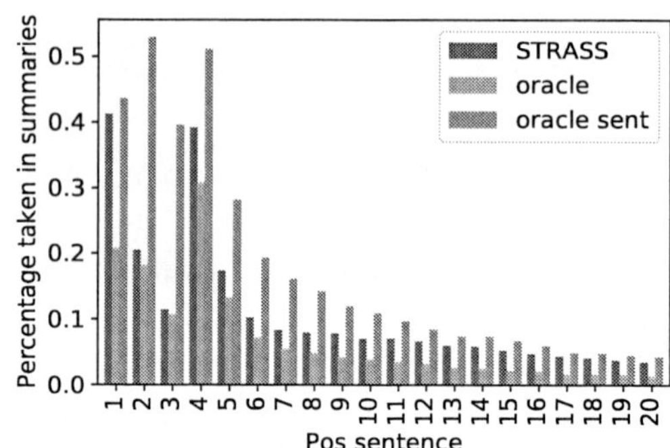

(b) Percentage of times that a sentence is taken in a generated summary in function of their position in the document on the CNN/DM dataset.

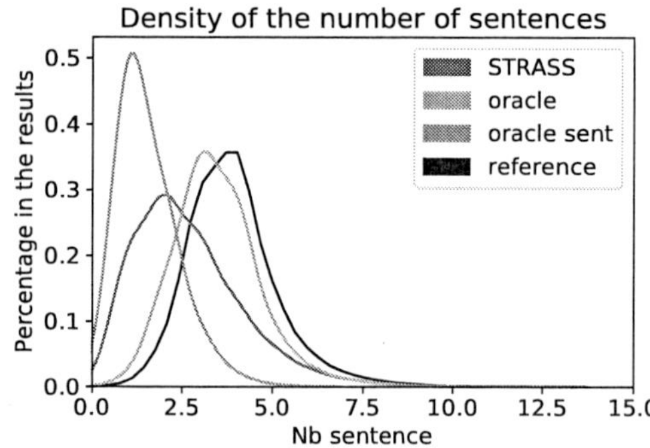

(c) Density of the number of sentences in the generated summaries for several models and the reference on the CNN/DM dataset.

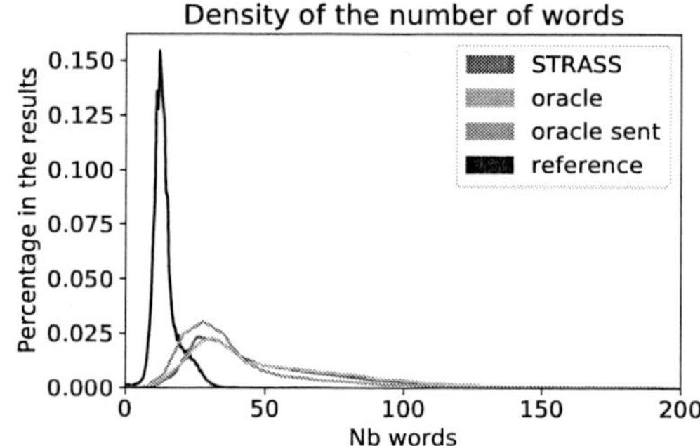

(d) Density of the number of words in the generated summaries for several models and the reference on the CNN/DM dataset.

Figure 4: Information about the length of the generated summaries for the CNN/DM dataset.

Attention and Lexicon Regularized LSTM for Aspect-based Sentiment Analysis

Lingxian Bao
Universitat Pompeu Fabra
`lingxian.bao@upf.edu`

Patrik Lambert
Universitat Pompeu Fabra
`patrik.lambert`
`@upf.edu`

Toni Badia
Universitat Pompeu Fabra
`toni.badia@upf.edu`

Abstract

Attention based deep learning systems have been demonstrated to be the state of the art approach for aspect-level sentiment analysis, however, end-to-end deep neural networks lack flexibility as one can not easily adjust the network to fix an obvious problem, especially when more training data is not available: e.g. when it always predicts *positive* when seeing the word *disappointed*. Meanwhile, it is less stressed that attention mechanism is likely to "over-focus" on particular parts of a sentence, while ignoring positions which provide key information for judging the polarity. In this paper, we describe a simple yet effective approach to leverage lexicon information so that the model becomes more flexible and robust. We also explore the effect of regularizing attention vectors to allow the network to have a broader "focus" on different parts of the sentence. The experimental results demonstrate the effectiveness of our approach.

1 Introduction

Sentiment analysis (also called opinion mining) has been one of the most active fields in NLP due to its important value to business and society. It is the field of study that tries to extract opinion (*positive, neutral, negative*) expressed in natural languages. Most sentiment analysis works have been carried out at document level (Pang et al., 2002; Turney, 2002) and sentence level (Wilson et al., 2004), but as opinion expressed by words is highly context dependent, one word may express opposite sentiment under different circumstances. Thus aspect-level sentiment analysis (ABSA) was proposed to address this problem. It finds the polarity of an opinion associated with a certain aspect, such as *food, ambiance, service,* or *price* in a restaurant domain.

Although deep neural networks yield significant improvement across a variety of tasks compared to

previous state of the art methods, end-to-end deep learning systems lack flexibility as one cannot easily adjust the network to fix an obvious problem: e.g. when the network always predicts *positive* when seeing the word *disappointed*, or when the network is not able to recognize the word *dungeon* as an indication of *negative* polarity. It could be even trickier in a low-resource scenario where more labeled training data is simply not available. Moreover, it is less stressed that attention mechanism is likely to over-fit and force the network to "focus" too much on a particular part of a sentence, while in some cases ignoring positions which provide key information for judging the polarity. In recent studies, both Niculae and Blondel (2017) and Zhang et al. (2019) proposed approaches to make the attention vector more sparse, however, it would only encourage the over-fitting effect in such scenario.

In this paper, we describe a simple yet effective approach to merge lexicon information with an attention LSTM model for ABSA in order to leverage both the power of deep neural networks and existing linguistic resources, so that the framework becomes more flexible and robust without requiring additional labeled data. We also explore the effect of regularizing attention vectors by introducing an attention regularizer to allow the network to have a broader "focus" on different parts of the sentence.

2 Related works

ABSA is a fine-grained task which requires the model to be able to produce accurate prediction given different aspects. As it is common that one sentence may contain opposite polarities associated to different aspects at the same time, attention-based LSTM (Wang et al., 2016) was first proposed to allow the network to be able to as-

Proceedings of the ACL 2019, Student Research Workshop, pages 253–259
Florence, Italy, July 28th-August 2nd, 2019. ©2019 Association for Computational Linguistics

sign higher weights to more relevant words given different aspects. Following this idea, a number of researches have been carried out to keep improving the attention network for ABSA (Ma et al., 2017; Tay et al., 2017; Cheng et al., 2017; He et al., 2018; Zhu and Qian, 2018).

On the other hand, a lot of works have been done focusing on leveraging existing linguistic resources such as sentiment to enhance the performance; however, most works are performed at document and sentence level. For instance, at document level, Teng et al. (2016) proposed a weighted-sum model which consists of representing the final prediction as a weighted sum of the network prediction and the polarities provided by the lexicon. Zou et al. (2018) described a framework to assign higher weights to opinion words found in the lexicon by transforming lexicon polarity to sentiment degree.

At sentence level, Shin et al. (2017) used two convolutional neural networks to separately process sentence and lexicon inputs. Lei et al. (2018) described a multi-head attention network where the attention weights are jointly learned with lexicon inputs. Wu et al. (2018) proposed a new labeling strategy which breaks a sentence into clauses by punctuation to produce more lower-level examples, inputs are then processed at different levels with linguistic information such as lexicon and POS, and finally merged back to perform sentence level prediction. Meanwhile, some other similar works that incorporate linguistic resources for sentiment analysis have been carried out (Rouvier and Favre, 2016; Qian et al., 2017).

Regarding the attention regularization, instead of using *softmax* and *sparesmax*, Niculae and Blondel (2017) proposed *fusemax* as a regularized attention framework to learn the attention weights; Zhang et al. (2019) introduced L_{max} and *Entropy* as regularization terms to be jointly optimized with the loss. However, both approaches share the same idea of shaping the attention weights to be sharper and more sparse so that the advantage of the attention mechanism is maximized.

In our work, different from the previously mentioned approaches, we incorporate polarities obtained from lexicons directly into the attention-based LSTM network to perform aspect-level sentiment analysis, so that the model improves in terms of robustness without requiring extra training examples. Additionally, we find that the at-

tention vector is likely to over-fit which forces the network to "focus" on particular words while ignoring positions that provide key information for judging the polarity; and that by adding lexical features, it is possible to reduce this effect. Following this idea, we also experimented reducing the over-fitting effect by introducing an attention regularizer. Unlike previously mentioned ideas, we want the attention weights to be less sparse. Details of our approach are in following sections.

3 Methodology

3.1 Baseline AT-LSTM

In our experiments, we replicate AT-LSTM proposed by Wang et al. (2016) as our baseline system. Comparing with a traditional LSTM network (Hochreiter and Schmidhuber, 1997), AT-LSTM is able to learn the attention vector and at the same time to take into account the aspect embeddings. Thus the network is able to assign higher weights to more relevant parts of a given sentence with respect to a specific aspect.

Formally, given a sentence S, let $\{w_1, w_2, ..., w_N\}$ be the word vectors of each word where N is the length of the sentence; $v_a \in R^{d_a}$ represents the aspect embeddings where d_a is its dimension; let $H \in R^{d \times N}$ be a matrix of the hidden states $\{h_1, h_2, ..., h_N \in R^d\}$ produced by LSTM where d is the number of neurons of the LSTM cell. Thus the attention vector α is computed as follows:

$$M = tanh(\begin{bmatrix} W_h H \\ W_v v_a \otimes e_N \end{bmatrix})$$

$$\alpha = softmax(w^T M)$$

$$r = H\alpha^T$$

where, $M \in R^{(d+d_a) \times N}, \alpha \in R^N, r \in R^d, W_h \in R^{d \times d}, W_v \in R^{d_a \times d_a}, w \in R^{d+d_a}$. α is a vector consisting of attention weights and r is a weighted representation of the input sentence with respect to the input aspect. $v_a \otimes e_N = [v_a, v_a, ..., v_a]$, that is, the operator repeatedly concatenates v_a for N times. Then, the final representation is obtained and fed to the output layer as below:

$$h^* = tanh(W_p r + W_x h_N)$$

$$\hat{y} = softmax(W_s h^* + b_s)$$

where, $h^* \in R^d$, W_p and W_x are projection parameters to be learned during training; W_s and b_s

are weights and biases in the output layer. The prediction $\hat{y}$ is then plugged into the cross-entropy loss function for training, and L_2 regularization is applied.

$$loss = -\sum_i y_i log(\hat{y}_i) + \lambda\|\Theta\|_2^2 \qquad (1)$$

where i is the number of classes (three way classification in our experiments); λ is the hyperparameter for L_2 regularization; Θ is the regularized parameter set in the network.

3.2 ATLX

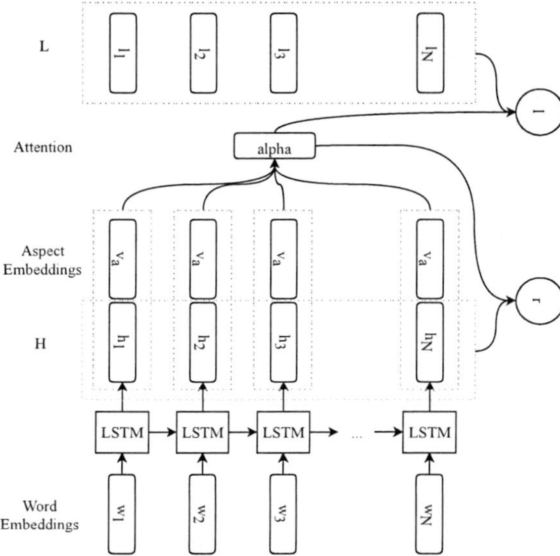

Figure 1: ATLX model diagram

3.2.1 Lexicon Build

Similar to Shin et al. (2017), but in a different way, we build our lexicon by merging 4 existing lexicons to one: MPQA, Opinion Lexicon, Opener and Vader. SentiWordNet was in the initial design but was removed from the experiments as unnecessary noise was introduced, e.g. *highly* is annotated as *negative*. For categorical labels such as *negative, weakneg, neutral, both, positive*, we convert them to values in $\{-1.0, -0.5, 0.0, 0.0, 1.0\}$ respectively. Regarding lexicons with real value annotations, for each lexicon, we adopt the annotated value standardized by the maximum polarity in that lexicon. Finally, the union U of all lexicons is taken where each word $w_l \in U$ has an associated vector $v_l \in R^n$ that represents the polarity given by each lexicon. n here is the number of lexicons; average values across

all available lexicons are taken for missing values. e.g. the lexical feature for word *adorable* is represented by $[1.0, 1.0, 1.0, 0.55]$, which are taken from MPQA(1.0), Opener(1.0), Opinion Lexicon(1.0) and Vader(0.55) respectively. For words outside U, a zero vector of dimension n is supplied.

3.2.2 Lexicon Integration

To merge the lexical features obtained from U into the baseline, we first perform a linear transformation to the lexical features in order to preserve the original sentiment distribution and have compatible dimensions for further computations. Later, the attention vector learned as in the baseline is applied to the transformed lexical features. In the end, all information is added together to perform the final prediction.

Formally, let $V_l \in R^{n \times N}$ be the lexical matrix for the sentence, V_l then is transformed linearly:

$$L = W_l \cdot V_l$$

where $L \in R^{d \times N}, W_l \in R^{d \times n}$. Later, the attention vector learned from the concatenation of H and $v_a \otimes e_N$ is applied to L:

$$l = L \cdot \alpha^T$$

where $l \in R^d, \alpha \in R^N$. Finally h^* is updated and passed to output layer for prediction:

$$h^* = tanh(W_p r + W_x h_N + W_l l)$$

where $W_l \in R^{d \times d}$ is a projection parameter as W_p and W_x. The model architecture is shown in Figure 1.

3.3 Attention Regularization

As observed in both Figure 2 and Figure 3, the attention weights in ATLX seem less sparse across the sentence, while the ones in the baseline are focusing only on the final part of the sentence. It is reasonable to think that the attention vector might be over-fitting in some cases, causing the network to ignore other relevant positions, since the attention vector is learned purely on training examples. Thus we propose a simple attention regularizer to further validate our hypothesis, which consists of adding into the loss function a parameterized standard deviation or negative entropy term for the attention weights. The idea is to avoid the attention vector to have heavy weights in few positions, instead, it is preferred to have higher weights for more positions. Formally, the attention regularized loss is computed as:

$$loss = -\sum_i y_i log(\hat{y}_i) + \lambda\|\Theta\|_2^2 + \epsilon \cdot R(\alpha) \quad (2)$$

compared to equation (1), a second regularization term is added, where ϵ is the hyper-parameter for the attention regularizer; R stands for the regularization term defined in (3) or (4); and α is the distribution of attention weights. Note that during implementation, the attention weights for batch padding positions are excluded from α.

We experiment two different regularizers, one uses standard deviation of α defined in equation (3); the other one uses the negative entropy of α defined in equation (4).

$$R(\alpha) = \sigma(\alpha) \quad (3)$$

$$R(\alpha) = -[-\sum_i^N \alpha_i \cdot log(\alpha_i)] \quad (4)$$

4 Experiments

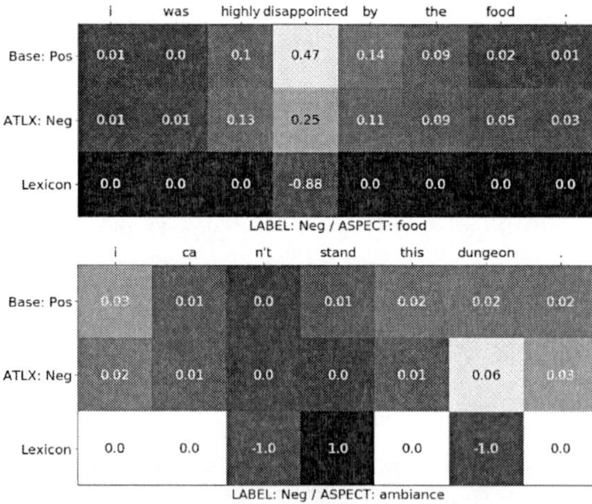

Figure 2: Comparison of attention weights between baseline and ATLX; The rows annotated as "Lexicon" indicates the average polarity per word given by U.

4.1 Dataset

Same as Wang et al. (2016), we experiment on SemEval 2014 Task 4, restaurant domain dataset. The data consists of reviews of restaurants with aspects: {*food, price, service, ambience, miscellaneous*} and associated polarities: {*positive, neutral, negative*}. The objective is to predict the polarity given a sentence and an aspect. There are

	Pos	Neu	Neg	In Corpus
MPQA	2298	440	4148	908
OL	2004	3	4780	732
Opener	2298	440	4147	908
Vader	3333	0	4170	656
Merged U	5129	404	7764	1234

Table 1: Lexicon statistics of positive, neutral, negative words and number of words covered in corpus.

3,518 training examples and 973 test examples in the corpus. To initialize word vectors with pre-trained word embeddings, the 300 dimensional Glove vectors trained on 840b tokens are used, as described in the original paper.

4.2 Lexicons

As shown in Table 1, we merge four existing and online available lexicons into one. The merged lexicon U as described in section 3.2.1 is used for our experiments. After the union, the following postprocess is carried out: {bar, try, too} are removed from U since they are unreasonably annotated as negative by MPQA and Opener; {$n't, not$} are added to U with -1 polarity for negation.

4.3 Evaluation

Cross validation is applied to measure the performance of each model. In all experiments, the training set is randomly shuffled and split into 6 folds with a fixed random seed. According to the code released by Wang et al. (2016), a development set containing 528 examples is used, which is roughly $\frac{1}{6}$ of the training corpus. In order to remain faithful to the original implementation, we thus evaluate our model with a cross validation of 6 folds.

As shown in Table 2, compared to the baseline system, ATLX is not only able to improve in terms of accuracy, but also the variance of the performance across different sets gets significantly reduced. On the other hand, by adding attention regularization to the baseline system without introducing lexical features, both the standard deviation regularizer (base^std) and the negative entropy regularizer (base^ent) are able to contribute positively; where base^ent yields largest improvement. By combining attention regularization and lexical features together, although the model is able to further improve, the difference is too small to draw strong conclusion.

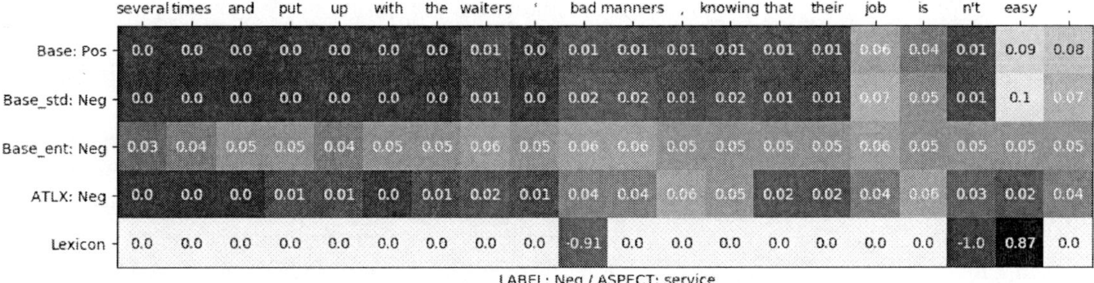

Figure 3: Comparison of attention weights between baseline, base^{std}, base^{ent} and ATLX.

	CV	σ^{CV}	TEST	σ^{TEST}
base	75.27	1.420	81.48	1.157
base^{std}	74.67	1.688	81.57	0.915
base^{ent}	**75.93**	1.467	82.24	0.863
ATLX	75.64	1.275	82.62	**0.498**
ATLX^{std}	75.64	1.275	82.68	0.559
ATLX^{ent}	75.53	**1.265**	**82.86**	1.115
ATLX*	74.99	1.638	82.03	1.409
base^{LX}	71.98	1.588	79.24	2.322

Table 2: Mean accuracy and standard deviation of cross validation results on 6 folds of development sets and one test set. Note that in our replicated baseline system, test accuracy ranges from 80.06 to 83.45; 83.1 was reported in the original paper.

5 Discussion

5.1 ATLX

As described in previously, the overall performance of the baseline gets enhanced by leveraging lexical features independent from the training data, which makes the model more robust and flexible. The example in Figure 2, although the baseline is able to pay relatively high attention to the word *disappointed* and *dungeon*, it is not able to recognize these words as clear indicators of *negative* polarity; while ATLX is able to correctly predict *positive* for both examples. On the other hand, it is worth mentioning that the computation of the attention vector α does not take lexical features V_l into account. Although it is natural to think that adding V_l as input for computing α would be a good option, the results of ATLX* in Table 2 suggest otherwise.

In order to understand where does the improvement of ATLX come from, lexical features or the way we introduce lexical features to the system? We conduct a support experiment to verify its impact (base^{LX}), which consists of naively concate-

nating input word vector with its associated lexical vector and feed the extended embedding to the baseline. As demonstrated in Table 2, by comparing baseline with base^{LX}, we see that the simple merge of lexical features with the network without carefully designed mechanism, the model is not able to leverage new information; and in contrast, the overall performance gets decreased.

5.2 Attention Regularization

As shown in Figure 3, when comparing ATLX with the baseline, we find that although the lexicon only provides non-neutral polarity information for three words, the attention weights of ATLX are less sparse and less spread out than in the baseline. Also, this effect is general as the standard deviation of the attention weights distribution for the test set in ATLX (0.0219) are significantly lower than in the baseline (0.0354).

Thus it makes us think that the attention weights might be over-fitting in some cases as it is purely learned on training examples. This could cause that by giving too much weight to particular words in a sentence, the network ignores other positions which could provide key information for classifying the polarity. For instance, the example in Figure 3 shows that the baseline which predicts *positive* is "focusing" on the final part of the sentence, mostly the word *easy*; while ignoring the *bad manners* coming before, which is key for judging the polarity of the sentence given the aspect *service*. In contrast, the same baseline model trained with attention regularized by standard deviation is able to correctly predict *negative* just by "focusing" a little bit more on the *"bad manners"* part.

However, the hard regularization by standard deviation might not be ideal as the optimal minimum value of the regularizer will imply that all words in the sentence have homogeneous weight,

Parameter name	Value
$\epsilon\ \text{base}^{\text{std}}$	1e-3
$\epsilon\ \text{base}^{\text{ent}}$	0.5
$\epsilon\ \text{ATLX}^{\text{std}}$	1e-4
$\epsilon\ \text{ATLX}^{\text{ent}}$	0.006

Table 3: Attention regularization parameter settings

which is the opposite of what the attention mechanism is able to gain.

Regarding the negative entropy regularizer, taking into account that the attention weights are output of $softmax$ which is normalized to sum up to 1, although the minimum value of this term would also imply homogeneous weight of $\frac{1}{N}$, it is interesting to see that with almost evenly distributed α, the model remains sensitive to few positions with relatively higher weights; e.g. in Figure 3, the same sentence with entropy regularization demonstrates that although most positions are closely weighted, the model is still able to differentiate key positions even with a weight difference of 0.01 and predict correctly.

6 Parameter Settings

In our experiments, apart from newly introduced parameter ϵ for attention regularization, we follow Wang et al. (2016) and their released code.

More specifically, we set batch size as 25; aspect embedding dimension d_a equals to 300, same as Glove vector dimension; number of LSTM cell d as 300; number of LSTM layers as 1; dropout with 0.5 keep probability is applied to h^*; AdaGrad optimizer is used with initial accumulate value equals to 1e-10; learning rate is set to 0.01; L2 regularization parameter λ is set to 0.001; network parameters are initialized from a random uniform distribution with min and max values as -0.01 and 0.01; all network parameters except word embeddings are included in the L2 regularizer. The hyperparmerter ϵ for attention regularization is shown in Table 3.

7 Conclusion and Future Works

In this paper, we describe our approach of directly leveraging numerical polarity features provided by existing lexicon resources in an aspect-based sentiment analysis environment with an attention LSTM neural network. Meanwhile, we stress that the attention mechanism may over-fit on particular positions, blinding the model from other relevant positions. We also explore two regularizers to reduce this overfitting effect. The experimental results demonstrate the effectiveness of our approach.

For future works, since the lexical features can be leveraged directly by the network to boost performance, a fine-grained lexicon which is domain and aspect specific in principle could further improve similar models. On the other hand, although the negative entropy regularizer is able to reduce the overfitting effect, a better attention framework could be researched, so that the attention distribution would be sharp and spare but at the same time, being able to "focus" on more positions.

References

Jiajun Cheng, Hui Wang, Shenglin Zhao, Xin Zhang, Irwin King, and Jiani Zhang. 2017. Aspect-level Sentiment Classification with HEAT (HiErarchical ATtention) Network. In *Proceedings of the 2017 ACM on Conference on Information and Knowledge Management - CIKM '17*, pages 97–106.

Ruidan He, Wee Sun Lee, Hwee Tou Ng, and Daniel Dahlmeier. 2018. Effective Attention Modeling for Aspect-Level Sentiment Classification. In *Proceedings of the 27th International Conference on Computational Linguistics (COLING)*, pages 1121–1131.

Sepp; Hochreiter and J?urgen Schmidhuber. 1997. Long Short Term Memory. *Neural Computation*, 9(8):1735–1780.

Zeyang Lei, Yujiu Yang, and Min Yang. 2018. Sentiment Lexicon Enhanced Attention-Based LSTM for Sentiment Classification. *AAAI-2018-short paper*, pages 8105–8106.

Dehong Ma, Sujian Li, Xiaodong Zhang, and Houfeng Wang. 2017. Interactive attention networks for aspect-level sentiment classification. In *IJCAI International Joint Conference on Artificial Intelligence*, pages 4068–4074.

Vlad Niculae and Mathieu Blondel. 2017. A Regularized Framework for Sparse and Structured Neural Attention. *NIPS*.

Bo Pang, Lillian Lee, and Shivakumar Vaithyanathan. 2002. Thumbs up?: sentiment classification using machine learning techniques. *Empirical Methods in Natural Language Processing (EMNLP)*, 10(July):79–86.

Qiao Qian, Minlie Huang, Jinhao Lei, and Xiaoyan Zhu. 2017. Linguistically Regularized LSTM for Sentiment Classification. In *Proceedings of the 55th Annual Meeting of the Association for Computational Linguistics (Volume 1: Long Papers)*, pages 1679–1689.

Mickael Rouvier and Benoit Favre. 2016. SENSEI-LIF at SemEval-2016 Task 4 : Polarity embedding fusion for robust sentiment analysis. In *Proceedings of the 10th International Workshop on Semantic Evaluation (SemEval-2016)*, pages 207–213.

Bonggun Shin, Timothy Lee, and Jinho D Choi. 2017. Lexicon Integrated CNN Models with Attention for Sentiment Analysis. *ACL*, pages 149–158.

Yi Tay, Luu Anh Tuan, and Siu Cheung Hui. 2017. Dyadic Memory Networks for Aspect-based Sentiment Analysis. In *Proceedings of the 2017 ACM on Conference on Information and Knowledge Management - CIKM '17*, pages 107–116.

Zhiyang Teng, Duy-Tin Vo, and Yue Zhang. 2016. Context-Sensitive Lexicon Features for Neural Sentiment Analysis. *EMNLP*, pages 1629–1638.

Peter D Turney. 2002. Thumbs up or thumbs down? Semantic Orientation applied to Unsupervised Classification of Reviews. *Proceedings of the 40th Annual Meeting of the Association for Computational Linguistics (ACL)*, (July):417–424.

Yequan Wang, Minlie Huang, Li Zhao, and Xiaoyan Zhu. 2016. Attention-based LSTM for Aspect-level Sentiment Classification. *Proceedings of the 2016 Conference on Empirical Methods in Natural Language Processing (EMNLP)*, pages 606–615.

Theresa Wilson, Theresa Wilson, Janyce Wiebe, Janyce Wiebe, Rebecca Hwa, and Rebecca Hwa. 2004. Just how mad are you? Finding strong and weak opinion clauses. *Proceedings of the National Conference on Artificial Intelligence*, pages 761–769.

Ou Wu, Tao Yang, Mengyang Li, and Ming Li. 2018. $$-hot Lexicon Embedding-based Two-level LSTM for Sentiment Analysis.

Jiajun Zhang, Yang Zhao, Haoran Li, and Chengqing Zong. 2019. Attention with sparsity regularization for neural machine translation and summarization. *IEEE/ACM Transactions on Audio Speech and Language Processing*, 27(3):507–518.

Peisong Zhu and Tieyun Qian. 2018. Enhanced Aspect Level Sentiment Classification with Auxiliary Memory. In *COLING*, pages 1077–1087.

Yicheng Zou, Tao Gui, Qi Zhang, and Xuanjing Huang. 2018. A Lexicon-Based Supervised Attention Model for Neural Sentiment Analysis. In *COLING*, pages 868–877.

A Supplemental Material

A.1 Resource Details

Lexical resources: MPQA[1], Opinion Lexicon[2], Opener[3], and Vader[4]. Glove vectors[5]. Code[6] released by Wang et al. (2016). Experiments described in this paper are implemented with TensorFlow[7].

---

[1] http://mpqa.cs.pitt.edu/#subj_lexicon
[2] https://www.cs.uic.edu/liub/FBS/sentiment-analysis.html#lexicon
[3] https://github.com/opener-project/VU-sentiment-lexicon/tree/master/VUSentimentLexicon/EN-lexicon
[4] https://github.com/cjhutto/vaderSentiment
[5] https://nlp.stanford.edu/projects/glove/
[6] https://www.wangyequan.com/publications/
[7] https://www.tensorflow.org/

Controllable Text Simplification with Lexical Constraint Loss

Daiki Nishihara[†], Tomoyuki Kajiwara[‡], Yuki Arase[†*]
[†]Graduate School of Information Science and Technology, Osaka University
[‡]Institute for Datability Science, Osaka University
[*]Artificial Intelligence Research Center (AIRC), AIST
[†]{nishihara.daiki, arase}@ist.osaka-u.ac.jp
[‡]kajiwara@ids.osaka-u.ac.jp

Abstract

We propose a method to control the level of a sentence in a text simplification task. Text simplification is a monolingual translation task translating a complex sentence into a simpler and easier to understand the alternative. In this study, we use the grade level of the US education system as the level of the sentence. Our text simplification method succeeds in translating an input into a specific grade level by considering levels of both sentences and words. Sentence level is considered by adding the target grade level as input. By contrast, the word level is considered by adding weights to the training loss based on words that frequently appear in sentences of the desired grade level. Although existing models that consider only the sentence level may control the syntactic complexity, they tend to generate words beyond the target level. Our approach can control both the lexical and syntactic complexity and achieve an aggressive rewriting. Experiment results indicate that the proposed method improves the metrics of both BLEU and SARI.

1 Introduction

Text simplification (Shardlow, 2014) is the task of rewriting a complex text into a simpler form while preserving its meaning. Its applications include reading comprehension assistance and language education support. Because each target user has different reading abilities and/or knowledge, we need a text simplification system that translates an input sentence into a sentence of an appropriate difficulty level for each user. According to the input hypothesis (Krashen, 1985), educational materials slightly beyond the learner's level effectively improve their reading abilities. On the contrary, materials that are too difficult for learners deteriorate their learning motivation. In the context of language education, teachers manually simplify

Grade	Examples
12	According to the Pentagon , 152 female troops have been killed while serving in Iraq and Afghanistan .
7	The **Pentagon** says 152 female troops have been killed while serving in Iraq and Afghanistan .
5	The **military** says 152 female have died .

Table 1: Example sentences with different grade levels. To control the sentence level, syntactic (underline) and/or lexical (bold) paraphrasing is performed.

sentences for each learner. To reduce the burden on teachers, automatic text simplification systems are desired (Petersen and Ostendorf, 2007).

As mentioned, text simplification translates a complex sentence into a simpler alternative. The transformation allows entailment and omission/replacement of phrases and words. Table 1 shows sentences in different grade levels. Sentence level depends on both the syntactic and lexical complexities. When simplifying a sentence of grade level 12 into grade level 7[1], paraphrasing "According to ∼ ," to "∼ says" reduces the syntactic complexity. In addition, when simplifying the sentence from the grade levels 12 to 5, paraphrasing "Pentagon" to "military" reduces the lexical complexity. Assuming an application to language education, we aim at automatically rewriting the input sentence to accommodate the level of difficulty appropriate for each grade level, as shown in Table 1.

Many previous studies (Specia, 2010; Wubben et al., 2012; Xu et al., 2016; Nisioi et al., 2017; Zhang and Lapata, 2017; Vu et al., 2018;

---

[1]In this study, we use grades K-12.

260

Proceedings of the ACL 2019, Student Research Workshop, pages 260–266
Florence, Italy, July 28th-August 2nd, 2019. ©2019 Association for Computational Linguistics

Guo et al., 2018; Zhao et al., 2018) in text simplification have trained machine translators on a monolingual parallel corpus consisting of complex-simple sentence pairs without considering the level of each sentence. Therefore, these text simplification models are ignorant regarding the sentence level. Scarton and Specia (2018) developed a pioneering text simplification model that can control the sentence level. They trained a text simplification model on a parallel corpus by attaching tags specifying 11 grade levels to each sentence (Xu et al., 2015). The trained model allows the generation of a sentence of a desired level specified by a tag attached to the input. This model may control the syntactic complexity such as the sentence length; however, it often outputs overly difficult words beyond the target grade level. To control the lexical complexity in text simplification, we propose a method for add weights to a training loss according to levels of words on top of (Scarton and Specia, 2018), and thus output only words under the desired level.

Experiment results indicate that the proposed method improves the BLEU and SARI scores by 1.04 and 0.15 compared to Scarton and Specia (2018). Moreover, our detailed analysis indicates that our method controls both the lexical and syntactic complexities and promotes an aggressive rewriting.

2 Related Work

2.1 Text Simplification

Text simplification can be regarded as a monolingual machine translation problem. Previous studies have trained a model to translate complex sentences into simpler sentences on parallel corpora between Wikipedia and Simple Wikipedia (W-SW) (Zhu et al., 2010; Coster and Kauchak, 2011). As in the field of machine translation, early studies (Specia, 2010; Wubben et al., 2012; Xu et al., 2016) were mainly based on a statistical machine translation (Koehn et al., 2007; Post et al., 2013). Inspired by the success of neural machine translation (Bahdanau et al., 2015), recent studies (Nisioi et al., 2017; Zhang and Lapata, 2017; Vu et al., 2018; Guo et al., 2018; Zhao et al., 2018) use the encoder-decoder model with the attention mechanism. These studies do not consider the level of each sentence.

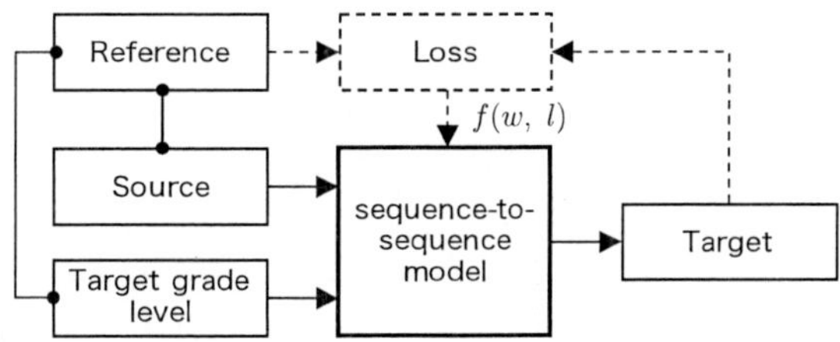

Figure 1: Our method adds a weight to the training loss based on levels of words w and target level l..

2.2 Controllable Text Simplification

In addition to W-SW, Newsela (Xu et al., 2015) is a famous dataset available for text simplification. Newsela is a parallel corpus with 11 grade levels. Scarton and Specia (2018) trained a level-controllable text simplification model on Newsela. Although their model is a standard attentional encoder-decoder model similar to (Nisioi et al., 2017), a special token <grade> indicating the grade level of the target sentence is attached to the beginning of the input sentence. This is a promising approach that has been successful in similar tasks (Johnson et al., 2017; Niu et al., 2018). As expected regarding the task of text simplification, this approach has improved both BLEU (Papineni et al., 2002) and SARI (Xu et al., 2016) compared to a baseline model (Nisioi et al., 2017) that does not consider the target level at all. This model allows the syntactic complexity to be controlled; however, it tends to output overly difficult words beyond the target grade level.

3 Loss Function with Word Level

To control the lexical complexity, our model weighs a training loss of a text simplification model considering words that frequently appear in the sentences of a specific grade level, as shown in Figure 1. Here, the weight $f(w, l)$ corresponds to the relevance of the word w at grade level l.

A sequence-to-sequence model commonly uses the cross-entropy loss. When a model outputs $o = [o_1, \cdots, o_N]$ (where N is the size of the vocabulary) at a certain time step, the cross-entropy loss is as follows:

$$L(o, y) = -y \log o^\top = -\log o_c \qquad (1)$$

where $y = [y_1, \cdots, y_N]$ is a one-hot vector in which only the c-th element of a correct word is 1 and others are all 0. Our model adds weights to the loss function (Equation 1) based on the level of words such that the model learns to output words of the desired level:

$$L'(\boldsymbol{o}, \boldsymbol{y}, w, l) = -f(w, l) \cdot \log o_c. \quad (2)$$

As $f(\cdot, \cdot)$, we use TFIDF or PPMI assuming that words frequently appear in sentences of level l also have the same level l.

TFIDF We compute the TFIDF regarding sentences of the same level as a document:

$$\text{TFIDF}(w, l) = P(w \mid l) \cdot \log \frac{D}{\text{DF}(w)} \quad (3)$$

where $P(w \mid l)$ is a probability that word w appears in a set of sentences of grade level l, D is the number of grade levels[2], and $\text{DF}(w)$ is the number of grade levels in which w appears. By so doing, TFIDF provides more weights to words that uniquely appear in the sentences of a specific level.

PPMI Pointwise mutual information (PMI) allows estimating the strength of a co-occurrence between w and l:

$$\text{PMI}(w, l) = \log \frac{P(w \mid l)}{P(w)}. \quad (4)$$

where $P(w)$ is a probability of word w being within the entire training corpus, whereas $P(w \mid l)$ is the same as Equation 3. Words with negative PMI scores have a negative correlation against l that means w tends to appear across different sentence levels. Hence, we ignore w with a negative PMI using a positive-PMI (PPMI) function:

$$\text{PPMI}(w, l) = \max(\text{PMI}(w, l), 0). \quad (5)$$

Both TFIDF and PPMI have a range of $[0, \infty)$, and thus we apply the Laplace smoothing:

$$f(w, l) = \text{Func}(w, l) + 1 \quad (6)$$
$$\text{Func} \in \{\text{PPMI, TFIDF}\} \quad (7)$$

4 Experiment

4.1 Dataset

We evaluated whether our method can control the grade levels in a text simplification using the Newsela corpus. The Newsela corpus provides

Grade	#Sentences	#Words	S-length
2	953	9,882	10.37
3	3,865	47,211	12.22
4	43,971	618,184	14.06
5	31,918	526,769	16.50
6	19,535	367,319	18.80
7	17,322	356,307	20.57
8	15,446	376,678	24.39
9	7,897	200,242	25.36
10	1,018	30,693	30.15
11	104	2,844	27.35
12	50,799	1,484,625	29.23
All	192,828	4,020,754	20.85

Table 2: Statistics for the Newsela corpus, where S-length shows the average number of words in a sentence.

news articles of different levels, which have been manually rewritten by human experts. It conforms to the grade levels in the US education system, where the levels range from 2 to 12.

We use the publicly available version of the Newsela corpus[3] that has been sentence-aligned by Xu et al. (2015) and divided into 94k, 1k, and 1k sentences for the training, development, and test, respectively, by Zhang and Lapata (2017). As in previous studies, we regard each sentence in an article as sharing the same level as the entire article. Zhang and Lapata (2017) first divided the set of articles and then extracted sentence pairs to avoid the same sentences appearing in both the training and test sets. Note that the Newsela corpus used in (Scarton and Specia, 2018) is different from the present corpus, and is preprocessed differently. Due to these differences, the training, development, and test sets used in (Scarton and Specia, 2018) are unreproducible. Therefore, we reimplemented (Scarton and Specia, 2018) and compared it to our method using our public corpus.

Table 2 shows statistics for the Newsela corpus, which clearly present the tendency that lower grade sentences are significantly shorter than those of higher grades. This indicates that aggressive omission of phrases is required to simplify sentences of grade 8 to 12 into those of grade 2 to 7.

---

[2]Here, $D = 11$ because we use grade levels 2 to 12.

[3]https://newsela.com/data/

	BLEU ↑	SARI ↑	BLEU$_{ST}$ ↓	MAE$_{LEN}$ ↓	MPMI ↑
source	21.37	2.82	100.0	10.73	0.08
reference	100.0	70.13	18.30	0.00	0.23
s2s	20.43	28.21	37.60	4.38	0.12
s2s+grade	20.82	29.44	31.96	3.77	0.15
s2s+grade+TFIDF	21.00	29.58	31.56	3.75	0.15
s2s+grade+PPMI	**21.86**	**29.59**	**31.38**	**3.69**	**0.19**

Table 3: Results on the Newsela test set.

4.2 Methods for Comparison

During this experiment, the following four methods were compared.

1. **s2s** is a baseline, plain sequence-to-sequence model based on the attention mechanism.

2. **s2s+grade** is our re-implementation of Scarton and Specia (2018), which is a state-of-the-art controllable text simplification.

3. **s2s+grade+TFIDF** is our model (Sec. 3) implemented on s2s+grade, which adds TFIDF-based word weighing to the loss function. TFIDF scores were pre-computed using the training data.

4. **s2s+grade+PPMI** is our other model (Sec. 3) implemented on s2s+grade, which adds PPMI-based word weighing in the loss function. PPMI scores were pre-computed using the training data.

4.3 Implementation Details

In this study, we implemented our model using Marian (Junczys-Dowmunt et al., 2018).[4] Both the encoder and decoder consist of 2 layers of Bi-LSTM with the $1,024$-dimensions of hidden layers and 512-dimensions of the embedding layer shared by the encoder and decoder including its output layer. Word embedding was randomly initialized. A dropout rate of 0.2 was applied to the hidden layer, and a dropout rate of 0.1 was applied to the embedding layer. Adam was used as an optimizer. Training was stopped when the perplexity measured on the development set stopped improving for 8 epochs.[5] All scores reported in this experiment are the averages of 3 trials with random initialization.

4.4 Automatic Evaluation Metrics

Following previous studies on text simplification, *e.g.*, Scarton and Specia (2018), BLEU[6] (Papineni et al., 2002) and SARI[7] (Xu et al., 2016) were used to evaluate the overall performance.

In addition, we investigate the scores of BLEU$_{ST}$, mean absolute error (MAE) of sentence length (MAE$_{LEN}$), and mean PMI (MPMI) for a detailed analysis. BLEU$_{ST}$ computes a BLEU score by taking the source and output sentences as input, which allows evaluating the degree of rewrites made by a model. The lower BLEU$_{ST}$ is, the more actively the model rewrites the source sentence.

In addition, MAE$_{LEN}$ approximately evaluates the syntactic complexity of the output based on its length:

$$\mathrm{MAE}_{\mathrm{Len}} = \frac{1}{N} \sum_{\substack{s_R \in \mathrm{Reference} \\ s_T \in \mathrm{Target}}} |\mathrm{Len}(s_R) - \mathrm{Len}(s_T)|, \tag{8}$$

where N is the number of sentences in the test set, and $\mathrm{Len}(\cdot)$ provides the number of words in a sentence. The lower the MAE$_{LEN}$ is, the more appropriate the length of the output.

MPMI evaluates to what extent the levels of the output words match with the target level:

$$\mathrm{MPMI} = \frac{1}{W} \sum_{s \in \mathrm{Target}} \sum_{w \in s} \mathrm{PMI}(w, l_s), \tag{9}$$

where W is the number of words appearing in the output and l_s is the grade level of sentence s. PMI scores were pre-computed using the training data. The higher the MPMI is, the more words of the target level are generated by the model.

---

[4]https://github.com/marian-nmt/marian/commit/02f4af4

[5]48.7 epochs on average to train s2s+grade+PPMI.

[6]We use the multi-bleu-detok.perl script from https://github.com/moses-smt/mosesdecoder

[7]https://github.com/cocoxu/simplification

Grade	Examples
Source 12	In its original **incarnation** during the ' 60s , African-American " freedom songs " aimed to **motivate** protesters to march into harm 's way and , on a broader scale , spread news of the struggle to a mainstream audience .
7	**s2s+grade:** In the 1960s , African-American " freedom songs are aimed to motivate protesters to march into harm 's way . **s2s+grade+PPMI:** In its original **people** in the 1960s , African-American " freedom songs are aimed to **inspire** protesters to march into harm 's way .
4	**s2s+grade:** In the 1960s , African-American " freedom songs are aimed to motivate protesters to march into harm 's way . **s2s+grade+PPMI:** African-American " freedom songs are aimed to **inspire** protesters to march into harm 's way .

Table 4: Example of model outputs. Here, s2s+grade+PPMI successfully simplified some complex words (highlighted in bold) and deleted the underlined phrases.

5 Results and Analysis

5.1 Overall Results

Table 3 shows the experiment results. The first two rows show the performances when the source sentence itself or the reference sentence is regarded as the model output, which sets the standard to interpret the scores.

Our method outperforms the state-of-the-art baseline in both the BLEU and SARI metrics. In particular, s2s+grade+PPMI improved the BLEU and SARI scores by 1.04 and 0.15 compared to s2s+grade, respectively.

An evaluation in BLEU_{ST} shows that our proposed models conduct an aggressive rewriting. In addition, s2s+grade+PPMI, which has the highest performance in both the BLEU and BLEU_{ST} metrics, conducts many appropriate rewrites that are far from the source and close to the reference. The s2s baseline, which does not consider the target level, applies conservative rewriting, whereas the proposed model, which considers it more properly conducts more aggressive rewriting.

The evaluations of MAE_{LEN} and MPMI show that s2s+grade+PPMI can best the control both syntactic and lexical complexities. From these results, we confirmed the effectiveness of the text simplification model that takes the word level into account.

Table 4 shows examples of the model outputs. Here, s2s+grade+PPMI paraphrases a complex word "incarnation" into "people" for grade level 7. In addition, the complex word "motivate" is simplified to "inspire" for grade level 4. Although

Grade	FKGL			MPMI	
	prev.	prop.	diff.	prev.	prop.
<8>	4.92	**5.33**	+0.41	0.11	**0.12**
<7>	4.87	**5.25**	+0.38	0.10	**0.12**
<6>	4.47	**4.56**	+0.09	0.12	**0.14**
<5>	3.51	**3.71**	+0.20	0.13	**0.15**
<4>	2.68	**2.69**	+0.01	0.16	**0.19**
<3>	**2.06**	1.89	−0.17	0.18	**0.23**
<2>	**1.81**	1.44	−0.37	0.20	**0.24**
MAE	1.52	**1.45**	—	—	—

Table 5: FKGL and MPMI of s2s+grade (prev.) and s2s+grade+PPMI (prop.) for each grade level. Models suitable for the target level are highlighted in bold.

both models can remove unimportant phrases "and , on ~", s2s+grade+PPMI successfully summarized shorter sentences for grade level 4.

5.2 Analysis for Each Grade Level

To analyze the level control in detail, we simplified each source sentence in the test set to all simpler grade levels[8]. This analysis does not allow an evaluation based on references such as BLEU because references are only given for some levels for each source sentence.

Table 5 shows FKGL (Kincaid et al., 1975) and MPMI for each target grade level for s2s+grade (prev.) and s2s+grade+PPMI (prop.). FKGL is

---

[8]We omitted grade levels <9>-<12> because the sentences with these grade levels do not exist in the reference sentences of the training set.

an automatic evaluation metric that estimates the textual readability. The FKGL scores correspond to grade levels of K-12.

An analysis of the FKGL revealed that both models were oversimplified. However, MAE with the target grade level shows that the proposed model is superior to the baseline model. Focusing on the FKGL differences, the proposed model generates simpler sentences for the simpler target grade levels than the baseline model, and vice versa. These results show that incorporating word levels into the model contributes to a level control in text simplification.

In the evaluation of MPMI, the proposed method consistently outperforms the state-of-the-art baseline at all target levels. As expected, we confirmed that the proposed method for weighting the cross-entropy losses based on PPMI encourages the use of words suitable for the target grade level.

6 Conclusion

We proposed a text simplification method that controls not only the sentence level but also the word level. Our method controls the word level by weighing words in the loss function, which frequently appear in text of a specific grade level. The evaluation results confirmed that our method improved both the BLEU and SARI scores, and achieved an aggressive rewriting compared to Scarton and Specia (2018). A detailed analysis indicated that our method achieved an accurate control of the level in converting the sentences into those of the target level.

In this study, we regard a document and the sentences contained within it to have the same grade level as in previous studies. In practice, however, this assumption may not hold. Although the readability and level in the units of document (Kincaid et al., 1975) and phrase (Pavlick and Callison-Burch, 2016; Maddela and Xu, 2018) have been studied, there have been no previous works focusing on the level of the sentences. This direction is an area of our future work.

Acknowledgments

This project is funded by Microsoft Research Asia, Microsoft Japan Co., Ltd., JST ACT-I Grant Number JPMJPR18UB, and JSPS KAKENHI Grant Number JP18K11435.

References

Dzmitry Bahdanau, KyungHyun Cho, and Yoshua Bengio. 2015. Neural Machine Translation by Jointly Learning to Align and Translate. In *Proceedings of International Conference on Learning Representations*.

William Coster and David Kauchak. 2011. Simple English Wikipedia: A New Text Simplification Task. In *Proceedings of the 49th Annual Meeting of the Association for Computational Linguistics*, pages 665–669.

Han Guo, Ramakanth Pasunuru, and Mohit Bansal. 2018. Dynamic Multi-Level Multi-Task Learning for Sentence Simplification. In *Proceedings of the 27th International Conference on Computational Linguistics*, pages 462–476.

Melvin Johnson, Mike Schuster, Quoc V Le, Maxim Krikun, Yonghui Wu, Zhifeng Chen, Nikhil Thorat, Fernanda Viégas, Martin Wattenberg, Greg Corrado, Macduff Hughes, and Jeffrey Dean. 2017. Google's Multilingual Neural Machine Translation System: Enabling Zero-Shot Translation. *Transactions of the Association for Computational Linguistics*, 5:339–351.

Marcin Junczys-Dowmunt, Roman Grundkiewicz, Tomasz Dwojak, Hieu Hoang, Kenneth Heafield, Tom Neckermann, Frank Seide, Ulrich Germann, Alham Fikri Aji, Nikolay Bogoychev, André F. T. Martins, and Alexandra Birch. 2018. Marian: Fast Neural Machine Translation in C++. In *Proceedings of the 56th Annual Meeting ofthe Association for Computational Linguistics, System Demonstrations*, pages 116–121.

J. Peter Kincaid, Robert P. Fishburne Jr., Richard L. Rogers, and Brad S. Chissom. 1975. Derivation of New Readability Formulas (Automated Readability Index, Fog Count and Flesch Reading Ease Formula) for Navy Enlisted Personnel. Technical report.

Philipp Koehn, Hieu Hoang, Alexandra Birch, Chris Callison-Burch, Marcello Federico, Nicola Bertoldi, Brooke Cowan, Wade Shen, Christine Moran, Richard Zens, Chris Dyer, Ondej Bojar, Alexandra Constantin, and Evan Herbst. 2007. Moses: Open Source Toolkit for Statistical Machine Translation. In *Proceedings of the 45th Annual Meeting of the Association for Computational Linguistics, Demo and Poster session*, pages 177–180.

S. D. Krashen. 1985. The Input Hypothesis: Issues and implications. *London: Longman*.

Mounica Maddela and Wei Xu. 2018. A Word-Complexity Lexicon and A Neural Readability Ranking Model for Lexical Simplification. In *Proceedings of the 2018 Conference on Empirical Methods in Natural Language Processing*, pages 3749–3760.

Sergiu Nisioi, Sanja Štajner, Simone Paolo Ponzetto, and Liviu P. Dinu. 2017. Exploring Neural Text Simplification Models. In *Proceedings of the 55th Annual Meeting of the Association for Computational Linguistics*, pages 85–91.

Xing Niu, Sudha Rao, and Marine Carpuat. 2018. Multi-Task Neural Models for Translating Between Styles Within and Across Languages. In *Proceedings of the 27th International Conference on Computational Linguistics*, pages 1008–1021.

Kishore Papineni, Salim Roukos, Todd Ward, and Wei-Jing Zhu. 2002. BLEU: a Method for Automatic Evaluation of Machine Translation. In *Proceedings of the 40th Annual Meeting of the Association for Computational Linguistics*, pages 311–318.

Ellie Pavlick and Chris Callison-Burch. 2016. Simple PPDB: A Paraphrase Database for Simplification. In *Proceedings of the 54th Annual Meeting of the Association for Computational Linguistics*, pages 143–148.

Sarah E Petersen and Mari Ostendorf. 2007. Text Simplification for Language Learners: A Corpus Analysis. In *Proceedings of Workshop on Speech and Language Technology in Education*, pages 69–72.

Matt Post, Juri Ganitkevitch, Luke Orland, Jonathan Weese, Cao Yuan, and Chris Callison-Burch. 2013. Joshua 5.0: Sparser, better, faster, server. In *Proceedings of the 8th Workshop on Statistical Machine Translation*, pages 206–212.

Carolina Scarton and Lucia Specia. 2018. Learning Simplifications for Specific Target Audiences. In *Proceedings of the 56th Annual Meeting of the Association for Computational Linguistics*, pages 712–718.

Matthew Shardlow. 2014. A Survey of Automated Text Simplification. *International Journal of Advanced Computer Science and Applications, Special Issue on Natural Language Processing 2014*, pages 58–70.

Lucia Specia. 2010. Translating from Complex to Simplified Sentences. In *Proceedings of the 9th International Conference on Computational Processing of the Portuguese Language*, pages 30–39.

Tu Vu, Baotian Hu, Tsendsuren Munkhdalai, and Hong Yu. 2018. Sentence Simplification with Memory-Augmented Neural Networks. In *Proceedings of the 2018 Conference of the North American Chapter of the Association for Computational Linguistics: Human Language Technologies*, pages 79–85.

Sander Wubben, Antal van den Bosch, and Emiel Krahmer. 2012. Sentence Simplification by Monolingual Machine Translation. In *Proceedings of the 50th Annual Meeting of the Association for Computational Linguistics*, pages 1015–1024.

Wei Xu, Chris Callison-Burch, and Courtney Napoles. 2015. Problems in Current Text Simplification Research: New Data Can Help. *Transactions of the Association for Computational Linguistics*, 3:283–297.

Wei Xu, Courtney Napoles, Ellie Pavlick, Quanze Chen, and Chris Callison-Burch. 2016. Optimizing Statistical Machine Translation for Text Simplification. *Transactions of the Association for Computational Linguistics*, 4:401–415.

Xingxing Zhang and Mirella Lapata. 2017. Sentence Simplification with Deep Reinforcement Learning. In *Proceedings of the 2017 Conference on Empirical Methods in Natural Language Processing*, pages 584–594.

Sanqiang Zhao, Rui Meng, Daqing He, Saptono Andi, and Parmanto Bambang. 2018. Integrating Transformer and Paraphrase Rules for Sentence Simplification. In *Proceedings of the 2018 Conference on Empirical Methods in Natural Language Processing*, pages 3164–3173.

Zhemin Zhu, Delphine Bernhard, and Iryna Gurevych. 2010. A Monolingual Tree-based Translation Model for Sentence Simplification. In *Proceedings of the 23rd International Conference on Computational Linguistics*, pages 1353–1361.

Normalizing Non-canonical Turkish Texts
Using Machine Translation Approaches

Talha Çolakoğlu
Istanbul Technical University
Istanbul, Turkey
colakoglut@itu.edu.tr

Umut Sulubacak
University of Helsinki
Helsinki, Finland
umut.sulubacak@helsinki.fi

A. Cüneyd Tantuğ
Istanbul Technical University
Istanbul, Turkey
tantug@itu.edu.tr

Abstract

With the growth of the social web, user-generated text data has reached unprecedented sizes. Non-canonical text normalization provides a way to exploit this as a practical source of training data for language processing systems. The state of the art in Turkish text normalization is composed of a token-level pipeline of modules, heavily dependent on external linguistic resources and manually-defined rules. Instead, we propose a fully-automated, context-aware machine translation approach with fewer stages of processing. Experiments with various implementations of our approach show that we are able to surpass the current best-performing system by a large margin.

1 Introduction

Supervised machine learning methods such as CRFs, SVMs, and neural networks have come to define standard solutions for a wide variety of language processing tasks. These methods are typically data-driven, and require training on a substantial amount of data to reach their potential. This kind of data often has to be manually annotated, which constitutes a bottleneck in development. This is especially marked in some tasks, where quality or structural requirements for the data are more constraining. Among the examples are text normalization and machine translation (MT), as both tasks require parallel data with limited natural availability.

The success achieved by data-driven learning methods brought about an interest in user-generated data. Collaborative online platforms such as social media are a great source of large amounts of text data. However, these texts typically contain non-canonical usages, making them hard to leverage for systems sensitive to training data bias. Non-canonical text normalization is the task of processing such texts into a canonical format. As such, normalizing user-generated data has the capability of producing large amounts of serviceable data for training data-driven systems.

As a denoising task, text normalization can be regarded as a translation problem between closely related languages. Statistical machine translation (SMT) methods dominated the field of MT for a while, until neural machine translation (NMT) became more popular. The modular composition of an SMT system makes it less susceptible to data scarcity, and allows it to better exploit unaligned data. In contrast, NMT is more data-hungry, with a superior capacity for learning from data, but often faring worse when data is scarce. Both translation methods are very powerful in generalization.

In this study, we investigate the potential of using MT methods to normalize non-canonical texts in Turkish, a morphologically-rich, agglutinative language, allowing for a very large number of common word forms. Following in the footsteps of unsupervised MT approaches, we automatically generate synthetic parallel data from unaligned sources of *"monolingual"* canonical and non-canonical texts. Afterwards, we use these datasets to train character-based translation systems to normalize non-canonical texts[1]. We describe our methodology in contrast with the state of the art in Section 3, outline our data and empirical results in Sections 4 and 5, and finally present our conclusions in Section 6.

2 Related Work

Non-canonical text normalization has been relatively slow to catch up with purely data-driven

---

[1] We have released the source code of the project at
https://github.com/talha252/tur-text-norm

Proceedings of the ACL 2019, Student Research Workshop, pages 267–272
Florence, Italy, July 28th-August 2nd, 2019. ©2019 Association for Computational Linguistics

learning methods, which have defined the state of the art in many language processing tasks. In the case of Turkish, the conventional solutions to many normalization problems involve rule-based methods and morphological processing via manually-constructed automata. The best-performing system (Eryiğit and Torunoğlu-Selamet, 2017) uses a cascaded approach with several consecutive steps, mixing rule-based processes and supervised machine learning, as first introduced in Torunoğlu and Eryiğit (2014). The only work since then, to the best of our knowledge, is a recent study (Göker and Can, 2018) reviewing neural methods in Turkish non-canonical text normalization. However, the reported systems still underperformed against the state of the art. To normalize noisy Uyghur text, Tursun and Cakici (2017) uses a noisy channel model and a neural encoder-decoder architecture which is similar to our NMT model. While our approaches are similar, they utilize a naive artificial data generation method which is a simple stochastic replacement rule of characters. In Matthews (2007), character-based SMT was originally used for transliteration, but later proposed as a possibly viable method for normalization. Since then, a number of studies have used character-based SMT for texts with high similarity, such as in translating between closely related languages (Nakov and Tiedemann, 2012; Pettersson et al., 2013), and non-canonical text normalization (Li and Liu, 2012; Ikeda et al., 2016). This study is the first to investigate the performance of character-based SMT in normalizing non-canonical Turkish texts.

3 Methodology

Our guiding principle is to establish a simple MT recipe that is capable of fully covering the conventional scope of normalizing Turkish. To promote a better understanding of this scope, we first briefly present the modules of the cascaded approach that has defined the state of the art (Eryiğit and Torunoğlu-Selamet, 2017). Afterwards, we introduce our translation approach that allows implementation as a lightweight and robust data-driven system.

3.1 Cascaded approach

The cascaded approach was first introduced by Torunoğlu and Eryiğit (2014), dividing the task into seven consecutive modules. Every token is processed by these modules sequentially (hence *cascaded*) as long as it still needs further normalization. A transducer-based morphological analyzer (Eryiğit, 2014) is used to generate morphological analyses for the tokens as they are being processed. A token for which a morphological analysis can be generated is considered fully normalized. We explain the modules of the cascaded approach below, and provide relevant examples.

Letter case transformation. Checks for valid non-lowercase tokens (*e.g.* "ACL", "Jane", "iOS"), and converts everything else to lowercase.

Replacement rules / Lexicon lookup. Replaces non-standard characters (*e.g.* 'ß'→'b'), expands shorthand (*e.g.* "slm"→"selam"), and simplifies repetition (*e.g.* "yaaaaa"→"ya").

Proper noun detection. Detects proper nouns by comparing unigram occurrence ratios of proper and common nouns, and truecases detected proper nouns (*e.g.* "umut"→"Umut").

Diacritic restoration. Restores missing diacritics (*e.g.* "yogurt"→"yoğurt").

Vowel restoration. Restores omitted vowels between adjacent consonants (*e.g.* "olck"→"olacak").

Accent normalization. Converts contracted, stylized, or phonetically transcribed suffixes to their canonical written forms (*e.g.* "yapcem"→"yapacağım")

Spelling correction. Corrects any remaining typing and spelling mistakes that are not covered by the previous modules.

While the cascaded approach demonstrates good performance, there are certain drawbacks associated with it. The risk of error propagation down the cascade is limited only by the accuracy of the ill-formed word detection phase. The modules themselves have dependencies to external linguistic resources, and some of them require rigorous manual definition of rules. As a result, implementations of the approach are prone to human error, and have a limited ability to generalize to different domains. Furthermore, the cascade only works on the token level, disregarding larger context.

3.2 Translation approach

In contrast to the cascaded approach, our translation approach can appropriately consider sentence-level context, as machine translation is a

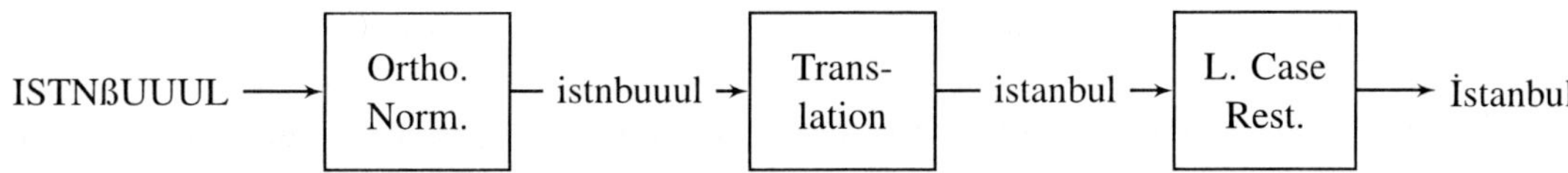

Figure 1: A flow diagram of the pipeline of components in our translation approach, showing the intermediate stages of a token from non-canonical input to normalized output.

sequence-to-sequence transformation. Though not as fragmented or conceptually organized as in the cascaded approach, our translation approach involves a pipeline of its own. First, we apply an orthographic normalization procedure on the input data, which also converts all characters to lowercase. Afterwards, we run the data through the translation model, and then use a recaser to restore letter cases. We illustrate the pipeline formed by these components in Figure 1, and explain each component below.

Orthographic normalization. Sometimes users prefer to use non-Turkish characters resembling Turkish ones, such as $\mu \rightarrow u$. In order to reduce the vocabulary size, this component performs lowercase conversion as well as automatic normalization of certain non-Turkish characters, similarly to the replacement rules module in the cascaded approach.

Translation. This component performs a lowercase normalization on the pre-processed data using a translation system (see Section 5 for the translation models we propose). The translation component is rather abstract, and its performance depends entirely on the translation system used.

Letter case restoration. As emphasized earlier, our approach leaves truecasing to the letter case restoration component that processes the translation output. This component could be optional in case normalization is only a single step in a downstream pipeline that processes lowercased data.

4 Datasets

As mentioned earlier, our translation approach is highly data-driven. Training translation and language models for machine translation, and performing an adequate performance evaluation comparable to previous works each require datasets of different qualities. We describe all datasets that we use in this study in the following subsections.

4.1 Training data

OpenSubs$_{Filtered}$ As a freely available large text corpus, we extract all Turkish data from the OpenSubtitles2018[2] (Lison and Tiedemann, 2016) collection of the OPUS repository (Tiedemann, 2012). Since OpenSubtitles data is rather noisy (e.g. typos and colloquial language), and our idea is to use it as a collection of well-formed data, we first filter it offline through the morphological analyzer described in Oflazer (1994). We only keep subtitles with a valid morphological analysis for each of their tokens, leaving a total of $\sim$105M sentences, or $\sim$535M tokens.

Train$_{ParaTok}$ In order to test our translation approach, we automatically generate a parallel corpus to be used as training sets for our translation models. To obtain a realistic parallel corpus, we opt for mapping real noisy words to their clean counterparts rather than noising clean words by probabilistically adding, deleting and changing characters. For that purpose, we develop a custom weighted edit distance algorithm which has a couple of new operations. Additional to usual insertion, deletion and substitution operations, we have defined duplication and constrained-insertion operations. Duplication operation is used to handle multiple repeating characters which are intentionally used to stress a word, such as *geliyooooooorum*. Also, to model keyboard errors, we have defined a constrained-insertion operation that allows to assign different weights of a character insertion with different adjacent characters.

To build a parallel corpus of clean and illformed words, firstly we scrape a set of $\sim$25M Turkish tweets which constitutes our noisy words source. The tweets in this set are tokenized, and non-word tokens like hashtags and URLs are eliminated, resulting $\sim$5M unique words. The words in OpenSubs$_{Filtered}$ are used as clean words source. To obtain an ill-formed word candidate list for each clean word, the clean words are matched with the noisy words by using our custom weighted edit

---

[2] http://www.opensubtitles.org/

Datasets	# Tokens	# Non-canonical tokens
Test_{IWT}	38,917	5,639 (14.5%)
Test_{2019}	7,948	2,856 (35.9%)
Test_{Small}	6,507	1,171 (17.9%)

Table 1: Sizes of each test datasets

distance algorithm, Since the lists do not always contain relevant ill-formed words, it would've been mistake to use the list directly to create word pairs. To overcome this, we perform tournament selection on candidate lists based on word similarity scores.

Finally, we construct $\text{Train}_{ParaTok}$ from the resulting $\sim$5.7M clean-noisy word pairs, as well as some artificial transformations modeling tokenization errors (*e.g.* "birşey"→"bir şey").

Huawei$_{MonoTR}$　　As a supplementary collection of canonical texts, we use the large Turkish text corpus from Yildiz et al. (2016). This resource contains $\sim$54M sentences, or $\sim$968M tokens, scraped from a diverse set of sources, such as e-books, and online platforms with curated content, such as news stories and movie reviews. We use this dataset for language modeling.

4.2　Test and development data

Test$_{IWT}$　　Described in Pamay et al. (2015), the ITU Web Treebank contains 4,842 manually normalized and tagged sentences, or 38,917 tokens. For comparability with Eryiğit and Torunoğlu-Selamet (2017), we use the raw text from this corpus as a test set.

Test$_{Small}$　　We report results of our evaluation on this test set of 509 sentences, or 6,507 tokens, introduced in Torunoğlu and Eryiğit (2014) and later used as a test set in more recent studies (Eryiğit and Torunoğlu-Selamet, 2017; Göker and Can, 2018).

Test$_{2019}$　　This is a test set of a small number of samples taken from Twitter, containing 713 tweets, or 7,948 tokens. We manually annotated this set in order to have a test set that is in the same domain and follows the same distribution of non-canonical occurrences as our primary training set.

Val$_{Small}$　　We use this development set of 600 sentences, or 7,061 tokens, introduced in Torunoğlu and Eryiğit (2014), as a validation set for our NMT and SMT experiments.

Table 1 shows all token and non-canonical token count of each test dataset as well as the ratio of non-canonical token count over all tokens.

5　Experiments and results

The first component of our system (i.e. Orthographic Normalization) is a simple character replacement module. We gather unique characters that appear in Twitter corpus which we scrape to generate $\text{Train}_{ParaTok}$. Due to non-Turkish tweets, there are some Arabic, Persian, Japanese and Hangul characters that cannot be orthographically converted to Turkish characters. We filter out those characters using their unicode character name leaving only characters belonging Latin, Greek and Cyrillic alphabets. Then, the remaining characters are mapped to their Turkish counterparts with the help of a library[3]. After manual review and correction of these characters mappings, we have 701 character replacement rules in this module.

We experiment with both SMT and NMT implementations as contrastive methods. For our SMT pipeline, we employ a fairly standard array of tools, and set their parameters similarly to Scherrer and Erjavec (2013) and Scherrer and Ljubešić (2016). For alignment, we use MGIZA (Gao and Vogel, 2008) with grow-diag-final-and symmetrization. For language modeling, we use KenLM (Heafield, 2011) to train 6-gram character-level language models on $\text{OpenSubs}_{Filtered}$ and Huawei_{MonoTR}. For phrase extraction and decoding, we use Moses (Koehn et al., 2007) to train a model on $\text{Train}_{ParaTok}$. Although there is a small possibility of transposition between adjacent characters, we disable distortion in translation. We use Val_{Small} for minimum error rate training, optimizing our model for word error rate.

We train our NMT model using the OpenNMT toolkit (Klein et al., 2017) on $\text{Train}_{ParaTok}$ without any parameter tuning. Each model uses an attentional encoder-decoder architecture, with 2-layer LSTM encoders and decoders. The input embeddings, the LSTM layers of the encoder, and the inner layer of the decoder all have a dimensionality of 500. The outer layer of the decoder has a dimensionality of 1,000. Both encoder and decoder LSTMs have a dropout probability of 0.3.

---

[3]The library name is *Unidecode* which can be found at `https://pypi.org/project/Unidecode/`

Model	Test$_{IWT}$	Test$_{2019}$	Test$_{Small}$
Eryiğit et al.	95.78%	80.25%	92.97%
(2017)	93.57%	75.39%	86.20%
SMT	**96.98%**	**85.23%**	**93.52%**
	95.21%	**78.10%**	**89.59%**
NMT	93.90%	74.04%	89.52%
	92.20%	67.87%	85.77%

Table 2: Case-insensitive (top) and case-sensitive (bottom) accuracy over all tokens.

Model	Test$_{IWT}$	Test$_{2019}$	Test$_{Small}$
Eryiğit et al.	79.16%	66.18%	74.72%
(2017)	70.54%	56.44%	53.80%
SMT	**87.43%**	**74.02%**	**76.00%**
	84.70%	**66.35%**	**68.40%**
NMT	71.34%	50.84%	58.67%
	68.91%	45.03%	51.84%

Table 3: Case-insensitive (top) and case-sensitive (bottom) accuracy scores over non-canonical tokens.

In our experimental setup, we apply a naïve tokenization on our data. Due to this, alignment errors could be caused by non-standard token boundaries (*e.g.* "A E S T H E T I C"). Similarly, it is possible that, in some cases, the orthography normalization step may be impairing our performances by reducing the entropy of our input data. Regardless, both components are frozen for our translation experiments, and we do not analyze the impact of errors from these components in this study.

For the last component, we train a case restoration model on Huawei$_{MonoTR}$ using the Moses recaser (Koehn et al., 2007). We do not assess the performance of this individual component, but rather optionally apply it on the output of the translation component to generate a recased output.

We compare the lowercased and fully-cased translation outputs with the corresponding ground truth, respectively calculating the case-insensitive and case-sensitive scores shown in Tables 2 and 3. We detect tokens that correspond to URLs, hashtags, mentions, keywords, and emoticons, and do not normalize them[4]. The scores we report are token-based accuracy scores, reflecting the percentages of correctly normalized tokens in each test set. These tables display performance evaluations on our own test set as well as other test sets used in the best-performing system so far Eryiğit and Torunoğlu-Selamet (2017), except the Big Twitter Set (BTS), which is not an open-access dataset.

The results show that, while our NMT model seem to have performed relatively poorly, our character-based SMT model outperforms Eryiğit and Torunoğlu-Selamet (2017) by a fairly large margin. The SMT system demonstrates that our unsupervised parallel data bootstrapping method and translation approach to non-canonical text normalization both work quite well in the case of Turkish. The reason for the dramatic underperformance of our NMT model remains to be investigated, though we believe that the language model we trained on large amounts of data is likely an important contributor to the success of our SMT model.

6 Conclusion and future work

In this study, we proposed a machine translation approach as an alternative to the cascaded approach that has so far defined the state of the art in Turkish non-canonical text normalization. Our approach is simpler with fewer stages of processing, able to consider context beyond individual tokens, less susceptible to human error, and not reliant on external linguistic resources or manually-defined transformation rules. We show that, by implementing our translation approach with basic pre-processing tools and a character-based SMT model, we were able to outperform the state of the art by a fairly large margin.

A quick examination of the outputs from our best-performing system shows that it has often failed on abbreviations, certain accent normalization issues, and proper noun suffixation. We are working on a more detailed error analysis to be able to identify particular drawbacks in our systems, and implement corresponding measures, including using a more sophisticated tokenizer. We also plan to experiment with character embeddings and character-based composite word embeddings in our NMT model to see if that would boost its performance. Finally, we are aiming for a closer look at out-of-domain text normalization in order to investigate ways to perform domain adaptation using our translation approach.

---

[4]The discrepancy between the reproduced scores and those originally reported in Eryiğit and Torunoğlu-Selamet (2017) is partly because we also exclude these from evaluation, and partly because the original study excludes all-uppercase tokens from theirs.

Acknowledgments

The authors would like to thank Yves Scherrer for his valuable insights, and the Faculty of Arts at the University of Helsinki for funding a research visit, during which this study has materialized.

References

Gülşen Eryiğit. 2014. ITU Turkish NLP web service. In *Proceedings of the Demonstrations at the 14th Conference of the European Chapter of the Association for Computational Linguistics*, pages 1–4.

Gülşen Eryiğit and Dilara Torunoğlu-Selamet. 2017. Social media text normalization for Turkish. *Natural Language Engineering*, 23(6):835–875.

Qin Gao and Stephan Vogel. 2008. Parallel implementations of word alignment tool. *Software engineering, testing, and quality assurance for natural language processing*, pages 49–57.

Sinan Göker and Burcu Can. 2018. Neural text normalization for turkish social media. In *2018 3rd International Conference on Computer Science and Engineering (UBMK)*, pages 161–166. IEEE.

Kenneth Heafield. 2011. KenLM: Faster and smaller language model queries. In *Proceedings of the sixth workshop on statistical machine translation*, pages 187–197. Association for Computational Linguistics.

Taishi Ikeda, Hiroyuki Shindo, and Yuji Matsumoto. 2016. Japanese text normalization with encoder-decoder model. In *Proceedings of the 2nd Workshop on Noisy User-generated Text (WNUT)*, pages 129–137.

Guillaume Klein, Yoon Kim, Yuntian Deng, Jean Senellart, and Alexander M. Rush. 2017. OpenNMT: Open-source toolkit for neural machine translation. In *Proc. ACL*.

Philipp Koehn, Hieu Hoang, Alexandra Birch, Chris Callison-Burch, Marcello Federico, Nicola Bertoldi, Brooke Cowan, Wade Shen, Christine Moran, Richard Zens, et al. 2007. Moses: Open source toolkit for statistical machine translation. In *Proceedings of the 45th annual meeting of the association for computational linguistics companion volume proceedings of the demo and poster sessions*, pages 177–180.

Chen Li and Yang Liu. 2012. Normalization of text messages using character- and phone-based machine translation approaches. In *Thirteenth Annual Conference of the International Speech Communication Association*.

Pierre Lison and Jörg Tiedemann. 2016. OpenSubtitles2016: Extracting large parallel corpora from movie and TV subtitles.

David Matthews. 2007. Machine transliteration of proper names. *Master's Thesis, University of Edinburgh, Edinburgh, United Kingdom*.

Preslav Nakov and Jörg Tiedemann. 2012. Combining word-level and character-level models for machine translation between closely-related languages. In *Proceedings of the 50th Annual Meeting of the Association for Computational Linguistics: Short Papers-Volume 2*, pages 301–305. Association for Computational Linguistics.

Kemal Oflazer. 1994. Two-level description of turkish morphology. *Literary and linguistic computing*, 9(2):137–148.

Tuğba Pamay, Umut Sulubacak, Dilara Torunoğlu-Selamet, and Gülşen Eryiğit. 2015. The annotation process of the itu web treebank. In *Proceedings of the 9th Linguistic Annotation Workshop*, pages 95–101.

Eva Pettersson, Beáta Megyesi, and Jörg Tiedemann. 2013. An smt approach to automatic annotation of historical text. In *Proceedings of the workshop on computational historical linguistics at NODALIDA 2013; May 22-24; 2013; Oslo; Norway. NEALT Proceedings Series 18*, 087, pages 54–69. Linköping University Electronic Press.

Yves Scherrer and Tomaž Erjavec. 2013. Modernizing historical Slovene words with character-based SMT. In *BSNLP 2013-4th Biennial Workshop on Balto-Slavic Natural Language Processing*.

Yves Scherrer and Nikola Ljubešić. 2016. Automatic normalisation of the Swiss German ArchiMob corpus using character-level machine translation. In *Proceedings of the 13th Conference on Natural Language Processing (KONVENS 2016)*, pages 248–255.

Jörg Tiedemann. 2012. Parallel data, tools and interfaces in opus. In *Proceedings of the Eight International Conference on Language Resources and Evaluation (LREC'12)*, Istanbul, Turkey. European Language Resources Association (ELRA).

Dilara Torunoğlu and Gülsen Eryiğit. 2014. A cascaded approach for social media text normalization of turkish. In *Proceedings of the 5th Workshop on Language Analysis for Social Media (LASM)*, pages 62–70.

Osman Tursun and Ruket Cakici. 2017. Noisy uyghur text normalization. In *Proceedings of the 3rd Workshop on Noisy User-generated Text*, pages 85–93.

Eray Yildiz, Caglar Tirkaz, H Bahadır Sahin, Mustafa Tolga Eren, and Omer Ozan Sonmez. 2016. A morphology-aware network for morphological disambiguation. In *Thirtieth AAAI Conference on Artificial Intelligence*.

ARHNet - Leveraging Community Interaction For Detection Of Religious Hate Speech In Arabic

Arijit Ghosh Chowdhury[*]
Manipal Institute of Technology
arijit10@gmail.com

Aniket Didolkar[*]
Manipal Institute of Technology
adidolkar123@gmail.com

Ramit Sawhney
Netaji Subhas Institute of Technology
ramits.co@nsit.net.in

Rajiv Ratn Shah
MIDAS, IIIT-Delhi
rajivratn@iiitd.ac.in

Abstract

The rapid widespread of social media has led to some undesirable consequences like the rapid increase of hateful content and offensive language. Religious Hate Speech, in particular, often leads to unrest and sometimes aggravates to violence against people on the basis of their religious affiliations. The richness of the Arabic morphology and the limited available resources makes this task especially challenging. The current state-of-the-art approaches to detect hate speech in Arabic rely entirely on textual (lexical and semantic) cues. Our proposed methodology contends that leveraging Community-Interaction can better help us profile hate speech content on social media. Our proposed ARHNet (Arabic Religious Hate Speech Net) model incorporates both Arabic Word Embeddings and Social Network Graphs for the detection of religious hate speech.

1 Introduction

Hate speech was a major tool employed to promote slavery in Colonial America, to aggravate tensions in Bosnia and in the rise of the Third Reich. The aim of such speech is to ridicule victims, to humiliate them and represent their grievances as less serious (Gelashvili, 2018). The relationship between religion and hate speech is complex and has been central to recent discussions of hate speech directed at religious people, especially members of religious minorities (Bonotti, 2017). This makes it important to develop automated tools to detect messages that use inflammatory sectarian language to promote hatred and violence against people.

Our work extends on the work done by (Albadi et al., 2018) in terms of exploring the merits of introducing community interaction as a feature in the detection of religious hate speech in Arabic. Most previous work in the area of hate speech detection has targeted mainly English content (Davidson et al., 2017) (Djuric et al., 2015) (Badjatiya et al., 2017). Author profiling using community graphs has been explored by (Mishra et al., 2018) for abuse detection on Twitter. We propose a novel Cyber Hate Detection approach using multiple twitter graphs and traditional word embeddings.

Social network graphs are increasingly being used as a powerful tool for NLP applications (Mahata et al., 2018; Shah et al., 2016b), leading to substantial improvement in performance for tasks like text categorization, sentiment analysis, and author attribute identification ((Hovy, 2015); (Yang and Eisenstein, 2015); (Yang et al., 2016). The idea of using this type of information is best explained by the concept of homophily, i.e., the phenomenon that people, both in real life as well as on the Internet, tend to associate more with those who appear similar. Here, similarity can be defined based on various parameters like location, age, language, etc. The basic idea behind leveraging community interaction is that if we have information about members of a community defined by some similarity measure, then we can infer information about a person based on which community they belong to. For our study, knowing that members of a particular community are prone to proliferating religious hate speech content, and knowing that the user is connected to this community, we can use this information beyond linguistic cues and more accurately predict the use of hateful/non-hateful language. Our work seeks to address two main questions:

Proceedings of the ACL 2019, Student Research Workshop, pages 273–280
Florence, Italy, July 28th-August 2nd, 2019. ©2019 Association for Computational Linguistics

- Is one community more prone to spreading hateful content than the other?

- Can such information be effectively leveraged to improve the performance of the current state of the art in the detection of religious hate speech within Arabic speaking users?

In this paper, we do an in-depth analysis of how adding community features may enhance the performance of classification models that detect religious hate speech in Arabic.

2 Related Work

Hate speech research has been conducted extensively for the English language. Amongst the first ones to apply supervised learning to the task of hate speech detection were (Yin and Davison, 2009) who used a linear SVM classifier to identify posts containing harassment based on local, contextual and sentiment-based (e.g., presence of expletives) features. Their best results were with all of these features combined. Notably, (Waseem and Hovy, 2016) created a dataset for detection of Hate Speech on Twitter. They noted that character n-grams are better predictive features than word n-grams for recognizing racist and sexist tweets. Their n-gram-based classification model was outperformed using Gradient Boosted Decision Trees classifier trained on word embeddings learned using LSTMs (Waseem and Hovy, 2016). There has been limited literature on the problem of Hate Speech detection on Arabic social media. (Magdy et al., 2015) trained an SVM classifier to predict whether a user is more likely to be an ISIS supporter or opposer based on features of the users tweets.

Social Network graphs have been leveraged in several ways for a variety of purposes in NLP. Given the graph representing the social network, such methods create low-dimensional representations for each node, which are optimized to predict the nodes close to it in the network. Among those that implement this idea are (Yang et al., 2016), who used representations derived from a social graph to achieve better performance in entity linking tasks, and Chen and Ku (Yang and Eisenstein, 2015), who used them for stance classification. A considerable amount of literature has also been devoted to sentiment analysis with representations built from demographic factors ((Yang and Eisenstein, 2015); (Chen and Ku, 2016)). Other tasks that have benefited from social representations are sarcasm detection (Amir et al., 2016) and political opinion prediction (Tlmcel and Leon, 2017).

To our knowledge, so far there has been no substantial research on using social network graphs as features to analyze and categorize tweets in Arabic. Our work proposes a novel architecture that builds on the current state of the art and improves its performance using community graph features.

3 Data

We conduct our experiments with the dataset provided by (Albadi et al., 2018). The authors collected the tweets referring to different religious groups and labeled them using crowdsourced workers. In November 2017, using Twitters search API 2, the authors collected 6000 Arabic tweets, 1000 for each of the six religious groups. They used this collection of tweets as their training dataset. Due to the unavailability of a hate lexicon and to ensure unbiased data collection process; they included in their query only impartial terms that refer to a religion name or the people practicing that religion. In January 2018, they collected another set of 600 tweets, 100 for each of the six religious groups, for their testing dataset. After an inter-annotator agreement of 81% , 2526 tweets were labeled as *Hate*.

The dataset was released as a list of 5570 tweet IDs along with their corresponding annotations. Using the python Twarc library, we could only retrieve 3950 of the tweets since some of them have now been deleted or their visibility limited. Of the ones retrieved, 1,685 (42.6%) are labelled as *hate*, and the remaining 2,265 (57.4%) as *Non-Hate*; this distribution follows the original dataset very closely (45.1%, 54.9%).

3.1 Preprocessing

We followed some of the Arabic-specific normalization steps proposed in (Albadi et al., 2018) along with some other Twitter-specific preprocessing techniques.

- Normalization of Hamza with alef seat to bare alef.

- Normalization of dotless yeh (alef maksura) to yeh.

- Normalization of teh marbuta to heh.

Hate
اليوم الثلاثاء لعنة الله على اليهود الذين هم أبناء الشيطان وعلى مساعديه الذين هم وقود الجحيم
TuesdayMorning curse of god on the jews who are the sons of the satan and on their helpers who are the fuel of hell
اللهم طهر الأرض من الشيعة المنافقين ومن يتبعهم
Oh god purify the land from the rawafid hypocrite Shia and those who follow them
الله يلعن فيتفا لعنه اليهود والنصاري
God cursed Vittafa cursed Jews and Christians
مؤله المسلم يقتل اخاه المسلم بالسلاح ويحاول قتل اليهودي بالدعاء تبا لعروبتكم حقيقه
Muslim Muslim kills his Muslim brother and tries to kill the Jew by praying to the Arabs

Table 1: Examples for Hate Speech.

Non-Hate
مؤسسة أرشيف المغرب تتسلم وثائق عن ذاكرة اليهودگ المغاربة
The Moroccan Archives Foundation receives documents on the memory of Moroccan Jews
يالله انزل المن والسلوي كما انزلته علي اليهود (المفضلون علي كل البشر) في التيه
God sent down the Manna and the Salafi as it sent down on the Jews (the favored of all human beings) in Hell
مؤسسة أرشيف المغرب تتسلم وثائق عن ذاكرة اليهود المغاربة الخميس المقبلگ بالرباط
Morocco's Shiv receives documents on the memory of Moroccan Jews next Thursday in Rabat
كلنا اولاد ادم مسلمين مسيحين يهود صهاينه بس لم نعد نحترم الانسانيه
We are all Adam's children, Muslims, Christian Jews, Zionists, but we no longer respect humanity

Table 2: Examples for Non-Hate Speech.

- Normalizing links, user mentions, and numbers to somelink, someuser, and somenumber, respectively.

- Normalizing hashtags by deleting underscores and the # symbol.

- Removing diacritics (the harakat), tatweel (stretching character), punctuations, emojis, non-Arabic characters, and one-letter words.

- Repeated characters were removed if the repetition was of count three or more.

- We used the list of 356 stopwords created by (Albadi et al., 2018). This list did not have negation words as they usually represent important sentiments.

- Stemming: We used the ISRI Arabic Stemmer provided by NLTK to handle inflected words and reduce them to a common reduced form.

4 Methodology

4.1 Community and Social Interaction Network

To leverage information about community interaction, we create an undirected unlabeled social network graph wherein nodes are the authors and edges are the connections between them.

We use two social network graphs in our study :

- **Follower Graph** : This is an unweighted undirected graph G with nodes v representing authors, with edges e such that for each $e \in E$, there exists $u, v \in$ the set of authors such that u follows v or vice versa.

- **Retweet Graph** : This is an unweighted undirected graph G with nodes v representing authors, with edges e such that for each $e \in E$, there exists $u, v \in$ the set of authors such that u has retweeted v or vice versa.

From these social network graphs, we obtain a vector representation, i.e., an embedding that we refer to as an *Interaction*, for each author using the *Node2Vec* framework (Grover and Leskovec, 2016). *Node2Vec* uses a skip-gram model (Mikolov et al., 2013) on a graph to create a representation for each of its nodes based on their positions and their neighbors. Given a graph with nodes $V = v1, v2, ..., vn$, Node2Vec seeks to maximize the following log probability:

$$\sum_{v \in V} Log P_r(N_s(v)|v)$$

where $N_s(v)$ denotes the network neighborhood of node v generated through sampling strategy s. The framework can learn low-dimensional embeddings for nodes in the graph. These embeddings can emphasize either their structural role or the local community they are a part of. This depends on the sampling strategies used to generate the neighborhood: if breadth-first sampling (BFS) is adopted, the model focuses on the immediate neighbors of a node; when depth-first sampling (DFS) is used, the model explores farther regions in the network, which results in embeddings that encode more information about structural role of a particular node . The balance between these two ways of sampling the neighbors is directly controlled by two node2vec parameters, namely p and q. The default value for these is 1, which ensures a node representation that gives equal weight to both structural and community-oriented information. In our work, we use the default value for both p and q. Additionally, since Node2Vec does not produce embeddings for single users without a community, these have been mapped to a single zero embedding. The dimensions of these embeddings were 64.

Figure 1 shows an example of a community. The nodes represent users and the edges represent an *Interaction* between them.

4.2 Classification

For every tweet $t_i \in D$, in the dataset, a binary valued value variable y_i is used, which can either be 0 or 1. The value 0 indicates that the text belongs to the *Non-Hate category* while 1 indicates *Hate Speech*.

The following steps are executed for every tweet $t_i \in D$:

1. *Word Embeddings.* All the words in our vocabulary are encoded to form 600-dimensional word embeddings obtained

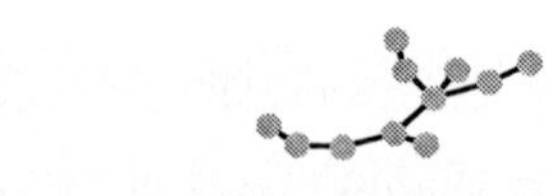
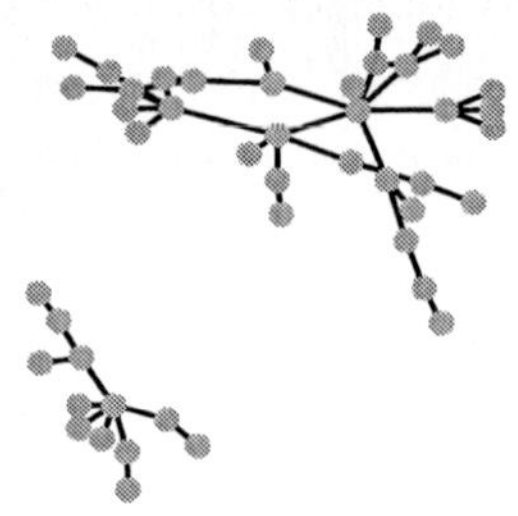

Figure 1: A community interaction snippet from $\mathcal{G}_{retweet}$

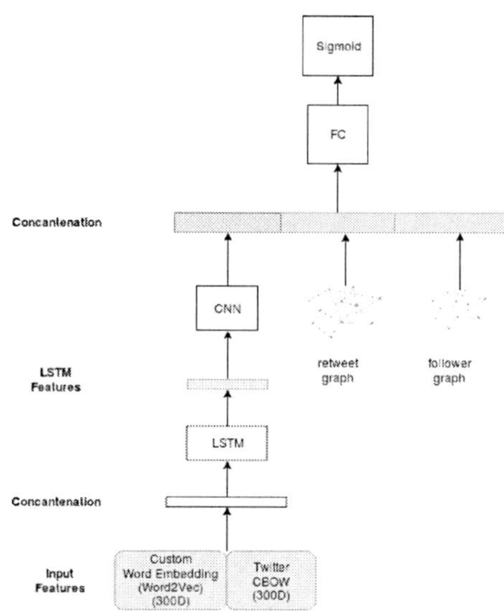

Figure 2: The ARHNet Architecture

by concatenating Twitter-CBOW 300-dimensional embedding with our trained embedding.

2. *Sentence Representation.* This is obtained by passing the word embeddings through the corresponding deep learning model.

3. *Node Embeddings.* The node embedding for the author of t_i is concatenated with the sentence representation to get the final representation.

4. *Dense Layer.* The final representation is passed through a dense layer which outputs

Architecture	Accuracy	Precision	Recall	F1	AUROC
AraHate-LR	0.75	0.72	0.74	0.73	0.82
AraHate-SVM	0.75	0.72	0.72	0.72	0.81
AraHate-GRU	0.77	0.65	0.89	0.75	0.84
GRU + self-attention	0.78	0.71	0.78	0.74	0.83
GRU + CNN	0.79	0.69	0.86	0.77	0.86
LSTM	0.76	0.65	0.86	0.74	0.82
LSTM + self-attention	0.78	0.68	0.82	0.75	0.86
LSTM + CNN	0.80	0.71	0.83	0.77	0.86
Bidirectional GRU	0.79	0.70	0.85	0.77	0.85
Bidirectional GRU + self-attention	0.80	0.74	0.80	0.77	0.87
Bidirectional GRU + CNN	0.79	0.71	0.81	0.76	0.85
Bidirectional LSTM	0.80	0.73	0.79	0.76	0.86
Bidirectional LSTM + self-attention	0.77	0.66	0.86	0.75	0.87
Bidirectional LSTM + CNN	0.81	0.74	0.81	0.77	0.86

Table 3: Performance of various deep learning models.

Architecture	Accuracy	Precision	Recall	F1	AUROC
GRU + NODE2VEC	0.79	**0.74**	0.76	0.75	0.85
GRU + self-attention + NODE2VEC	0.78	0.67	0.87	0.75	0.84
GRU + CNN + NODE2VEC	0.80	0.68	0.87	0.77	0.85
LSTM + NODE2VEC	0.75	0.63	0.86	0.73	0.81
LSTM + self-attention + NODE2VEC	0.78	0.70	0.79	0.74	0.84
LSTM + CNN + NODE2VEC (ARHNet)	0.79	0.69	**0.89**	**0.78**	**0.86**
Bi-GRU + NODE2VEC	0.79	0.67	0.86	0.75	0.85
Bi-GRU + self-attention + NODE2VEC	0.79	0.70	0.82	0.76	0.86
Bi-GRU + CNN + NODE2VEC	**0.81**	0.72	0.84	0.77	0.86
Bi-LSTM + NODE2VEC	0.80	0.73	0.81	0.77	0.86
Bi-LSTM + self-attention + NODE2VEC	0.78	0.68	0.82	0.75	0.85
Bi-LSTM + CNN + NODE2VEC	0.80	0.73	0.81	0.77	0.86

Table 4: Performance of various deep learning models with community features.

a score that is converted to a probability distribution using a sigmoid activation.

4.3 Baselines

An extensive comparison with state-of-the-art generic and specific models the case for our proposed methodology. To make a fair comparison between all the methodologies, the experiments are conducted concerning the baselines in (Albadi et al., 2018) have used a simple GRU model as their best performing model. Their GRU model uses 240 hidden features. They have also compared results with Logistic Regression and Support Vector Machine Models. The Logistic regression classifier was trained using character n-gram features (n =1-4) with L2 regularization. The SVM classifier was also trained us-ing character n-gram features (n = 1-4) with linear kernel and L2 regularization, similar to (Albadi et al., 2018). For the GRU model, they have used the Twitter-CBOW 300-dimensional embedding model(Soliman et al., 2017) for obtaining word embeddings. The output of the embedding layer was fed into a dropout layer with probability 0.5. They used batches of size 32 and Adam as their optimizer. We refer the models trained by (Albadi et al., 2018) as the AraHate baselines. We conduct our experiments with LSTM (Liu et al., 2016) and CNN-LSTM (Zhou et al., 2015) models. LSTMs can capture long term dependencies better than RNNs and GRUs, and a CNN-LSTM network utilizes the ability of a CNN to extract higher-level phrase representations, which are fed into an LSTM. We did not increase the complexity of the baselines beyond this to not risk overfitting on a small dataset.

4.4 Models and Hyperparameters

First, we prepared the vocabulary by assigning integer indexes to unique words in our dataset. Tweets were then converted into sequences of integer indexes. These sequences were padded with zeros so that the tweets in each batch have the same length during training. They were then fed into an embedding layer which maps word indexes to word embeddings. We trained our word embeddings using GenSim [1]. We also used the Twitter-CBOW 300-dimension embedding model provided by AraVec (Soliman et al., 2017) which contains over 331k word vectors that have been trained on about 67M Arabic tweets. We concatenated our own trained embeddings with the AraVec embeddings to obtain 600-dimensional embeddings Similar to (Albadi et al., 2018), The output of the embedding layer was fed into a dropout layer with a rate of 0.5 to prevent overfitting.

For both LSTM and GRU, the word embeddings were passed to both unidirectional and bidirectional LSTM with 240 features each. In the GRU-CNN/LSTM-CNN models, we used 2 Convolutional Layers with a Kernel Size of 3 and Relu Activation in the middle. We obtained the final representation by taking the maximum along the temporal dimension. For self-attention, the output of the GRU/LSTM was passed to a self-attention layer. For the self-attention models, we used 240 features.

We compared each of these models with their counterparts obtained by concatenating Node2Vec embeddings to the representations obtained by the above deep learning models. The final representation was then passed into a Sigmoid Layer. We performed training in batches of size 32, and we used Adam as our optimizer for all experiments.

5 Results And Discussion

In our experiments, we have beaten the scores of (Albadi et al., 2018) in all 5 metrics. We obtained a highest f1-score of 0.78 as compared to 0.77 in (Albadi et al., 2018). This is achieved in our LSTM + CNN + CISNet model. The ARHNet model outperforms baselines in terms of Recall, F1 and AUROC metrics while

GRU-NODE2VEC demonstrates the highest precision, and the Bi-GRU-CNN-NODE2VEC model achieves the highest accuracy. Our methodology effectively improves upon the current state of the art and is successful in demonstration of how community interaction can be leveraged to tackle downstream NLP tasks like detection of religious hate speech. Albadi et al. (2018) reached an 0.81 agreement score between annotators. Our methodology, therefore, matches human performance in terms of unambiguously categorizing texts that contain religious hate speech from texts that don't.

To summarize, our approach highlights the validity of using Community Interaction Graphs as features of classification in Arabic. Despite having a sparse representation of users, our proposed methodology has shown improvements on Accuracy and F1 over previously state of the art models on a reduced dataset.

6 Conclusion

In this paper, we explored the effectiveness of community-interaction information about authors for the purpose of categorizing religious hate speech in the Arabic Twittersphere and build upon existing work in the linguistic aspects of social media (Shah et al., 2016c,a; Mahata et al., 2015). Working with a dataset of 3950 tweets annotated for *Hate* and *Non-Hate*, we first comprehensively replicated three established and currently best-performing hate speech detection methods based on character n-grams and GRUs as our baselines. We then constructed a graph of all the authors of tweets in our dataset and extracted community-based information in the form of dense low-dimensional embeddings for each of them using Node2Vec. We showed that the inclusion of community graph embeddings significantly improves system performance over the baselines and advances the state of the art in this task. Users prone to proliferate hate do tend to form social groups online, and this stresses the importance of utilizing community-based information for automatic religious hate speech detection.

References

N. Albadi, M. Kurdi, and S. Mishra. 2018. Are they our brothers? analysis and detection of religious hate speech in the arabic twittersphere. In *2018 IEEE/ACM International Conference on Advances*

---

in Social Networks Analysis and Mining (ASONAM), pages 69–76.

Silvio Amir, Byron C. Wallace, Hao Lyu, Paula Carvalho, and Mário J. Silva. 2016. Modelling context with user embeddings for sarcasm detection in social media. *CoRR*, abs/1607.00976.

Pinkesh Badjatiya, Shashank Gupta, Manish Gupta, and Vasudeva Varma. 2017. Deep learning for hate speech detection in tweets. *CoRR*, abs/1706.00188.

Matteo Bonotti. 2017. Religion, hate speech and non-domination. *Ethnicities*, 17:259–274.

Wei-Fan Chen and Lun-Wei Ku. 2016. UTCNN: a deep learning model of stance classification on social media text. In *Proceedings of COLING 2016, the 26th International Conference on Computational Linguistics: Technical Papers*, pages 1635–1645, Osaka, Japan. The COLING 2016 Organizing Committee.

Thomas Davidson, Dana Warmsley, Michael W. Macy, and Ingmar Weber. 2017. Automated hate speech detection and the problem of offensive language. *CoRR*, abs/1703.04009.

Nemanja Djuric, Jing Zhou, Robin Morris, Mihajlo Grbovic, Vladan Radosavljevic, and Narayan Bhamidipati. 2015. Hate speech detection with comment embeddings. In *Proceedings of the 24th International Conference on World Wide Web*, WWW '15 Companion, pages 29–30, New York, NY, USA. ACM.

Teona Gelashvili. 2018. Hate speech on social media: Implications of private regulation and governance gaps. Student Paper.

Aditya Grover and Jure Leskovec. 2016. node2vec: Scalable feature learning for networks. *CoRR*, abs/1607.00653.

Dirk Hovy. 2015. Demographic factors improve classification performance. In *Proceedings of the 53rd Annual Meeting of the Association for Computational Linguistics and the 7th International Joint Conference on Natural Language Processing (Volume 1: Long Papers)*, pages 752–762, Beijing, China. Association for Computational Linguistics.

Pengfei Liu, Xipeng Qiu, and Xuanjing Huang. 2016. Recurrent neural network for text classification with multi-task learning. *CoRR*, abs/1605.05101.

Walid Magdy, Kareem Darwish, and Ingmar Weber. 2015. #failedrevolutions: Using twitter to study the antecedents of ISIS support. *CoRR*, abs/1503.02401.

Debanjan Mahata, Jasper Friedrichs, Rajiv Ratn Shah, and Jing Jiang. 2018. Detecting personal intake of medicine from twitter. *IEEE Intelligent Systems*, 33(4):87–95.

Debanjan Mahata, John R Talburt, and Vivek Kumar Singh. 2015. From chirps to whistles: discovering event-specific informative content from twitter. In *Proceedings of the ACM web science conference*, page 17. ACM.

Tomas Mikolov, Ilya Sutskever, Kai Chen, Greg Corrado, and Jeffrey Dean. 2013. Distributed representations of words and phrases and their compositionality. *CoRR*, abs/1310.4546.

Pushkar Mishra, Marco Del Tredici, Helen Yannakoudakis, and Ekaterina Shutova. 2018. Author profiling for abuse detection. In *COLING*.

Rajiv Ratn Shah, Anupam Samanta, Deepak Gupta, Yi Yu, Suhua Tang, and Roger Zimmermann. 2016a. Prompt: Personalized user tag recommendation for social media photos leveraging personal and social contexts. In *2016 IEEE International Symposium on Multimedia (ISM)*, pages 486–492. IEEE.

Rajiv Ratn Shah, Yi Yu, Suhua Tang, Shin'ichi Satoh, Akshay Verma, and Roger Zimmermann. 2016b. Concept-level multimodal ranking of flickr photo tags via recall based weighting. In *Proceedings of the 2016 ACM Workshop on Multimedia COMMONS*, pages 19–26. ACM.

Rajiv Ratn Shah, Yi Yu, Akshay Verma, Suhua Tang, Anwar Dilawar Shaikh, and Roger Zimmermann. 2016c. Leveraging multimodal information for event summarization and concept-level sentiment analysis. *Knowledge-Based Systems*, 108:102–109.

Abu Bakr Soliman, Kareem Eissa, and Samhaa R. El-Beltagy. 2017. Aravec: A set of arabic word embedding models for use in arabic nlp. *Procedia Computer Science*, 117:256 – 265. Arabic Computational Linguistics.

C. Tlmcel and F. Leon. 2017. Predicting political opinions in social networks with user embeddings. In *2017 13th IEEE International Conference on Intelligent Computer Communication and Processing (ICCP)*, pages 213–219.

Zeerak Waseem and Dirk Hovy. 2016. Hateful symbols or hateful people? predictive features for hate speech detection on twitter. In *Proceedings of the NAACL Student Research Workshop*, pages 88–93, San Diego, California. Association for Computational Linguistics.

Yi Yang, Ming-Wei Chang, and Jacob Eisenstein. 2016. Toward socially-infused information extraction: Embedding authors, mentions, and entities. *CoRR*, abs/1609.08084.

Yi Yang and Jacob Eisenstein. 2015. Putting things in context: Community-specific embedding projections for sentiment analysis. *CoRR*, abs/1511.06052.

Dawei Yin and Brian D. Davison. 2009. Detection of harassment on web 2.0.

Chunting Zhou, Chonglin Sun, Zhiyuan Liu, and Francis C. M. Lau. 2015. A C-LSTM neural network for text classification. *CoRR*, abs/1511.08630.

Investigating Political Herd Mentality: A Community Sentiment Based Approach

Anjali Bhavan[*]
Delhi Technological University
anjalibhavan98@gmail.com

Rohan Mishra[*]
Delhi Technological University
rohan.mishra1997@gmail.com

Pradyumna Prakhar Sinha[*]
Delhi Technological University
pradyumna014@gmail.com

Ramit Sawhney
Netaji Subhash Institute of Technology
ramits.co@nsit.net.in

Rajiv Ratn Shah
MIDAS, IIIT-Delhi
rajivratn@iiitd.ac.in

Abstract

Analyzing polarities and sentiments inherent in political speeches and debates poses an important problem today. This experiment aims to address this issue by analyzing publicly-available Hansard transcripts of the debates conducted in the UK Parliament. Our proposed approach, which uses community-based graph information to augment hand-crafted features based on topic modeling and emotion detection on debate transcripts currently surpasses the benchmark results on the same dataset. Such sentiment classification systems could prove to be of great use in today's politically turbulent times, for public knowledge of politicians stands on various relevant issues proves vital for good governance and citizenship. The experiments also demonstrate that continuous feature representations learned from graphs can improve performance on sentiment classification tasks significantly.

1 Introduction

One of the key aspects of a functional, free society is being presented with comprehensive options in electing government representatives. The decision is aided by the positions politicians take on relevant issues like water, housing, etc. Hence, it becomes important to relay political standings to the general public in a comprehensible manner. The Hansard transcripts of speeches delivered in the UK Parliament are one such source of information. However, owing to the voluminous quantity,

* Indicates equal contribution.

esoteric language and opaque procedural jargon of Parliament, it is tougher for the non-expert citizen to assess the standings of their elected representative. Therefore, conducting stance classification studies on such data is a challenging task with potential benefits. However, the documents tend to be highly tedious and difficult to comprehend, and thus become a barrier to information about political issues and leanings.

Sentiment analysis of data from various relevant sources (social media, newspapers, transcripts, etc.) has often given several insights about public opinion, issues of contention, general trends and so on (Carvalho et al., 2011; Loukis et al., 2014). Such techniques have even been used for purposes like predicting election outcomes and the reception of newly-launched products. Since these insights have wide-ranging consequences, it becomes imperative to develop rigorous standards and state-of-the-art techniques for them.
One aspect that helps with analyzing such patterns and sentiments is studying about the interconnections and networks underlying such data. Homophily, or the tendency of people to associate with like-minded individuals, is the fundamental aspect of depicting relationships between users of a social network (for instance). Constructing graphs to map such complex relationships and attributes in data could help one arrive at ready insights and conclusions. This comes particularly useful when studying parliamentary debates and sessions; connecting speakers according to factors like party or position affiliations pro-

Proceedings of the ACL 2019, Student Research Workshop, pages 281–287
Florence, Italy, July 28th-August 2nd, 2019. ©2019 Association for Computational Linguistics

vides information on how a speaker is likely to respond to an issue being presented. Attempts to analyze social media data based on such approaches have been made (Deitrick and Hu, 2013).

2 Related Work

The analysis of political content and parliamentary debates have opened an exciting line of research in recent years and has shown promising results in tasks of stance classification (Hasan and Ng, 2013) and opinion mining (Karami et al., 2018). A large part of the work initially concentrated on legislative speeches, but the focus has shifted to social media content analysis in recent times. This shift in focus has been particularly rapid with the proliferation of social media data and research (?Shah and Zimmermann, 2017; Shah et al., 2016b; Mahata et al., 2018; Shah et al., 2016c,a).

Lauderdale and Herzog (2016) presented their method of determining political positions from legislative speech. The datasets were sourced from Irish and US Senate debates. Rheault et al. (2016) examined the emotional polarity variations in speeches delivered in the British parliament over a hundred years. They observed a correlation between the variations in emotional states of a particular period of time and the national economic situation. Thomas et al. (2006) studied the relationships between segments of speeches delivered in the Congress and the overall tone: of opposition or support. A significant amount of research exists on the political temperament across social media websites like Facebook and Twitter. Stieglitz and Dang-Xuan (2012) studied the relationship between the inherent sentiment of politically relevant tweets and the retweet activity. Ceron et al. (2014) proposed methods for determining the political alignments of citizens and tested them on French and Italian-context datasets. Many new findings based on the contemporary political landscape continue to be developed and presented. Wang and Liu (2018) analyzed US President Donald Trump's speeches delivered during his 2016 election campaign. Rudkowsky et al. (2018) proposed the usage of word embeddings in the place of the traditional Bag-of-Words (BOW) approach for text analysis, and demonstrated experiments on Austrian parliamentary speeches. There have been some approaches to model interactions among members of a network to help in the task of sentiment analysis. Moreover, there have been applications that extract information about each user by representing them as a node in the social graph and creating low dimensional representation usually induced by neural architectures (Grover and Leskovec, 2016). Mishra et al. (2018) and Qian et al. (2018) use such social graph-based features to gain considerable improvement in the task of abuse detection in social media. However there has been no work done to model the interaction between the members of the Parliament for the task of stance classification.

For studying transcripts of speeches delivered in the House of Commons in the UK Parliament, Abercrombie and Batista-Navarro (2018b) curated a dataset consisting of parliamentary motions and debates as provided in the Hansard transcripts, along with other information like party affiliations and polarities of the motions being discussed. This was followed by carrying out studies on the dataset and developing a sentiment analysis model which also demonstrated the results of motion-independent (one-step) and motion-dependent classification of polarities Abercrombie and Batista-Navarro (2018a). This dataset is used for further analysis in our experiments.

3 Dataset

In the UK, transcripts of parliamentary debates are publicly available along with information related to *division votes* as well as manually annotated sentiment labels. To investigate the effectiveness of our pipeline, experiments were conducted using the *HanDeSeT* dataset as created by (Abercrombie and Batista-Navarro, 2018b). The dataset consists of 607 politicians and their speeches over various motions, with a total of 1251 samples. The speeches are divided into five utterances, and other features such as *Debate ID, Debate title, Motion subject with polarities: manual annotation and ruling-opposing-based, Motion and Speaker party affiliations, Speech Polarities: manual and vote-based, Rebellion percentage.*

Sentiment polarity is present in both speeches and motions. Hence labels are provided for motion polarities as well. Two label types are provided for motions: a manually-annotated one predicting positive or negative polarity, and a government/opposition one decided as follows: if the speaker who proposes the motion belongs to the ruling government, the polarity is positive; if the speaker belongs to the opposition then the polarity is negative. Two label types are provided for speeches as well: one manually-annotated, and the other a speaker-vote label extracted from the division related to the corresponding debate.

4 Methodology

The models described in Abercrombie and Batista-Navarro (2018a) extracted n-gram features (uni-grams, bi-grams, tri-grams, and their combinations) from the utterances for sentiment classification. The stance-based relationships between the members are modeled, and their effectiveness is analyzed. This study aims to develop on the limitations of using only text-based features and by doing so present a sound, coherent model for sentiment classification for parliamentary speeches. The methodology consists of the following subsections: *preprocessing*, to describe the initial data preprocessing methods undertaken; *feature extraction*, which discusses the feature sets used for our model, and *model description* and training, to elaborate on our model and training procedures.

4.1 Preprocessing

The dataset was preprocessed for further analysis. This was required so unnecessary words; characters etc. could be removed and not add further noise to the dataset. The text was lower-cased, and all punctuation marks and other special characters were removed. Following this, stopword removal was done using NLTK. Finally, a few custom stopwords specific to the parliamentary procedure were removed. These were taken from Abercrombie and Batista-Navarro (2018b). Finally, the utterances were concatenated and prepared for feature extraction and model training.

4.2 Feature Extraction

4.2.1 Textual Features

Various textual features were extracted for classification and normalized using the L2 norm. These are listed below.

- *TF-IDF*: Term Frequency-inverse Document Frequency (TF-IDF) features were extracted from n-grams (upto 3) in the text. N-gram features are immensely useful for factoring in contextual information surrounding the components of a text (whether characters or words) and are widely used for text analysis, language processing, etc.

- LDA-based topic modeling: Topic modeling is used to derive information related to the underlying "topics" contained in a text. In order to extract such topic-based features from the utterances, the Latent Dirichlet Allocation (LDA) (Blei et al., 2003) model was used. The probability distribution over the most commonly occurring 30 topics was used as features for each speech.

- *NRC Emotion*: The NRC Emotion Lexicon (Mohammad and Turney, 2013) is a publicly available lexicon that contains commonly occurring words along with their affect category (anger, fear, anticipation, trust, surprise, sadness, joy, or disgust) and two polarities (negative or positive). The score along these 10 features was computed for the utterances.

4.2.2 Graph-based features

For our analysis, two graphs were constructed from the dataset. The graph consists of nodes that represent the members who participate in the proceedings of the Parliament. The edges among the members are conditioned upon their accord or discord on debates regarding policies. Two members of the same or varying political parties either agree on a policy or differ on it. Therefore, the two graphs are constructed.

- *simGraph*: In order to model the similarity on stances among members, $G_{sim}(v, e)$ is a weighted undirected graph induced on the dataset with vertices v corresponding to the members m of political parties where an edge e between two vertices v and u is defined as $weight(e) =| f(v) \cap f(u) |$ where $f(v)$ is the set of stances taken by the member that is represented by node v.

- *oppGraph*: Similarly, to model the differences among the members, $G_{opp}(v, e)$ is induced on the dataset such that an edge e between two vertices v and u is defined as $weight(e) =| (f(v) \setminus f(u)) \cap (f(u) \setminus f(v)) |$ where $f(v)$ is the set of stances taken by the member that is represented by node v.

node2vec: To obtain community based embeddings, feature representations were generated using *node2vec* (Grover and Leskovec, 2016).

Table 1: Statistical properties of constructed graphs

Properties	Values	
	simGraph	oppGraph
Number of nodes	607	607
Number of edges	5,431	2,893
Density of graphs	0.0295	0.0157
Average weight	1.047	1.037

node2vec is similar to word2vec (Mikolov et al., 2013b) and uses the same loss function to assign similar representations to nodes that are in the context of each other. To obtain the context of a node, node2vec samples a neighborhood for each of the nodes by constructing a fixed number of random walks of constant length. The traversal strategy for these random walks is determined by the hyper-parameters Return Parameter p and In-out Parameter q which have the ability to moderate the sampling between a depth-first strategy and a breadth-first strategy. The return parameter p controls the likelihood of immediately revisiting a node in the walk, while the in-out parameter q allows the search to differentiate between inward and outward nodes.

Formally, given a graph $G = (V, E)$, we learn a function $f : V \rightarrow \mathbb{R}^d$ that maps nodes to feature representations where d is the dimension of the representation. In order to do so, for every node $u \in V$, we define a neighbourhood $N_S(u) \subseteq V$ is generated using the sampling strategy S.

The skip-gram model (Mikolov et al., 2013a) is then employed to maximize the following objective function:

$$\max_f \sum logPr(N_s(u)|f(u)). \qquad (1)$$

Combining Graph Embeddings: To combine embeddings generated for each member in the two graphs, a dense neural network was used. The embeddings were projected onto a linear layer and fine-tuned upon the classification task. The penultimate layer of the model was used as the graph embedding corresponding to each user.

The network consisted of two input layers for the two embedding sets, followed by single dense layers with hidden layer size 16 and activation ReLU. These two layers were then combined, and the resultant combination passed through two dense layers (layer size 16, activation ReLU), before being passed through a final dense softmax layer. The network was optimized using Adam, and trained over 20 epochs with batch size 64.

4.2.3 Other features

Of all the feature sets explored in Abercrombie and Batista-Navarro (2018a), the feature set all the meta-features had the best results consistently across all the three models. Hence, we used these in addition to our textual and community-based graph features. The meta-features consisted of speaker party affiliation, debate IDs and motion party affiliation.

4.3 Baseline models

The original experiments consisted of 3 models for classification: a one-step model and two two-step models. We consider the two-step models as our baselines, which are described below.

- manAnnot: a two-step model in which motion polarity classification is first performed based on manually-annotated positive or negative sentiments, corresponding to model 2a in the original experiments;

- govAnnot: a two-step model in which motion polarity classification is first performed based on government or opposition labeling, corresponding to model 2b in the original experiments.

In the case of the two two-step models, the dataset is divided into two parts based on the predicted polarities. These two divided datasets are then used for training and classification separately. Two classifiers were used in both the steps: Support Vector Machine (SVM) with the linear kernel and Multi-Layer Perceptron (MLP) with 1 hidden layer containing 100 neurons.

4.4 Proposed model

In the original experiment, the best results were obtained from the two-step models with the MLP classifier. A similar two-step approach is followed here as well, with MLP as the chosen classifier. The network consists of 1 hidden layer with 100 neurons.

5 Experiments

Experiments on two models are presented:

1. manAnnot: here, the dataset is divided into two parts based on predicted motion polarity from manually annotated labels.

Table 2: Observations for manModel

Feature Combinations	without graph-based features				with graph-based features			
	Acc.(%)	Prec.	Recall	F1	Acc.(%)	Prec.	Recall	F1
TF-IDF+meta	89.38	0.897	0.887	0.884	92.26	0.920	0.917	0.917
LDA+meta	86.34	0.875	0.839	0.850	92.34	0.930	0.902	0.915
NRC+meta	86.43	0.860	0.859	0.858	92.25	0.932	0.903	0.916
TF-IDF+LDA+meta	88.59	0.885	0.867	0.874	91.70	0.915	0.910	0.912
TF-IDF+NRC+meta	88.73	0.896	0.867	0.879	91.94	0.918	0.914	0.914
LDA+NRC+meta	85.86	0.861	0.828	0.842	**92.66**	**0.938**	**0.905**	**0.920**
TF-IDF+LDA+NRC+meta	90.89	0.908	0.900	0.908	91.78	0.917	0.909	0.919

Table 3: Observations for govModel

Feature Combinations	without graph-based features				with graph-based features			
	Acc.(%)	Prec.	Recall	F1	Acc.(%)	Prec.	Recall	F1
TF-IDF+meta	90.25	0.902	0.900	0.898	**92.72**	**0.927**	**0.924**	**0.923**
LDA+meta	88.42	0.879	0.880	0.877	92.09	0.917	0.923	0.918
NRC+meta	86.91	0.875	0.848	0.858	92.73	0.927	0.919	0.921
TF-IDF+LDA+meta	89.06	0.887	0.882	0.883	92.33	0.920	0.925	0.920
TF-IDF+NRC+meta	88.97	0.892	0.883	0.885	92.80	0.923	0.911	0.914
LDA+NRC+meta	86.35	0.864	0.851	0.855	92.41	0.923	0.922	0.920
TF-IDF+LDA+NRC+meta	89.22	0.896	0.876	0.883	92.33	0.920	0.922	0.918

2. govAnnot: Here, the dataset is separated into two parts based on the speaker's affiliation: if the speaker presenting the motion belongs to the ruling government, then the motion polarity is positive, or otherwise negative.

The hyperparameters (for each of the feature sets and the classifier) were tuned using grid search. L-BFGS (Liu and Nocedal, 1989) was used for optimization in the neural network. Model training and evaluation was carried out using stratified 10-fold cross-validation. Stratification was performed to account for the slight imbalance in the dataset. Two types of labels are presented in the dataset: vote-based and manually-annotated. We use the manually-annotated labels for our experiments.

For the graph-based features, a grid search was performed which yielded the following parameters for generating embeddings:

- simGraph: p = 10, q = 1, walk length = 15, number of walks = 15, window size = 10. The feature vector obtained from these parameters yielded an accuracy of 79.51%.

- oppGraph: p = 0.1, q = 10, walk length = 5, number of walks = 10, window size = 10. The feature vector obtained from these parameters yielded an accuracy of 69.53%.

6 Results and Discussion

Table 2 and Table 3 present the results on the two models respectively. The values of accuracy, precision, recall, and F1-score are presented on feature sets with and without graph-based features.

In the case of both models, the usage of graph-based features outperforms the results obtained without using them. The difference is large in the case of the feature set comprising of LDA, NRC, and meta-features in the model with manually-annotated labels: the F1 scores obtained with and without graph features differ by 7.8%.

It can be observed that by using graph-based features The baselines for both have been surpassed by using graph-based features along with the other textual and meta-features. Our best results for manAnnot are obtained by using the combination of LDA, NRC, and graph-based features along with meta-features. The best results for gov-Annot are obtained by using the combination of TF-IDF and meta-features along with graph-based features.

7 Conclusion

We presented a method for sentiment analysis of parliamentary debate transcripts, which could go a long way in helping determine the position an elected representative might assume on issues of great importance to the general public. The experiments were carried out on the Hansard parliamentary debates dataset (Abercrombie and Batista-Navarro, 2018b). We performed experiments on a variety of textual analysis methods (e.g. topic modeling, emotion classification, n-grams), and combined them with community-based graph features obtained by representational learning on the dataset using node2vec. Our results surpass the state-of-the-art results using both govAnnot and manAnnot. Also, the F1 and accuracy values of the models using graph-based features are higher than those without graph-based features, the difference being considerable in some cases. This gives sufficient demonstration for the ability of representational learning to enhance performances on tasks like sentiment analysis.

8 Future Work

Future work in this area could involve the following aspects:

- Application of the proposed approach to tasks other than sentiment classification, for instance analysis of mental health and suicide ideation on social media.

- Constructing different graphs and analyzing other training and feature extraction methods for enhancing performance and deriving better inferences.

- Application of the proposed approach for analyzing data in different contexts; an example could be the analysis of the recently-conducted elections in India.

- Extend the proposed methodology to other problems (Mahata and Talburt, 2015; Mahata et al., 2015a,b) based on social media.

References

Gavin Abercrombie and Riza Batista-Navarro. 2018a. 'aye'or'no'? speech-level sentiment analysis of hansard uk parliamentary debate transcripts. In *Proceedings of the Eleventh International Conference on Language Resources and Evaluation (LREC-2018)*, pages 33–40.

Gavin Abercrombie and Riza Theresa Batista-Navarro. 2018b. Identifying opinion-topics and polarity of parliamentary debate motions. In *Proceedings of the 9th Workshop on Computational Approaches to Subjectivity, Sentiment and Social Media Analysis*, pages 280–285.

David M Blei, Andrew Y Ng, and Michael I Jordan. 2003. Latent dirichlet allocation. *Journal of machine Learning research*, 3(Jan):993–1022.

Paula Carvalho, Luís Sarmento, Jorge Teixeira, and Mário J Silva. 2011. Liars and saviors in a sentiment annotated corpus of comments to political debates. In *Proceedings of the 49th Annual Meeting of the Association for Computational Linguistics: Human Language Technologies: short papers-Volume 2*, pages 564–568. Association for Computational Linguistics.

Andrea Ceron, Luigi Curini, Stefano M Iacus, and Giuseppe Porro. 2014. Every tweet counts? how sentiment analysis of social media can improve our knowledge of citizens political preferences with an application to italy and france. *New media & society*, 16(2):340–358.

William Deitrick and Wei Hu. 2013. Mutually enhancing community detection and sentiment analysis on twitter networks. *Journal of Data Analysis and Information Processing*, 1(03):19.

Aditya Grover and Jure Leskovec. 2016. node2vec: Scalable feature learning for networks. In *Proceedings of the 22nd ACM SIGKDD international conference on Knowledge discovery and data mining*, pages 855–864. ACM.

Kazi Saidul Hasan and Vincent Ng. 2013. Stance classification of ideological debates: Data, models, features, and constraints. In *Proceedings of the Sixth International Joint Conference on Natural Language Processing*, pages 1348–1356.

Amir Karami, London S Bennett, and Xiaoyun He. 2018. Mining public opinion about economic issues: Twitter and the us presidential election. *International Journal of Strategic Decision Sciences (IJSDS)*, 9(1):18–28.

Benjamin E Lauderdale and Alexander Herzog. 2016. Measuring political positions from legislative speech. *Political Analysis*, 24(3):374–394.

Dong C Liu and Jorge Nocedal. 1989. On the limited memory bfgs method for large scale optimization. *Mathematical programming*, 45(1-3):503–528.

Euripides Loukis, Yannis Charalabidis, and Aggeliki Androutsopoulou. 2014. An analysis of multiple social media consultations in the european parliament from a public policy perspective.

Debanjan Mahata, Jasper Friedrichs, Rajiv Ratn Shah, and Jing Jiang. 2018. Detecting personal intake of medicine from twitter. *IEEE Intelligent Systems*, 33(4):87–95.

Debanjan Mahata and John R Talburt. 2015. A framework for collecting, extracting and managing event identity information from twitter. In *ICIQ*.

Debanjan Mahata, John R Talburt, and Vivek Kumar Singh. 2015a. From chirps to whistles: Discovering event-specific informative content from twitter. In *Proceedings of the ACM web science conference*, page 17. ACM.

Debanjan Mahata, John R Talburt, and Vivek Kumar Singh. 2015b. Identification and ranking of event-specific entity-centric informative content from twitter. In *International Conference on Applications of Natural Language to Information Systems*, pages 275–281. Springer.

Tomas Mikolov, Kai Chen, Greg Corrado, and Jeffrey Dean. 2013a. Efficient estimation of word representations in vector space. *arXiv preprint arXiv:1301.3781*.

Tomas Mikolov, Ilya Sutskever, Kai Chen, Greg S Corrado, and Jeff Dean. 2013b. Distributed representations of words and phrases and their compositionality. In *Advances in neural information processing systems*, pages 3111–3119.

Pushkar Mishra, Marco Del Tredici, Helen Yannakoudakis, and Ekaterina Shutova. 2018. Author profiling for abuse detection. In *Proceedings of the 27th International Conference on Computational Linguistics*, pages 1088–1098.

Saif M Mohammad and Peter D Turney. 2013. Nrc emotion lexicon. *National Research Council, Canada*.

Jing Qian, Mai ElSherief, Elizabeth M Belding, and William Yang Wang. 2018. Leveraging intra-user and inter-user representation learning for automated hate speech detection. *arXiv preprint arXiv:1804.03124*.

Ludovic Rheault, Kaspar Beelen, Christopher Cochrane, and Graeme Hirst. 2016. Measuring emotion in parliamentary debates with automated textual analysis. *PloS one*, 11(12):e0168843.

Elena Rudkowsky, Martin Haselmayer, Matthias Wastian, Marcelo Jenny, Štefan Emrich, and Michael Sedlmair. 2018. More than bags of words: Sentiment analysis with word embeddings. *Communication Methods and Measures*, 12(2-3):140–157.

Rajiv Shah and Roger Zimmermann. 2017. *Multimodal analysis of user-generated multimedia content*. Springer.

Rajiv Ratn Shah, Anupam Samanta, Deepak Gupta, Yi Yu, Suhua Tang, and Roger Zimmermann. 2016a. Prompt: Personalized user tag recommendation for social media photos leveraging personal and social contexts. In *2016 IEEE International Symposium on Multimedia (ISM)*, pages 486–492. IEEE.

Rajiv Ratn Shah, Yi Yu, Suhua Tang, Shin'ichi Satoh, Akshay Verma, and Roger Zimmermann. 2016b. Concept-level multimodal ranking of flickr photo tags via recall based weighting. In *Proceedings of the 2016 ACM Workshop on Multimedia COMMONS*, pages 19–26. ACM.

Rajiv Ratn Shah, Yi Yu, Akshay Verma, Suhua Tang, Anwar Dilawar Shaikh, and Roger Zimmermann. 2016c. Leveraging multimodal information for

event summarization and concept-level sentiment analysis. *Knowledge-Based Systems*, 108:102–109.

Stefan Stieglitz and Linh Dang-Xuan. 2012. Political communication and influence through microblogging – an empirical analysis of sentiment in twitter messages and retweet behavior. In *2012 45th Hawaii International Conference on System Sciences*, pages 3500–3509. IEEE.

Matt Thomas, Bo Pang, and Lillian Lee. 2006. Get out the vote: Determining support or opposition from congressional floor-debate transcripts. In *Proceedings of the 2006 conference on empirical methods in natural language processing*, pages 327–335. Association for Computational Linguistics.

Yaqin Wang and Haitao Liu. 2018. Is trump always rambling like a fourth-grade student? an analysis of stylistic features of donald trumps political discourse during the 2016 election. *Discourse & Society*, 29(3):299–323.

Transfer Learning Based Free-Form Speech Command Classification for Low-Resource Languages

Yohan Karunanayake
University of Moratuwa
Sri Lanka
yohan.13@cse.mrt.ac.lk

Uthayasanker Thayasivam
University of Moratuwa
Sri Lanka
rtuthaya@uom.lk

Surangika Ranathunga
University of Moratuwa
Sri Lanka
surangikar@uom.lk

Abstract

Current state-of-the-art speech-based user interfaces use data intense methodologies to recognize free-form speech commands. However, this is not viable for low-resource languages, which lack speech data. This restricts the usability of such interfaces to a limited number of languages. In this paper, we propose a methodology to develop a robust domain-specific speech command classification system for low-resource languages using speech data of a high-resource language. In this transfer learning-based approach, we used a Convolution Neural Network (CNN) to identify a fixed set of intents using an ASR-based character probability map. We were able to achieve significant results for Sinhala and Tamil datasets using an English based ASR, which attests the robustness of the proposed approach.

1 Introduction

Speech command recognizable user interfaces are becoming popular since they are more natural for end-users to interact with. Google Assistant[1], and Amazon Alexa[2] can be highlighted as few such commercial services, which are ranging from smartphones to home automation. These are capable of identifying the intent of free-form speech commands given by the user. To enable this kind of service, Automatic Speech Recognition (ASR) systems and Natural Language Understanding (NLU) systems work together with a very high level of accuracy (Ram et al., 2018).

If ASR or NLU components have suboptimal results, it directly affects the final output (Yaman et al., 2008; Rao et al., 2018). Hence, to get good results in ASR systems, it is common to use

very large speech corpora (Hannun et al., 2014; Amodei et al., 2016; Chiu et al., 2018). However, low-resource languages (LRL) do not have this luxury. Here, languages that have a limited presence on the Internet and those that lack electronic resources for speech and/or language processing are referred to as low-resource languages (LRLs) (Besacier et al., 2014). Because of this reason despite the applicability, speech-based user interfaces are limited to common languages. For LRLs researchers have focused on narrower scopes such as recognition of digits or keywords (Manamperi et al., 2018; Chen et al., 2015). However, free-form commands are difficult to manage in this way since there can be overlappings between commands.

Buddhika et al. (2018); Chen et al. (2018) show some direct speech classification approaches to its intents. In particular, Buddhika et al. (2018) have given some attention for the low resource setting. Additionally, Transfer learning is used to exploit the issue of limited data in some of the ASR based research (Huang et al., 2013; Kunze et al., 2017).

In this paper, we present an improved and effective methodology to classify domain-specific free-form speech commands while utilizing this direct classification and transfer learning approaches. Here, we use a character probability map from an ASR model trained on English to identify intents. Performance of this methodology is evaluated using Sinhala (Buddhika et al., 2018) and newly collected Tamil datasets. The proposed approach can reach to a reasonable accuracy using limited training data.

Rest of the paper is organized as follows. Section 2 presents related work, section 3 describes methodology used. Section 4 and 5 provides details of the datasets and experiments. Section 6 presents a detailed analysis of the obtained results. Finally Section 7 concludes the paper.

---

[1] https://assistant.google.com
[2] https://developer.amazon.com/alexa

Proceedings of the ACL 2019, Student Research Workshop, pages 288–294
Florence, Italy, July 28th-August 2nd, 2019. ©2019 Association for Computational Linguistics

2 Related Work

Most of the previous research has used separate ASR and NLU components to classify speech intents. In this approach, transcripts generated from the ASR module are fed as input for a separate text classifier (Yaman et al., 2008; Rao et al., 2018). Here, an erroneous transcript from the ASR module can affect the final results of this cascaded system (Yaman et al., 2008; Rao et al., 2018). In this approach, two separately trained subsystems are connected to work jointly. As a solution for these issues, Yaman et al. (2008) proposed a joint optimization technique and use of the n-best list of the ASR output. Later He and Deng (2013) extended this work by developing a generalized framework. However, these systems require a large amount of speech data, corresponding transcript, and their class labels. Further, the ASR component used in these systems requires language models and phoneme dictionaries to function, which are difficult to find for low-resource languages.

This cascading approach is effective when there is a highly accurate ASR in the target language. Rao et al. (2018) present such a system to navigate in an entertainment platform for English. Here, they have used a separate ASR system to convert speech into text. More importantly, they highlight that a lower performance of ASR affects the entire system.

More recently, researchers have presented some approaches that aim to go beyond cascading ASR components. In this way, they have tried to eliminate the use of intermediate text representations and have used automatically generated acoustic level features for classification. Liu et al. (2017) proposed topic identification in speech without the need for manual transcriptions and phoneme dictionaries. Here, the input features are bottleneck features extracted from a conventional ASR system trained with transcribed multilingual data. Then these features are classified through CNN and SVM classifiers. Additionally Lee et al. (2015) have highlighted that effectiveness of this kind of bottleneck features of speech when comparing different speech queries.

Chen et al. (2018); Buddhika et al. (2018) present two different direct classification approaches to determine the intent of a given spoken utterance. Chen et al. (2018) have used a neural network based acoustic model and a CNN based classifier. However, this requires transcripts of the speech data to train the acoustic model, thus accuracy depends on the availability of a large amount of speech data. One advantage of this approach is that we can optimize the final model once we combined the two models. Buddhika et al. (2018) classified speech directly using MFCC (Mel-frequency Cepstral Coefficients) of the speech signals as features. In this approach, they have used only 10 hours of speech data to achieve reasonable accuracy.

3 Methodology

In section 2, we showed that research work of Liu et al. (2017); Chen et al. (2018); Buddhika et al. (2018) has benefited from direct speech classification approach. Additionally, as shown in the work of Lee et al. (2015); Liu et al. (2017), it is beneficial to use automatically discovered acoustic related features. Therefore our key idea is reusing a well trained ASR neural network on high resource language as a feature transformation module. This is known as transfer learning (Pan and Yang, 2010). Here, we try to reuse the knowledge learned from one task to another associated task. Current well trained neural network based end-to-end ASR models are capable of converting given spoken utterance into the corresponding character sequence. Therefore these ASR models can convert speech into some character representation. Our approach is to reuse this ability in low-resource speech classification.

We used DeepSpeech (DS) (Hannun et al., 2014) model as the ASR model. DS model consists of 5 hidden layers including a bidirectional recurrent layer. Input for the model is a time-series of audio features for every timeslice. MFCC coefficients are used as features. Model converts this input sequence $x^{(i)}$ into a sequence of character probabilities $y^{(i)}$, with $\hat{y}_t = \mathbb{P}(c_t|x)$, where $c_t = \in \{a, b, c, .., z, space, apostrophe, blank\}$ in English model. These probability values are calculated by a softmax layer. Finally, the corresponding transcript is generated using the probabilities via beam search decoding with or without combining a language model.

Here, we selected intermediate probability values as the transfer learning features from the model. Any feature generated after this layer is ineffective since it is affected by the beam search and it only outputs the best possible character sequence. Before the final softmax layer, there is a bi-directional recurrent layer, which is very critical for detecting sequence features in speech. Without this layer, the model is useless (Hannun et al., 2014; Amodei et al., 2016). Hence, the only possible way to extract features is after the softmax layer. Additionally, this layer provides normalized probability values for each time step. Figure 1 shows a visualization of this intermediate character probability map for a Sinhala speech query containing 'ශේෂය කීයද - śēṣaya kīyada'.

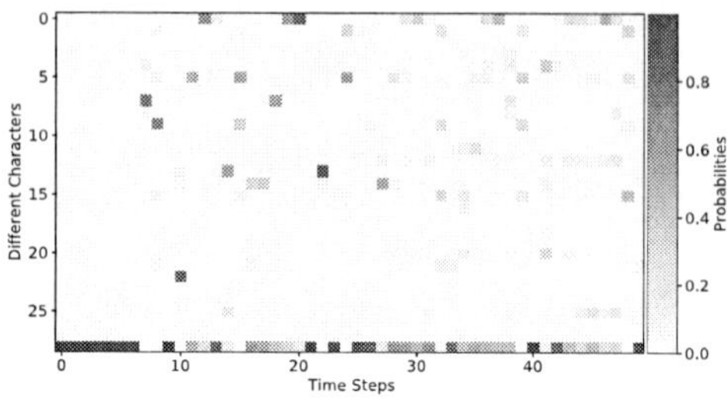

Figure 1: Visualization of probability output for Sinhala utterance

In this considering scenario, we need to identify a fixed set of intents related to a specific domain. Instead of converting these probability values into a text representation, we classify these obtained features directly in to intents as in (Liu et al., 2017; Chen et al., 2018). We experimented with different classifier models such as Support Vector Machines (SVM), Feed Forward Networks (FFN), which used in previous works. Further, in the work of Liu et al. (2017); Chen et al. (2018), they have shown the effectiveness of Convolutional Neural Networks - CNN to classify intermediate features of the speech. Because of this, we evaluated the performance of CNN. Additionally, We examined the effectiveness of 1-dimensional(1D) and 2-dimensional(2D) convolution for feature classification. Figure 2 shows the architecture of the final CNN based model. Please refer to 'Supplementary Material' for the detail of model parameters.

4   Datasets

We used two different free-form speech command datasets to measure the accuracy of the proposed methodology. The first one is a Sinhala dataset and contains audio clips in the banking domain (Buddhika et al., 2018). Since it was difficult to find such other datasets for low-resource languages, we created another dataset in the Tamil language,

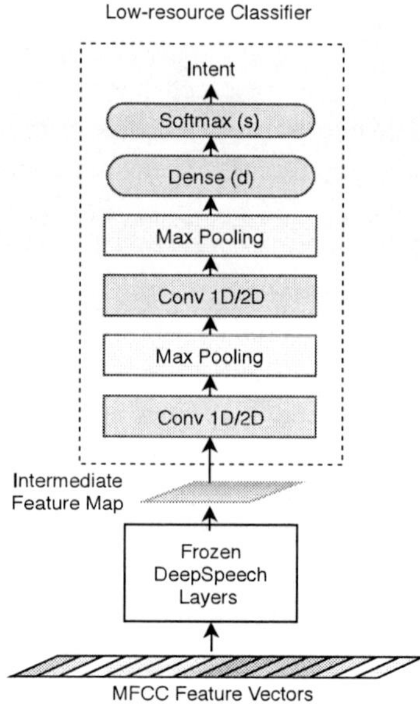

Figure 2: Architecture of the final model

which contains the same intentions as Sinhala dataset. Both Sinhala and Tamil are morphologically different languages. Table 1 summarizes the details.

Intent	Sinhala		Tamil	
	I	S	I	S
1. Request Acc. balance	8	1712	7	101
2. Money deposit	7	1306	7	75
3. Money withdraw	8	1548	5	62
4. Bill payments	5	1004	4	46
5. Money transfer	7	1271	4	49
6. Credit card payments	4	795	4	67
Total	39	7624	31	400
Unique words	32		46	

Table 1: Details of the data sets (I-Inflections, S-Number of samples)

Original Sinhala dataset contained 10 hours of speech data from 152 males and 63 females students in the age between 20 to 25 years. We had to revalidate the dataset since it included some miss-classified, too lengthy and erroneous speech queries. The final data set contained 7624 samples totaling 7.5 hours. Tamil dataset contains 0.5 hours of speech data from 40 males and females students in the same age group. There were 400 samples in the Tamil dataset. The length of each audio clip is less than 7 seconds.

5   Experiments

For the transfer learning task, we considered the DeepSpeech (DS) model 1 (Hannun et al., 2014).

	Benchmark		Current			
Approach	SVM	6L FFN	TL + SVM	TL + FFN	TL + 1D CNN	TL + 2D CNN
Features	MFCC		DS Intermediate			
Accuracy Sinhala	48.79%	63.23%	70.04%	74.67%	**93.16%**	92.09%
Accuracy Tamil	29.25%	26.98%	23.77%	35.50%	37.57%	**76.30%**

Table 2: Summary of results with different approaches and overall accuracy values

This model and some other neural network based ASR modes provide a probability map for each character in each time step. Due to high computational demand for training, we adopted an already available pre-trained DS model by Mozilla[3]. This model uses the first 26 MFCC features as input. Model is trained on American English and achieves an 11% word error rate on the LibriSpeech clean test corpus.

Given the DS English model, we extract the intermediate probability features for a given speech sample and then fed them into the classifier. Further, we employed a Bayesian optimization based algorithm for hyperparameter tuining (Bergstra et al., 2013). Since datasets are small we used 5 fold cross-validation to evaluate the accuracy.

We selected method presented in (Buddhika et al., 2018) as our benchmark. In their work, they have used the first 13 MFCC features as input for the SVM, FFN classifiers. Since we had to validate the Sinhala dataset, we reevaluate the accuracy values on the validated dataset using 5-fold cross-validation. Additionally, we performed the same experiments on newly collected Tamil dataset to examine the language independence of the proposing method. Table 2 summarizes the outcomes of these different approaches. In all experiments, class distribution among all data splits was nearly equal.

In this work, we are concerned about the amount of available data. Hence, we evaluated the accuracy change of the best performing approaches with the size of training samples. We perform this on the Sinhala dataset since it has more than 4000 data samples. We drew multiple random samples with a particular size and performed 5-fold cross-validation. Here, the number of random samples is 20. Table 3 summarizes the experiment results.

In another experiment, we examined the end-to-end text output of the DS English model for a given Sinhala speech query. Table 4 presents some of these outputs.

[3]https://github.com/mozilla/DeepSpeech

6 Result and Discussion

We were able to achieve 93.16% and 76.30% overall accuracy for Sinhala and Tamil datasets respectively using 5-fold cross-validation. Table 2 provides a comparison of previous and our approaches. It shows clearly that the proposed method is more viable than the previous direct speech feature classification approach. One possible reason can be the reduction of noise in speech signals. In this situation, the DS model is capable of removing these noises since it is already trained on noisy data. Another reason is that reduction of the feature space. Additionally, in this way, we can have more accurate results using small dataset.

Intent	Sinhala			Tamil		
	F1	P	R	F1	P	R
1	0.96	0.94	0.99	0.87	0.89	0.87
2	0.93	0.97	0.89	0.80	0.78	0.84
3	0.91	0.87	0.95	0.75	0.89	0.66
4	0.89	0.93	0.87	0.64	0.75	0.63
5	0.96	0.97	0.95	0.60	0.76	0.51
6	0.92	0.95	0.89	0.79	0.74	0.89
Average	0.93	0.93	0.93	0.76	0.81	0.76

Table 3: Classification results of best performing models (F1- F1-Score, P- Precision, R- Recall)

Table 3 shows the averaged precision, recall and F1-score values for each intent class and two datasets. In the Sinhala dataset, all classes achieve more than 0.9 F1-score, except for type 4 intent. Type 1 intent shows the highest F1-score among all and, this must be because of the higher number of data samples available for this class. Despite that, type 6 intent also reports 0.93 f1-score even with a lower number of data samples. Tamil data shows a slightly different result. Intent types 4,5 report the lowest score in the Tamil dataset and the number of speech queries from these classes are comparatively low in the dataset. Further, we can observe that the Tamil classifier is incapable of accurately identifying positive intent classes 4 and 5 (since lower recall value).

Compared to Sinhala data with a sample size of 500, Tamil dataset reports high overall accuracy with 400 samples. Tamil dataset contains codemixed speech quires since it is more natural when in speaking. These words are in English. Additionally, the feature generator model (DS model) is also trained in English data. This can result in more overall accuracy in Tamil data set. Additionally, type 6 intent commands contain English words in both datasets and this can result for higher precision value.

Further, sentences with more overlapping words with other sentences (different intent type) and with limited length tend to misclassify more. Hence classes, type 3,4 in Sinhala, type 2,4 in Tamil dataset show lower accuracy.

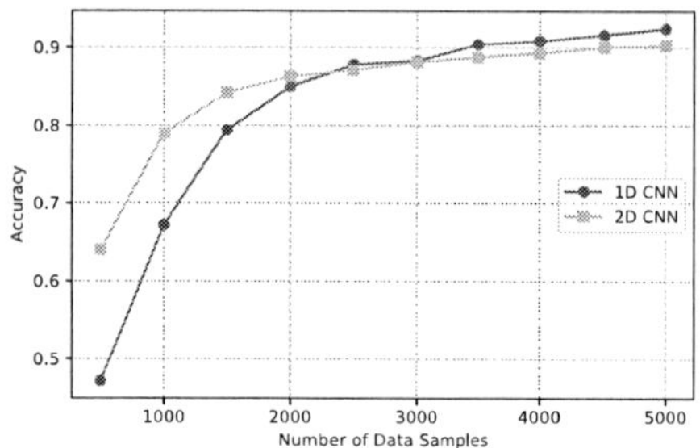

Figure 3: CNN classifier accuracy variance with the number of samples (Sinhala dataset)

Figure 3 summarize the overall accuracy change of best performing classifiers with samples size. As it shows having 1000 samples is enough to achieve nearly 80% overall accuracy. After that, it reaches saturation. Furthermore, it reports 77% overall accuracy for Tamil dataset with 320 training samples. This highlights the effectiveness of the proposed transfer learning approach in limited data situations.

Additionally, Figure 3 shows the most effective CNN model type with the number of available data samples to classify sequential feature maps. As it shows, it is useful to use 2D CNN based classifiers when there is a very limited amount of data. However, when there are relatively more data (More than 4000 samples in Sinhala dataset) 1D CNN based classifiers gives higher results. We can see this effect on Tamil dataset also. As table 2 shows 1D CNN model accuracy is low compared to 2D CNN model with 400 data samples.

Further, we examined the speech decoding capability of the English model. See Table 4. Here 'Utterance' is the pronounced Sinhal sentence, 'Eng. Transcript' is the ideal English transcript. 'DS output' lists the generated transcripts from the

Utterance	ශේෂය කීයද	ඉතිරිය කීයද
Eng. Transcript	'sheshaya keeyada'	'ithiriya keeyada'
DS Output	'she s reci ete' 'sheis heki edit' 'sheis ae an'	'it cillety edet' 'it tia gaviade' 'it lid en'

Table 4: DS transcript for some Sinhala utterances

full model. In these generated outputs, the first few characters are decoded correctly. But, in the latter part, this decoding is compromised by the possible character sequences of the English language since it is trained in English. From this, we can infer that this character probability map is closer to text representation than the MFCC features. Hence, this can improve the classification accuracy.

7 Conclusion

In this study, we proposed a method to identify the intent of free-form commands in a low-resource language. We used an ASR model trained on the English language to classify the Sinhala and Tamil low-resource datasets. The proposed method outperforms previous work and, even with a limited number of samples, it can reach to a reasonable accuracy.

CNN base classifiers perform well in the classification of character probability maps generated by ASRs. Further, 1D CNN models work better with a higher number of samples, while 2D CNN models work better with a small amount of data. In the future, we plan to extend this study by incorporating more data from different languages and domains.

Acknowledgments

This research was funded by a Senate Research Committee (SRC) Grant of the University of Moratuwa. We thank for the support received from the LK Domain Registry. We thank Mr. P. Thananjay for assistance with data validation.

References

Dario Amodei, Sundaram Ananthanarayanan, Rishita Anubhai, Jingliang Bai, Eric Battenberg, Carl Case, Jared Casper, Bryan Catanzaro, Qiang Cheng, Guoliang Chen, et al. 2016. Deep speech 2: End-to-end speech recognition in english and mandarin. In *International Conference on Machine Learning*, pages 173–182.

James Bergstra, Dan Yamins, and David D Cox. 2013. Hyperopt: A python library for optimizing the hyperparameters of machine learning algorithms. In *Proceedings of the 12th Python in science conference*, pages 13–20. Citeseer.

Laurent Besacier, Etienne Barnard, Alexey Karpov, and Tanja Schultz. 2014. Automatic speech recognition for under-resourced languages: A survey. *Speech Communication*, 56:85–100.

Darshana Buddhika, Ranula Liyadipita, Sudeepa Nadeeshan, Hasini Witharana, Sanath Javasena, and Uthayasanker Thayasivam. 2018. Domain specific intent classification of sinhala speech data. In *2018 International Conference on Asian Language Processing (IALP)*, pages 197–202. IEEE.

Nancy F Chen, Chongjia Ni, I-Fan Chen, Sunil Sivadas, Haihua Xu, Xiong Xiao, Tze Siong Lau, Su Jun Leow, Boon Pang Lim, Cheung-Chi Leung, et al. 2015. Low-resource keyword search strategies for tamil. In *2015 IEEE International Conference on Acoustics, Speech and Signal Processing (ICASSP)*, pages 5366–5370. IEEE.

Yuan-Ping Chen, Ryan Price, and Srinivas Bangalore. 2018. Spoken language understanding without speech recognition. In *2018 IEEE International Conference on Acoustics, Speech and Signal Processing (ICASSP)*, pages 6189–6193. IEEE.

Chung-Cheng Chiu, Tara N Sainath, Yonghui Wu, Rohit Prabhavalkar, Patrick Nguyen, Zhifeng Chen, Anjuli Kannan, Ron J Weiss, Kanishka Rao, Ekaterina Gonina, et al. 2018. State-of-the-art speech recognition with sequence-to-sequence models. In *2018 IEEE International Conference on Acoustics, Speech and Signal Processing (ICASSP)*, pages 4774–4778. IEEE.

Awni Hannun, Carl Case, Jared Casper, Bryan Catanzaro, Greg Diamos, Erich Elsen, Ryan Prenger, Sanjeev Satheesh, Shubho Sengupta, Adam Coates, et al. 2014. Deep speech: Scaling up end-to-end speech recognition. *arXiv preprint arXiv:1412.5567*.

Xiaodong He and Li Deng. 2013. Speech-centric information processing: An optimization-oriented approach. *Proceedings of the IEEE*, 101(5):1116–1135.

Jui-Ting Huang, Jinyu Li, Dong Yu, Li Deng, and Yifan Gong. 2013. Cross-language knowledge transfer using multilingual deep neural network with shared hidden layers. In *2013 IEEE International Conference on Acoustics, Speech and Signal Processing*, pages 7304–7308. IEEE.

Julius Kunze, Louis Kirsch, Ilia Kurenkov, Andreas Krug, Jens Johannsmeier, and Sebastian Stober. 2017. Transfer learning for speech recognition on a budget. In *Proceedings of the 2nd Workshop on Representation Learning for NLP*, pages 168–177.

Lin-shan Lee, James Glass, Hung-yi Lee, and Chun-an Chan. 2015. Spoken content retrievalbeyond cascading speech recognition with text retrieval. *IEEE/ACM Transactions on Audio, Speech, and Language Processing*, 23(9):1389–1420.

Chunxi Liu, Jan Trmal, Matthew Wiesner, Craig Harman, and Sanjeev Khudanpur. 2017. Topic identification for speech without asr. In *Proc. Interspeech 2017*, pages 2501–2505.

Wageesha Manamperi, Dinesha Karunathilake, Thilini Madhushani, Nimasha Galagedara, and Dileeka Dias. 2018. Sinhala speech recognition for interactive voice response systems accessed through mobile phones. In *2018 Moratuwa Engineering Research Conference (MERCon)*, pages 241–246. IEEE.

Sinno Jialin Pan and Qiang Yang. 2010. A survey on transfer learning. *IEEE Transactions on knowledge and data engineering*, 22(10):1345–1359.

Ashwin Ram, Rohit Prasad, Chandra Khatri, Anu Venkatesh, Raefer Gabriel, Qing Liu, Jeff Nunn, Behnam Hedayatnia, Ming Cheng, Ashish Nagar, et al. 2018. Conversational ai: The science behind the alexa prize. *arXiv preprint arXiv:1801.03604*.

Jinfeng Rao, Ferhan Ture, and Jimmy Lin. 2018. Multi-task learning with neural networks for voice query understanding on an entertainment platform. In *Proceedings of the 24th ACM SIGKDD International Conference on Knowledge Discovery & Data Mining*, pages 636–645. ACM.

Sibel Yaman, Li Deng, Dong Yu, Ye-Yi Wang, and Alex Acero. 2008. An integrative and discriminative technique for spoken utterance classification. *IEEE Transactions on Audio, Speech, and Language Processing*, 16(6):1207–1214.

A Supplemental Material

Table 5 present hyperparameters for low-resourced models described in the section 3

Layer	Sinhala Models		Tamil Models	
	1D CNN	2D CNN	1D CNN	2D CNN
1. Conv	Filters 38 Kernel Size 19	Filters 16 Kernel Size 1x8	Filters 39 Kernel Size 18	Filters 14 Kernel Size 5x1
2. Max Pooling	Size 18 Stride 7	Size 6x1 Stride 5x5	Size 25 Stride 5	Size 13x1 Stride 5x1
3. Conv	Filters 28 Kernel Size 22	Filters 17 Kernel Size 20x8	Filters 26 Kernel Size 19	Filters 13 Kernel Size 11x20
4. Max Pooling	Size 22 Stride 10	Size 19x2 Stride 16x8	Size 20 Stride 5	Size 17x1 Stride 2x7
5. Dense	Units 131	Units 118	Units 84	Units 127
6. Softmax	6	6	6	6

Table 5: Hyperparameters for CNN classifier models

Embedding Strategies for Specialized Domains: Application to Clinical Entity Recognition

Hicham El Boukkouri[1,2], Olivier Ferret[3], Thomas Lavergne[1,2], Pierre Zweigenbaum[1]

[1]LIMSI, CNRS, Université Paris-Saclay, Orsay, France,
[2]Univ. Paris-Sud,
[3]CEA, LIST, Gif-sur-Yvette, F-91191 France.
{elboukkouri, lavergne, pz}@limsi.fr, olivier.ferret@cea.fr

Abstract

Using pre-trained word embeddings in conjunction with Deep Learning models has become the *de facto* approach in Natural Language Processing (NLP). While this usually yields satisfactory results, off-the-shelf word embeddings tend to perform poorly on texts from specialized domains such as clinical reports. Moreover, training specialized word representations from scratch is often either impossible or ineffective due to the lack of large enough in-domain data. In this work, we focus on the clinical domain for which we study embedding strategies that rely on general-domain resources only. We show that by combining off-the-shelf contextual embeddings (ELMo) with static word2vec embeddings trained on a small in-domain corpus built from the task data, we manage to reach and sometimes outperform representations learned from a large corpus in the medical domain.[1]

1 Introduction

Today, the NLP community can enjoy an ever-growing list of embedding techniques that include factorization methods (e.g. GloVe (Pennington et al., 2014)), neural methods (e.g. word2vec (Mikolov et al., 2013), fastText (Bojanowski et al., 2017)) and more recently dynamic methods that take into account the context (e.g. ELMo (Peters et al., 2018), BERT (Devlin et al., 2018)).

The success of these methods can be arguably attributed to the availability of large general-domain corpora like Wikipedia, Gigaword (Graff et al., 2003) or the BooksCorpus (Zhu et al., 2015). Unfortunately, similar corpora are often unavailable for specialized domains, leaving the NLP practitioner with only two choices: either using

general-domain word embeddings that are probably not fit for the task at hand or training new embeddings on the available in-domain corpus, which may probably be too small and result in poor performance.

In this paper, we focus on the clinical domain and explore several ways to improve pre-trained embeddings built from a small corpus in this domain by using different kinds of general-domain embeddings. More specifically, we make the following contributions:

- we show that word embeddings trained on a small in-domain corpus can be improved using off-the-shelf contextual embeddings (ELMo) from the general domain. We also show that this combination performs better than the contextual embeddings alone and improves upon static embeddings trained on a large in-domain corpus;

- we define two ways of combining contextual and static embeddings and conclude that the naive concatenation of vectors is consistently outperformed by the addition of the static representation directly into the internal linear combination of ELMo;

- finally, we show that ELMo models can be successfully fine-tuned on a small in-domain corpus, bringing significant improvements to strategies involving contextual embeddings.

2 Related Work

Former work by Roberts (2016) analyzed the trade-off between corpus size and similarity when training word embeddings for a clinical entity recognition task. The author's conclusion was that while embeddings trained with word2vec on in-domain texts performed generally better, a combination of both in-domain and general domain em-

---

[1]Python code for reproducing our experiments is available at: https://github.com/helboukkouri/acl_srw_2019

Proceedings of the ACL 2019, Student Research Workshop, pages 295–301
Florence, Italy, July 28th-August 2nd, 2019. ©2019 Association for Computational Linguistics

3. Echocardiogram on **DATE[Nov 6 2007] , showed ejection fraction of 55% , mild mitral insufficiency , and 1+ tricuspid insufficiency with mild pulmonary hypertension .

DERMOPLAST TOPICAL TP Q12H PRN Pain DOCUSATE SODIUM 100 MG PO BID PRN Constipation IBUPROFEN 400-600 MG PO Q6H PRN Pain

The patient had headache that was relieved only with oxycodone . A CT scan of the head showed microvascular ischemic changes . A followup MRI which also showed similar changes . This was most likely due to her multiple myeloma with hyperviscosity .

Table 1: Examples of entity mentions (Problem, Treatment, and Test) from the i2b2 2010 dataset[*].
[*] This table is reproduced from (Roberts, 2016).

beddings worked the best. Subsequent work by Zhu et al. (2018) obtained state-of-the-art results on the same task using contextual embeddings (ELMo) that were pre-trained on a large in-domain corpus made of medical articles from Wikipedia and clinical notes from MIMIC-III (Johnson et al., 2016). More recently, these embeddings were outperformed by BERT representations pre-trained on MIMIC-III, proving once more the value of large in-domain corpora (Si et al., 2019).[2]

While interesting for the clinical domain, these strategies may not always be applicable to other specialized fields since large in-domain corpora like MIMIC-III will rarely be available. To deal with this issue, we explore embedding combinations[3]. In this respect, we consider both static forms of combination explored in (Yin and Schütze, 2016; Muromägi et al., 2017; Bollegala et al., 2018) and more dynamic modes of combination that can be found in (Peters et al., 2018) and (Kiela et al., 2018). In this work, we show in particular how a combination of general-domain contextual embeddings, fine-tuning, and in-domain static embeddings trained on a small corpus can be employed to reach a similar performance using resources that are available for any domain.

3 Evaluation Task: i2b2/VA 2010 Clinical Concept Detection

We evaluate our embedding strategies on the Clinical Concept Detection task of the 2010 i2b2/VA challenge (Uzuner et al., 2011).

3.1 Data

The data consists of discharge summaries and progress reports from three different institutions: Partners Healthcare, Beth Israel Deaconess Medical Center, and the University of Pittsburgh Medical Center. These documents are labeled and split into 394 training files and 477 test files for a total of $30,946 + 45,404 \approx 76,000$ sequences [4].

3.2 Task and Model

The goal of the Clinical Concept Detection task is to extract three types of medical entities: problems (e.g. the name of a disease), treatments (e.g. the name of a drug) and tests (e.g. the name of a diagnostic procedure). Table 1 shows examples of entity mentions and Table 2 shows the distribution of each entity type in the training and test sets.

Entity type	Train set	Test set
Problem	11,967	18,550
Treatment	8,497	13,560
Test	7,365	12,899
Total	27,829	45,009

Table 2: Distribution of medical entity types.

To solve this task, we choose a bi-LSTM-CRF as is usual in entity recognition tasks (Lample et al., 2016; Chalapathy et al., 2016; Habibi et al., 2017). Our particular architecture uses 3 bi-LSTM layers with 256 units, a dropout rate of 0.5 and is implemented using the AllenNLP framework (Gardner et al., 2018). During training, the exact span F1 score is monitored on 5,000 randomly sampled sequences for early-stopping.

---

[2]In this work, we will be focusing on contextualized embeddings from ELMo.

[3]This is more generally related to the notion of "meta-embeddings" and ensemble of embeddings as highlighted by Yin and Schütze (2016).

[4]Due to limitations introduced by the Institutional Review Board (IRB), only part of the original 2010 data can now be obtained for research at `https://www.i2b2.org/NLP/DataSets/`. Our work uses the full original dataset.

4 Embedding Strategies

We focus on two kinds of embedding algorithms: static embeddings (word2vec) and contextualized embeddings (ELMo). The first kind assigns to each token a fixed representation (hence the name "static"), is relatively fast to train but does not manage out-of-vocabulary words and polysemy. The second kind, on the other hand, produces a contextualized representation. As a result, the word embedding is adapted dynamically to the context and polysemy is managed. Moreover, in the particular case of ELMo, word embeddings are character-level, which implies that the model is able to produce vectors whether or not the word is part of the training vocabulary.

Despite contextualized embeddings usually performing better than static embeddings, they still require large amounts of data to be trained successfully. Since this data is often unavailable in specialized domains, we explore strategies that combine off-the-shelf contextualized embeddings with static embeddings trained on a small in-domain corpus.

4.1 Static Embeddings

First, we use word2vec[5] to train embeddings on a small corpus built from the task data:

i2b2 (2010) 394 documents from the training set to which we added 826 more files from a set of unlabeled documents. This is a small (1 million tokens) in-domain corpus. Similar corpora will often be available in other specialized domains as it is always possible to build a corpus from the training documents.

Then, we also train embeddings on each of two general-domain corpora:

Wikipedia (2017) encyclopedia articles from the 01/10/2017 data dump[6]. This is a large (2 billion tokens) corpus from the general domain that has limited coverage of the medical field.

Gigaword (2003) newswire text data from many sources including the New York Times. This is a large (2 billion tokens) corpus from the general domain with almost no coverage of the medical field.

---

[5]We used the following parameters: cbow=1, size=256, window=5, min-count=5, iter=10.

[6]Similar dumps can be downloaded at https://dumps.wikimedia.org/enwiki/.

4.2 Contextualized Embeddings

We use two off-the-shelf ELMo models[7]:

ELMo_small a general-domain model trained on the 1 Billion Word Benchmark corpus (Chelba et al., 2013). This is the small version of ELMo that produces 256-dimensional embeddings.

ELMo_original the original ELMo model. This is a general-domain model trained on a mix of Wikipedia and newswire data. It produces 1024-dimensional embeddings.

Additionally, we also build embeddings by fine-tuning each model on the i2b2 corpus. The fine-tuning is achieved by resuming the training of the ELMo language model on the new data (i2b2). At each epoch, the validation perplexity is monitored and ultimately the best model is chosen:

ELMo_small$_{finetuned}$ the result of fine-tuning ELMo_small for 10 epochs.

ELMo_original$_{finetuned}$ the result of fine-tuning ELMo_original for 5 epochs.

4.3 Embedding Combinations

There are many possible ways to combine embeddings. In this work, we explore two methods:

Concatenation a simple concatenation of vectors coming from two different embeddings. This is denoted $\mathbf{X} \oplus \mathbf{Y}$ (e.g. i2b2$\oplus$Wikipedia).

Mixture in the particular case where ELMo embeddings were combined with word2vec vectors, we can directly add the word2vec embedding in the linear combination of ELMo. We denote this combination strategy $\mathbf{X} + \!\!+ \mathbf{Y}$ (e.g. ELMo_small$+\!\!+$i2b2).

The mixture method generalizes the way ELMo representations are combined. Given a word w, if we denote the three internal representations produced by ELMo (i.e. the CharCNN, 1st bi-LSTM and 2nd bi-LSTM representations) by h_1, h_2, h_3, we recall that the model computes the word's embedding as:

$$\text{ELMo}(w) = \gamma(\alpha_1 h_1 + \alpha_2 h_2 + \alpha_3 h_3)$$

---

[7]All the models with their descriptions are available at https://allennlp.org/elmo.

Embedding Strategy	X	i2b2 $\oplus$ X	i2b2 $+\!\!+$ X
i2b2	82.06 ± 0.32	-	-
Wikipedia	83.30 ± 0.25	83.35 ± 0.62	-
Gigaword	82.54 ± 0.41	83.10 ± 0.37	-
ELMo_small	80.79 ± 0.95	84.18 ± 0.26	84.94 ± 0.94
ELMo_original	84.28 ± 0.66	85.25 ± 0.21	85.64 ± 0.33
ELMo_small$_{finetuned}$	83.86 ± 0.87	84.81 ± 0.40	85.93 ± 1.01
ELMo_original$_{finetuned}$	85.90 ± 0.50	$\mathbf{86.18} \pm 0.48$	$\mathbf{86.23} \pm 0.58$

Table 3: Performance of various strategies involving a general-domain resource and a small in-domain corpus (i2b2). The values are Exact Span F1 scores given as Mean $\pm$ Std (bold: best result for each kind of combination).

where γ and $\{\alpha_i, i = 1, 2, 3\}$ are tunable task-specific coefficients[8]. Given h_{w2v}, the word2vec representation of the word w, we compute a "mixture" representation as:

$$\text{ELMo}_{\text{mix}}(w) = \gamma(\alpha_1 h_1 + \alpha_2 h_2 + \alpha_3 h_3 + \beta h_{w2v})$$

where β is a new tunable coefficient[9].

5 Results and Discussion

We run each experiment with 10 different random seeds and report performance in mean and standard deviation (std). Values are expressed in terms of strict F1 measure that we compute using the official script from the i2b2/VA 2010 challenge.

5.1 Using General-domain Resources

Table 3 shows the results we obtain using general-domain resources only. The top part of the table shows the performance of word2vec embeddings trained on i2b2 as well as two general-domain corpora: Wikipedia and Gigaword. We see that i2b2 performs the worst despite being trained on in-domain data. This explicitly showcases the challenge faced by specialized domains and confirms that training embeddings on small in-domain corpora tends to perform poorly. As for the general domain embeddings, we can observe that Wikipedia is slightly better than Gigaword. This can be explained by the fact that the former has some medical-related articles which implies a better coverage of the clinical vocabulary compared to the newswire corpus Gigaword[10]. We can also see that combining general-domain word2vec embeddings with i2b2 results in weak improvements that are slightly higher for Gigaword probably for the same reason.

The middle part of the table shows the results we obtain using off-the-shelf contextualized representations. Looking at the embeddings alone, we see that ELMo_small performs worse than i2b2 while ELMo_original is better than all word2vec embeddings. Again, the reason for the small model's performance might be related to the different training corpora. In fact, ELMo_original, aside from being a larger model, was trained on Wikipedia articles which may include some medical articles. Another interesting point is that both the mean and variance of the performance when using off-the-shelf ELMo models improve notably when combined with word2vec embeddings trained on i2b2. This improvement is even greater for the small model, probably because it has less coverage of the medical domain. Furthermore, we see that the performance improves again, although to a lesser extent when the word2vec embedding is mixed with ELMo instead of combined through concatenation.

The bottom part of the table shows the results obtained after fine-tuning both ELMo models. We see that fine-tuning improves all the results (but to varying extents), with the best performance being achieved using combinations—either concatenation or mixture—of i2b2's word2vec and the larger fine-tuned ELMo.

Two points are worth being noted. First, it is interesting to see that we achieve good results with a model that only uses an off-the-shelf model and a small in-domain corpus built from the task data. This is a valuable insight since the same strategy could be applied for any specialized

---

[8]In practice, the coefficients go through a softmax before being used in the linear combination.

[9]In particular cases where the ELMo model produces 1024-dimensional embeddings, we duplicate the 256-dimensional word2vec embeddings so that the dimensions match before mixing.

[10]We count 14.42% out-of-vocabulary tokens in Gigaword against 5.82% for Wikipedia.

domain. Second, we see that the smaller 256-dimensional ELMo model, which initially performed very poorly ($\approx$ 80 F1), improved drastically ($\approx$ +6 F1) using our best strategy and does not lag very far behind the original 1024-dimensional model. This is also valuable since many practitioners do not have the computational resources that are required for using the larger versions of recent models like ELMo or BERT.

5.2 Using In-domain Resources

It is natural to wonder how our results fare against models trained on large in-domain corpora. Fortunately, there are two such corpora in the clinical domain:

MIMIC III (2016) a collection of medical notes from a large database of Intensive Care Unit encounters at a large hospital (Johnson et al., 2016)[11]. This is a large (1 billion tokens) in-domain corpus.

PubMed (2018) a collection of scientific article abstracts in the biomedical domain[12]. This is a large (4 billion tokens) corpus from a close but somewhat different domain.

Both Zhu et al. (2018) and Si et al. (2019) trained the ELMo (original) on MIMIC, with the former resorting to only a part of MIMIC mixed with some curated Wikipedia articles. Table 4 reports their results, to which we add the performance of strategies using word2vec embeddings trained on MIMIC and PubMed, and an open-source ELMo model trained on PubMed[13].

We can see yet again that word2vec embeddings perform less well than ELMo models trained on the same corpora. We also see that combining the two kinds of embeddings still brings some improvement (see ELMo (PubMed) + MIMIC). And more importantly, we observe that by using only general-domain resources, we perform very close to the ELMo models trained on a large in-domain corpus (MIMIC) with a maximum difference in F1 measure of $\approx$ 1.5 points.

Embedding Strategy	F1
MIMIC	84.29 $\pm$ 0.30
PubMed	84.06 $\pm$ 0.14
ELMo (PubMed)	86.29 $\pm$ 0.61
ELMo (PubMed) + MIMIC	87.17 $\pm$ 0.54
ELMo_original$_{finetuned}$ + i2b2	86.23 $\pm$ 0.58
ELMo (Clinical) (Zhu et al., 2018)	86.84 $\pm$ 0.16
ELMo (MIMIC) (Si et al., 2019)	**87.80**

Table 4: Comparison of strategies using large in-domain corpora with the best strategy using a small in-domain corpus and general-domain resources. The values are Exact Span F1 scores.

5.3 Using GloVe and fastText

In order to make sure that the observed phenomena are not the result of using the word2vec method in particular, we reproduce the same experiments using GloVe and fastText[14]. The corresponding results are reported in Table 5 and Table 6.

We can see that GloVe and fastText are always outperformed by word2vec when trained on a single corpus only. This is not true anymore when combining these embeddings with representations from ELMo. In fact, in this case, the results are mostly comparable to the performance obtained when using word2vec, with a slight improvement when using fastText. This small improvement may be explained by the fact that the fastText method is able to manage Out-Of-Vocabulary tokens while GloVe and word2vec are not.

More importantly, these additional experiments validate the initial results obtained with word2vec: static embeddings pre-trained on a small in-domain corpus (i2b2) can be combined with general domain contextual embeddings (ELMo), through either one of the proposed methods, to reach a performance that is comparable to the state-of-the-art[15].

5.4 Limitations

We can list the following limitations for this work:

- we tested only one specialized domain on one task using one NER architecture. Although

[11]The MIMIC-III corpus can be downloaded at `https://mimic.physionet.org/gettingstarted/access/`.

[12] The PubMed-MEDLINE corpus can be downloaded at `https://www.nlm.nih.gov/databases/download/pubmed_medline.html`.

[13]Since we did not train this model ourselves, we are not sure whether the training corpus is equivalent to the PubMed corpus we use for training word2vec embeddings.

[14]We used the following parameters: (GloVe) `size=256, window=15, min-count=5, iter=10`; (fastText) `skipgram, size=256, window=5, min-count=5, neg=5, loss=ns, minn=3, maxn=6, iter=10`.

[15]Our single best model gets a F1 score of 87.10.

Embedding Strategy	X	i2b2 $\oplus$ X	i2b2 $+\!\!\!+$ X
i2b2	80.21 $\pm$ 0.37	-	-
Wikipedia	81.82 $\pm$ 0.52	81.29 $\pm$ 0.42	-
Gigaword	81.38 $\pm$ 0.33	81.47 $\pm$ 0.18	-
ELMo_small	80.79 $\pm$ 0.95	83.04 $\pm$ 1.03	84.30 $\pm$ 0.72
ELMo_original	84.28 $\pm$ 0.66	85.00 $\pm$ 0.32	85.12 $\pm$ 0.26
ELMo_small$_{finetuned}$	83.86 $\pm$ 0.87	84.42 $\pm$ 0.75	85.19 $\pm$ 0.75
ELMo_original$_{finetuned}$	85.90 $\pm$ 0.50	86.05 $\pm$ 0.16	**86.46** $\pm$ 0.36

Table 5: Performance of the strategies from Table 3 using GloVe instead of word2vec (bold: GloVe > word2vec)

Embedding Strategy	X	i2b2 $\oplus$ X	i2b2 $+\!\!\!+$ X
i2b2	81.98 $\pm$ 0.41	-	-
Wikipedia	82.32 $\pm$ 0.37	81.84 $\pm$ 1.48	-
Gigaword	81.77 $\pm$ 0.36	82.40 $\pm$ 0.32	-
ELMo_small	80.79 $\pm$ 0.95	**84.44** $\pm$ 0.42	**85.47** $\pm$ 0.61
ELMo_original	84.28 $\pm$ 0.66	**85.57** $\pm$ 0.46	**85.77** $\pm$ 0.47
ELMo_small$_{finetuned}$	83.86 $\pm$ 0.87	**85.18** $\pm$ 0.67	**86.27** $\pm$ 0.35
ELMo_original$_{finetuned}$	85.90 $\pm$ 0.50	**86.49** $\pm$ 0.28	**86.82** $\pm$ 0.29

Table 6: Performance of the strategies from Table 3 using fastText instead of word2vec (bold: fastText > word2vec)

the results look promising, they should be validated by a wider set of experiments;

- our best strategies use the task corpus (i2b2) to adapt general off-the-shelf embeddings to the target domain, then combine two different types of embeddings as an ensemble to boost performance. This may not work if the task corpus is really small (we recall that our corpus is $\approx$ 1 million tokens).

6 Conclusion and Future Work

While embedding methods are improving on a regular basis, specialized domains still lack large enough corpora to train these embeddings successfully. We address this issue and propose embedding strategies that only require general-domain resources and a small in-domain corpus. In particular, we show that using a combination of general-domain ELMo, fine-tuning and word2vec embeddings trained on a small in-domain corpus, we achieve a performance that is not very far behind that of models trained on large in-domain corpora. Future work may investigate other contextualized representations such as BERT, which has proven to be superior to ELMo—at least on our task—in the recent work by Si et al. (2019). Another inter-

esting research direction could be exploiting external knowledge (e.g. ontologies) that may be easier to find in specialized fields than large corpora.

Acknowledgments

This work has been funded by the French National Research Agency (ANR) and is under the ADDICTE project (ANR-17-CE23-0001). We are also thankful to Kirk Roberts for having kindly provided assistance regarding his 2016 paper.

References

Piotr Bojanowski, Edouard Grave, Armand Joulin, and Tomas Mikolov. 2017. Enriching word vectors with subword information. *Transactions of the Association for Computational Linguistics*, 5:135–146.

Danushka Bollegala, Koheu Hayashi, and Ken ichi Kawarabayashi. 2018. Think globally, embed locally — locally linear meta-embedding of words. In *Proceedings of IJCAI-ECAI*, pages 3970–3976.

Raghavendra Chalapathy, Ehsan Zare Borzeshi, and Massimo Piccardi. 2016. Bidirectional LSTM-CRF for clinical concept extraction. In *Proceedings of the Clinical Natural Language Processing Workshop (ClinicalNLP)*, pages 7–12, Osaka, Japan. The COLING 2016 Organizing Committee.

Ciprian Chelba, Tomas Mikolov, Mike Schuster, Qi Ge, Thorsten Brants, Phillipp Koehn, and Tony Robinson. 2013. One billion word benchmark for measuring progress in statistical language modeling. *arXiv preprint arXiv:1312.3005*.

Jacob Devlin, Ming-Wei Chang, Kenton Lee, and Kristina Toutanova. 2018. Bert: Pre-training of deep bidirectional transformers for language understanding. *arXiv preprint arXiv:1810.04805*.

Matt Gardner, Joel Grus, Mark Neumann, Oyvind Tafjord, Pradeep Dasigi, Nelson F. Liu, Matthew Peters, Michael Schmitz, and Luke Zettlemoyer. 2018. AllenNLP: A deep semantic natural language processing platform. In *Proceedings of Workshop for NLP Open Source Software (NLP-OSS)*, pages 1–6, Melbourne, Australia. Association for Computational Linguistics.

David Graff, Junbo Kong, Ke Chen, and Kazuaki Maeda. 2003. English gigaword. *Linguistic Data Consortium, Philadelphia*, 4(1):34.

Maryam Habibi, Leon Weber, Mariana Neves, David Luis Wiegandt, and Ulf Leser. 2017. Deep learning with word embeddings improves biomedical named entity recognition. *Bioinformatics*, 33(14):i37–i48.

Alistair EW Johnson, Tom J Pollard, Lu Shen, H Lehman Li-wei, Mengling Feng, Mohammad Ghassemi, Benjamin Moody, Peter Szolovits, Leo Anthony Celi, and Roger G Mark. 2016. MIMIC-III, a freely accessible critical care database. *Scientific data*, 3:160035.

Douwe Kiela, Changhan Wang, and Kyunghyun Cho. 2018. Dynamic meta-embeddings for improved sentence representations. In *Proceedings of the 2018 Conference on Empirical Methods in Natural Language Processing (EMNLP 2018)*, pages 1466–1477, Brussels, Belgium.

Guillaume Lample, Miguel Ballesteros, Sandeep Subramanian, Kazuya Kawakami, and Chris Dyer. 2016. Neural architectures for named entity recognition. In *Proceedings of the 2016 Conference of the North American Chapter of the Association for Computational Linguistics: Human Language Technologies*, pages 260–270, San Diego, California. Association for Computational Linguistics.

Tomas Mikolov, Kai Chen, Greg Corrado, and Jeffrey Dean. 2013. Efficient estimation of word representations in vector space. In *International Conference on Learning Representations (ICLR 20013), workshop track*.

Avo Muromägi, Kairit Sirts, and Sven Laur. 2017. Linear ensembles of word embedding models. In *21st Nordic Conference on Computational Linguistics (NoDaLiDa 2017)*, pages 96–104, Gothenburg, Sweden.

Jeffrey Pennington, Richard Socher, and Christopher Manning. 2014. Glove: Global vectors for word representation. In *Proceedings of the 2014 conference on empirical methods in natural language processing (EMNLP)*, pages 1532–1543.

Matthew E. Peters, Mark Neumann, Mohit Iyyer, Matt Gardner, Christopher Clark, Kenton Lee, and Luke Zettlemoyer. 2018. Deep contextualized word representations. In *Proc. of NAACL*.

Kirk Roberts. 2016. Assessing the corpus size vs. similarity trade-off for word embeddings in clinical NLP. In *Proceedings of the Clinical Natural Language Processing Workshop (ClinicalNLP)*, pages 54–63.

Yuqi Si, Jingqi Wang, Hua Xu, and Kirk Roberts. 2019. Enhancing clinical concept extraction with contextual embedding. *arXiv preprint arXiv:1902.08691*.

Özlem Uzuner, Brett R South, Shuying Shen, and Scott L DuVall. 2011. 2010 i2b2/VA challenge on concepts, assertions, and relations in clinical text. *Journal of the American Medical Informatics Association*, 18(5):552–556.

Wenpeng Yin and Hinrich Schütze. 2016. Learning word meta-embeddings. In *Proceedings of the 54th Annual Meeting of the Association for Computational Linguistics (ACL 2016)*, pages 1351–1360, Berlin, Germany.

Henghui Zhu, Ioannis Ch. Paschalidis, and Amir Tahmasebi. 2018. Clinical concept extraction with contextual word embedding. In *Proceedings of the Machine Learning for Health (ML4H) Workshop at NeurIPS 2018*.

Yukun Zhu, Ryan Kiros, Rich Zemel, Ruslan Salakhutdinov, Raquel Urtasun, Antonio Torralba, and Sanja Fidler. 2015. Aligning books and movies: Towards story-like visual explanations by watching movies and reading books. In *Proceedings of the IEEE international conference on computer vision*, pages 19–27.

Enriching Neural Models with Targeted Features for Dementia Detection

Flavio Di Palo and **Natalie Parde**
Department of Computer Science
University of Illinois at Chicago
{fdipal2, parde}@uic.edu

Abstract

Alzheimer's disease (AD) is an irreversible brain disease that can dramatically reduce quality of life, most commonly manifesting in older adults and eventually leading to the need for full-time care. Early detection is fundamental to slowing its progression; however, diagnosis can be expensive, time-consuming, and invasive. In this work we develop a neural model based on a CNN-LSTM architecture that learns to detect AD and related dementias using targeted and implicitly-learned features from conversational transcripts. Our approach establishes the new state of the art on the DementiaBank dataset, achieving an F1 score of 0.929 when classifying participants into AD and control groups.

1   Introduction

Older adults constitute a growing subset of the population. In the United States, adults over age 65 are expected to comprise one-fifth of the population by 2030, and a larger proportion of the population than those under 18 by 2035 (United States Census Bureau, 2018). In Japan—perhaps the most extreme example of shifting age demographics—42.4% of the population is expected to be aged 60 or over by 2050 (United Nations, 2017). This will necessitate that age-related physical and cognitive health issues become a foremost concern not only because they will impact such a large population, but because there will be a proportionally smaller number of human caregivers available to diagnose, monitor, and remediate those conditions. Artificial intelligence offers the potential to fill many of these deficits, and already, elder-focused research is underway to test intelligent systems that monitor and assist with activities of daily living (Lotfi et al., 2012), support mental health (Wada et al., 2004), promote physical well-being (Sarma et al., 2014), and encourage

cognitive exercise (Parde and Nielsen, 2019).

Perhaps some of the most pressing issues beleaguering an aging population are Alzheimer's disease (AD) and other age-related dementias. Our interest lies in fostering early diagnosis of these conditions. Although there are currently no cures, with early diagnosis the symptoms can be managed and their impact on quality of life may be minimal. However, there can be many barriers to early diagnosis, including cost, location, mobility, and time.

Here, we present preliminary work towards automatically detecting whether individuals suffer from AD using only conversational transcripts. This solution addresses the above barriers by providing a diagnosis technique that could eventually be employed free of cost and in the comfort of one's home, at whatever time works best. Our contributions are as follows:

1. We introduce a hybrid Convolutional Neural Network (CNN) and Long Short Term Memory Network (LSTM) approach to dementia detection that takes advantage of both targeted and implicitly learned features to perform classification.

2. We explore the effects of a bi-directional LSTM and attention mechanism on both our model and the current state-of-the-art for dementia detection.

3. We empirically demonstrate that our technique outperforms the current state of the art, and suggest directions for future work that we expect to further improve performance.

2   Related Work

The task of automatically detecting dementia in conversational transcripts is not new. In Fraser et al. (2016), the authors tackled the task using

Proceedings of the ACL 2019, Student Research Workshop, pages 302–308
Florence, Italy, July 28th-August 2nd, 2019. ©2019 Association for Computational Linguistics

features associated with many linguistic phenomena, including part of speech tags, syntactic complexity, psycholinguistic characteristics, vocabulary richness, and many others. They trained a logistic regression model to distinguish between dementia-affected and healthy patients, achieving an accuracy of 81%. In our work here we consider some of the features found to be informative in this work; in particular, psycholinguistic features.

Habash et al. (2012) studied Alzheimer's-related dementia (AD) specifically. The authors selected 14 linguistic features to perform syntactic, semantic, and disfluency modeling. In doing so, they checked for the presence of filler words, repetitions, and incomplete words, and additionally incorporated counts indicating the number of syllables used per minute. Using this feature set, the authors trained a decision tree classifier to make predictions for 80 conversational samples from 31 AD and 57 non-AD patients. Their model achieved an accuracy of 79.5%.

Orimaye et al. (2014) considered syntactic features, computed from syntactic tree structures, and various lexical features to evaluate four machine learning algorithms for dementia detection. The algorithms considered included a decision tree, naïve Bayes, SVM with a radial basis kernel, and a neural network. On a dataset containing 242 AD and 242 healthy individuals, they found that compared to other algorithms, SVM exhibited the best performance with an accuracy score of 74%, a recall of 73%, and a precision of 75%.

Yancheva and Rudzicz (2016) used automatically-generated topic models to extract a small number of semantic features (12), which they then used to train a random forest classifier. Their approach achieved an F1 Score of 0.74 in binary classification of control patients versus dementia-affected patients. This is comparable to results (F1 Score=0.72) obtained with a much larger set of lexicosyntactic and acoustic features. Ultimately, Yancheva and Rudzicz found that combining these varied feature types improved their F1 Score to 0.80.

Finally, Karlekar et al. (2018) proposed a CNN-LSTM neural language model and explored the effectiveness of part-of-speech (POS) tagging the conversational transcript to improve classification accuracy for AD patients. They divided patient interviews into single utterances, and rather than classifying at the patient level, they made their predictions at the utterance level. Their model achieved an accuracy of 91%. Unfortunately, the dataset on which their classifier was trained is imbalanced, and no other performance metrics were reported. This makes it difficult to fully understand the capabilities of their model. Here, in addition to our other contributions, we extend their work by considering a full-interview classification scenario and providing more detailed classification metrics to assess the classifier's quality.

3 Data

We use a subset of DementiaBank (Becker et al., 1994) for our work here. DementiaBank is a dataset gathered as part of a protocol administered by the Alzheimer and Related Dementias Study at the University of Pittsburgh School of Medicine. It contains spontaneous speech from individuals who do (AD group) and do not (control group) present different kinds of dementia. Participants in the dataset performed several different tasks:

- **Fluency:** Participants were asked to name words belonging to a given category or that start with a given letter.

- **Recall:** Participants were asked to recall a story from their past experience.

- **Sentence:** Participants were asked to construct a simple sentence with a given word, or were asked if a given sentence made sense.

- **Cookie Theft:** Participants were asked to verbally describe an eventful image illustrating, among other elements, a child attempting to steal a cookie. For this task, the participant's and interviewer's speech utterances were recorded and manually transcribed according to the TalkBank CHAT protocol (MacWhinney, 1992).

Of these tasks, Cookie Theft provides the largest source of unstructured text. Thus, it is the data subset that we use for our work here. In total, the Cookie Theft sub-corpus consists of 1049 transcripts from 208 patients suffering from dementia (AD group) and 243 transcripts from 104 healthy elderly patients (control, or CT, group), for a total of 1229 transcripts. Dataset statistics are provided in Table 1. For each participant, DementiaBank also provides demographic information including

	Total	AD	CT
Number of Participants	312	208	104
Number of Transcripts	1229	1049	243
Median Interview Length	73	65	97

Table 1: Dataset statistics including the number of participants, the number of transcripts, and the median interview length. Interview length is computed as the number of words spoken by the patient during the interview.

age, gender, education, and race. We use all available transcripts, and randomly separate them into 81% training, 9% validation, and 10% testing.

4   Methods

We propose a neural network architecture designed to classify patients into the two groups mentioned previously: those suffering from dementia, and those who are not. The architecture takes as input transcriptions of the patients' spoken conversations. The transcripts are of moderate length (the average participant spoke 73 words across 16.8 utterances). We consider all participant speech in a single block rather than splitting the interview into separate utterances, allowing the model to consider the entire interview context in a manner similar to a real diagnosis scenario.

4.1   Model Architecture

The model architecture proposed is a CNN-LSTM (Zhou et al., 2015) with several modifications:

- We introduced a dense neural network at the end of the LSTM layer to also take into consideration linguistic features that have been considered significant by previous research (Karlekar et al., 2018; Salsbury et al., 2011).

- Rather than a classic unidirectional LSTM, we used a bi-directional LSTM and inserted an attention mechanism on the hidden states of the LSTM. In this way we expect our model to identify specific linguistic patterns related to dementia detection. In addition, the attention mechanism has proven to lead to performance improvements when long sequences are considered (Yang et al., 2016).

- We added class weights to the loss function during training to take into account the dataset imbalance.

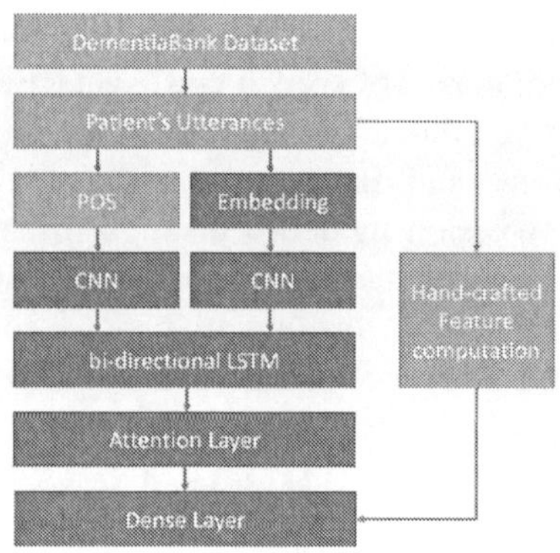

Figure 1: Model architecture.

We illustrate the architecture in Figure 1. We preprocess each full interview transcript from DementiaBank by removing interviewer utterances and truncating the length of the remaining text to 73 words. This is done so that (a) each instance is of a uniform text size, and (b) the instances are of relatively substantial length, thereby providing adequate material with which to assess the health of the patient. Seventy-three words represents the median (participant-only) interview length; thus, 50% of instances include the full interview (padded as needed), and 50% of instances are truncated to their first 73 words. The interviews are tokenized into single word tokens, and POS tags[1] are computed for each token.

The model takes two inputs: the tokenized interview, and the corresponding POS tag list. Word embeddings for the interview text tokens are computed using pre-trained 300 dimensional GloVe embeddings trained on the Wikipedia 2014 and Gigaword 5 dataset (Pennington et al., 2014). The POS tag for each word is represented as a one-hot-encoded vector. The word embeddings and POS vectors are input to two different CNNs utilizing the same architecture, and the output of the two CNNs is then flattened and given as input to a bi-directional LSTM with an attention mechanism.

The output of the bi-directional LSTM is then given as input to a dense neural network which also takes into consideration linguistic features that have proven to be effective in previous literature, as well as some demographic features (see further discussion in Section 4.2). The final outcome of the model is obtained with a single neuron at the end of the dense layer having a sigmoid

---

[1] We compute POS tags using NLTK (https://www.nltk.org/).

activation function. We implement the model using Keras.[2] The advantage of our hybrid architecture that considers both implicitly-learned and engineered features is that it can jointly incorporate information that may be useful but latent to the human observer and information that directly encodes findings from clinical and psycholinguistic literature.

4.2 Targeted Features

Previous research has shown the effectiveness of neural models trained on conversational transcripts at identifying useful features for dementia classification (Lyu, 2018; Karlekar et al., 2018; Olubolu Orimaye et al., 2018). Nevertheless, other information that has proven to be crucial to the task cannot be derived from interview transcripts themselves. Inspired by Karlekar et al.'s (2018) finding that adding POS tags as features improved the performance of their neural model, we sought to enrich our model with other engineered features that have proven effective in prior dementia detection work. We describe those features Table 2.

Each of the token-level (psycholinguistic or sentiment) features was averaged across all tokens in the instance, allowing us to obtain a participant-level feature vector to be coupled with the participant-level demographic features. These features were then concatenated with the output of our model's attention layer and the resulting vector was given as input to a dense portion of the neural network that performed the final classification. Sentiment scores were obtained using NLTK's sentiment library and psycholinguistic scores were obtained from an open source repository[3] based on the work of Fraser et al. (2016). As noted earlier, demographic information was included with the DementiaBank dataset.

4.3 Class Weight Correction

Since the DementiaBank dataset is unbalanced (more participants suffer from dementia than not), we noticed that even when high accuracy was achieved by previously proposed models, they resulted in poor precision scores. This was because those classifiers were prone to producing false positive outcomes. To combat this issue, we tuned the loss function of our model such that it more

---

[2] https://keras.io/
[3] https://github.com/vmasrani/dementia_classifier

	Feature	Description
Psych.	*Age of Acquisition*	The age at which a particular word is usually learned.
	Concreteness	A measure of a word's tangibility.
	Familiarity	A measure of how often one might expect to encounter a word.
	Imageability	A measure of how easily a word can be visualized.
Sent.	*Sentiment*	A measure of a word's sentiment polarity.
Demo.	*Age*	The participant's age at the time of the visit.
	Gender	The participant's gender.

Table 2: Targeted psycholinguistic, sentiment, and demographic features considered by the model.

severely penalized misclassifying the less frequent class.

5 Evaluation

5.1 Baseline Approach

We selected the C-LSTM model developed by Karlekar et al. (2018) as our baseline approach. This model represents the current state of the art for dementia detection on the DementiaBank dataset (Lyu, 2018).

5.2 Experimental Setup

We split the dataset into 81% training, 9% validation, and 10% testing. Each data sample represents a patient interview and its associated demographic characteristics. In order to have a more robust evaluation, we split the dataset multiple times. Thus, each model has been trained, validated, and tested using three different random shufflings of the data with different random seeds. The results presented are the average of the results that each model achieved over the three test sets.

To measure performance we consider Accuracy, Precision, Recall, F1 Score, Area Under the Curve (AUC), and the number of True Negative (TN), False Positive (FP), False Negative (FN), and True Positive (TP) classifications achieved by each approach on the test set. All metrics except AUC used a classification threshold of 0.5.

We compared six different models on the described task: two main architectures (ours and the state of the art approach developed by Karlekar et al. (2018)), each with several variations. The baseline version of Karlekar et al.'s (2018) model

Approach	Accuracy	Precision	Recall	F1	AUC	TN	FP	FN	TP
C-LSTM	0.8384	0.8683	0.9497	0.9058	0.9057	6.3	15.6	5.3	102.6
C-LSTM-ATT	0.8333	0.8446	0.9778	0.9061	0.9126	2.6	19.3	2.3	105.6
C-LSTM-ATT-W	0.8512	0.9232	0.8949	0.9084	0.9139	14.0	8.0	11.3	96.6
OURS	0.8495	0.8508	**0.9965**	0.9178	0.9207	1.0	16.6	0.3	95.0
OURS-ATT	0.8466	0.8525	0.9895	0.9158	**0.9503**	1.3	16.3	1.0	94.3
OURS-ATT-W	**0.8820**	**0.9312**	0.9298	**0.9305**	0.9498	11.0	6.6	6.6	88.6

Table 3: Performance of evaluated models.

(C-LSTM) is used directly, without any modification. Our architecture is OURS. For both architectures we then consider the effects of switching to a bidirectional LSTM and adding an attention mechanism (-ATT) and the effects of class weight correction inside the loss function (-W).

5.3 Results

We report performance metrics for each model in Table 3. As is demonstrated, our proposed model achieves the highest performance in Accuracy, Precision, Recall, F1, and AUC. It outperforms the state of the art (C-LSTM) by 5.2%, 7.1%, 4.9%, 2.6%, and 3.7%, respectively.

5.4 Additional Findings

In addition to presenting the results above, we conducted further quantitative and qualitative analyses regarding the targeted features to uncover additional insights and identify key areas for follow-up work. We describe these analyses in the subsections below.

5.4.1 Quantitative Analysis

To further assess the individual contributions of the targeted features, we performed a follow-up ablation study using our best-performing model. We systematically retrained the model after removing one type (psycholinguistic, sentiment, or demographic) of targeted feature at a time, and report our findings in Table 4.

Removing sentiment features left the model mostly unchanged in terms of AUC. However, it produced slightly fewer true negatives and slightly more false positives. Reducing false positives is important, particularly in light of the class imbalance; thus, the sentiment features give rise to a small but meaningful contribution to the model's overall performance. Interestingly, it appears that the demographic and psycholinguistic features inform the model in similar and perhaps interchangeable ways: removing one group but retaining the other yields similar performance to that of a model utilizing both. Future experiments can tease apart the contributions of individual psycholinguistic characteristics at a finer level. Extending the psycholinguistic resources employed by our model such that they exhibit greater coverage may also result in increased performance from those features specifically.

5.4.2 Qualitative Analysis

In Table 5 we present two samples misclassified by our model (one false positive, and one false negative). We make note of a key distinction between the two: surprisingly, the false positive includes many interjections indicative of "stalling" behaviors, whereas the false negative is quite clear. Neither of these is representative of other (correctly predicted) samples in their respective classes; rather, participants with dementia often exhibit more stalling or pausing behaviors, observable in text as an overuse of words such as "uh," "um," or "oh." We speculate that our model was fooled into misclassifying these samples as a result of this style reversal. Follow-up work incorporating stylistic features (e.g., syntactic variation or sentence structure patterns) may reduce errors of this nature. Finally, we note that many prosodic distinctions between the two classes that pass through text mostly unnoticed may be more effectively encoded using audio features. We plan to experiment with these as well as features from other modalities in the future, in hopes of further improving performance.

6 Discussion

The introduction of sentiment-based, psycholinguistic, and demographic features improved the performance of the model, demonstrating that implicitly-learned features (although impressive) still cannot encode conversational characteristics of dementia to the extent that other, more targeted features can. Likewise, in both C-LSTM and our approach, the introduction of a bi-directional

Approach	Accuracy	Precision	Recall	F1	AUC	TN	FP	FN	TP
OURS-ATT-W NO PSYCH.	0.8790	0.8870	**0.9825**	0.9319	0.9499	12.0	5.6	1.6	93.6
OURS-ATT-W NO SENT.	**0.8970**	**0.9239**	0.9615	**0.9321**	**0.9501**	7.6	10.0	3.6	91.6
OURS-ATT-W NO DEMO.	0.8908	0.9005	0.9789	0.9308	0.9473	10.33	7.33	2	93.3

Table 4: Ablation study performed using our best-performing model (OURS-ATT-W).

False Positive	Uh, oh I can oh you don't want me to memorize it. Oh okay, the the little girl is asking for the cookie from the boy who is about to fall on his head And she is going I guess "shush" or give me one The mother laughs we don't think she might be on drugs because uh laughs she is off someplace because the sink is running over and uh it is summer outside because the window is open and the grasses or the bushes look healthy. And uh that's it.
False Negative	Oh, the water is running off the sink Mother is calmly drying a dish The uh stool is going to fall over and the little boy is on top of it getting in the cookie jar. And the little girl is reaching for a cookie. She has her hands to her her finger to her lip as if she is telling the boy not to tell. The curtains seem to be waving a bit, the water is running. that's it.

Table 5: Samples misclassified by our model. False Positives are control patients classified as AD patients, while False Negatives are AD-patients classified as control patients.

LSTM with an attention mechanism led to performance improvements on classifier AUC. This improvement suggests that these additions allowed the model to better focus on specific patterns indicative of participants suffering from dementia.

In contrast, the benefits of adding class weights to the model's loss function were less clear. We introduced this correction as a mechanism to encourage our classifier to make fewer false positive predictions, and although this worked, the model also became less capable of identifying true positives. Given the nature of our classification problem, this trade-off is rather undesirable, and additionally this correction did not improve the general quality of the classifier—the AUC for both our model and C-LSTM remained almost unchanged. However, regardless of the inclusion of class weights for the loss function, our measures regarding the AUC, Precision, Recall, F1 Score, and Accuracy show that overall our model is able to outperform the previous state of the art (C-LSTM) at predicting whether or not participants are suffering from dementia based on their conversational transcripts.

7   Conclusion

In this work we introduced a new approach to classify conversational transcripts as belonging to individuals with or without dementia. Our contributions were as follows:

1. We introduced a hybrid architecture that allowed us to take advantage of both engineered features and deep-learning techniques on conversational transcripts.

2. We explored the effects of a bi-directional LSTM and attention mechanism on both our model and the current state of the art for dementia detection.

3. We examined the effects of loss function modification to take into consideration the class imbalance in the DementiaBank dataset.

Importantly, the model that we present in this work represents the new state of the art for AD detection on the DementiaBank dataset. Our source code is available publicly online.[4] In the future, we plan to explore additional psycholinguistic, sentiment-based, and stylistic features for this task, as well as to experiment with features from other modalities. Finally, we plan to work towards interpreting the neural features implicitly learned by the model, in order to understand some of the latent characteristics it captures in AD patients' conversational transcripts.

---

[4]`https://github.com/flaviodipalo/AlzheimerDetection`

References

James T Becker, François Boiler, Oscar L Lopez, Judith Saxton, and Karen L McGonigle. 1994. The natural history of alzheimer's disease: description of study cohort and accuracy of diagnosis. *Archives of Neurology*, 51(6):585–594.

Kathleen C. Fraser, Jed A. Meltzer, and Frank Rudzicz. 2016. Linguistic features identify alzheimer's disease in narrative speech. *Journal of Alzheimer's disease: JAD*, 49 2:407–22.

Anthony Habash, Curry Guinn, Doug Kline, and Laurie Patterson. 2012. *Language Analysis of Speakers with Dementia of the Alzheimer's Type*. Ph.D. thesis, University of North Carolina Wilmington.

Sweta Karlekar, Tong Niu, and Mohit Bansal. 2018. Detecting linguistic characteristics of alzheimer's dementia by interpreting neural models. In *Proceedings of the 2018 Conference of the North American Association for Computational Linguistics (NAACL 2018)*.

Ahmad Lotfi, Caroline Langensiepen, Sawsan M. Mahmoud, and M. J. Akhlaghinia. 2012. Smart homes for the elderly dementia sufferers: identification and prediction of abnormal behaviour. *Journal of Ambient Intelligence and Humanized Computing*, 3(3):205–218.

G. Lyu. 2018. A review of alzheimer's disease classification using neuropsychological data and machine learning. In *2018 11th International Congress on Image and Signal Processing, BioMedical Engineering and Informatics (CISP-BMEI)*, pages 1–5.

Brian MacWhinney. 1992. The childes project: tools for analyzing talk. *Child Language Teaching and Therapy*, 8(2):217–218.

Sylvester Olubolu Orimaye, Jojo Wong, and Chee Piau Wong. 2018. Deep language space neural network for classifying mild cognitive impairment and alzheimer-type dementia. *PLOS ONE*, 13:e0205636.

Sylvester Olubolu Orimaye, Jojo Sze-Meng Wong, and Karen Jennifer Golden. 2014. Learning predictive linguistic features for Alzheimer's disease and related dementias using verbal utterances. In *Proceedings of the Workshop on Computational Linguistics and Clinical Psychology: From Linguistic Signal to Clinical Reality*, pages 78–87, Baltimore, Maryland, USA. Association for Computational Linguistics.

Natalie Parde and Rodney D. Nielsen. 2019. AI meets Austen: Towards human-robot discussions of literary metaphor. In *Artificial Intelligence in Education*, Cham. Springer International Publishing.

Jeffrey Pennington, Richard Socher, and Christopher D. Manning. 2014. Glove: Global vectors for word representation. In *Empirical Methods in Natural Language Processing (EMNLP)*, pages 1532–1543.

Tom Salsbury, Scott A. Crossley, and Danielle S. McNamara. 2011. Psycholinguistic word information in second language oral discourse. *Second Language Research*, 27(3):343–360.

Bandita Sarma, Amitava Das, and Rodney Nielsen. 2014. A framework for health behavior change using companionable robots. In *Proceedings of the 8th International Natural Language Generation Conference (INLG)*, pages 103–107, Philadelphia, Pennsylvania, U.S.A. Association for Computational Linguistics.

United Nations. 2017. World population ageing. *Department of Economic and Social Affairs, Population Division*.

United States Census Bureau. 2018. Older people projected to outnumber children for first time in U.S. history. *Public Information Office*.

K. Wada, T. Shibata, T. Saito, and K. Tanie. 2004. Effects of robot-assisted activity for elderly people and nurses at a day service center. *Proceedings of the IEEE*, 92(11):1780–1788.

Maria Yancheva and Frank Rudzicz. 2016. Vectorspace topic models for detecting Alzheimer's disease. In *Proceedings of the 54th Annual Meeting of the Association for Computational Linguistics (Volume 1: Long Papers)*, pages 2337–2346, Berlin, Germany. Association for Computational Linguistics.

Zichao Yang, Diyi Yang, Chris Dyer, Xiaodong He, Alexander J. Smola, and Eduard H. Hovy. 2016. Hierarchical attention networks for document classification. In *Proceedings of the 2016 Conference of the North American Association for Computational Linguistics (NAACL 2016)*.

Chunting Zhou, Chonglin Sun, Zhiyuan Liu, and Francis Chi-Moon Lau. 2015. A c-lstm neural network for text classification. *CoRR*, abs/1511.08630.

English-Indonesian Neural Machine Translation for Spoken Language Domains

Meisyarah Dwiastuti

Charles University, Faculty of Mathematics and Physics

Prague, Czech Republic

meisyarah.dwiastuti@gmail.com

Abstract

In this work, we conduct a study on Neural Machine Translation (NMT) for English-Indonesian (EN-ID) and Indonesian-English (ID-EN). We focus on spoken language domains, namely colloquial and speech languages. We build NMT systems using the Transformer model for both translation directions and implement domain adaptation, in which we train our pre-trained NMT systems on speech language (in-domain) data. Moreover, we conduct an evaluation on how the domain-adaptation method in our EN-ID system can result in more formal translation outputs.

1 Introduction

Neural machine translation (NMT) has become the state-of-the-art method in the research area of machine translation (MT) in the past few years (Bojar et al., 2018). As a data-driven method, NMT suffers from the need of a big amount of data to build a robust translation model (Koehn and Knowles, 2017). The lack of parallel corpora for some languages is one of the reasons why the research of NMT for these languages has not grown. Indonesian is one of the examples of such under-researched language. Despite the huge number of speakers (more than 200 million people), there have been only a few works on Indonesian MT, even towards the heavily researched language like English. While the lack of data was an issue for NMT research in this language (Trieu et al., 2017; Adiputra and Arase, 2017), the recent release of OpenSubtitles2018 corpus (Lison et al., 2018) containing more than 9 millions Indonesian-English sentence pairs gives us an opportunity to broaden the study of Indonesian NMT systems.

One of interesting linguistic problems is language style, which is the way a language is used depending on some circumstances, such as when

and where it is spoken, who is speaking, or to whom it is addressed. We are interested in studying the formality of MT output, focusing on spoken language domains. Given a small dataset of speech-styled language and a significantly larger dataset of less formal language, we would like to investigate the effect of domain adaptation method in learning the formality level of MT output. Learning formality level through domain adaptation will help MT systems generate formality-specific translations.

In this paper, we conduct a study of NMT for English-Indonesian (EN-ID) and Indonesian-English (ID-EN) directions. This study has the following objectives:

1. to present a set of baseline results for EN-ID and ID-EN NMT systems on spoken language domains.

2. to examine the effectiveness of domain adaptation in:

    (a) boosting the performance of the NMT systems for both directions.

    (b) learning the formality change in spoken language EN-ID NMT systems.

To accomplish both objectives, we build the NMT systems for both EN-ID and ID-EN directions using the Transformer model (Vaswani et al., 2017). This model relies on self-attention to compute the representation of the sequence. To the best of our knowledge, there has not been any work on building NMT for those language pairs using the Transformer model.

We perform experiments using domain adaptation. We consider formal speech language as our in-domain data, and colloquial dialogue-styled language from movie subtitles as our out-of-domain data. We adopt the domain-adaptation

Proceedings of the ACL 2019, Student Research Workshop, pages 309–314
Florence, Italy, July 28th-August 2nd, 2019. ©2019 Association for Computational Linguistics

method used by Luong and Manning (2015) to fine-tune the trained model using in-domain data. For each translation direction, we run five experiments: three in which we do not perform domain adaptation and two when we do. We evaluate the effectiveness of the domain adaptation method using automatic evaluation, BLEU (Papineni et al., 2002), and report the score obtained from each experiment on in-domain test set. Moreover, we analyze how domain adaptation affects formality change in the translations of EN-ID NMT systems by performing a human evaluation.

2   Background

In this section, we provide background information on Indonesian language and the approaches used in our experiments.

2.1   Indonesian language

Similarly to English, Indonesian's writing system uses the Latin alphabet without any diacritics. The typical word order in Indonesian is Subject-Verb-Object (SVO). The language does not make use of any grammatical case nor gender. The grammatical tenses do not change the form of the verbs. Most of the word constructions are derivational morphology. The complexity of its morphology includes affixation, clitics, and reduplication.

In spoken language, while formal speech is similar to written language, people tend to use non-standard spelling in colloquial language by changing the word forms or simply using informal words. For example, '*bagaimana*' (how) → '*gimana*' or '*tidak*' (no) → '*nggak*'. Although the measure of formality level can be relative to some people depending on their culture, there are words that are only used in formal situation. For example, the use of pronouns like *saya*' (I), '*Anda*' (you), or certain words like '*dapat*' (can) or '*mengkehendaki*' (would like).

2.2   Neural Machine Translation

Neural machine translation (NMT) uses an encoder-decoder architecture, in which the encoder encodes the source sentence $x = (x_1, ..., x_n)$ to a continuous representation sequence $z = (z_1, ..., z_k)$ and the decoder translates the representation z into a sentence $y = (y_1, ..., y_m)$ in the target language.

Several previous works implemented recurrent neural networks (RNN) in their encoder-decoder architecture (Sutskever et al., 2014; Cho et al., 2014; Bahdanau et al., 2015; Luong and Manning, 2015). While Bahdanau et al. (2015) used bidirectional RNN for their encoder and Luong and Manning (2015) used multilayer RNN in their architecture, both works implemented an attention mechanism in their decoder, which was able to handle the problem in translating long sentences.

The model that we use in this paper is Transformer model (Vaswani et al., 2017), which gets rid of all the recurrent operations found in the previous approach. Instead, it relies on self-attention mechanism to compute the continuous representation on both the encoder and the decoder. In order to keep track of the token order within the sequence, the model appends *positional-encoding* of the tokens to the input and output embeddings. Both of the encoder and the decoder are composed of stacked *multi-head* self-attention and fully-connected layers.

Our choice of the Transformer model is motivated by its good performance reported recently in various translation tasks, such as bilingual translation of various language directions (Bojar et al., 2018), multilingual translation (Lakew et al., 2018), and also for the low-resource with multisource setting (Tubay and Costa-jussà, 2018). While some works empirically compare the performance of Transformer and RNN-based models (Vaswani et al., 2017; Lakew et al., 2018; Tang et al., 2018), this is not the aim of this paper. We leave the comparison of both methods for EN-ID and ID-EN NMT as future research.

2.3   Domain-adaptation

One of the challenges in translation is that words can be translated differently depending on the context or domain (Koehn and Knowles, 2017). While in-domain data is limited, we expect using available large amounts of out-of-domain data to train our model and implementing a domain-adaptation method will give the model a robust performance. Therefore, we implement the method of Luong and Manning (2015). First, we train our model on general domain data consisting of around 9 millions parallel sentences. After that we fine-tune the model using in-domain data, which means the model training is continued on only in-domain data for a few more steps.

3 Experimental Setup

We run experiments on both EN-ID and ID-EN pairs with different training scenarios as follows:

1. **IN (baseline)**: using only small in-domain data (speech language)

2. **OUT**: using only large out-of-domain data (colloquial language)

3. **OUT+DA**: using only large out-of-domain data, then fine-tune the model using only in-domain data

4. **MIX**: using a mixture of in-domain and out-of-domain data

5. **MIX+DA**: using a mixture of in-domain and out-of-domain data, then fine-tune the model using only in-domain data

3.1 Dataset

We use OpenSubtitles2018 (Lison et al., 2018) parallel corpus as our out-of-domain data and TEDtalk (Cettolo et al., 2012) as in-domain data. OpenSubtitles2018 corpus contains movie subtitles which can represent colloquial language in dialogue style. On the other hand, TEDtalk corpus contains speech language which has higher level of formality than colloquial language. The details of the dataset setting is shown in Table 1. As the training data, we use all the sentences from OpenSubtitles2018 and the train set of TEDtalk. For training the baseline system (IN), we use only TEDtalk train set. For OUT and MIX, we use OpenSubtitles2018 train set and both sets in the first phase of training, respectively. Then, for the second phase of training (fine-tuning), we use TEDtalk train set while keeping the vocabulary from the first phase train set.

As development set, we use TEDtalk tst2013 and tst2014. As test set, we use TEDtalk tst2015-16 and tst2017-plus. We notice that the test set tst2017-plus provided at the website[1] contains a small part of the train data. Therefore, we remove these common sentences from the test set and obtain tst2017-plus-mod with 1035 sentences not overlapping with the training data.

---

[1]https://wit3.fbk.eu/mt.php?release=2017-01-more, accessed on 25th February 2019

Part	Dataset	#sentences
Train	OpenSubtitles2018	9,273,809
	TEDtalk train	107,329
Dev	TEDtalk tst2013	1034
	TEDtalk tst2014	878
Test	TEDtalk tst2015-16	980
	TEDtalk tst2017-plus-mod	1035

Table 1: Dataset used in our experiments

3.2 Training details

We run our experiments using Tensor2Tensor (T2T) (Vaswani et al., 2018) on a GeForce GTX 1080 machine using a single GPU. We use Transformer model with hyperparameter set `transformer_base` (Vaswani et al., 2017). Some hyperparameters follow the suggestion of Popel and Bojar (2018): maximum sequence length=150, batch size=1500, learning rate=0.2, learning rate warmup steps=8000. We optimize our model using the Adafactor optimizer (Shazeer and Stern, 2018). For the vocabulary, we use the default subword units implemented in T2T, SubwordTextEncoder (STE), which is shared between source and target languages with approximate size of 32,678 units. Our data is not tokenized.

We run the baseline and the first phase of our domain-adaptation experiments training for 300,000 and 500,000 steps, respectively, and save the checkpoint hourly. However, we find an overfit on baseline systems during the training so we stop early and select the model from the checkpoint resulting the highest BLEU score on development set. For the second phase of training in domain-adaptation experiments, we set the steps to 50,000 in order to avoid overfit to the in-domain data and save the checkpoint every 10 minutes. We use the last value of learning rate in the first training phase for the second training phase.

During decoding, we use beam search with beam size of 4 and alpha value (length normalization penalty) of 0.6. We evaluate our model on the development set during the training and the test set after the model selection using case-sensitive BLEU score computed by the built-in command `t2t-bleu`.

3.3 Formality level evaluation

We conduct a manual evaluation for the formality level of translations resulted from our best EN-ID system. The purpose of this evaluation is to

System	EN-ID	ID-EN
IN	22.03	23.06
OUT	20.75	22.81
OUT+DA	27.47	26.93
MIX	24.84	25.18
MIX+DA	**29.10**	**28.18**

Table 2: BLEU scores of our English-Indonesian (EN-ID) and Indonesian-English (ID-EN) NMT systems on test set. The bold texts mark the best scores.

see whether the domain-adapted system generates more formal translation based on human evaluation. The evaluation is inspired by human assessment of Niu et al. (2017). We randomly select 50 translation pairs from the test set generated by the first and second phases of our EN-ID system. We make sure each pair does not consist of the same sentences. Then 48 Indonesian native speakers vote which sentence is more formal between two of them. An option of "neutral or difficult to distinguish" is also available. The voters are not aware that the sentence pairs are generated by MT systems in order to keep the purity of the evaluation based on formality level and not biased to the translation quality.

4 Result

4.1 NMT performance

Table 2 shows the BLEU evaluation of our systems. For both EN-ID and ID-EN directions, the result shows similar patterns: (1) System trained with only in-domain data (IN) works better than with only out-of-domain data (OUT) although the training-data sizes are significantly different. (2) Domain adaptation (fine-tuning) helps to improve the BLEU score in both cases when the model is first trained without and with in-domain data (OUT and MIX respectively). Despite the best performance of our mixture system, the domain adaptation method has higher impact on the out-of-domain system.

While IN systems suffer from overfit, both training and evaluation loss in OUT and MIX systems still slightly decrease in the end of the training which indicates the training steps still can be increased.

4.2 Formality level

We use the evaluation approach described in Subsection 3.3 on translation output of MIX and

Sentence 1	
Source	*You* have to listen to one another.
MIX	*Kau* harus mendengarkan satu sama lain.
MIX+DA	*Anda* harus mendengarkan satu sama lain.
Sentence 2	
Source	*I* enjoy **fashion** magazines and <u>pretty</u> things.
MIX	*Aku* menikmati majalah **fashion** dan hal-hal <u>cantik</u>.
MIX+DA	*Saya* menikmati majalah **adibusana** dan hal-hal yang <u>cukup</u>.
Sentence 3	
Source	It *could* even **be disseminated** <u>intentionally</u>.
MIX	Itu bahkan *bisa* **dibubarkan** <u>secara</u> sengaja.
MIX+DA	Hal ini bahkan *dapat* **diabaikan** <u>dengan</u> sengaja.
Sentence 4	
Source	They *come* from these cells.
MIX	Mereka *datang* dari sel-sel ini.
MIX+DA	Mereka *berasal* dari sel-sel ini.

Figure 1: Sample outputs of our EN-ID non-adapted (MIX) and domain-adapted (MIX+DA) systems, in which more than 50% of human assessors vote translation by the domain-adapted system as more formal.

MIX+DA from the test set. Out of 50 pairs, 35 MIX+DA sentences are voted by the majority (>50% of the voters) as more formal than their pairs. For the remaining pairs, the majority either select MIX sentences as more formal (12 pairs) or the MIX+DA sentences are still the most selected but the frequency is less than 50% of the voters (3 pairs). We consider the latter condition has no difference to being indistinct, although none of the pairs with "difficult to distinguish" option are selected by the majority,

Among those 35 MIX+DA sentence pairs, we analyze 13 pairs that are voted by more than 85% voters to observe which segment of the sentences might trigger the voters to label them as more formal. Figure 1 shows sample output sentence pairs with such condition. Interestingly, 9 of those pairs show similar pattern, namely they contain the change of pronouns to the formal one. For instance, "*kau*" → "*Anda*" or "*aku*" → "*saya*" in Sentence 1 and 2, respectively, in the figure. Note that English does not use honorifics that can give such context change in the translation.

Among 2015 translation pairs from the test set, we find 316 translations which change the pronouns to be more formal, 448 translations which already use formal pronouns before domain-adapted thus do not change, and, surprisingly, no translation that still uses informal pronouns after being domain-adapted. This indicates the style of using honorifics is successfully transferred from speech styled language.

Sentence 3 and 4 are of the remaining pairs that do not have such pattern. In sentence 3, there are 3 different segments in the translations. Although native speaker might easily find that "*dapat*" is more formal than "*bisa*", just like the use of "could" and "can" in English, we cannot find how to measure each of the lexical differences affects the formality level. Meanwhile, in a pair that only has one word difference like in sentence 4, we can infer that the highlighted words are the trigger of the formality of the sentences, if we assume that the translation is correct (which is true in this sample). Nevertheless, the focus on finding segments that trigger the formality of the whole translation outputs can be an interesting future work.

5   Related Work

Most works on ID-EN or EN-ID MT were based on phrase-based SMT (Yulianti et al., 2011; Larasati, 2012; Sujaini et al., 2014), in which other approaches were incorporated to the basic SMT to enhance the performance, such as by combining SMT with rule-based system or adding linguistics information. Neural method was used as a language model to replace statistical n-gram language model in EN-ID SMT (Hermanto et al., 2015), not as an end-to-end MT system like our models.

While we can not find any previous work on end-to-end Indonesian NMT paired with English, such work has been performed with some Asian languages. Trieu et al. (2017) built NMT systems for Indonesian-Vietnamese and Adiputra and Arase (2017) for Japanese-Indonesian NMT. Those works used RNN-based encoder-decoder architecture, while we use self-attention based model.

Our analysis of formality level is related to politeness or formality control in NMT output (Sennrich et al., 2016; Niu et al., 2017). Both works added a mark on the source side as an expected formality level on the translation output. While the former focused only on the use of honorifics, the latter had a wider definition of formality based on the calculation of formality score. Although the finding of our work is similar to the expected output of Sennrich et al. (2016), it differs from both works as we use domain-adaptation method instead of a formality mark.

6   Conclusions and Future Research

We have presented the use of Neural Machine Translation (NMT) using Transformer model for English-Indonesian language pair in the spoken language domains, namely colloquial language and speech language. We demonstrate that the domain-adaptation method we use does not only improve the model performance, but is also able to generate translation in more formal language. The most notable formality style transferred is the use of honorifics.

There are still many open research directions for EN-ID and ID-EN NMT systems. In this work, we mostly use the default value of hyperparameters for our Transformer model. An empirical study to explore different set of hyperparameters can be an interesting future work with a goal to build the state-of-the-art model for both language directions. The work can be also followed by model comparison with the previous state-of-the-art RNN-based NMT systems. Besides investigating segments of the translations that may trigger the formality, it is also interesting to conduct further analysis on the style transfer learned by the domain adaptation method in our EN-ID system, not restricted to the formality level.

Acknowledgments

We thank Martin Popel for thoughtful discussions, Ondřej Bojar for the help in the initial work, the mentor and anonymous reviewers for helpful comments. We gratefully acknowledge the support of European Masters Program in Language and Communication Technologies (LCT) and Erasmus Mundus scholarship.

References

Cosmas Krisna Adiputra and Yuki Arase. 2017. Performance of Japanese-to-Indonesian Machine Translation on Different Models. *23rd Annual Meeting of the Speech Processing Society of Japan (NLP2017)*, pages 757–760.

Dzmitry Bahdanau, Kyunghyun Cho, and Yoshua Bengio. 2015. Neural Machine Translation by Jointly Learning to Align and Translate. *ICLR 2015*, pages 1–15.

Ondřej Bojar, Christian Federmann, Mark Fishel, Yvette Graham, Barry Haddow, Matthias Huck, Philipp Koehn, and Christof Monz. 2018. Findings of the 2018 Conference on Machine Translation (WMT18). In *Proceedings of the Third Confer-*

ence on Machine Translation, pages 272–307, Belgium, Brussels. Association for Computational Linguistics.

Mauro Cettolo, Christian Girardi, and Marcello Federico. 2012. Inventory of transcribed and translated talks.

Kyunghyun Cho, Bart van Merrienboer, Caglar Gulcehre, Dzmitry Bahdanau, Fethi Bougares, Holger Schwenk, and Yoshua Bengio. 2014. Learning phrase representations using rnn encoder–decoder for statistical machine translation. In *Proceedings of the 2014 Conference on Empirical Methods in Natural Language Processing (EMNLP)*, pages 1724–1734, Doha, Qatar. Association for Computational Linguistics.

Andi Hermanto, Teguh Bharata Adji, and Noor Akhmad Setiawan. 2015. Recurrent neural network language model for english-indonesian machine translation: Experimental study. In *2015 International Conference on Science in Information Technology (ICSITech)*. IEEE.

Philipp Koehn and Rebecca Knowles. 2017. Six challenges for neural machine translation. *CoRR*, abs/1706.03872.

Surafel Melaku Lakew, Mauro Cettolo, and Marcello Federico. 2018. A Comparison of Transformer and Recurrent Neural Networks on Multilingual Neural Machine Translation. *CoRR*, abs/1806.06957.

Septina Dian Larasati. 2012. Towards an Indonesian-English SMT System : A Case Study of an Under-Studied and Under-Resourced Language , Indonesian. pages 123–129.

Pierre Lison, Jörg Tiedemann, and Milen Kouylekov. 2018. OpenSubtitles2018: Statistical rescoring of sentence alignments in large, noisy parallel corpora. In *Proceedings of the 11th Language Resources and Evaluation Conference*, Miyazaki, Japan. European Language Resource Association.

Minh-Thang Luong and Christopher D. Manning. 2015. Stanford neural machine translation systems for spoken language domain. In *International Workshop on Spoken Language Translation*, Da Nang, Vietnam.

Xing Niu, Marianna Martindale, and Marine Carpuat. 2017. A study of style in machine translation: Controlling the formality of machine translation output. In *Proceedings of the 2017 Conference on Empirical Methods in Natural Language Processing*, pages 2814–2819. Association for Computational Linguistics.

Kishore Papineni, Salim Roukos, Todd Ward, and Wei-Jing Zhu. 2002. BLEU: A Method for Automatic Evaluation of Machine Translation. In *Proceedings of the 40th Annual Meeting on Association for Computational Linguistics, ACL '02*, pages 311–318, Stroudsburg, PA, USA. Association for Computational Linguistics.

Martin Popel and Ondrej Bojar. 2018. Training tips for the transformer model. *CoRR*, abs/1804.00247.

Rico Sennrich, Barry Haddow, and Alexandra Birch. 2016. Controlling politeness in neural machine translation via side constraints. In *Proceedings of the 2016 Conference of the North American Chapter of the Association for Computational Linguistics: Human Language Technologies*, pages 35–40, San Diego, California. Association for Computational Linguistics.

Noam Shazeer and Mitchell Stern. 2018. Adafactor: Adaptive learning rates with sublinear memory cost. *CoRR*, abs/1804.04235.

Herry Sujaini, Kuspriyanto Kuspriyanto, Arry Akhmad Arman, and Ayu Purwarianti. 2014. A novel part-of-speech set developing method for statistical machine translation. *TELKOMNIKA (Telecommunication Computing Electronics and Control)*, 12(3):581.

Ilya Sutskever, Oriol Vinyals, and Quoc V. Le. 2014. Sequence to sequence learning with neural networks. *CoRR*, abs/1409.3215.

Gongbo Tang, Matthias Müller, Annette Rios, and Rico Sennrich. 2018. Why self-attention? A targeted evaluation of neural machine translation architectures. *CoRR*, abs/1808.08946.

Hai-Long Trieu, Duc-Vu Tran, and Le-Minh Nguyen. 2017. Investigating phrase-based and neural-based machine translation on low-resource settings. In *Proceedings of the 31st Pacific Asia Conference on Language, Information and Computation*, pages 384–391. The National University (Phillippines).

Brian Tubay and Marta R. Costa-jussà. 2018. Neural machine translation with the transformer and multi-source romance languages for the biomedical WMT 2018 task. In *Proceedings of the Third Conference on Machine Translation: Shared Task Papers, WMT 2018, Belgium, Brussels, October 31 - November 1, 2018*, pages 667–670.

Ashish Vaswani, Samy Bengio, Eugene Brevdo, François Chollet, Aidan N. Gomez, Stephan Gouws, Llion Jones, Lukasz Kaiser, Nal Kalchbrenner, Niki Parmar, Ryan Sepassi, Noam Shazeer, and Jakob Uszkoreit. 2018. Tensor2tensor for neural machine translation. *CoRR*, abs/1803.07416.

Ashish Vaswani, Noam Shazeer, Niki Parmar, Jakob Uszkoreit, Llion Jones, Aidan N. Gomez, Lukasz Kaiser, and Illia Polosukhin. 2017. Attention is all you need. *CoRR*, abs/1706.03762.

Evi Yulianti, Indra Budi, Achmad Nizar Hidayanto, Hisar Maruli Manurung, and Mirna Adriani. 2011. Developing indonesian-english hybrid machine translation system. In *Proceedings of the 2011 International Conference on Advanced Computer Science and Information Systems*, pages 265–270.

Improving Neural Entity Disambiguation with Graph Embeddings

Özge Sevgili[†], Alexander Panchenko[‡, †, *], and Chris Biemann[†]

[†]Universität Hamburg, Hamburg, Germany
[‡]Skolkovo Institute of Science and Technology, Moscow, Russia
[*]Diffbot Inc., Menlo Park, CA, USA
{sevgili,panchenko,biemann}@informatik.uni-hamburg.de

Abstract

Entity Disambiguation (ED) is the task of linking an ambiguous entity mention to a corresponding entry in a knowledge base. Current methods have mostly focused on unstructured text data to learn representations of entities, however, there is structured information in the knowledge base itself that should be useful to disambiguate entities. In this work, we propose a method that uses graph embeddings for integrating structured information from the knowledge base with unstructured information from text-based representations. Our experiments confirm that graph embeddings trained on a graph of hyperlinks between Wikipedia articles improve the performances of simple feed-forward neural ED model and a state-of-the-art neural ED system.

1 Introduction

The inherent and omnipresent ambiguity of language at the lexical level results in ambiguity of words, named entities, and other lexical units. Word Sense Disambiguation (WSD) (Navigli, 2009) deals with individual ambiguous words such as nouns, verbs, and adjectives. The task of Entity Linking (EL) (Shen et al., 2015) is devoted to the disambiguation of mentions of named entities such as persons, locations, and organizations. Basically, EL aims to resolve such ambiguity by creating an automatic reference between an ambiguous entity mention/span in a context and an entity in a knowledge base. These entities can be Wikipedia articles and/or DBpedia (Mendes et al., 2011)/Freebase (Bollacker et al., 2008) entries. EL can be divided into two subtasks: (i) Mention Detection (MD) or Name Entity Recognition (NER) (Nadeau and Sekine, 2007) finds entity references from a given raw text; (ii) and Entity Disambiguation (ED) assigns entity references for a given mention in context. This work deals with the entity disambiguation task.

The goal of an ED system is resolving the ambiguity of entity mentions, such as *Mars, Galaxy, and Bounty are all delicious*. It is hard for an algorithm to identify whether the entity is an astronomical structure[1] or a brand of milk chocolate[2].

Current neural approaches to EL/ED attempt to use context and word embeddings (and sometimes entity embeddings on mentions in text) (Kolitsas et al., 2018; Sun et al., 2015). Whereas these and most other previous approaches employ embeddings trained from text, we aim to create entity embeddings based on structured data (i.e. hyperlinks) using graph embeddings and integrate them into the ED models.

Graph embeddings aim at representing nodes in a graph, or subgraph structure, by finding a mapping between a graph structure and the points in a low-dimensional vector space (Hamilton et al., 2017). The goal is to preserve the features of the graph structure and map these features to the geometric relationships, such as distances between different nodes, in the embedding space. Using fixed-length dense vector embeddings as opposed to operating on the knowledge bases' graph structure allows the access of the information encoded in the graph structure in an efficient and straightforward manner in modern neural architectures.

Our claim is that including graph structure features of the knowledge base has a great potential to make an impact on ED. In our first experiment, we present a method based on a simple neural network with the inputs of a context, entity mention/span, explanation of a candidate entity, and a candidate entity. Each entity is represented by graph embeddings, which are created using the knowledge base, DBpedia (Mendes et al., 2011)

---

[1]http://dbpedia.org/resource/Galaxy
[2]http://dbpedia.org/resource/Galaxy_(chocolate)

315

Proceedings of the ACL 2019, Student Research Workshop, pages 315–322
Florence, Italy, July 28th-August 2nd, 2019. ©2019 Association for Computational Linguistics

containing hyperlinks between entities. We perform ablation tests on the types of inputs, which allows us to judge the impact of the single inputs as well as their interplay. In a second experiment, we enhance a state-of-the-art neural entity disambiguation system called end2end (Kolitsas et al., 2018) with our graph embeddings: The original system relies on character, word and entity embeddings; we replace respectively complement these with our graph embeddings. Both experiments confirm the hypothesis that structured information in the form of graph embeddings are an efficient and effective way of improving ED.

Our **main contribution** is a creation of a simple technique for integration of structured information into an ED system with graph embeddings. There is no obvious way to use large structured knowledge bases directly in a neural ED system. We provide a simple solution based on graph embeddings and confirm experimentally its effectiveness.

2   Related Work

Entity Linking   Traditional approaches to EL focus on defining the similarity measurement between a mention and a candidate entity (Mihalcea and Csomai, 2007; Strube and Ponzetto, 2006; Bunescu and Paşca, 2006). Similarly, Milne and Witten (2008) define a measurement of entity-entity relatedness. Current state-of-the-art approaches are based on neural networks (Huang et al., 2015; Ganea and Hofmann, 2017; Kolitsas et al., 2018; Sun et al., 2015), where are based on character, word and/or entity embeddings created by a neural network with a motivation of their capability to automatically induce features, as opposed to hand-crafting them. Then, they all use these embeddings in neural EL/ED.

Yamada et al. (2016) and Fang et al. (2016) utilize structured data modelling entities and words in the same space and mapping spans to entities based on the similarity in this space. They expand the objective function of word2vec (Mikolov et al., 2013a,b) and use both text and structured information. Radhakrishnan et al. (2018) extend the work of Yamada et al. (2016) by creating their own graph based on co-occurrences statistics instead of using the knowledge graph directly. Contrary to them, our model learns a mapping of spans and entities, which reside in different spaces and use graph embeddings trained on the knowledge graph for representing structured information.

Kolitsas et al. (2018) address both MD and ED in their end2end system. They build a context-aware neural network based on character, word, and entity embeddings coupled with attention and global voting mechanisms. Their entity embeddings, proposed by Ganea and Hofmann (2017), are computed by the empirical conditional word-entity distribution based on the co-occurrence counts on Wikipedia pages and hyperlinks.

Graph Embeddings   There are various methods to create graph embedding, which can be grouped into the methods based on matrix factorization, random walks, and deep learning (Goyal and Ferrara, 2018). Factorization-based models depend on the node adjacency matrix and dimensionality reduction method (Belkin and Niyogi, 2001; Roweis and Saul, 2000; Tang et al., 2015). Random-walk-based methods aim to preserve many properties of graph (Perozzi et al., 2014; Grover and Leskovec, 2016). Deep-learning-based ones reduce dimensionality automatically and model non-linearity (Wang et al., 2016; Kipf and Welling, 2017). In our case, efficiency is crucial and time complexity of factorization-based models is high. The disadvantage of the deep-learning-based models is that they require extensive hyperparameter optimization. To keep it simple, efficient, and to minimize the numbers of hyperparameters to tune, yet still effective, we select random-walk-based methods, where two prominent representatives are DeepWalk (Perozzi et al., 2014) and node2vec (Grover and Leskovec, 2016).

3   Learning Graph-based Entity Vectors

In order to make information from a semantic graph available for an entity linking system, we make use of graph embeddings. We use DeepWalk (Perozzi et al., 2014) to create the representation of entities in the DBPedia. DeepWalk is scalable, which makes it applicable on a large graph. It uses random walks to learn latent representations and provides a representation of each node on the basis of the graph structure.

First, we created a graph whose nodes are unique entities; attributes are explanations of entities, i.e. long abstracts; edges are the page links between entities with the information from DBpedia. Second, a vector representation per entity is generated by training DeepWalk on the edges of this graph. For this, we used all default hyper-parameters of DeepWalk, e.g. *number-*

Entity	Most similar 3 entities
Michael_Jordan_(basketball)	Charles_Barkley, Scottie_Pippen, Larry_Bird
Michael_I._Jordan	David_Blei, Machine_learning , Supervised_learning
Michael_Jordan_(footballer)	Dagenham_&_Redbridge_F.C., Stevenage_F.C., Yeovil_Town_F.C.

Table 1: **Graph entity embeddings:** Top three most similar entities for the name "Michael Jordan" based on our 400-dimensional DeepWalk embeddings.

walks is 10, *walk-length* is 40, and *window-size* is 5. To exemplify the result, the most similar 3 entities of disambiguated versions of Michael_Jordan, in the trained model with 400-dimension vectors are shown in Table 1. The first entity, Michael_Jordan_(basketball), is a well-known basketball player, and his all most similar entities are all basketball players and of similar age. The second entity, Michael_I._Jordan is a scientist, and again the most similar entities are either scientists in the same field or the topics of his study field. The last entity, Michael_Jordan_(footballer), is a football player whose most similar entities are football clubs. This suggests that our graph entity embeddings can differentiate different entities with the same name.

4 Experiment 1: Entity Disambiguation with Text and Graph Embeddings

In our first experiment, we build a simple neural ED system based on a feed-forward network and test the utility of the graph embeddings as compared to text-based embeddings.

4.1 Description of the Neural ED Model

The inputs of an ED task are a context and a possibly ambiguous entity span, and the output is a knowledge base entry. For example, *Desire contains a duet with Harris in the song Joey* and *Desire* given as an input and the output is *Bob Dylan's album* entity[3].

Our model in this experiment is a feed-forward neural network. Its input is a concatenation of document vectors of a context, a span, and an explanation of the candidate entity, i.e. long abstract, and graph embedding of a candidate entity

[3]http://dbpedia.org/page/Desire_(Bob_Dylan_album)

as in Figure 1, and output is a prediction value denoting whether the candidate entity is correct in this context. For learning representations, we employ doc2vec (Le and Mikolov, 2014) for text and DeepWalk (Perozzi et al., 2014) for graphs, both methods have shown good performance on other tasks. We will describe the input components in more detail in the following.

Creating Negative Samples: It is not computationally efficient to use all entities in our graph as a candidate for every context-span as negative examples for training because of the high number of entities (about 5 million). Thus, we need to filter some possible entities for each context-span in order to generate negative samples. We use spans to find out possible entities. If any lemma in the span is contained in an entity's name, the entity is added to the candidates for this mention. For example, if the span is *undergraduates*, the entity Undergraduate_degree is added to the candidates.

For training, we generate negative samples by filtering this candidate list and limited the number of candidates per positive sample. We employ two techniques to filter the candidate list. First, we shuffle the candidate list and randomly select n candidates. The other is to select the closest candidates by the following score formula: $score = \frac{\# \ of \ intersection \times page \ rank}{length}$, where $\# \ of \ intersection$ means the number of the common words between span/entity mention and candidate entity, $page \ rank$ is the page rank value (Page et al., 1999) on the entire graph for the candidate entity, and length is the number of tokens in the entity's name/title, e.g. the length of the entity Undergraduate_degree is 2. Before taking candidates with highest n scores, we have pruned the most similar candidates to the correct entity on the basis of the cosine between their respective graph embeddings. The reason for pruning is to assure that the entities are distinctive enough from each other so that a classifier can learn the distinction.

Word and Context Vectors: Document embedding techniques like doc2vec (Le and Mikolov, 2014) assign each document a single vector, which gets adjusted with respect to all words in the document and all document vectors in the dataset. Additionally, doc2vec provides the *infer_vector* method, which takes a word sequence and returns its representation. We employ this function for representing contexts (including the entity span),

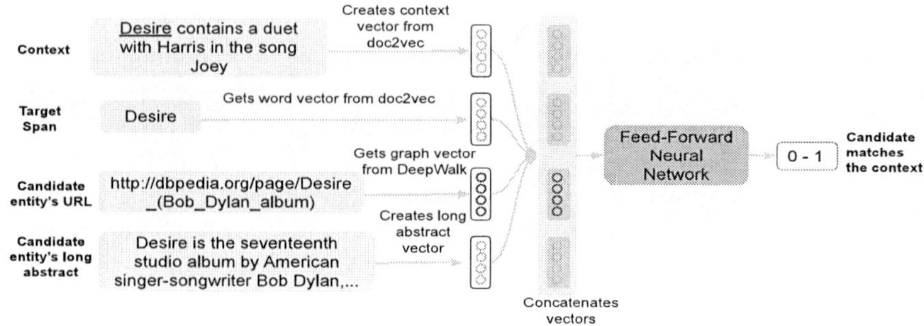

Figure 1: **Architecture of our feed-forward neural ED system:** using Wikipedia hyperlink graph embeddings as an additional input representation of entity candidates.

entity explanations (long abstracts), and multi-word spans.

4.2 Experimental Setup

Datasets: An English Wikipedia 2017 dump has been used to train doc2vec, using the gensim implementation (Řehůřek and Sojka, 2010). There are about 5 million entities (nodes), and 112 million page links (edges), in our graph.

DBpedia Spotlight (Mendes et al., 2011) (331 entities), *KORE50* (Hoffart et al., 2012) (144 entities), and *Reuters-128* (Röder et al., 2014) (881 entities) datasets as described in (Rosales-Méndez et al., 2018) are used to train and test our architecture. We have used 80% of these data for training, 10% for development, and the remaining for testing.

Implementation Details: We fixed context, span, and long abstract embedding dimensionality to 100, the default parameter defined in the implementation of gensim (Řehůřek and Sojka, 2010). The size of the graph embeddings is 400. We optimize the graph embedding size based on the development set with the range $100 - 400$. The overall input size is 700 when concatenating context, span, long abstract, and graph entity embeddings.

The number of negative samples per positive sample is 10. We have 3 hidden layers with equal sizes of 100. In the last layer, we have applied the *tanh* activation function. We have used *Adam* (Kingma and Ba, 2014) optimizer with a learning rate of 0.005 and 15000 epochs. All hyperparameters are determined by preliminary experiments.

4.3 Evaluation

The evaluation shows the impact of graph embeddings in a rather simple learning architecture.

In this experiment, an ablation test is performed to analyze the effect of graph embeddings. We have two types of training sets, where the creation of negative samples differs (in one of them, we have filtered negative samples randomly, whereas, in the other, we filtered them by selecting the closest ones, as explained in Section 4.1). In Figure 2, the upper part shows the Accuracy, Precision, Recall, and F1 values of the training set filtered randomly while the lower part results refer to the training set filtered by selecting closest neighbors. The first bar in the charts contains the result of the input, which concatenates context and long abstract embeddings (in this condition the input size becomes 200), here entity information only comes from its long abstract. The second bar presents the results of the input combination, context, word/span, and long abstract embeddings (the size of the input is 300). In the third bar, the input is the concatenation of context, long abstract, and graph embeddings (the input size is 600). Finally, the last bar indicates results for the concatenation of all types of inputs, for an input size of 700. For each configuration, we run the model 5 times and get the mean and standard deviation values. In Figure 2, charts show the mean values and the lines on the charts indicate standard deviation.

Comparing the first and third bars (or the second and last bars) in Figure 2, we can clearly see the results are increased when the input includes the graph embeddings for both variants of negative sampling. Comparing the third and last bars (or the first and second bars), we observe that including the span representation slightly decreases results for both sampling variants. We attribute this to the presence of the context embedding, which already includes the span, thus this increases the number of parameters of the network without sub-

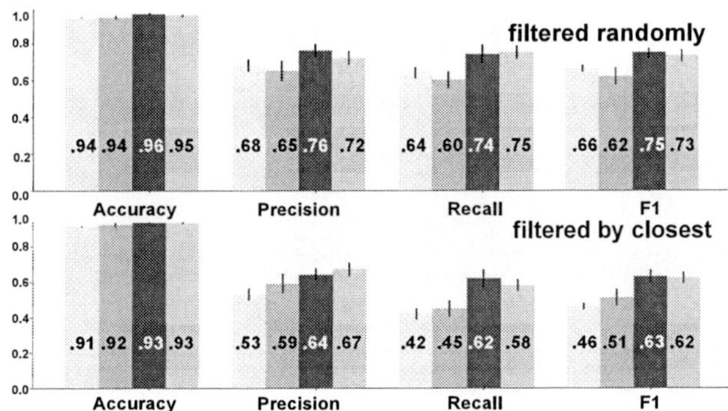

Figure 2: **Entity disambiguation performance**: various representations of our neural feed-forward ED system (cf. Figure 1). Reported are scores on the positive class filtered randomly and closest neighbors: context+long abstract,   context+long abstract+span,   context+long abstract+graph,   context+long abstract+span+graph.

stantially adding new information. Appending the graph embeddings improves the results about $0.09 - 0.17$ in F1, $0.13 - 0.2$ in recall, $0.07 - 0.12$ in precision and $0.01 - 0.02$ in accuracy scores. In general, the randomly sampled dataset is easier as it contains less related candidates.

5 Experiment 2: Integrating Graph Embeddings in the end2end ED System

5.1 Description of the Neural ED Model

For the second experiment, we have used the end2end state-of-the-art system for EL/ED (Kolitsas et al., 2018) and expanded it with our graph embeddings. In this neural end-to-end entity disambiguation system, standard text-based entity embeddings are used. In the experiment described in this section, we replace or combine them (keeping the remaining architecture unchanged) with our graph embeddings build as described in Section 3.

We replaced end2end's entity vector with our graph embeddings and the concatenation of their entity vector and our graph embeddings. We use the GERBIL (Usbeck et al., 2015) benchmark platform for an evaluation.

5.2 Experimental Setup

Datasets: We train the neural end2end system in its default configuration with the combination of *MSNBC* (Cucerzan, 2007) (747 entities), *ACE2004* (Ratinov et al., 2011) (306 entities), *AQUAINT* (Ratinov et al., 2011) (727 entities), *ClueWeb*, and *Wikipedia* datasets. We test the system on the GERBIL (Usbeck et al., 2015) platform using *DBpedia Spotlight* (Mendes et al., 2011)

(331 entities) and *Reuters-128* (Röder et al., 2014) (881 entities) datasets.

Implementation Details: We have not changed hyper-parameters for training the end2end system[4] (We used their base model + global for ED setting). We create graph embeddings with the same technique used before, however, to keep everything the same, we decided to also use 300 dimensions for the graph embeddings in this experiment to match the dimensionality of end2end's space.

We create the embeddings file with the same format they used. They give an id for each entity and call it "wiki id". First, we generate a map between this wiki id and our graph id (id of our entity). Then, we replace each entity vector corresponding to the wiki id with our graph embeddings, which refers to the entity. Sometimes there is no corresponding graph entity for the entity in the end2end system, in this case, we supply a zero vector.

They have a stopping condition, which applies after 6 consecutive evaluations with no significant improvement in the Macro F1 score. We have changed this hyperparameter to 10, accounting for our observation that the training converges slower when operating on graph embeddings.

5.3 Evaluation

Table 2 reports ED performance evaluated on *DBpedia Spotlight* and *Reuters-128* datasets. There are three models, end2end trained using their text entity vectors, our graph embeddings and the combination of them. Training datasets and implementation details are the same for all models. We train

---

[4]https://github.com/dalab/end2end_neural_el

319

	DBpedia Spotlight dataset					
Model	Macro F1	Macro Precision	Macro Recall	Micro F1	Micro Precision	Micro Recall
text embeddings	0.762	0.790	0.742	0.781	0.815	0.750
graph embeddings	0.796	**0.860**	0.758	0.783	**0.847**	0.730
text and graph embeddings	**0.798**	0.835	**0.775**	**0.797**	0.835	**0.763**
	Reuters-128 dataset					
Model	Macro F1	Macro Precision	Macro Recall	Micro F1	Micro Precision	Micro Recall
text embeddings	0.593	0.654	0.575	0.634	0.687	0.589
graph embeddings	0.607	**0.694**	0.574	**0.660**	**0.747**	0.592
text and graph embeddings	**0.614**	0.687	**0.590**	0.650	0.707	**0.602**

Table 2: **Entity disambiguation performance**: The end2end (Kolitsas et al., 2018) system based on the original text-based embeddings, our graph embeddings and a combination of both evaluated using the GERBIL platform on *DBpedia Spotlight* and *Reuters-128* datasets.

the models for 10 times and removed the models that did not converge (1 non-converging run for each single type of embedding and 2 for the combination). Table 2 shows the mean values. The standard deviations of the models are between $0.02 - 0.05$ in the *DBpedia Spotlight* dataset and $0.01 - 0.03$ in the *Reuters-128* dataset over all scores. Scores are produced using the GERBIL platform; these are Micro-averaged over the set of annotations in the dataset and Macro-averaged over the average performance per document. The results are improved by including graph embeddings. When we compare two models, trained by graph embeddings and trained by entity vectors, the results are improved up to 0.03 in Macro F1 scores and Micro Precision, and up to 0.07 in Macro Precision. However, the improvement of the combination model is higher in Macro F1 and Recall. Micro-averaged results follow a similar trend. When we look at the scores of *Reuters-128* (Röder et al., 2014) dataset, the combination model improves Macro F1 and Recall and Micro Recall up to 0.02, 0.015, and 0.013 respectively. In the Micro-averaged evaluation, the combination model scores slightly below the model using graph embeddings alone.

To summarize the evaluation, our graph embeddings alone already lead to improvements over the original text-based embeddings, and their combination is even more beneficial. This suggests that test-based and graph-based representations in fact encode somewhat complementary information.

6 Conclusion and Future Work

We have shown how to integrate structured information into the neural ED task using two differ-ent experiments. In the first experiment, we use a simple neural network to gauge the impact of different text-based and graph-based embeddings. In the second experiment, we replace respectively complemented the representation of candidate entities in the ED component of a state-of-the-art EL system. In both setups, we demonstrate that graph embeddings lead to en par or better performance. This confirms our research hypothesis that it is possible to use structured resources for modeling entities in ED tasks and the information is complementary to a text-based representation alone. Our code and datasets are available online[5].

For future work, we plan to examine graph embeddings on other relationships, e.g. taxonomic or otherwise typed relations such as works-for, married-with, and so on, generalizing the notion to arbitrary structured resources. It might make a training step on the distance measure depending on the relation necessary. On the disambiguation architecture, modeling such direct links could give rise to improvements stemming from the mutual disambiguation of entities as e.g. done in (Ponzetto and Navigli, 2010). We will explore ways to map them into the same space to reduce the number of parameters. In another direction, we will train task-specific sentence embeddings.

Acknowledgments

We thank the SRW mentor Matt Gardner and anonymous reviewers for their most useful feedback on this work. The work was partially supported by a Deutscher Akademischer Austauschdienst (DAAD) doctoral stipend and the DFG-funded JOIN-T project BI 1544/4.

---

[5] https://github.com/uhh-lt/kb2vec

References

Mikhail Belkin and Partha Niyogi. 2001. Laplacian eigenmaps and spectral techniques for embedding and clustering. In *Proceedings of the 14th International Conference on Neural Information Processing Systems: Natural and Synthetic*, NIPS'01, pages 585–591, Cambridge, MA, USA. MIT Press.

Kurt Bollacker, Colin Evans, Praveen Paritosh, Tim Sturge, and Jamie Taylor. 2008. Freebase: A collaboratively created graph database for structuring human knowledge. In *Proceedings of the 2008 ACM SIGMOD International Conference on Management of Data*, SIGMOD '08, pages 1247–1250, New York, NY, USA. ACM.

Razvan Bunescu and Marius Paşca. 2006. Using encyclopedic knowledge for named entity disambiguation. In *11th Conference of the European Chapter of the Association for Computational Linguistics*, pages 9–16, Trento, Italy. Association for Computational Linguistics.

Silviu Cucerzan. 2007. Large-scale named entity disambiguation based on Wikipedia data. In *Proceedings of the 2007 Joint Conference on Empirical Methods in Natural Language Processing and Computational Natural Language Learning (EMNLP-CoNLL)*, pages 708–716, Prague, Czech Republic. Association for Computational Linguistics.

Wei Fang, Jianwen Zhang, Dilin Wang, Zheng Chen, and Ming Li. 2016. Entity disambiguation by knowledge and text jointly embedding. In *Proceedings of The 20th SIGNLL Conference on Computational Natural Language Learning*, pages 260–269, Berlin, Germany. Association for Computational Linguistics.

Octavian-Eugen Ganea and Thomas Hofmann. 2017. Deep joint entity disambiguation with local neural attention. In *Proceedings of the 2017 Conference on Empirical Methods in Natural Language Processing*, pages 2619–2629, Copenhagen, Denmark. Association for Computational Linguistics.

Palash Goyal and Emilio Ferrara. 2018. Graph embedding techniques, applications, and performance: A survey. *Knowledge-Based Systems*, 151(1 July):78–94.

Aditya Grover and Jure Leskovec. 2016. Node2vec: Scalable feature learning for networks. In *Proceedings of the 22Nd ACM SIGKDD International Conference on Knowledge Discovery and Data Mining*, KDD '16, pages 855–864, New York, NY, USA. ACM.

William L. Hamilton, Rex Ying, and Jure Leskovec. 2017. Representation learning on graphs: Methods and applications. *IEEE Data Eng. Bull.*, 40:52–74.

Johannes Hoffart, Stephan Seufert, Dat Ba Nguyen, Martin Theobald, and Gerhard Weikum. 2012. KORE: keyphrase overlap relatedness for entity disambiguation. In *Proceedings of the 21st ACM International Conference on Information and Knowledge Management*, CIKM '12, pages 545–554, New York, NY, USA. ACM.

Hongzhao Huang, Larry P. Heck, and Heng Ji. 2015. Leveraging deep neural networks and knowledge graphs for entity disambiguation. *CoRR*, abs/1504.07678.

Diederik P. Kingma and Jimmy Ba. 2014. Adam: A method for stochastic optimization. Proceedings of the 3rd International Conference for Learning Representations (ICLR), San Diego, CA, USA, 2015.

Thomas N. Kipf and Max Welling. 2017. Semi-supervised classification with graph convolutional networks. In *Proceedings of the 5th International Conference on Learning Representations, (ICLR)*, Toulon, France.

Nikolaos Kolitsas, Octavian-Eugen Ganea, and Thomas Hofmann. 2018. End-to-end neural entity linking. In *Proceedings of the 22nd Conference on Computational Natural Language Learning*, pages 519–529, Brussels, Belgium. Association for Computational Linguistics.

Quoc Le and Tomas Mikolov. 2014. Distributed representations of sentences and documents. In *Proceedings of the 31st International Conference on International Conference on Machine Learning - Volume 32*, ICML'14, pages II–1188–II–1196. JMLR.org.

Pablo N. Mendes, Max Jakob, Andrés García-Silva, and Christian Bizer. 2011. DBpedia spotlight: Shedding light on the web of documents. In *Proceedings of the 7th International Conference on Semantic Systems*, I-Semantics '11, pages 1–8, New York, NY, USA. ACM.

Rada Mihalcea and Andras Csomai. 2007. Wikify!: Linking documents to encyclopedic knowledge. In *Proceedings of the Sixteenth ACM Conference on Conference on Information and Knowledge Management*, CIKM '07, pages 233–242, New York, NY, USA. ACM.

Tomas Mikolov, Kai Chen, Greg Corrado, and Jeffrey Dean. 2013a. Efficient estimation of word representations in vector space. In *Workshop Proceedings of the International Conference on Learning Representations (ICLR)*. 2013, Scottsdale, AZ, USA.

Tomas Mikolov, Ilya Sutskever, Kai Chen, Greg S. Corrado, and Jeffrey Dean. 2013b. Distributed representations of words and phrases and their compositionality. In *Proceedings of the 26th International Conference on Neural Information Processing Systems - Volume 2*, NIPS'13, pages 3111–3119, Lake Tahoe, NV, USA. Curran Associates Inc.

David Milne and Ian H. Witten. 2008. Learning to link with Wikipedia. In *Proceedings of the 17th ACM*

Conference on Information and Knowledge Management, CIKM '08, pages 509–518, New York, NY, USA. ACM.

David Nadeau and Satoshi Sekine. 2007. A survey of named entity recognition and classification. *Linguisticae Investigationes*, 30(1):3–26.

Roberto Navigli. 2009. Word sense disambiguation: A survey. *ACM Computing Surveys*, 41(2):10:1–10:69.

Lawrence Page, Sergey Brin, Rajeev Motwani, and Terry Winograd. 1999. The PageRank citation ranking: Bringing order to the web. Technical Report 1999-66, Stanford InfoLab. Previous number = SIDL-WP-1999-0120.

Bryan Perozzi, Rami Al-Rfou, and Steven Skiena. 2014. DeepWalk: Online learning of social representations. In *Proceedings of the 20th ACM SIGKDD International Conference on Knowledge Discovery and Data Mining*, KDD '14, pages 701–710, New York, NY, USA. ACM.

Simone P. Ponzetto and Roberto Navigli. 2010. Knowledge-rich word sense disambiguation rivaling supervised systems. In *Proceedings of the 48th Annual Meeting of the Association for Computational Linguistics*, pages 1522–1531, Uppsala, Sweden. Association for Computational Linguistics.

Priya Radhakrishnan, Partha Talukdar, and Vasudeva Varma. 2018. ELDEN: Improved entity linking using densified knowledge graphs. In *Proceedings of the 2018 Conference of the North American Chapter of the Association for Computational Linguistics: Human Language Technologies, Volume 1 (Long Papers)*, pages 1844–1853, New Orleans, LA, USA. Association for Computational Linguistics.

Lev Ratinov, Dan Roth, Doug Downey, and Mike Anderson. 2011. Local and global algorithms for disambiguation to Wikipedia. In *Proceedings of the 49th Annual Meeting of the Association for Computational Linguistics: Human Language Technologies - Volume 1*, HLT '11, pages 1375–1384, Portland, OR, USA. Association for Computational Linguistics.

Radim Řehůřek and Petr Sojka. 2010. Software Framework for Topic Modelling with Large Corpora. In *Proceedings of the LREC 2010 Workshop on New Challenges for NLP Frameworks*, pages 45–50, Valletta, Malta. European Language Resources Association (ELRA).

Michael Röder, Ricardo Usbeck, Sebastian Hellmann, Daniel Gerber, and Andreas Both. 2014. N^3 - A collection of datasets for named entity recognition and disambiguation in the NLP interchange format. In *Proceedings of the Ninth International Conference on Language Resources and Evaluation (LREC'14)*, pages 3529–3533, Reykjavik, Iceland. European Language Resources Association (ELRA).

Henry Rosales-Méndez, Aidan Hogan, and Barbara Poblete. 2018. VoxEL: A benchmark dataset for multilingual entity linking. In *International Semantic Web Conference (2)*, volume 11137 of *Lecture Notes in Computer Science*, pages 170–186, Monterey, CA, USA. Springer.

Sam T. Roweis and Lawrence K. Saul. 2000. Nonlinear dimensionality reduction by locally linear embedding. *Science*, 290:2323–2326.

Wei Shen, Jianyong Wang, and Jiawei Han. 2015. Entity linking with a knowledge base: Issues, techniques, and solutions. *IEEE Trans. Knowl. Data Eng.*, 27(2):443–460.

Michael Strube and Simone P. Ponzetto. 2006. WikiRelate! Computing semantic relatedness using Wikipedia. In *Proceedings of the 21st National Conference on Artificial Intelligence - Volume 2*, AAAI'06, pages 1419–1424, Boston, MA, USA. AAAI Press.

Yaming Sun, Lei Lin, Duyu Tang, Nan Yang, Zhenzhou Ji, and Xiaolong Wang. 2015. Modeling mention, context and entity with neural networks for entity disambiguation. In *Proceedings of the 24th International Conference on Artificial Intelligence*, IJCAI'15, pages 1333–1339, Buenos Aires, Argentina. AAAI Press.

Jian Tang, Meng Qu, Mingzhe Wang, Ming Zhang, Jun Yan, and Qiaozhu Mei. 2015. LINE: Large-scale information network embedding. In *Proceedings of the 24th International Conference on World Wide Web*, WWW '15, pages 1067–1077, Republic and Canton of Geneva, Switzerland. International World Wide Web Conferences Steering Committee.

Ricardo Usbeck, Michael Röder, Axel-Cyrille Ngonga Ngomo, Ciro Baron, Andreas Both, Martin Brümmer, Diego Ceccarelli, Marco Cornolti, Didier Cherix, Bernd Eickmann, Paolo Ferragina, Christiane Lemke, Andrea Moro, Roberto Navigli, Francesco Piccinno, Giuseppe Rizzo, Harald Sack, René Speck, Raphaël Troncy, Jörg Waitelonis, and Lars Wesemann. 2015. GERBIL: General entity annotator benchmarking framework. In *Proceedings of the 24th International Conference on World Wide Web*, WWW '15, pages 1133–1143, Florence, Italy. International World Wide Web Conferences Steering Committee.

Daixin Wang, Peng Cui, and Wenwu Zhu. 2016. Structural deep network embedding. In *Proceedings of the 22Nd ACM SIGKDD International Conference on Knowledge Discovery and Data Mining*, KDD '16, pages 1225–1234, New York, NY, USA. ACM.

Ikuya Yamada, Hiroyuki Shindo, Hideaki Takeda, and Yoshiyasu Takefuji. 2016. Joint learning of the embedding of words and entities for named entity disambiguation. In *Proceedings of The 20th SIGNLL Conference on Computational Natural Language Learning*, pages 250–259, Berlin, Germany. Association for Computational Linguistics.

Hierarchical Multi-label Classification of Text with Capsule Networks

Rami Aly, **Steffen Remus**, and **Chris Biemann**

Language Technology group
Universität Hamburg, Hamburg, Germany
`{5aly,remus,biemann}@informatik.uni-hamburg.de`

Abstract

Capsule networks have been shown to demonstrate good performance on structured data in the area of visual inference. In this paper we apply and compare simple shallow capsule networks for hierarchical multi-label text classification and show that they can perform superior to other neural networks, such as CNNs and LSTMs, and non-neural network architectures such as SVMs. For our experiments, we use the established Web of Science (WOS) dataset and introduce a new real-world scenario dataset, the BlurbGenreCollection (BGC). Our results confirm the hypothesis that capsule networks are especially advantageous for rare events and structurally diverse categories, which we attribute to their ability to combine latent encoded information.

1 Introduction

In hierarchical multi-label classification (HMC), samples are classified into one or multiple class labels that are organized in a structured label hierarchy (Silla and Freitas, 2011). HMC has been thoroughly researched for traditional classifiers (Sun and Lim, 2001; Silla and Freitas, 2011), but with the increase of available data, the desire for more specific and specialized hierarchies increases. However, since traditional approaches fail to generalize adequately, more sophisticated and robust classification methods are receiving more attention. Complex neural network classifiers on the contrary are computationally expensive, difficult to analyze, and the amount of hyperparameters is significantly higher as compared to other classification approaches. This makes it difficult to apply the *local classifier approach* (Silla and Freitas, 2011), where multiple classifiers are employed to cover different parts of the hierarchy. Therefore, in this paper we focus on the *global approach* – one classifier that is able to capture the entire hierarchy at once. There are indications

that capsule networks (Hinton et al., 2011; Sabour et al., 2017) are successful at finding, adapting, and agreeing on latent structures in the underlying data in the area of image recognition as well as recently in the field of natural language processing (Zhao et al., 2018). This insight motivates our research question: To which extent can the capabilities of capsule networks be transferred and applied to HMC in order to capture the categories' underlying structures?

In our experiments[1] we compare HMC-adjusted capsule networks to several baseline neural as well as non-neural architectures on the *BlurbGenreCollection* (BGC), a dataset which we collected and that consists of so-called blurbs of books and their hierarchically structured writing genres. Additionally, we test our hypothesis on the *Web of Science* (WOS) dataset (Kowsari et al., 2017). The main benefit of capsules is their ability to encode information of each category separately by associating each capsule with one category. Combining encoded features independently for each capsule, and thus category, enables capsule networks to handle label combinations better than previous approaches. This property is especially relevant for HMC since documents that for instance only belong to a parent category, e.g. *Fiction*, often share similar features such as the most frequent words or n-grams with documents that additionally classify into one of the parent's child labels, e.g. *Mystery & Suspense* or *Fantasy*. This makes it difficult for traditional classifiers to distinguish between parent and child labels correctly, especially if the specific combination of labels was never observed during training. This paper contributes in two ways: Firstly, we introduce the new openly accessible *BlurbGenreCollection* dataset for the English language. This dataset is created and only minimally adjusted on basis

---

[1]Code for replicating results: `https://github.com/uhh-lt/BlurbGenreCollection-HMC`

Proceedings of the ACL 2019, Student Research Workshop, pages 323–330
Florence, Italy, July 28th-August 2nd, 2019. ©2019 Association for Computational Linguistics

of a vertical search webpage for books and thus presents a real-world scenario task. Secondly, we thoroughly analyze the properties of capsule networks for HMC. To the best of our knowledge, capsule networks have not yet been applied and tested in the HMC domain.

2   Related Work

Neural networks for HMC: In hierarchical multi-label classification (HMC) samples are assigned one or multiple class labels, which are organized in a structured label hierarchy (Silla and Freitas, 2011). For text classification (TC), we treat a document as a sample and its categories as labels. *Convolutional Neural Networks* (CNNs) and different types of *Recurrent Neural Networks* (RNNs) (Goodfellow et al., 2016; Kim, 2014), most notably long short-term memory units (LSTMs, Hochreiter and Schmidhuber, 1997) have shown to be highly efficient in TC tasks. For HMC, Cerri et al. (2014) use concatenated multi-layer perceptrons (MLP), where each MLP is associated to one level of the class hierarchy. Kowsari et al. (2017) use multiple concatenated deep learning architectures (CNN, LSTM, and MLP) to HMC on a dataset with a rather shallow hierarchy with only two levels. Similar to Kiritchenko et al. (2005), Baker and Korhonen (2017) treat the HMC task as a multi-label classification problem that considers every label in the hierarchy, but they additionally leverage the co-occurrence of labels within the hierarchy to initialize the weights of their CNN's final layer (Kurata et al., 2016).

Capsule Networks: Capsule networks encapsulate features into groups of neurons, so-called capsules (Hinton et al., 2011; Sabour et al., 2017). Originally introduced for a handwritten digit image classification task where each digit has been associated with a capsule, capsules have shown to learn more robust representations for each class as they capture parent-child relationships more accurately. They reached on-par performance with more complex CNN architectures, even outperforming them in several classification tasks such as the *affNIST* and *MultiMNIST* dataset (Sabour et al., 2017). First attempts to use capsules for sentiment analysis were carried out by (Wang et al., 2018) on the basis of an RNN, however, they did not employ the routing algorithm, thus highly limiting the capabilities of capsules. Zhao et al.

(2018) show that capsule networks can outperform traditional neural networks for TC by a great margin when training on single-labeled and testing on multi-labeled documents of the Reuters-21578 dataset since the routing of capsules behaves like a parallel attention mechanism regarding the selection of categories. By connecting a BiLSTM to a capsule network for relation extraction, Zhang et al. (2018) show that capsule networks improve at extracting n-ary relations, with $n > 2$, per sentence and thus confirm the observation of (Zhao et al., 2018) in a different context. For multi-task learning, Xiao et al. (2018) use capsule networks to improve the differentiation between tasks. They encapsulate features in different capsules and use the routing algorithm to cluster features for each task. Further applications to NLP span aggression, toxicity and emotion detection (Srivastava et al., 2018; Rathnayaka et al., 2018), embedding creation for knowledge graph completion (Nguyen et al., 2019), and knowledge transfer of user intents (Xia et al., 2018). Despite the suitable properties of capsule networks to classify into hierarchical structured categories, they have not yet been applied to HMC. This work aims to fill the gap by applying and thoroughly analyzing capsules' properties at HMC.

3   Capsule Network for HMC

For each category in the hierarchy, an associated capsule outputs latent information of the category in form of a vector as opposed to a single scalar value used in traditional neural networks. The vector is equivariant with its length defining the pseudo-probability of its activation and its orientation representing different cases of a category's existence. This distributional representation in the form of a vector instead of a scalar makes capsules exponentially more informative than traditional perceptrons (Sabour et al., 2017).

The input of capsules in the first capsule layer of a capsule network is called *primary capsules* and can be of arbitrary dimension, typically coming from a convolutional layer or from the hidden state of a recurrent network. The output vector of a primary capsule represents latent information such as local order and semantic representations of words (Zhao et al., 2018). Each capsule j in the next layer, called *classification capsules*, take as input the weighted sum $s_j = \sum_i c_{j|i} \hat{u}_{j|i}$ of the prediction vectors of all primary capsules *i*. A capsule's prediction vector $\hat{u}_{j|i}$ is generated by multiplying the output $u_{j|i}$ by a weight matrix W_{ij}. Since the length of a vector of a classification capsule should be interpreted as the probability of the corresponding category, a squashing function $v_j = squash(s_j)$ is applied, which scales the output of each classification capsule non-linearly between zero and one. The coupling coefficients $c_{j|i}$ that determine the contribution of each primary capsule's output to a classification capsule are calculated using a dynamic routing heuristic (Sabour et al., 2017). It iteratively decides the routes of capsules and thus how to cluster features for each category. The pseudocode for the full routing algorithm is written in Algorithm 1.

Routing algorithm
Result: v_j
Initialization: $\forall i \in Primary. \forall j \in$
$\quad Classification : b_{j|i} \leftarrow 0.$

for *r iterations* **do**
$\quad \forall i \in Primary : c_i \leftarrow \text{softmax}(b_i)$
$\quad \forall j \in Clas. : v_j \leftarrow \text{squash}(\sum_i c_{j|i}\hat{u}_{j|i})$
$\quad \forall i \in Primary. \forall j \in Clas. : b_{j|i} \leftarrow$
$\quad\quad b_{j|i} + \hat{u}_{j|i} \cdot v_j$
end

Algorithm 1: Routing algorithm as described in (Sabour et al., 2017)

The coupling coefficients are generated by applying the softmax function to the log prior probabilities that primary capsule i should be coupled to classification capsule j. The probability is higher when the primary capsule's prediction vector is more similar to the classification capsule's output. Therefore, primary capsules try to predict the output of the capsule in the subsequent layer. Since v_j is partially determined by $u_{j|i}$, their similarity increases for the next iteration. Thus a convergence is guaranteed.

This routing algorithm is superior regarding its ability to combine and generalize information compared to primitive routing algorithms such as max-pooling layers, as the latter only stores the most prominent features while the others are ignored. This leads to CNNs having more difficulty differentiating between classes with highly similar features (Sabour et al., 2017), but since most label combinations appear rarely and categories often share features with their parents, it is a desirable property to exploit for hierarchical classification.

Architecture: The HMC task is converted to a

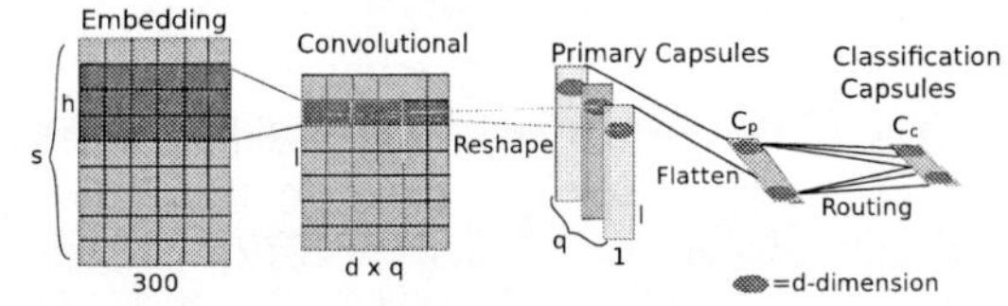

Figure 1: Architecture of our capsule network with d being the dimensionality of a capsule's output.

multi-label classification task using the hierarchy of labels: All explicitly labeled classes must also include all ancestor labels of the hierarchy. The architecture of our capsule network is shown in Figure 1 and consists of four layers. We designed a minimal capsule network, similar to CapsNet-1 in (Xiao et al., 2018) in order to benefit from capsules and dynamic routing while maintaining high comparability to a similarly simple CNN. In our network, the primary capsules take as input the output created by a preceding convolutional layer. For each classification capsule, the routing algorithm is then used to cluster the outputs of all c_p primary capsules. The pseudo-probability $||v_j||$ is then assigned to the category associated with the effective classification capsule. We follow Sabour et al. (2017), and use their *margin loss* function.

Leveraging Label Co-occurrence: We further follow the layer weight initialization introduced by (Kurata et al., 2016) in order to leverage label co-occurrences during the learning process of a neural network. Since label co-occurrences such as {*Fiction, Mystery & Suspense*} or {*Fiction, Fantasy*} naturally occur in HMC because of parent-child relationships between categories, we aim to bias the learning process of the capsule network in respect to the co-occurrences in the dataset by initializing W with label co-occurrences. Weights between a primary capsule and the co-occurring classification capsules are initialized using a uniform distribution while all other values are set to zero.

Label Correction: A classifier may assign labels to classes that do not conform with the underlying hierarchy of the categories as the activation function as well as the routing algorithm look at each category separately. For instance, if the capsule network only assigns the label *Fantasy* then the prediction is inconsistent with the hierarchy as its parent *Fiction* has not been labeled. Inconsistencies with respect to the hierarchical structure of categories are corrected by a post-processing step.

We applied three different ways of label correction: Correction by *extension, removal* and *threshold*. The former two systematically add parent or remove parentless labels to make the prediction consistent (Baker and Korhonen, 2017). Therefore, the first method adds *Fiction* to the predictions while the second one removes the prediction *Fantasy* (and all its children) in its entirety. Correction by threshold calculates the average confidence of all ancestors for an inconsistent prediction and adds them if above the threshold (Kiritchenko et al., 2005).

4 Experiments

Datasets: We test our hypothesis on two different datasets with fundamentally different properties, the BlurbGenreCollection[2] (BGC), and the WOS-11967 (Web of Science, Kowsari et al., 2017).

The BGC dataset consists of book blurbs (short advertising texts) and several book-related meta-information such as author, date of publication, number of pages, and so on. Each blurb is categorized into one or multiple categories in a hierarchy. With their permission, we crawled the Penguin Random House website and performed cleaning steps, such as: removing categories that do not rely on content (e.g. audiobooks), and removing category combinations that appear less than five times. The dataset follows the well-known dataset properties as described in (Lewis et al., 2004): Firstly, at least one writing-genre is assigned to each book and secondly, every ancestor of a book's label is assigned to it as well. It is important to note that the most specific genre of a book does not have to be a leaf. For instance, the most specific category of a book could be *Children's Books*, although Children's Books has further sub-genres, such as *Middle Grade books*. Furthermore, in this dataset, each child-label has exactly one parent, forming all-together a hierarchy in form of a forest. Nonetheless, the label distribution remains highly unbalanced and diverse, with a total of $1,342$ different label co-occurrences from a pool of 146 different labels arranged on 4 hierarchy levels.

The WOS dataset consists of abstracts of published papers from the Web of Science. The hi-

	BGC	WOS-11967
Number of texts	91,892	11,967
Average number of tokens	93.56	125.90
Total number of classes	146	40
Classes on level 1;2;3;4	7; 46; 77; 16	7; 33; -; -
Average number of labels	3.01	2
Total number of label co-occurrences	1342	33
Co-occurrence entropy (normalized)	0.7345	0.9973
Samples per category standard deviation	4374.19	529.43

Table 1: Quantitative characteristics of both datasets. Normalized entropy is the quotient between entropy and the log of co-occurrence cardinality.

erarchy of the WOS dataset is shallower, but significantly broader, with fewer classes in total. In addition to having only as many co-occurrences as leaf nodes, measuring the entropy of label combinations shows that the dataset is unnaturally balanced – a consequence of the dataset's requirement to assign exactly two labels to each example. Table 1 shows further important quantitative characteristics of both datasets.

Feature selection: Since CNNs and our capsule network require a fixed input length, we limit the texts to the first 100 tokens, which covers the complete input for over 90% of the dataset. We remove stop-words, most punctuation and low-frequency words (< 2). For the BGC, we kept special characters like exclamation marks as they can be frequently found in blurbs that have a younger target audience and hence could provide useful information. We are using pre-trained fastText embeddings[3] provided by Bojanowski et al. (2017) and adjust them during training.

Baselines: We employ a one-vs-rest classification strategy using one SVM (Cortes and Vapnik, 1995) for each label with linear kernels and tf-idf values in a bag-of-words fashion as feature vectors. Also, we apply the CNN as described by Kim (2014) and an LSTM with recurrent dropout (Gal and Ghahramani, 2016).[4] For all experiments we use the initialization strategy as described in (Baker and Korhonen, 2017), which takes label co-occurrences for initializing the weights of the final layer, and the label correction method by thresh-

---

[2] The dataset is available at https://www.inf.uni-hamburg.de/en/inst/ab/lt/resources/data/blurb-genre-collection.html

[3] https://fasttext.cc/docs/en/pretrained-vectors.html

[4] All neural networks use the Adam optimizer, a dropout probability of 0.5 and a minibatch size of 32. LSTM and CNN use the binary cross entropy loss. Further hyperparameters for (BGC, WOS) – CNN: filters: (1500, 1000), windows: {3,4,5}, l. rate: (0.0005, 0.001), l. decay: (0.9, 1), epochs: (30, 20); LSTM: hidden units: (1500, 1000), l. rate: (0.005, 0.001), epochs: (15, 25); capsule network: num capsules: (55, 32), windows: (90, 50), primary/class. cap. dim.: 8/16, l. rate: (0.001, 0.002), l. decay: (0.4, 0.95), epochs: 4

	BGC				WOS-11967			
Model	Recall	Precision	F_1	Subset Acc.	Recall	Precision	F_1	Subset Acc.
SVM	61.11	**85.37**	71.23	35.79	72.43	89.84	80.20	56.47
CNN	64.75 ± 0.41	83.87 ± 0.09	73.08 ± 0.27	37.26 ± 0.52	$\mathbf{84.06 \pm 0.93}$	$\mathbf{91.68 \pm 1.00}$	$\mathbf{87.71 \pm 0.58}$	75.16 ± 1.66
LSTM	69.12 ± 1.24	75.49 ± 3.54	72.16 ± 1.01	$\mathbf{37.99 \pm 1.52}$	83.78 ± 1.69	87.56 ± 1.04	85.63 ± 1.22	$\mathbf{76.80 \pm 2.15}$
Caps. Network	$\mathbf{71.73 \pm 0.63}$	77.21 ± 0.54	$\mathbf{74.37 \pm 0.35}$	37.70 ± 0.68	80.67 ± 1.27	82.75 ± 2.42	81.69 ± 0.70	64.97 ± 0.49

Table 2: All results with their corresponding 95% confidence intervals, measured across three runs.

old with a confidence value of 0.2.[5] The dataset is split into 64% train, 16% validation and 20% test. For evaluation, we measure subset accuracy, micro-averaged recall, precision, and F_1 as defined in (Sorower, 2010; Silla and Freitas, 2011).

5 Results

Results are shown in Table 2. Regarding the BGC dataset, the capsule network yields the highest F_1 and recall, the SVM the highest precision, while the LSTM showed the best result in subset accuracy. On WOS, all neural network architectures beat the baseline SVM model by a substantial margin. However, both, the SVM and the capsule network, are substantially outperformed by the CNN and LSTM. In Figure 2 we further observe a performance decline for deeper levels of the hierarchy. On BGC, the capsule network performs best on every level of the hierarchy with an increasing margin for more specific labels.

5.1 Identification of label co-occurrences

We argue that the pronounced performance difference between the datasets is due to the ability of capsules to handle label combinations better than the CNN and LSTM. We observe, as shown in Figure 4, that capsule networks are beneficial for examples with many label assignments. While the capsule network performs worse on BGC for a label set cardinality of 1 and 2, it starts to perform better at a cardinality of 3 and almost doubles the F_1 of all baselines for 9 and 11. The number of examples decreases exponentially with the label set cardinality, so that the ability of networks to combine labels is becoming increasingly important.

In contrast, in the WOS dataset, exactly one parent-child label combination is assigned to each example, resulting in a label set cardinality of two for the whole dataset. There are comparably few label combinations, which occur with a high frequency in the dataset (cf. Table 1). The benefit of capsules can thus not apply here.

---

[5]These options consistently performed well in preliminary experiments.

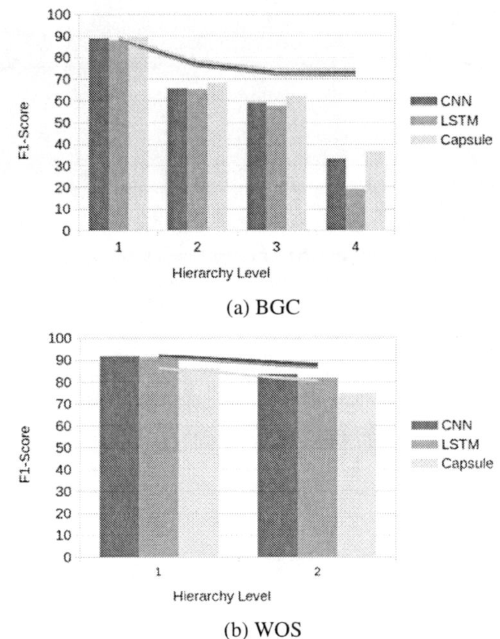

(a) BGC

(b) WOS

Figure 2: Scores on different levels for the BGC (a) and WOS (b). The lines are the cumulative scores.

To verify this hypothesis, we conduct a further test exclusively on BGC examples with label combinations that have not been observed during training (5, 943 samples). As shown in Table 3, the capsule network again achieves the highest F_1 score, outperforming the other networks, especially in terms of recall. In order to create hierarchical inconsistencies in the WOS dataset, we test two modifications on the training data while the test data is kept the same: *a)* 50% of all child labels are removed, and *b)* for each sample, either the child or the parent label is kept. Results of this study are shown in Table 4. Removing 50% of the children labels results in the capsule network being more similar to the CNN and LSTM in terms of subset accuracy. However, for the second modification, where label combinations are completely omitted for training, the capsule network significantly outperforms both networks. Figure 3 shows that different primary capsules are routed to the classification capsule representing the parent cat-

327

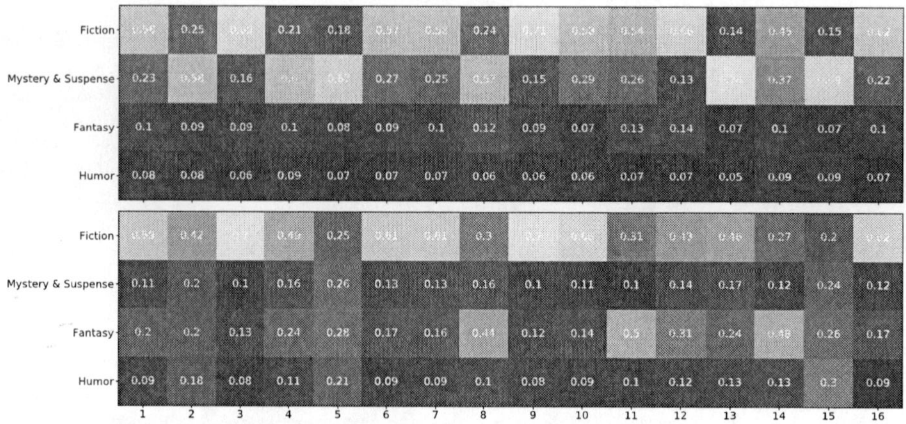

Figure 3: Connection strength between primary capsules (x-axis) and classification capsules (y-axis) for two BGC samples: top belonging to {*Fiction, Mystery & Suspense*} and bottom to {*Fiction, Fantasy*} with *Fiction* being their parent category. A reduced number of primary capsules and categories was used for visualization purposes.

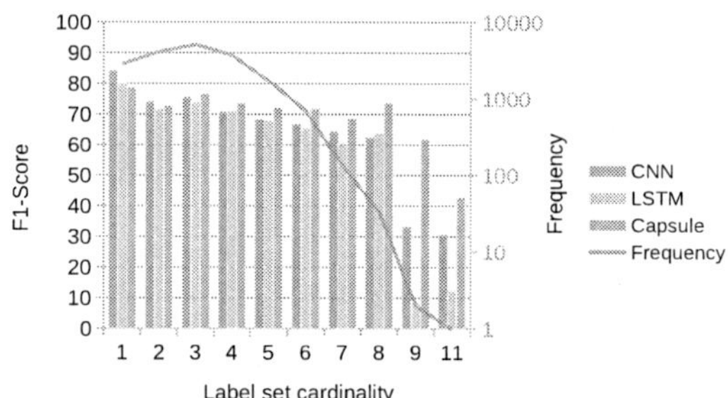

Figure 4: Test F_1-scores of classifiers for different label cardinalities.

BGC, unobserved	R	P	F_1
CNN	46.21	**68.95**	55.34
LSTM	45.79	60.48	52.13
Capsule Net.	**53.30**	61.21	**56.98**

Table 3: Performance results on the test set with label combinations not seen during training.

egory *Fiction* than to the children. Some primary capsules learn features for specific children categories. For instance Primary Capsule 5 is not inclined to any category for the bottom sample because of missing features for *Mystery & Suspense* in this sample. Some capsules distribute their connection strength to the parent and child category evenly, likely due to the categories' similarities. To combine encoded features for each category separately while using the softmax to ensure that primary capsules encapsulate features of specific categories appears to be the main cause of these significant performance differences. These observations also align with previous work, especially see (Sabour et al., 2017; Zhao et al., 2018).

Modified WOS	50% Child Labels		Either Parent or Child	
	F_1	Acc	F_1	Acc
CNN	**75.15**	**36.28**	41.93	16.36
LSTM	73.00	35.09	38.74	5.28
Capsule Net.	71.59	35.21	**67.23**	**34.27**

Table 4: Results on the modified WOS training data. Firstly, by removing 50% of the children labels and secondly, by removing label combinations completely.

6 Conclusion

This first application of capsule networks to the HMC task indicates that the beneficial properties of capsules can be successfully utilized. By associating each category in the hierarchy with a separate capsule, as well as using a routing algorithm to combine in capsules encoded features, capsule networks have shown to identify and combine categories with similar features more accurately than the baselines. The introduced dataset, the BlurbGenreCollection (BGC), is compiled from a real-world scenario and is indicative of the promising properties of capsule networks for HMC tasks, since most hierarchically organized datasets consist of substantial amounts of rare label combinations, where algorithms are very likely to be confronted with unseen label combinations.

This initial attempt shows the advantage of simplistic capsule networks over traditional methods for HMC. Future architectures could for example employ a cascade of capsule layers with each capsule in one layer being associated to a category of one specific level in the hierarchy.

References

Simon Baker and Anna Korhonen. 2017. Initializing neural networks for hierarchical multi-label text classification. In *Proceedings of the 16th Biomedical Natural Language Processing Workshop*, pages 307–315, Vancouver, Canada.

Piotr Bojanowski, Edouard Grave, Armand Joulin, and Tomas Mikolov. 2017. Enriching word vectors with subword information. *Transactions of the Association for Computational Linguistics*, 5(1):135–146.

Ricardo Cerri, Rodrigo C. Barros, and André C.P.L.F. de Carvalho. 2014. Hierarchical multi-label classification using local neural networks. *Journal of Computer and System Sciences*, 80(1):39 – 56.

Corinna Cortes and Vladimir Vapnik. 1995. Support-vector networks. *Machine learning*, 20(3):273–297.

Yarin Gal and Zoubin Ghahramani. 2016. A theoretically grounded application of dropout in recurrent neural networks. In *Advances in neural information processing systems 2016*, pages 1019–1027, Barcelona, Spain.

Ian Goodfellow, Yoshua Bengio, and Aaron Courville. 2016. *Deep Learning*. MIT Press. http://www.deeplearningbook.org.

Geoffrey E. Hinton, Alex Krizhevsky, and Sida D. Wang. 2011. Transforming auto-encoders. In *International Conference on Artificial Neural Networks*, pages 44–51, Espoo, Finland.

Sepp Hochreiter and Jürgen Schmidhuber. 1997. Long short-term memory. *Neural computation*, 9(8):1735–1780.

Yoon Kim. 2014. Convolutional neural networks for sentence classification. In *Proceedings of the 2014 Conference on Empirical Methods in Natural Language Processing (EMNLP)*, pages 1746–1751, Doha, Qatar.

Svetlana Kiritchenko, Stan Matwin, and A. Fazel Famili. 2005. Functional annotation of genes using hierarchical text categorization. In *BioLINK SIG: Linking Literature, Information and Knowledge for Biology*, Detroit, MI, USA. Workshop track.

Kamran Kowsari, Donald E. Brown, Mojtaba Heidarysafa, Kiana Jafari Meimandi, Matthew S. Gerber, and Laura E. Barnes. 2017. HDLTex: Hierarchical deep learning for text classification. In *IEEE International Conference on Machine Learning and Applications*, pages 364–371, Cancún, Mexico.

Gakuto Kurata, Bing Xiang, and Bowen Zhou. 2016. Improved neural network-based multi-label classification with better initialization leveraging label co-occurrence. In *Proceedings of the 2016 Conference of the North American Chapter of the Association for Computational Linguistics: Human Language Technologies*, pages 521–526, New Orleans, LA, USA.

David D. Lewis, Yiming Yang, Tony G. Rose, and Fan Li. 2004. RCV1: A new benchmark collection for text categorization research. *Journal of Machine Learning Research*, 5(Apr):361–397.

Dai Quoc Nguyen, Thanh Vu, Tu Dinh Nguyen, Dat Quoc Nguyen, and Dinh Q. Phung. 2019. A capsule network-based embedding model for knowledge graph completion and search personalization. In *Proceedings of the 2019 Conference of the North American Chapter of the Association for Computational Linguistics: Human Language Technologies*, Minneapolis, MN, USA.

Prabod Rathnayaka, Supun Abeysinghe, Chamod Samarajeewa, Isura Manchanayake, and Malaka Walpola. 2018. Sentylic at IEST 2018: Gated recurrent neural network and capsule network based approach for implicit emotion detection. In *Proceedings of the 9th Workshop on Computational Approaches to Subjectivity, Sentiment and Social Media Analysis*, pages 254–259, Brussels, Belgium.

Sara Sabour, Nicholas Frosst, and Geoffrey E. Hinton. 2017. Dynamic routing between capsules. In *Advances in Neural Information Processing Systems 30*, pages 3856–3866, Long Beach, CA, USA.

Carlos N. Silla and Alex A. Freitas. 2011. A survey of hierarchical classification across different application domains. *Data Mining and Knowledge Discovery*, 22(1-2):31–72.

Mohammad S. Sorower. 2010. A literature survey on algorithms for multi-label learning. Oregon State University, Corvallis, OR, USA.

Saurabh Srivastava, Prerna Khurana, and Vartika Tewari. 2018. Identifying aggression and toxicity in comments using capsule network. In *Proceedings of the First Workshop on Trolling, Aggression and Cyberbullying (TRAC-2018)*, pages 98–105, Santa Fe, NM, USA.

Aixin Sun and Ee-Peng Lim. 2001. Hierarchical text classification and evaluation. In *Proceedings of the 2001 IEEE International Conference on Data Mining*, ICDM '01, pages 521–528, San Jose, CA, USA.

Yequan Wang, Aixin Sun, Jialong Han, Ying Liu, and Xiaoyan Zhu. 2018. Sentiment analysis by capsules. In *Proceedings of the 2018 World Wide Web Conference*, pages 1165–1174, Lyon, France.

Congying Xia, Chenwei Zhang, Xiaohui Yan, Yi Chang, and Philip Yu. 2018. Zero-shot user intent detection via capsule neural networks. In *Proceedings of the 2018 Conference on Empirical Methods in Natural Language Processing*, pages 3090–3099, Brussels, Belgium.

Liqiang Xiao, Honglun Zhang, Wenqing Chen, Yongkun Wang, and Yaohui Jin. 2018. MCapsNet: Capsule network for text with multi-task learning. In *Proceedings of the 2018 Conference on Empirical Methods in Natural Language Processing*, page 4565–4574, Brussels, Belgium.

Ningyu Zhang, Shumin Deng, Zhanlin Sun, Xi Chen, Wei Zhang, and Huajun Chen. 2018. Attention-based capsule networks with dynamic routing for relation extraction. In *Proceedings of the 2018 Conference on Empirical Methods in Natural Language Processing*, page 986–992, Brussels, Belgium.

Wei Zhao, Jianbo Ye, Min Yang, Zeyang Lei, Suofei Zhang, and Zhou Zhao. 2018. Investigating capsule networks with dynamic routing for text classification. In *Proceedings of the 2018 Conference on Empirical Methods in Natural Language*, pages 3110 – 3119, Brussels, Belgium.

Convolutional Neural Networks for Financial Text Regression

Neşat Dereli[†] and **Murat Saraçlar**[‡]
[†]Institute of Graduate Studies in Science and Engineering
[‡]Electrical and Electronics Engineering Department
Boğaziçi University, Istanbul, Turkey
`nesat.dereli@boun.edu.tr, murat.saraclar@boun.edu.tr`

Abstract

Forecasting financial volatility of a publicly-traded company from its annual reports has been previously defined as a text regression problem. Recent studies use a manually labeled lexicon to filter the annual reports by keeping sentiment words only. In order to remove the lexicon dependency without decreasing the performance, we replace bag-of-words model word features by word embedding vectors. Using word vectors increases the number of parameters. Considering the increase in number of parameters and excessive lengths of annual reports, a convolutional neural network model is proposed and transfer learning is applied. Experimental results show that the convolutional neural network model provides more accurate volatility predictions than lexicon based models.

1 Introduction

Most financial analysis methods and portfolio management techniques are based on risk classification and risk prediction. Stock return volatility is a solid indicator of the financial risk of a company. Therefore, forecasting stock return volatility successfully creates an invaluable advantage in financial analysis and portfolio management. While most of the studies are focusing on historical data and financial statements when predicting financial volatility of a company, some studies introduce new fields of information by analyzing soft information which is embedded in textual sources.

Kogan et al. (2009) defined the problem of forecasting financial volatility from annual reports as a text regression task and other studies contributed to the task because of its value (Wang et al., 2013; Tsai and Wang, 2014; Rekabsaz et al., 2017). There are also alternative soft information sources used for financial forecast like news (Tetlock et al., 2008; Nuij et al., 2014; Kazemian et al., 2014; Ding et al., 2015), online forums (Narayanan et al., 2009; Nguyen and Shirai, 2015), blogs (Bar-Haim et al., 2011) and bank reports (Nopp and Hanbury, 2015). However, annual reports are more informative and contain less noise since they are regulated by the government. On the other hand, annual reports are not suitable for short-term forecasting.

Volatility prediction using annual reports of companies is also a proper test-bed for natural language processing (NLP) since both volatility data and annual report data are freely available and no manual labeling is needed. In U.S., annual report filings, known as 10-K reports, are mandated by the government in a strictly specified format.

Previous works focus on sentiment polarity while forecasting the volatility. Their models are built on top of a financial lexicon (Loughran and McDonald, 2011) and most improvements are obtained by expanding the lexicon. However, a manually created lexicon should be updated over time and the solutions, depending on the lexicon, are not persistent.

In this paper, we propose an artificial neural network (ANN) solution which does not use a lexicon or any other manually labeled source. The convolutional neural network (CNN) model is designed similar to Bitvai and Cohn (2015) and Kim (2014). Nonetheless, annual reports contain excessively long text compared to movie reviews and this results in a more difficult task. To overcome this difficulty, max-over-time pooling layer is replaced by local max-pooling layer and transfer learning is applied.

The rest of the paper is organized as follows. In Section 2, we defined the problem. Section 3 introduces the model and its architecture. The details of our experimental settings, the results of the experiments and the analyses are presented in Section 4. Our work is concluded in Section 5.

Proceedings of the ACL 2019, Student Research Workshop, pages 331–337
Florence, Italy, July 28th-August 2nd, 2019. ©2019 Association for Computational Linguistics

2   Problem Definition

In this section, stock return volatility which is aimed to be predicted is defined. Later, the dataset which is used in this work is introduced. Finally, evaluation measures are described.

2.1   Stock Return Volatility

Stock return volatility is defined as the standard deviation of adjusted daily closing prices of a target stock over a period of time (Kogan et al., 2009; Tsai and Wang, 2014; Rekabsaz et al., 2017; Hacısalihzade, 2017). Let S_t be the adjusted closing stock price for the day t. Then, the stock return for the day t is $R_t = \frac{S_t}{S_{t-1}} - 1$. Stock return volatility $v_{[t-\tau,t]}$ for τ days is given as

$$v_{[t-\tau,t]} = \sqrt{\sum_{i=0}^{\tau} \frac{(R_{t-i} - \bar{R})^2}{\tau}}.$$

2.2   Dataset

In this work, the dataset from Tsai et al. (2016), which is published online[1], is used because it includes up-to-date years and has enough reports for each year. Note that the datasets shared by Kogan et al. (2009) and Rekabsaz et al. (2017) are different than the dataset shared by Tsai et al. (2016) even if the same year is compared since the number of reports differ from each other. Hence, a direct performance comparison is not meaningful.

The dataset from Tsai et al. (2016) includes 10-K reports available on the U.S. Security Exchange Commission (SEC) Electronic Data Gathering, Analysis and Retrieval (EDGAR) website[2]. Following previous works (Kogan et al., 2009; Wang et al., 2013; Tsai and Wang, 2014; Tsai et al., 2016), section 7, Management's Discussion and Analysis (MD&A) is used instead of the complete 10-K report.

The dataset includes a volatility value for each report of 12 months after the report is published. The volatility value in the dataset is the natural logarithm of stock return volatility and used as the prediction target. We checked randomly sampled reports from SEC EDGAR and calculated volatility values by using adjusted closing stock prices from Yahoo Finance[3]. Both were consistent with the dataset.

<hr>

[1] https://clip.csic.org/10K/data
[2] https://www.sec.gov/edgar.shtml
[3] https://finance.yahoo.com

2.3   Evaluation

Mean Square Error (MSE) is chosen as the main evaluation metric which is calculated by

$$MSE = \frac{1}{n} \sum_{i=1}^{n} (y_i - \hat{y}_i)^2$$

where $y_i = \ln(v_i)$.

Spearman's rank correlation coefficient is a measure which is used to evaluate the ranking performance of a model. Real volatility values and predicted volatility values can be used to calculate Spearman's rank correlation coefficient. Each set contains samples which consist of a company identifier and the volatility value of the company. Spearman's rank correlation coefficient of two sets is equal to Pearson's correlation coefficient of the rankings of the sets. The rankings of a set can be generated by sorting the volatility values of the set in an ascending order and enumerating them. The rankings of a set contains samples which consist of a company identifier and a volatility rank of the company. Spearman's rank correlation coefficient of the sets X and Y can be calculated by

$$\rho_{X,Y} = \frac{\text{cov}(rank_X, rank_Y)}{\sigma_{rank_X} \sigma_{rank_Y}}$$

where $rank_X$ and $rank_Y$ represent the rankings of the sets X and Y respectively.

In all experiments, MSE is used as the loss function which means each model tries to optimize MSE. On the other hand, Spearman's rank correlation coefficient is reported only to evaluate the ranking performance of different models.

3   Model

The architecture of the network is presented in Figure 1 which is similar to previous works using CNN for NLP (Collobert et al., 2011; Kim, 2014; Bitvai and Cohn, 2015). Before reports are fed into embedding layer, their lengths are fixed to m words and reports with less than m words are padded. The output matrix of the embedding layer, $E \in \mathbb{R}^{km}$, consists of k-dimensional word vectors where the unknown word vector is initialized randomly and the padding vector is initialized as zero vector. Each element of the word vector represents a feature of the word.

The convolution layer consist of different kernel sizes where each kernel size represents a different n-gram. Figure 1 shows tri-gram, four-gram

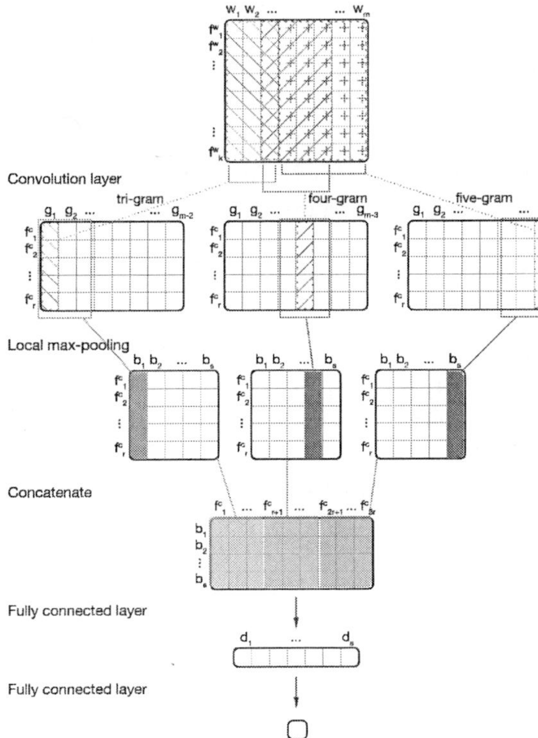

Figure 1: Network architecture of our baseline model (CNN-simple). A word embedded report through a single channel convolution layer with kernel sizes 3, 4 and 5 followed by a local max-pooling and two fully connected layers.

and five-gram examples. Let $n \in \mathbb{N}$ be the kernel width of a target n-gram. Each convolution feature $f_i^c \in \mathbb{R}^{m-n+1}$ is generated from a distinct kernel weight, $weight_i^n \in \mathbb{R}^{kn}$, and bias, $bias_i \in \mathbb{R}$. Rectified linear unit (ReLU) is used as the non-linear activation function at the output of the convolution layer,

$$f_{ij}^c = ReLU(weight_i^n \cdot w_{j:j+n-1} + bias_i).$$

Note that the convolution features, f_i^c have $m - n + 1$ dimension and they contain different information than word features, f_i^w. Convolution features are concatenated as

$$f_i^c = [f_{i1}^c, f_{i2}^c, ..., f_{i+n-1}^c].$$

g_i in Figure 1 represents each n-gram element thus there are $m - n + 1$ n-gram elements for each individual n-gram. Next step is local max-pooling layer which basically applies max-over-time pooling to smaller word sequence instead of the complete text (Le et al., 2018). Each sequence length

is h and there are s outputs for each sequence,

$$b_i = \max(g_{ih:i(h+1)-1})$$

where $b_i \in \mathbb{R}^r$. After the local max-pooling layer is applied to all convolution layer output matrices, they are merged by concatenating feature vectors. Later, dropout is applied to the merged matrix and finally it is fed into two sequential fully connected layers. The presented neural network is implemented by using Pytorch[4] deep learning framework.

4 Experiments and Results

This section states preprocessing operations which are applied to the dataset. Pretrained word embeddings which are used in this work are described. Later, details of the setup of our experiments and the model variations are presented. Finally, the results of the experiments and the analysis of the results are discussed.

4.1 Preprocessing

MD&A section of the 10-K reports in the dataset are already tokenized by removing punctuation, replacing numerical values with # and downcasing the words. As in previous works, reports are stemmed by using the Porter stemmer (Porter, 1980), supported by Natural Language Toolkit (NLTK)[5]. Stemming decreases the vocabulary size of the word embeddings and thus reduces the parameters of the model. Stemming is also required to use word vectors trained by Tsai et al. (2016) since the corpora which is used to train the word embeddings consists of stemmed reports.

4.2 Word Embedding

Word embedding is a method, used to represent words with vectors to embed syntactic and semantic information. Instead of random initialization of the embedding layer of the model, initialization with pretrained word embeddings enables the model to capture contextual information faster and better. In our work, we used pretrained word embeddings supported by Tsai et al. (2016). They used MD&A section of 10-K reports from 1996 to 2013 to train the word embeddings with a vector dimension of 200 by word2vec[6] continuous bag-of-words (CBOW) (Mikolov et al., 2013).

[4]https://pytorch.org
[5]https://www.nltk.org
[6]https://code.google.com/archive/p/word2vec/

Model	2008	2009	2010	2011	2012	2013	Avg
EXP-SYN (Tsai 2016)	0.6537	**0.2387**	0.1514	0.1217	0.2290	0.1861	0.2634
CNN-simple (baseline)	**0.3716**	0.4708	**0.1471**	0.1312	0.2412	0.2871	0.2748
CNN-STC	0.5358	0.3575	0.3001	0.1215	0.2164	0.1497	0.2801
CNN-NTC-multichannel	0.5077	0.4353	0.1892	0.1605	0.2116	0.1268	0.2718
CNN-STC-multichannel	0.4121	0.4040	0.2428	0.1574	0.2082	0.1676	0.2653
CNN-NTC	0.4672	0.3169	0.2156	**0.1154**	**0.1944**	**0.1238**	**0.2388**

Table 1: Performance of different models, measured by Mean Square Error (MSE). **Boldface** shows the best result among presented models for the corresponding column.

4.3 Setup

The hyper-parameters of the CNN models are decided by testing them with our baseline CNN model. All weights of the baseline model are non-static and randomly initialized. Final hyper-parameters are selected as mini-batch size 10, fixed text length 20000, convolution layer kernels 3, 4 and 5 with 100 output features, probability of dropout layer 0.5, and learning rate 0.001.

Kogan et al. (2009) showed that using reports of the last two years for training performs better than using reports of the last 5 years. Rekabsaz et al. (2017) presented similarity heat-map of ten consecutive years and stated that groups consist of three to four consecutive years are highly similar. Our experiments also show that including reports which are four years older than test year into training set does not always help and sometimes even causes noise.

In this work, reports of three consecutive years were used for training while reports of the last year were used for validation to determine the best epoch. After the best epoch is determined, it is used as fixed epoch and the oldest year is ignored while the first step is repeated to train a new network without using validation set but fixed epoch instead. For example, reports of 2006 to 2008 are used as training set while reports of 2009 is used for validation. If the best result is achieved after 30 epochs, a new network is trained with reports of 2007 to 2009 through 30 fixed epochs. Finally, the trained network is tested for the year 2010.

Ignoring years older than four years prevent their noise effect but also reduces training set size. Experiments of this work show that old reports decrease the performance of the embedding layer but increase the performance of the convolution layer. The embedding layer can be biased easier than convolution layer since convolution layer learns features from larger structures (n-grams).

Nonetheless, even training only the convolution layer using all years from 1996 to test year is time-consuming. Therefore, transfer learning is used by sharing the convolution layer weights which are trained on comparatively larger range of years. Yang et al. (2017) showed that relatedness of the transfer domains has a direct effect on the amount of improvement. Convolution layer weights are trained by freezing the embedding layer which is initialized with pretrained word embeddings and using years 1996 to 2006 for 120 epoch with early stopping. Other hyper-parameters are kept as described above.

4.4 Extended Models

Using transfer learning convolution layer, four different models are built. Since convolution layer weights are trained using pretrained word embeddings, those models perform well only when their embedding layers are initialized with pretrained word embeddings. Following Kim (2014), multichannel embedding layers are applied to some models.

- **CNN-STC:** A model with single channel non-static pretrained embedding layer and a transferred convolution layer which is static.

- **CNN-NTC:** Same as CNN-STC but its transferred convolution layer is non-static.

- **CNN-STC-multichannel:** A model with two channel of embedding layers, both are pretrained but one is static and other one is non-static. Transferred convolution layer is also static.

- **CNN-NTC-multichannel:** Same as CNN-STC-multichannel but its transferred convolution layer is non-static

Model	2008	2009	2010	2011	2012	2013	Avg
CNN-simple (baseline)	0.3884	0.0814	**0.5758**	0.5842	0.7064	0.7060	0.5070
CNN-STC	0.3875	**0.5226**	0.5570	0.5737	**0.7149**	**0.7341**	**0.5816**
CNN-NTC-multichannel	0.3727	0.4293	0.5187	0.5625	0.6531	0.7332	0.5449
CNN-STC-multichannel	0.3424	0.4042	0.4641	0.4924	0.4945	0.6305	0.4713
CNN-NTC	**0.3921**	0.4713	0.5500	**0.5910**	0.6978	0.7234	0.5709

Table 2: Ranking performance of different models, measured by Spearman's rank correlation coefficient. **Boldface** shows the best result among presented models for the corresponding column.

4.5 Results

Table 1 indicates that performance of our CNN-simple (baseline) model is comparable with EXP-SYN, the best model represented by Tsai et al. (2016), which uses a manually created lexicon and POS tagger. Furthermore, the best predictions for the years 2008 and 2010 are achieved by the CNN-simple model. Our best model, CNN-NTC, decreases the average error by 10% and produces the best predictions for the last three years of the experiment.

Ranking performance is valuable for some real world applications such as portfolio management. Furthermore, better ranking performance indicates better explanation of label distribution. Table 2 shows ranking performance of each model which is presented in this work. Spearman's rank correlation coefficient is bounded between -1 and 1. Higher Spearman's rank correlation coefficient means the model captures larger proportion of variability in the labels. It can be seen that ranking performance of CNN-NTC is as good as its regression performance. On the other hand, CNN-STC can model future distribution of stock return volatilities better than future values of stock return volatilities. It is important to note that our models use MSE as loss function and optimize MSE. Changing the loss function may improve ranking performance results and performance orders of the models.

4.6 Analysis

The embedding weights of CNN-NTC are compared with the pretrained word embeddings to determine the most changed words. While comparing the most changed word vectors, the words with yearly frequency less than 250 and more than 5000 are filtered out. Table 3 presents the top 10 most changed words and cosine distances to their pretrained vectors. Note that presented words are stemmed. Since words are in lowercase, the

Word	Cosine Distance
anoth	0.2565
concern	0.2436
etc	0.2431
accordingli	0.2353
entir	0.2349
stabil	0.2328
increment	0.2308
thu	0.2306
situat	0.2167
guaranti	0.2120

Table 3: Top-10 most changed words, extracted from non-static embedding layer.

word *ETC* may cause confusion. It is an abbreviation and stands for Exchanged-Traded Commodity which is a common word in finance domain and stemmed version includes its plural form *ETCs* also. The stemmed words *concern*, *stabil* and *guaranti* are sentiment words and contained by finance sentiment lexicon (Loughran and McDonald, 2011). Having 3 sentiment words out of 10 words shows that our model uses sentiment information but not solely depend on sentiment words.

We also analyzed most changed sentiment word, *concern*, by extracting the 10 nearest words of pretrained word embeddings and CNN-NTC embedding weights separately (Table 4). It can be observed that *pertain*, *about* and *fear* are replaced with *safeti*, *trend* and *dmaa*. Stem words *safeti* and *trend* are related with the stem word *concern*. The word *pertain* is semantically very close to the word *concern*, they are even used interchangeably sometimes. However, *concern* can be replaced with *pertain* only if it does not have any sentiment polarity. It can be seen that expanding the lexicon using word embeddings, like previous works did (Tsai and Wang, 2014; Tsai et al., 2016; Rekabsaz et al., 2017), can be problematic and may end up with a lexicon expansion contain-

Static Embedding on 'concern'		Non-static Embedding on 'concern'	
Word	Cosine Distance	Word	Cosine Distance
regard	0.2772	regard	0.3233
privaci	0.5287	privaci	0.5433
inform	0.5587	safeti	0.5550
debat	0.5706	inform	0.5562
implic	0.5817	trend	0.5568
heighten	0.5825	heighten	0.5692
pertain	0.5844	inquiri	0.5959
about	0.5901	dmaa	0.6013
inquiri	0.5919	debat	0.6025
fear	0.5954	implic	0.6033

Table 4: Top-10 most similar words to *concern* comparing their word vectors.

ing semantically close but sentimentally far words.

Another interesting word in the list is *DMAA*. It stands for dimethylamylamine which is an energy-boosting dietary supplement. In 2012, the U.S. Food and Drug Administration (FDA) warned DMAA manufacturers. In 10-K report of Vitamin Shoppe, Inc. published on February 26, 2013, concern of the company about DMAA is stated:

> "If it is determined that **DMAA** does not comply with applicable regulatory and legislative requirements, we could be required to recall or remove from the market all products containing **DMAA** and we could become subject to lawsuits related to any alleged non-compliance, any of which recalls, removals or lawsuits could materially and adversely affect our business, financial condition and results of operations."

It shows that the CNN model focuses on correct word features but also can overfit easier. In financial text regression task, the word *DMAA* is quite related with the word concern but it is not a common word and also sector specific.

5 Conclusion

The previous studies depend on a financial sentiment lexicon which is initially created by manual work. This paper reduced both dependencies by using word vectors in the model. Word vectors are used in previous studies to expand the lexicon but they are not included to the model directly. On the contrary, our work includes word vectors directly to the model as main input.

In addition, transfer learning is applied to the convolution layer since effect of temporal information on distinct layers differs. Evolving word vectors are analyzed after model benchmarks. The analysis demonstrates that CNN model tracks sentiment polarity of the words successfully and it does not depend on sentiment words only. However, it is also observed that CNN models can overfit easier.

This work is focused on text source and did not include any historical market data or any other metadata. Further research on including metadata to CNN model for the same task may increase the value and analysis.

Acknowledgments

The numerical calculations reported in this paper were performed at TUBITAK ULAKBIM, High Performance and Grid Computing Center (TRUBA resources). We would like to thank to Can Altay, Çağrı Aslanbaş, Ilgaz Çakın, Ömer Adıgüzel, Zeynep Yiyener and the anonymous reviewers for their feedback and suggestions.

References

Roy Bar-Haim, Elad Dinur, Ronen Feldman, Moshe Fresko, and Guy Goldstein. 2011. Identifying and following expert investors in stock microblogs. In *Proceedings of the 2011 Conference on Empirical Methods in Natural Language Processing*, pages 1310–1319, Edinburgh, Scotland, UK. Association for Computational Linguistics.

Zsolt Bitvai and Trevor Cohn. 2015. Non-linear text regression with a deep convolutional neural network. In *Proceedings of the 53rd Annual Meeting of the Association for Computational Linguistics and the*

7th International Joint Conference on Natural Language Processing (Volume 2: Short Papers), pages 180–185, Beijing, China. Association for Computational Linguistics.

Ronan Collobert, Jason Weston, Léon Bottou, Michael Karlen, Koray Kavukcuoglu, and Pavel Kuksa. 2011. Natural language processing (almost) from scratch. *J. Mach. Learn. Res.*, 12:2493–2537.

Xiao Ding, Yue Zhang, Ting Liu, and Junwen Duan. 2015. Deep learning for event-driven stock prediction. In *Proceedings of the 24th International Conference on Artificial Intelligence*, IJCAI'15, pages 2327–2333. AAAI Press.

S.S. Hacısalihzade. 2017. *Control Engineering and Finance*, Lecture Notes in Control and Information Sciences, page 49. Springer International Publishing.

Siavash Kazemian, Shunan Zhao, and Gerald Penn. 2014. Evaluating sentiment analysis evaluation: A case study in securities trading. In *Proceedings of the 5th Workshop on Computational Approaches to Subjectivity, Sentiment and Social Media Analysis*, pages 119–127, Baltimore, Maryland. Association for Computational Linguistics.

Yoon Kim. 2014. Convolutional neural networks for sentence classification. In *Proceedings of the 2014 Conference on Empirical Methods in Natural Language Processing (EMNLP)*, pages 1746–1751, Doha, Qatar. Association for Computational Linguistics.

Shimon Kogan, Dimitry Levin, Bryan R. Routledge, Jacob S. Sagi, and Noah A. Smith. 2009. Predicting risk from financial reports with regression. In *Proceedings of Human Language Technologies: The 2009 Annual Conference of the North American Chapter of the Association for Computational Linguistics*, pages 272–280, Boulder, Colorado. Association for Computational Linguistics.

Hoa Le, Christophe Cerisara, and Alexandre Denis. 2018. Do convolutional networks need to be deep for text classification ?

Tim Loughran and Bill McDonald. 2011. When is a liability not a liability? textual analysis, dictionaries, and 10-ks. *The Journal of Finance*, 66(1):35–65.

Tomas Mikolov, Ilya Sutskever, Kai Chen, Greg S Corrado, and Jeff Dean. 2013. Distributed representations of words and phrases and their compositionality. In C. J. C. Burges, L. Bottou, M. Welling, Z. Ghahramani, and K. Q. Weinberger, editors, *Advances in Neural Information Processing Systems 26*, pages 3111–3119. Curran Associates, Inc.

Ramanathan Narayanan, Bing Liu, and Alok Choudhary. 2009. Sentiment analysis of conditional sentences. In *Proceedings of the 2009 Conference on Empirical Methods in Natural Language Processing*, pages 180–189, Singapore. Association for Computational Linguistics.

Thien Hai Nguyen and Kiyoaki Shirai. 2015. Topic modeling based sentiment analysis on social media for stock market prediction. In *Proceedings of the 53rd Annual Meeting of the Association for Computational Linguistics and the 7th International Joint Conference on Natural Language Processing (Volume 1: Long Papers)*, pages 1354–1364, Beijing, China. Association for Computational Linguistics.

Clemens Nopp and Allan Hanbury. 2015. Detecting risks in the banking system by sentiment analysis. In *Proceedings of the 2015 Conference on Empirical Methods in Natural Language Processing*, pages 591–600, Lisbon, Portugal. Association for Computational Linguistics.

Wijnand Nuij, Viorel Milea, Frederik Hogenboom, Flavius Frasincar, and Uzay Kaymak. 2014. An automated framework for incorporating news into stock trading strategies. *IEEE Trans. on Knowl. and Data Eng.*, 26(4):823–835.

MF Porter. 1980. An algorithm for suffix stripping. *Program: Electronic Library and Information Systems*, 14.

Navid Rekabsaz, Mihai Lupu, Artem Baklanov, Alexander Dür, Linda Andersson, and Allan Hanbury. 2017. Volatility prediction using financial disclosures sentiments with word embedding-based ir models. In *Proceedings of the 55th Annual Meeting of the Association for Computational Linguistics (Volume 1: Long Papers)*, pages 1712–1721, Vancouver, Canada. Association for Computational Linguistics.

Paul C. Tetlock, Maytal Saar-Tsechansky, and Sofus Macskassy. 2008. More than words: Quantifying language to measure firms' fundamentals. *The Journal of Finance*, 63(3):1437–1467.

Ming-Feng Tsai and Chuan-Ju Wang. 2014. Financial keyword expansion via continuous word vector representations. In *Proceedings of the 2014 Conference on Empirical Methods in Natural Language Processing (EMNLP)*, pages 1453–1458, Doha, Qatar. Association for Computational Linguistics.

Ming-Feng Tsai, Chuan-Ju Wang, and Po-Chuan Chien. 2016. Discovering finance keywords via continuous-space language models. *ACM Trans. Manage. Inf. Syst.*, 7(3):7:1–7:17.

Chuan-Ju Wang, Ming-Feng Tsai, Tse Liu, and Chin-Ting Chang. 2013. Financial sentiment analysis for risk prediction. In *Proceedings of the Sixth International Joint Conference on Natural Language Processing*, pages 802–808, Nagoya, Japan. Asian Federation of Natural Language Processing.

Zhilin Yang, Ruslan Salakhutdinov, and William W. Cohen. 2017. Transfer learning for sequence tagging with hierarchical recurrent networks.

Sentiment Analysis on Naija-Tweets

Taiwo Kolajo[*]
Covenant University, Ota, Nigeria
taiwo.kolajo@stu.cu.edu.ng
Federal University Lokoja, Kogi State, Nigeria
taiwo.kolajo@fulokoja.edu.ng

Olawande Daramola
CPUT, Cape Town, South Africa
daramolaj@cput.ac.za

Ayodele Adebiyi
Covenant University, Ota, Nigeria
ayo.adebiyi@covenantuniversity.edu.ng
Landmark University, Omu-Aran, Nigeria
ayo.adebiyi@lmu.edu.ng

Abstract

Examining sentiments in social media poses a challenge to natural language processing because of the intricacy and variability in the dialect articulation, noisy terms in form of slang, abbreviation, acronym, emoticon, and spelling error coupled with the availability of real-time content. Moreover, most of the knowledge-based approaches for resolving slang, abbreviation, and acronym do not consider the issue of ambiguity that evolves in the usage of these noisy terms. This research work proposes an improved framework for social media feed pre-processing that leverages on the combination of integrated local knowledge bases and adapted Lesk algorithm to facilitate pre-processing of social media feeds. The results from the experimental evaluation revealed an improvement over existing methods when applied to supervised learning algorithms in the task of extracting sentiments from Nigeria-origin tweets with an accuracy of 99.17%.

1 Introduction

Sentiment Analysis is being used to automatically detect speculations, emotions, opinions, and evaluations in social media content (Thakkar and Patel, 2015). Unlike carefully created news and other literary web contents, social media streams present various difficulties for analytics algorithms because of their extensive scale, short nature, slang, abbreviation, grammatical and spelling errors (Asghar et al., 2017). Most of the knowledge-based approaches for resolving these noisy terms do not consider the issue of ambiguity that evolves in their usage (Sabbir et al., 2017). These challenges, which inform this research work, make it necessary to seek improvement on the performance of existing solutions for pre-processing of social media streams (Carter et al., 2013; Ghosh et al., 2017; Kuflik et al., 2017).

Due to language complexity, analysing sentiments in social media presents a challenge to natural language processing (Vyas and Uma, 2018). Moreover, social media content is characterized with a short length of messages, use of dynamically evolving, irregular, informal, and abbreviated words. These make it difficult for techniques that build on them to perform effectively and efficiently (Singh and Kumari, 2016; Zhan and Dahal, 2017).

The short nature of social media streams coupled with no restriction in the choice of language has informed the usage of abbreviation, slang, and acronym (Atefeh and Khreich, 2015; Kumar, 2016). These noisy but useful terms have their implicit meanings and form part of the rich context that needs to be addressed in order to fully make sense of social media streams (Bontcheva and Rout, 2014). Just like there is ambiguity in the use of normal language there is also ambiguity in the usage of slang/abbreviation/acronym because they often have context-based meanings, which must be rightly interpreted in order to improve the

338

Proceedings of the ACL 2019, Student Research Workshop, pages 338–343
Florence, Italy, July 28th-August 2nd, 2019. ©2019 Association for Computational Linguistics

results of social media analysis. There is a dearth of social media streams preprocessing geared at resolving slang, abbreviation and acronym as well as ambiguity issues that erupt as a result of their usage (Mihanovic et al., 2014; Matsumoto et al., 2016).

2　Related Work

Many researchers have studied the effect and impact of pre-processing (which ranges from tokenization, removal of stop-words, lemmatization, fixing of slangs, redundancy elimination) on the accuracy of result of techniques building on them for sentiment analysis and unanimously agreed that when social media stream data are well interpreted and represented, it leads to significant improvement of sentiment analysis result.

Haddi et al. (2013) presented the role of text pre-processing in sentiment analysis. The pre-processing stages include removal of HTML tags, stop word removal, negation handling, stemming, and expansion of abbreviation using pattern recognition and regular expression techniques. The problem here is that representing abbreviation based on co-occurrence does not take care of ambiguity. The impact of pre-processing methods on Twitter sentiment classification was explored by Bao et al. (2014) by using the Stanford Twitter Sentiment Dataset. The result of the study showed an improvement in accuracy when negation transformation, URLs feature reservation and repeated letters normalization is employed while lemmatization and stemming reduce the accuracy of sentiment classification. In the same vein, Uysal and Gunal (2014) and Singh and Kumari (2016) investigated the role of text pre-processing and found out that an appropriate combination of pre-processing tasks improves classification accuracy.

Smailovic et al. (2014) and Ansari et al. (2017) investigated sentiments analysis on twitter dataset. Their pre-processing method along with tokenization, stemming and lemmatization includes replacement of user mention, URLs, negation, exclamation, and question marks with tokens. Letter repetition was replaced with one or two occurrences of the letter. From the result of their experiments, it was concluded that pre-processing twitter data improves techniques building on them.

The pre-processing method adopted by Ouyang et al. (2017) and Ramadhan et al. (2017) includes deletion of URLs, mentions, stop-words, punctuation, and stemming. Ramadhan et al. (2017) added the handling of slang conversion in their work although the authors did not state how the slang conversion was done. Jianqiang and Xiaolin (2017) discussed the effect of pre-processing and found that expanding acronyms and replacing negation improve classification while removal of stop-words, numbers or URLs do not yield any significant improvement. On the contrary, Symeonidis et al. (2018) evaluated classification accuracy based on pre-processing techniques and found out that removing numbers, lemmatization, and replacing negation improve accuracy. Zhang et al. (2017) presented Arc2Vec framework for learning acronyms in twitter using three embedding models. However, the authors did not take care of contextual information. From the review, most research efforts have not been directed towards the handling all of slang/abbreviation/acronym as well as resolving ambiguity in the usage of noisy terms based on contextual information.

3　Methodology

3.1　Data Collection

The dataset (referred to as Naija-tweets in this paper) was extracted from tweets of Nigeria origin. The dataset focused on politics in Nigeria. A user interface was built around an underlying API provided by Twitter to collect tweets based on politics-related keywords such as "politics", "governments", "policy", "policymaking", and "legislation". The total tweets extracted was 10,000. These were manually classified into positive (1) or negative (0) by three experts in sentiment analysis. 80% was used as training data while 10% was used as test data and 10% for dev set. The general preprocessing method (GTPM), Arc2Vec Framework and the proposed preprocessing method (PTPM) are depicted in figure 1 (a), (b) and (c) respectively.

3.2　Data Preprocessing

From the data stream collected, Tags, URLs, mentions and non-ASCII characters were automatically removed using a regular expression. This was followed by tokenization and normalization. Thereafter, slangs, abbreviation, acronyms, and emoticons were filtered from the tweets using corpora of English words in natural language toolkit (NLTK). The filtered slangs/abbreviation/acronyms are then passed to the Integrated Knowledge Base (IKB) for further processing.

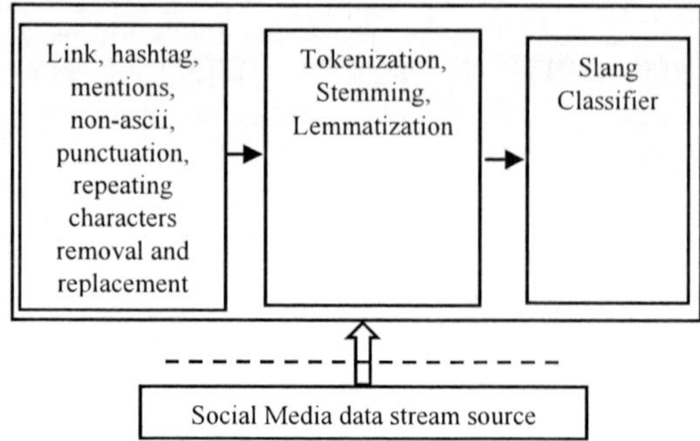

Figure 1a: General Textual Preprocessing Method

3.3 Data Enrichment

The IKB is an API centric resource that communicates with three (3) internet sources which are Naijalingo, Urban dictionary, and Internetslang.com. Naijalingo is included in order to take care of adulterated English commonly found in social media feeds in Nigeria and some parts of Anglophone West Africa. Moreover, the presence of Naijalingo is very important in order to resolve ambiguity in the usage of slang/abbreviation/acronym in tweets originated from Nigeria.

The PTPM framework will allow the integrations of any other local knowledge base that may suit some other contexts in order to capture slang/abbreviation/acronym that has locally defined meaning. The IKB API is also responsible for slang/abbreviation/acronym disambiguation, spelling correction and emoticon replacement. The IKB is to cater for slangs, abbreviation or acronyms, and emoticons found in tweets and to provide a single platform where all these knowledge sources can be easily referenced. About two million slang/abbreviation/acronym and emoticons terms were crawled from these knowledge sources and stored on MongoDB. All lexicons that were used for the enrichment of the collected tweets in the IKB were derived from Naijalingo, Urban dictionary, and Internet slang knowledge sources. A lexicon of noisy terms (slang/acronym/abbreviation) in the IKB has four elements which are (1) slang/acronym/abbreviation term, (2) a descriptive phrase, (3) example (i.e. how it is being used) and (4) related terms from the three knowledge sources. Each term can have multiple entries which

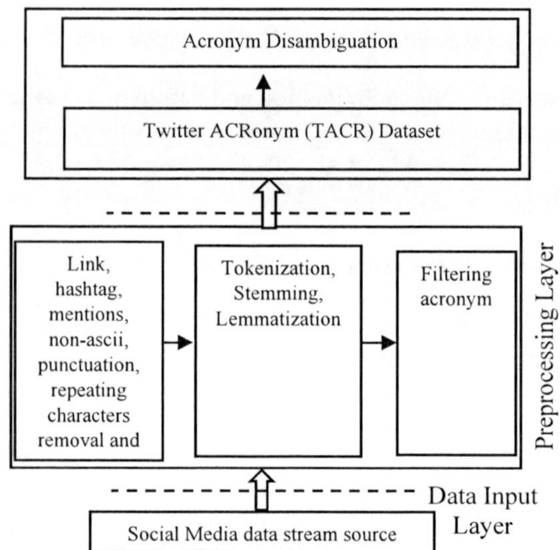

Figure 1b: Arc2Vec Preprocessing Framework

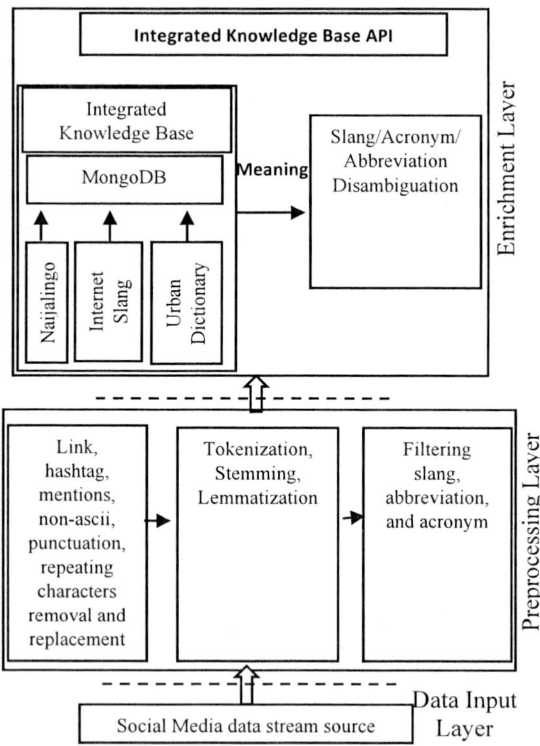

Figure 1c: Proposed Textual Preprocessing Method

imply that each term can be associated with any number of descriptive phrases. Each term is seen as a key-value pair where each term is the key and a network of associated descriptive phrases represent the value.

3.4 Resolving Ambiguity in Slang/Abbreviation/Acronym

The next stage is to extract meanings of slang/abbreviation/acronym terms from IKB. Ambiguous slang/abbreviation/acronym terms were resolved by leveraging adapted Lesk algorithm based on the context in which they appear in the tweet. For ambiguous slang/abbreviation/acronym, there is a need to obtain the best sense from the pool of various definitions in the IKB based on how it is used in the tweet (see Listing 1).

Usage examples (st) with a total number, n, mapped to various definitions of the slang/abbreviation/acronym term ($sabt$) that is to be interpreted are extracted from the IKB, where there are no usage examples mapped to definitions for a particular $sabt$ in the ikb, the definitions are used instead. The tweet (sjk) in which this slang/abbreviation/acronym term appears and the extracted usage examples (st) is represented as a set data structure. After this, intersection operation between the tweet and each of the usage examples ($relatedness(st,sjk)$) is performed. Then the usage example (sti) with the highest intersection value ($best\_score$) is selected. A lookup of the meaning attached to the selected usage example from the IKB is performed ($map\ sense\_i\ with\ definition$), the definition is then used to replace the slang in the tweet as the best possible semantically meaningful elaboration of each slang/abbreviation/acronym based on how it is being used in the tweet.

3.5 Feature Extraction

For feature extraction, a total of 3,000 unigrams and 8,000 bigrams were used for vector representation. Each tweet was represented as a feature vector of these unigrams and bigrams. For convolutional neural network, Glove twitter 27B 200d was used for the dataset vector representation.

4 Result

The proposed PTPM framework was benchmarked with the General Textual Pre-processing Method (GTPM) and Arc2Vec Framework by running them on three classifiers. The GTPM (i.e. general pre-processing method) does not take care of slang/abbreviation/acronym ambiguity issue while that of Arc2Vec framework only took care of

Listing 1. Adapted Lesk Pseudocode

```
Input: tweet text
Output: enriched tweet text
// Procedure to disambiguate ambiguous
// slang/acronyms/abbreviation in tweets
// by adapting Lesk algorithm over usage
// examples of slangs/acronym/abbreviation
// found in the integrated knowledge base (ikb)
Notations:
 slngs: slangs; acrs: acronyms; abbrs: abrreviations
 sab: slang/acronym/abbreviation;
 sabt: slang/acronym/abbreviation term
 st: ith usage example of target word sabt found in the
     ikb
procedure disambiguate_all_slngs/acrs/abbrs
     for all sab(word) in input do //the input is the
         //extracted      slang/abbreviation/acronym
         //from tweet
         best_sense=disambiguate_each_
               slng/acr/abbr(sabt)
         display best_sense
     end for
end procedure
function disambiguate_each_ slng/acr/abbr(sabt)
     // target word represent
     //slang/acronym/abbreviation in the tweet
     st → ith usage example of target word sabt
     found in the ikb
     sjk → the current tweet being processed
     sense  → { s1, s2, …sn | m ≥1}  // sense
     is the set of senses of st found in the ikb

     for all st of the target word sabt do
         // sti is the ith usage example of target
         //word sabt found in the ikb
         score i = 0
         for i= 1 to n do
                  // n is the total number of
                  //usage examples for each
                  //slang/acronym/abbreviation
                  //in tweet
                  for sjk of word sabt
                       temp_score k =
                       relatedness(st,sjk)
                  end for
                  best_score =
                  max(temp_score)
                  score i += best_score
         end for
     end for
     return si ∈ Sense
     // si is the ith usage example from the ikb that
     best matches
     // slang/acronym/abbreviation in the tweet
     map si with defi (where defi ∈ definition)
     replace sabt in tweet with defi
end function
```

Acronym. The classifiers used for the benchmarking were support vector machine (SVM), multi-layer perceptron (MLP), and convolutional neural networks (CNN) to extract sentiments from tweets. The essence of running both the general pre-processing method – GTPM, Arc2Vec framework, and the proposed SMFP framework on the classifiers was to compare the results of capturing of slangs/acronym/abbreviation and resolving ambiguity in social media streams slang/acronym/abbreviation have been undertaken, and whether it has not been undertaken. The goal is to ascertain the impact of this on the algorithms building on them. The result of the sentiment classification of naija_tweets dataset is shown in Tables 1 and 2

Method	Algorithm	Accuracy (%) Unigram	Accuracy (%) Bigram	Accuracy (%) Unigram + Bigram
GTPM	SVM	77.50	67.50	72.50
Arc2Vec		66.97	66.58	66.32
PTPM		**80.00**	**70.00**	**87.50**
GTPM	MLP	74.80	93.00	**99.00**
Arc2Vec		62.78	90.36	75.04
PTPM		**75.00**	**95.00**	**99.00**

Table 1. Sentiment Classification Results by SVM, Arc2Vec, and MLP

In Table 1, the result of the experiment did not only reveal that the PTPM outperformed the GTPM and Arc2Vec but there is also an improvement in the accuracy of the result obtained. This underscores the importance of using a localized knowledge base in pre-processing social media feeds to fully capture the noisy terms that are domiciled in the social media feeds originating from a particular location.

Method	Algorithm (Kernel size = 3)	Accuracy (%) 1-Con-NN	Accuracy (%) 2-Con-NN	Accuracy (%) 3-Con-NN	Accuracy (%) 3-Con-NN
GTPM	CNN	97.78	97.78	94.72	**93.61**
Arc2Vec		83.00	93.00	73.4	70.74
PTPM		**99.17**	**98.61**	**96.94**	93.33

Table 2. Sentiment Classification Results by CNN

The result presented in Table 2 also supports our argument that there should be the inclusion of localized knowledge source in pre-processing social media feeds originating from a specific location in order to better interpret slang/abbreviation/acronym emanating from such social media feeds content. It is also worthy to note that convolutional neural networks performed better than support vector machines and multilayer perceptron algorithms in tweet sentiment analysis with the accuracy of 99.17%.

5   Conclusion

This paper provides an improved approach to pre-processing of social media streams by (1) integrating localized knowledge sources as extension to knowledge-based approaches, (2) capturing the rich semantics embedded in slangs, abbreviation and acronym, and (3) resolving ambiguity in the usage of slangs, abbreviation and acronym to better interpret and understand social media streams content. The result shows that in addition to normal preprocessing techniques of the social media stream, understanding, interpreting and resolving ambiguity in the usage of slangs/abbreviation/acronyms lead to improved accuracy of algorithms building on them as evident in the experimental result.

Acknowledgements

The research was supported by Covenant University Centre for Research, Innovation, and Discovery (CUCRID); Landmark University, Omu-Aran, Osun State, Nigeria; The World Academy of Sciences for Research and Advanced Training Fellowship, FR Number: 3240301383; and the Cape Peninsula University of Technology, South Africa.

References

Ansari, A. F., Seenivasan, A., and Anandan, A. (2017). Twitter Sentiment Analysis. https://github.com/abdulfatir/twitter-sentiment-analysis

Asghar, M. Z., Kundi, F. M., Ahmad, S., Khan A., and Khan, F. (2017). T-SAF: Twitter sentiment analysis framework using a hybrid classification scheme. Expert System, 1-19.

Atefeh, F. and Khreich, W. (2015). A survey of techniques for event detection in twitter. Computational Intelligence, 31(1), 132-164.

Bao, Y., Quan, C., Wang, L., and Ren, F. (2014). The role of text pre-processing in twitter sentiment analysis. In: D. S. Huang, K. H. Jo, and L. Wang (Eds.), Intelligent Computing Methodologies. ICIC

2014. Lecture Notes in Computer Science 8589, 615-629. Taiyuan, China: Springer.

Bontcheva, K. and Rout, D. (2014). Making sense of social media streams through semantics: A survey. Semantic Web, 5(5), 373-403. Available from: semantic-web-journal.org>swj303_0.pdf

Carter, S., Weerkamp, W., and Tsagkias, E. (2013). Microblog language identification: Overcoming the limitations of short, unedited and idiomatic text. Language Resources and Evaluation Journal, 47(1), 195-215.

Ghosh, S., Ghosh, S., and Das, D. (2017). Sentiment identification in code-mixed social media text. https://arxiv.org/pdf/1707.01184.pdf

Haddi, E., Liu, X., and Shi, Y. (2013). The role of text pre-processing in sentiment analysis. Procedia Computer Science, 17, 26-32.

Jianqiang, Z., and Xiaolin, G. (2017). Comparison research on text pre-processing methods on twitter sentiment analysis. IEEE Access, 5, 2870-2879.

Kuflik, T., Minkov, E., Nocera, S., Grant-Muller, S., Gal-Tzur, A., and Shoor I. (2017). Automating a framework to extract and analyse transport related social media content: the potential and challenges. Transport Research Part C, 275-291.

Kumar, M.G.M. (2016). Review on event detection techniques in social multimedia. Online Information Review, 40(3), 347-361.

Matsumoto, K., Yoshida, M., Tsuchiya, S., Kita, K., and Ren, F. (2016). Slang Analysis Based on Variant Information Extraction Focusing on the Time Series Topics. International Journal of Advanced Intelligence, 8(1), 84-98.

Mihanovic, A., Gabelica, H., and Kristic, Z. (2014). Big Data and Sentiment Analysis using KNIME: Online reviews vs. social media. MIPRO 2014, 26-30 May, Opatija, Croatia, (pp. 1464-1468).

Ouyang, Y., Guo, B., Zhang, J., Yu, Z., and Zhou, X. (2017). Senti-story: Multigrained sentiment analysis and event summarization with crowdsourced social media data. Personal and Ubiquitous Computing, 21(1), 97-111.

Ramadhan, W. P., Novianty, A., and Setianingsih, C. (2017, September). Sentiment analysis using multinomial logistic regression. Proceedings of the 2017 International Conference on Control, Electronics, Renewable Energy and Communications (ICCEREC) (pp.46-49). Yogyakarta, Indonesia: IEEE.

Sabbir, A. K. M., Jimeno-Yepes, A., and Kavuluru, R. (2017, October). Knowledge-based biomedical word sense disambiguation with neural concept embeddings. 2017 IEEE 17th International Conference on Bioinformatics and Bioengineering (BIBE). Washington, DC, USA: IEEE.

Singh, T., and Kumari, M. (2016). Role of text pre-processing in twitter sentiment analysis. Procedia Computer Science 89, 549-554. Available from: https://doi.org/10.1016/j.procs.2016.06.095

Smailovic, J., Grcar, M., Lavrac, N. Znidarsic, M. (2014). Stream-based active learning for sentiment analysis. Information Sciences, 285, 181-203.

Symeonidis, S., Effrosynidis, D., and Arampatzis, A. (2018). A comparative evaluation of pre-processing techniques and their interactions for twitter sentiment analysis. Expert Systems with Applications, 110, 298-310.

Thakkar, H., and Patel, D. (2015). Approaches for sentiment analysis on twitter: A state-of-art study. arXuv preprint arXiv:1512.01043, 1-8.

Uysal, A. K., and Gunal, S. (2014). The impact of pre-processing on text classification. Information Processing and Management, 50(1), 104-112.

Vyas, V., and Uma, V. (2018). An extensive study of sentiment analysis tools and binary classification of tweets using rapid miner. Procedia Computer Science, 125, 329-335.

Zhan, J., and Dahal, B. (2017). Using deep learning for short text understanding. Journal of Big Data, 4:34. doi: 10.1186/s40537-017-0095-2

Zhang, Z., Luo, S., and Ma, S. (2017). Arc2Vec: Learning acronym representations in twitter. In: L. Polkowski et al. (Eds.) IJCRS 2017, Part I, LNAI 10313, 280-288

Fact or Factitious? Contextualized Opinion Spam Detection

Stefan Kennedy, Niall Walsh,* Kirils Sloka, Andrew McCarren and Jennifer Foster
School of Computing
Dublin City University
{15902803,15384141,13405888}@mail.dcu.ie
{Andrew McCarren,Jennifer.Foster}@dcu.ie

Abstract

In recent years, it has been shown that falsification of online reviews can have a substantial, quantifiable effect on the success of the subject. This creates a large enticement for sellers to participate in review deception to boost their own success, or hinder the competition. Most current efforts to detect review deception are based on supervised classifiers trained on syntactic and lexical patterns. However, recent neural approaches to classification have been shown to match or outperform state-of-the-art methods. In this paper, we perform an analytic comparison of these methods, and introduce our own results. By fine-tuning Google's recently published transformer-based architecture, BERT, on the fake review detection task, we demonstrate near state-of-the-art performance, achieving over 90% accuracy on a widely used deception detection dataset.

1 Introduction

Online reviews of products and services have become significantly more important over the last two decades. Reviews influence customer purchasing decisions through review score and volume of reviews (Maslowska et al., 2017). It is estimated that as many as 90% of consumers read reviews before a purchase (Kumar et al., 2018) and that the conversion rate of a product increases by up to 270% as it gains reviews. For high price products, reviews can increase conversion rate by 380% (Askalidis and Malthouse, 2016).

With the rise of consumer reviews comes the problem of deceptive reviews. It has been shown that in competitive, ranked conditions it is worthwhile for unlawful merchants to create fake reviews. For TripAdvisor, in 80% of cases, a hotel could become more visible than another hotel using just 50 deceptive reviews (Lappas et al., 2016). Fake reviews are an established problem – 20% of

---

Yelp reviews are marked as fake by Yelp's algorithm (Luca and Zervas, 2016).

First introduced by Jindal and Liu (2007), the problem of fake review detection has been tackled from the perspectives of opinion spam detection and deception detection. It is usually treated as a binary classification problem using traditional text classification features such as word and part-of-speech n-grams, structural features obtained from syntactic parsing (Feng et al., 2012), topic models (Hernández-Castañeda et al., 2017), psycho-linguistic features obtained using the *Linguistic Inquiry and Word Count* (Ott et al., 2011; Hernández-Castañeda et al., 2017; Pennebaker et al., 2015) and non-verbal features related to reviewer behaviour (You et al., 2018; Wang et al., 2017; Aghakhani et al., 2018; Stanton and Irissappane, 2019)

We revisit the problem of fake review detection by comparing the performance of a variety of neural and non-neural approaches on two freely available datasets, a small set of hotel reviews where the deceptive subset has been obtained via crowdsourcing (Ott et al., 2011) and a much larger set of Yelp reviews obtained automatically (Rayana and Akoglu, 2015). We find that features based on reviewer characteristics can be used to boost the accuracy of a strong bag-of-words baseline. We also find that neural approaches perform at about the same level as the traditional non-neural ones. Perhaps counter-intuitively, the use of pretrained non-contextual word embeddings do not tend to lead to improved performance in most of our experiments. However, our best performance is achieved by fine-tuning BERT embeddings (Devlin et al., 2018) on this task. On the hotel review dataset, bootstrap validation accuracy is 90.5%, just behind the 91.2% reported by Feng et al. (2012) who combine bag-of-words with constituency tree fragments.

Proceedings of the ACL 2019, Student Research Workshop, pages 344–350
Florence, Italy, July 28th-August 2nd, 2019. ©2019 Association for Computational Linguistics

2 Data

Collecting data for classifying opinion spam is difficult because human labelling is only slightly better than random (Ott et al., 2011). Thus, it is difficult to find large-scale ground truth data. We experiment with two datasets:

- OpSpam (Ott et al., 2011): This dataset contains 800 gold-standard, labelled reviews. These reviews are all deceptive and were written by paid, crowd-funded workers for popular Chicago hotels. Additionally this dataset contains 800 reviews considered truthful, that were mined from various online review communities. These truthful reviews cannot be considered gold-standard, but are considered to have a reasonably low deception rate.

- Yelp (Rayana and Akoglu, 2015): This is the largest ground truth, deceptively labelled dataset available to date. The deceptive reviews in this dataset are those that were filtered by Yelp's review software for being manufactured, solicited or malicious. Yelp acknowledges that their recommendation software makes errors[1]. Yelp removed 7% of its reviews and marked 22% as not recommended[2]. This dataset is broken into three review sets, one containing 67,395 hotel and restaurant reviews from Chicago, one containing 359,052 restaurant reviews from NYC and a final one containing 608,598 restaurant reviews from a number of zip codes. There is overlap between the zip code dataset and the NYC dataset, and it is known that there are significant differences between product review categories (Blitzer et al., 2007) (hotels and restaurants) so we will only use the zip code dataset in training our models. Due to the memory restrictions of using convolutional networks, we filter the reviews with an additional constraint of being shorter than 321 words. This reduces the size of our final dataset by 2.63%. There are many more genuine reviews than deceptive, so we extract 78,346 each of genuine and deceptive classes to create a balanced dataset. The entire dataset contains 451,906 unused reviews.

3 Methods

We train several models to distinguish between fake and genuine reviews. The non-neural of these are logistic regression, and support vector machines (Cortes and Vapnik, 1995), and the neural are feed-forward networks, convolutional networks and long short-term memory networks (LeCun and Bengio, 1998; Jacovi et al., 2018; Hochreiter and Schmidhuber, 1997). We experiment with simple bag-of-word input representations and, for the neural approaches, we also use pre-trained word2vec embeddings (Le and Mikolov, 2014). In contrast with word2vec vectors which provide the same vector for a particular word regardless of its sentential context, we also experiment with contextualised vectors. Specifically, we utilize the BERT model developed by Google (Devlin et al., 2018) for fine-tuning pre-trained representations.

4 Experiments

4.1 Feature Engineering

Following Wang et al. (2017), we experiment with a number of features on the Yelp dataset:

- Structural features including review length, average word and sentence length, percentage of capitalized words and percentage of numerals.

- Reviewer features including maximum review count in one day, average review length, standard deviation of ratings, and percentage of positive and negative ratings.

- Part-of-Speech (POS) tags as percentages.

- Positive and negative word sentiment as percentages.

Feature selection using logistic regression found that some features were not predictive of deception. In particular POS tag percentages and sentiment percentages were not predictive. Metadata about the author of the review was the most predictive of deception, and the highest classification performance occurred when including only reviewer features in conjunction with bag-of-word vectors. Separation of these features displayed in Figure 1 shows that a large number (greater than 2) of reviews in one day indicates that a reviewer is deceptive. Conversely a long (greater than 1000)

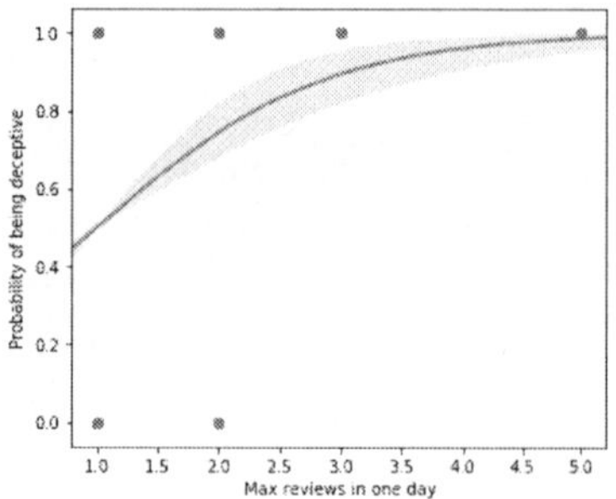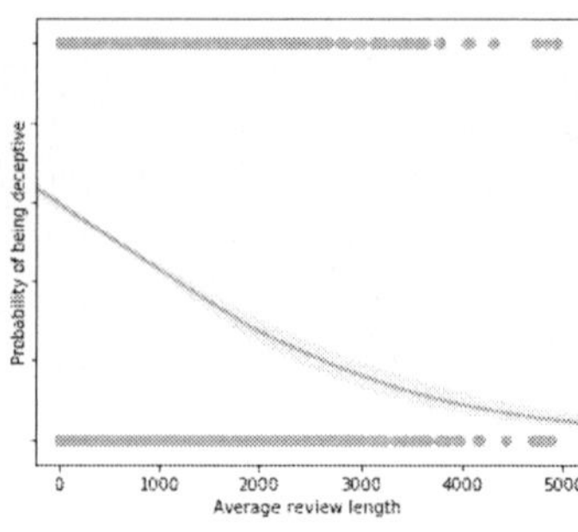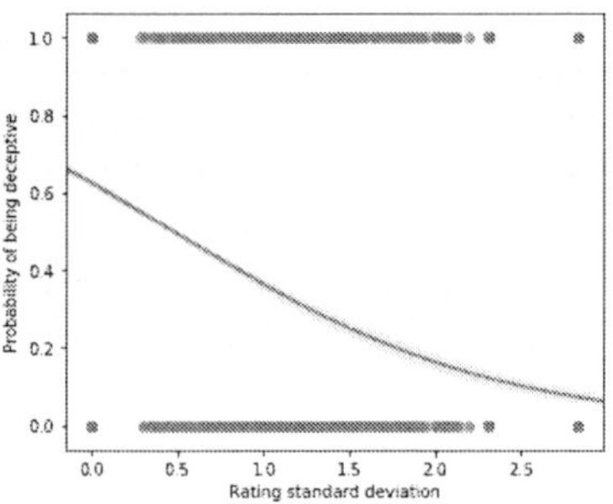

Figure 1: Separability of three most significant metadata features. Max reviews in one day is computed over randomly sampled, equal numbers of each class. The vertical axis represents deceptive as 1.0 and genuine as 0.0.

average character length of reviews is indicative that a reviewer is genuine. The standard deviation of a user's ratings is also included as a large deviation is an indicator of a review being genuine. For the remainder of experiments, we concatenate the word representations with a scaled (from 0 to 1) version of these user features. Note that reviewer features are not available for the OpSpam dataset.

4.2 Experimental Details

Evaluation

For the smaller OpSpam dataset we report results with both 5-Fold cross validation and bootstrap validation repeated 10 times. For small datasets and a small number of splits, K-Fold is known to be subject to high variance. Additionally bootstrap validation is known to be subject to high bias in some contexts (Kohavi, 1995). We therefore report results for both forms of validation. In all forms of validation we create stratified train and test sets. For the larger Yelp dataset we use the balanced set described in section 2. As this dataset is substantially large enough we use 10-Fold cross validation only to obtain results.

Non-Neural Models

For both OpSpam and Yelp datasets we design our models with similar methods. In the logistic regression and SVM experiments, words are represented in TF-IDF format, and in the case of Yelp only the most relevant 10,000 words are represented. Repeated experiments found that both linear and non-linear SVM kernels produced comparable performance. Applying grid search with the Yelp dataset found that a linear kernel could reach the highest accuracy.

Neural Models

For the Yelp dataset, neural classifiers use early stopping with a patience of 6 epochs of waiting for an improvement in validation loss. The same filtered, balanced dataset is used as input to all classifiers, and we use a hold out set of 1000 samples (6.38% of the balanced data) to verify performance.

Word2vec We use word2vec embeddings pretrained with a dimensionality of 300 on a Google News dataset[3]. This model was pretrained using a skip-gram architecture.

FFNNs We model FFNNs using a network containing two hidden dense layers. For both layers we use ReLU activation and l2 regularization, and we use sigmoid activation on the output layer. For the Yelp data, user features are directly concatenated to the BoW representation. For word2vec embeddings, the embeddings are first flattened to a single dimension before concatenation. The model used for OpSpam contains 32 units in the first hidden layer, and 16 units in the second. The model used for Yelp contains 16 units in the first hidden layer, and 8 units in the second. Models for both datasets use a dropout rate of 0.25 between the two hidden layers.

CNNs Convolutional networks are modelled in different ways for BoW and word2vec embedding representations. As BoW is represented in a single dimension, we create a convolutional layer with a kernel height of 1 unit and width of 10 units. This kernel slides horizontally along the BoW vector. For word2vec embeddings we position word vectors vertically in the order they occur, as has been implemented in earlier research (Kim, 2014). In

---

[3]https://code.google.com/archive/p/word2vec/

this case the kernel has a width equal to the dimensionality of the word vectors and slides vertically along the word axis. We use a kernel height of 10, containing 10 words in each kernel position. Both BoW and word2vec embedding models use 50 filters. Following the convolutions the result is passed through a pooling layer, and a dropout rate of 0.5 is applied before the result is flattened. In the case of Yelp this flattened result is concatenated with the user features of the review. Two hidden dense layers follow this, both using ReLU activation and l2 regularization. Both hidden layers contain 8 units and are followed by an output layer that uses sigmoid activation. For the OpSpam dataset, the BoW model uses a pool size of (1, 10) and the word2vec embedding implementation uses a pool size of (5, 1). For the Yelp dataset both BoW and word2vec embedding models use global max pooling.

LSTMs In the implementation of LSTMs, models for both BoW and word2vec embeddings directly input word representations to an LSTM layer. Numerous repeated runs with different numbers of LSTM layers and units found that the optimal accuracy occurs at just one layer of 10 units. We model implementations for both OpSpam and Yelp datasets using this number of layers and units. In the case of the Yelp dataset, the output of the LSTM layer is concatenated with user features. This is followed by 2 hidden dense layers using ReLU activation and l2 regularization, each containing 8 units, followed by an output layer using sigmoid activation.

BERT We fine-tune the `bert-base-uncased` model on the OpSpam dataset and perform stratified validation using both 5-Fold validation and bootstrap validation repeated 10 times. For fine-tuning we use a learning rate of 2e-5, batch size of 16 and 3 training epochs.

Two implementations of fine-tuning are used to verify results. One implementation is the BERT implementation published by Google alongside the pretrained models, and the other uses the 'op-for-op' reimplementation of BERT created by Hugging Face[4].

---

[4]https://github.com/huggingface/pytorch-pretrained-BERT

4.3 Results

The results of performing validation on these models are shown in Tables 1, 2 and 3. Table 1 shows that SVMs slightly outperform logistic regression, and that the Yelp dataset represents a much harder challenge than the OpSpam one.

Contrary to expectations, Table 2 shows that pretrained word2vec embeddings do not improve performance, and in the case of OpSpam BoW can substantially outperform them. We do not yet know why this might be case.

The BERT results in Table 3 show that the Google TensorFlow implementation performs substantially better than PyTorch in our case. This is an unexpected result and more research needs to be carried out to understand the differences. We also report that Google's TensorFlow implementation outperforms all other classifiers tested on the OpSpam dataset, providing tentative evidence of contextualized embeddings outperforming all non-contextual pre-trained word2vec embeddings and BoW approaches.

By inspecting the results of evaluation on a single 5-Fold test set split for the BERT experiments, we see that there are an approximately equal number of false negatives (15), and false positives (14). There appears to be a slight tendency for the model to perform better when individual sentences are longer, and when the review is long. In the case of our 29 incorrect classifications the number of words in a sentence was 16.0 words, compared to 18.4 for correct classifications. Entire reviews tend to be longer in correct classifications with an average length of 149.0 words, compared to 117.6 for incorrect classifications. Meanwhile the average word length is approximately 4.25 for both correct and incorrect classifications.

5 Application of Research

We have developed a frontend which retrieves business information from Yelp and utilizes our models to analyze reviews. Results are displayed in an engaging fashion using data visualization and explanations of our prediction. We display a deception distribution of all reviews for the product. This includes how many reviews are classified as deceptive or genuine, shown in buckets at 10% intervals of confidence. This allows users to quickly determine if the distribution is different to a typical, expected one. This tool also enables users to view frequency and average rating of re-

	OpSpam		Yelp
	5-Fold	Bootstrap	10-Fold
Logistic Reg	0.856	0.869	0.713
SVM	0.864	0.882	0.721

Table 1: Non-neural Classifier Accuracy

	OpSpam				Yelp	
	BoW		word2vec		BoW	word2vec
	5-Fold	Bootstrap	5-Fold	Bootstrap		
FFNN	0.888	0.883	0.587	0.605	0.708	0.704
CNN	0.669	0.639	0.800	0.822	0.722	0.731
LSTM	0.876	0.876	0.761	0.769	0.731	0.727

Table 2: Neural classifier accuracy using bag-of-words (BoW) and non-contextual (word2vec) word embeddings

	TensorFlow	PyTorch
K-Fold	0.891	0.862
Bootstrap	0.905	0.867

Table 3: Accuracy performance of BERT implementations in TensorFlow and PyTorch (OpSpam)

views over time. This information can be used to spot unusual behaviour at a given time, such as a sudden increase in activity, where that activity is creating a positive or negative rating score. The aim of this web application is to highlight the ability of our models to detect fake reviews, and allows interactions that drill down on specific details such as the impact of individual words on the overall evaluation. Additional features enrich the evaluation by performing statistical analysis on the users who wrote the retrieved reviews. We use badges to show the significance of this analysis, where a badge is given to show a deceptive or genuine indicator. Reviews can receive badges for the user's average review length, standard deviation of review scores and maximum number of reviews in one day. This adds a layer of transparency to the data, allowing us to give a more informative verdict on the review itself.

The models developed in this research are publicized through our API. The web application provides an option to set the model used in requests, providing easy access to experimentation. This is an open-source[5] project implemented in the React[6] Javascript web interface library and Flask[7]

Figure 2: Search page of web interface.

Python server library respectively.

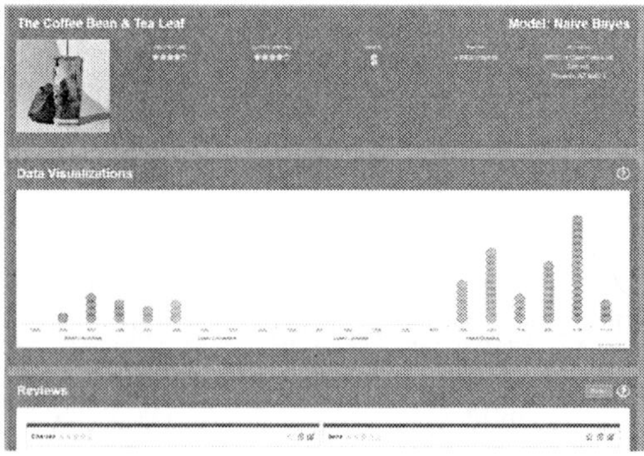

Figure 3: Sample Visualization of Reviews

6 Conclusion

We have conducted a series of classification experiments on two freely available deceptive review datasets. The dataset created by crowd-sourcing deceptive reviews results in an easier task than the real-world, potentially noisy, dataset produced by Yelp. On the Yelp dataset, we find that features

[5]https://github.com/CPSSD/LUCAS
[6]https://reactjs.org
[7]http://flask.pocoo.org

that encode reviewer behaviour are important in both a neural and non-neural setting. The best performance on the OpSpam dataset, which is competitive with the state-of-the-art, is achieved by fine-tuning with BERT. Future work involves understanding the relatively poor performance of the pretrained non-contextual embeddings, and experimenting with conditional, more efficient generative adversarial networks.

Acknowledgments

We thank the reviewers for their helpful comments. The work presented in this paper is the final year project of the first three authors, conducted as part of their undergraduate degree in Computational Problem Solving and Software Development in Dublin City University. We thank the ADAPT Centre for Digital Content Technology for providing computing resources. The ADAPT Centre for Digital Content Technology is funded under the Science Foundation Ireland Research Centres Programme (Grant 13/RC/2106) and is co-funded under the European Regional Development Fund.

References

H. Aghakhani, A. Machiry, S. Nilizadeh, C. Kruegel, and G. Vigna. 2018. Detecting deceptive reviews using generative adversarial networks. In *2018 IEEE Security and Privacy Workshops (SPW)*, pages 89–95.

Georgios Askalidis and Edward Malthouse. 2016. The value of online customer reviews. In *Proceedings of the ACM conference on Recommender Systems*.

John Blitzer, Mark Dredze, and Fernando Pereira. 2007. Biographies, bollywood, boom-boxes and blenders: Domain adaptation for sentiment classification. In *Proceedings of the 45th annual meeting of the association of computational linguistics*, pages 440–447.

Corinna Cortes and Vladimir Vapnik. 1995. Support-vector networks. *Machine Learning*, 20(3):273–297.

Jacob Devlin, Ming-Wei Chang, Kenton Lee, and Kristina Toutanova. 2018. BERT: pre-training of deep bidirectional transformers for language understanding. *CoRR*, abs/1810.04805.

Song Feng, Ritwik Banerjee, and Yejin Choi. 2012. Syntactic stylometry for deception detection. In *Proceedings of the 50th Annual Meeting of the Association for Computational Linguistics (Volume 2: Short Papers)*, pages 171–175, Jeju Island, Korea. Association for Computational Linguistics.

Ángel Hernández-Castañeda, Hiram Calvo, Alexander Gelbukh, and Jorge J. Flores. 2017. Cross-domain deception detection using support vector networks. *Soft Comput.*, 21(3):585–595.

Sepp Hochreiter and Jürgen Schmidhuber. 1997. Long short-term memory. *Neural Comput.*, 9(8):1735–1780.

Alon Jacovi, Oren Sar Shalom, and Yoav Goldberg. 2018. Understanding convolutional neural networks for text classification. pages 56–65.

Nitin Jindal and Bing Liu. 2007. Review spam detection. In *Proceedings of the 16th International Conference on World Wide Web*, WWW '07, pages 1189–1190, New York, NY, USA. ACM.

Yoon Kim. 2014. Convolutional neural networks for sentence classification. In *Proceedings of the 2014 Conference on Empirical Methods in Natural Language Processing (EMNLP)*, pages 1746–1751, Doha, Qatar. Association for Computational Linguistics.

Ron Kohavi. 1995. A study of cross-validation and bootstrap for accuracy estimation and model selection. In *Proceedings of the 14th International Joint Conference on Artificial Intelligence - Volume 2*, IJCAI'95, pages 1137–1143, San Francisco, CA, USA. Morgan Kaufmann Publishers Inc.

Naveen Kumar, Deepak Venugopal, Liangfei Qiu, and Subodha Kumar. 2018. Detecting review manipulation on online platforms with hierarchical supervised learning. *Journal of Management Information Systems*, 35(1):350–380.

Theodoros Lappas, Gaurav Sabnis, and Georgios Valkanas. 2016. The impact of fake reviews on online visibility: A vulnerability assessment of the hotel industry. *Information Systems Research*, 27:940–961.

Quoc V. Le and Tomas Mikolov. 2014. Distributed representations of sentences and documents. In *Proceedings of the 31th International Conference on Machine Learning, ICML 2014, Beijing, China, 21-26 June 2014*, pages 1188–1196.

Yann LeCun and Yoshua Bengio. 1998. Convolutional networks for images, speech, and time series. pages 255–258. MIT Press, Cambridge, MA, USA.

Michael Luca and Georgios Zervas. 2016. Fake it till you make it: Reputation, competition, and yelp review fraud. *Management Science*, 62:3412–3427.

Ewa Maslowska, Edward C. Malthouse, and Vijay Viswanathan. 2017. Do customer reviews drive purchase decisions? the moderating roles of review exposure and price. *Decis. Support Syst.*, 98(C):1–9.

Myle Ott, Yejin Choi, Claire Cardie, and Jeffrey T. Hancock. 2011. Finding deceptive opinion spam by any stretch of the imagination. In *Proceedings of the 49th Annual Meeting of the Association for Computational Linguistics: Human Language Technologies*, pages 309–319, Portland, Oregon, USA. Association for Computational Linguistics.

James W Pennebaker, Ryan L Boyd, Kayla Jordan, and Kate Blackburn. 2015. The development and psychometric properties of liwc2015. Technical report.

Shebuti Rayana and Leman Akoglu. 2015. Collective opinion spam detection: Bridging review networks and metadata. In *Proceedings of the 21th ACM SIGKDD International Conference on Knowledge Discovery and Data Mining*, KDD '15, pages 985–994, New York, NY, USA. ACM.

Gray Stanton and Athirai Aravazhi Irissappane. 2019. Gans for semi-supervised opinion spam detection. *CoRR*, abs/1903.08289.

Zehui Wang, Yuzhu Zhang, and Tianpei Qian. 2017. Fake review detection on yelp.

Zhenni You, Tieyun Qian, and Bing Liu. 2018. An attribute enhanced domain adaptive model for cold-start spam review detection. In *Proceedings of the 27th International Conference on Computational Linguistics*, pages 1884–1895, Santa Fe, New Mexico, USA. Association for Computational Linguistics.

Scheduled Sampling for Transformers

Tsvetomila Mihaylova
Instituto de Telecomunicações
Lisbon, Portugal
tsvetomila.mihaylova@lx.it.pt

André F. T. Martins
Instituto de Telecomunicações & Unbabel
Lisbon, Portugal
andre.martins@unbabel.com

Abstract

Scheduled sampling is a technique for avoiding one of the known problems in sequence-to-sequence generation: exposure bias. It consists of feeding the model a mix of the teacher forced embeddings and the model predictions from the previous step in training time. The technique has been used for improving the model performance with recurrent neural networks (RNN). In the Transformer model, unlike the RNN, the generation of a new word attends to the full sentence generated so far, not only to the last word, and it is not straightforward to apply the scheduled sampling technique. We propose some structural changes to allow scheduled sampling to be applied to Transformer architecture, via a two-pass decoding strategy. Experiments on two language pairs achieve performance close to a teacher-forcing baseline and show that this technique is promising for further exploration.

1 Introduction

Recent work in Neural Machine Translation (NMT) relies on a sequence-to-sequence model with global attention (Sutskever et al., 2014; Bahdanau et al., 2014), trained with maximum likelihood estimation (MLE). These models are typically trained by teacher forcing, in which the model makes each decision conditioned on the gold history of the target sequence. This tends to lead to quick convergence but is dissimilar to the procedure used at decoding time, when the gold target sequence is not available and decisions are conditioned on previous model predictions.

Ranzato et al. (2015) point out the problem that using teacher forcing means the model has never been trained on its own errors and may not be robust to them—a phenomenon called *exposure bias*. This has the potential to cause problems at translation time, when the model is exposed to its own (likely imperfect) predictions.

A common approach for addressing the problem with exposure bias is using a scheduled strategy for deciding when to use teacher forcing and when not to (Bengio et al., 2015). For a recurrent decoder, applying scheduled sampling is trivial: for generation of each word, the model decides whether to condition on the gold embedding from the given target (teacher forcing) or the model prediction from the previous step.

In the Transformer model (Vaswani et al., 2017), the decoding is still autoregressive, but unlike the RNN decoder, the generation of each word conditions on the whole prefix sequence and not only on the last word. This makes it non-trivial to apply scheduled sampling directly for this model. Since the Transformer achieves state-of-the-art results and has become a default choice for many natural language processing problems, it is interesting to adapt and explore the idea of scheduled sampling for it, and, to our knowledge, no way of doing this has been proposed so far.

Our contributions in this paper are:

- We propose a new strategy for using scheduled sampling in Transformer models by making two passes through the decoder in training time.

- We compare several approaches for conditioning on the model predictions when they are used instead of the gold target.

- We test the scheduled sampling with transformers in a machine translation task on two language pairs and achieve results close to a teacher forcing baseline (with a slight improvement of up to 1 BLEU point for some models).

2 Related Work

Bengio et al. (2015) proposed scheduled sampling

Proceedings of the ACL 2019, Student Research Workshop, pages 351–356
Florence, Italy, July 28th-August 2nd, 2019. ©2019 Association for Computational Linguistics

for sequence-to-sequence RNN models: a method where the embedding used as the input to the decoder at time step $t+1$ is picked randomly between the gold target and the `argmax` of the model's output probabilities at step t. The Bernoulli probability of picking one or the other changes over training epochs according to a schedule that makes the probability of choosing the gold target decrease across training steps. The authors propose three different schedules: linear decay, exponential decay and inverse sigmoid decay.

Goyal et al. (2017) proposed an approach based on scheduled sampling which backpropagates through the model decisions. At each step, when the model decides to use model predictions, instead of the `argmax`, they use a weighted average of all word embeddings, weighted by the prediction scores. They experimented with two options: a softmax with a temperature parameter, and a stochastic variant using Gumbel Softmax (Jang et al., 2016) with temperature. With this technique, they achieve better results than the standard scheduled sampling. Our works extends Bengio et al. (2015) and Goyal et al. (2017) by adapting their frameworks to Transformer architectures.

Ranzato et al. (2015) took ideas from scheduled sampling and the REINFORCE algorithm (Williams, 1992) and combine the teacher forcing training with optimization of the sequence level loss. In the first epochs, the model is trained with teacher forcing and for the remaining epochs they start with teacher forcing for the first t time steps and use REINFORCE (sampling from the model) until the end of the sequence. They decrease the time for training with teacher forcing t as training continues until the whole sequence is trained with REINFORCE in the final epochs. In addition to the work of Ranzato et al. (2015) other methods that are also focused on sequence-level training are using for example actor-critic (Bahdanau et al., 2016) or beam search optimization (Wiseman and Rush, 2016). These methods directly optimize the metric used at test time (e.g. BLEU). Another proposed approach to avoid exposure bias is SEARN (Daumé et al., 2009). In SEARN, the model uses its own predictions at training time to produce sequence of actions, then a search algorithm determines the optimal action at each step and a policy is trained to predict that action. The main drawback of these approaches is that the training becomes much slower. By contrast, in this paper we

focus on methods which are comparable in training time with a force-decoding baseline.

3 Scheduled Sampling with Transformers

In the case with recurrent neural networks (RNN) in the training phase we generate one word at a time step, and we condition the generation of this word to the previous word from the gold target sequence. This sequential decoding makes it simple to apply scheduled sampling - at each time step, with some probability, instead of using the previous word in the gold sequence, we use the word predicted from the model on the previous step.

The Transformer model (Vaswani et al., 2017), which achieves state-of-the-art results for a lot of natural language processing tasks, is also an autoregressive model. The generation of each word conditions on all previous words in the sequence, not only on the last generated word. The model is based on several *self-attention layers*, which directly model relationships between all words in the sentence, regardless of their respective position. The order of the words is achieved by position embeddings which are summed with the corresponding word embeddings. Using position masking in the decoder ensures that the generation of each word depends only on the previous words in the sequence and not on the following ones. Because generation of a word in the Transformer conditions on all previous words in the sequence and not just the last word, it is not trivial to apply scheduled sampling to it, where, in training time, we need to choose between using the gold target word or the model prediction. In order to allow usage of scheduled sampling with the Transformer model, we needed to make some changes in the Transformer architecture.

3.1 Two-decoder Transformer

The model we propose for applying scheduled sampling in transformers makes two passes on the decoder. Its architecture is illustrated on Figure 1. We make no changes in the encoder of the model. The decoding of the scheduled transformer has the following steps:

1. **First pass on the decoder: get the model predictions.** On this step, the decoder conditions on the gold target sequence and predicts scores for each position as a standard trans-

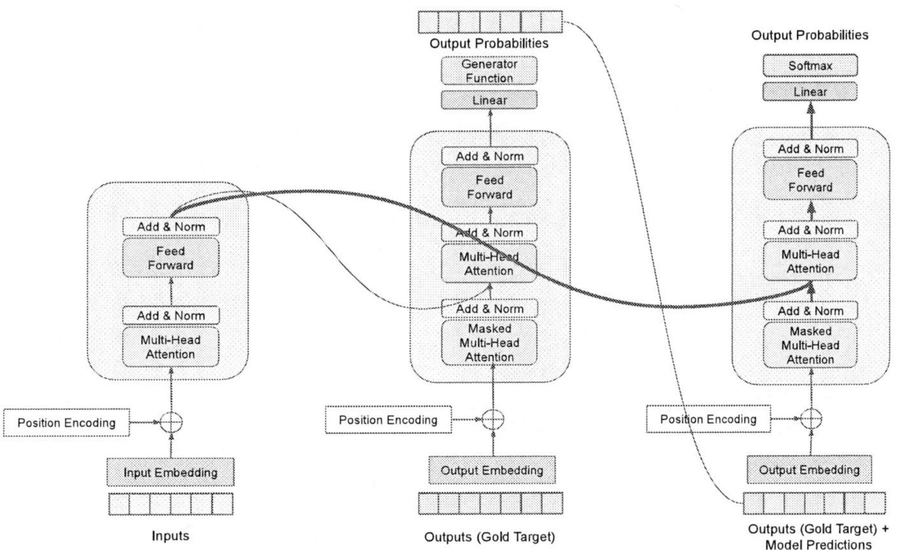

Figure 1: Transformer model adapted for use with scheduled sampling. The two decoders on the image share the same parameters. The first pass on the decoder conditions on the gold target sequence and returns the model predictions. The second pass conditions on a mix of the target sequence and model predictions and returns the result. The thicker lines show the path that is backpropagated in all experiments, i.e. we always make backpropagation through the second decoder pass. The thin arrows are only backpropagated in a part of the experiments. (*The image is based on the transformer architecture from the paper of Vaswani et al. (2017).*)

former model. Those scores are passed to the next step.

2. **Mix the gold target sequence with the predicted sequence.** After obtaining a sequence representing the prediction from the model for each position, we imitate scheduled sampling by mixing the target sequence with the model predictions: For each position in the sequence, we select with a given probability whether to use the gold token or the prediction from the model. The probability for using teacher forcing (i.e. the gold token) is a function of the training step and is calculated with a selected schedule. We pass this "new reference sequence" as the reference for the second decoder. The vectors used from the model predictions can be either the embedding of the highest-scored word, or a mix of the embeddings according to their scores. Several variants of building the vector from the model predictions for each position are described below.

3. **Second pass on the decoder: the final predictions.** The second pass of the decoder uses as output target the mix of words in the gold sequence and the model predictions.

The outputs of this decoder pass are the actual result from the models.

It is important to mention that the two decoders are identical and share the same parameters. We are using the same decoder for the first pass, where we condition on the gold sequence and the second pass, where we condition on the mix between the gold sequence and the model predictions.

3.2 Embedding Mix

For each position in the sequence, the first decoder pass gives a score for each vocabulary word. We explore several ways of using those scores when the model predictions are used.

- The most obvious case is to not mix the embeddings at all and pass the `argmax` from the model predictions, i.e. use the embedding of the vocabulary word with the highest score from the decoder.

- We also experiment with mixing the `top-k` embeddings. In our experiments, we use the weighted average of the embeddings of the top-5 scored vocabulary words.

- Inspired by the work of Goyal et al. (2017), we experiment with passing a mix of the embeddings with `softmax` with temperature.

Using a higher temperature parameter makes a better approximation of the `argmax`.

$$\bar{e}_{i-1} = \sum_y e(y) \frac{\exp(\alpha s_{i-1}(y))}{\sum_{y'} \exp(\alpha s_{i-1}(y'))}$$

where $\bar{e}_{i-1}$ is the vector which will be used at the current position, obtained by a sum of the embeddings of all vocabulary words, weighted by a softmax of the scores s_{i-1}.

- An alternative of using argmax is sampling an embedding from the softmax distribution. Also based on the work of Goyal et al. (2017), we use the Gumbel Softmax (Maddison et al., 2016; Jang et al., 2016) approximation to sample the embedding:

$$\bar{e}_{i-1} = \sum_y e(y) \frac{\exp(\alpha(s_{i-1}(y)) + G_y)}{\sum_{y'} \exp(\alpha(s_{i-1}(y') + G_{y'}))}$$

where $U \sim \mathrm{Uniform}(0,1)$ and $G = -\log(-\log U)$.

- Finally, we experiment with passing a `sparsemax` mix of the embeddings (Martins and Astudillo, 2016).

3.3 Weights update

We calculate Cross Entropy Loss based on the outputs from the second decoder pass. For the cases where all vocabulary words are summed (Softmax, Gumbel softmax, Sparsemax), we try two variants of updating the model weights.

- Only backpropagate through the decoder which makes the final predictions, based on mix between the gold target and the model predictions.

- Backpropagate through the second, as well as through the first decoder pass which predicts the model outputs. This setup resembles the differentiable scheduled sampling proposed by Goyal et al. (2017).

4 Experiments

We report experiments with scheduled sampling for Transformers for the task of machine translation. We run the experiments on two language pairs:

- IWSLT 2017 German−English (DE−EN, Cettolo et al. (2017)).

Encoder model type	Transformer
Decoder model type	Transformer
# Enc. & dec. layers	6
Heads	8
Hidden layer size	512
Word embedding size	512
Batch size	32
Optimizer	Adam
Learning rate	1.0
Warmup steps	20,000
Maximum training steps	300,000
Validation steps	10,000
Position Encoding	True
Share Embeddings	True
Share Decoder Embeddings	True
Dropout	0.2 (DE-EN)
Dropout	0.1 (JA-EN)

Table 1: Hyperparameters shared across models

- KFTT Japanese−English (JA−EN, Neubig (2011)).

We use byte pair encoding (BPE; (Sennrich et al., 2016)) with a joint segmentation with 32,000 merges for both language pairs.

Hyperparameters used across experiments are shown in Table 1. All models were implemented in a fork of OpenNMT-py (Klein et al., 2017). We compare our model to a **teacher forcing baseline**, i.e. a standard transformer model, without scheduled sampling, with the hyperparameters given in Table 1. We did hyperparameter tuning by trying several different values for dropout and warmup steps, and choosing the best BLEU score on the validation set for the baseline model.

With the scheduled sampling method, the teacher forcing probability continuously decreases over the course of training according to a predefined function of the training steps. Among the decay strategies proposed for scheduled sampling, we found that linear decay is the one that works best for our data:

$$t(i) = \max\{\epsilon, k - ci\}, \tag{1}$$

where $0 \leq \epsilon < 1$ is the minimum teacher forcing probability to be used in the model and k and c provide the offset and slope of the decay. This function determines the teacher forcing ratio t for training step i, that is, the probability of doing teacher forcing at each position in the sequence.

Experiment	DE−EN		JA−EN	
	Dev	**Test**	**Dev**	**Test**
Teacher Forcing Baseline	35.05	**29.62**	18.00	19.46
No backprop				
Argmax	23.99	20.57	12.88	15.13
Top-k mix	35.19	29.42	**18.46**	20.24
Softmax mix $\alpha = 1$	35.07	29.32	17.98	20.03
Softmax mix $\alpha = 10$	35.30	29.25	17.79	19.67
Gumbel Softmax mix $\alpha = 1$	**35.36**	29.48	18.31	20.21
Gumbel Softmax mix $\alpha = 10$	35.32	29.58	17.94	**20.87**
Sparsemax mix	35.22	29.28	18.14	20.15
Backprop through model decisions				
Softmax mix $\alpha = 1$	33.25	27.60	15.67	17.93
Softmax mix $\alpha = 10$	27.06	23.29	13.49	16.02
Gumbel Softmax mix $\alpha = 1$	30.57	25.71	15.86	18.76
Gumbel Softmax mix $\alpha = 10$	12.79	10.62	13.98	17.09
Sparsemax mix	24.65	20.15	12.44	16.23

Table 2: Experiments with scheduled sampling for Transformer. The table shows BLEU score for the best checkpoint on BLEU, measured on the validation set. The first group of experiments do not have a backpropagation pass through the first decoder. The results from the second group are from model runs with backpropagation pass through the second as well as through the first decoder.

The results from our experiments are shown In Table 2. The scheduled sampling which uses only the highest-scored word predicted by the model does not have a very good performance. The models which use mixed embeddings (the top-k, softmax, Gumbel softmax or sparsemax) and only backpropagate through the second decoder pass, perform slightly better than the baseline on the validation set, and one of them is also slightly better on the test set. The differentiable scheduled sampling (when the model backpropagates through the first decoder) have much lower results. The performance of these models starts degrading too early, so we expect that using more training steps with teacher forcing at the beginning of the training would lead to better performance, so this setup still needs to be examined more carefully.

5   Discussion and Future Work

In this paper, we presented our approach to applying the scheduled sampling technique to Transformers. Because of the specifics of the decoding, applying scheduled sampling is not straightforward as it is for RNN and required some changes in the way the Transformer model is trained, by using a two-step decoding. We experimented with several schedules and mixing of the embeddings in the case where the model predictions were used. We tested the models for machine translation on two language pairs. The experimental results showed that our scheduled sampling strategy gave better results on the validation set for both language pairs compared to a teacher forcing baseline and, in one of the tested language pairs (JA−EN), there were slightly better results on the test set.

One possible direction for future work is experimenting with more schedules. We noticed that when the schedule starts falling too fast, for example, with the exponential or inverse sigmoid decay, the performance of the model degrades too fast. Therefore, we think it is worth exploring more schedules where the training does more pure teacher forcing at the beginning of the training and then decays more slowly, for example, inverse sigmoid decay which starts decreasing after more epochs. We will also try the experiments on more language pairs.

Finally, we need to explore the poor performance on the differential scheduled sampling setup (with backpropagating through the two decoders). In this case, the performance of the model starts decreasing earlier and the reason for this needs to be examined carefully. We expect this setup to give better results after adjusting the decay schedule to allow more teacher forcing training before starting to use model predictions.

Acknowledgments

This work was supported by the European Research Council (ERC StG DeepSPIN 758969), and by the Fundação para a Ciência e Tecnologia through contracts UID/EEA/50008/2019 and CMUPERI/TIC/0046/2014 (GoLocal). We would like to thank Gonçalo Correia and Ben Peters for their involvement on an earlier stage of this project.

References

Dzmitry Bahdanau, Philemon Brakel, Kelvin Xu, Anirudh Goyal, Ryan Lowe, Joelle Pineau, Aaron Courville, and Yoshua Bengio. 2016. An actor-critic algorithm for sequence prediction. *arXiv preprint arXiv:1607.07086*.

Dzmitry Bahdanau, Kyunghyun Cho, and Yoshua Bengio. 2014. Neural machine translation by jointly learning to align and translate. *arXiv preprint arXiv:1409.0473*.

Samy Bengio, Oriol Vinyals, Navdeep Jaitly, and Noam Shazeer. 2015. Scheduled sampling for sequence prediction with recurrent neural networks. In *Advances in Neural Information Processing Systems*, pages 1171–1179.

Mauro Cettolo, Marcello Federico, Luisa Bentivogli, Niehues Jan, Stüker Sebastian, Sudoh Katsuitho, Yoshino Koichiro, and Federmann Christian. 2017. Overview of the iwslt 2017 evaluation campaign. In *International Workshop on Spoken Language Translation*, pages 2–14.

Hal Daumé, John Langford, and Daniel Marcu. 2009. Search-based structured prediction. *Machine learning*, 75(3):297–325.

Kartik Goyal, Chris Dyer, and Taylor Berg-Kirkpatrick. 2017. Differentiable scheduled sampling for credit assignment. *arXiv preprint arXiv:1704.06970*.

Eric Jang, Shixiang Gu, and Ben Poole. 2016. Categorical reparameterization with gumbel-softmax. *arXiv preprint arXiv:1611.01144*.

G. Klein, Y. Kim, Y. Deng, J. Senellart, and A. M. Rush. 2017. OpenNMT: Open-Source Toolkit for Neural Machine Translation. *ArXiv e-prints*.

Chris J Maddison, Andriy Mnih, and Yee Whye Teh. 2016. The concrete distribution: A continuous relaxation of discrete random variables. *arXiv preprint arXiv:1611.00712*.

Andre Martins and Ramon Astudillo. 2016. From softmax to sparsemax: A sparse model of attention and multi-label classification. In *International Conference on Machine Learning*, pages 1614–1623.

Graham Neubig. 2011. The kyoto free translation task.

Marc'Aurelio Ranzato, Sumit Chopra, Michael Auli, and Wojciech Zaremba. 2015. Sequence level training with recurrent neural networks. *arXiv preprint arXiv:1511.06732*.

Rico Sennrich, Barry Haddow, and Alexandra Birch. 2016. Neural machine translation of rare words with subword units. *arXiv preprint arXiv:1508.07909*.

Ilya Sutskever, Oriol Vinyals, and Quoc V Le. 2014. Sequence to sequence learning with neural networks. In *Advances in neural information processing systems*, pages 3104–3112.

Ashish Vaswani, Noam Shazeer, Niki Parmar, Jakob Uszkoreit, Llion Jones, Aidan N Gomez, Łukasz Kaiser, and Illia Polosukhin. 2017. Attention is all you need. In *Advances in Neural Information Processing Systems*, pages 5998–6008.

Ronald J Williams. 1992. Simple statistical gradient-following algorithms for connectionist reinforcement learning. *Machine learning*, 8(3-4):229–256.

Sam Wiseman and Alexander M Rush. 2016. Sequence-to-sequence learning as beam-search optimization. In *Proceedings of the 2016 Conference on Empirical Methods in Natural Language Processing*, pages 1296–1306.

BREAKING! Presenting Fake News Corpus For Automated Fact Checking

Archita Pathak
University at Buffalo (SUNY)
New York, USA
architap@buffalo.edu

Rohini K. Srihari
University at Buffalo (SUNY)
New York, USA
rohini@buffalo.edu

Abstract

Popular fake news articles spread faster than mainstream articles on the same topic which renders manual fact checking inefficient. At the same time, creating tools for automatic detection is as challenging due to lack of dataset containing articles which present fake or manipulated stories as compelling facts. In this paper, we introduce manually verified corpus of compelling fake and questionable news articles on the USA politics, containing around 700 articles from Aug-Nov, 2016. We present various analyses on this corpus and finally implement classification model based on linguistic features. This work is still in progress as we plan to extend the dataset in the future and use it for our approach towards automated fake news detection.

1 Introduction

Fake news is a widespread menace which has resulted into protests and violence around the globe. A study published by Vosoughi et al. of MIT states that falsehood diffuses significantly farther, faster, deeper and more broadly than the truth in all categories of information. They also stated that effects were more pronounced for false political news than for false news about terrorism, natural disaster, science, urban legends or financial information. According to Pew Research Center's survey [1] of 2017, 64% of US adults said to have great deal of confusion about the facts in the current events. Major events around the globe saw sudden jump in deceitful stories on internet during sensitive events because of which social media organizations and government institutions have scrambled together to tackle this problem as soon as possible. However, fake news detection has its own challenges.

---

[1] http://www.journalism.org/2016/12/15/many-americans-believe-fake-news-is-sowing-confusion/

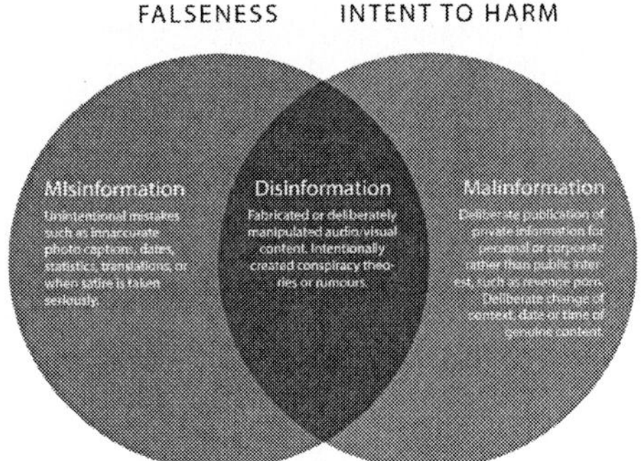

Figure 1: Conceptual framework for examining information disorder presented by Wardle and Derakhshan

First and foremost is the consensus on the definition of fake news which is a topic of discussion in several countries. Considering the complexity of defining fake news, Wardle and Derakhshan instead created a conceptual framework for examining information disorder as shown in Figure - 1. Based on this model, EU commission in 2018 categorized fake news as disinformation with the characteristics being *verifiably false or misleading information that is created, presented and disseminated for economic gain or to intentionally deceive the public, and in any event to cause public harm*. Since our work focuses on false information written intentionally to deceive people in order to cause social unrest, we will be following the definition defined by EU to categorize fake articles into various categories as defined in Section 3 of this paper.

The second challenge is the lack of structured and clean dataset which is a bottleneck for fake opinion mining, automated fact checking and creating computationally-intensive learning models

357

Proceedings of the ACL 2019, Student Research Workshop, pages 357–362
Florence, Italy, July 28th-August 2nd, 2019. ©2019 Association for Computational Linguistics

for feature learning. In the following section, we elaborate on this challenge more, specify related works and how our work is different from others.

2 Related Works

There have been several datasets released previously for fake news, most notably Buzzfeed[2] and Stanford (Allcott and Gentzkow, 2017) datasets containing list of popular fake news articles from 2016. However, these datasets only contain webpage links of these articles and most of them don't exist anymore. Fake news challenge, 2017[3] released a fake news dataset for stance detection, i.e, identifying whether a particular news headline represents the content of news article, but almost 80% of the dataset does not meet the definition that we are following in our work. Many of the articles were satire or personal opinions which cannot be flagged as *intentionally deceiving the public*. (Wang, 2017) released a benchmark dataset containing manually labelled 12, 836 short statements, however it contains short statements by famous personalities and not malicious false stories about certain events that we are interested in. Finally, the dataset created by using BS detector[4] contains articles annotated by news veracity detector tool and hence, cannot be trusted, as the labels are not verified manually and there are many anomalies like movie or food reviews being flagged as fake.

In this paper, we overcome these issues by manually selecting popular fake and questionable stories about US politics during Aug-Nov, 2016. The corpus has been designed in such a way that the writing style matches mainstream articles. In the following sections, we define our motivation for creating such corpus, provide details on it and present a classification model trained on this corpus to segregate articles based on writing style. We also discuss properties of fake news articles that we observed while developing this corpus.

Other notable works like FEVER dataset (Thorne et al., 2018), TwoWingOS (Yin and Roth, 2018) etc. are focused on claim extraction and verification which is currently out of scope of this paper. In this work, we are solely focused on creating a clean corpus for fake news articles and performing classification of articles into "question-

able" and "mainstream" based on writing style. Fact checking, fake news opinion mining and fake claim extraction and verification fall under future work of this paper. For classification task, previous works include Potthast et al. who used stylometric approach on Buzzfeed dataset and achieved an F1 score of 0.41; Pérez-Rosas et al. who used Amazon Mechanical Turk to manually generate fake news based on real news content and achieved an F1 score of 0.76 to detect fake news, and Ruchansky et al. who used Twitter and Weibo datasets and achieved F1 scores of 0.89 and 0.95 on respective datasets. In our work, we were able to achieve an F1 score of 0.97 on the corpus we have created, hence setting benchmark for the writing-style based classification task on this corpus.

3 Motivation

Fake news detection is a complicated topic fraught with many difficulties such as freedom of expression, confirmation bias and different types of dissemination techniques. In addition to these, there are three more ambiguities that one needs to overcome to create an unbiased automated fake news detector - 1. harmless teenagers writing false stories for monetary gains[5]; 2. AI tools generating believable articles[6] and; 3. mainstream channels publishing unverifiable stories[7]. Considering these elements, our motivation for this problem is to design a system with the focus on understanding the inference of the assertions, automatically fact check and explain the users why a particular article was tagged as questionable by the system. In order to do so, our first priority was to create an efficient corpus for this task. As we will see in the following sections, we have manually selected the articles that contain malicious assertions about a particular topic (2016 US elections), written with an intent of inciting hatred towards a particular entity of the society. The uniqueness of the articles in this corpus lies in the fact that a reader might believe them if not specifically informed about them being fake, hence confusing them whether the article was written by mainstream media or fake news

---

[2]https://www.buzzfeednews.com/article/craigsilverman/these-are-50-of-the-biggest-fake-news-hits-on-facebook-in

[3]http://www.fakenewschallenge.org/

[4]https://www.kaggle.com/mrisdal/fake-news/data/

[5]https://www.wired.com/2017/02/veles-macedonia-fake-news/

[6]https://www.technologyreview.com/s/612960/an-ai-tool-auto-generates-fake-news-bogus-tweets-and-plenty-of-gibberish/

[7]https://indianexpress.com/article/cities/delhi/retract-reports-that-claim-najeeb-is-isis-sympathiser-delhi-hc-to-media-5396414/

channel. This uniqueness will ultimately help in creating a detector which is not biased towards mainstream news articles on the same topic (2016 elections in this case.)

4 Corpus

4.1 Creation and Verification

The final corpus consists of 26 known fake articles from Stanford's dataset along with 679 questionable articles taken from BS detector's kaggle dataset. All the articles are in English and talk about 2016 US presidential elections. We, first, went through the Stanford's list of fake articles links and found the webpages that still exist. We then picked the first 50-70 assertive sentences from these articles. After that, we read the articles from BS detector's kaggle dataset and selected those articles which are written in a very compelling way and succeeded in making us believe its information. We then manually verified the claims made by these articles by doing simple Google searches and categorized them as shown in Table - 1. Based on the type of assertions, we have come up with two types of labels:

Primary Label: based on the assertions they make, articles are divided into 3 categories: 1. False but compelling (innovated lies having journalistic style of writing); 2. Half baked information i.e, partial truth (manipulating true events to suit agenda); and 3. Opinions/commentary presented as facts (written in a third person narrative with no disclaimer of the story being a personal opinion).

Secondary Label: is of 2 types: 1. articles extracted from Stanford's dataset have been tagged as *fake* as per their own description and; 2. articles taken from kaggle dataset are tagged as *questionable*. We believe tagging something fake, when they do contain some elements of truth, will be an extreme measure and we leave this task to the experts.

Finally, the corpus was cleaned by removing articles with first person narrative; removing images and video links and keeping only textual content; removing tweets, hyperlinks and other gibberish like *Read additional information here, [MORE], [CLICK HERE]* etc.

4.2 Analysis

Features: We used NLTK package to explore basic features of the content of news articles in terms

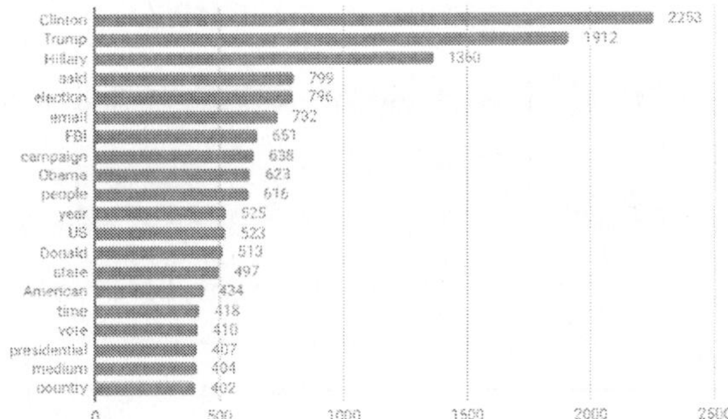

Figure 2: Top 20 most common keywords

of sentence count, word count etc. Number of assertions ranges from 2 to 124 with word count varying from 74-1430. Maximum number of stop words in the longest article is 707. Since keywords form an important representation of the dataset, we extracted top 20 most common keywords from the corpus as shown in Figure - 2.

Comparison with mainstream article: Mainstream articles from publishers like New York Times were extracted from *all the news*[8] kaggle dataset, which contains news articles from 15 US mainstream publishers. We selected articles from Oct - Nov, 2016 covering US politics during the time of election. There were total 6679 articles retrieved from this dataset which were then categorized into two labels as per our corpus's schema. Table - 2 compares characteristics of top 3 sentences from mainstream news articles with our corpus. We can observe that there are not many dissimilarities except the information presented in both the articles.

Observed Characteristics: Although articles in our corpus have many similarities with mainstream articles, there are some underlying patterns that can be noticed by reading all of them together at once. Following are the observations that we made while verifying the claims presented in these articles.

1. All of the news articles were trying to create sympathy for a particular entity by manipulating real stories. They were either trying to sympathize with Donald Trump by mentioning media rhetoric against him, or with Hillary Clinton by mentioning Trump's past.

2. Similarly, they also made false claims against above mentioned entities, by referring leaked

---

[8]https://www.kaggle.com/snapcrack/all-the-news

URL	Authors	Content	Headline	Primary Label	Secondary Label
URL of article	Can contain anonymous writers	Collection of assertions	Headline of the article	1. False 2. Partial truth 3. Opinions	1. Fake 2. Questionable

Table 1: Corpus schema. No cleaning has been performed on headlines as they are intentionally made catchy for attention seeking.

Attributes	Mainstream	Questionable
Word count range (min to max)	20-100	21-100
Character count range (min to max)	89-700	109-691
Uppercase words count range (min to max)	0-14	0-8
Mainstream Example	WASHINGTON - An exhausted Iraqi Army faces daunting obstacles on the battlefield that will most likely delay for months a major offensive on the Islamic State stronghold of Mosul, American and allied officials say. The delay is expected despite American efforts to keep Iraqs creaky war machine on track. Although President Obama vowed to end the United States role in the war in Iraq, in the last two years the American military has increasingly provided logistics to prop up the Iraqi military, which has struggled to move basics like food, water and ammunition to its troops.	
Questionable Example	WASHINGTON - Hillary Clinton is being accused of knowingly allowing American weapons into the hands of ISIS terrorists. Weapons that Hillary Clinton sent off to Qatar ostensibly designed to give to the rebels in Libya eventually made their way to Syria to assist the overthrow of the Assad regime. The folks fighting against Assad were ISIS and al-Qaeda jihadists.	

Table 2: Comparing basic features of top 3 sentences from mainstream articles and questionable articles.

documents from WikiLeaks or other similar sources. In our verification, we found that in most of these articles, only few claims matched the leaked story and rest were invented.

3. Articles first tell false stories against a certain entity and then asks the reader questions such as "Do you think mainstream media is conspiring against you by hiding this story?", "Do you think Google is making algorithms to create an illusion of reality?" After asking such questions, they either leave the reader hanging in contemplation or ask them to "share [the article] if you believe so."

4. The above point then leads to what (Nyhan and Reifler, 2010) describes as *backfire effect* in which correcting readers actually makes them believe false stories.

5. Fake news writers have learnt/are learning to use mainstream writing style such as, mentioning city name before starting the article, mentioning abbreviations like (SC) for Security Council, (AI) for Amnesty Investor, using elaborate vocabulary etc.

Split	Random		K-Fold	
	Questionable (1)	Mainstream (0)	Questionable (1)	Mainstream (0)
Train	406	5334	396	5343
Test	90	1345	100	1336

Table 3: To meet the real world scenario, train data and test data have been split with an approximate ratio of 1:10.

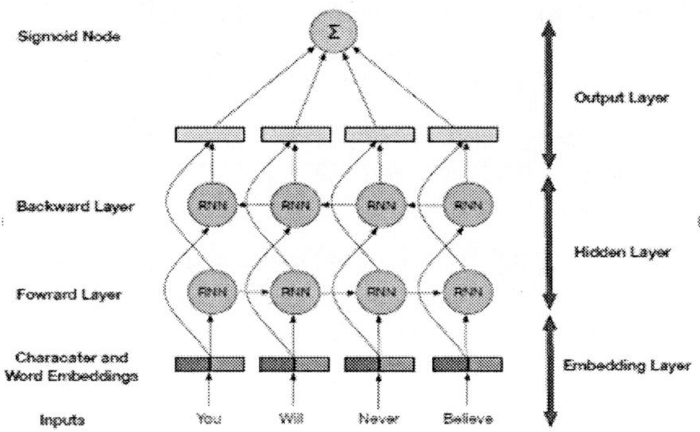

Figure 3: Bi-directional architecture

5 Classification Task

5.1 Model

After creating this corpus, we trained a classification model on the content to see if it can learn any writing patterns which are not visible to human eye and create benchmark results. Our model, as shown in Figure - 3, is inspired by the works of (Anand et al., 2016) and uses bi-directional LSTM and character embedding to classify articles into questionable (1) and mainstream (0) by learning writing style. We have not performed any pre-processing like removing punctuation, stop words etc. to make sure the model learns every context of the content. 1-D CNN has been used to create character embedding which has been proven to be very efficient in learning orthographic and morphological features of text (Zhang et al., 2015). This layer takes one-hot vector of each character and uses filter size of [196, 196, 300]. We have used 3 layers of 1-D CNN with pool size 2 and kernel stride of 3. Finally, we have performed maxpooling across the sequence to identify features that produces strong sentiments. This layer is then connected to bi-directional LSTM which contains one forward and one backward layer with 128 units each.

This model was trained with top 3 sentences, containing 20-100 words, and retrieved from total 7175 articles. As per the example shown in Table - 2, it can be assumed that top 3 sentences are enough for a normal reader to understand what the article is talking about. Dataset splitting for training and testing was inspired by the findings in the study conducted by (Guess et al., 2019) of Princeton and NYU earlier this year which stated that Americans who shared false stories during 2016 Presidential elections were far more likely to be over 65. Current US age demographic suggests that 15% of the population are over 65 [9]. Therefore, we have decided to have the ratio of questionable to mainstream news articles approximately 1:10, as shown in Table - 3.

5.2 Training and Results

We first trained our model by randomly splitting our dataset into training, validation and test set of sizes 4592, 1148 and 1435 respectively. However, since the dataset is unbalanced, stratified k-fold cross-validation mechanism is also implemented with 5 folds. (Kohavi, 1995) states that stratification, which ensures that each fold represents the entire dataset, is generally a better scheme both in terms of bias and variance. The model was trained on an average number of $2, 296, 000$ characters. We have evaluated our models on various metrics as shown in Figure - 4. For this problem, we will be majorly focused on ROC and F1 scores. In both the cases, stratified k-fold outperforms random sampling significantly. Training with only random sampling resulted into under-representation of data points leading to many false positives. This can also be because writing style of questionable and mainstream articles are very similar. On the other hand, 5-fold cross validation performed significantly well in learning the patterns and avoiding the problems of false positives.

---

[9]https://www.census.gov/quickfacts/fact/table/US/PST045217

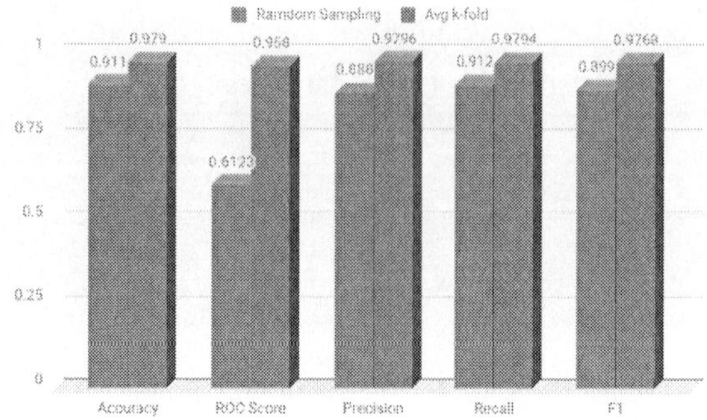

Figure 4: Evaluation results of our model over various metrics. Performance of model using Stratified K-Fold is exceptionally good in terms of ROC score and F1 score.

6 Conclusion

In this paper, we have introduced a novel corpus of articles containing false assertions which are written in a very compelling way. We explain how this corpus is different from previously published datasets and explore the characteristics of the corpus. Finally, we use a deep learning classification model to learn the invisible contextual patterns of the content and produce benchmark results on this dataset. Our best model was able to achieve state of the art ROC score of 97%. This is a work in progress and we are planning to extend this corpus by adding more topics and metadata. Future work also involves claim extraction and verification which can be further used to design an unbiased automated detector of intentionally written false stories.

7 Acknowledgement

I would like to extend my gratitude to my doctorate advisor, Dr. Rohini K. Srihari, for taking interest into my work and guiding me into the right direction. I would also like to thank my mentor assigned by ACL-SRW, Arkaitz Zubiaga, and anonymous reviewers for their invaluable suggestions and comments on this paper.

References

Hunt Allcott and Matthew Gentzkow. 2017. Social media and fake news in the 2016 election. *Journal of economic perspectives*, 31(2):211–36.

Ankesh Anand, Tanmoy Chakraborty, and Noseong Park. 2016. We used neural networks to detect clickbaits: You won't believe what happened next! *CoRR*, abs/1612.01340.

Andrew Guess, Jonathan Nagler, and Joshua Tucker. 2019. Less than you think: Prevalence and predictors of fake news dissemination on facebook. *Science Advances*, 5(1).

Ron Kohavi. 1995. A study of cross-validation and bootstrap for accuracy estimation and model selection. In *Proceedings of the 14th International Joint Conference on Artificial Intelligence - Volume 2*, IJCAI'95, pages 1137–1143, San Francisco, CA, USA. Morgan Kaufmann Publishers Inc.

Brendan Nyhan and Jason Reifler. 2010. When corrections fail: The persistence of political misperceptions. *Political Behavior*, 32(2):303–330.

Verónica Pérez-Rosas, Bennett Kleinberg, Alexandra Lefevre, and Rada Mihalcea. 2017. Automatic detection of fake news. *CoRR*, abs/1708.07104.

Martin Potthast, Johannes Kiesel, Kevin Reinartz, Janek Bevendorff, and Benno Stein. 2017. A stylometric inquiry into hyperpartisan and fake news. *CoRR*, abs/1702.05638.

Natali Ruchansky, Sungyong Seo, and Yan Liu. 2017. CSI: A hybrid deep model for fake news. *CoRR*, abs/1703.06959.

James Thorne, Andreas Vlachos, Christos Christodoulopoulos, and Arpit Mittal. 2018. FEVER: a large-scale dataset for fact extraction and verification. *CoRR*, abs/1803.05355.

Soroush Vosoughi, Deb Roy, and Sinan Aral. 2018. The spread of true and false news online. *Science*, 359(6380):1146–1151.

William Yang Wang. 2017. "liar, liar pants on fire": A new benchmark dataset for fake news detection. *CoRR*, abs/1705.00648.

Claire Wardle and Hossein Derakhshan. 2017. Information disorder: Toward an interdisciplinary framework for research and policy making. *Council of Europe report, DGI (2017)*, 9.

Wenpeng Yin and Dan Roth. 2018. Twowingos: A two-wing optimization strategy for evidential claim verification. *CoRR*, abs/1808.03465.

Xiang Zhang, Junbo Zhao, and Yann LeCun. 2015. Character-level convolutional networks for text classification. In C. Cortes, N. D. Lawrence, D. D. Lee, M. Sugiyama, and R. Garnett, editors, *Advances in Neural Information Processing Systems 28*, pages 649–657. Curran Associates, Inc.

Cross-domain and Cross-lingual Abusive Language Detection: a Hybrid Approach with Deep Learning and a Multilingual Lexicon

Endang Wahyu Pamungkas, Viviana Patti
Dipartimento di Informatica
University of Turin, Italy
{pamungka,patti}@di.unito.it

Abstract

The development of computational methods to detect abusive language in social media within variable and multilingual contexts has recently gained significant traction. The growing interest is confirmed by the large number of benchmark corpora for different languages developed in the latest years. However, abusive language behaviour is multifaceted and available datasets are featured by different topical focuses. This makes abusive language detection a domain-dependent task, and building a robust system to detect general abusive content a first challenge. Moreover, most resources are available for English, which makes detecting abusive language in low-resource languages a further challenge. We address both challenges by considering ten publicly available datasets across different domains and languages. A hybrid approach with deep learning and a multilingual lexicon to cross-domain and cross-lingual detection of abusive content is proposed and compared with other simpler models. We show that training a system on general abusive language datasets will produce a cross-domain robust system, which can be used to detect other more specific types of abusive content. We also found that using the domain-independent lexicon HurtLex is useful to transfer knowledge between domains and languages. In the cross-lingual experiment, we demonstrate the effectiveness of our joint-learning model also in out-domain scenarios.

1 Introduction

Detecting online abusive language in social media messages is gaining increasing attention from scholars and stakeholders, such as governments, social media platforms and citizens. The spread of online abusive content negatively affects the targeted victims, has a chilling effect on the democratic discourse on social networking platforms and negatively impacts those who speak for freedom and non-discrimination. *Abusive language* is usually used as an umbrella term (Waseem et al., 2017), covering several sub-categories, such as cyberbullying (Van Hee et al., 2015; Sprugnoli et al., 2018), hate speech (Waseem and Hovy, 2016; Davidson et al., 2017), toxic comments (Wulczyn et al., 2017), offensive language (Zampieri et al., 2019a) and online aggression (Kumar et al., 2018). Several datasets have been proposed having different topical focuses and specific targets, e.g., misogyny or racism. This diversity makes the task to detect general abusive language difficult. Some studies attempted to bridge some of these subtasks by proposing cross-domain classification of abusive content (Wiegand et al., 2018a; Karan and Šnajder, 2018; Waseem et al., 2018).

Another prominent challenge in abusive language detection is the multilinguality issue. Even if in the last year abusive language datasets were developed for other languages, including Italian (Bosco et al., 2018; Fersini et al., 2018b), Spanish (Fersini et al., 2018b), and German (Wiegand et al., 2018b), most studies so far focused on English. Since most popular social media such as Twitter and Facebook goes multilingual, fostering their users to interact in their primary language, there is a considerable urgency to develop a robust approach for abusive language detection in a multilingual environment, also for guaranteeing a better compliance to governments demands for counteracting the phenomenon (see, e.g., the recently issued EU commission *Code of Conduct on countering illegal hate speech online* (EU Commission, 2016). Cross-lingual classification is an approach to transfer knowledge from resource-rich languages to resource-poor ones. It has been applied to sentiment analysis (Zhou et al., 2016), a related task to abusive language detection. However, there is still not much work focused on cross-

Proceedings of the ACL 2019, Student Research Workshop, pages 363–370
Florence, Italy, July 28th-August 2nd, 2019. ©2019 Association for Computational Linguistics

Dataset	Label	Language	Topical Focus	Train	Test	PIR
Harassment (Golbeck et al., 2017)	**H - harassing,** N - non-harassing	EN	Harassing content, including racist and misogynistic contents, offensive profanities and threats	14,252	6,108	0.26
Waseem (Waseem and Hovy, 2016)	**racism, sexism,** none	EN	Racism and Sexism	11,542	4,947	0.31
OffensEval (Zampieri et al., 2019b)	**OFF - offensive,** NOT - not offensive	EN	Offensive content, including insults, threats, and posts containing profane language or swear words	13,240	860	0.33
HatEval (Basile et al., 2019)	**1 - hateful,** 0 - not hateful	EN, ES	Hate speech against women and immigrants	9,000 (EN) 4,500 (ES)	2,971 (EN) 1,600 (ES)	0.42 0.41
AMI Evalita (Fersini et al., 2018a)	**1 - misogynous,** 0 - not misogynous	EN, IT	Misogynous content	4,000 (EN) 4,000 (IT)	1,000 (EN) 1,000 (IT)	0.45 0.47
AMI IberEval (Fersini et al., 2018b)	**1 - misogynous,** 0 - not misogynous	EN, ES	Misogynous content	3,251 (EN) 3,307 (ES)	726 (EN) 831 (ES)	0.47 0.50
GermEval (Wiegand et al., 2018b)	**offensive,** other	DE	Offensive content, including insults, abuse, and profanity	5,009	3,532	0.34

Table 1: Twitter abusive language datasets in four languages: original labels, language(s) featured, topical focus, distribution of train and test set and positive instance rate (PIR).

lingual abusive language classification.

In this study, we conduct an extensive experiment to explore cross-domain and cross-lingual abusive language classification in social media data, by proposing a hybrid approach with deep learning and a multilingual lexicon. We exploit several available Twitter datasets in different domains and languages. We present three main contributions in this work. First, we characterize the available datasets as capturing various phenomena related to abusive language, and investigate this characterization in cross-domain classification. Second, we explored the use of a domain-independent, multilingual lexicon of abusive words called *HurtLex* (Bassignana et al., 2018) in both cross-domain and cross-lingual settings. Last, we take advantage of the availability of multilingual word embeddings to build a joint-learning approach in the cross-lingual setting. All code and resources are available at `https://github.com/dadangewp/ACL19-SRW`.

2 Related Work

Some work has been done in the cross-domain classification of abusive language. Wiegand et al. (2018a) proposed to use high-level features by combining several linguistic features and lexicons of abusive words in the cross-domain classification of abusive microposts from different sources. Waseem et al. (2018) use multi-task learning for domain transfer in a cross-domain hate speech detection task. Recently, Karan and Šnajder (2018) also addressed cross-domain classification in several abusive language datasets, testing the framework of Frustratingly Simple Domain Adaptation (FEDA) (Daume III, 2007) to transfer knowledge between domains.

Meanwhile, cross-lingual abusive language detection has not been explored yet by NLP scholars. We only found a few works describing participating systems developed for recent shared tasks on the identification of misogynous (Basile and Rubagotti, 2018) and offensive language (van der Goot et al., 2018), where some experiment in a cross-lingual setting is proposed. Basile and Rubagotti (2018) used the *bleaching* approach (van der Goot et al., 2018) to conduct cross-lingual experiments between Italian and English when participating to the automatic misogyny identification task at EVALITA 2018 (Fersini et al., 2018a). Schneider et al. (2018) used multilingual embeddings in a cross-lingual experiment related to GermEval 2018 (Wiegand et al., 2018b).

3 Data

We consider ten different publicly abusive language datasets and benchmark corpora from shared tasks. Some shared tasks (HatEval, AMI Evalita and AMI IberEval) provided data in two languages. Table 1 summarizes the datasets' characteristics. We binarize the label of these datasets into abusive (bold) and not-abusive. For the cross-lingual experiments, we include datasets from four languages: English, Italian, Spanish, and German. We split all datasets into training and testing by keeping the original split when provided, and splitting the distribution randomly (70% for training and 30% for testing) otherwise.

Dataset		LSVC + BoW				LSVC + BoW + HL				LSTM + WE				LSTM + WE + HL			
Test	Train	P	R	F_1	Δ	P	R	F_1	Δ	P	R	F_1	Δ	P	R	F_1	Δ
Harassment	Waseem	.325	.233	.271	.103	.337	.264	.296	.079	.291	.467	.359	.033	.290	.524	**.373**	.045
	HatEval	.389	.119	.183	.191	.374	.116	.177	.198	.341	.308	.324	.068	.332	.379	**.354**	.064
	OffensEval	.320	.508	.393	-.019	.322	.516	.396	-.021	.333	.443	.380	.012	.314	.567	**.404**	.014
	Harassment	.547	.284	.374		.540	.288	.375		.510	.319	.392		.464	.380	.418	
Waseem	Harassment	.729	.022	.043	.688	.720	.034	.065	.669	.464	.111	.179	.587	.491	.149	**.229**	.520
	HatEval	.620	.109	.186	.545	.672	.113	.194	.540	.496	.213	.299	.467	.453	.318	**.374**	.375
	OffensEval	.461	.390	**.422**	.309	.453	.391	.420	.314	.444	.282	.345	.421	.419	.411	.415	.334
	Waseem	.817	.662	.731		.819	.665	.734		.760	.771	.766		.711	.790	.749	
HatEval	Harassment	.485	.181	.264	.339	.513	.229	.317	.290	.523	.308	.387	.216	.514	.394	**.446**	.158
	Waseem	.505	.490	.497	.106	.477	.558	.514	.093	.481	.636	**.548**	.055	.494	.609	.546	.058
	OffensEval	.450	.646	.531	.072	.451	.656	.534	.073	.452	.603	.516	.087	.457	.704	**.554**	.050
	HatEval	.449	.919	.603		.453	.919	.607		.444	.939	.603		.441	.955	.604	
OffensEval	Harassment	.301	.104	.155	.422	.321	.113	.167	.406	.525	.133	.213	.395	.406	.179	**.249**	.349
	Waseem	.440	.246	.316	.261	.462	.254	**.328**	.245	.403	.225	.289	.319	.400	.175	.244	.354
	HatEval	.372	.225	.281	.296	.381	.233	.289	.284	.392	.371	.381	.227	.371	.529	**.436**	.162
	OffensEval	.616	.542	.577		.626	.529	.573		.667	.558	.608		.551	.654	.598	

Table 2: Results on cross-domain abusive language identification (only in English).

We also provide further information about the captured phenomena of every dataset. Based on this information, we can compare the nature and topical focus of the dataset, which potentially affect the cross-domain experimental results. Some datasets have a broader coverage than the others, focussing on more general phenomena, such as OffensEval (Zampieri et al., 2019b), and GermEval (Wiegand et al., 2018b). However, there are also some shared phenomena between datasets, such as racism and sexism in Waseem (Waseem and Hovy, 2016) and HatEval (Basile et al., 2019). AMI datasets contain the most specific phenomenon, only focusing on misogyny. The positive instance rate (PIR) denotes the ratio of abusive instances to all instances of the dataset.

4   Cross-domain Classification

In this experiment, we investigate the performance of machine learning classifiers which are trained on a particular dataset and tested on different datasets ones. We focus on investigating the influence of captured phenomena coverage between datasets. We hypothesize that a classifier which is trained on a broader coverage dataset and tested on narrower coverage dataset will give better performance than the opposite. Furthermore, we analyse the impact of using the HurtLex lexicon (Bassignana et al., 2018) to transfer knowledge between domains. HurtLex is a multilingual lexicon of hate words, originally built from 1,082 Italian hate words compiled in a manual fashion by the linguist Tullio De Mauro (De Mauro, 2016). This lexicon is semi-automatically extended and translated into 53 languages by using BabelNet (Navigli and Ponzetto, 2012), and the lexical items are divided into 17 categories such as homophobic slurs, ethnic slurs, genitalia, cognitive and physical disabilities, animals and more[1].

Model. In this experiment, we employ two models. First, we exploit a simple traditional machine learning approach by using linear support vector classifier (LSVC) with unigram representation as a feature. Second, we utilize a long short-term memory (LSTM) neural model consisting of several layers, starting with a word embedding layer (32-dimensions) without any pre-trained model initialization[2]. This embedding layer is followed by LSTM networks (16-units), whose output is passed to a dense layer with ReLU activation function and dropout (0.4). The last section is a dense layer with sigmoid activation to produce the final prediction. We experiment with HurtLex by concatenating its 17 categories as one hot encoding representation to both LSVC-based and LSTM-based systems.

Data and Evaluation We use four English datasets, namely Harassment, Waseem, HatEval, and OffensEval [3]. We evaluate the system performance based on precision, recall, and F-score on the positive class (abusive class).

Results. Table 2 shows the results of the cross-domain experiment. We test every dataset with three systems which are trained on three other datasets. We also run in-domain scenario to compare the delta between in-domain and out-domain performance and measure the drop in per-

---

[1]http://hatespeech.di.unito.it/resources.html

[2]We experimented the use of pre-trained models (i.e. GloVe, word2vec, and FastText), but the result is lower compared to a self-trained model based on training set.

[3]AMI datasets are excluded due to the low number of instances.

formance. Not surprisingly, the performance on out-domain datasets is always lower (except in two cases when the Harassment dataset is used as test set). Overall, LSTM-based systems performed better than LSVC-based systems. The use of HurtLex also succeeded in improving the performance on both LSVC-based and LSTM-based systems. We can see that HurtLex is able to improve the recall in most of the cases. Our further investigation shows that systems with HurtLex are able to detect more abusive contents, noted by the increases of true positives. The OffensEval training set always achieves the best performance when tested on three other datasets. On the other hand, the Harassment dataset always presents the larger drop in performance when used as training data. Training the models on the Harassment dataset lead to a very low result even in the in-domain setting. The highest result on the Harassment dataset is only .418 F-score, achieved by LSTM with HurtLex [4], while when trained on the other datasets our models are able to reach above .600 F-score. Upon further investigation, we found, that Golbeck et al. (2017) only used a limited set of keywords, which contributes to limit their dataset coverage. Overall, we argue that there are good arguments in favor of our hypothesis that a system trained on datasets with a broader coverage of phenomena will be more robust to detect other kinds of abusive language (see the OffensEval results).

5   Cross-lingual Classification

We aim to experiment with cross-lingual abusive language classification. As far as our knowledge goes, there is still no work which focuses on investigating the feasibility of cross-lingual classification in the abusive language area. We will explore two scenarios, in-domain and out-domain classification, in four different languages, namely English, Spanish, Italian, and German. Again, we will test HurtLex in this experiment.

Model. We build four systems for each in-domain and out-domain experiments. One system of each scenario is built based on LSVC with unigram features, while three other systems are built based on a LSTM architecture. Here we describe three systems which are based on LSTM:

(a). **LSTM + WE.** First, we exploit LSTM with

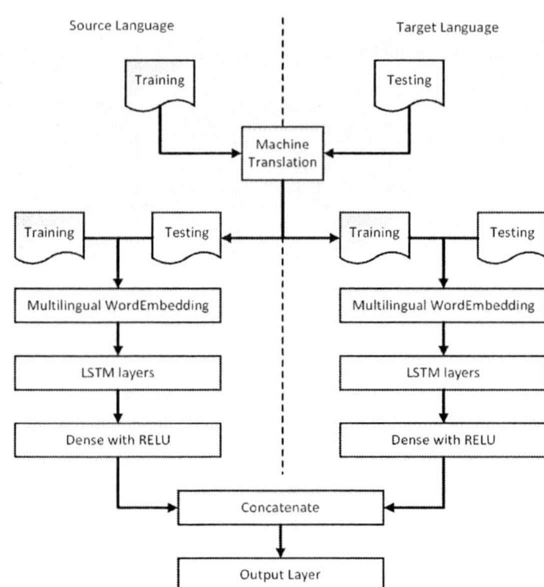

Figure 1: Joint-learning model architecture.

monolingual word embedding. We adopt a similar model as in cross-domain classification where we use machine translation (Google Translate[5]) to translate training data from source to target language. In this model, we use pre-trained word embedding from FastText[6].

(b). **JL + ME.** We also propose a joint-learning model with multilingual word embedding. We take advantage of the availability of multilingual word embeddings[7] to build a joint-learning model. Figure 1 summarize how the data is transformed and learned in this model. We create bilingual training data automatically by using Google Translate to translate the data in both directions (training from source to target language and testing from target to source language), then using it as training data for the two LSTM-based architectures (similar architecture of the model in cross-domain experiment). We concatenate these two architectures before the output layer, which produces the final prediction. In the, we expect to reduce some of the noise from the translation while keeping the original structure of the training set.

---

[4]Marwa et al. (2018) claimed to get a higher result, but that paper did not give a complete information about system configuration they used.

[5]http://translate.google.com/
[6]https://fasttext.cc/
[7]https://github.com/facebookresearch/MUSE

Dataset		LSVC + BoW				LSTM + WE				JL + ME			JL + ME + HL		
Test	Train	P	R	F_1	Δ	P	R	F_1	Δ	P	R	F_1	P	R	F_1
EN-Evalita	IT-Evalita	.491	.739	.590	.004	.479	.824	.605	.019	.480	.935	**.635**	.501	.761	.605
	ES-IberEval	.561	.704	.624	-.030	.551	.615	.581	.081	.550	.711	.620	.543	.763	**.635**
	EN-Evalita	.557	.637	.594		.518	.917	.662		-	-	-	-	-	-
IT-Evalita	EN-Evalita	.209	.125	.156	.698	.179	.129	.150	.682	.453	.520	.484	.491	.502	**.497**
	ES-IberEval	.611	.611	.611	.243	.583	.287	.385	.447	.698	.387	.506	.666	.654	**.660**
	IT-Evalita	.786	.934	.854		.714	.996	.832		-	-	-	-	-	-
ES-IberEval	EN-Evalita	.640	.545	.589	.151	.524	.829	.642	.118	.627	.721	.670	.604	.798	**.687**
	IT-Evalita	.575	.528	.550	.190	.474	.455	.464	.296	.587	.636	.610	.586	.696	**.637**
	ES-IberEval	.739	.742	.740		.761	.759	.760		-	-	-	-	-	-

Table 3: Results on in-domain (AMI) cross-lingual abusive language identification (EN, ES,IT).

Dataset		LSVC + BoW				LSTM + WE				JL + ME			JL + ME + HL		
Test	Train	P	R	F_1	Δ	P	R	F_1	Δ	P	R	F_1	P	R	F_1
EN-Waseem	ES-HatEval	.498	.353	.413	.318	.519	.524	.522	.244	.591	.414	.487	.532	.523	**.528**
	IT-Evalita	.470	.248	.325	.406	.481	.199	.282	.484	.497	.156	.238	.566	.311	**.401**
	DE-GermEval	.547	.323	.406	.325	.505	.388	**.439**	.327	.545	.182	.273	.350	.456	.396
	EN-Waseem	.817	.662	.731		.760	.771	.766		-	-	-	-	-	-
ES-HatEval	EN-Waseem	.464	.286	.354	.308	.489	.323	.389	.284	.332	.708	**.452**	.426	.351	.384
	IT-Evalita	.517	.234	.323	.239	.620	.443	.517	.156	.626	.506	.559	.602	.647	**.623**
	DE-GermEval	.495	.429	.459	.203	.450	.503	.475	.198	.510	.341	.409	.516	.446	**.478**
	ES-HatEval	.606	.730	.662		.615	.744	.673		-	-	-	-	-	-
IT-Evalita	EN-Waseem	.311	.700	.431	.423	.300	.709	.422	.410	.306	.836	**.448**	.301	.743	.428
	ES-HatEval	.502	.538	.519	.335	.424	.724	.534	.298	.439	.829	**.574**	.462	.724	.564
	DE-GermEval	.569	.268	.364	.490	.486	.377	.425	.407	.369	.730	.490	.593	.590	**.592**
	IT-Evalita	.786	.934	.854		.714	.996	.832		-	-	-	-	-	-
DE-GermEval	EN-Waseem	.442	.178	.254	.196	.421	.189	.261	.311	.436	.136	.208	.456	.188	**.266**
	ES-HatEval	.438	.254	.321	.129	.398	.607	.481	.091	.361	.726	**.482**	.395	.359	.377
	IT-Evalita	.371	.656	.474	-.024	.369	.730	.490	.082	.362	.862	**.510**	.354	.909	.509
	DE-GermEval	.578	.369	.450		.799	.446	.572		-	-	-	-	-	-

Table 4: Results on out-domain cross-lingual abusive language identification (EN, ES, IT, DE).

(c). **JL + ME + HL.** Finally, we also experiment the use of HurtLex in our joint-learning model, by simply concatenating its representation into both LSTM model in source and target language.

Dataset and Evaluation We use the AMI datasets (with topical focus on misogyny identification) for the in-domain experiment, in three languages, i.e. English (EN-Evalita), Spanish (ES-Ibereval), and Italian (IT-Evalita). For English, we decide to use the Evalita one due to its larger size. For the out-domain experiment, we use Waseem (EN), HatEval (ES), AMI-Evalita (IT-Evalita in the table, IT), and GermEval (DE). We use precision, recall, and F-score in positive class as evaluation metric.

Results. Table 3 shows the results of the in-domain experiments, while out-domain results can be seen in Table 4. For the in-domain experiment, our joint-learning based systems are able to outperform two other systems based on LSVC and LSTM with monolingual embeddings. Furthermore, HurtLex succeeded to improve the system performance, except when systems are tested on English datasets. LSCV models were outperformed by deep learning-based systems in the out-domain experiment. Our joint-learning based sys-

tem always gives the best performance on all settings (except when trained on GermEval and tested on Waseem, where LSTM with monolingual embeddings performs better). HurtLex is only able to improve 7 out of 12 results based on F-score, where in most cases it succeeds to improve the recall. This result is consistent with in cross-domain experiments in Section 3. The out-domain results are generally lower than in-domain ones. A lot of variables could influence the difficulty of the out-domain scenario, which calls for deeper investigations. Some of them are discussed in Section 6.

6 Discussion

We discuss some of the challenges which contribute to make the cross-domain and cross-lingual abusive language detection tasks difficult. In particular we will focus on some issues related to the presence of swear words in these kinds of texts.

The different uses of swear words. As described in Section 3, the datasets we considered have different focuses w.r.t. the abusive phenomena captured, and this impacts on the lexical distribution in each dataset. Based on a further analysis we observed that in datasets with a general topical focus such as OffensEval, the abusive tweets are marked by some common swear words such as "fuck", "shit", and "ass". While in datasets featured by a specific hate target, such as the AMI dataset (misogyny), the lexical keywords in abusive tweets are dominated by specific sexist slurs such as "bitch", "cunt", and "whore". This finding is consistent with the study of (ElSherief et al., 2018), which conducted an analysis on hate speech in social media based on its target. Furthermore, the pragmatics of swearing could also change from one dataset to another, depending on the topical features.

Translation issues. As we expected, the use of automatic machine translation (via Google Translate) in our pipeline can give rise to errors in the cross-lingual setting. In particular, we observed errors in translations from English to other languages (Italian and Spanish) on some swear words, which are usually important clues to detect abusive content. See for instance the following cases from the EN-AMI Evalita dataset:

> *Original tweet (EN):*
> Punch that girl right in the **skank**
> *Translated tweet (IT):*
> Pugno quella ragazza proprio nella **Skank**
>
> *Original tweet (EN):*
> Apparently, you can turn a **hoe** into a housewife
> *Translated tweet (ES):*
> Aparentemente, puedes convertir una **azada** en una ama de casa.

Translating swearing is indeed challenging. In the first example, Google Translate is unable to provide an Italian translation for the English word "skank" (a proper translation could be "sciacquetta" or "sciattona", which means "slut"). We found 134 occurrences of the word "skank" in EN-AMI Evalita and 185 in the EN-HatEval dataset. The second example shows, instead, a problem related to context and disambiguation issues. Indeed, the word "hoe" here is used informally in its derogatory sense, meaning *"A woman who engages in sexual intercourse for money"* (synonyms: slut, whore, floozy)[8]. But, disregarding the context, it is translated in Spanish by relying on a different conventional meaning (hoe as *agricultural and horticultural hand tool*). The term

---

[8] https://www.urbandictionary.com/define.php?term=Hoe

"hoe" is also very frequent in the EN-AMI Evalita (292 occurrences) and EN-HatEval dataset (348 occurrences).

7   Conclusion and Future Work

In this study, we conduct an exploratory experiment on abusive language detection in cross-domain and cross-lingual classification scenarios. We focus on social media data, exploiting several datasets across different domains and languages. Based on the cross-domain experiments, we found that training a system on datasets featured by more general abusive phenomena will produce a more robust system to detect other more specific kinds of abusive languages. We also observed that HurtLex is able to transfer knowledge between domains by improving the number of true positives. In the cross-lingual experiment, our joint-learning systems outperformed the other systems in most cases also in the out-domain setting. The results presented here succeed to shed some light regarding the issues and difficulties of this research direction. As future work, we aim at exploring more deeply the issue related to different coverage, topical focuses and abusive phenomena characterizing the datasets in this field, taking a semantic ontology-based approach to clearly represent the relations between concepts and linguistic phenomena involved. This will allow us to further explore and refine the idea that combining some datasets can produce a more robust system to detect abusive language across different domains. We also found that detecting out-domain abusive content cross-lingual is really challenging, and the use of domain-independent resources to transfer knowledge between domains and languages an interesting issue to be further explored. Finally, we will further investigate the different uses and contexts of swearing, which seems to play a key role in the abusive language detection task (Holgate et al., 2018), with impact also on experiments in cross-domain and cross-lingual settings.

Acknowledgements

We would like to deeply thank Valerio Basile for his valuable and useful feedback on earlier versions of this paper. The work of Endang W. Pamungkas and Viviana Patti was partially funded by Progetto di Ateneo/CSP 2016 (*Immigrants, Hate and Prejudice in Social Media*, S1618_L2_BOSC_01).

References

Angelo Basile and Chiara Rubagotti. 2018. Crotone-milano for AMI at evalita2018. A performant, cross-lingual misogyny detection system. In *Proceedings of the Sixth Evaluation Campaign of Natural Language Processing and Speech Tools for Italian. Final Workshop (EVALITA 2018) co-located with the Fifth Italian Conference on Computational Linguistics (CLiC-it 2018), Turin, Italy, December 12-13, 2018.*

Valerio Basile, Cristina Bosco, Elisabetta Fersini, Debora Nozza, Viviana Patti, Francisco Manuel Rangel Pardo, Paolo Rosso, and Manuela Sanguinetti. 2019. SemEval-2019 task 5: Multilingual detection of hate speech against immigrants and women in twitter. In *Proceedings of the 13th International Workshop on Semantic Evaluation*, pages 54–63, Minneapolis, Minnesota, USA. ACL.

Elisa Bassignana, Valerio Basile, and Viviana Patti. 2018. Hurtlex: A multilingual lexicon of words to hurt. In *Proceedings of the Fifth Italian Conference on Computational Linguistics (CLiC-it 2018), Torino, Italy, December 10-12, 2018.*

Cristina Bosco, Felice Dell'Orletta, Fabio Poletto, Manuela Sanguinetti, and Maurizio Tesconi. 2018. Overview of the EVALITA 2018 hate speech detection task. In *Proceedings of the Sixth Evaluation Campaign of Natural Language Processing and Speech Tools for Italian. Final Workshop (EVALITA 2018) co-located with the Fifth Italian Conference on Computational Linguistics (CLiC-it 2018), Turin, Italy, December 12-13, 2018.*, volume 2263 of *CEUR Workshop Proceedings*. CEUR-WS.org.

Hal Daume III. 2007. Frustratingly easy domain adaptation. In *Proceedings of the 45th Annual Meeting of the Association of Computational Linguistics*, pages 256–263, Prague, Czech Republic. Association for Computational Linguistics.

Thomas Davidson, Dana Warmsley, Michael W. Macy, and Ingmar Weber. 2017. Automated hate speech detection and the problem of offensive language. In *Proceedings of the Eleventh International Conference on Web and Social Media, ICWSM 2017, Montréal, Québec, Canada, May 15-18, 2017.*, pages 512–515. AAAI Press.

Tullio De Mauro. 2016. Le parole per ferire. *Internazionale*. 27 settembre 2016.

Mai ElSherief, Vivek Kulkarni, Dana Nguyen, William Yang Wang, and Elizabeth M. Belding. 2018. Hate lingo: A target-based linguistic analysis of hate speech in social media. In *Proceedings of the Twelfth International Conference on Web and Social Media, ICWSM 2018, Stanford, California, USA, June 25-28, 2018.*, pages 42–51. AAAI Press.

EU Commission. 2016. Code of conduct on countering illegal hate speech online.

Elisabetta Fersini, Debora Nozza, and Paolo Rosso. 2018a. Overview of the evalita 2018 task on automatic misogyny identification (AMI). In *Proceedings of the Sixth Evaluation Campaign of Natural Language Processing and Speech Tools for Italian. Final Workshop (EVALITA 2018) co-located with the Fifth Italian Conference on Computational Linguistics (CLiC-it 2018), Turin, Italy, December 12-13, 2018.*, volume 2263 of *CEUR Workshop Proceedings*. CEUR-WS.org.

Elisabetta Fersini, Paolo Rosso, and Maria Anzovino. 2018b. Overview of the task on automatic misogyny identification at ibereval 2018. In *Proceedings of the Third Workshop on Evaluation of Human Language Technologies for Iberian Languages (IberEval 2018) co-located with 34th Conference of the Spanish Society for Natural Language Processing (SEPLN 2018), Sevilla, Spain, September 18th, 2018.*, volume 2150 of *CEUR Workshop Proceedings*, pages 214–228. CEUR-WS.org.

Jennifer Golbeck, Zahra Ashktorab, Rashad O. Banjo, Alexandra Berlinger, Siddharth Bhagwan, Cody Buntain, Paul Cheakalos, Alicia A. Geller, Quint Gergory, Rajesh Kumar Gnanasekaran, Raja Rajan Gunasekaran, Kelly M. Hoffman, Jenny Hottle, Vichita Jienjitlert, Shivika Khare, Ryan Lau, Marianna J. Martindale, Shalmali Naik, Heather L. Nixon, Piyush Ramachandran, Kristine M. Rogers, Lisa Rogers, Meghna Sardana Sarin, Gaurav Shahane, Jayanee Thanki, Priyanka Vengataraman, Zijian Wan, and Derek Michael Wu. 2017. A large labeled corpus for online harassment research. In *Proceedings of the 2017 ACM on Web Science Conference, WebSci 2017, Troy, NY, USA, June 25 - 28, 2017*, pages 229–233. ACM.

Rob van der Goot, Nikola Ljubesic, Ian Matroos, Malvina Nissim, and Barbara Plank. 2018. Bleaching text: Abstract features for cross-lingual gender prediction. In *Proceedings of the 56th Annual Meeting of the Association for Computational Linguistics, ACL 2018, Melbourne, Australia, July 15-20, 2018, Volume 2: Short Papers*, pages 383–389. Association for Computational Linguistics.

Eric Holgate, Isabel Cachola, Daniel Preoţiuc-Pietro, and Junyi Jessy Li. 2018. Why swear? analyzing and inferring the intentions of vulgar expressions. In *Proceedings of the 2018 Conference on Empirical Methods in Natural Language Processing*, pages 4405–4414, Brussels, Belgium. Association for Computational Linguistics.

Mladen Karan and Jan Šnajder. 2018. Cross-domain detection of abusive language online. In *Proceedings of the 2nd Workshop on Abusive Language Online (ALW2)*, pages 132–137, Brussels, Belgium. Association for Computational Linguistics.

Ritesh Kumar, Atul Kr. Ojha, Shervin Malmasi, and Marcos Zampieri. 2018. Benchmarking aggression identification in social media. In *Proceedings of the*

First Workshop on Trolling, Aggression and Cyber-bullying (TRAC-2018)*, pages 1–11, Santa Fe, New Mexico, USA. Association for Computational Linguistics.

Tolba Marwa, Ouadfel Salima, and Meshoul Souham. 2018. Deep learning for online harassment detection in tweets. In *2018 3rd International Conference on Pattern Analysis and Intelligent Systems (PAIS)*, pages 1–5. IEEE.

Roberto Navigli and Simone Paolo Ponzetto. 2012. Babelnet: The automatic construction, evaluation and application of a wide-coverage multilingual semantic network. *Artificial Intelligence*, 193:217–250.

Julian Moreno Schneider, Roland Roller, Peter Bourgonje, Stefanie Hegele, and Georg Rehm. 2018. Towards the automatic classification of offensive language and related phenomena in german tweets. In *14th Conference on Natural Language Processing KONVENS 2018*, page 95.

Rachele Sprugnoli, Stefano Menini, Sara Tonelli, Filippo Oncini, and Enrico Piras. 2018. Creating a WhatsApp dataset to study pre-teen cyberbullying. In *Proceedings of the 2nd Workshop on Abusive Language Online (ALW2)*, pages 51–59, Brussels, Belgium. Association for Computational Linguistics.

Cynthia Van Hee, Els Lefever, Ben Verhoeven, Julie Mennes, Bart Desmet, Guy De Pauw, Walter Daelemans, and Veronique Hoste. 2015. Detection and fine-grained classification of cyberbullying events. In *Proceedings of the International Conference Recent Advances in Natural Language Processing*, pages 672–680, Hissar, Bulgaria. INCOMA Ltd. Shoumen, BULGARIA.

Zeerak Waseem, Thomas Davidson, Dana Warmsley, and Ingmar Weber. 2017. Understanding abuse: A typology of abusive language detection subtasks. In *Proceedings of the First Workshop on Abusive Language Online*, pages 78–84, Vancouver, BC, Canada. Association for Computational Linguistics.

Zeerak Waseem and Dirk Hovy. 2016. Hateful symbols or hateful people? predictive features for hate speech detection on twitter. In *Proceedings of the NAACL Student Research Workshop*, pages 88–93, San Diego, California. Association for Computational Linguistics.

Zeerak Waseem, James Thorne, and Joachim Bingel. 2018. Bridging the gaps: Multi task learning for domain transfer of hate speech detection. *Online Harassment*, page 29.

Michael Wiegand, Josef Ruppenhofer, Anna Schmidt, and Clayton Greenberg. 2018a. Inducing a lexicon of abusive words – a feature-based approach. In *Proceedings of the 2018 Conference of the North American Chapter of the Association for Computational Linguistics: Human Language Technologies,*

Volume 1 (Long Papers), pages 1046–1056, New Orleans, Louisiana. Association for Computational Linguistics.

Michael Wiegand, Melanie Siegel, and Josef Ruppenhofer. 2018b. Overview of the germeval 2018 shared task on the identification of offensive language. In *14th Conference on Natural Language Processing KONVENS 2018*, page 1.

Ellery Wulczyn, Nithum Thain, and Lucas Dixon. 2017. Ex machina: Personal attacks seen at scale. In *Proceedings of the 26th International Conference on World Wide Web*, pages 1391–1399. International World Wide Web Conferences Steering Committee.

Marcos Zampieri, Shervin Malmasi, Preslav Nakov, Sara Rosenthal, Noura Farra, and Ritesh Kumar. 2019a. Predicting the type and target of offensive posts in social media. In *Proceedings of the 2019 Conference of the North American Chapter of the Association for Computational Linguistics: Human Language Technologies, Volume 1 (Long and Short Papers)*, pages 1415–1420, Minneapolis, Minnesota. Association for Computational Linguistics.

Marcos Zampieri, Shervin Malmasi, Preslav Nakov, Sara Rosenthal, Noura Farra, and Ritesh Kumar. 2019b. SemEval-2019 task 6: Identifying and categorizing offensive language in social media (OffensEval). In *Proceedings of the 13th International Workshop on Semantic Evaluation*, pages 75–86, Minneapolis, Minnesota, USA. Association for Computational Linguistics.

Xinjie Zhou, Xiaojun Wan, and Jianguo Xiao. 2016. Cross-lingual sentiment classification with bilingual document representation learning. In *Proceedings of the 54th Annual Meeting of the Association for Computational Linguistics (Volume 1: Long Papers)*, pages 1403–1412, Berlin, Germany. Association for Computational Linguistics.

De-Mixing Sentiment from Code-Mixed Text

Yash Kumar Lal[*†]   **Vaibhav Kumar**[*‡]   **Mrinal Dhar**[*◦]
Manish Shrivastava[◦]   **Philipp Koehn**[†]
[†]Johns Hopkins University, [‡]Carnegie Mellon University, [◦]Bloomberg LP,
[◇]International Institute of Information Technology
{yash, phi}@jhu.edu,
vaibhav2@andrew.cmu.edu, mrinaldhar@gmail.com,
manish.shrivastava@iiit.ac.in

Abstract

Code-mixing is the phenomenon of mixing the vocabulary and syntax of multiple languages in the same sentence. It is an increasingly common occurrence in today's multilingual society and poses a big challenge when encountered in different downstream tasks. In this paper, we present a hybrid architecture for the task of Sentiment Analysis of English-Hindi code-mixed data. Our method consists of three components, each seeking to alleviate different issues. We first generate subword level representations for the sentences using a CNN architecture. The generated representations are used as inputs to a Dual Encoder Network which consists of two different BiLSTMs - the Collective and Specific Encoder. The Collective Encoder captures the overall sentiment of the sentence, while the Specific Encoder utilizes an attention mechanism in order to focus on individual sentiment-bearing sub-words. This, combined with a Feature Network consisting of orthographic features and specially trained word embeddings, achieves state-of-the-art results - 83.54% accuracy and 0.827 F1 score - on a benchmark dataset.

1   Introduction

Sentiment Analysis (SA) is crucial in tasks like user modeling, curating online trends, running political campaigns and opinion mining. The majority of this information comes from social media websites such as Facebook and Twitter. A large number of Indian users on such websites can speak both English and Hindi with bilingual proficiency. Consequently, English-Hindi code-mixed content has become ubiquitous on the Internet, creating the need to process this form of natural language.

Code-mixing is defined as "the embedding of linguistic units such as phrases, words and mor-

phemes of one language into an utterance of another language" (Myers-Scotton, 1993). Typically, a code-mixed sentence retains the underlying grammar and script of one of the languages it is comprised of.

Due to the lack of a formal grammar for a code-mixed hybrid language, traditional approaches don't work well on such data. The spelling variations of the same words according to different writers and scripts increase the issues faced by traditional SA systems. To alleviate this issue, we introduce the first component of our model - it uses CNNs to generate subword representations to provide increased robustness to informal peculiarities of code-mixed data. These representations are learned over the code-mixed corpus.

Now, let's consider the expression: x **but** y, where x and y are phrases holding opposite sentiments. However, the overall expression has a positive sentiment. Standard LSTMs work well in classifying the individual phrases but fail to effectively combine individual emotions in such compound sentences (Socher et al., 2013). To address this issue, we introduce a second component into our model which we call the Dual Encoder Network. This network consists of two parallel BiLSTMs, which we call the Collective and Specific Encoder. The Collective Encoder takes note of the overall sentiment of the sentence and hence, works well on phrases individually. On the other hand, the Specific Encoder utilizes an attention mechanism which focuses on individual sentiment bearing units. This helps in choosing the correct sentiment when presented with a mixture of sentiments, as in the expression above.

Additionally, we introduce a novel component, which we call the Feature Network. It uses surface features as well as monolingual sentence vector representations. This helps our entire system work well, even when presented with a lower amount of

---

*Equal Contribution

Proceedings of the ACL 2019, Student Research Workshop, pages 371–377
Florence, Italy, July 28th-August 2nd, 2019. ©2019 Association for Computational Linguistics

training examples as compared to established approaches.

We perform extensive experiments to evaluate the effectiveness of this system in comparison to previously proposed approaches and find that our method outperforms all of them for English-Hindi code-mixed sentiment analysis, reporting an accuracy of 83.54% and F1 score of 0.827. An ablation of the model also shows the effectiveness of the individual components.

2 Related Work

Mohammad et al. (2013) employ surface-form and semantic features to detect sentiments in tweets and text messages using SVMs. Keeping in mind a lack of computational resources, Giatsoglou et al. (2017) came up with a hybrid framework to exploit lexicons (polarized and emotional words) as well as different word embedding approaches in a polarity classification model. Ensembling simple word embedding based models with surface-form classifiers has also yielded slight improvements (Araque et al., 2017).

Extending standard NLP tasks to code-mixed data has presented peculiar challenges. Methods for POS tagging of code-mixed data obtained from online social media such as Facebook and Twitter has been attempted (Vyas et al., 2014) . Shallow parsing of code-mixed data curated from social media has also been tried (Sharma et al., 2016). Work has also been done to support word level identification of languages in code-mixed text (Chittaranjan et al., 2014).

Sharma et al. (2015) tried an approach based on lexicon lookup for text normalization and sentiment analysis of code-mixed data. Pravalika et al. (2017) used a lexicon lookup approach to perform domain specific sentiment analysis. Other attempts include using sub-word level compositions with LSTMs to capture sentiment at morpheme level (Joshi et al., 2016), or using contrastive learning with Siamese networks to map code-mixed and standard language text to a common sentiment space (Choudhary et al., 2018).

3 Model Architecture

An overview of this architecture can be found in Figure 3. Our approach is built on three components. The first generates sub-word level representations for words using Convolutional Neural Networks (CNNs). This produces units that are more atomic than words, which serve as inputs for a sequential model.

In Section 3.2, we describe our second component, a dual encoder network made of two Bi-directional Long Short Term Memory (BiLSTM) Networks that: (1) captures the overall sentiment information of a sentence, and (2) selects the more important sentiment-bearing parts of the sentence in a differential manner.

Finally, we introduce a Feature Network, in Section 3.3, built on surface features and a monolingual vector representation of the sentence. It augments our base neural network to boost classification accuracy for the task.

3.1 Generating Subword Representations

Word embeddings are now commonplace but are generally trained for one language. They are not ideal for code-mixed data given the transcription of one script into another, and spelling variations in social media data. As a single character does not inherently provide any semantic information that can be used for our purpose, we dismiss character-level feature representations as a possible choice of embeddings.

Keeping in mind the fact that code-mixed data has innumerable inconsistencies, we use characters to generate subword embeddings (Joshi et al., 2016). This increases the robustness of the model, which is important for noisy social media data. Intermediate sub-word feature representations are learned by filters during the convolution operation.

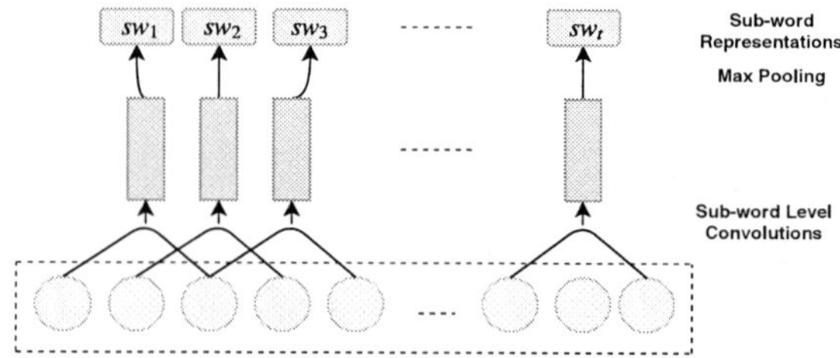

Figure 1: CNNs for Generating Sub-Word Representations

Let S be the representation of the sentence. We generate the required embedding by passing the characters of a sentence individually into 3 layer 1-D CNN. We perform a convolution of S with a filter F of length m, before adding a bias b and applying a non-linear activation function g. Each such operation generates a sub-word level feature map f_{sw}.

$$f_{sw}[i] = g((S[:, i : i + m - 1] * F) + b) \qquad (1)$$

Here, $S[:, i : i + m - 1]$ is a matrix of $(i)^{th}$ to $(i + m - 1)^{th}$ character embeddings and g is the ReLU activation function. Thereafter, a final max-pooling operation over p feature maps generates a representation for individual subwords:

$$sw_i = max(f_{sw}[p * (i : i + p - 1)]) \qquad (2)$$

A graphical representation of the architecture can be seen in Figure 1

3.2 Dual Encoder

We utilize a combination of two different encoders in our model.

3.2.1 Collective Encoder

The collective encoder, built over a BiLSTM, aims to learn a representation for the overall sentiment of the sentence. A graphical representation of this encoder is in Figure 2(A). It takes as input the subword representation of the sentence. The last hidden state of the BiLSTM i.e. h_t, encapsulates the overall summary of the sentence's sentiment, which is denoted by cmr^c.

3.2.2 Specific Encoder

The specific encoder is similar to the collective encoder, in that it takes as input a subword representation of the sentence and is built over LSTMs, with one caveat - an affixed attention mechanism. This allows for selection of subwords which contribute the most towards the sentiment of the input text. It can be seen in Figure 2(B).

Identifying which subwords play a significant role in deciding the sentiment is crucial. The specific encoder generates a context vector cmr^s to this end. We first concatenate the forward and backward states to obtain a combined annotation $(k_1, k_2, \ldots, k_t)$. Taking inspiration from (Yang et al., 2016), we quantify the significance of a sub-word by measuring the similarity of an additional hidden representation u_i of each sub-word against a sub-word level context vector X. Then, a normalized significance weight α_i is obtained.

$$u_i = tanh(W_i k_i + b_i) \qquad (3)$$

$$\alpha_i = \frac{exp(u_i^T X)}{\sum exp(u_i^T X)} \qquad (4)$$

The context vector X can be looked at as a high-level representation of the question "is it a significant sentiment-bearing unit" evaluated across the sub-words. It is initialized randomly and learned jointly during training. Finally, we calculate a vector cmr^s as a weighted sum of the sub-word annotations.

$$cmr^s = \sum \alpha_i k_i \qquad (5)$$

Using such a mechanism helps our model to adaptively select the more important sub-words from the less important ones.

3.2.3 Fusion of the Encoders

We concatenate the outputs obtained from both these encoders and use it as inputs to further fully connected layers. Information obtained from both the encoders is utilized to come up with a unified representation of sentiment present in a sentence,

$$cmr^{sent} = [cmr^c; cmr^s] \qquad (6)$$

where cmr^{sent} represents the unified representation of the sentiment. A representation of the same can be found in Figure 3.

3.3 Feature Network

We also use linguistic features to augment the neural network framework of our model.

- Capital words: Number of words that have only capital letters

- Extended words: Number of words with multiple contiguous repeating characters.

- Aggregate positive and negative sentiments: Using SentiWordNet (Esuli and Sebastiani, 2006) for every word bar articles and conjunctions, and combining the sentiment polarity values into net positive aggregate and net negative aggregate features.

- Repeated exclamations and other punctuation: Number of sets of two or more contiguous punctuation.

- Exclamation at end of sentence: Boolean value.

- Monolingual Sentence Vectors: Bojanowski et al. (2017)'s method is used to train word vectors for Hindi words in the code-mixed sentences.

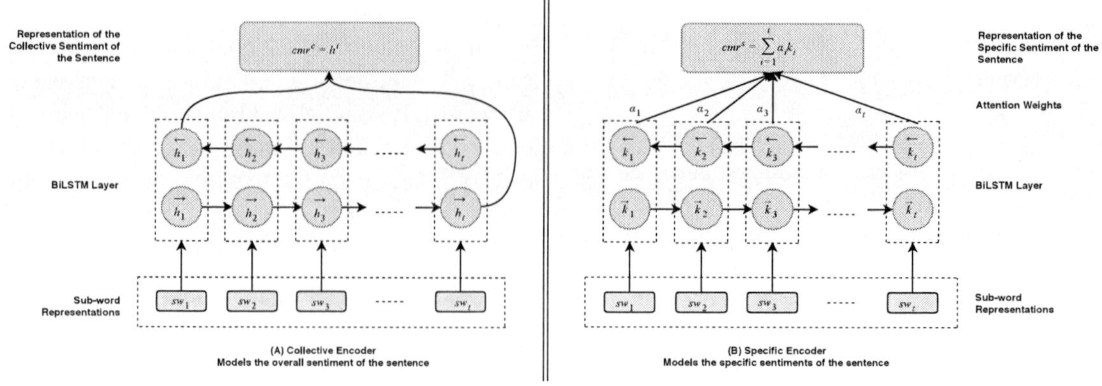

Figure 2: Parts of the Dual Encoder Network

Method	Accuracy	F1-score
SVM (Uni+Bigram) (Pang and Lee, 2008)	52.96%	0.3773
NBSVM (Uni+Bigram) (Wang and Manning, 2012)	62.5%	0.5375
MNB (Uni+Bigram) (Wang and Manning, 2012)	66.36%	0.6046
MNB (Tf-Idf) (Wang and Manning, 2012)	63.53%	0.4783
Lexicon Lookup (Sharma et al., 2015)	51.15%	0.252
Char-LSTM (Joshi et al., 2016)	59.8%	0.511
Subword-LSTM (Joshi et al., 2016)	69.7%	0.658
FastText (Joulin et al., 2017)	46.39%	0.505
SACMT (Choudhary et al., 2018)	77.3%	0.759
CMSA (Proposed)	**83.54%**	**0.827**

Table 1: Comparing against previous approaches

3.4 CMSA

The entire model is shown in Figure 3. Sub-word representations are fed into both the specific and the collective encoder. The outputs of the encoders are concatenated with each other, and further with the result of the Feature Network. Subsequently, these are passed through multiple fully connected layers to make the prediction. This architecture allows us to capture sentiment on the morphemic, syntactic and semantic levels simultaneously and learn which parts of a sentence provide the most value to its sentiment.

This system enables us to combine the best of neural networks involving attention mechanisms with surface and semantic features that are traditionally used for sentiment analysis.

4 Experiments And Results

4.1 Dataset

We use the dataset released by (Joshi et al., 2016). It is made up of 3879 code-mixed English-Hindi sentences which were collected from public Facebook pages popular in India.

4.2 Baselines

We compare our approach with the following:

- **SVM** (Pang and Lee, 2008): Uses SVMs with ngrams as features.

- **NBSVM** (Wang and Manning, 2012): Uses Naive Bayes and SVM with ngrams as features.

- **MNB** (Wang and Manning, 2012): Uses Multinomial Naive Bayes with various features.

- **Lexicon Lookup** (Sharma et al., 2015): The code-mixed sentences are first transliterated from Roman to Devanagari. Thereafter, sentiment analysis is done using a lexicon based approach.

- **Char-LSTM and Sub-word-LSTM** (Joshi et al., 2016): Character and sub-word level

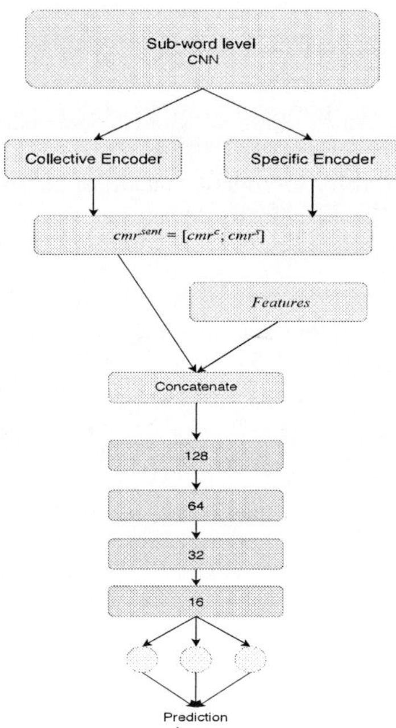

Figure 3: Complete Architecture of CMSA.

embeddings are passed to LSTM for classification.

- **FastText** (Joulin et al., 2017): Word Embeddings utilized for classification. It has the ability to handle OoV words as well.

- **SACMT** (Choudhary et al., 2018): Siamese networks are used to map code-mixed and standard sentences to a common sentiment space.

5   Results and Analysis

From Table 1, it is clear that that CMSA outperforms the state-of-the-art techniques by 6.24% in accuracy and 0.068 in F1-score. We observe that sentence vectors (FastText) alone are not suitable for this task. A possible reason for this is the presence of two different languages.

There is a significant difference in accuracy between Subword-LSTM and Char-LSTM, as seen in Table 1, which confirms our assumption about subword-level representations being better for this task as compared to character-level embeddings. Amongst the baselines, SACMT performed the best. However, mapping two sentences into a common space does not seem to be enough for sentiment classification. With a combination of differ-

ent components, our proposed method is able to overcome the shortcomings of each of these baselines and achieve significant gains.

5.1   Effect of different Encoders

Method	Accuracy	F1-score
Specific Encoder	80.2%	0.801
Collective Encoder	77.3%	0.795
Specific + Collective (CMSA)	**83.54%**	**0.827**

Table 2: Different encoding mechanisms with Feature Network

We experiment with different encoders used in the dual encoder network. From Table 2, we can see that CMSA > Collective Encoder > Specific Encoder, for both accuracy and F1 score. A combination of the two encoders provides a better sentiment classification model which validates our initial hypothesis of using two separate encoders.

5.2   Effect of Different Model Components

System	Accuracy	F1-score
Dual Encoder	75.74%	0.705
Feature Network only	57.9%	0.381
CMSA	**83.54%**	**0.827**

Table 3: Effect of different model components

From Table 3, we see the performance trend as follows: CMSA > Dual Encoder > Feature Network. Although the feature network alone does not result in better overall performance, it is still comparable to Char-LSTM (Table 2). However, the combination of feature network with dual encoder helps in boosting the overall performance.

5.3   Effect of Training Examples

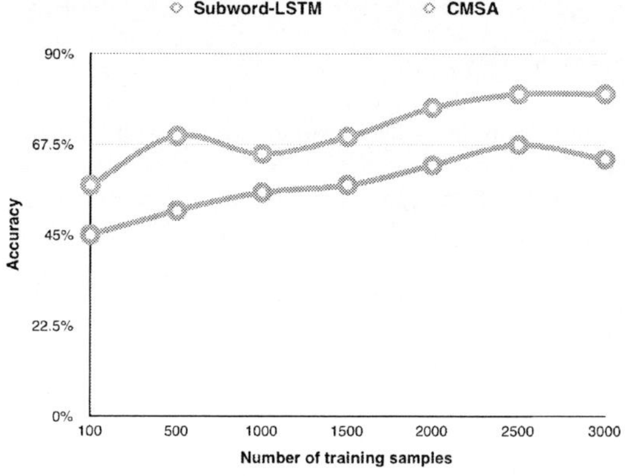

Figure 4: Performance on varying training data size

We experimented with varying numbers of training examples used for learning the model parameters. Different models were trained on 500, 1000, 1500 and 2000 examples. We observed that the performance of CMSA was greater than Subword-LSTM and SACMT at each point. This can be seen in Figure 4. One of the reasons for the same is the feature network in CMSA which helps in better performance even with lesser number of training examples.

6 Conclusion

We propose a hybrid approach that combines recurrent neural networks utilizing attention mechanisms, with surface features, yielding a unified representation that can be trained to classify sentiments. We conduct extensive experiments on a real world code-mixed social media dataset, and demonstrate that our system is able to achieve an accuracy of 83.54% and an F1-score of 0.827, outperforming state-of-the-art approaches for this task. In the future, we'd like to look at varying the attention mechanism in the model, and evaluating how it performs with a larger training set.

References

Oscar Araque, Ignacio Corcuera-Platas, J. Fernando Snchez-Rada, and Carlos A. Iglesias. 2017. Enhancing deep learning sentiment analysis with ensemble techniques in social applications. *Expert Systems with Applications*, 77:236 – 246.

Piotr Bojanowski, Edouard Grave, Armand Joulin, and Tomas Mikolov. 2017. Enriching word vectors with subword information. *Transactions of the Association for Computational Linguistics*, 5:135–146.

Gokul Chittaranjan, Yogarshi Vyas, Kalika Bali, and Monojit Choudhury. 2014. Word-level language identification using crf: Code-switching shared task report of msr india system.

Nurendra Choudhary, Rajat Singh, Ishita Bindlish, and Manish Shrivastava. 2018. Sentiment analysis of code-mixed languages leveraging resource rich languages.

Andrea Esuli and Fabrizio Sebastiani. 2006. Sentiwordnet: A publicly available lexical resource for opinion mining. In *In Proceedings of the 5th Conference on Language Resources and Evaluation (LREC06*, pages 417–422.

Maria Giatsoglou, Manolis G. Vozalis, Konstantinos Diamantaras, Athena Vakali, George Sarigiannidis, and Konstantinos Ch. Chatzisavvas. 2017. Sentiment analysis leveraging emotions and word embeddings. *Expert Systems with Applications*, 69:214 – 224.

Aditya Joshi, Ameya Prabhu, Manish Shrivastava, and Vasudeva Varma. 2016. Towards sub-word level compositions for sentiment analysis of hindi-english code mixed text. In *Proceedings of the 26th International Conference on Computational Linguistics (COLING)*.

Armand Joulin, Edouard Grave, Piotr Bojanowski, and Tomas Mikolov. 2017. Bag of tricks for efficient text classification. In *Proceedings of the 15th Conference of the European Chapter of the Association for Computational Linguistics: Volume 2, Short Papers*, pages 427–431.

Saif M. Mohammad, Svetlana Kiritchenko, and Xiaodan Zhu. 2013. Nrc-canada: Building the state-of-the-art in sentiment analysis of tweets. *CoRR*, abs/1308.6242.

Carol Myers-Scotton. 1993. Common and uncommon ground: Social and structural factors in codeswitching. *Language in society*, 22(4):475–503.

Bo Pang and Lillian Lee. 2008. Opinion mining and sentiment analysis. *Found. Trends Inf. Retr.*, 2(1-2):1–135.

A. Pravalika, V. Oza, N. P. Meghana, and S. S. Kamath. 2017. Domain-specific sentiment analysis approaches for code-mixed social network data. In *2017 8th International Conference on Computing, Communication and Networking Technologies (ICCNT)*, pages 1–6.

A. Sharma, S. Gupta, R. Motlani, P. Bansal, M. Srivastava, R. Mamidi, and D. M. Sharma. 2016. Shallow Parsing Pipeline for Hindi-English Code-Mixed Social Media Text.

Shashank Sharma, PYKL Srinivas, and Rakesh Chandra Balabantaray. 2015. Text normalization of code mix and sentiment analysis. *2015 International Conference on Advances in Computing, Communications and Informatics (ICACCI)*, pages 1468–1473.

Richard Socher, Alex Perelygin, Jean Wu, Jason Chuang, Christopher D Manning, Andrew Ng, and Christopher Potts. 2013. Recursive deep models for semantic compositionality over a sentiment treebank. In *Proceedings of the 2013 conference on empirical methods in natural language processing*, pages 1631–1642.

Yogarshi Vyas, Spandana Gella, Jatin Sharma, Kalika Bali, and Monojit Choudhury. 2014. Pos tagging of english-hindi code-mixed social media content. In *Proceedings of the 2014 Conference on Empirical Methods in Natural Language Processing (EMNLP)*.

Sida Wang and Christopher D. Manning. 2012. Baselines and bigrams: Simple, good sentiment and topic classification. In *Proceedings of the 50th Annual Meeting of the Association for Computational Linguistics: Short Papers - Volume 2*, ACL '12.

Zichao Yang, Diyi Yang, Chris Dyer, Xiaodong He, Alexander J. Smola, and Eduard H. Hovy. 2016. Hierarchical attention networks for document classification. In *HLT-NAACL*.

Unsupervised Learning of
Discourse-Aware Text Representation for Essay Scoring

Farjana Sultana Mim[1]   **Naoya Inoue**[1,2]   **Paul Reisert**[2,1]
Hiroki Ouchi[2,1]   **Kentaro Inui**[1,2]

[1]Tohoku University [2]RIKEN Center for Advanced Intelligence Project (AIP)

{mim, naoya-i, inui} @ecei.tohoku.ac.jp
{paul.reisert, hiroki.ouchi} @riken.jp

Abstract

Existing document embedding approaches mainly focus on capturing sequences of words in documents. However, some document classification and regression tasks such as essay scoring need to consider discourse structure of documents. Although some prior approaches consider this issue and utilize discourse structure of text for document classification, these approaches are dependent on computationally expensive parsers. In this paper, we propose an unsupervised approach to capture discourse structure in terms of coherence and cohesion for document embedding that does not require any expensive parser or annotation. Extrinsic evaluation results show that the document representation obtained from our approach improves the performance of essay Organization scoring and Argument Strength scoring.

1 Introduction

Document embedding is important for many NLP tasks such as document classification (e.g., essay scoring and sentiment classification) (Le and Mikolov, 2014; Liu et al., 2017; Wu et al., 2018; Tang et al., 2015) and summarization. While embedding approaches can be supervised, semi-supervised and unsupervised, recent studies have largely focused on unsupervised and semi-supervised approaches in order to utilize large amounts of unlabeled text and avoid expensive annotation procedures.

In general, a document is a discourse where sentences are logically connected to each other to provide comprehensive meaning. Discourse has two important properties: *coherence* and *cohesion* (Halliday, 1994). Coherence refers to the semantic relatedness among sentences and logical order of concepts and meanings in a text. For example, *"I saw Jill on the street. She was going home."* is coherent whereas *"I saw Jill on the street. She has two sisters."* is incoherent. Cohesion refers to the use of linguistic devices that hold a text together. Example of these linguistic devices include conjunctions such as discourse indicators (DIs) (e.g., *"because" and "for example"*), coreference (*e.g., "he" and "they"*), substitution, ellipsis etc.

Some text classification and regression tasks need to consider discourse structure of text in addition to dependency relations and predicate-argument structures. One example of such tasks is essay scoring, where discourse structure (e.g., coherence and cohesion) plays a crucial role, especially when considering *Organization* and *Argument Strength* criteria, since they refer to logical-sequence awareness in texts. Organization refers to how good an essay structure is, where well-structured essays logically develop arguments and state positions by supporting them (Persing et al., 2010). Argument Strength means how strongly an essay argues in favor of its thesis to persuade the readers (Persing and Ng, 2015).

An example of the relation between coherence and an essay's Organization is shown in Figure 1. The high-scored essay (i.e., Organization score of 4) first states its position regarding the prompt and then provides several reasons to strengthen the claim. It is considered coherent because it follows a logical order. However, the low-scored essay is not clear on its position and what it is arguing about. Therefore, it can be considered incoherent since it lacks logical sequencing.

Previous studies on document embedding have primarily focused on capturing word similarity, word dependencies and semantic information of documents (Le and Mikolov, 2014; Liu et al., 2017; Wu et al., 2018; Tang et al., 2015). However, less attention has been paid to capturing discourse structure for document embedding in an unsupervised manner and no prior work applies unsupervised document representation learning to essay scoring. In short, it has not yet been explored how some of the discourse properties can

378

Proceedings of the ACL 2019, Student Research Workshop, pages 378–385
Florence, Italy, July 28th-August 2nd, 2019. ©2019 Association for Computational Linguistics

be included in text embedding without an expensive parser and how document embeddings affect essay scoring tasks.

In this paper, we propose an unsupervised method to capture discourse structure in terms of cohesion and coherence for document embedding. We train a document encoder with unlabeled data which learns to discriminate between coherent/cohesive and incoherent/incohesive documents. We then use the pre-trained document encoder to obtain feature vectors of essays for Organization and Argument Strength score prediction, where the feature vectors are mapped to scores by regression. The advantage of our approach is that it is fully unsupervised and does not require any expensive parser or annotation. Our results show that capturing discourse structure in terms of cohesion and coherence for document representation helps to improve the performance of essay Organization scoring and Argument Strength scoring. We make our implementation publicly available.[1]

2 Related Work

The focus of this study is the unsupervised encapsulation of discourse structure (coherence and cohesion) into document representation for essay scoring. A popular approach for document representation is the use of fixed-length features such as bag-of-words (BOW) and bag-of-ngrams due to their simplicity and highly competitive results (Wang and Manning, 2012). However, such approaches fail to capture the semantic similarity of words and phrases since they treat each word or phrase as a discrete token.

Several methods for document representation learning have been introduced in recent years. One popular unsupervised method is doc2vec (Le and Mikolov, 2014), where a document is mapped to a unique vector and every word in the document is also mapped to a unique vector. Then, the document vector and and word vectors are either concatenated or averaged to predict the next word in a context. Liu et al. (2017) used a convolutional neural network (CNN) to capture longer range semantic structure within a document where the learning objective predicted the next word. Wu et al. (2018) proposed Word Mover's Embedding (WME) utilizing Word Mover's Distance (WMD) that considers both word alignments and pre-trained word vectors to learn feature representation of documents. Tang et al. (2015) proposed a semi-supervised method called Predictive Text Embedding (PTE) where both labeled information and different levels of word co-occurrence were encoded in a large-scale heterogeneous text network, which was then embedded into a low dimensional space. Although these approaches have been proven useful for several document classification and regression tasks, their focus is not on capturing the discourse structure of documents.

One exception is the study by Ji and Smith (2017) who illustrated the role of discourse structure for document representation by implementing a discourse structure (defined by RST) aware model and showed that their model improves text categorization performance (e.g., sentiment classification of movies and Yelp reviews, and prediction of news article frames). The authors utilized an RST-parser to obtain the discourse dependency

---

[1]Our implementation is publicly available at `https://github.com/FarjanaSultanaMim/DiscoShuffle`

tree of a document and then built a recursive neural network on top of it. The issue with their approach is that texts need to be parsed by an RST parser which is computationally expensive. Furthermore, the performance of RST parsing is dependent on the genre of documents (Ji and Smith, 2017).

Previous studies have modeled text coherence (Li and Jurafsky, 2016; Joty et al., 2018; Mesgar and Strube, 2018). Farag et al. (2018) demonstrated that state-of-the-art neural automated essay scoring (AES) is not well-suited for capturing adversarial input of grammatically correct but incoherent sequences of sentences. Therefore, they developed a neural local coherence model and jointly trained it with a state-of-the-art AES model to build an adversarially robust AES system. Mesgar and Strube (2018) used a local coherence model to assess essay scoring performance on a dataset of holistic scores where it is unclear which criteria of the essay the score considers.

We target Organization and Argument Strength dimension of essays which are related to coherence and cohesion. Persing et al. (2010) proposed heuristic rules utilizing various DIs, words and phrases to capture the organizational structure of texts. Persing and Ng (2015) used several features such as part-of-speech, n-grams, semantic frames, coreference, and argument components for calculating Argument Strength in essays. Wachsmuth et al. (2016) achieved state-of-the-art performance on Organization and Argument Strength scoring of essays by utilizing argumentative features such as sequence of argumentative discourse units (e.g., *(conclusion, premise, conclusion)*). However, Wachsmuth et al. (2016) used an expensive argument parser to obtain such units.

3 Base Model

3.1 Overview

Our base model consists of (i) a base document encoder, (ii) auxiliary encoders, and (iii) a scoring function. The base document encoder produces a vector representation $\mathbf{h}^{\mathrm{base}}$ by capturing a sequence of words in each essay. The auxiliary encoders capture additional essay-related information that is useful for essay scoring and produce a vector representation $\mathbf{h}^{\mathrm{aux}}$. By taking $\mathbf{h}^{\mathrm{base}}$ and $\mathbf{h}^{\mathrm{aux}}$ as input, the scoring function outputs a score.

Specifically, these encoders first produce the representations, $\mathbf{h}^{\mathrm{base}}$ and $\mathbf{h}^{\mathrm{aux}}$. Then, these representations are concatenated into one vector, which is mapped to a feature vector $\mathbf{z}$.

$$\mathbf{z} = \tanh(\mathbf{W} \cdot [\mathbf{h}^{\mathrm{base}}; \mathbf{h}^{\mathrm{aux}}]) \, , \qquad (1)$$

where $\mathbf{W}$ is a weight matrix. Finally, $\mathbf{z}$ is mapped to a scalar value by the sigmoid function.

$$y = \mathrm{sigmoid}(\mathbf{w} \cdot \mathbf{z} + b) \, ,$$

where $\mathbf{w}$ is a weight vector, b is a bias value, and y is a score in the range of $(0, 1)$. In the following subsections, we describe the details of each encoder.

3.2 Base Document Encoder

The base document encoder produces a document representation $\mathbf{h}^{\mathrm{base}}$ in Equation 1. For the base document encoder, we use the Neural Essay Assessor (NEA) model proposed by Taghipour and Ng (2016). This model uses three types of layers: an embedding layer, a Bi-directional Long Short-Term Memory (BiLSTM) (Schuster and Paliwal, 1997) layer and a mean-over-time layer.

Given the input essay of T words $w_{1:T} = (w_1, w_2, \cdots, w_T)$, the embedding layer (Emb) produces a sequence of word embeddings $\mathbf{w}_{1:T} = (\mathbf{w}_1, \mathbf{w}_2, \cdots, \mathbf{w}_T)$.

$$\mathbf{w}_{1:T} = \mathrm{Emb}(w_{1:T}) \, ,$$

where each word embedding is a d^{word} dimensional vector, i.e. $\mathbf{w}_i \in \mathbb{R}^{d^{\mathrm{word}}}$.

Then, taking $\mathbf{x}_{1:T}$ as input, the BiLSTM layer produces a sequence of contextual representations $\mathbf{h}_{1:T} = (\mathbf{h}_1, \mathbf{h}_2, \cdots, \mathbf{h}_T)$.

$$\mathbf{h}_{1:T} = \mathrm{BiLSTM}(\mathbf{x}_{1:T}) \, ,$$

where each representation $\mathbf{h}_i$ is $\mathbb{R}^{d^{\mathrm{hidden}}}$.

Finally, taking $\mathbf{h}_{1:T}$ as input, the mean-over-time layer produces a vector averaged over the sequence.

$$\mathbf{h}^{\mathrm{mean}} = \frac{1}{T} \sum_{t=1}^{T} \mathbf{h}_t \, . \qquad (2)$$

We use this resulting vector as the base document representation, i.e. $\mathbf{h}^{\mathrm{base}} = \mathbf{h}^{\mathrm{mean}}$.

3.3 Auxiliary Encoders

The auxiliary encoders produce a representation of essay-related information $\mathbf{h}^{\mathrm{aux}}$ in Equation 1. We provide two encoders that capture different types of essay-related information.

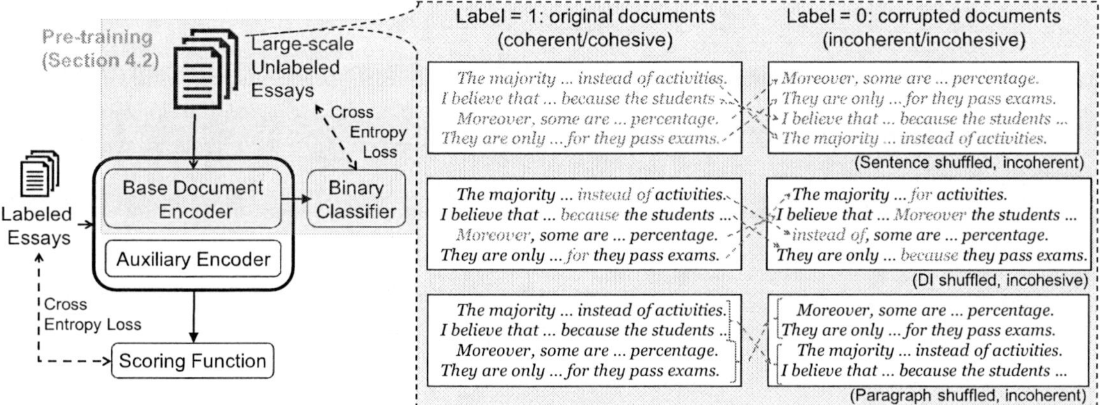

Figure 2: Proposed method for unsupervised learning of discourse-aware text representation utilizing coherent/incoherent and cohesive/incohesive texts and use of the discourse-aware text embeddings for essay scoring.

Paragraph Function Encoder (PFE). Each paragraph in an essay plays a different role. For instance, the first paragraph tends to introduce the topic of the essay, and the last paragraph tends to sum up the whole content and make some conclusions. Here, we capture such paragraph functions.

Specifically, we obtain paragraph function labels of essays using Persing et al. (2010)'s heuristic rules.[2] Persing et al. (2010) specified four paragraph function labels: Introduction (**I**), Body (**B**), Rebuttal (**R**) and Conclusion (**C**). We represent these labels as vectors and incorporate them into the base model. The paragraph function label encoder consists of two modules, an embedding layer and a BiLSTM layer.

We assume that an essay consists of M paragraphs, and the i-th paragraph has already been assigned a function label p_i. Given the sequence of paragraph function labels of an essay $p_{1:M} = (p_1, p_2, ..., p_M)$, the embedding layer (Emb^{para}) produces a sequence of label embeddings, i.e. $\boldsymbol{p}_{1:M} = \text{Emb}^{\text{para}}(p_{1:M})$, where each embedding $\boldsymbol{p}_i$ is $\mathbb{R}^{d^{\text{para}}}$. Then, taking $\boldsymbol{p}_{1:M}$ as input, the BiLSTM layer produces a sequence of contextual representations $\mathbf{h}_{1:M} = \text{BiLSTM}(\boldsymbol{p}_{1:M})$, where $\mathbf{h}_i$ is $\mathbb{R}^{d^{\text{PFE}}}$. We use the last hidden state $\mathbf{h}_M$ as the paragraph function label sequence representation, i.e. $\mathbf{h}^{\text{aux}} = \mathbf{h}_M$.

Prompt Encoder (PE). As shown in Figure 1, essays are written for a given prompt, where the prompt itself can be useful for essay scoring.

Based on this intuition, we incorporate prompt information.

The prompt encoder uses an embedding layer and a Long Short-Term Memory (LSTM) (Hochreiter, Sepp and Schmidhuber, Jürgen, 1997) layer to produce a prompt representation. Formally, we assume that the input is a prompt of N words, $w_{1:N} = (w_1, w_2, \cdots, w_N)$. First, the embedding layer maps the input prompt $w_{1:N}$ to a sequence of word embeddings, $\mathbf{w}_{1:N}$, where $\mathbf{w}_i$ is $\mathbb{R}^{d^{\text{prompt}}}$. Then, taking $\mathbf{w}_{1:N}$ as input, the LSTM layer produces a sequence of hidden states, $\mathbf{h}_{1:N} = (\mathbf{h}_1, \mathbf{h}_2, \cdots, \mathbf{h}_N)$, where $\mathbf{h}_i$ is $\mathbb{R}^{d^{\text{PE}}}$. The last hidden state is regarded as the resulting representation, i.e. $\mathbf{h}^{\text{aux}} = \mathbf{h}_N$.

4 Proposed Method

4.1 Overview

Figure 2 summarizes the proposed method. First, we pre-train a base document encoder (Section 3.2) in an unsupervised manner. The pretraining is motivated by the following hypotheses: (i) artificially corrupted incoherent/incohesive documents lack logical sequencing, and (ii) training a base document encoder to differentiate between the original and incoherent/incohesive documents makes the encoder logical sequence-aware.

The pre-training is done in two steps. First, we pre-train the document encoder with large-scale unlabeled essays. Second, we pre-train the encoder using only the unlabeled essays of target corpus used for essay scoring. We expect that this fine-tuning alleviates the domain mismatch between the large-scale essays and target essays

---

381

(e.g., essay length). Finally, the pre-trained encoder is then re-trained on the annotations of essay scoring tasks in a supervised manner.

4.2 Pre-training

We artificially create incoherent/incohesive documents by corrupting them with random shuffling methods: (i) *sentences*, (ii) *only DIs* and (iii) *paragraphs*. Figure 2 shows examples of original and corrupted documents. We shuffle DIs since they are important for representing the logical connection between sentences. For example, *"Mary did well although she was ill"* is logically connected, but *"Mary did well but she was ill."* and *"Mary did well. She was ill."* lack logical sequencing because of improper and lack of DI usage, respectively. Paragraph shuffling is also important since coherent essays have sequences like *Introduction-Body-Conclusion* to provide a logically consistent meaning of the text.

Specifically, we treat the pre-training as a binary classification task where the encoder classifies documents as coherent/cohesive or not.

$$P(y(d) = 1|d) = \sigma(\mathbf{w}^{\text{unsup}} \cdot \mathbf{h}^{\text{mean}}) \ ,$$

where y is a binary function mapping from a document d to $\{0, 1\}$, in which 1 represents the document is coherent/cohesive and 0 represents not. The base document representation $\mathbf{h}^{\text{mean}}$ (Eq. 2) is multiplied with a weight vector $\mathbf{w}^{\text{unsup}}$, and the sigmoid function σ returns a probability that the given document d is coherent/cohesive.

To train the model parameters, we minimize the binary cross-entropy loss function,

$$\mathcal{L} = -\sum_{i=1}^{N} y_i \log(P(y(d_i) = 1|d_i)) +$$

$$(1 - y_i)\log(1 - P(y(d_i) = 1|d_i)) \ ,$$

where y_i is a gold-standard label of coherence/cohesion of d_i and N is the total number of documents. Note that y_i is automatically assigned in the corruption process where an original document has a label of 1 and an artificially corrupted document has a label of 0.

5 Experiments

5.1 Setup

We use five-fold cross-validation for evaluating our models with the same split as Persing et al.

(2010); Persing and Ng (2015) and Wachsmuth et al. (2016). The reported results are averaged over five folds. However, our results are not directly comparable since our training data is smaller as we reserve a development set (100 essays) for model selection while they do not. We use the mean squared error as an evaluation measure.

Data We use the International Corpus of Learner English (ICLE) (Granger et al., 2009) for essay scoring which contains 6,085 essays and 3.7 million words. Most of the ICLE essays (91%) are argumentative and vary in length, having 7.6 paragraphs and 33.8 sentences on average (Wachsmuth et al., 2016). Some essays have been annotated with different criteria among which 1,003 essays are annotated with Organization scores and 1,000 essays are annotated with Argument Strength scores. Both scores range from 1 to 4 at half-point increments. For our scoring task, we utilize the 1,003 essays.

To pre-train the document encoder, we use 35,222 essays from four datasets, (i) the Kaggle's Automated Student Assessment Prize (ASAP) dataset[3] (12,976) (ii) TOEFL11 (Blanchard et al., 2013) dataset (12,100), (iii) The International Corpus Network of Asian Learners of English (IC-NALE) (Ishikawa, 2013) dataset (5,600), and (iv) the ICLE essays not used for Organization and Argument Strength scoring (4,546).[4]

See Appendix A and B for further details on the hyperparameters and preprocessing.

5.2 Results and Discussion

From two baseline models, we report the best model for each task (*Base+PFE* for Organization, *Base+PE* for Argument Strength).

Table 1 indicates that the proposed unsupervised pre-training improves the performance of Organization and Argument Strength scoring. These results support our hypothesis that training with random corruption of documents helps a document encoder learn logical sequence-aware text representations. In most cases, fine-tuning the encoder for each scoring task again helps to improve the performance.

The results indicate that paragraph shuffling

---

[3]https://www.kaggle.com/c/asap-aes
[4]During pre-training with paragraph shuffled essays, we use only 16,646 essays (TOEFL11 and ICLE essays) since ASAP and ICNALE essays have a single paragraph.

Model	Shuffle Type	Fine-tuning	Mean Squared Error	
			Organization	Argument Strength
Baseline	-	-	0.182	0.248
Proposed	Sentence		0.187	**0.244**
	Sentence	✓	0.186	**0.244***
	Discourse Indicator		0.187	**0.242**
	Discourse Indicator	✓	0.193	**0.246**
	Paragraph		**0.172***	**0.236***
	Paragraph	✓	**0.169***	**0.231***
Persing et al. (2010)			0.175	-
Persing et al. (2015)			-	0.244
Wachsmuth et al. (2016)			0.164	0.226

Table 1: Performance of essay scoring. '*' indicates a statistical significance (Wilcoxon signed-rank test, $p < 0.05$) against the baseline model. Base+PFE and Base+PE are used in Organization and Argument Strength, respectively.

is the most effective in both scoring tasks (statistically significant by Wilcoxon's signed rank test, $p < 0.05$). This could be attributed to the fact that paragraph sequences create a more clear organizational and argumentative structure. Suppose that an essay first introduces a topic, states their position, supports their position and then concludes. Then, the structure of the essay would be regarded as "well-organized". Moreover, the argument of the essay would be considered "strong" since it provides support for their position. The results suggest that such levels of abstractions (e.g., *Introduction-Body-Body-Conclusion*) are well captured at a paragraph-level, but not at a sentence-level or DI-level alone.

Furthermore, a manual inspection of DIs identified by the system suggest room for improvement in DI shuffling. First, the identification of DIs is not always reliable. Almost half of DIs identified by our simple pattern matching algorithm (see Appendix B) were not actually DIs (e.g., *we have survived so far only external difficulties*). Second, we also found that some DI-shuffled documents are sometimes cohesive. This happens when original document counterparts have two or more DIs with the more or less same meaning (e.g., *since* and *because*). We speculate that this confuses the document encoder in the pre-training process.

6 Conclusion and Future Work

We proposed an unsupervised strategy to capture discourse structure (i.e., coherence and cohesion) for document embedding. We train a document encoder with coherent/cohesive and randomly corrupted incoherent/incohesive documents to make it logical-sequence aware. Our method does not require any expensive annotation or parser. The experimental results show that the proposed learning strategy improves the performance of essay Organization and Argument Strength scoring.

Our future work includes adding more unannotated data for pre-training and trying other unsupervised objectives such as swapping clauses before and after DIs (e.g., A because B → B because A). We also intend to perform intrinsic evaluation of the learned document embedding space. Moreover, we plan to evaluate the effectiveness of our approach on more document regression or classification tasks.

7 Acknowledgements

This work was supported by JST CREST Grant Number JPMJCR1513 and JSPS KAKENHI Grant Number 19K20332. We would like to thank the anonymous ACL reviewers for their insightful comments. We also thank Ekaterina Kochmar for her profound and useful feedback.

References

Daniel Blanchard, Joel Tetreault, Derrick Higgins, Aoife Cahill, and Martin Chodorow. 2013. TOEFL11: A corpus of non-native English. *ETS Research Report Series*, 2013(2):i–15.

Youmna Farag, Helen Yannakoudakis, and Ted Briscoe. 2018. Neural automated essay scoring and coherence modeling for adversarially crafted input. *arXiv preprint arXiv:1804.06898*.

Sylviane Granger, Estelle Dagneaux, Fanny Meunier, and Magali Paquot. 2009. International corpus of learner English.

Miochael AK Halliday. 1994. An introduction to functional grammar 2nd edition. *London: Arnold.*

Hochreiter, Sepp and Schmidhuber, Jürgen. 1997. Long short-term memory. *Neural computation*, 9(8):1735–1780.

S Ishikawa. 2013. ICNALE: the international corpus network of Asian learners of English. *Retrieved on November*, 21:2014.

Yangfeng Ji and Noah Smith. 2017. Neural discourse structure for text categorization. *arXiv preprint arXiv:1702.01829*.

Shafiq Joty, Muhammad Tasnim Mohiuddin, and Dat Tien Nguyen. 2018. Coherence modeling of asynchronous conversations: A neural entity grid approach. In *Proceedings of the 56th Annual Meeting of the Association for Computational Linguistics (Volume 1: Long Papers)*, volume 1, pages 558–568.

Quoc Le and Tomas Mikolov. 2014. Distributed representations of sentences and documents. In *International Conference on Machine Learning*, pages 1188–1196.

Jiwei Li and Dan Jurafsky. 2016. Neural net models for open-domain discourse coherence. *arXiv preprint arXiv:1606.01545*.

Chundi Liu, Shunan Zhao, and Maksims Volkovs. 2017. Unsupervised Document Embedding With CNNs. *arXiv preprint arXiv:1711.04168*.

Mohsen Mesgar and Michael Strube. 2018. A Neural Local Coherence Model for Text Quality Assessment. In *Proceedings of the 2018 Conference on EMNLP*, pages 4328–4339.

Isaac Persing, Alan Davis, and Vincent Ng. 2010. Modeling organization in student essays. In *Proceedings of the 2010 Conference on EMNLP*, pages 229–239. ACL.

Isaac Persing and Vincent Ng. 2015. Modeling argument strength in student essays. In *Proceedings of the 53rd Annual Meeting of the ACL the 7th International Joint Conference on Natural Language Processing*, volume 1, pages 543–552.

Mike Schuster and Kuldip K Paliwal. 1997. Bidirectional recurrent neural networks. *IEEE Transactions on Signal Processing*, 45(11):2673–2681.

Kaveh Taghipour and Hwee Tou Ng. 2016. A neural approach to automated essay scoring. In *Proceedings of the 2016 Conference on EMNLP*, pages 1882–1891.

Jian Tang, Meng Qu, and Qiaozhu Mei. 2015. Pte: Predictive text embedding through large-scale heterogeneous text networks. In *Proceedings of the 21th ACM SIGKDD International Conference on Knowledge Discovery and Data Mining*, pages 1165–1174. ACM.

Henning Wachsmuth, Khalid Al Khatib, and Benno Stein. 2016. Using argument mining to assess the argumentation quality of essays. In *Proceedings of COLING 2016, the 26th International Conference on Computational Linguistics: Technical Papers*, pages 1680–1691.

Sida Wang and Christopher D Manning. 2012. Baselines and bigrams: Simple, good sentiment and topic classification. In *Proceedings of the 50th Annual Meeting of the ACL: Short Papers-Volume 2*, pages 90–94. Association for Computational Linguistics.

Lingfei Wu, Ian EH Yen, Kun Xu, Fangli Xu, Avinash Balakrishnan, Pin-Yu Chen, Pradeep Ravikumar, and Michael J Witbrock. 2018. Word Mover's Embedding: From Word2Vec to Document Embedding. *arXiv preprint arXiv:1811.01713*.

Will Y Zou, Richard Socher, Daniel Cer, and Christopher D Manning. 2013. Bilingual word embeddings for phrase-based machine translation. In *Proceedings of the 2013 Conference on EMNLP*, pages 1393–1398.

A   Hyperparameters

We use BiLSTM with 200 hidden units in each layer for the base document encoder ($d^{\text{hidden}} = 200$). For the paragraph function encoder, we use a BiLSTM with hidden units of 200 in each layer ($d^{\text{PFE}} = 200$). For the prompt encoder, an LSTM with an output dimension of 300 is used ($d^{\text{PE}} = 300$). We use the 50-dimensional pre-trained word embeddings released by Zou et al. (2013) in our base document encoder ($d^{\text{word}} = 50, d^{\text{prompt}} = 50$).

We use the Adam optimizer with a learning rate of 0.001 and a batch size of 32. We use early stopping with patience 15 (5 for pre-training), and train the network for 100 epochs. The vocabulary consists of the 90,000 and 15,000 most frequent words for pre-training and essay scoring, respectively. Out-of-vocabulary words are mapped to special tokens. We perform hyperparameter tuning and choose the best model. We tuned norm clipping maximum values (3,5,7) and dropout rates (0.3, 0.5, 0.7, 0.9) for all models on the development set.

B   Preprocessing

We lowercase the tokens and specify an essay's paragraph boundaries with special tokens. During sentence/DI shuffling for pre-training, paragraph boundaries are not used. We collect 847 DIs from the Web.[5] We exclude the DI "and" since it is not always used for initiating logic (e.g milk, banana *and* tea). In essay scoring data, we found 176 DIs and average DIs per essay is around 24. In the pre-training data, the number of DIs found is 204 and the average DIs per essay is around 13. We identified DIs by simple string-pattern matching.

[5] `http://www.studygs.net/wrtstr6.htm`, `http://home.ku.edu.tr/~doregan/Writing/Cohesion.html` etc.

Multimodal Logical Inference System for Visual-Textual Entailment

Riko Suzuki[1]
suzuki.riko@is.ocha.ac.jp

Hitomi Yanaka[1,2]
hitomi.yanaka@riken.jp

Masashi Yoshikawa[3]
yoshikawa.masashi.
yh8@is.naist.jp

Koji Mineshima[1]
mineshima.koji@ocha.ac.jp

Daisuke Bekki[1]
bekki@is.ocha.ac.jp

[1]Ochanomizu University, Tokyo, Japan
[2]RIKEN Center for Advanced Intelligence Project, Tokyo, Japan
[3]Nara Institute of Science and Technology, Nara, Japan

Abstract

A large amount of research about multimodal inference across text and vision has been recently developed to obtain visually grounded word and sentence representations. In this paper, we use logic-based representations as unified meaning representations for texts and images and present an unsupervised multimodal logical inference system that can effectively prove entailment relations between them. We show that by combining semantic parsing and theorem proving, the system can handle semantically complex sentences for visual-textual inference.

1 Introduction

Multimodal inference across image data and text has the potential to improve understanding information of different modalities and acquiring new knowledge. Recent studies of multimodal inference provide challenging tasks such as visual question answering (Antol et al., 2015; Hudson and Manning, 2019; Acharya et al., 2019) and visual reasoning (Suhr et al., 2017; Vu et al., 2018; Xie et al., 2018).

Grounded representations from image-text pairs are useful to solve such inference tasks. With the development of large-scale corpora such as Visual Genome (Krishna et al., 2017) and methods of automatic graph generation from an image (Xu et al., 2017; Qi et al., 2019), we can obtain structured representations for images and sentences such as scene graph (Johnson et al., 2015), a visually-grounded graph over object instances in an image.

While graph representations provide more interpretable representations for text and image than embedding them into high-dimensional vector spaces (Frome et al., 2013; Norouzi et al., 2014), there remain two challenges: (i) to capture complex logical meanings such as negation and quantification, and (ii) to perform logical inferences on them.

Figure 1: An example of visual-textual entailment. An image paired with logically complex statements, namely, negation (1), numeral (2), and quantification (3), leads to a true (✓) or false (✗) judgement.

For example, consider the task of checking if each statement in Figure 1 is true or false under the situation described in the image. The statements (1) and (2) are false, while (3) is true. To perform this task, it is necessary to handle semantically complex phenomena such as negation, numeral, and quantification.

To enable such advanced visual-textual inferences, it is desirable to build a framework for representing richer semantic contents of texts and images and handling inference between them. We use logic-based representations as unified meaning representations for texts and images and present an unsupervised inference system that can prove entailment relations between them. Our visual-textual inference system combines semantic parsing via Combinatory Categorial Grammar (CCG; Steedman (2000)) and first-order theorem proving (Blackburn and Bos, 2005). To describe information in images as logical formulas, we propose a method of transforming graph representations into logical formulas, using the idea of predicate circumscription (McCarthy, 1986), which complements information implicit in images using the closed world assumption. Experiments show that our system can perform visual-textual inference with semantically complex sentences.

Proceedings of the ACL 2019, Student Research Workshop, pages 386–392
Florence, Italy, July 28th-August 2nd, 2019. ©2019 Association for Computational Linguistics

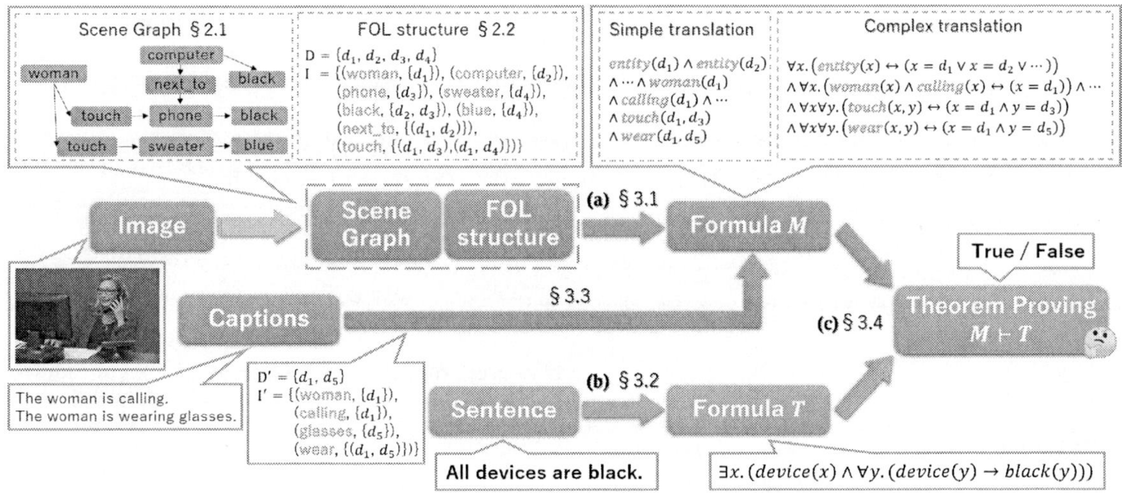

Figure 2: Overview of the proposed system. In this work, we assume the input image is processed into an FOL structure or scene graph a priori. The system consists of three parts: (a) **Graph Translator** converts an image annotated with a scene graph/FOL structure to formula M; (b) **Semantic parser** maps a sentence to formula T via CCG parsing; (c) **Inference Engine** checks whether M entails T by FOL theorem proving.

2 Background

There are two types of grounded meaning representations for images: scene graphs and first-order logic (FOL) structures. Both characterize objects and their semantic relationships in images.

2.1 Scene Graph

A *scene graph*, as proposed in Johnson et al. (2015), is a graphical representation that depicts objects, their attributes, and relations among them occurring in an image. An example is given in Figure 2. Nodes in a scene graph correspond to objects with their categories (e.g. *woman*) and edges correspond to the relationships between objects (e.g. *touch*). Such a graphical representation has been shown to be useful in high-level tasks such as image retrieval (Johnson et al., 2015; Schuster et al., 2015) and visual question answering (Teney et al., 2017). Our proposed method builds on the idea that these graph representations can be translated into logical formulas and be used in complex logical reasoning.

2.2 FOL Structure

In logic-based approaches to semantic representations, *FOL structures* (also called *FOL models*) are used to represent semantic information in images (Hürlimann and Bos, 2016), An FOL structure is a pair (D, I) where D is a domain (also called *universe*) consisting of all the entities in an

image and I is an interpretation function that maps a 1-place predicate to a set of entities and a 2-place predicate to a set of pairs of entities, and so on; for instance, we write $I(\mathsf{man}) = \{d_1\}$ if the entity d_1 is a man, and $I(\mathsf{next\_to}) = \{(d_1, d_2)\}$ if d_1 is next to d_2. FOL structures have clear correspondence with the graph representations of images in that they both capture the categories, attributes and relations holding of the entities in an image. For instance, the FOL structure and scene graph in the upper left of Figure 2 have exactly the same information. Thus, the translation from graphs to formulas can also work for FOL structures (see §3.1).

3 Multimodal Logical Inference System

Figure 2 shows the overall picture of the proposed system. We use formulas of FOL with equality as unified semantic representations for text and image information. We use 1-place and 2-place predicates for representing attributes and relations, respectively. The language of FOL consists of (i) a set of atomic formulas, (ii) equations of the form $t = u$, and (iii) complex formulas composed of negation ($\neg$), conjunction ($\wedge$), disjunction ($\vee$), implication ($\rightarrow$), and universal and existential quantification ($\forall$ and $\exists$). The expressive power of the FOL language provides a structured representation that captures not only objects and their semantic relationships but also those complex expressions including negation, quantification and numerals.

$$\text{Tr}_s(D) = \text{entity}(d_1) \wedge \ldots \wedge \text{entity}(d_n)$$

$$\text{Tr}_s(P) = P(d_1) \wedge \ldots \wedge P(d_{n'})$$

$$\text{Tr}_s(R) = R(d_{i_1}, d_{j_1}) \wedge \ldots \wedge R(d_{i_n}, d_{j_n})$$

$$\text{Tr}_c(D) = \forall x.(\text{entity}(x) \leftrightarrow (x = d_1 \vee \ldots \vee x = d_n))$$

$$\text{Tr}_c(P) = \forall x.(P(x) \leftrightarrow (x = d_1 \vee \ldots \vee x = d_{n'}))$$

$$\text{Tr}_c(R) = \forall x \forall y.(R(x,y) \leftrightarrow ((x = d_{i_1} \wedge y = d_{j_1}) \vee \ldots \\ \vee (x = d_{i_m} \wedge y = d_{j_m})))$$

Table 1: Definition of two types of translation, TR_s and TR_c. Here we assume that $D = \{d_1, \ldots, d_n\}$, $P = \{d_1, \ldots, d_{n'}\}$, and $R = \{(d_{i_1}, d_{j_1}), \ldots, (d_{i_m}, d_{j_m})\}$.

The system takes as input an image I and a sentence S and determines whether I entails S, in other words, S is true with respect to the situation described in I. In this work, we assume the input image I is processed into a scene graph/FOL structure G_I using an off-the-shelf converter (Xu et al., 2017; Qi et al., 2019).

To determine entailment relations between sentences and images, we proceed in three steps. First, **graph translator** maps a graph G_I to a formula M. We develop two ways of translating graphs to FOL formulas (§3.1). Second, **semantic parser** takes a sentence S as input and return a formula T via CCG parsing. We improve a semantic parser in CCG for handling numerals and quantification (§3.2). Additionally, we develop a method for utilizing image captions to extend G_I with information obtainable from their logical formulas (§3.3). Third, **inference engine** checks whether M entails T, written $M \vdash T$, using FOL theorem prover (§3.4). Note that FOL theorem provers can accept multiple premises, $M_1, \ldots, M_n$, converted from images and/or sentences and check if $M_1, \ldots, M_n \vdash T$ holds or not. Here we focus on single-premise visual inference.

3.1 Graph Translator

We present two ways of translating graphs (or equivalently, FOL structures) to formulas: a simple translation (Tr_s) and a complex translation (Tr_c). These translations are defined in Table 1. For example, consider a graph consisting of the domain $D = \{d_1, d_2\}$, where we have $\text{man}(d_1), \text{hat}(d_2), \text{red}(d_2)$ as properties and $\text{wear}(d_1, d_2)$ as relations. The simple translation TR_s gives the formula (S) below, which simply conjoins all the atomic information.

(S) $\text{man}(d_1) \wedge \text{hat}(d_2) \wedge \text{red}(d_2) \wedge \text{wear}(d_1, d_2)$

1. $A \in \mathcal{P}$, $\neg A \in \mathcal{N}$, if A is an atomic formula.
2. $A, \neg A \in \mathcal{P}$, if A is an equation of the form $t = u$.
3. $A \wedge B$, $A \vee B \in \mathcal{P}$, if $A \in \mathcal{P}$ and $B \in \mathcal{P}$.
4. $A \wedge B$, $A \vee B \in \mathcal{N}$, if $A \in \mathcal{N}$ or $B \in \mathcal{N}$.
5. $A \to B \in \mathcal{P}$, if $A \in \mathcal{N}$ and $B \in \mathcal{P}$.
6. $A \to B \in \mathcal{N}$, if $A \in \mathcal{P}$ or $B \in \mathcal{N}$.
7. $\forall x.A$, $\exists x.A \in \mathcal{P}$, if $A \in \mathcal{P}$.
8. $\forall x.A$, $\exists x.A \in \mathcal{N}$, if $A \in \mathcal{N}$.

Table 2: Positive ($\mathcal{P}$) and negative ($\mathcal{N}$) formulas

However, this does not capture the *negative* information that d_1 is the only entity that has the property man; similarly for the other predicates. To capture it, we use the complex translation Tr_c, which gives the following formula:

(C) $\forall x.(\text{man}(x) \leftrightarrow x = d_1) \wedge$
$\forall y.(\text{hat}(y) \leftrightarrow y = d_2) \wedge$
$\forall z.(\text{red}(z) \leftrightarrow z = d_2) \wedge$
$\forall x \forall y.(\text{wear}(x,y) \leftrightarrow (x = d_1 \wedge y = d_2))$

This formula says that d_1 is the only man in the domain, d_2 is the only hat in the domain, and so on. This way of translation can be regarded as an instance of Predicate Circumscription (McCarthy, 1986), which complement negative information using the closed world assumption. The translation Tr_c is useful for handling formulas with negation and universal quantification.

One drawback here is that since (C) involves complex formulas, it increases the computational cost in theorem proving. To remedy this problem, we use two types of translation selectively, depending on the polarity of the formula to be proved. Table 2 shows the definition to classify each FOL formula $A \in \mathcal{L}$ into positive ($\mathcal{P}$) and negative ($\mathcal{N}$) one. For instance, the formulas $\exists x \exists y.(\text{cat}(x) \wedge \text{dog} \wedge \text{touch}(x,y))$, which correspond to *A cat touches a dog*, is a positive formula, while $\neg \exists x.(\text{cat}(x) \wedge \text{white}(x))$, which corresponds to *No cats are white*, is a negative formula.

3.2 Semantic Parser

We use ccg2lambda (Mineshima et al., 2015), a semantic parsing system based on CCG to convert sentences to formulas, and extend it to handle numerals and quantificational sentences. In our system, a sentence with numerals, e.g., *There are (at least) two cats*, is compositionally mapped to the following FOL formula:

(Num) $\exists x \exists y.(\text{cat}(x) \wedge \text{cat}(y) \wedge (x \neq y))$

Also, to capture the existential import of universal sentences, the system maps the sentence *All cats are white* to the following one:

(Q) $\exists x.\mathsf{cat}(x) \land \forall y.(\mathsf{cat}(y) \to \mathsf{white}(y))$

3.3 Extending Graphs with Captions

Compared with images, captions can describe a variety of properties and relations other than spatial and visual ones. By integrating caption information into FOL structures, we can obtain semantic representations reflecting relations that can be described only in the caption.

We convert captions into FOL structures (= graphs) using our semantic parser. We only consider the cases where the formulas obtained are composed of existential quantifiers and conjunctions. For extending FOL structures with caption information, it is necessary to analyze co-reference between the entities occurring in sentences and images. We add a new predicate to an FOL structure if the co-reference is uniquely determined.

As an illustration, consider the captions and the FOL structure (D, I) which represents the image shown in Figure 2.[1] The captions, (1a) and (2a), are mapped to the formulas (1a) and (2b), respectively, via semantic parsing.

(1) a. The woman is calling.

b. $\exists x.(\mathsf{woman}(x) \land \mathsf{calling}(x))$

(2) a. The woman is wearing glasses.

b. $\exists x \exists y.(\mathsf{woman}(x) \land \mathsf{glasses}(y)$
$\land \mathsf{wear}(x, y))$

Then, the information in (1b) and (2b) can be added to (D, I), because there is only one woman d_1 in (D, I) and thus the co-reference between *the woman* in the caption and the entity d_1 is uniquely determined. Also, a new entity d_5 for glasses is added because there are no such entities in the structure (D, I). Thus we obtain the following new structure (D^*, I^*) extended with the information in the captions.

$D^* := D \cup \{d_5\}$

$I^* := I \cup \{(\mathsf{glasses}, \{d_5\}), (\mathsf{calling}, \{d_1\}),$
$(\mathsf{wear}, \{(d_1, d_5)\})\}$

---

[1]Note that there is a unique correspondence between FOL structures and scene graphs. For the sake of illustration, we use FOL structures in this subsection.

Pattern	Phenomena
There is a $\langle attr \rangle$ $\langle attr \rangle$ $\langle obj \rangle$.	Con
There are at least $\langle number \rangle$ $\langle obj \rangle$.	Num
All $\langle obj \rangle$ are $\langle attr \rangle$.	Q
$\langle obj \rangle$ $\langle rel \rangle$ $\langle obj \rangle$.	Rel
No $\langle obj \rangle$ is $\langle attr \rangle$.	Neg
All $\langle obj \rangle$ $\langle attr \rangle$ or $\langle attr \rangle$.	Con, Q
Every $\langle obj \rangle$ is not $\langle rel \rangle$ $\langle obj \rangle$.	Num, Rel, Neg

Table 3: Examples of sentence templates. $\langle obj \rangle$: objects, $\langle attr \rangle$: attributes, $\langle rel \rangle$: relations.

3.4 Inference Engine

Theorem prover is a method for judging whether a formula M entails a formula T. We use Prover9[2] as an FOL prover for inference. We set timeout (10 sec) to judge that M does not entail T.

4 Experiment

We evaluate the performance of the proposed visual-textual inference system. Concretely, we formulate our task as image retrieval using query sentences and evaluate the performance in terms of the number of correctly returned images. In particular, we focus on semantically complex sentences containing numerals, quantifiers, and negation, which are difficult for existing graph representations to handle.

Dataset: We use two datasets: Visual Genome (Krishna et al., 2017), which contains pairs of scene graphs and images, and GRIM dataset (Hürlimann and Bos, 2016), which annotates an FOL structure of an image and two types of captions (true and false sentences with respect to the image). Note that our system is fully unsupervised and does not require any training data; in the following, we describe only test set creation procedure.

For the experiment using Visual Genome, we randomly extracted 200 images as test data, and a separate set of 4,000 scene graphs for creating query sentences; we made queries by the following steps. First, we prepared sentence templates focusing on five types of linguistic phenomena: logical connective (**Con**), numeral (**Num**), quantifier (**Q**), relation (**Rel**) and negation (**Neg**). See Table 3 for the templates. Then, we manually extracted object, attribute and relation types from the frequent ones (appearing more than 30 times) in the extracted 4,000 graphs, and created queries by

---

[2]http://www.cs.unm.edu/ mccune/prover9/

Sentences	Phenomena	Count
There is a long red bus.	Con	3
There are at least three men.	Num	32
All windows are closed.	Q	53
Every green tree is tall.	Q	18
A man is wearing a hat.	Rel	12
No umbrella is colorful.	Neg	197
There is a train which is not red.	Neg	6
There are two cups or three cups.	Con, Num	5
All hairs are black or brown.	Con, Q	46
A gray or black pole has two signs.	Con, Num, Rel	6
Three cars are not red.	Num, Neg	28
All women wear a hat.	Q, Rel	2
A man is not walking on a street.	Rel, Neg	76
A clock on a tower is not black.	Rel, Neg	7
Two women aren't having black hair.	Num, Rel, Neg	10
Every man isn't eating anything.	Q, Rel, Neg	67

Table 4: Examples of query sentences In §4.1; Count shows the number of images describing situations under which each sentence is true.

replacing $\langle obj \rangle$, $\langle attr \rangle$ and $\langle rel \rangle$ in the templates with them. As a result, we obtained 37 semantically complex queries as shown in Table 4. To assign correct images to each query, two annotators judged whether each of the test images entails the query sentence. If the two judgments disagreed, the first author decided the correct label.

In the experiment using GRIM, we adopted the same procedure to create a test dataset and obtained 19 query sentences and 194 images.

One of the issues in this dataset is that annotated FOL structures contain only spatial relations such as *next_to* and *near*; to handle queries containing general relations such as *play* and *sing*, our system needs to utilize annotated captions (§3.3). To evaluate if our system can effectively extract information from captions, we split **Rel** of above linguistic phenomena into spatial relation (**Spa-Rel**; relations about spatial information) and general relation (**Gen-Rel**; other relations), and report the scores separately in terms of these categories.

4.1 Experimental Results on Visual Genome

Firstly, we evaluate the performance in terms of our **Graph translator**'s conversion algorithm. As described in §3.1, there are two translation algorithms; simple one that conjunctively enumerates all relation in a graph (**SIMPLE** in the following), and one that selectively employs translation based on Predicate Circumscription (**HYBRID**).

Table 5 shows image retrieval scores per linguistic phenomenon, macro averages of F1 scores of queries labeled with the respective phenomena.

Phenomena (#)		SIMPLE	HYBRID
Con	(17)	36.40	41.66
Num	(9)	43.07	45.45
Q	(9)	8.59	**28.18**
Rel	(11)	25.13	**35.10**
Neg	(11)	66.38	**73.39**

Table 5: Experimental results on Visual Genome (F1). "#" stands for the number of query sentences categorized into that phenomenon.

HYBRID shows better performance for all phenomena than SIMPLE one, improving by 19.59% on **Q**, 9.97% on **Rel** and 7.01% on **Neg**, over SIMPLE, suggesting that the proposed complex translation is useful for inference using semantically complex sentences including quantifier and negation. Figure 3 shows retrieved results for a query (a) *Every green tree is tall* and (b) *No umbrella is colorful*, each containing universal quantifier and negation, respectively. Our system successfully performs inference on these queries, returning the correct images, while excluding wrong ones (note that the third picture in (a) contains short trees).

(a) *Every green tree is tall.*

(b) *No umbrella is colorful.*

Figure 3: Predicted images of our system; Images in green entail the queries, while those in red do not.

Error Analysis: One of the reasons for the lower F1 of **Q** is the gap of annotation rule between Visual Genome and our test set. Quantifiers in natural language often involve vagueness (Pezzelle et al., 2018). for example, the interpretation of *everyone* depends on what counts as an entity in the domain. Difficulties in fixing the interpretation of quantifiers caused the lower performance.

The low F1 in **Rel** is primarily due to lexical gaps between formulas of a query and an image. For example, sentences *All women wear a hat* and *All women have a hat* are the same in their meaning. However, if a scene graph contains only *wear* relation, our system can handle the former query, while not the other. In future work, we will extend our system with a knowledge insertion mechanism (Martínez-Gómez et al., 2017).

4.2 Experimental Results on GRIM

We test our system on GRIM dataset. As noted above, the main issue on this dataset is the lack of relations other than spatial ones. We evaluate if our system can be enhanced using the information contained in captions. The F1 scores of the Hybrid system with captions are the same with the one without captions on the sets except for **Gen-Rel**;[3] on the subset, the F1 score of the former improves by 60% compared to the latter, which suggests that captions can be integrated into FOL structures for the improved performance.

5 Conclusion

We have proposed a logic-based system to achieve advanced visual-textual inference, demonstrating the importance of building a framework for representing the richer semantic content of texts and images. In the experiment, we have shown that our CCG-based pipeline system, consisting of graph translator, semantic parser and inference engine, can perform visual-textual inference with semantically complex sentences, without requiring any supervised data.

Acknowledgement

We thank the two anonymous reviewers for their encouragement and insightful comments. This work was partially supported by JST CREST Grant Number JPMJCR1301, Japan.

References

Manoj Acharya, Kushal Kafle, and Christopher Kanan. 2019. TallyQA: Answering complex counting questions. In *The Association for the Advancement of Artificial Intelligence (AAAI2019)*.

Stanislaw Antol, Aishwarya Agrawal, Jiasen Lu, Margaret Mitchell, Dhruv Batra, C. Lawrence Zitnick, and Devi Parikh. 2015. VQA: Visual Question Answering. In *International Conference on Computer Vision*.

Patrick Blackburn and Johan Bos. 2005. *Representation and Inference for Natural Language: A First Course in Computational Semantics*. Center for the Study of Language and Information, Stanford, CA, USA.

Andrea Frome, Greg S Corrado, Jon Shlens, Samy Bengio, Jeff Dean, Marc Aurelio Ranzato, and Tomas Mikolov. 2013. DeViSE: A Deep Visual-Semantic Embedding Model. In *Neural Information Processing Systems conference*, pages 2121–2129.

Drew A. Hudson and Christopher D. Manning. 2019. Gqa: A new dataset for real-world visual reasoning and compositional question answering. In *The IEEE Conference on Computer Vision and Pattern Recognition (CVPR)*.

Manuela Hürlimann and Johan Bos. 2016. Combining lexical and spatial knowledge to predict spatial relations between objects in images. In *Proceedings of the 5th Workshop on Vision and Language*, pages 10–18. Association for Computational Linguistics.

Justin Johnson, Ranjay Krishna, Michael Stark, Li-Jia Li, David A. Shamma, Michael S. Bernstein, and Li Fei-Fei. 2015. Image retrieval using scene graphs. In *IEEE/ CVF International Conference on Computer Vision and Pattern Recognition*, pages 3668–3678. IEEE Computer Society.

Ranjay Krishna, Yuke Zhu, Oliver Groth, Justin Johnson, Kenji Hata, Joshua Kravitz, Stephanie Chen, Yannis Kalantidis, Li-Jia Li, David A Shamma, Michael Bernstein, and Li Fei-Fei. 2017. Visual genome: Connecting language and vision using crowdsourced dense image annotations. *International Journal of Computer Vision*, 123(1):32–73.

Pascual Martínez-Gómez, Koji Mineshima, Yusuke Miyao, and Daisuke Bekki. 2017. On-demand Injection of Lexical Knowledge for Recognising Textual Entailment. In *Proceedings of The European Chapter of the Association for Computational Linguistics*, pages 710–720.

John McCarthy. 1986. Applications of circumscription to formalizing common-sense knowledge. *Artificial Intelligence*, 28(1):89–116.

Koji Mineshima, Pascual Martínez-Gómez, Yusuke Miyao, and Daisuke Bekki. 2015. Higher-order logical inference with compositional semantics. In *Proceedings of the 2015 Conference on Empirical Methods in Natural Language Processing*, pages 2055–2061. Association for Computational Linguistics.

Mohammad Norouzi, Tomas Mikolov, Samy Bengio, Yoram Singer, Jonathon Shlens, Andrea Frome, Greg Corrado, and Jeffrey Dean. 2014. Zero-Shot Learning by Convex Combination of Semantic Embeddings. In *International Conference on Learning Representations*.

Sandro Pezzelle, Ionut-Teodor Sorodoc, and Raffaella Bernardi. 2018. Comparatives, quantifiers, proportions: a multi-task model for the learning of quantities from vision. In *Proceedings of the 2018 Conference of the North American Chapter of the Association for Computational Linguistics: Human Language Technologies*, pages 419–430. Association for Computational Linguistics.

Mengshi Qi, Weijian Li, Zhengyuan Yang, Yunhong Wang, and Jiebo Luo. 2019. Attentive relational networks for mapping images to scene graphs. In *The IEEE Conference on Computer Vision and Pattern Recognition*.

Sebastian Schuster, Ranjay Krishna, Angel Chang, Li Fei-Fei, and Christopher D. Manning. 2015. Generating semantically precise scene graphs from textual descriptions for improved image retrieval. In *Proceedings of the Fourth Workshop on Vision and Language*, pages 70–80. Association for Computational Linguistics.

---

[3]**Con**: 91.41%, **Num**: 95.24%, **Q**: 78.84%, **Spa-Rel**: 88.57%, **Neg**: 62.57%.

Mark Steedman. 2000. *The Syntactic Process*. MIT Press, Cambridge, MA, USA.

Alane Suhr, Mike Lewis, James Yeh, and Yoav Artzi. 2017. A corpus of natural language for visual reasoning. In *Proceedings of the 55th Annual Meeting of the Association for Computational Linguistics (Volume 2: Short Papers)*, pages 217–223, Vancouver, Canada. Association for Computational Linguistics.

Damien Teney, Lingqiao Liu, and Anton van den Hengel. 2017. Graph-structured representations for visual question answering. In *The IEEE Conference on Computer Vision and Pattern Recognition*, pages 3233–3241.

Hoa Trong Vu, Claudio Greco, Aliia Erofeeva, Somayeh Jafaritazehjan, Guido Linders, Marc Tanti, Alberto Testoni, Raffaella Bernardi, and Albert Gatt. 2018. Grounded textual entailment. In *Proceedings of the 27th International Conference on Computational Linguistics*, pages 2354–2368.

Ning Xie, Farley Lai, Derek Doran, and Asim Kadav. 2018. Visual entailment task for visually-grounded language learning. *arXiv preprint arXiv:1811.10582*.

Danfei Xu, Yuke Zhu, Christopher B. Choy, and Li Fei-Fei. 2017. Scene Graph Generation by Iterative Message Passing. In *The IEEE Conference on Computer Vision and Pattern Recognition*.

Deep Neural Models for Medical Concept Normalization in User-Generated Texts

Zulfat Miftahutdinov
Kazan Federal University,
Kazan, Russia
zulfatmi@gmail.com

Elena Tutubalina
Kazan Federal University,
Kazan, Russia
Samsung-PDMI Joint AI Center,
PDMI RAS, St. Petersburg, Russia
elvtutubalina@kpfu.ru

Abstract

In this work, we consider the *medical concept normalization* problem, i.e., the problem of mapping a health-related entity mention in a free-form text to a concept in a controlled vocabulary, usually to the standard thesaurus in the Unified Medical Language System (UMLS). This is a challenging task since medical terminology is very different when coming from health care professionals or from the general public in the form of social media texts. We approach it as a sequence learning problem with powerful neural networks such as recurrent neural networks and contextualized word representation models trained to obtain semantic representations of social media expressions. Our experimental evaluation over three different benchmarks shows that neural architectures leverage the semantic meaning of the entity mention and significantly outperform an existing state of the art models.

1 Introduction

User-generated texts (UGT) on social media present a wide variety of facts, experiences, and opinions on numerous topics, and this treasure trove of information is currently severely under-explored. We consider the problem of discovering medical concepts in UGTs with the ultimate goal of mining new symptoms, adverse drug reactions (ADR), and other information about a disorder or a drug.

An important part of this problem is to translate a text from "social media language" (e.g., "can't fall asleep all night" or "head spinning a little") to "formal medical language" (e.g., "insomnia" and "dizziness" respectively). This is necessary to match user-generated descriptions with medical concepts, but it is more than just a simple matching of UGTs against a vocabulary. We call the task of mapping the language of UGTs to medical termi-

nology *medical concept normalization*. It is especially difficult since in social media, patients discuss different concepts of illness and a wide array of drug reactions. Moreover, UGTs from social networks are typically ambiguous and very noisy, containing misspelled words, incorrect grammar, hashtags, abbreviations, smileys, different variations of the same word, and so on.

Traditional approaches for concept normalization utilized lexicons and knowledge bases with string matching. The most popular knowledge-based system for mapping texts to UMLS identifiers is MetaMap (Aronson, 2001). This linguistic-based system uses lexical lookup and variants by associating a score with phrases in a sentence. The state-of-the-art baseline for clinical and scientific texts is DNorm (Leaman et al., 2013). DNorm adopts a pairwise learning-to-rank technique using vectors of query mentions and candidate concept terms. This model outperforms MetaMap significantly, increasing the macro-averaged F-measure by 25% on an NCBI disease dataset. However, while these tools have proven to be effective for patient records and research papers, they achieve moderate results on social media texts (Nikfarjam et al., 2015; Limsopatham and Collier, 2016).

Recent works go beyond string matching: these works have tried to view the problem of matching a one- or multi-word expression against a knowledge base as a supervised sequence labeling problem. Limsopatham and Collier (2016) utilized convolutional neural networks (CNNs) for phrase normalization in user reviews, while Tutubalina et al. (2018), Han et al. (2017), and Belousov et al. (2017) applied recurrent neural networks (RNNs) to UGTs, achieving similar results. These works were among the first applications of deep learning techniques to medical concept normalization.

The goal of this work is to study the use of deep neural models, i.e., contextualized word represen-

393

Proceedings of the ACL 2019, Student Research Workshop, pages 393–399
Florence, Italy, July 28th-August 2nd, 2019. ©2019 Association for Computational Linguistics

Entity from UGTs	Medical Concept
no sexual interest	Lack of libido
nonsexual being	Lack of libido
couldnt remember long periods of time or things	Poor long-term memory
loss of memory	Amnesia
bit of lower back pain	Low Back Pain
pains	Pain
like i went downhill	Depressed mood
just lived day by day	Apathy
dry mouth	Xerostomia

Table 1: Examples of extracted social media entities and their associated medical concepts.

tation model BERT (Devlin et al., 2018) and Gated Recurrent Units (GRU) (Cho et al., 2014) with an attention mechanism, paired with *word2vec* word embeddings and contextualized ELMo embeddings (Peters et al., 2018). We investigate if a joint architecture with special provisions for domain knowledge can further improve the mapping of entity mentions from UGTs to medical concepts. We combine the representation of an entity mention constructed by a neural model and distance-like similarity features using vectors of an entity mention and concepts from the UMLS. We experimentally demonstrate the effectiveness of the neural models for medical concept normalization on three real-life datasets of tweets and user reviews about medications with two evaluation procedures.

2 Problem Statement

Our main research problem is to investigate the content of UGTs with the aim to learn the transition between a laypersons language and formal medical language. Examples from Table 1 show that an automated model has to account for the semantics of an entity mention. For example, it has to be able to map not only phases with shared n-grams *no sexual interest* and *nonsexual being* into the concept "Lack of libido" but also separate the phase *bit of lower back pain* from the broader concept "Pain" and map it to a narrower concept.

While focusing on user-generated texts on social media, in this work we seek to answer the following research questions.

RQ1: Do distributed representations reveal important features for medication use in user-generated texts?

RQ2: Can we exploit the semantic similarity between entity mentions from user comments and medical concepts? Do the neural models produce better results than the existing effective baselines? [current research]

RQ3: How to integrate linguistic knowledge about concepts into the models? [current research]

RQ4: How to jointly learn concept embeddings from UMLS and representations of health-related entities from UGTs? [future research]

RQ5: How to effectively use of contextual information to map entity mentions to medical concepts? [future research]

To answer RQ1, we began by collecting UGTs from popular medical web portals and investigating distributed word representations trained on 2.6 millions of health-related user comments. In particular, we analyze drug name representations using clustering and chemoinformatics approaches. The analysis demonstrated that similar word vectors correspond to either drugs with the same active compound or to drugs with close therapeutic effects that belong to the same therapeutic group. It is worth noting that chemical similarity in such drug pairs was found to be low. Hence, these representations can help in the search for compounds with potentially similar biological effects among drugs of different therapeutic groups (Tutubalina et al., 2017).

To answer RQ2 and RQ3, we develop several models and conduct a set of experiments on three benchmark datasets where social media texts are extracted from user reviews and Twitter. We present this work in Sections 3 and 4. We discuss RQ4 and RQ5 with research plans in Section 5.

3 Methods

Following state-of-the-art research (Limsopatham and Collier, 2016; Sarker et al., 2018), we view concept normalization as a classification problem.

To answer RQ2, we investigate the use of neural networks to learn the semantic representation of an entity before mapping its representation to a medical concept. First, we convert each mention into a vector representation using one of the following (well-known) neural models:

(1) bidirectional LSTM (Hochreiter and Schmidhuber, 1997) or GRU (Cho et al., 2014) with an attention mechanism and a hyperbolic tangent activation function on top of 200-dimensional word embeddings obtained to answer RQ1;

(2) a bidirectional layer with attention on top of deep contextualized word representations ELMo (Peters et al., 2018);

(3) a contextualized word representation model BERT (Devlin et al., 2018), which is a multilayer bidirectional Transformer encoder.

We omit technical explanations of the neural network architectures due to space constraints and refer to the studies above.

Next, the learned representation is concatenated with a number of semantic similarity features based on prior knowledge from the UMLS Metathesaurus. Lastly, we add a softmax layer to convert values to conditional probabilities.

The most attractive feature of the biomedical domain is that domain knowledge is prevailing in this domain for dozens of languages. In particular, UMLS is undoubtedly the largest lexico-semantic resource for medicine, containing more than 150 lexicons with terms from 25 languages. To answer RQ3, we extract a set of features to enhance the representation of phrases. These features contain cosine similarities between the vectors of an input phrase and a concept in a medical terminology dictionary. We use the following strategy, which we call TF-IDF (MAX), to construct representations of a concept and a mention: represent a medical code as a set of terms; for each term, compute the cosine distance between its TF-IDF representation and the entity mention; then choose the term with the largest similarity.

4 Experiments

We perform an extensive evaluation of neural models on three datasets of UGTs, namely **CADEC** (Karimi et al., 2015), **PsyTAR** (Zolnoori et al., 2019), and **SMM4H 2017** (Sarker et al., 2018). The basic task is to map a social media phrase to a relevant medical concept.

4.1 Data

CADEC. CSIRO Adverse Drug Event Corpus (CADEC) (Karimi et al., 2015) is the first richly annotated and publicly available corpus of medical forum posts taken from *AskaPatient*[1]. This dataset contains 1253 UGTs about 12 drugs divided into two categories: Diclofenac and Lipitor. All posts were annotated manually for 5 types of entities: ADR, Drug, Disease, Symptom, and Finding. The annotators performed terminology association using the Systematized Nomenclature Of Medicine Clinical Terms (SNOMED CT). We removed "conceptless" or ambiguous mentions for the purposes of evaluation. There were 6,754 entities and 1,029 unique codes in total.

PsyTAR. Psychiatric Treatment Adverse Reactions (PsyTAR) corpus (Zolnoori et al., 2019) is the second open-source corpus of user-generated posts taken from AskaPatient. This dataset includes 887 posts about four psychiatric medications from two classes: (i) Zoloft and Lexapro from the Selective Serotonin Reuptake Inhibitor (SSRI) class and (ii) Effexor and Cymbalta from the Serotonin Norepinephrine Reuptake Inhibitor (SNRI) class. All posts were annotated manually for 4 types of entities: ADR, withdrawal symptoms, drug indications, and sign/symptoms/illness. The corpus consists of 6556 phrases mapped to 618 SNOMED codes.

SMM4H 2017. In 2017, Sarker et al. (2018) organized the Social Media Mining for Health (SMM4H) shared task which introduced a dataset with annotated ADR expressions from *Twitter*. Tweets were collected using 250 keywords such as generic and trade names for medications along with misspellings. Manually extracted ADR expressions were mapped to Preferred Terms (PTs) of the Medical Dictionary for Regulatory Activities (MedDRA). The training set consists of 6650 phrases mapped to 472 PTs. The test set consists of 2500 mentions mapped to 254 PTs.

4.2 Evaluation Details

We evaluate our models based on classification accuracy, averaged across randomly divided five folds of the CADEC and PsyTAR corpora. For SMM4H 2017 data, we adopted the official training and test sets (Sarker et al., 2018). Analysis of randomly split folds shows that *Random KFolds* create a high overlap of expressions in exact matching between subsets (see the baseline results in Table 2). Therefore, we set up a

---

specific train/test split procedure for 5-fold cross-validation on the CADEC and PsyTAR corpora: we removed duplicates of mentions and grouped medical records we are working with into sets related to specific medical codes. Then, each set has been split independently into k folds, and all folds have been merged into the final k folds named *Custom KFolds*. Random folds of CADEC are adopted from (Limsopatham and Collier, 2016) for a fair comparison. Custom folds of CADEC are adopted from our previous work (Tutubalina et al., 2018). PsyTAR folds are available on Zenodo.org[2]. We have also implemented a simple *baseline* approach that uses exact lexical matching with lowercased annotations from the training set.

4.3 Results

Table 2 shows our results for the concept normalization task on the Random and Custom KFolds of the CADEC, PsyTAR, and SMM4H 2017 corpora.

To answer RQ2, we compare the performance of examined neural models with the baseline and state-of-the-art methods in terms of accuracy. Attention-based GRU with ELMo embeddings showed improvement over GRU with *word2vec* embeddings, increasing the average accuracy to 77.85 (+3.65). The semantic information of an entity mention learned by BERT helps to improve the mapping abilities, outperforming other models (avg. accuracy 83.67). Our experiments with recurrent units showed that GRU consistently outperformed LSTM on all subsets, and attention mechanism provided further quality improvements for GRU. From the difference in accuracy on the Random and Custom KFolds, we conclude that future research should focus on developing extrinsic test sets for medical concept normalization. In particular, the BERT model's accuracy on the CADEC Custom KFolds decreased by 9.23% compared to the CADEC Random KFolds.

To answer RQ3, we compare the performance of models with additional similarity features (marked by "w/") with others. Indeed, joint models based on GRU and similarity features gain 2-5% improvement on sets with Custom KFolds. The joint model based on BERT and similarity features stays roughly on par with BERT on all sets. We also tested different strategies for con-

structing representations using word embeddings and TF-IDF for all synonyms' tokens that led to similar improvements for GRU.

5 Future Directions

RQ4. Future research might focus on developing an embedding method that jointly maps extracted entity mentions and UMLS concepts into the same continuous vector space. The methods could help us to easily measure the similarity between words and concepts in the same space. Recently, Yamada et al. (2016) demonstrated that co-trained vectors improve the quality of both word and entity representations in entity linking (EL) which is a task closely related to concept normalization. We note that most of the recent EL methods focus on the disambiguation sub-task, applying simple heuristics for candidate generation. The latter is especially challenging in medical concept normalization due to a significant language difference between medical terminology and patient vocabulary.

RQ5. Error analysis has confirmed that models often misclassify closely related concepts (e.g., "Emotionally detached" and "Apathy") and antonymous concepts (e.g., "Hypertension" and "Hypotension"). We suggest to take into account not only the distance-like similarity between entity mentions and concepts but the mention's context, which is not used directly in recent studies on concept normalization. The context can be represented by the set of adjacent words or entities. As an alternative, one can use a conditional random field (CRF) to output the most likely sequence of medical concepts discussed in a review.

6 Related Work

In 2004, the research community started to address the needs to automatically detect biomedical entities in free texts through shared tasks. Huang and Lu (2015) survey the work done in the organization of biomedical NLP (BioNLP) challenge evaluations up to 2014. These tasks are devoted to the normalization of (1) genes from scientific articles (BioCreative I-III in 2005-2011); (2) chemical entity mentions (BioCreative IV CHEMDNER in 2014); (3) disorders from abstracts (BioCreative V CDR Task in 2015); (4) diseases from clinical reports (ShARe/CLEF eHealth 2013; SemEval 2014 task 7). Similarly, the *CLEF Health* 2016

---

[2]`https://doi.org/10.5281/zenodo.3236318`

Method	CADEC		PsyTAR		SMM4H
	Random	Custom	Random	Custom	Official
Baseline: match with training set annotation	66.09	0.0	56.04	2.63	67.12
DNorm (Limsopatham and Collier, 2016)	73.39	-	-	-	-
CNN (Limsopatham and Collier, 2016)	81.41	-	-	-	-
RNN (Limsopatham and Collier, 2016)	79.98	-	-	-	-
Attentional Char-CNN (Niu et al., 2018)	84.65	-	-	-	-
Hierarchical Char-CNN (Han et al., 2017)	-	-	-	-	87.7
Ensemble (Sarker et al., 2018)	-	-	-	-	88.7
GRU+Attention	82.19	66.56	73.12	65.98	83.16
GRU+Attention w/ TF-IDF (MAX)	84.23	70.05	75.53	68.59	86.28
ELMo+GRU+Attention	85.06	71.68	77.58	68.34	86.60
ELMo+GRU+Attention w/ TF-IDF (MAX)	85.71	74.70	79.52	70.05	87.52
BERT	88.69	79.83	83.07	77.52	89.28
BERT w/ TF-IDF (MAX)	88.84	79.25	82.37	77.33	89.64

Table 2: The performance of the proposed models and the state-of-the-art methods in terms of accuracy.

and 2017 labs addressed the problem of ICD coding of free-form death certificates (without specified entity mentions). Traditionally, linguistic approaches based on dictionaries, association measures, and syntactic properties have been used to map texts to a concept from a controlled vocabulary (Aronson, 2001; Van Mulligen et al., 2016; Mottin et al., 2016; Ghiasvand and Kate, 2014; Tang et al., 2014). Leaman et al. (2013) proposed the DNorm system based on a pairwise learning-to-rank technique using vectors of query mentions and candidate concept terms. These vectors are obtained from a tf-idf representation of all tokens from training mentions and concept terms. Zweigenbaum and Lavergne (2016) utilized a hybrid method combining simple dictionary projection and mono-label supervised classification from ICD coding. Nevertheless, the majority of biomedical research on medical concept extraction primarily focused on scientific literature and clinical records (Huang and Lu, 2015). Zolnoori et al. (2019) applied a popular dictionary look-up system cTAKES on user reviews. cTAKES based on additional PsyTAR's dictionaries achieves twice better results (0.49 F1 score on the exact matching). Thus, dictionaries gathered from layperson language can efficiently improve automatic performance.

The 2017 SMM4H shared task (Sarker et al., 2018) was the first effort for the evaluation of NLP methods for the normalization of health-related text from social media on publicly released data. Recent advances in neural networks have been utilized for concept normalization: recent studies have employed convolutional neural networks (Limsopatham and Collier, 2016; Niu et al., 2018) and recurrent neural networks (Belousov et al., 2017; Han et al., 2017). These works have trained neural networks from scratch using only entity mentions from training data and pre-trained word embeddings. To sum up, most methods have dealt with encoding information an entity mention itself, ignoring the broader context where it occurred. Moreover, these studies did not examine an evaluation methodology tailored to the task.

7 Conclusion

In this work, we have performed a fine-grained evaluation of neural models for medical concept normalization tasks. We employed several powerful models such as BERT and RNNs paired with pre-trained word embeddings and ELMo embeddings. We also developed a joint model that combines (i) semantic similarity features based on prior knowledge from UMLS and (ii) a learned representation that captures extensional semantic information of an entity mention. We have carried out experiments on three datasets using 5-fold cross-validation in two setups. Each dataset contains phrases and their corresponding SNOMED or MedDRA concepts. Analyzing the results, we have found that similarity features help to improve mapping abilities of joint models based on recurrent neural networks paired with pre-trained word embeddings or ELMo embeddings while staying roughly on par with the advanced language representation model BERT in terms of accuracy. Different setups of evaluation procedures affect the performance of models significantly: the accuracy of BERT is 7.25% higher on test sets with a simple random split than on test sets with the proposed custom split. Moreover, we have discussed some interesting future research directions and challenges to be overcome.

Acknowledgments

We thank Sergey Nikolenko for helpful discussions. This research was supported by the Russian Science Foundation grant no. 18-11-00284.

References

Alan R Aronson. 2001. Effective mapping of biomedical text to the UMLS Metathesaurus: the MetaMap program. In *Proceedings of the AMIA Symposium*, page 17. American Medical Informatics Association.

M. Belousov, W. Dixon, and G. Nenadic. 2017. Using an ensemble of generalised linear and deep learning models in the smm4h 2017 medical concept normalisation task. *CEUR Workshop Proceedings*, 1996:54–58.

Kyunghyun Cho, Bart van Merrienboer, Çaglar Gülçehre, Fethi Bougares, Holger Schwenk, and Yoshua Bengio. 2014. Learning phrase representations using RNN encoder-decoder for statistical machine translation. *CoRR*, abs/1406.1078.

Jacob Devlin, Ming-Wei Chang, Kenton Lee, and Kristina Toutanova. 2018. Bert: Pre-training of deep bidirectional transformers for language understanding. *arXiv preprint arXiv:1810.04805*.

Omid Ghiasvand and Rohit J Kate. 2014. Uwm: Disorder mention extraction from clinical text using crfs and normalization using learned edit distance patterns. In *SemEval@ COLING*, pages 828–832.

S. Han, T. Tran, A. Rios, and R. Kavuluru. 2017. Team uknlp: Detecting adrs, classifying medication intake messages, and normalizing adr mentions on twitter. *CEUR Workshop Proceedings*, 1996:49–53.

S. Hochreiter and J. Schmidhuber. 1997. Long Short-Term Memory. *Neural Computation*, 9(8):1735–1780. Based on TR FKI-207-95, TUM (1995).

Chung-Chi Huang and Zhiyong Lu. 2015. Community challenges in biomedical text mining over 10 years: success, failure and the future. *Briefings in bioinformatics*, 17(1):132–144.

Sarvnaz Karimi, Alejandro Metke-Jimenez, Madonna Kemp, and Chen Wang. 2015. Cadec: A corpus of adverse drug event annotations. *Journal of biomedical informatics*, 55:73–81.

Robert Leaman, Rezarta Islamaj Doğan, and Zhiyong Lu. 2013. DNorm: disease name normalization with pairwise learning to rank. *Bioinformatics*, 29(22):2909–2917.

Nut Limsopatham and Nigel Collier. 2016. Normalising Medical Concepts in Social Media Texts by Learning Semantic Representation. In *ACL*.

Luc Mottin, Julien Gobeill, Anaïs Mottaz, Emilie Pasche, Arnaud Gaudinat, and Patrick Ruch. 2016. Bitem at clef ehealth evaluation lab 2016 task 2: Multilingual information extraction. In *CLEF (Working Notes)*, pages 94–102.

Azadeh Nikfarjam, Abeed Sarker, Karen OConnor, Rachel Ginn, and Graciela Gonzalez. 2015. Pharmacovigilance from social media: mining adverse drug reaction mentions using sequence labeling with word embedding cluster features. *Journal of the American Medical Informatics Association*, 22(3):671–681.

Jinghao Niu, Yehui Yang, Siheng Zhang, Zhengya Sun, and Wensheng Zhang. 2018. Multi-task character-level attentional networks for medical concept normalization. *Neural Processing Letters*, pages 1–18.

Matthew E. Peters, Mark Neumann, Mohit Iyyer, Matt Gardner, Christopher Clark, Kenton Lee, and Luke Zettlemoyer. 2018. Deep contextualized word representations. In *Proc. of NAACL*.

Abeed Sarker, Maksim Belousov, Jasper Friedrichs, Kai Hakala, Svetlana Kiritchenko, Farrokh Mehryary, Sifei Han, Tung Tran, Anthony Rios, Ramakanth Kavuluru, et al. 2018. Data and systems for medication-related text classification and concept normalization from twitter: insights from the social media mining for health (smm4h)-2017 shared task. *Journal of the American Medical Informatics Association*, 25(10):1274–1283.

Yaoyun Zhang1 Jingqi Wang1 Buzhou Tang, Yonghui Wu1 Min Jiang, and Yukun Chen3 Hua Xu. 2014. Uth_ccb: a report for semeval 2014–task 7 analysis of clinical text. *SemEval 2014*, page 802.

Elena Tutubalina, Zulfat Miftahutdinov, Sergey Nikolenko, and Valentin Malykh. 2018. Medical concept normalization in social media posts with recurrent neural networks. *Journal of biomedical informatics*, 84:93–102.

EV Tutubalina, Z Sh Miftahutdinov, RI Nugmanov, TI Madzhidov, SI Nikolenko, IS Alimova, and AE Tropsha. 2017. Using semantic analysis of texts for the identification of drugs with similar therapeutic effects. *Russian Chemical Bulletin*, 66(11):2180–2189.

E Van Mulligen, Zubair Afzal, Saber A Akhondi, Dang Vo, and Jan A Kors. 2016. Erasmus MC at CLEF eHealth 2016: Concept recognition and coding in French texts. CLEF.

Ikuya Yamada, Hiroyuki Shindo, Hideaki Takeda, and Yoshiyasu Takefuji. 2016. Joint learning of the embedding of words and entities for named entity disambiguation. In *Proceedings of The 20th SIGNLL Conference on Computational Natural Language Learning*, pages 250–259.

Maryam Zolnoori, Kin Wah Fung, Timothy B Patrick, Paul Fontelo, Hadi Kharrazi, Anthony Faiola, Yi Shuan Shirley Wu, Christina E Eldredge, Jake Luo, Mike Conway, et al. 2019. A systematic approach for developing a corpus of patient reported adverse drug events: A case study for ssri and snri medications. *Journal of biomedical informatics*, 90:103091.

Pierre Zweigenbaum and Thomas Lavergne. 2016. Hybrid methods for icd-10 coding of death certificates. *EMNLP 2016*, page 96.

Using Semantic Similarity as Reward for Reinforcement Learning in Sentence Generation

Go Yasui[1]   **Yoshimasa Tsuruoka[1]**   **Masaaki Nagata[2]**

[1]The University of Tokyo
7-3-1 Hongo, Bunkyo-ku, Tokyo, Japan
`{gyasui,tsuruoka}@logos.t.u-tokyo.ac.jp`

[2]NTT Communication Science Laboratories, NTT Corporation
2-4 Hikaridai, Seika-cho, Soraku-gun, Kyoto, 619-0237 Japan
`masaaki.nagata.et@hco.ntt.co.jp`

Abstract

Traditional model training for sentence generation employs cross-entropy loss as the loss function. While cross-entropy loss has convenient properties for supervised learning, it is unable to evaluate sentences as a whole, and lacks flexibility. We present the approach of training the generation model using the estimated semantic similarity between the output and reference sentences to alleviate the problems faced by the training with cross-entropy loss. We use the BERT-based scorer fine-tuned to the Semantic Textual Similarity (STS) task for semantic similarity estimation, and train the model with the estimated scores through reinforcement learning (RL). Our experiments show that reinforcement learning with semantic similarity reward improves the BLEU scores from the baseline LSTM NMT model.

1 Introduction

Sentence generation using neural networks has become a vital part of various natural language processing tasks including machine translation (Sutskever et al., 2014) and abstractive summarization (Rush et al., 2015). Most previous work on sentence generation employ cross-entropy loss between the model outputs and the ground-truth sentence to guide the maximum-likelihood training on the token-level. Differentiability of cross-entropy loss is useful for computing gradients in supervised learning; however, it lacks flexibility and may penalize the generation model for a slight shift or change in token sequence even if the sequence retains the meaning.

For instance, consider the sentence pair, "I watched a movie last night." and "I saw a film last night.". As the simple cross-entropy loss lacks the ability to properly assess semantically similar tokens, these sentences are penalized for having two token mismatches. As another example, the sentence pair "He often walked to school." and "He walked to school often." would be severely punished by the token misalignment, despite having identical meanings.

To tackle the inflexible nature of model evaluation during training, we propose an approach of using semantic similarity between the output sequence and the ground-truth sequence to train the generation model. In the proposed framework, semantic similarity of sentence pairs is estimated by a BERT-based (Devlin et al., 2018) regression model fine-tuned against Semantic Textual Similarity (Agirre et al., 2012) dataset, and the resulting score is passed back to the model using reinforcement learning strategies.

Our experiment on translation datasets suggests that the proposed method is better at improving the BLEU score than the traditional cross-entropy learning. However, since the model outputs had limited paraphrastic variations, the results are also inconclusive in supporting the effectiveness of applying the proposed method to sentence generation.

2 Related Work

2.1 Sentence Generation

Recurrent neural networks have become popular models of choice for sentence generation (Sutskever et al., 2014). These sentence generation models are generally implemented as an architecture known as an Encoder-Decoder model.

The decoder model, the portion of Encoder-

Proceedings of the ACL 2019, Student Research Workshop, pages 400–406
Florence, Italy, July 28th-August 2nd, 2019. ©2019 Association for Computational Linguistics

Decoder responsible for generating tokens, is usually an RNN. For an intermediate representation X, output token distribution at time t $\hat{y}_t$ for the RNN decoder π_θ can be written as

$$s_{t+1} = \Phi_\theta \left(\hat{y}_t, s_t, X \right) \tag{1}$$

$$\hat{y}_{t+1} \sim \pi_\theta \left(y_t \mid \hat{y}_t, s_t, X \right) \tag{2}$$

where s_t is the hidden state of the decoder at time t, Φ_θ is the state update function, and θ is the model parameter. Since a simple RNN is known to lack the ability to handle long-term dependencies, recurrent models with more sophisticated update mechanisms such as Long Short-term Memory (LSTM) (Hochreiter and Schmidhuber, 1997) and Gate Recurrent Unit (GRU) (Cho et al., 2014) are used in more recent works.

Sentence generation models are typically trained using cross-entropy loss as follows:

$$L_{CE} = - \sum_{t=1}^{T} \log \pi_\theta \left(y_t \mid y_{t-1}, s_t, X \right), \tag{3}$$

where $Y = \{y_1, y_2, ..., y_T\}$ is the ground-truth sequence.

While cross-entropy loss is an effective loss function for multi-class classification problems such as sentence generation, there are a few drawbacks. Cross-entropy loss is computed by comparing the output distribution and the target distribution on every timestep, and this token-wise nature is intolerant of slight shift or reordering in output tokens. As the ground-truth distributions Y are usually one-hot distributions cross-entropy loss is also intolerant to distribution mismatch even when the two distributions represent similar but different tokens.

2.2 Reinforcement Learning for Sentence Generation

One way to avoid the problems of cross-entropy loss is to use a different criterion during the model training. Reinforcement learning, a framework in which the agent must choose a series of discrete actions to maximize the reward returned from its surrounding environment, is one of such approaches. The advantages of using RL are that the reward for an action does not have to be returned spontaneously and that the reward function does not have to be differentiable by the parameter of the agent model.

Because of these advantages, RL has often been used as a means to train sentence generation model against sentence-level metrics (Pasunuru and Bansal, 2018; Ranzato et al., 2015). Sentence-level metrics commonly used in RL settings, such as BLEU, ROUGE and METEOR, are typically not differentiable, and thus are not usable under the regular supervised training.

One of the common RL algorithms used in sentence generation is REINFORCE (Williams, 1992). REINFORCE is a relatively simple policy gradient algorithm. In the context of sentence generation, the goal of the agent is to maximize the expectation of the reward provided as the function r as in the following:

$$Maximize \, \mathbb{E}_{\hat{y}_1,...,\hat{y}_T \sim \pi_\theta(\hat{y}_1,...,\hat{y}_T)} \left[r \left(\hat{y}_1, ..., \hat{y}_T \right) \right], \tag{4}$$

where $\hat{Y} = \{\hat{y}_1, \hat{y}_2, ..., \hat{y}_T\}$ is a series of decoder output tokens.

The loss function is the negative of the reward expectation, but the expectation is typically approximated by a single sample sequence as follows:

$$L_{RL} = \sum_{t} \log \pi_\theta \left(y_t \mid \hat{y}_{t-1}, s_t \right) \left(r \left(\hat{y}_{1,...,T} \right) - r_b \right), \tag{5}$$

where r_b is the baseline reward which counters the large variance of reward caused by sampling. r_b can be any function that does not contain the parameter of the sentence generation model, but usually is kept to a simple model or function to not hinder the training.

2.3 Semantic Textual Similarity

Semantic Textual Similarity (STS) (Agirre et al., 2012; Cer et al., 2017) is an NLP task of evaluating the degree of similarity between two given texts. Similarity scores must be given as continuous real values from 0 (completely dissimilar) and 5 (completely equivalent), and the model performance is measured by computing the Pearson correlation between the machine score and the human score. As STS scores are assigned as similarity scores between whole sentences and not tokens, slight token differences can lower the STS score drastically. For example, the first sentence pair shown in Table 1, "A man is playing a guitar." and "A girl is playing a guitar.", only has a single token mismatch, "man" and "girl". However, the score given to the pair is 2.8, because that single mismatch causes clear contrasts in meanings between the sentences.

Table 1: Examples of STS similarity scores in STS-B dataset.

Score	Sentence Pair
2.8	A man is playing a guitar.
	A girl is playing a guitar.
4.2	A panda bear is eating some bamboo.
	A panda is eating bamboo.

On the other hand, STS scores are tolerant of modifications that do not change the meaning of sentence. This leniency is illustrated by the second sentence pair in Table 1, "A panda bear is eating some bamboo." and "A panda is eating bamboo.". Such a sentence pair would receive an unfavourable score in similarity evaluation using token-wise comparison, because every word after "panda" would be considered as a mismatched token. In contrast, the STS score given to the pair is 4.2. Omission of words "bear" and "some" in the latter sentence does not alter the meaning from the first sentence, and thus the pair is considered semantically similar.

STS is similar to other semantic comparison tasks such as textual entailment (Dagan et al., 2010) and paraphrase identification (Dolan et al., 2004). One key distinction that STS has from these two tasks is that STS expects the model to output continuous scores with interpretable intermediate values rather than discrete binary values describing whether or not given sentence pairs have certain semantic relationships.

2.4 BERT

Bidirectional Encoder Representations from Transformer (BERT) (Devlin et al., 2018) is a pre-training model based on the transformer model (Vaswani et al., 2017). Previous pre-training models such as ELMo (Peters et al., 2017) and OpenAI-GPT (Radford et al., 2018) used unidirectional language models to learn general language representations and this limited their ability to capture token relationships in both directions. Instead, BERT employs a bidirectional self-attention architecture to capture the language representations more thoroughly.

Upon its release, BERT broke numerous state-of-the-art records such as those on a general language understanding task GLUE (Wang et al., 2018), question answering task SQuAD v1.1 (Rajpurkar et al., 2016), and grounded com-monsense inference task SWAG (Zellers et al., 2018). STS is one of the tasks included in GLUE.

3 Models

3.1 Sentence Generation Model

The sentence generation model π_θ used for this research is a neural machine translation (NMT) model consisting of a single-layer LSTM encoder-decoder model with attention mechanism and the softmax output layer. The model also incorporates input feeding to make itself aware of the alignment decision in the previous decoding step (Luong et al., 2015). The encoder LSTM is bidirectional while the decoder LSTM is unidirectional.

3.2 STS Estimator

The STS estimator model r_ψ consists of two modules. As described in Eq. (6), one is the BERT encoder with pooling layer B and the other is a linear output layer (with weight vector W_ψ and bias b_ψ) with ReLU activation r_ψ.

$$B\left(Y_1, Y_2\right) = \mathrm{Pool}\left(\mathrm{BERT}\left(Y_1, Y_2\right)\right), \qquad (6)$$

$$r_\psi\left(Y_1, Y_2\right) = \mathrm{ReLU}\left(W_\psi \cdot B\left(Y_1, Y_2\right) + b_\psi\right). \qquad (7)$$

The BERT encoder reads tokenized sentence pairs (Y_1, Y_2) joined by a separation (SEP) token and outputs intermediate representations that are then fed into the linear layer through a pooling layer. The output layer projects the input into scalar values representing the estimated STS scores for input sentence pairs.

The model r_ψ is trained using the mean squared error (MSE) to fit the corresponding real-valued label v as written in Eq. (8).

$$L_{BERT} = \left|r_\psi\left(Y_1, Y_2\right) - v\right|^2. \qquad (8)$$

While the use of the BERT-based STS estimator as an evaluation mechanism allows the sentence generation model to train its outputs against sentence-wise evaluation criteria, there is a downside to this framework.

The BERT encoder expects the input sentences to be sequences of tokens. As with most sentence generation models, the outputs of the encoder-decoder model described in the previous subsection are sequences of output probability distributions of tokens.

Obtaining a single token from a probability distribution equates to performing indifferentiable operations like argmax and sampling. Consequently, the regular backpropagation algorithm cannot be applied the training of generation model. Furthermore, the scores provided by the STS estimator r_ψ are sentence-wise while the sequence generation is done token by token. There is no direct way to evaluate the effect of a single instance of token generation on a sentence-wise outcome in the setting of supervised learning. As mentioned in Section 2.2, RL is an approach that can provide solutions to these problems.

3.3 Baseline Estimator

Following the previous work (Ranzato et al., 2015), the baseline estimator Ω_ω is defined as follows:

$$\Omega_\omega\left(s_t\right) = \sigma\left(W_\omega \cdot s_t + b_\omega\right), \qquad (9)$$

where W_r is a weight vector, b_ω is a bias, and σ is the logistic sigmoid function.

3.4 Model Training

Overall, the model training is separated into three stages.

The first stage is the training of BERT-based STS estimator r_ψ. The model r_ψ, with its pre-trained BERT encoder, is fine-tuned using a STS dataset with the loss function described in Eq. (8). The parameter of the STS estimator is frozen from this point onward.

The second stage is the training of the NMT model using the cross-entropy loss shown in Eq. (3). This stage is necessary to allow the model training to converge. The action space in sentence generation is extremely large and applying RL from scratch would lead to slow and unstable training.

The final stage is the RL stage where we apply REINFORCE to NMT model. The loss function for REINFORCE is rewritten from Eq. (5) as follows:

$$L_{RL} = \sum_t R_t \log \pi_\theta\left(y_t \mid \hat{y}_{t-1}, s_t\right), \qquad (10)$$

$$R_t = \left(\frac{1}{5} r_\psi\left(\hat{Y}, Y\right) - \Omega_\omega\left(s_t\right)\right), \qquad (11)$$

where R_t is the difference between the reward r_ψ and the expected reward Ω_ω. r_ψ is multiplied by $\frac{1}{5}$ as Ω_ω is bounded in $[0, 1]$. Because using only

L_{RL} in the RL stage reportedly leads to unstable training (Wu et al., 2016) the loss used in this step is a linear combination of L_{CE} and L_{RL} as follows:

$$L = \lambda L_{CE} + (1 - \lambda) L_{RL}, \qquad (12)$$

where $\lambda \in [0, 1]$ is a hyperparameter. The value of λ typically is a small non-zero value.

During the RL stage, the reward prediction model Ω_ω is trained using the MSE loss as follows:

$$L_{BSE} = \left|\frac{1}{5} r_\psi\left(\hat{Y}, Y\right) - \Omega_\omega\left(s_t\right)\right|^2. \qquad (13)$$

The reward predictor does not share its parameter with the NMT model.

4 Experiment

4.1 Dataset

The dataset used for fine-tuning the STS estimator is STS-B (Cer et al., 2017). The tokenizer used is a wordpiece tokenizer for BERT.

For machine translation, we used De-En parallel corpora from multi30k-dataset (Elliott et al., 2016) and WIT3 (Cettolo et al., 2012). The multi30k-dataset is comprised of textual descriptions of images while the WIT3 consists of transcribed TED talks. Each corpus provides a single validation set and multiple test sets. We chose the best models based on their scores for the validation sets and used the two newest test sets from each corpus for testing. Both corpora are tokenized using the sentencepiece BPE tokenizer with a vocabulary size of 8,000 for each language. All letters are turned to lowercase and any consecutive spaces are turned into a single space before tokenization. The source and target vocabularies are kept separate.

4.2 Training Settings

The BERT model used for the experiment is BERT-base-uncased, and is trained with a maximum sequence length of 128, batch size of 32, learning rate of 2×10^{-5} up to 6 epochs.

For the supervised (cross-entropy) training of the NMT model, we set size of hidden states for all LSTM to 256 for each direction, and use SGD with an initial learning rate of 1.0, momentum of 0.75, the learning rate decay of 0.5, and the dropout rate of 0.2. With the batch size of 128 and the maximum sequence length of 100, the

NMT model typically reached the highest estimated STS score on the validation set after less than 10 epochs.

In the RL stage, initial learning rates are set to 0.01 and 1.0×10^{-3} for the NMT model and the baseline estimator model respectively. λ is set to 0.005. The batch size is reduced to 100 but other hyperparameters are kept the same as in the supervised stage.

For a comparison, we also train a separate translation model with RL using GLEU (Wu et al., 2016). GLEU score is calculated by taking the minimum of n-gram recall and n-gram precision between output tokens and target tokens. While the GLEU score is known to correlate well with the BLEU score on the corpus-level, it also avoids some of the undesirable characteristics that the BLEU score has on the sentence-level. During the RL stage for the GLEU model, the reward measure $\frac{1}{5} r_\psi \left(\hat{Y}, Y \right)$ in Eq. (11) and Eq. (13) is replaced by $GLEU \left(\hat{Y}, Y \right)$. Other training procedures and hyperparameters are kept the same as those of the model trained using STS.

5   Results and Discussion

The BLEU scores of Cross-entropy, RL-GLEU and RL-STS models are shown in Table 2 and the sample outputs of the models during the training are displayed in Table 3.

As shown in Table 2 applying the RL step with STS improved BLEU scores for all test sets, even though the model was not directly optimized to increase the BLEU score. It can be inferred that estimated semantic similarity scores have positive correlation with the BLEU score.

As BLEU is scored using matching n-grams between the candidate and ground-truth sentences, it can be considered a better indicator of semantic similarity between sentences than cross-entropy loss. One interesting observation made during the training was that after entering the RL stage, the cross-entropy loss against the training data increased yet the BLEU scores improved. This suggests that RL using STS reward is a better training strategy for improving the semantic accuracy of output tokens than the plain cross-entropy loss training.

Table 2 also shows that RL-GLEU has better BLEU scores than RL-STS. This is inevitable considering that STS, unlike GLEU and BLEU, is not based on n-gram matching and may permit output tokens not present in a target sequence as long as the output sequence stays semantically similar to the target sequence. Such property can lead to n-gram mismatches and lower BLEU scores. It is important to note that the leniency of STS evaluation does not severely affect BLEU scores.

In fact, training with RL using STS did alter outputs of the model in ways that suggest the leniency of STS as a training objective. For instance, sentences shown in Table 3 demonstrate the cases where the RL swapped a few tokens or added an extra token to the output sentences without drastically changing the meaning of the original sentence.

Nevertheless, this kind of alterations were not abundant perhaps because of the fact that the model is never encouraged to output paraphrastic sentences during the supervised learning phase. The degree of effectiveness of our approach would be more apparent in the setting where the model outputs are more diverse, such as paraphrasing.

Another interesting characteristic of the outputs of RL-STS is that they sometimes did not properly terminate. This occurred even in cases where the cross-entropy model was able to form a complete sentence. One possible cause of this problem is the way the output sequence is tokenized before it is fed to the BERT-based estimator. Because an end-of-sentence (EOS) token is not one of the special tokens used in pretraining of BERT, any EOS token was stripped before inserting a SEP token. Consequently, the RL-STS model was not able to receive proper feedback for producing the EOS token. This can perhaps be avoided by introducing an additional loss term in Eq. (10) to penalize sequences that are not terminated.

6   Conclusion

In this paper, we focused on the disadvantages of using cross-entropy loss for sentence generation, namely its inability to handle similar tokens and its intolerance towards token reordering. To solve these problems, we proposed an approach of using the BERT-based semantic similarity estimator trained using STS dataset to evaluate the degree of meaning overlap between output sentences and ground-truth sentences. As the estimated STS scores are indifferentiable, we also incorporated REINFORCE into the training to backpropagate the gradient using RL strategies. The proposed

Table 2: BLEU and estimated STS scores for test sets in multi30k-dataset and WIT3. mscoco2017 and flickr2017 are test sets for multi30k-dataset, while TED2014 and TED2015 are test sets for WIT3. RL-GLEU and RL-STS denote models trained with REINFORCE using GLEU reward and STS reward respectively.

Model	mscoco2017		flickr2017		TED2014		TED2015	
	BLEU	STS	BLEU	STS	BLEU	STS	BLEU	STS
Cross-entropy	16.44	2.76	22.22	3.03	12.54	2.63	13.43	2.80
RL-GLEU	20.13	2.93	25.83	3.15	13.97	2.71	14.59	2.89
RL-STS	18.31	2.96	24.70	3.21	13.58	2.87	14.56	2.99

Table 3: Sample outputs of the models for the training set

Model	Output Sentences	
Ground-truth	I'll show you what I mean.	So how do we solve?
Cross-entropy	I'll show you what I mean.	So how do we solve?
RL-GLEU	I'll show you what I mean.	So how do we solve?
RL-STS	I'm going to show you what I mean.	So how do we solve problems?

method proved successful in improving the BLEU score over the baseline model trained using only the cross-entropy loss. The findings from the comparison of model outputs suggest that the STS allows lenient evaluation without severely degrading BLEU scores. However, the extent of effectiveness of the proposed method is yet to be determined. Further analysis of the method using different datasets such as those for abstractive summarization and paraphrasing, as well as human evaluation are necessary to reach a proper conclusion.

Acknowledgments

We would like to thank Kazuma Hashimoto and anonymous reviewers for helpful comments and suggestions.

References

Eneko Agirre, Mona Diab, Daniel Cer, and Aitor Gonzalez-Agirre. 2012. Semeval-2012 task 6: A pilot on semantic textual similarity. In *SemEval*.

Daniel Cer, Mona Diab, Eneko Agirre, Inigo Lopez-Gazpio, and Lucia Specia. 2017. SemEval-2017 Task 1: Semantic Textual Similarity Multilingual and Crosslingual Focused Evaluation. In *SemEval*.

Mauro Cettolo, Christian Girardi, and Marcello Federico. 2012. Wit^3: Web inventory of transcribed and translated talks. In *EAMT*.

Kyunghyun Cho, Bart van Merrienboer, Caglar Gulcehre, Dzmitry Bahdanau, Fethi Bougares, Holger Schwenk, and Yoshua Bengio. 2014. Learning Phrase Representations using RNN EncoderDecoder for Statistical Machine Translation. In *EMNLP*.

Ido Dagan, Bill Dolan, Bernardo Magnini, and Dan Roth. 2010. Recognizing textual entailment: Rational, evaluation and approaches–erratum. *Natural Language Engineering*, 16(1).

Jacob Devlin, Ming-Wei Chang, Kenton Lee, and Kristina Toutanova. 2018. BERT: Pre-training of Deep Bidirectional Transformers for Language Understanding. *arXiv:1810.04805 [cs]*.

Bill Dolan, Chris Quirk, and Chris Brockett. 2004. Unsupervised construction of large paraphrase corpora: Exploiting massively parallel news sources. In *COLING*.

Desmond Elliott, Stella Frank, Khalil Sima'an, and Lucia Specia. 2016. Multi30k: Multilingual english-german image descriptions. In *VL*.

Sepp Hochreiter and Jrgen Schmidhuber. 1997. Long Short-Term Memory. *Neural Computation*, 9(8):1735–1780.

Thang Luong, Hieu Pham, and Christopher D. Manning. 2015. Effective Approaches to Attention-based Neural Machine Translation. In *EMNLP*.

Ramakanth Pasunuru and Mohit Bansal. 2018. Multi-reward reinforced summarization with saliency and entailment. In *NAACL*.

Matthew Peters, Waleed Ammar, Chandra Bhagavatula, and Russell Power. 2017. Semi-supervised sequence tagging with bidirectional language models. In *ACL*.

Alec Radford, Karthik Narasimhan, Time Salimans, and Ilya Sutskever. 2018. Improving language understanding with unsupervised learning. Technical report, Technical report, OpenAI.

Pranav Rajpurkar, Jian Zhang, Konstantin Lopyrev, and Percy Liang. 2016. Squad: 100,000+ questions for machine comprehension of text. *arXiv preprint arXiv:1606.05250*.

Marc'Aurelio Ranzato, Sumit Chopra, Michael Auli, and Wojciech Zaremba. 2015. Sequence Level Training with Recurrent Neural Networks. *arXiv:1511.06732 [cs]*. ArXiv: 1511.06732.

Alexander M Rush, Sumit Chopra, and Jason Weston. 2015. A neural attention model for abstractive sentence summarization. In *EMNLP*.

Ilya Sutskever, Oriol Vinyals, and Quoc V Le. 2014. Sequence to Sequence Learning with Neural Networks. In *NIPS*.

Ashish Vaswani, Noam Shazeer, Niki Parmar, Jakob Uszkoreit, Llion Jones, Aidan N Gomez, Ł ukasz Kaiser, and Illia Polosukhin. 2017. Attention is all you need. In *NIPS*.

Alex Wang, Amanpreet Singh, Julian Michael, Felix Hill, Omer Levy, and Samuel Bowman. 2018. GLUE: A Multi-Task Benchmark and Analysis Platform for Natural Language Understanding. In *EMNLP Workshop BlackboxNLP*.

Ronald J. Williams. 1992. Simple statistical gradient-following algorithms for connectionist reinforcement learning. *Machine Learning*, 8(3):229–256.

Yonghui Wu, Mike Schuster, Zhifeng Chen, Quoc V. Le, Mohammad Norouzi, Wolfgang Macherey, Maxim Krikun, Yuan Cao, Qin Gao, Klaus Macherey, Jeff Klingner, Apurva Shah, Melvin Johnson, Xiaobing Liu, ukasz Kaiser, Stephan Gouws, Yoshikiyo Kato, Taku Kudo, Hideto Kazawa, Keith Stevens, George Kurian, Nishant Patil, Wei Wang, Cliff Young, Jason Smith, Jason Riesa, Alex Rudnick, Oriol Vinyals, Greg Corrado, Macduff Hughes, and Jeffrey Dean. 2016. Google's neural machine translation system: Bridging the gap between human and machine translation. *CoRR*.

Rowan Zellers, Yonatan Bisk, Roy Schwartz, and Yejin Choi. 2018. Swag: A large-scale adversarial dataset for grounded commonsense inference. *arXiv preprint arXiv:1808.05326*.

Sentiment Classification using Document Embeddings trained with Cosine Similarity

Tan Thongtan
Department of Computer Engineering
Mahidol University International College
Mahidol University
Thailand
tan.thongtan1@gmail.com

Tanasanee Phienthrakul
Department of Computer Engineering
Faculty of Engineering
Mahidol University
Thailand
tanasanee.phi@mahidol.ac.th

Abstract

In document-level sentiment classification, each document must be mapped to a fixed length vector. Document embedding models map each document to a dense, low-dimensional vector in continuous vector space. This paper proposes training document embeddings using cosine similarity instead of dot product. Experiments on the IMDB dataset show that accuracy is improved when using cosine similarity compared to using dot product, while using feature combination with Naïve Bayes weighted bag of n-grams achieves a new state of the art accuracy of 97.42%. Code to reproduce all experiments is available at https://github.com/tanthongtan/dv-cosine.

1 Introduction

In document classification tasks such as sentiment classification (in this paper we focus on binary sentiment classification of long movie reviews, i.e. determining whether each review is positive or negative), the choice of document representation is usually more important than the choice of classifier. The task of text representation aims at mapping variable length texts into fixed length vectors, as to be valid inputs to a classifier. Document embedding models achieve this by mapping each document to a dense, real-valued vector.

This paper aims to improve existing document embedding models (Le and Mikolov, 2014; Li et al., 2016a) by training document embeddings using cosine similarity instead of dot product. For example, in the basic model of trying to predict - given a document - the words/n-grams in the document, instead of trying to maximize the dot product between a document vector and vectors of the words/n-grams in the document over the training set, we'll be trying to maximize the cosine similarity instead.

The motivation behind this is twofold. Firstly, cosine similarity serves as a regularization mechanism; by ignoring vector magnitudes, there is less incentive to increase the magnitudes of the input and output vectors, whereas in the case of dot product, vectors of frequent document-n-gram pairs can be made to have a high dot product simply by increasing the magnitudes of each vector. The weights learned should be smaller overall.

Secondly, as cosine similarity is widely used to measure document similarity (Singhal, 2001; Dai et al., 2015), we believe our method should more directly maximize the cosine similarity between similar document vectors. The angle between similar documents should be lower, and that may encode useful information for distinguishing between different types of documents. We'll compare the performance of our model on the IMDB dataset (Maas et al., 2011) with dot product and to determine if our model serves anything beyond simple regularization, we'll also compare it to dot product using L2 regularization.

2 Related Work

Here we review methods of text representation, in which there are two main categories: **bag of words models** and **neural embedding models**.

The **bag of words** model (Joachims, 1998) represents text as a fixed length vector of length equal to the number of distinct n-grams in the vocabulary. **Naive Bayes - Support Vector Machine (NB-SVM)** (Wang and Manning, 2012) utilizes naïve bayes weighted bag of n-grams vectors for representing texts, feeding these vectors into a logistic regression or support vector machine classifier.

The first example of a **neural embedding model** is **word embeddings** which was proposed by Bengio et al. in 2003, while objective functions

Proceedings of the ACL 2019, Student Research Workshop, pages 407–414
Florence, Italy, July 28th-August 2nd, 2019. ©2019 Association for Computational Linguistics

utilizing the negative sampling technique for efficient training of word embeddings were proposed in 2013 by Mikolov et al. (word2vec). The aim of word embeddings is to map each word to a real vector, whereby the dot product between two vectors represents the amount of similarity in meaning between the words they represent. There are two versions of word2vec: continuous bag of words (CBOW), in which a neural network is trained to predict the next word in a piece of text given the word's context, and skip-gram, where it will try to predict a word's context given the word itself.

In a 2017 paper Arora et al. produce **Sentence Embeddings** by computing the weighted average of word vectors, where each word is weighted using smooth inverse frequency, and removing the first principle component.

Paragraph Vector (Le and Mikolov, 2014) may be seen as a modification to word embeddings in order to embed as vectors paragraphs as opposed to words. Paragraph vector comes in two flavors: the Distributed Memory Model of Paragraph Vectors (PV-DM), and the Distributed Bag of Words version of Paragraph Vector (PV-DBOW). PV-DM is basically the same as CBOW except that a paragraph vector is additionally averaged or concatenated along with the context and that whole thing is used to predict the next word. In the PV-DBOW model a paragraph vector alone is used/trained to predict the words in the paragraph.

Document Vector by predicting n-grams (DV-ngram) (Li et al., 2016a) trains paragraph vectors to predict not only the words in the paragraph, but n-grams in the paragraph as well. **Weighted Neural Bag of n-grams (W-Neural-BON)** (Li et al., 2016b) uses an objective function similar to the one in DV-ngram, except that each log probability term is weighted using a weighing scheme which is similar to taking the absolute values of naive bayes weights.

In (Li et al., 2017), they introduce three main methods of **embedding n-grams**. The first is context guided n-gram representation (CGNR), which is training n-gram vectors to predict its context n-grams. The second is label guided n-gram representation (LGNR), which is predicting given an n-gram the label of the document to which it belongs. The last is text guided n-gram representation (TGNR), which is predicting given an n-gram the document to which it belongs.

Embeddings from Language Models (ELMo) (Peters et al., 2018) learns contextualized word embeddings by training a bidirectional LSTM (Hochreiter and Schmidhuber, 1997) on the language modelling task of predicting the next word as well as the previous word. **Bidirectional Encoder Representations from Transformers (BERT)** (Devlin et al., 2018) uses the masked language model objective, which is predicting the masked word given the left and right context, in order to pre-train a multi-layer bidirectional Transformer (Vaswani et al., 2017). BERT also jointly pre-trains text-pair representations by using a next sentence prediction objective.

For the rest of this section we'll look at other research which replaces dot product with cosine similarity. In the context of fully-connected neural networks and convolutional neural networks, (Luo et al., 2017) uses cosine similarity instead of dot product in computing a layer's pre-activation as a regularization mechanism. Using a special dataset where each instance is a paraphrase pair, (Wieting et al., 2015) trains word vectors in such a way that the cosine similarity between the resultant document vectors of a paraphrase pair is directly maximized.

3   Proposed Model

In learning neural n-gram and document embeddings, a dot product between the input vector and the output vector is generally used to compute the similarity measure between the two vectors, i.e. 'similar' vectors should have a high dot product. In this paper we explore using cosine similarity instead of dot product in computing the similarity measure between the input and output vectors. More specifically we focus on modifications to the PV-DBOW and the similar DV-ngram models. The cosine similarity between a paragraph vector and vectors of n-grams in the paragraph is maximized over the training set.

3.1   Architecture

A neural network is trained to be useful in predicting, given a document, the words and n-grams in the document, in the process of doing so learning useful document embeddings. Formally, the objective function to be minimized is defined as follows:

$$\sum_{d \in D} \sum_{w_o \in W_d} -\log p(w_o|d) \qquad (1)$$

where d is a document, D is the set of all documents in the dataset, w_o is an n-gram and W_d is the set of all n-grams in the document d. $p(w_o|d)$ is defined using softmax:

$$p(w_o|d) = \frac{e^{\alpha \cos \theta_{w_o}}}{\sum_{w \in W} e^{\alpha \cos \theta_w}} \quad (2)$$

$$= \text{softmax}(\alpha \cos \theta_{w_o}) \quad (3)$$

We have $\cos \theta_w$ defined as follows:

$$\cos \theta_w = \frac{\boldsymbol{v}_d^T \boldsymbol{v}_w}{\|\boldsymbol{v}_d\| \|\boldsymbol{v}_w\|} \quad (4)$$

where $\boldsymbol{v}_d$ and $\boldsymbol{v}_w$ are vector representations of the document d and the word/n-gram w respectively and are parameters to be learned. α is a hyperparameter. W is the set of all n-grams in the vocabulary.

Normally, the softmax of the dot product between the input and output vector is used to model the conditional probability term as follows:

$$p(w_o|d) = \frac{e^{\boldsymbol{v}_d^T \boldsymbol{v}_{w_o}}}{\sum_{w \in W} e^{\boldsymbol{v}_d^T \boldsymbol{v}_w}} \quad (5)$$

Whereas dot product ranges from negative infinity to positive infinity, since cosine similarity ranges from -1 to 1, using the cosine similarity term alone as an input to the softmax function may not be sufficient in modeling the conditional probability distribution. Therefore, we add a scaling hyperparameter α to increase the range of possible probability values for each conditional probability term.

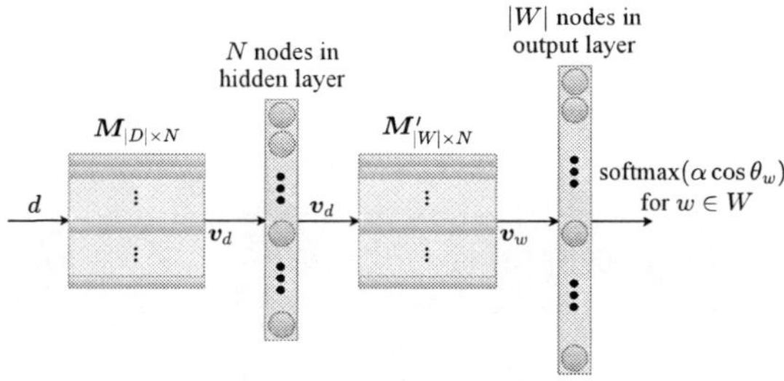

Figure 1: Proposed Architecture.

Figure 1 shows the architecture of the neural network used in learning the document embeddings. There is a hidden layer with N nodes corresponding to the dimensionality of the paragraph vectors and an output layer with $|W|$ nodes corresponding to the number of distinct n-grams found in the dataset. There are two weight parameter matrices to be learned: M, which may be seen as a

collection of $|D|$ document vectors each having N dimensions, and M', which is a collection of $|W|$ n-gram vectors each also having N dimensions.

An input document id d is used to select its vector representation $\boldsymbol{v}_d$ which is exactly output through the N nodes of the first hidden layer. The output of each node in the output layer represents the probability $p(w|d)$ of its corresponding n-gram w, and is calculated as in (2) using softmax.

3.2 Negative Sampling

Since the weight update equations for minimizing (1) implies that we must update each output vector corresponding to each feature in the feature set W, with extremely large vocabularies, this computation is impractical. In (Mikolov et al., 2013), the negative sampling technique is introduced as a means to speed up the learning process and it can be shown that the updates for the negative sampling version of (1) as shown in (6) approximates the weight updates carried out in minimizing (1). Therefore in practice, the document embeddings are obtained by minimizing the following objective function with stochastic gradient descent and backpropagation (Rumelhart et al., 1986):

$$\sum_{d \in D} \sum_{w_o \in W_d} \left[- \log \sigma \left(\alpha \cos \theta_{w_o} \right) \right.$$

$$\left. - \sum_{w_n \in W_{neg}} \log \sigma \left(-\alpha \cos \theta_{w_n} \right) \right] \quad (6)$$

where W_{neg} is a set of negatively sampled words; the size of the set or the negative sampling size as well as the distribution used to draw negatively sampled words/n-grams are hyperparameters. σ is the sigmoid function.

By contrast, in the case of dot product the objective function is:

$$\sum_{d \in D} \sum_{w_o \in W_d} \left[- \log \sigma \left(\boldsymbol{v}_d^T \boldsymbol{v}_{w_o} \right) \right.$$

$$\left. - \sum_{w_n \in W_{neg}} \log \sigma \left(-\boldsymbol{v}_d^T \boldsymbol{v}_{w_n} \right) \right] \quad (7)$$

while in the case of L2R dot product, the objective function used is:

$$\sum_{d \in D} \sum_{w_o \in W_d} \left[- \log \sigma \left(\boldsymbol{v}_d^T \boldsymbol{v}_{w_o} \right) + \frac{\lambda}{2} \|\boldsymbol{v}_d\|^2 + \frac{\lambda}{2} \|\boldsymbol{v}_{w_o}\|^2 \right.$$

$$\left. - \sum_{w_n \in W_{neg}} \left(\log \sigma \left(-\boldsymbol{v}_d^T \boldsymbol{v}_{w_n} \right) + \frac{\lambda}{2} \|\boldsymbol{v}_{w_n}\|^2 \right) \right]$$

$$(8)$$

Features	Dot Product (DV-ngram) (%)	Dot Product with L2R (%)	Cosine Similarity (%)
Unigrams	89.60	87.15 (-2.45)	**90.75 (+1.15)**
Unigrams+Bigrams	91.27	91.72 (+0.45)	**92.56 (+1.29)**
Unigrams+Bigrams+Trigrams	92.14	92.45 (+0.31)	**93.13 (+0.99)**

Table 1: Experimental Results.

where λ is the regularization strength.

4 Experiments

The models are benchmarked on the IMDB dataset (Maas et al., 2011), which contains 25,000 training documents, 25,000 test documents, and 50,000 unlabeled documents. The IMDB dataset is a binary sentiment classification dataset consisting of movie reviews retrieved from IMDB; training documents in the dataset are highly polar. For labeled documents, there is a 1:1 ratio between negative and positive documents. The document vectors are learned using all the documents in the dataset (train, test and unlabeled documents). The dataset consists of mainly long movie reviews.

In order to train the document vectors on unigrams to trigrams, the reviews are preprocessed in such a way that tokens representing bigrams and trigrams are simply appended to the original unigrams of the review itself. An L2-regularized logistic regression (LR) classifier is used to classify the documents at the end of each epoch using the predefined train-test split. However, the results reported in this paper include only the accuracy obtained from classifying documents in the final epoch. For any java implementations of the LR classifier we use the LIBLINEAR library (Fan et al., 2008) while for python implementations we use Sci-kit learn (Pedregosa et al., 2011). Code to reproduce all experiments is available at https://github.com/tanthongtan/dv-cosine.

4.1 Optimal Hyperparameters

Grid search was performed using 20% of the training data as a validation set in order to determine the optimal hyperparameters as well as whether to use a constant learning rate or learning rate annealing. Table 2 shows the optimal hyperparameters for the models on the IMDB dataset. We did not tune the N hyperparameter or the negative sampling size and left it the same as in (Li et al., 2016a) and (Lau and Baldwin, 2016). We did however tune the number of iterations from

[10, 20, 40, 80, 120], learning rate from [0.25, 0.025, 0.0025, 0.001] and α from [4, 6, 8]. A sensible value of α should be around 6, since looking at the graph of the sigmoid function, for input values greater than 6 and less than -6, the sigmoid function doesn't change much and has values of close to 1 and 0, respectively. In the case of using L2 regularized dot product, λ (regularization strength) was chosen from [1, 0.1, 0.01].

Hyperparameter	Dot Prod.	L2R Dot Prod.	Cos. Sim.
N (dimensionality)	500	500	500
Neg. Sampling Size	5	5	5
Iterations	10	20	120
Learning Rate	0.25	0.025	0.001
α	-	-	6
λ	-	0.01	-
LR annealing	true	false	false

Table 2: Optimal Hyperparameters.

The optimal learning rate in the case of cosine similarity is extremely small, suggesting a chaotic error surface. Since the learning rate is already small to begin with, no learning rate annealing is used. The model in turn requires a larger number of epochs for convergence. For the distribution for sampling negative words, we used the n-gram distribution raised to the $3/4^{th}$ power in accordance with (Mikolov et al., 2013). The weights of the networks were initialized from a uniform distribution in the range of [-0.001, 0.001].

4.2 Results

Each experiment was carried out 5 times and the mean accuracy is reported in Table 1. This is to account for random factors such as shuffling document and word ids, and random initialization. From here we see that using cosine similarity instead of dot product improves accuracy across the board. The results are most apparent in the case of unigrams + bigrams. However it is not to suggest that switching from dot product to cosine similarity alone improves accuracy as other minor ad-

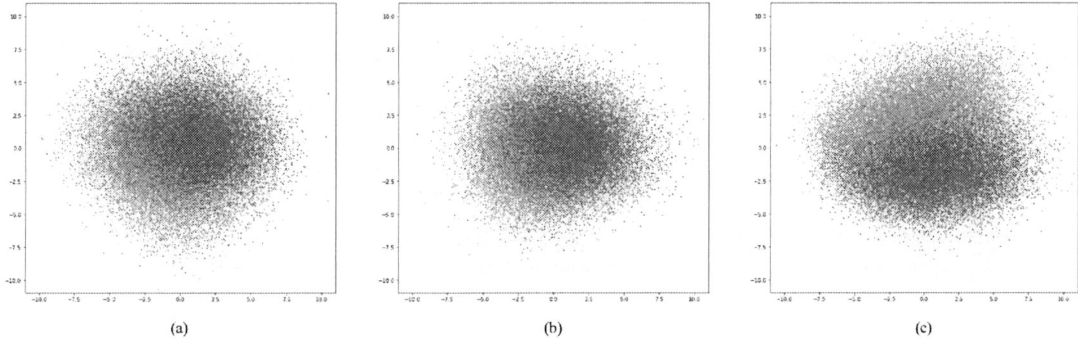

Figure 2: PCA visualization of embeddings trained with (a) dot product, (b) L2R dot product and (c) cos. similarity.

justments and hyperparameter tuning as explained was done. However it may imply that using cosine similarity allows for a higher potential accuracy as was achieved in these experiments.

Regardless, we believe the comparisons are fair since each model is using its own set of optimal hyperparameters, but for the full sake of comparison, leaving everything the same and only switching out dot product for cosine similarity ($\alpha = 1$) as well as switching it out and using a sensible value of α at $\alpha = 6$ both achieve an accuracy of around 50%. This is because our model fails whenever the learning rate is too large. As seen during grid search, whenever the initial learning rate was 0.25, accuracy was always poor.

Introducing L2 regularization to dot product improves accuracy for all cases except a depreciation in the case of using unigrams only, lucikily cosine similarity does not suffer from this same depreciation.

4.3 Discussion

From table 3, the mean Euclidean norm of embeddings trained with cosine similarity is lower than that of L2R dot product which is in turn lower than in the case of using dot product; this suggests that the method employing cosine similarity acts as a regularization mechanism, preventing the weights from getting too large. Large magnitudes of document vectors may be harder for the end classifier to fit in such a way that generalizes well, which may be why cosine similarity and L2R dot product perform better than dot product on the IMDB dataset.

As predicted, the mean cosine similarity between all pairs of vectors in the same class (Same Mean Cos. Sim.) is higher in the case of cosine similarity than the other two models. Unfortu-

nately, the mean for all pairs in different classes (Diff. Mean Cos. Sim.) is higher as well. Further analysis and hopefully some formalism as to why cosine similarity performs better is a planned future work.

Embedding Statistic	Dot Prod.	L2R Dot Prod.	Cos. Sim.
Same Mean Cos. Sim.	0.23	0.20	0.35
Diff. Mean Cos. Sim.	0.21	0.17	0.32
Mean Norm	8.91	6.30	5.35

Table 3: Embedding statistics.

Figure 2 shows the projection of the embeddings along their first two principle components, different colors corresponding to different classes. Cosine similarity shows slightly better seperability between the two classes, while dot product and L2R dot product are quite similar.

4.4 Feature Combination

Another contribution of this paper is demonstrating the effectiveness of concatenating naive bayes weighted bag of n-grams with DV-ngram, L2R dot product, or document vectors trained with cosine similarity, the last achieving state of the art accuracy on the IMDB dataset. We note that all models utilize unigrams to trigrams and additional unlabeled data if possible. Table 4 shows a comparison between our proposed models (shown in bold) and previous state of the arts and other published results.

5 Conclusion and Future Work

Our proposed model trains document embeddings using cosine similarity as the similarity measure and we show that sentiment classification performance on the IMDB dataset is improved when

Model	IMDB Dataset Accuracy (%)
NB-SVM Bigrams (Wang and Manning, 2012)	91.22
NB-SVM Trigrams (Mesnil et al., 2015)	91.87
DV-ngram (Li et al., 2016a)	92.14
Dot Product with L2 Regularization	**92.45**
Paragraph Vector (Le and Mikolov, 2014)	92.58
Document Vectors using Cosine Similarity	**93.13**
W-Neural-BON Ensemble (Li et al., 2016b)	93.51
TGNR Ensemble (Li et al., 2017)	93.51
TopicRNN (Dieng et al., 2017)	93.76
One-hot bi-LSTM (Johnson and Zhang, 2016)	94.06
Virtual Adversarial (Miyato et al., 2016)	94.09
BERT large finetune UDA (Xie et al., 2019)	95.80
NB-weighted-BON + DV-ngram	**96.95**
NB-weighted-BON + L2R Dot Product	**97.17**
NB-weighted-BON + Cosine Similarity	**97.42**

Table 4: Comparison with other models.

utilizing these embeddings as opposed to those trained using dot-product. Cosine similarity may help reduce overfitting to the embedding task, and this regularization in turn produces more useful embeddings. We also show that concatenating these embeddings with Naïve bayes weighed bag of n-grams results in high accuracy on the IMDB dataset.

An important future development is to carry out experiments on other datasets. It is essential that we benchmark on more than one dataset, to prevent superficially good results by overfitting hyperparameters or the cosine similarity model itself to the IMDB dataset. Other tasks and datasets include: (1) sentiment analysis - the Stanford sentiment treebank dataset (Socher et al., 2013), the polarity dataset v2.0 (Pang and Lee, 2004), (2) topic classification - AthR, XGraph, BbCrypt (Wang and Manning, 2012), and (3) semantic relatedness tasks - datasets from the SemEval semantic textual similarity (STS) tasks (Agirre et al., 2015)

References

Eneko Agirre, Carmen Banea, Claire Cardie, Daniel Cer, Mona Diab, Aitor Gonzalez-Agirre, Weiwei Guo, Inigo Lopez-Gazpio, Montse Maritxalar, Rada Mihalcea, German Rigau, Larraitz Uria, and Janyce Wiebe. 2015. Semeval-2015 task 2: Semantic textual similarity, english, spanish and pilot on interpretability. In *Proceedings of the 9th International Workshop on Semantic Evaluation*, pages 252–263.

Sanjeev Arora, Yingyu Liang, and Tengyu Ma. 2017. A simple but tough-to-beat baseline for sentence embeddings. In *Proceedings of the 5th International Conference on Learning Representations*.

Yoshua Bengio, Réjean Ducharme, Pascal Vincent, and Christian Jauvin. 2003. A neural probabilistic language model. *Journal of Machine Learning Research*, 3(Feb):1137–1155.

Andrew M. Dai, Christopher Olah, and Quoc V. Le. 2015. Document embedding with paragraph vectors. *arXiv preprint arXiv:1507.07998*.

Jacob Devlin, Ming-Wei Chang, Kenton Lee, and Kristina Toutanova. 2018. Bert: Pre-training of deep bidirectional transformers for language understanding. *arXiv preprint arXiv:1810.04805*.

Adji B. Dieng, Chong Wang, Jianfeng Gao, and John Paisley. 2017. Topicrnn: A recurrent neural network with long-range semantic dependency. In *Proceedings of the 5th International Conference on Learning Representations*.

Rong-En Fan, Kai-Wei Chang, Cho-Jui Hsieh, Xiang-Rui Wang, and Chih-Jen Lin. 2008. Liblinear: A library for large linear classification. *Journal of Machine Learning Research*, 9(Aug):1871–1874.

Sepp Hochreiter and Jürgen Schmidhuber. 1997. Long short-term memory. *Neural Computation*, 9(8):1735–1780.

Thorsten Joachims. 1998. Text categorization with support vector machines: Learning with many relevant features. In *Proceedings of the 10th European Conference on Machine Learning*, pages 137–142.

Rie Johnson and Tong Zhang. 2016. Supervised and semi-supervised text categorization using lstm for region embeddings. In *Proceedings of the 4th International Conference on Learning Representations*.

Jey Han Lau and Timothy Baldwin. 2016. An empirical evaluation of doc2vec with practical insights into document embedding generation. *arXiv preprint arXiv:1607.05368*.

Quoc V. Le and Tomas Mikolov. 2014. Distributed representations of sentences and documents. In *Proceedings of the 31st International Conference on Machine Learning*, pages 1188–1196.

Bofang Li, Tao Liu, Xiaoyong Du, Deyuan Zhang, and Zhe Zhao. 2016a. Learning document embeddings by predicting n-grams for sentiment classification of long movie reviews. In *Proceedings of the 4th International Workshop on Learning Representations*.

Bofang Li, Tao Liu, Zhe Zhao, Puwei Wang, and Xiaoyong Du. 2017. Neural bag-of-ngrams. In *Proceedings of the 31st AAAI Conference on Artificial Intelligence*, pages 3067–3074.

Bofang Li, Zhe Zhao, Tao Liu, Puwei Wang, and Xiaoyong Du. 2016b. Weighted neural bag-of-n-grams model: New baselines for text classification. In *Proceedings of the 26th International Conference on Computational Linguistics*, pages 1591–1600.

Chunjie Luo, Jianfeng Zhan, Lei Wang, and Qiang Yang. 2017. Cosine normalization: Using cosine similarity instead of dot product in neural networks. *arXiv preprint arXiv:1702.05870*.

Andrew L. Maas, Raymond E. Daly, Peter T. Pham, Dan Huang, Andrew Y. Ng, and Christopher Potts. 2011. Learning word vectors for sentiment analysis. In *Proceedings of the 49th Annual Meeting of the Association for Computational Linguistics*, pages 142–150.

Grégoire Mesnil, Tomas Mikolov, Marc'Aurelio Ranzato, and Yoshua Bengio. 2015. Ensemble of generative and discriminative techniques for sentiment analysis of movie reviews. In *Proceedings of the 3rd International Workshop on Learning Representations*.

Tomas Mikolov, Ilya Sutskever, Kai Chen, Greg S. Corrado, and Jeff Dean. 2013. Distributed representations of words and phrases and their compositionality. In *Proceedings of the 26th International Conference on Neural Information Processing Systems*, pages 3111–3119.

Takeru Miyato, Andrew M. Dai, and Ian Goodfellow. 2016. Adversarial training methods for semisupervised text classification. In *Proceedings of the 4th International Conference on Learning Representations*.

Bo Pang and Lillian Lee. 2004. A sentimental education: Sentiment analysis using subjectivity summarization based on minimum cuts. In *Proceedings of the 42nd Annual Meeting of the Association for Computational Linguistics*, page 271.

Fabian Pedregosa, Gaël Varoquaux, Alexandre Gramfort, Vincent Michel, Bertrand Thirion, Olivier Grisel, Mathieu Blondel, Peter Prettenhofer, Ron Weiss, Vincent Dubourg, et al. 2011. Scikit-learn: Machine learning in python. *Journal of Machine Learning Research*, 12(Oct):2825–2830.

Matthew E. Peters, Mark Neumann, Mohit Iyyer, Matt Gardner, Christopher Clark, Kenton Lee, and Luke Zettlemoyer. 2018. Deep contextualized word representations. In *Proceedings of the 2018 Conference of the North American Chapter of the Association for Computational Linguistics: Human Language Technologies*, pages 2227–2237.

David E. Rumelhart, Geoffrey E. Hinton, and Ronald J. Williams. 1986. Learning representations by backpropagating errors. *Nature*, 323(6088):533–536.

Amit Singhal. 2001. Modern information retrieval: A brief overview. *IEEE Data Engineering Bulletin*, 24(4):35–43.

Richard Socher, Alex Perelygin, Jean Wu, Jason Chuang, Christopher D. Manning, Andrew Ng, and Christopher Potts. 2013. Recursive deep models for semantic compositionality over a sentiment treebank. In *Proceedings of the 2013 Conference on Empirical Methods in Natural Language Processing*, pages 1631–1642.

Ashish Vaswani, Noam Shazeer, Niki Parmar, Jakob Uszkoreit, Llion Jones, Aidan N. Gomez, Ł ukasz Kaiser, and Illia Polosukhin. 2017. Attention is all you need. In *Proceedings of the 31st International Conference on Neural Information Processing Systems*, pages 5998–6008.

Sida Wang and Christopher D. Manning. 2012. Baselines and bigrams: Simple, good sentiment and topic classification. In *Proceedings of the 50th Annual Meeting of the Association for Computational Linguistics*, pages 90–94.

John Wieting, Mohit Bansal, Kevin Gimpel, and Karen Livescu. 2015. Towards universal paraphrastic sentence embeddings. In *Proceedings of the 4th International Conference on Learning Representations*.

Qizhe Xie, Zihang Dai, Eduard Hovy, Minh-Thang Luong, and Quoc V. Le. 2019. Unsupervised data augmentation. *arXiv preprint arXiv:1904.12848*.

A Obtaining the weight update equations in the case of cosine similarity

To obtain the weight update equations for the input and output vectors of our model in each iteration of stochastic gradient descent, we must find the gradient of the error function at a given training example, which may be considered a document, n-gram pair.

Let:

$$E = -\log \sigma \left(\alpha \cos \theta_{w_o} \right) - \sum_{w_n \in W_{neg}} \log \sigma \left(-\alpha \cos \theta_{w_n} \right) \quad (9)$$

where:

$$\cos \theta_w = \frac{\boldsymbol{v}_d^T \boldsymbol{v}_w}{\|\boldsymbol{v}_d\| \|\boldsymbol{v}_w\|} \quad (10)$$

be the objective function at a single training example (d, w_o). Then, to find the gradient of E first differentiate E with respect to $\cos \theta_w$:

$$\frac{\partial E}{\partial \cos \theta_w} = \alpha \left(\sigma \left(\alpha \cos \theta_w \right) - t \right) \quad (11)$$

where $t = 1$ if $w = w_o$; 0 otherwise. We then obtain the derivative of E w.r.t. the output n-gram vectors:

$$\frac{\partial E}{\partial \boldsymbol{v}_w} = \frac{\partial E}{\partial \cos \theta_w} \cdot \frac{\partial \cos \theta_w}{\partial \boldsymbol{v}_w} \quad (12)$$

$$\frac{\partial E}{\partial \boldsymbol{v}_w} = \alpha \left(\sigma \left(\alpha \cos \theta_w \right) - t \right)$$
$$\cdot \left(\frac{\boldsymbol{v}_d}{\|\boldsymbol{v}_d\| \|\boldsymbol{v}_w\|} - \frac{\boldsymbol{v}_w \left(\boldsymbol{v}_d^T \boldsymbol{v}_w \right)}{\|\boldsymbol{v}_d\| \|\boldsymbol{v}_w\|^3} \right) \quad (13)$$

This leads to the following weight update equation for the output vectors:

$$\boldsymbol{v}_w^{(new)} = \boldsymbol{v}_w^{(old)} - \eta \frac{\partial E}{\partial \boldsymbol{v}_w} \quad (14)$$

where η is the learning rate. This equation needs to be applied to all $w \in \{w_o\} \cup W_{neg}$ in each iteration.

Next, the errors are backpropagated and the input document vectors are updated. Differentiating E with respect to $\boldsymbol{v}_d$:

$$\frac{\partial E}{\partial \boldsymbol{v}_d} = \sum_{w \in \{w_o\} \cup W_{neg}} \frac{\partial E}{\partial \cos \theta_w} \cdot \frac{\partial \cos \theta_w}{\partial \boldsymbol{v}_d} \quad (15)$$

$$= \sum_{w \in \{w_o\} \cup W_{neg}} \alpha \left(\sigma \left(\alpha \cos \theta_w \right) - t \right)$$
$$\cdot \left(\frac{\boldsymbol{v}_w}{\|\boldsymbol{v}_d\| \|\boldsymbol{v}_w\|} - \frac{\boldsymbol{v}_d \left(\boldsymbol{v}_d^T \boldsymbol{v}_w \right)}{\|\boldsymbol{v}_d\|^3 \|\boldsymbol{v}_w\|} \right) \quad (16)$$

Thus, we obtain the weight update equation for the input vector in each iteration:

$$\boldsymbol{v}_d^{(new)} = \boldsymbol{v}_d^{(old)} - \eta \frac{\partial E}{\partial \boldsymbol{v}_d} \quad (17)$$

B Weight update equations in the case of dot product

This section contains the weight update equations for the input and output vectors of the dot product model in each iteration of stochastic gradient descent.

The following weight update equations for the output vectors:

$$\boldsymbol{v}_w^{(new)} = \boldsymbol{v}_w^{(old)} - \eta \left(\sigma \left(\boldsymbol{v}_d^T \boldsymbol{v}_w \right) - t \right) \cdot \boldsymbol{v}_d \quad (18)$$

where $t = 1$ if $w = w_o$; 0 otherwise, needs to be applied to all $w \in \{w_o\} \cup W_{neg}$ in each iteration.

The following weight update equation needs to be applied to the input vector in each iteration:

$$\boldsymbol{v}_d^{(new)} = \boldsymbol{v}_d^{(old)} - \eta \sum_{w \in \{w_o\} \cup W_{neg}} \left(\sigma \left(\boldsymbol{v}_d^T \boldsymbol{v}_w \right) - t \right) \cdot \boldsymbol{v}_w$$
$$(19)$$

C Weight update equations in the case of L2R dot product

This section contains the weight update equations for the input and output vectors of the L2R dot product model in each iteration of stochastic gradient descent.

The following weight update equations for the output vectors:

$$\boldsymbol{v}_w^{(new)} = \boldsymbol{v}_w^{(old)} - \eta \left(\sigma \left(\boldsymbol{v}_d^T \boldsymbol{v}_w \right) - t \right) \cdot \boldsymbol{v}_d$$
$$- \eta \lambda \boldsymbol{v}_w \quad (20)$$

where $t = 1$ if $w = w_o$; 0 otherwise, needs to be applied to all $w \in \{w_o\} \cup W_{neg}$ in each iteration.

The following weight update equation needs to be applied to the input vector in each iteration:

$$\boldsymbol{v}_d^{(new)} = \boldsymbol{v}_d^{(old)} - \eta \sum_{w \in \{w_o\} \cup W_{neg}} \left(\sigma \left(\boldsymbol{v}_d^T \boldsymbol{v}_w \right) - t \right) \cdot \boldsymbol{v}_w$$
$$- \eta \lambda \boldsymbol{v}_d \quad (21)$$

Detecting Adverse Drug Reactions from Biomedical Texts With Neural Networks

Ilseyar Alimova
Kazan Federal University,
Kazan, Russia
ISAlimova@kpfu.ru

Elena Tutubalina
Kazan Federal University,
Kazan, Russia
Samsung-PDMI Joint AI Center,
PDMI RAS, St. Petersburg, Russia
elvtutubalina@kpfu.ru

Abstract

Detection of adverse drug reactions in post-approval periods is a crucial challenge for pharmacology. Social media and electronic clinical reports are becoming increasingly popular as a source for obtaining health-related information. In this work, we focus on extraction information of adverse drug reactions from various sources of biomedical text-based information, including biomedical literature and social media. We formulate the problem as a binary classification task and compare the performance of four state-of-the-art attention-based neural networks in terms of the F-measure. We show the effectiveness of these methods on four different benchmarks.

1 Introduction

Detection of adverse drug reactions (ADRs) in the post-marketing period is becoming increasingly popular, as evidenced by the growth of ADR monitoring systems (Singh et al., 2017; Shareef et al., 2017; Hou et al., 2016). Information about adverse drug reactions can be found in the texts of social media, health-related forums, and electronic health records. We formulated the problem as a binary classification task. The ADR classification task addresses two sub-tasks: (a) detecting the presence of ADRs in a textual message (message-level task) and (b) detecting the class of an entity within a message (entity-level task). In this paper, we focus on the latter task. Different from the message-level classification task, which aims to determine whether a textual fragment such as tweet or an abstract of a paper includes an ADR mention or not, the objective of the entity-level task is to detect whether a given entity (a single word or a multi-word expression) conveys adverse drug effect in the context of a message. For example, in "He was unable to sleep last night because

of pain", the health condition 'pain' trigger insomnia. Meanwhile, in "after 3 days on this drug I was unable to sleep due to symptoms like a very bad attack of RLS", there is an entity 'unable to sleep' associated with drug use and can be classified as ADR.

Inspired by recent successful methods, we investigated various deep neural network models for entity-level ADR classification (Alimova and Tutubalina, 2018). Our previous experiments showed that Interactive Attention Neural network (IAN) (Ma et al., 2017) outperforms other models based on LSTM (Hochreiter and Schmidhuber, 1997). In this paper, we continue our study and compare IAN with the following attention-based neural networks for entity-level ADR classification: (i) Attention-over-Attention (AOA) model (Huang et al., 2018); (ii) Attentional Encoder Network (AEN) (Song et al., 2019); (iii) Attention-based LSTM with Aspect Embedding (ATAE-LSTM) (Wang et al., 2016). We conduct extensive experiments on four benchmarks which consist of scientific abstracts and user-generated texts about drug therapy.

2 Related Work

Different approaches are utilized to identify adverse drug reactions (Sarker et al., 2015; Gupta et al., 2018b; Harpaz et al., 2010). First works were limited in the number of study drugs and targeted ADRs due to limitations of traditional lexicon-based approaches (Benton et al., 2011; Liu and Chen, 2013). In order to eliminate these shortcomings, rule-based methods have been proposed (Nikfarjam and Gonzalez, 2011; Na et al., 2012). These methods capture the underlying syntactic and semantic patterns from social media posts. Third group of works utilized popular machine learning models, such as support vec-

415

Proceedings of the ACL 2019, Student Research Workshop, pages 415–421
Florence, Italy, July 28th-August 2nd, 2019. ©2019 Association for Computational Linguistics

tor machine (SVM) (Liu and Chen, 2013; Sarker et al., 2015; Niu et al., 2005; Bian et al., 2012; Alimova and Tutubalina, 2017), conditional random fields (CRF) (Aramaki et al., 2010; Miftahutdinov et al., 2017), and random forest (RF) (Rastegar-Mojarad et al., 2016). The most popular hand-crafted features are n-grams, parts of speech tags, semantic types from the Unified Medical Language System (UMLS), the number of negated contexts, the belonging lexicon based features for ADRs, drug names, and word embeddings (Dai et al., 2016). One of the tracks of the shared task SMM4H 2016 was devoted to ADR classification on a tweet level. The two best-performing systems applied machine learning classifier ensembles and obtained 41.95% F-measure for ADR class (Rastegar-Mojarad et al., 2016; Zhang et al., 2016). Two other participants utilized SVM classifiers with different sets of feature and obtained 35.8% and 33% F-measure (Ofoghi et al., 2016; Jonnagaddala et al., 2016). During SMM4H 2017, the best performance was achieved by SVM classifiers with a variety of surface-form, sentiment, and domain-specific features (Kiritchenko et al., 2018). This classifier obtained 43.5% F-measure for 'ADR' class. Sarker and Gonsales outperformed these result utilizing SVM with a more rich set of features and the tuning of the model parameters and obtained 53.8% F-measure for ADR class (Sarker and Gonzalez, 2015). However, these results are still behind the current state-of-the-art for general text classification (Lai et al., 2015).

Modern approaches for the extracting of ADRs are based on neural networks. Saldana adopted CNN for the detection of ADR relevant sentences (Miranda, 2018). Huynh T. et al. applied convolutional recurrent neural network (CRNN), obtained by concatenating CNN with a recurrent neural network (RNN) and CNN with the additional weights (Huynh et al., 2016). Gupta S. et al. utilized a semi-supervised method based on co-training (Gupta et al., 2018a). Chowdhury et al. proposed a multi-task neural network framework that in addition to ADR classification learns extract ADR mentions (Chowdhury et al., 2018).

Methods for sentiment analysis are actively adopted in the medical domain as well as in other domains (Serrano-Guerrero et al., 2015; Rusnachenko and Loukachevitch, 2018; Ivanov et al., 2015; Solovyev and Ivanov, 2014). In the field of aspect-level sentiment analysis, neural networks are popularly utilized (Zhang et al., 2018). Ma et al. proposed Interactive Attention Network which interactively learns attentions in the contexts and targets, and generates the representations for targets and contexts separately (Ma et al., 2017). The model compared with different modifications of Long Short Term Memory (LSTM) models and performed greatest results with 78.6% and 72.1% of accuracy on restaurant and laptop corpora respectively. Song et al. introduced Attentional Encoder Network(AEN) (Song et al., 2019). AEN eschews recurrence and employs attention based encoders for the modeling between context and target. The model obtained 72.1% and 69% f accuracy on restaurant and laptop corpora respectively. Wang et al. utilized Attention-based LSTM, which takes into account aspect information during attention (Wang et al., 2016). This neural network achieved 77.2% and 68.7% of accuracy restaurant and laptop corpora respectively. The Attention-over-Attention neural network proposed by Huang et al. models aspects and sentences in a joint way and explicitly captures the interaction between aspects and context sentences (Huang et al., 2018). This approach achieved the best results among the described articles wit 81.2% and 74.5% of accuracy on restaurant and laptop corpora.

To sum up this section, we note that there has been little work on utilizing neural networks for entity-level ADR classification task. Most of the works used classical machine learning models, which are limited to linear models and manual feature engineering (Liu and Chen, 2013; Sarker et al., 2015; Niu et al., 2005; Bian et al., 2012; Alimova and Tutubalina, 2017; Aramaki et al., 2010; Miftahutdinov et al., 2017; Rastegar-Mojarad et al., 2016). Most methods for extracting ADR so far dealt with extracting information from the mention itself and a small window of words on the left and on the right as a context, ignoring the broader context of the text document where it occurred (Korkontzelos et al., 2016; Dai et al., 2016; Alimova and Tutubalina, 2017; Bian et al., 2012; Aramaki et al., 2010). Finally, in most of the works experiments were conducted on a single corpus.

3   Corpora

We conducted our experiments on four corpora: CADEC, PsyTAR, Twitter, TwiMed. Further, we briefly describe each dataset.

CADEC CSIRO Adverse Drug Event Corpus (CADEC) consists of annotated user reviews written about Diclofenac or Lipitor on askapatient.com (Karimi et al., 2015). There are five types of annotations: 'Drug', 'Adverse effect', 'Disease', 'Symptom', and 'Finding'. We grouped diseases, symptoms, and findings as a single class called 'non-ADR'.

PsyTAR Psychiatric Treatment Adverse Reactions (PsyTAR) corpus (Zolnoori et al., 2019) is the first open-source corpus of user-generated posts about psychiatric drugs taken from AskaPatient.com. This dataset includes reviews about four psychiatric medications: Zoloft, Lexapro, Effexor, and Cymbalta. Each review annotated with 4 types of entities: adverse drug reactions, withdrawal symptoms, drug indications, sign/symptoms/illness.

TwiMed TwiMed corpus consists of sentences extracted from PubMed and tweets. This corpus contains annotations of diseases, symptoms, and drugs, and their relations. If the relationship between disease and drug was labeled as 'Outcome-negative', we marked disease as ADR, otherwise, we annotate it as 'non-ADR' (Alvaro et al., 2017).

Twitter Twitter corpus include tweets about drugs. There are three annotations: 'ADR', 'Indication' and 'Other'. We consider 'Indication' and 'Other' as 'non-ADR' (Nikfarjam et al., 2015).

Summary statistics of corpora are presented in Table 1. As shown in this table, the CADEC and PsyTAR corpora contain a much larger number of annotations than the TwiMed and Twitter corpora.

4 Models

4.1 Interactive Attention Network

The Interactive Attention Network (IAN) network consists of two parts, each of which creates a representation of the context and the entity using the vector representation of the words and the LSTM layer (Ma et al., 2017). The obtained vectors are averaged and used to calculate the attention vector. IAN uses attention mechanisms to detect the important words of the target entity and its full context. In the first layer of attention, the vector of context and the averaged vector of the entity and in the second, the vector of the entity and the averaged vector of context are applied. The resulting vectors are concatenated and transferred to the

layer with the softmax activation function for classification.

4.2 Attention-over-Attention

Attention-over-Attention (AOA) model was introduced by Huang et al. (Huang et al., 2018). This model consists of two parts which handle left and right contexts, respectively. Using word embeddings as input, BiLSTM layers are employed to obtain hidden states of words for a target and its context, respectively. Given the hidden semantic representations of the context and target the attention weights for the text is calculated with AOA module. At the first step, the AOA module calculates a pair-wise interaction matrix. On the second step, with a column-wise softmax and row-wise softmax, the module obtains target-to-sentence attention and sentence-to-target attention. The final sentence-level attention is calculated by a weighted sum of each individual target-to-sentence attention using column-wise averaging of sentence-to-target attention. The final sentence representation is a weighted sum of sentence hidden semantic states using the sentence attention from AOA module.

4.3 Attentional Encoder Network

The Attentional Encoder Network (AEN) eschews complex recurrent neural networks and employs attention based encoders for the modeling between context and target (Song et al., 2019). The model architecture consists of four main parts: embedding layer, attentional encoder layer, target-specific attention layer, and output layer. The embedding layer encodes context and target with pre-trained word embedding models. The attentional encoder layer applies the Multi-Head Attention and the Point-wise Convolution Transformation to the context and target embedding representation. The target-specific attention layer employs another Multi-Head Attention to the introspective context representation and context-perceptive target representation obtained on the previous step. The output layer concatenates the average pooling outputs of previous layers and uses a fully connected layer to project the concatenated vector into the space of the targeted classes.

4.4 Attention-based LSTM with Aspect Embedding

The main idea of Attention-based LSTM with Aspect Embedding (ATAE-LSTM) is based on ap-

Table 1: Summary statistics of corpora.

Corpus	Documents	ADR	non-ADR	Max sentence length
CADEC (Karimi et al., 2015)	1231	5770	550	236
PsyTAR (Zolnoori et al., 2019)	891	4525	2987	264
TwiMed-Pubmed (Alvaro et al., 2017)	1000	264	983	150
TwiMed-Twitter (Alvaro et al., 2017)	637	329	308	42
Twitter (Nikfarjam et al., 2015)	645	569	76	37

pending the input aspect embedding into each context word input vector (Wang et al., 2016). The concatenated vectors are fed to the LSTM layer in order to obtain the hidden semantic representations. With the resulting hidden states and the aspect embedding, the attention mechanism produces an attention weight vector and a weighted hidden representation, which is applied for final classification.

5 Experiments

In this section, we compare the performance of the discussed neural networks with Interactive Attention Neural Network.

5.1 Settings

We utilized vector representation trained on social media posts from (Miftahutdinov et al., 2017). Word embedding vectors were obtained using *word2vec* trained on a Health corpus consists of 2.5 million reviews written in English. We used an embedding size of 200, local context length of 10, the negative sampling of 5, vocabulary cutoff of 10, Continuous Bag of Words model. Coverage statistics of word embedding model vocabulary: CADEC – 93.5%, Twitter – 80.4%, PsyTAR – 54%, TwiMed-Twitter – 81.2%, TwiMed-Pubmed – 76.4%. For the out of vocabulary words, the representations were uniformly sampled from the range of embedding weights. We used a maximum of 15 epochs to train IAN and ATAE-LSTM and 30 epochs to train AEN and AOA on each dataset. We set the batch size to 32 for each corpus. The number of hidden units for LSTM layer is 300, the learning rate is 0.01, l2 regularization is 0.001. We applied the implementation of the model from this repository[1].

5.2 Experiments and Results

All models were evaluated by 5-fold cross-validation. We utilized the F-measure to evaluate

[1]https://github.com/songyouwei/ABSA-PyTorch

the quality of the classification.

The results are presented in Table 2. The results show that IAN outperformed other models on all corpora. IAN obtained the most significant increase in results compared to other models on Cadec and Twitter-Pubmed corpora with 81.5% and 87.4% of the macro F-measures, respectively. We assume that the superiority of the IAN results in comparison with other models is due to the small number of parameters being trained and the small size of the corpora.

The AOA model achieved the second-place result on all corpora except Twitter. The AOA results for PsyTAR (81.5%) and Twimed-Twitter (79.5%) corpora state on par with IAN model, while for the rest corpora, the results are significantly lower. This leads to the conclusion that the model is unstable for highly imbalanced corpora.

The ATAE-LSTM model with 78.6% of macro F-measure outperformed AEN and AOA models results on Twitter corpora and achieved comparable with AOA results on Twimed-Pubmed corpora (80.1%). This result shows that ATAE-LSTM applicable to a small size imbalanced corpora.

The AEN model achieved comparable with other models results on PsyTAR (80.2%) corpora and significantly lower results on Twitter (66.7%), Cadec (49%) and Twimed-Pubmed (74.3%) corpora. 72.4% of F-measure on Twimed-Twitter corpus states on par with the ATAE-LSTM model (73.5%). This leads to the conclusion that the presence of multiple attention layers did not give the improvement in results.

6 Conclusion and Feature Research Directions

We have performed a fine-grained evaluation of state-of-the-art attention-based neural network models for entity-level ADR classification task. We have conducted extensive experiments on four benchmarks. Analyzing the results, we have found that that increasing the number of attention layers

Model	Twitter	Cadec	PsyTAR	Twimed-Twitter	Twimed-PubMed
IAN	.794	**.815**	**.817**	**.819**	**.874**
AEN	.667	.490	.802	.742	.743
AOA	.752	.752	.815	.795	.803
ATAE-LSTM	.786	.702	.807	.735	.801

Table 2: Macro F-measure classification results of the compared methods for each datasets.

did not give an improvement in results. Addition an aspect vector to the input layer also did not give significant benefits. IAN model showed the best results for entity-level ADR classification task in all of our experiments.

There are three future research directions that require, from our point of view, more attention. First, we plan to add knowledge-based features as input for IAN model and evaluate their efficiency. Second, apply these models to the entity-level ADR classification task for texts in other languages. Finally, we plan to explore the potential of new state-of-the-art text classification methods based on BERT language model.

Acknowledgments

This research was supported by the Russian Science Foundation grant no. 18-11-00284.

References

Ilseyar Alimova and Elena Tutubalina. 2017. Automated detection of adverse drug reactions from social media posts with machine learning. In *International Conference on Analysis of Images, Social Networks and Texts*, pages 3–15. Springer.

I.S. Alimova and E. V. Tutubalina. 2018. Entity-level classification of adverse drug reactions: a comparison of neural network models. *Proceedings of the Institute for System Programming of the RAS*, 30(5):177–196.

Nestor Alvaro, Yusuke Miyao, and Nigel Collier. 2017. Twimed: Twitter and pubmed comparable corpus of drugs, diseases, symptoms, and their relations. *JMIR public health and surveillance*, 3(2).

Eiji Aramaki, Yasuhide Miura, Masatsugu Tonoike, Tomoko Ohkuma, Hiroshi Masuichi, Kayo Waki, and Kazuhiko Ohe. 2010. Extraction of adverse drug effects from clinical records. In *MedInfo*, pages 739–743.

Adrian Benton, Lyle Ungar, Shawndra Hill, Sean Hennessy, Jun Mao, Annie Chung, Charles E Leonard, and John H Holmes. 2011. Identifying potential adverse effects using the web: A new approach to medical hypothesis generation. *Journal of biomedical informatics*, 44(6):989–996.

Jiang Bian, Umit Topaloglu, and Fan Yu. 2012. Towards large-scale twitter mining for drug-related adverse events. In *Proceedings of the 2012 international workshop on Smart health and wellbeing*, pages 25–32. ACM.

Shaika Chowdhury, Chenwei Zhang, and Philip S Yu. 2018. Multi-task pharmacovigilance mining from social media posts. *arXiv preprint arXiv:1801.06294*.

Hong-Jie Dai, Musa Touray, Jitendra Jonnagaddala, and Shabbir Syed-Abdul. 2016. Feature engineering for recognizing adverse drug reactions from twitter posts. *Information*, 7(2):27.

Shashank Gupta, Manish Gupta, Vasudeva Varma, Sachin Pawar, Nitin Ramrakhiyani, and Girish Keshav Palshikar. 2018a. Co-training for extraction of adverse drug reaction mentions from tweets. In *European Conference on Information Retrieval*, pages 556–562. Springer.

Shashank Gupta, Sachin Pawar, Nitin Ramrakhiyani, Girish Keshav Palshikar, and Vasudeva Varma. 2018b. Semi-supervised recurrent neural network for adverse drug reaction mention extraction. *BMC bioinformatics*, 19(8):212.

Rave Harpaz, Herbert S Chase, and Carol Friedman. 2010. Mining multi-item drug adverse effect associations in spontaneous reporting systems. In *BMC bioinformatics*, volume 11, page S7. BioMed Central.

S. Hochreiter and J. Schmidhuber. 1997. Long Short-Term Memory. *Neural Computation*, 9(8):1735–1780. Based on TR FKI-207-95, TUM (1995).

Yongfang Hou, Xinling Li, Guizhi Wu, and Xiaofei Ye. 2016. National adr monitoring system in china. *Drug Safety*, 39(11):1043–1051.

Binxuan Huang, Yanglan Ou, and Kathleen M Carley. 2018. Aspect level sentiment classification with attention-over-attention neural networks. In *International Conference on Social Computing, Behavioral-Cultural Modeling and Prediction and Behavior Representation in Modeling and Simulation*, pages 197–206. Springer.

Trung Huynh, Yulan He, Alistair Willis, and Stefan Rüger. 2016. Adverse drug reaction classification with deep neural networks. In *Proceedings of COLING 2016, the 26th International Conference on Computational Linguistics: Technical Papers*, pages 877–887.

V Ivanov, E Tutubalina, N Mingazov, and I Alimova. 2015. Extracting aspects, sentiment and categories of aspects in user reviews about restaurants and cars. In *Proceedings of International Conference Dialog*, volume 2, pages 22–34.

Jitendra Jonnagaddala, Toni Rose Jue, and Hong-Jie Dai. 2016. Binary classification of twitter posts for adverse drug reactions. In *Proceedings of the Social Media Mining Shared Task Workshop at the Pacific Symposium on Biocomputing, Big Island, HI, USA*, pages 4–8.

Sarvnaz Karimi, Alejandro Metke-Jimenez, Madonna Kemp, and Chen Wang. 2015. Cadec: A corpus of adverse drug event annotations. *Journal of biomedical informatics*, 55:73–81.

Svetlana Kiritchenko, Saif M Mohammad, Jason Morin, and Berry de Bruijn. 2018. Nrc-canada at smm4h shared task: Classifying tweets mentioning adverse drug reactions and medication intake. *arXiv preprint arXiv:1805.04558*.

Ioannis Korkontzelos, Azadeh Nikfarjam, Matthew Shardlow, Abeed Sarker, Sophia Ananiadou, and Graciela H Gonzalez. 2016. Analysis of the effect of sentiment analysis on extracting adverse drug reactions from tweets and forum posts. *Journal of biomedical informatics*, 62:148–158.

Siwei Lai, Liheng Xu, Kang Liu, and Jun Zhao. 2015. Recurrent convolutional neural networks for text classification. In *AAAI*, volume 333, pages 2267–2273.

Xiao Liu and Hsinchun Chen. 2013. Azdrugminer: an information extraction system for mining patient-reported adverse drug events in online patient forums. In *International Conference on Smart Health*, pages 134–150. Springer.

Dehong Ma, Sujian Li, Xiaodong Zhang, and Houfeng Wang. 2017. Interactive attention networks for aspect-level sentiment classification. *arXiv preprint arXiv:1709.00893*.

Z.Sh. Miftahutdinov, E.V. Tutubalina, and A.E. Tropsha. 2017. Identifying disease-related expressions in reviews using conditional random fields. *Computational Linguistics and Intellectual Technologies: Papers from the Annual conference Dialogue*, 1(16):155–166.

Diego Saldana Miranda. 2018. Automated detection of adverse drug reactions in the biomedical literature using convolutional neural networks and biomedical word embeddings. *arXiv preprint arXiv:1804.09148*.

Jin-Cheon Na, Wai Yan Min Kyaing, Christopher SG Khoo, Schubert Foo, Yun-Ke Chang, and Yin-Leng Theng. 2012. Sentiment classification of drug reviews using a rule-based linguistic approach. In *International Conference on Asian Digital Libraries*, pages 189–198. Springer.

Azadeh Nikfarjam and Graciela H Gonzalez. 2011. Pattern mining for extraction of mentions of adverse drug reactions from user comments. In *AMIA Annual Symposium Proceedings*, volume 2011, page 1019. American Medical Informatics Association.

Azadeh Nikfarjam, Abeed Sarker, Karen OConnor, Rachel Ginn, and Graciela Gonzalez. 2015. Pharmacovigilance from social media: mining adverse drug reaction mentions using sequence labeling with word embedding cluster features. *Journal of the American Medical Informatics Association*, 22(3):671–681.

Yun Niu, Xiaodan Zhu, Jianhua Li, and Graeme Hirst. 2005. Analysis of polarity information in medical text. In *AMIA annual symposium proceedings*, volume 2005, page 570. American Medical Informatics Association.

BAHADORREZA Ofoghi, SAMIN Siddiqui, and KARIN Verspoor. 2016. Read-biomed-ss: Adverse drug reaction classification of microblogs using emotional and conceptual enrichment. In *Proceedings of the Social Media Mining Shared Task Workshop at the Pacific Symposium on Biocomputing*.

Majid Rastegar-Mojarad, Ravikumar Komandur Elayavilli, Yue Yu, and Hongfang Liu. 2016. Detecting signals in noisy data-can ensemble classifiers help identify adverse drug reaction in tweets. In *Proceedings of the Social Media Mining Shared Task Workshop at the Pacific Symposium on Biocomputing*.

N. Rusnachenko and N. Loukachevitch. 2018. Using convolutional neural networks for sentiment attitude extraction from analytical texts. *In Proceedings of CEUR Workshop, CLLS-2018 Conference*.

Abeed Sarker, Rachel Ginn, Azadeh Nikfarjam, Karen OConnor, Karen Smith, Swetha Jayaraman, Tejaswi Upadhaya, and Graciela Gonzalez. 2015. Utilizing social media data for pharmacovigilance: a review. *Journal of biomedical informatics*, 54:202–212.

Abeed Sarker and Graciela Gonzalez. 2015. Portable automatic text classification for adverse drug reaction detection via multi-corpus training. *Journal of biomedical informatics*, 53:196–207.

Jesus Serrano-Guerrero, Jose A Olivas, Francisco P Romero, and Enrique Herrera-Viedma. 2015. Sentiment analysis: A review and comparative analysis of web services. *Information Sciences*, 311:18–38.

SM Shareef, CDM Naidu, Shrinivas R Raikar, Y Venkata Rao, and U Devika. 2017. Development, implementation, and analysis of adverse drug reaction monitoring system in a rural tertiary care teaching hospital in narketpally, telangana. *International Journal of Basic & Clinical Pharmacology*, 4(4):757–760.

Preeti Singh, Manju Agrawal, Rajesh Hishikar, Usha Joshi, Basant Maheshwari, and Ajay Halwai. 2017. Adverse drug reactions at adverse drug reaction monitoring center in raipur: Analysis of spontaneous reports during 1 year. *Indian journal of pharmacology*, 49(6):432.

V. Solovyev and V. Ivanov. 2014. Dictionary-based problem phrase extraction from user reviews. *Lecture Notes in Computer Science (including subseries Lecture Notes in Artificial Intelligence and Lecture Notes in Bioinformatics)*, 8655 LNAI:225–232.

Youwei Song, Jiahai Wang, Tao Jiang, Zhiyue Liu, and Yanghui Rao. 2019. Attentional encoder network for targeted sentiment classification. *arXiv preprint arXiv:1902.09314*.

Yequan Wang, Minlie Huang, Li Zhao, et al. 2016. Attention-based lstm for aspect-level sentiment classification. In *Proceedings of the 2016 conference on empirical methods in natural language processing*, pages 606–615.

Lei Zhang, Shuai Wang, and Bing Liu. 2018. Deep learning for sentiment analysis: A survey. *Wiley Interdisciplinary Reviews: Data Mining and Knowledge Discovery*, page e1253.

Zhifei Zhang, JY Nie, and Xuyao Zhang. 2016. An ensemble method for binary classification of adverse drug reactions from social media. In *Proceedings of the Social Media Mining Shared Task Workshop at the Pacific Symposium on Biocomputing*.

Maryam Zolnoori, Kin Wah Fung, Timothy B Patrick, Paul Fontelo, Hadi Kharrazi, Anthony Faiola, Yi Shuan Shirley Wu, Christina E Eldredge, Jake Luo, Mike Conway, et al. 2019. A systematic approach for developing a corpus of patient reported adverse drug events: A case study for ssri and snri medications. *Journal of biomedical informatics*, 90:103091.

Annotating and Analyzing Semantic Role of Elementary Units and Relations in Online Persuasive Arguments

Ryo Egawa
Tokyo University of
Agriculture and Technology
Koganei, Tokyo, Japan
egawa@katfuji.lab.tuat.ac.jp

Gaku Morio[*]
Hitachi, Ltd.
Central Research Laboratory
Kokubunji, Tokyo, Japan

Katsuhide Fujita
Tokyo University of
Agriculture and Technology
Koganei, Tokyo, Japan
katfuji@cc.tuat.ac.jp

Abstract

For analyzing online persuasions, one of the important goals is to semantically understand how people construct comments to persuade others. However, analyzing the semantic role of arguments for online persuasion has been less emphasized. Therefore, in this study, we propose a novel annotation scheme that captures the semantic role of arguments in a popular online persuasion forum, so-called *ChangeMyView*. Through this study, we have made the following contributions: (i) proposing a scheme that includes five types of elementary units (EUs) and two types of relations; (ii) annotating *ChangeMyView* which results in 4612 EUs and 2713 relations in 345 posts; and (iii) analyzing the semantic role of persuasive arguments. Our analyses captured certain characteristic phenomena for online persuasion.

1 Introduction

Changing a person's opinion is a difficult process because one has to first understand his/her opinion and reasons. Recent studies in the field of argument mining and persuasion detection have investigated the feature of persuasiveness in the documents of a persuasive forum (Tan et al., 2016; Hidey et al., 2017). Many existing studies analyzing the features of persuasion have focused on lexical features (Tan et al., 2016; Habernal and Gurevych, 2016) and argumentative features such as post-to-post interaction (Ji et al., 2018), concessions (Musi et al., 2018), and semantic types of argument components. Although these analyses are important, we argue that it is also important to understand the fine-grained strategy by analyzing the semantic roles of arguments.

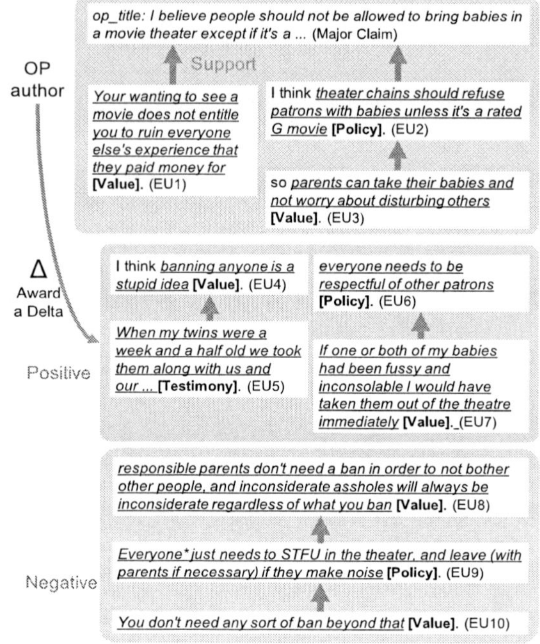

Figure 1: An overview of our annotation in *ChangeMyView*. EUs have five types and the relations between the EUs have two types (refer to Section 3.2).

In this study, we investigate the semantic roles of arguments in a persuasive forum by proposing an annotation scheme on a data set of *ChangeMyView* (Tan et al., 2016). *ChangeMyView* is a subreddit in which users post an opinion (named a *View*) to change their perspective through comments of a challenger. When the *View* is changed, the user who posted the original post (OP) awards a Delta point (Δ) to the challenger who changed the *View*. Figure 1 is an overview of our annotation in *ChangeMyView* in which the Positive post is an awarded post that won a Δ and the Negative post is a non-awarded one.

To parse arguments from *ChangeMyView*, we considered five types of elementary unit (EU) (i.e.,

---

*The work of this paper was performed when he was a student at Tokyo University of Agriculture and Technology (to contact: morio@katfuji.lab.tuat.ac.jp).

Proceedings of the ACL 2019, Student Research Workshop, pages 422–428
Florence, Italy, July 28th-August 2nd, 2019. ©2019 Association for Computational Linguistics

Fact, Testimony, Value, Policy, and Rhetorical Statement) and two types of relation between EUs (i.e., Support and Attack). Moreover, We demonstrated that EUs and these relations are effective for characterizing persuasive arguments.

The contributions of this study can be summarized as follows: (i) We have proposed an annotation scheme for EUs and its relations for *ChangeMyView*; (ii) We annotated 4612 EUs and 2713 relations in 115 threads, and we computed an interannotator agreement using Krippendorff's alpha. Note that $\alpha_{EU} = .677$ and $\alpha_{Rel} = .532$ are better than those of existing studies; (iii) A significant difference in the distribution of each EU exists between OP and reply posts; however, no significant difference in the types of EU and relation is observed between persuasive and non-persuasive arguments.

2   Related Work

Recent studies in argument mining investigated the characteristics of an argument by considering the role of argumentative discourse units and relations (Ghosh et al., 2014; Peldszus and Stede, 2015; Stab and Gurevych, 2014). Moreover, recent studies have focused on the semantics of argument components (Park et al., 2015; Al Khatib et al., 2016; Becker et al., 2016). For example, Hollihan and Baaske (2004) proposed three types of claims, i.e., fact, value, and policy, in which fact can be verified with objective evidence, value is an interpretation or judgment, and policy is an assertion of what should be done. Park et al. (2015) extended this argument model with types of claims such as testimony and reference. Al Khatib et al. (2016) proposed the argument model for analyzing the argumentation strategy in news editorials. This model separated an editorial into argumentative discourse units of six different types, such as Common Ground, Assumption, and Testimony. Because persuasion is often based on facts and testimony, this type of semantic classification of claim is valid for our study.

Several studies have focused on the semantics for analyzing the characteristics of persuasive arguments. Wachsmuth et al. (2018) investigated the rhetorical strategy for effectively persuading to the other, and Hidey et al. (2017) focused on the semantics of premise and claim.

3   Annotation Study

3.1   Data Source

In our study, a dataset of *ChangeMyView* (Tan et al., 2016) is introduced. *ChangeMyView* is a forum in which users initiate the discussion by posting an Original Post (OP) and describing their *View* (or we call it as Major Claim) in the title. An OP user has to describe his/her reason behind the *View*. Then, certain challengers post a reply to change the OP's *View*. If the challenger succeeds at changing the OP's *View*, the OP user awards a Δ to the challenger.

In this study, we extracted 115 threads from the *ChangeMyView* dataset through a simple random sampling. Each thread contained a triple of OP, Positive (which won a Δ), and Negative (which is a non-awarded one). Therefore, we used 345 posts (115 × (OP, Positive, Negative)) for our annotation.

3.2   Annotation Scheme

We defined the five types of EUs and two types of relations between the EUs. This scheme enables us to capture the semantic roles of elementary units and how we build an argument based on the semantic units.

3.2.1   Type of Elementary Units

There are five types of EUs that are similar to the scheme of Park et al. (2015) pertaining to eRulemaking comments. The motivation for the introduction of the scheme is based on our expectation that we can feature persuasive arguments by considering personal experience, facts, and value judgments. The five types of EUs are defined as follows:

Fact: This is a proposition describing objective facts as perceived without any distortion by personal feelings, prejudices, or interpretations. Unlike Testimony, this proposition can be verified with objective evidence; therefore, it captures the evidential facts for persuasion. Certain examples of Fact are as follows: *"they did exactly this in the U.K. about thirty or so years ago"* and *"this study shows that women are 75% less likely to speak up in a space when outnumbered"*.

Testimony: This is an objective proposition related to the author's personal state or experience. This proposition characterizes how users utilize their experience for persuasions. Certain examples of Testimony are as follows: *"I do not have* *children"* and *"I've heard suggestions of an exorbitant tax on ammunition"*.

Value: This is a proposition that refers to subjective value judgments without providing a statement on what should be done. This proposition is nearly similar to an opinion. Certain examples of Value are as follows: *"this is completely unworkable"* and *"it is absolutely terrifying"*.

Policy: This is a proposition that offers a specific course of action to be taken or what should be done. It typically contains modal verbs, such as *should*, or imperative forms. Certain examples of Policy are as follows: *"everyone needs to be respectful of other patrons"* and *"intelligent students should be able to see that"*.

Finally, because *ChangeMyView* users usually utilize a rhetorical question (Blankenship and Craig, 2006) to increase their persuasion, this study provides a novel EU type that is useful for determining a rhetorical strategy.

Rhetorical Statement: This unit implicitly states the subjective value judgment by expressing figurative phrases, emotions, or rhetorical questions. Therefore, we can regard it as a subset of Value [1]. Certain examples of Rhetorical Statement are as follows: *"You can observe this phenomenon yourself!"* and *"if one is paying equal fees to all other students why is one not allowed equal access and how is this a good thing?"*.

3.2.2 Type of Relations

The two types of relations between EUs are defined as follows:

Support: An EU X has support relation to the other EU Y if X provides positive reasoning for Y. It is typically linked by connectives such as *therefore*. An example of support relation is as follows: **X**: *"Every state in the U.S. allows homeschooling"* (Fact) support **Y**: *"if you are ideologically opposed to the public school system, you are free to opt out"* (Value).

Attack: An EU X has attack relation to the other EU Y if X provides negative reasoning for Y. It is typically linked by connectives such as *however*. An example of attack relation is as follows: **X**: *"Young men are the most likely demographic to get into an accident"* (Value) attack **Y**: *"that does not warrant discriminating against every individual in the group"* (Value).

---

[1]Unlike Value, we allow the Rhetorical Statement to be an incomplete sentence because it is usually expressed implicitly.

3.3 Annotation Process

The annotation task includes two subtasks: (1) segmentation and classification of EUs and (2) relation identification. We recruited 19 non-native students who are English proficient as annotators with all annotations being performed over original English texts. Each annotator was asked to read the guideline as well as the entire post before the actual annotation. Moreover, we held several meetings for each subtask to train the annotators. Furthermore, because the annotators are non-native speakers, to ensure the understanding of the posts is consistent among the annotators, the posts are translated into their language. The translation was conducted by two annotators per document: one for the translation and the other for the validation. Note that the translated documents are only used as a reference for the annotators.

In the EU annotation, three annotators independently annotated 87 threads, whereas the remaining 28 threads were annotated by eight expert annotators who were selected from 19 annotators. From the 87 threads, using a majority vote, a gold standard is established by merging three annotation results. To extract accurate minimal EU boundary and remove irrelevant tokens, such as *therefore* and punctuation, we considered the token-level annotation rather than the sentence-level. Token-level annotation enables us to distinguish an inference step that one of the propositions can be a claim and the other can be a premise. Here is an example of inference step: <*"Empire Theatres in Canada has a "Reel Babies" showing for certain movies"* [Fact]> so <*"parents can take their babies and not worry about disturbing others"* [Value]>. Moreover, all EU boundaries, except a Rhetorical Statement, should contain a complete sentence to render EU propositions.

In the relation annotation, two annotators independently annotated 50 threads, whereas the remaining 65 threads were annotated by eight expert annotators. In the 50 threads, to establish the gold standard by merging two annotation results, expert annotators were assigned to each thread. We modeled the structure of each argument with a *one-claim* approach (Stab and Gurevych, 2016) that considers an argument as the pairing of a single claim and a set of premises that justify the claim. Major Claim has to be a root node of an argument in OP posts, and each claim has a stance attribute to the OP's *View*.

Post type	#Fact	#Testimony	#Value	#Policy	#RS	#Total	#Support	#Attack	#Total
OP	52	134	914	44	157	1301	864	128	992
Positive	127	134	1338	55	327	1981	924	108	1032
Negative	78	86	882	41	243	1330	595	94	689

Table 1: Annotation results of EUs and relations

3.4 Annotation Result

Table 1 shows an overview of the annotated corpus. Our corpus contains 4612 EUs and 2713 relations between units in 345 posts. As can be seen from the table, 68% of EUs were Values and 15% of EUs were Rhetorical Statements. Although the Value ratio is 45% in the dataset of Park and Cardie (2018), Value occupies most of the EUs in our corpus. We estimate this because Value often gives a subjective opinion by the characteristics of persuasive forum. Moreover, 88% of relations were Support relations. This result indicates an Attack inference seldom appears in online persuasions.

We computed an inter-annotator agreement (IAA) using Krippendorff's α. Consequently, the IAA of EUs is $\alpha_{EU} = 0.677$ and that of relations is $\alpha_{Rel} = 0.532$. Note that the IAA values are higher than the result of Park and Cardie (2018) in the eRulemaking annotation with respect to EUs ($\alpha = 0.648$) and relations ($\alpha = 0.441$). [2] Furthermore, our IAA of EUs is higher than the result of Hidey et al. (2017) ($\alpha = 0.65$) in the *ChangeMyView* annotation [3]. We consider the higher agreement is because of the token-level annotations as the sentence-level annotations cannot accurately distinguish an inference step.

Most of the disagreement in EU annotation occurred between Value and the other types. In Value vs. Fact situation, a disagreement occurred when a unit is described in a general way, such as "many people" and "generally", and incorrectly marked as a Fact, although the unit should be Value. Moreover, in Value vs. Testimony situation, a disagreement occurred when a unit is incorrectly interpreted as a Value. For example, "I am an atheist" was incorrectly marked as Value, although it should be labeled Testimony because the unit describes a personal state.

4 Corpus Analysis

To examine the features of persuasive arguments, we analyzed the EUs and the relation between units in each case, i.e., *OP vs. Reply (Positive and Negative)* and *Positive vs. Negative*.

We investigated how the number of EU in a post contributes to the persuasive strategy. We used the Mann-Whitney U test and identified that there exists a significant difference in Testimony and Rhetorical Statement in OP vs. Reply. Testimony is more likely to appear in OP (10.3%) than in Reply (6.6%) and Rhetorical Statement is more likely to appear in Reply (17.2%) than in OP (12.1%). Therefore, an OP author tends to describe their *View* based on their own experience or state and Rhetorical Statement tends to appear more in Reply as the reply post is for trying to change the OP's *View*. This result is consistent with intuition; however, there is no significant difference between positive and negative in any type of the EU and the p-value of Testimony, Policy, and Rhetorical Statement is $p > 0.85$. This indicates that the frequency of occurrence of the EU cannot be a persuasive feature.

Figure 2 shows the annotation result of Relations between units in each post, in which *source* means the type of supporting EU and *target* means the type of supported unit. Most of the targets is Value type. Note that Testimony is reasoning more in OP than in reply and Rhetorical Statement is reasoning more in reply than in OP; moreover, the relation between Values is more in positive than in negative.

Next, to investigate the logical strength of an argument (Wachsmuth et al., 2017), we examine *degree* and *depth*. The degree means the number of supporting EUs to a supported unit. For example, in Figure 1, Major Claim is supported by EU1 and EU2; thus, the $degree = 2$ and the $depth = 2$. However, EU4 is only supported by EU5; thus, the $degree = 1$ and the $depth = 1$. Figures 3 and 4 show the resulting histogram of degree and depth in each post, respectively. According to the results, each post has no significant difference and it

---

[2]Note that the relation annotation of Park and Cardie (2018) is only limited to the Support relation.

[3]Note that the IAA result of relations cannot be compared because the labeling of relations is not conducted in Hidey et al. (2017)

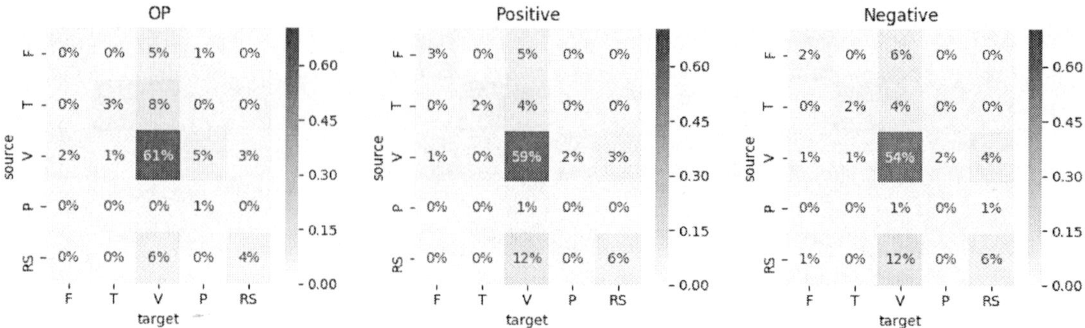

Figure 2: Transition matrix of Support and Attack relations

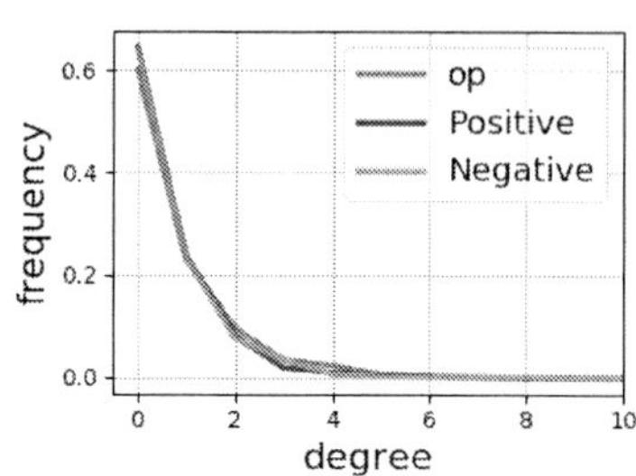

Figure 3: Histogram of the degree in each post.

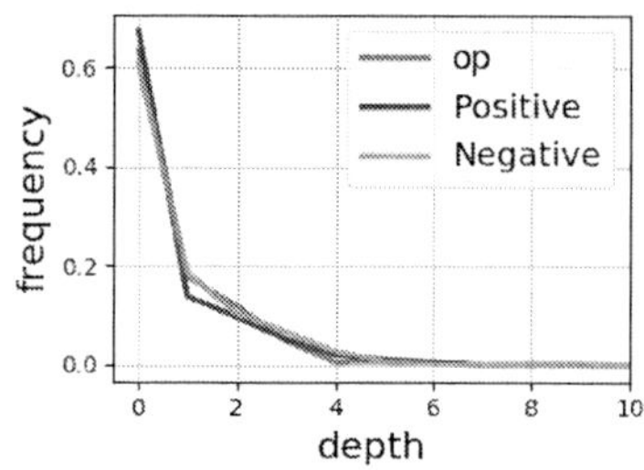

Figure 4: Histogram of the depth in each post.

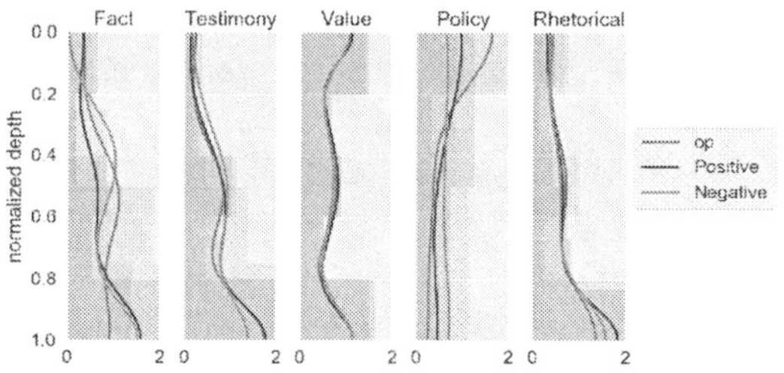

Figure 5: The distribution of positions in an argument in each type of EU.

as follows:

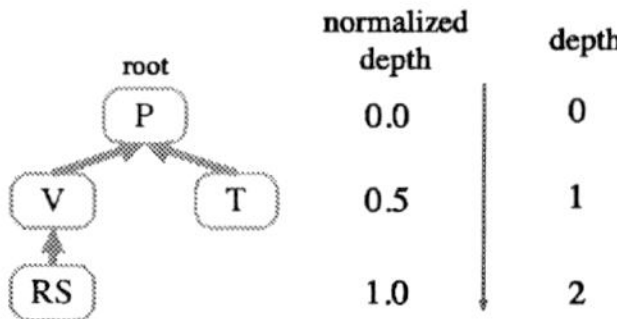

is a power-law distribution. Most of the EUs have two or less relations, and the depths of arguments are less than three. This indicates that the logical strength of argument may not contribute to persuasiveness. Moreover, because it indicates that there are many arguments that have a stance attribute to the OP's *View*, how they interact with the OP may contribute to persuasion.

To clarify the role of EUs as arguments, we investigated the position of each type of EUs in an argument. Figure 5 shows a histogram of the position in the argument, where the position means normalized depth at the root node to 0.0 and at the terminal node to 1.0. For instance, normalized depth of the following argument can be described

In Positive and Negative post, Fact and Testimony often appear at near the terminal node of an argument structure, which indicates that trying to persuade is based on facts and personal experiences. Moreover, Value and Policy appear at near the root node, which indicates trying to change the *View* by finally describing an opinion or what should be done as a conclusion. These results are consistent with intuitive results; moreover, an interesting result is that Rhetorical Statement tends to appear at near the terminal node of the argument. This indicates that people tend to use rhetorical phrases for appealing to the emotions first and then assert their opinion as their persuasive strategy.

Furthermore, the statistical tests were conducted to examine whether the difference in OP vs. Reply and Positive vs. Negative post exists. We used the Kolomogorov-Smirnov (KS) test and Levene test on each case. In OP vs. Reply, a significant difference exists in the position distribution of Fact by KS test ($p < 0.05$), and Policy by Levene test ($p < 0.01$). This indicates that people tend to make an assertion based on objective facts as a persuasion strategy.

5 Conclusion

In this study, we proposed an annotation scheme for capturing the semantic role of EUs and relations in online persuasions. We annotated five types of EUs and two types of relations that resulted in 4612 EU and 2713 relation annotations. The analyses revealed that the existence of Rhetorical Statement and the position of Fact in an argument structure characterizes the persuasive posts that try to change the *View*. In future studies, we will focus on the following: (i) the expansion of our corpus data by annotating the post-to-post interaction and (ii) the application of our data to training sets of machine learning, i.e., automatically identifying the argument structure and detecting the persuasive posts.

Acknowledgment

This work was supported by JST AIP-PRISM (JPMJCR18ZL) and JST CREST (JPMJCR15E1), Japan.

References

Khalid Al Khatib, Henning Wachsmuth, Johannes Kiesel, Matthias Hagen, and Benno Stein. 2016. A news editorial corpus for mining argumentation strategies. In *Proceedings of COLING 2016, the 26th International Conference on Computational Linguistics: Technical Papers*, pages 3433–3443, Osaka, Japan. The COLING 2016 Organizing Committee.

Maria Becker, Alexis Palmer, and Anette Frank. 2016. Argumentative texts and clause types. In *Proceedings of the Third Workshop on Argument Mining (ArgMining2016)*, pages 21–30, Berlin, Germany. Association for Computational Linguistics.

Kevin L. Blankenship and Traci Y. Craig. 2006. Rhetorical question use and resistance to persuasion: An attitude strength analysis. *Journal of Language and Social Psychology*, 25(2):111–128.

Debanjan Ghosh, Smaranda Muresan, Nina Wacholder, Mark Aakhus, and Matthew Mitsui. 2014. Analyzing argumentative discourse units in online interactions. In *Proceedings of the First Workshop on Argumentation Mining*, pages 39–48, Baltimore, Maryland. Association for Computational Linguistics.

Ivan Habernal and Iryna Gurevych. 2016. Which argument is more convincing? analyzing and predicting convincingness of web arguments using bidirectional lstm. In *Proceedings of the 54th Annual Meeting of the Association for Computational Linguistics (Volume 1: Long Papers)*, pages 1589–1599, Berlin, Germany. Association for Computational Linguistics.

Christopher Hidey, Elena Musi, Alyssa Hwang, Smaranda Muresan, and Kathy McKeown. 2017. Analyzing the semantic types of claims and premises in an online persuasive forum. In *Proceedings of the 4th Workshop on Argument Mining*, pages 11–21. Association for Computational Linguistics.

T.A. Hollihan and K.T. Baaske. 2004. *Arguments and Arguing: The Products and Process of Human Decision Making, Second Edition*. Waveland Press.

Lu Ji, Zhongyu Wei, Xiangkun Hu, Yang Liu, Qi Zhang, and Xuanjing Huang. 2018. Incorporating argument-level interactions for persuasion comments evaluation using co-attention model. In *Proceedings of the 27th International Conference on Computational Linguistics*, pages 3703–3714, Santa Fe, New Mexico, USA. Association for Computational Linguistics.

Elena Musi, Debanjan Ghosh, and Smaranda Muresan. 2018. Changemyview through concessions: Do concessions increase persuasion? *CoRR*, abs/1806.03223.

Joonsuk Park, Cheryl Blake, and Claire Cardie. 2015. Toward machine-assisted participation in erulemaking: An argumentation model of evaluability. In *Proceedings of the 15th International Conference on Artificial Intelligence and Law*, ICAIL '15, pages 206–210, New York, NY, USA. ACM.

Joonsuk Park and Claire Cardie. 2018. A corpus of erulemaking user comments for measuring evaluability of arguments. In *Proceedings of the 11th Language Resources and Evaluation Conference*, Miyazaki, Japan. European Language Resource Association.

Andreas Peldszus and Manfred Stede. 2015. Joint prediction in mst-style discourse parsing for argumentation mining. In *Proceedings of the 2015 Conference on Empirical Methods in Natural Language Processing*, pages 938–948, Lisbon, Portugal. Association for Computational Linguistics.

Christian Stab and Iryna Gurevych. 2014. Annotating argument components and relations in persuasive essays. In *COLING 2014, 25th International Conference on Computational Linguistics, Proceedings of the Conference: Technical Papers, August 23-29, 2014, Dublin, Ireland*, pages 1501–1510.

Christian Stab and Iryna Gurevych. 2016. Parsing argumentation structures in persuasive essays. *CoRR*, abs/1604.07370.

Chenhao Tan, Vlad Niculae, Cristian Danescu-Niculescu-Mizil, and Lillian Lee. 2016. Winning arguments: Interaction dynamics and persuasion strategies in good-faith online discussions. *CoRR*, abs/1602.01103.

Henning Wachsmuth, Nona Naderi, Ivan Habernal, Yufang Hou, Graeme Hirst, Iryna Gurevych, and Benno Stein. 2017. Argumentation quality assessment: Theory vs. practice. In *Proceedings of the 55th Annual Meeting of the Association for Computational Linguistics (Volume 2: Short Papers)*, pages 250–255. Association for Computational Linguistics.

Henning Wachsmuth, Manfred Stede, Roxanne El Baff, Khalid Al Khatib, Maria Skeppstedt, and Benno Stein. 2018. Argumentation synthesis following rhetorical strategies. In *Proceedings of the 27th International Conference on Computational Linguistics*, pages 3753–3765, Santa Fe, New Mexico, USA. Association for Computational Linguistics.

A Japanese Word Segmentation Proposal

Stalin Aguirre
National Polytechnic School of Ecuador
Faculty of Systems Engineering
stalin.aguirre@epn.edu.ec

Josafá de Jesus Aguiar Pontes
National Polytechnic School of Ecuador
Faculty of Systems Engineering
josafa.aguiar@epn.edu.ec

Abstract

Current Japanese word segmentation methods, that use a morpheme-based approach, may produce different segmentations for the same strings. This occurs when these strings appear in different sentences. The cause is the influence of different contexts around these strings affecting the probabilistic models used in segmentation algorithms. This paper presents an alternative to the current morpheme-based scheme for Japanese word segmentation. The proposed scheme focuses on segmenting inflections as single words instead of separating the auxiliary verbs and other morphemes from the stems. Some morphological segmentation rules are presented for each type of word and these rules are implemented in a program which is properly described. The program is used to generate a segmentation of a sentence corpus, whose consistency is calculated and compared with the current morpheme-based segmentation of the same corpus. The experiments show that this method produces a much more consistent segmentation than the morpheme-based one.

1 Introduction

In computational linguistics, the first step in text-processing tasks is segmenting an input text into words. Most languages make use of white spaces as word boundaries, facilitating this segmentation step. However, Japanese is one of the few languages that does not use a word delimiter. This particular problem has been the focus of many researchers because its solution is key to subsequent processing tasks, such as Part-of-Speech (PoS) tagging, machine translation or file indexing.

Segmenting a text requires the definition of a segmentation unit (Indurkhya and Damerau, 2010). This unit must be strictly defined to describe all the elements in a language. But languages are not perfect and have changed abruptly throughout the years, making it difficult or nearly impossible to define such a unit. The consensus has been that the unit to be used was the *word*, because it defines the majority of the elements in a language, elements that have a meaning and can stand by themselves (Katamba, 1994).

Even though there still are some constructions that do not fit in the word definition (Bauer, 1983), this segmentation unit is useful in languages that use spaces because they separate the majority of words in a text. For Japanese, however, this is not the case. It is a language that does not use spaces in its written form.

私たちの性格はまったく異なる。
(Our personalities are completely different.)

Furthermore, Japanese is an agglutinative language, which means that some constructions (specially inflected words) are formed by consecutively attaching morphemes to a stem (Kamermans, 2010). These long words are very important because they can work as full sentences without the need to add context that was previously stated, as illustrated in the following example:

待たされていました。
(I have been kept waiting.)

待つ (*wait*)
待たされる (*be kept waiting*)
待たされている (*being kept waiting*)
待たされています (*being kept waiting*) (*P)[1]
待たされていました (*been kept waiting*) (*P)

Given the nature of the language and the lack of a need for native speakers to explicitly separate words, there is no standard on how to segment a written text. Because of this, the segmentation unit and rules for text processing tasks are set by each researcher, although most of them have

---

[1] *P: Polite form

Proceedings of the ACL 2019, Student Research Workshop, pages 429–435
Florence, Italy, July 28th-August 2nd, 2019. ©2019 Association for Computational Linguistics

chosen a morpheme-based approach (Matsumoto et al., 1991; Kudo, 2005; Matsumoto et al., 2007).

The downside about this morpheme approach is that, in many cases, there is no consistency when segmenting the same string. The cause seems to be the influence of different contexts on the probabilistic models used in segmentation algorithms. In other words, by producing short morphemes as candidates, there are many segmentation possibilities from which the final one may change due to the context. This inconsistency problem is visible in n-gram data produced by Kudo and Kazawa (2009) and Yata (2010). Within these files, there are various entries of the same string as result of different segmentations, as shown in Table 1. This problem directly affects any later processing task that relies on the resulting segmentation. In machine translation, for example, different segmentations for the same word would produce different incorrect translations.

File	N-gram	Frequency
3gm-0034	行き まし た	2681486
4gm-0056	行 き まし た	290
4gm-0056	行き ま し た	384

Table 1: The word 行きました (*went*) (*P) as found in n-gram data files produced by Yata (2010).

Inflected words follow a limited set of rules. These rules properly define all possible inflections (Kamermans, 2010). As such, they can only lead to one possible correct segmentation. Taking this premise, the Proposed approach aims for a more consistent segmentation by focusing on the treatment of inflected words to limit their segmentation possibilities to a single one in all cases. Thus, reducing word segmentation inconsistency errors.

The present work is structured as follows: Section 2 describes the rules that lead the Proposed segmentation method. Section 3 describes the implementation of the algorithm that applies these rules; Section 4 introduces the evaluation parameters and the results obtained with the Proposed method, a comparison of these metrics with a morpheme-based method and discussion of the results; and Section 5 presents the conclusions of the work.

2 Segmentation Definition

Most Japanese constructions are created by directly connecting an affix to a word. A few of these constructions are considered separated words when translating them into English, such as: 日本式 (*Japan style*, from 日本 *Japan* and 式 *style*) or 外国語 (*foreign language*, from 外国 *foreign* and 語 *language*). Other constructions have a single word as translation, such as: 日本語 (*Japanese* (language) from 日本 *Japan* and 語 *language*). However, this word construction rule in Japanese can be found in "basic" words as well. For example: 大人 (*adult*, from 大 *great* and 人 *person*) or 女子 (*girl*, from 女 *woman* and 子 *child*), which are kept as single words in both languages. This means that we cannot generalize how these constructions should always get segmented, either as single words or multiple words.

As such, we have established a few segmentation rules where some affixes were connected to the words they modify by the use of symbols, regardless of the number of words it forms when translating them into English. For prefix concatenation, the backtick symbol (`) was used, on the other hand, for suffix concatenation, the hyphen symbol (-) was used. In general, the words that were considered for these affix concatenation rules were nouns and verbs.

Overall, the base of the segmentation for this work was the IPADIC (Asahara and Matsumoto, 2003) dictionary. This means that what was considered as *word* was each entry in this dictionary, with the exception of the verb and adjective entries. For these inflectional words, what was considered as word were the union of the inflectional word stems and the morphemes or auxiliary verbs that form the inflection, as described by Pontes (2013). In the case of the inflectional words, only the most common inflections are shown below [2].

Based on this word definition, the following rules were set:

2.1 Nouns

Most regular nouns were kept as single words according to the entries that belonged to this tag within the IPADIC. Some PoS included in this category were: common nouns, proper names, pronouns, pronoun contractions, adverbial nouns, verbal nouns (nouns that can be followed by す る or related verbs), adjectival nouns (nouns that can be followed by な), Arabic numbers (wide and short length), counters and Chinese numbers.

---

[2] When mentioning an inflection based on an auxiliary verb, it also refers to all the inflections of such auxiliary.

- Names and pronouns were connected to personal suffixes.

  和子-さん   (*Ms. Kazuko*)

- Common nouns were connected to non-inflectional affixes.

フィリピン-人	(*Filipino*) (demonym)
貧困-者	(*Pauper*)
ドイツ-語	(*German*) (language)
数\`年	(*Several years*)

- Pronouns were connected to plural suffixes.

私-たち	(*We*)
彼-等	(*They*)

- Nouns were connected to honorific prefixes.

  ご\`注文   (*Order*) (*P)

- Nouns were connected to more than one affix when it was the case. The main noun was always right after the backtick or just before the first hyphen.

  お\`手伝い-さん-たち   (*Servants*) (*P)

- Nouns connected to the 的 character to adjectivize them were treated as suffixes. For the possible inflections of the 的 character, refer to Section 2.4.

  世界-的な   (*Global*)

2.2 Verbs

Verbs are the most varied words in terms of inflections. This is due to the possibility of concatenating many auxiliary verbs to a single stem, producing really long words. In current segmentation methods, each inflectional word gets segmented by its stem and by each auxiliary verb. This scheme can be found in linguistic texts but it might not be the best way to segment these words because of the inconsistency problem illustrated in Table 1. For this method, the inflections were treated as single words.

- Present affirmative.

  会う   (*Meet*)

- Negative form with auxiliary ない.

  合わない   (*Do not meet*)

- Polite form with auxiliary ます.

  会います   (*Meet*) (*P)

- Past form with auxiliary た.

  描いた   (*Drew*)

- Continuative form with auxiliary て.

  話して   (*Talk and ...*)

- Continuative form using the auxiliary いる.

  走ている   (*Is running*)

- Desire with auxiliary たい.

  買いたい   (*Would like to buy*)

- Hypothetical with auxiliary ば.

  読めば   (*Should (you) read ...*)

- Passive with the auxiliary される.

  待たされる   (*Be kept waiting*)

2.3 Adjectival Verbs

Adjectival verbs, also called *i-adjectives*, work the same as verbs. They keep a static stem while their suffixes change. These suffixes are formed by inflected auxiliary verbs from which a few are the same as the ones for verbs. Just like verbs, the inflections are treated as single words.

- Attributive form with い.

  欲しい   (*Wanted, Desired*)

- Adverbial form with く.

  楽しく   (*Happily*)

- Past form with かった.

  寒かった   (*Was cold*)

- Negative form with auxiliary ない.

  面白くない   (*Not interesting*)

2.4 Adjectival Nouns

Adjectival nouns, usually known as *na-adjectives*, can be connected to just three morphemes which are directly connected to the stem in this method.

- Copula な to directly modify a noun.

  大変な   (*Terrible*)

- Continuative particle で to chain adjectives.

  知的で   (*Intelligent and ...*)

- Nominalising particle さ.

  深刻さ   (*Seriousness*)

3 Implementation

3.1 The Dictionaries

The dictionaries needed for this work were a list of non-inflectional words and various lists of inflectional word stems:

The **Non-Inflectional Word Dictionary (NIWD)** was formed by unifying the IPADIC files into a single list; omitting verb, adjectival verb, adjectival noun and symbol files. For the final dictionary file, a column with frequency counts was added. These counts were obtained from n-gram data produced by Yata (2010) and assigned to each entry. For this, the n-gram data was first cleaned by removing the white spaces separating the n-gram tokens, and the counts of the repeated entries were summed. Once cleaned, the whole n-gram data was sorted. Then, each entry of the dictionary was searched within the cleaned data to extract its frequency count.

The **Inflectional Word Dictionary (IWD)** included lists of the stems for all the inflectional words obtained by Pontes (2013). This dictionary was divided in two sets. The first set contained the adjectives classified in: noun adjectives (*na*, な), verbal adjectives (*i*, い) and irregular adjectives (*ii*, いい). The second set covered all verbs classified in eleven groups: *u* (う), *bu* (ぶ), *gu* (ぐ), *ku* (く), *mu* (む), *nu* (ぬ), *ru* (る), *su* (す) and *tsu* (つ) for first group verbs, and *ichidan* (える, いる) for second group verbs. One additional group was added for the honorific verbs that end in *aru* (ある).

3.2 The Inflection Automaton

Due to the large number of possible inflected words in the Japanese language, as shown by Pontes (2013), it was not practical to store them all in memory. Instead, a Deterministic Finite Automaton (DFA) was built to validate them.

The objective of the DFA was identifying whether an input string corresponds to an inflected word or not. This was done by checking if the string was formed by a stem (by making use of the IWD) and a correct inflectional suffix. The inflectional suffixes that were implemented in the DFA involved treating each character as a transition to a new state. The states were final if all the previous transitions formed a valid inflection. The transitions and states were created following the inflectional patterns obtained by (Pontes, 2013).

The process that the DFA implemented was:

1. Receive a string, set *position* to the start of the string.

2. Take a substring from *position* to *i*, where *i* grows by 1 in each iteration.

3. Look for the substring in the IWD. If not found, take the next substring and repeat this step. If there is no next substring, the string is not an inflected word, as it does not contain a stem.

4. If the substring is found, set the initial state to the corresponding stem group and move *position* to the end of the substring within the original string.

5. Read each next character from *position* and use it as a transition to a new state. If the next character is not a valid transition, go to step 3.

6. When there are no more characters left and the last state reached is an accepting state, the string is considered an inflected word. If the last state reached is not an accepting state, go to step 3.

Given that irregular verbs (suru する and kuru くる) do not have static stems, the method started at step 5 by setting the initial state to *suru* and, if not found, to *kuru*.

If the string was not recognized as an inflected word by the DFA, it verified if the first character of the string was a honorific prefix (お, ご or 御), and if so, a substring starting from the second character was sent to step 1.

3.3 The Segmentation Program

The main program implemented the NIWD and the DFA for word and inflection recognition respectively, which were part of a unigram language model for word segmentation (Jurafsky and Martin, 2000). This probabilistic model was accompanied with a few grammar rules for overriding the final segmentation decision. To refine the program, 2,500 sentences from the Tatoeba (Ho and Simon, 2006) sentence corpus were used as validation data.

The steps that were followed by the program were:

1. Split the input text into phrases by using delimiter symbols such as parenthesis, punctuation, etc., as separators.

2. For each phrase, take substrings of all sizes
   > 0, and from all positions $<$ phrase length.

3. For each substring, verify if it is an inflected
   word with the DFA. If it is not, look for it in
   the NIWD. If it is not found, verify if it is
   a number or a foreign word in Katakana or
   other alphabets. If it is not, repeat this step
   with the next substring.

4. If the substring was verified or found in step
   3, save it as a candidate word and assign it
   a frequency count by looking for its value
   within n-gram data like the one produced by
   Yata (2010), and accumulate the frequency
   count in a variable.

5. Once all candidate words are available, calculate their score by taking the negative logarithm of the frequency count assigned to each
   word, divided to the accumulated frequency
   count.

6. Create a graph where its nodes represent
   the positions between each character of the
   phrase.

7. For each node, select all the candidate words
   whose last character position is right before
   the node. Check if any of the grammar rules
   apply to them in order to directly choose one
   or remove them. If no rules applied, choose
   the one with the least score value.

8. Set the chosen word as the edge that connects
   the node before the position of the first character of the candidate word, and the current
   node.

9. When all the edges are set, obtain each previous edge that connects the current node, starting from the last one and going backwards.

10. Return the obtained edges in order while
    adding a separation symbol between them
    such as a backtick (') or hyphen (-) for affixes
    or a white space for other words.

4 Evaluation

Two evaluations were established for the Proposed
method. The first one checked how correctly
it segments a test corpus in comparison with a
gold segmentation. The second one compared the
consistency of its segmentation of a corpus with
MeCab's (Kudo, 2005) for the same corpus.

4.1 Segmentation Evaluation

For this evaluation, we used 1,000 sentences from
the Tatoeba (Ho and Simon, 2006) sentence corpus, which were manually segmented to create a
gold segmentation corpus.

A Baseline method by Pontes (2013), that segments words based on longest string matches, was
used for comparison. Both methods' outputs are
comparable given that the Baseline also uses the
IWD for inflected word segmentation. MeCab, on
the other hand, is not. It produces a morpheme-
based segmentation for inflected words.

The metrics used for evaluating both segmentation methods were: recall, precision, and f-
measure (Wong et al., 2009). From these metrics, the following abbreviations were considered:
number of correctly segmented words (CW), total number of words in gold corpus (GW), total
number of segmented words (SW). The obtained
results are shown in Table 2.

Table 2: Results from evaluating the segmentation
methods.

Method	GW	SW	CW
Proposed	9757	9798	9656
Baseline	9757	9190	8069

Method	Recall	Precision	F-Measure
Proposed	98.96%	98.55%	98.76%
Baseline	82.70%	87.80%	85.17%

The Proposed method outperforms the Baseline
method. This score is apparently high, but notice
that it is not statistically significant, as the time
allowed us to manually prepare and revise only
1,000 sentences. Definitely, a larger corpus is necessary in order to provide a higher confidence level
on the evaluation of our Japanese word segmentation method. For the next evaluation, however,
we do count with a larger corpus for testing as explained below.

4.2 Consistency Evaluation

To evaluate the consistency of the segmentation
method, a corpus of 185,393 sentences from the
Tatoeba (Ho and Simon, 2006) sentence corpus
was used. This corpus was segmented with four
segmentation methods which were: the Proposed
method that attaches affixes to words as defined
in Section 2.1 (PMA), the Proposed method that
does not attach affixes to words (PM), the Baseline method (BM) and MeCab.

PMA, PM and the Baseline method consider inflected words as single words, which means, all the auxiliary verbs that forms the inflections are directly connected to the stems.

For each corpus segmentation, the following process was applied:

Generate the n-gram data. Generate up to 7-gram data of a corpus segmentation by using the SRILM toolkit (Stolcke, 2004).

Clean the n-gram data. Remove the white spaces that separate the n-gram tokens and sort the whole n-gram data.

Create a list of repeated entries. Extract the repeated entries (RE) from the clean n-gram data by the use of regular expressions and produce a *repetition list*. Count the number of RE to calculate the inconsistency.

Count the RE that contain inflected words. Apply the DFA on the repetition list in order to obtain a subset of entries that contain inflected words and count them.

Due to the large amount of entries and the lack of context in n-gram data, it was not reasonable to say that the inflected words detected were the correct words in the corpus. Therefore, we made three different sets for inflected word count approximation: inflected words of more than one character within the entry (IW1), inflected words of more than two characters within the entry (IW2) and inflected words found as the whole entry (IWW). Table 3 shows an example of each set.

Table 3: Repeated n-gram entries, generated from MeCab's segmentation, that contain inflected words as found by the DFA.

Set	Clean N-gram Entry	Inflected Word Found
IW1	にいるか	いる
IW2	は思ったより	思った
IWW	変われる	変われる

In order to calculate the inconsistency of each method, the entries of the RE, IW1, IW2 and IWW lists of all the methods were summed. The share of the inconsistency from each method is shown in Table 4.

The evaluation of the four methods shows that both Proposed methods produce the least RE, which means that they are more consistent overall. Regarding the RE that contain inflected words, the Baseline method has the least inconsistency.

Table 4: Number of n-gram entries and inconsistency error distribution for each method.

Method	N-gram Entries
PMA	5,803,353
PM	5,808,828
BM	5,717,438
MeCab	6,245,224

Method	RE	IW1	IW2	IWW
PMA	14.58%	16.46%	17.42%	19.94%
PM	15.40%	17.20%	18.12%	20.66%
BM	16.23%	13.25%	13.46%	8.12%
MeCab	53.79%	53.09%	51.00%	51.28%
Total	100%	100%	100%	100%

The total number of n-gram entries produced from MeCab's segmentation is approximately 8% higher than the one produced by the second higher (PM). However, such a rate is insignificant compared to the rate of RE within the n-gram data, in which MeCab is around 300% more inconsistent than each one of the other three methods.

5 Conclusion

We have demonstrated that by considering inflectional words (with all their auxiliary verbs) as single words, the number of possible segmentations for those words in different contexts gets reduced. Therefore, the resulting segmentation is more consistent and more accurate. Tasks that use word segmentation would also see an improvement, such as language models and machine translation systems.

This approach relies on the fact that it is possible to define all the inflectional rules of the Japanese language. The same method could be applied to other words that can be defined by rules, or to other unsegmented languages whose rules can be defined the same way.

Acknowledgments

We give our most sincere thanks to the Japanese professor at Catholic University of Ecuador 出麻樹子 (Makiko Ide) for her very valuable contribution. She voluntarily helped us prepare the gold segmentation corpus which was a very important part of the project.

References

Masayuki Asahara and Yuji Matsumoto. 2003. Ipadic version 2.7.0 user's manual. [online] Open Source Development Network. Available at: https://ja.osdn.net/projects/ipadic/docs/ipadic-2.7.0-manual-en.pdf [Accessed 25 Apr. 2019].

Laurie Bauer. 1983. *Some basic concepts*, Cambridge Textbooks in Linguistics, page 7–41. Cambridge University Press.

Trang Ho and Allan Simon. 2006. Tatoeba. [online] Tatoeba: Collection of Sentences and Translations. Available at: https://tatoeba.org [Accessed 25 Apr. 2019].

Nitin Indurkhya and Fred J. Damerau. 2010. *Handbook of Natural Language Processing*, 2nd edition. Chapman & Hall/CRC.

Daniel Jurafsky and James H. Martin. 2000. *Speech and Language Processing: An Introduction to Natural Language Processing, Computational Linguistics, and Speech Recognition*, 1st edition. Prentice Hall PTR, Upper Saddle River, NJ, USA.

Michiel Kamermans. 2010. *An Introduction to Japanese - Syntax, Grammar and Language*. SJGR Publishing.

Francis Katamba. 1994. *English Words*. Routledge.

Taisei Kudo. 2005. Mecab : Yet another part-of-speech and morphological analyzer.

Taku Kudo and Hideto Kazawa. 2009. Japanese web n-gram version 1 ldc2009t08. [online] Linguistic Data Consortium. Available at: https://catalog.ldc.upenn.edu/LDC2009T08 [Accessed 25 Apr. 2019].

Yuji Matsumoto, Sadao Kurohashi, Yutaka Nyoki, Hitoshi Shinho, and Makoto Nagao. 1991. User's guide for the juman system, a user-extensible morphological analyzer for Japanese. *Nagao Laboratory, Kyoto University*.

Yuji Matsumoto, Kazuma Takaoka, and Masayuki Asahara. 2007. Chasen morphological analyzer version 2.4. 0 user's manual. *Nara Institute of Science and Technology*.

Josafá Pontes. 2013. A corpus of inflected japanese verbs and adjectives. [Unpublished].

Andreas Stolcke. 2004. Srilm — an extensible language modeling toolkit. *Proceedings of the 7th International Conference on Spoken Language Processing (ICSLP 2002)*, 2.

Kam-Fai Wong, Wenjie Li, Ruifeng Xu, and Zhengsheng Zhang. 2009. *Introduction to Chinese Natural Language Processing*, volume 2.

Susumu Yata. 2010. N-gram corpus - japanese web corpus 2010. [online] S-yata.jp. Available at: http://www.s-yata.jp/corpus/nwc2010/ngrams/ [Accessed 25 Apr. 2019].

Author Index

Association for Computational Linguistics
209 N. Eighth Street
Stroudsburg, Pennsylvania 18360

ISBN 978-1-5108-9097-8